Fodor's

NEW YORK CITY

**FODOR'S
TRAVEL PUBLICATIONS**

NEW YORK • TORONTO
LONDON • SYDNEY • AUCKLAND

WITHDRAWN

WWW.FODORS.COM

CONTENTS

KEY TO SYMBOLS

- Map reference
- Address
- Telephone number
- Opening times
- Admission prices
- Underground station
- Bus number
- Train station
- Ferry/boat
- Driving directions
- Tourist office
- Tours
- Guidebook
- Restaurant
- Café
- Bar
- Shop
- Number of rooms
- Air conditioning
- Swimming pool
- Gym
- Other useful information
- ▷ Cross reference
- ★ Walk/drive start point

114

69
216

UNDERSTANDING NEW YORK

Understanding New York is an introduction to the city, its geography, economy, history and its people. Living New York gets under the skin of New York today, while The Story of New York takes you through the city's past.

New York City is an international center for entertainment, fashion, creative arts and finance. It has great shopping, dynamic theater, superb concert halls and clubs, world-class museums, gorgeous parks and gardens, and sports events all year long. The variety and quality of restaurants is incomparable. As a world financial center, it soars and plummets with the fluctuations on Wall Street. New Yorkers move fast, talk fast and are passionate about politics and style. They come in all shapes, sizes, colors and ethnicities; the city's multiculturalism is part of its charm. Although known for being brusque, New Yorkers are often surprisingly warm. Sometimes infuriating, the city is never dull. And chances are, with its vibrant whirl of activity, it's nothing like home.

THE MANHATTAN LAYOUT

Manhattan is just one of five boroughs that comprise New York City. The others, sometimes known as the Outer Boroughs, are the Bronx, Brooklyn, Queens and Staten Island. Manhattan is the long, narrow island jutting southwest off the mainland and is the smallest borough at 13.5 miles (22km) long and 2.25 miles (3.5km) wide. On the east side of the island is the East River. On the west is the Hudson River. To the north is the Harlem River. Upper New York Bay—the city's fine harbor—is to the south.

In Manhattan, most streets are numbered and laid out in a grid. The exception to this is Lower Manhattan, south of 14th Street, which grew up before the grid system was established. On the grid, "avenues" run from north to south, and "streets" run east and west. Broadway cuts across town diagonally from northwest to southeast. First Avenue is on the eastern side of town, while Twelfth Avenue is on the western side. Fifth Avenue divides the city into the East Side and the West Side (except south of Washington Square, where Broadway becomes the east–west divide).

No matter where you are in Manhattan, if you are heading north you're going "uptown" and if you're heading south you're going "downtown." If you want to travel east or west, you want to go "crosstown."

CLIMATE

From January to March, New York can be very cold, with occasional blizzards. But cheaper air fares and hotel rooms can make it worth your while to visit then—and sometimes the weather can be temperate. The best times to visit are in late April and May, when temperatures are generally no lower than 61°F (16°C), and attractions are crowded only at peak times, and in September to early November, when temperatures range from 50°F (10°C) to 77°F (25°C). The city is hot and humid in July and August, with extremes of 95°F (35°C) or higher, but almost everything is air-conditioned.

STREET LIFE

Walking is the best way to fully appreciate the city, with its architectural splendors, intriguing sculptures, pretty fountains, beautiful parks and iconic landmarks. The street life is entertaining and colorful. Spanish, Chinese, Russian, Yiddish, Korean, Greek and English are just a few of the languages spoken by New Yorkers.

MANHATTAN'S NEIGHBORHOODS AT A GLANCE

LOWER MANHATTAN

Financial District The oldest part of the city and nexus of the securities industry anchored by the New York Stock Exchange and Wall Street.

TriBeCa Short for *Triangle Below Canal*, it is defined by Canal and Barclay streets and Broadway and the Hudson River. A mixed-use neighborhood of gritty warehouse lofts, loft-style restaurants and galleries.

Chinatown The area stretching over about 30 blocks, from Kenmare and Delancey streets to East Broadway and Worth Street, and from Broadway to Allen Street. Throngs of people shop for fish, meat, vegetables and herbal remedies or dine in the affordable restaurants.

Little Italy A section of Mulberry Street, with tourist-restaurants plus some genuine delis and pastry stores.

SoHo An ultra-expensive, chic shopping mall that is crowded with non-residents on weekends.

Lower East Side From 14th Street to Fulton and Franklin and from the East River to Broadway, the area takes in Chinatown, Little Italy and the East Village neighborhoods. Haunt of young professionals and artists.

DOWNTOWN AND CHELSEA

Greenwich Village/West Village 14th Street to Houston Street and from the Hudson River to Bowery and Fourth Avenue. Boutiques line the west end of Bleecker Street.

NoHo Between SoHo and Greenwich Village (from Houston to Eighth streets and Mercer to Bowery/Third Avenue), this youth-oriented neighborhood has plenty of fashionable shopping, bars and restaurants.

East Village Filled with restaurants, bars and a youth-oriented street scene.

Union Square/Flatiron District Hot neighborhood south of the Flatiron Building on 22nd Street and around Madison Square with bars, restaurants and clubs. From 14th to 23rd streets and Park Avenue to Sixth Avenue.

Chelsea Center of the gay community. Numerous warehouse/garage galleries along 24th Street, and a lively club and restaurant scene. Stretches from 14th to 30th streets and from Sixth Avenue to the Hudson River.

MIDTOWN

Hell's Kitchen The latest neighborhood undergoing gentrification (from Eighth Avenue to the Hudson River between 30th and 59th streets).

Midtown Commercial heart of the city between 34th and 59th streets on the West Side and from 40th to 59th streets on the East Side.

Times Square/Theater District The area around 42nd Street and Broadway is now occupied by major corporations and national chain stores, as well as new hotels, clubs and theaters.

CENTRAL PARK AND AROUND

Upper East Side From 59th to 96th streets and from Fifth Avenue to the East River. Madison Avenue is the ultra-chic shopping street.

East/Spanish Harlem From 96th to 142nd streets, and between Park Avenue and the East River. A mixed neighborhood of Italians, African-Americans and Hispanics.

Upper West Side Broadway cuts right through this section that extends from 59th to 125th streets between the Hudson River and Central Park West.

Harlem Stretching from 110th Street to the Harlem River and from Fifth to St. Nicholas avenues, Harlem is the city's most famous black community.

EXCURSIONS

The Bronx North of and linked to Manhattan by bridges and subway. Home of the New York Botanical Garden, the Bronx Zoo and Yankee Stadium.

Brooklyn Southeast of Manhattan and connected by bridges, a tunnel and subway, it is New York's most populous borough. Take in great views of Manhattan from Brooklyn Heights.

Queens A 20-minute subway trip east from Manhattan takes you to Queens, one of New York's fastest-growing and most ethnically diverse areas.

Staten Island The most southerly and least populous borough, with attractions such as Historic Richmond Town. Good views of Manhattan and the Statue of Liberty from the ferry.

LOWER MANHATTAN

Charging Bull sculpture at Bowling Green (▷ 91) by Arturo Di Modica (1989) reminds many stock-market traders who pass by daily that better times are ahead.

Century 21 (▷ 94) For seriously discounted designer wear and a crowd scene worthy of the annals of shopping.

Dean & DeLuca (▷ 95) Everything in this fancy food emporium is absolutely the best of its kind. A sensuous browsing and tasting experience.

The Immigrants (▷ 66) by Luis Sanguino (1973) is a heart-rending sculpture in Battery Park evoking the hardships of early immigrants.

J & R (▷ 96) Audiophiles and technophiles can satisfy every craving for audio components and CDs, computers and peripherals, cameras and other gadgets at good prices.

Nobu (▷ 104) Nobu Matsuhisa's sushi is inspirational at this stylish restaurant.

Pravda (▷ 100) Sixty-five vodkas, plus caviar and Russian snacks may tempt you to visit this trendsetter bar.

Soho Grand (▷ 105) First of the hip downtown hostelries where pets get the red-carpet welcome.

The Sphere (▷ 66) Fritz Koenig's 22-ton symbol of global peace, rescued from the plaza between the twin towers after 9/11, is now a memorial to the victims.

Staten Island Ferry (▷ 56) A free trip across the harbor giving fabulous views of the city. Just hop on.

Statue of Liberty (▷ 84–85) America's symbol of freedom is by Frédéric-Auguste Bartholdi (1885). Take the ferry to Liberty Island for a close-up look or to climb the 354 steps to the crown.

DOWNTOWN AND CHELSEA

Babbo (▷ 134) Mario Batali's flagship is the place to sample his lusty cuisine.

Flatiron Building (▷ 113) New York's first skyscraper got its nickname from its triangular shape.

Jeffrey (▷ 125) The shoe department at this expensive clothing store is stellar, and the best place to see high-designer selections in a single location.

Marcel (▷ 141) Chic on the cheap (by New York hotel standards) is the order of the day here.

Tabla (▷ 139) Seductive neo-Indian cuisine is presented by master spice blender Floyd Cardoz.

MIDTOWN

42nd Street/Times Square (▷ 172–173 and 168–170) Architecture as performing art—the luminous facades of pulsating color are best at night.

B & H Photo (▷ 176) The professional place for cameras, video equipment and film, all at great prices.

Le Bernardin (▷ 186) Everything about this seafood specialist is perfect—the service, the flowers and the exquisitely refined, thoughtful cuisine.

Chrysler Building (▷ 148–149) An art deco masterpiece, this is a shrine to the Chrysler automobile.

DB Bistro Moderne (▷ 187) Eating at one of Daniel Boulud's restaurants is a must for every food-loving visitor. This is the most relaxed and joyous of them all.

Empire State Building (▷ 152–154) Take the elevator to the 86th-floor Observation Deck for stunning views of

Above Fine specimens at the American Museum of Natural History
Opposite The Chrysler Building—a city icon

Manhattan, the rivers and far into the distance, especially at night when the city is illuminated.

FAO Schwarz (▷ 177) The ultimate toy store, as seen in the film *Big* with Tom Hanks.

Flute (▷ 180) A luxury subterranean retreat serving 20 different champagnes by the glass, this bar is perfect for pre- or post-theater.

Four Seasons (▷ 188) Established in 1959, this modern restaurant is the darling of the city's movers and shakers. Christian Albin's cuisine is another bonus.

Four Seasons (▷ 191) A hotel legendary for its service and its immense bathtubs.

International Center of Photography (▷ 151) More than 60,000 photographs by top names are on display in this exhibition space.

King Cole Bar (▷ 181) Where the Bloody Mary was invented, Maxfield Parrish's mural adds vibrant color to this bar in the St. Regis Hotel.

Library (▷ 192) A boutique hotel and book-lovers' haunt notable for its hip minimalist design and good service.

Metro (▷ 192) One of the best value hotels in the city, Metro is art deco and stylish.

Museum of Modern Art (▷ 162–163) Now doubled in size after architect Yoshio Taniguchi's expansion, MoMA displays masterworks of modern sculpture and painting.

New York Public Library (▷ 159) Archetypal Beaux Arts magnificence was funded by donations and bequests.

Le Parker Meridien (▷ 193) This very French uptown hotel with hip downtown style has a pool with a view and a rooftop jogging track.

P. J. Clarke's (▷ 183) A beloved New York saloon, this is home to a rakish crowd.

Prometheus (▷ 166) by Paul Manship (1934) is Rockefeller Center's famous gold-leaf and bronze statue overlooking the ice-skating rink.

Rainbow Grill Bar (▷ 183) The bartenders mix a great cocktail at this romantic only-in-New York locale.

Ritz Carlton (▷ 243) The opulent Central Park star offers superb service, the latest techno amenities and the only La Prairie spa in the United States.

St. Regis (▷ 195) A gilded Beaux Arts beauty, this hotel is just off Fifth Avenue.

Rockefeller Center and Grand Central Terminal (▷ 164–167 and 156–157) These two architectural gems are worth a self-guided tour.

Salon De Ning (▷ 183) Who can resist a rooftop bar in Midtown?

Tiffany (▷ 178) Superb silver, crystal and other luxury gifts are the attraction at this famous American name, in the jewelry business since 1837.

Top of the Tower (▷ 184) A nostalgic 26th-floor piano-bar overlooking the East River.

CENTRAL PARK AND AROUND

Alice in Wonderland (▷ 213) by José de Creeft (1959) perches on a giant mushroom while the March Hare holds out a watch and the Mad Hatter looks on.

American Museum of Natural History (▷ 204–207) Not only for dinosaur fossils and moon rocks, this is also a stunning modern planetarium complex.

Barneys (▷ 230) For cutting-edge fashion. Don't miss the handbag department.

Bloomingdale's (▷ 230) This department store is so very New York.

Carlyle (▷ 242) This hotel is considered the city's most discreet retreat.

Central Park (▷ 208–213) New York's green lung is Frederick Law Olmsted's masterpiece of landscape architecture, housing the Metropolitan Museum of Art.

Frick Collection (▷ 215) A large collection of masterpieces by Rembrandt, Vermeer, El Greco and Goya is housed in Henry Clay Frick's splendid mansion.

Guggenheim Museum (▷ 216–217) Frank Lloyd Wright's only New York building is a whirling wonder both inside and out.

Jean-Georges (▷ 239) All of Jean-Georges Vongerichten's restaurants (Jo Jo, 66, Mercer Kitchen and Spice Market) showcase his brilliance, but this is his flagship.

MO Bar (▷ 243) This romantic hot spot is in the Mandarin Oriental Hotel.

Per Se (▷ 240) Thrilling cuisine by Thomas Keller, of French Laundry, Napa Valley fame, makes this currently the city's most coveted reservation.

Sherry-Lehmann (▷ 232) An education; the inventory of international wine selections is worth $10 million.

Trump International Hotel and Tower (▷ 243) Enjoy breathtaking views of Central Park from this stylish hotel.

TOP EXPERIENCES

Empire State Building (▷ 152–154) The Observation Deck offers a panoramic view of all Manhattan, which is very romantic at sunset.

A Broadway show Seeing one is a quintessential New York experience and various discount pricing schemes make it more affordable (▷ 170, Tips; 283).

Bronx Zoo (▷ 256–257) Always entertaining—the people are sometimes as interesting as the animals.

Waldorf-Astoria Hotel (▷ 195) A study in opulence. Ogle the amazing floral displays in the lobby.

A walk across Brooklyn Bridge (▷ 68–69) This landmark bridge offers a terrific view of the skyscrapers in Lower Manhattan and the East River.

Statue of Liberty and Ellis Island (▷ 84–85 and 72–74) Take the ferry ride to see Lady Liberty, and if you're feeling energetic climb the steps to the crown, and the Ellis Island memorial to 12 million immigrants.

Guggenheim Museum (▷ 216–217) Frank Lloyd Wright's spiral-shaped building showcases an exceptional collection of modern and contemporary art.

Central Park (▷ 208–213) Stroll along the paths and down the tree-lined Mall to Bethesda Fountain and the lake beyond to experience New York's quiet side.

Shopping along Fifth Avenue (▷ 155) Savor one of the world's finest shopping streets with visits to Saks Fifth Avenue, Tiffany & Co, FAO Schwartz and many more.

Cathedral of St. John the Divine (▷ 227) The largest Gothic church in the world is vast, with chapels dedicated to different national, ethnic and social groups.

Chinatown (▷ 70–71) Explore the largest, busiest and most colorful ethnic neighborhood and eat in a Chinese restaurant.

Times Square (▷ 168–170) New York's popular landmark offers flashy neon signs, animated advertisements and an exciting vibe that makes this bustling cultural scene memorable.

Yankee Stadium (▷ 258–259) **and Citi Field** These are the places to go for great baseball when either the New York Yankees or the New York Mets (▷ 267) are in town.

Frick Collection (▷ 215) The opulent home of steel magnate Henry Clay Frick is filled with fine Old Master paintings, French furniture and museum quality artworks that showcase the wealthy lifestyle of New York during the gilded age.

Metropolitan Museum of Art (▷ 209–211) Magnificent displays of fabulous art from cultures around the world feature an astonishing number of masterpieces. The daily Museum Highlights Tour provides an excellent introduction to the collection.

Below *Walk or bicycle across the one-mile (1.6km) wooden, pedestrian walkway of Brooklyn Bridge to glimpse a spectacular view of the Manhattan skyline*

LIVING NEW YORK

Manhattan is only 13.5 miles (22km) long and 2.25 miles (3.5km) wide. Geologically it consists of bedrock made of gneiss, marble or mica schist. These two factors, plus population density, have played major roles in shaping the city's land- and streetscape, making it more vertical than most. Tall buildings line the streets, and people think nothing of riding elevators to their 50th-floor offices. Daily the population swells as commuters pour into Manhattan from the suburbs, creating a crowded environment that throbs with energy. Commuters access the city via ferry, tunnels and bridges, the most graceful of which are the Brooklyn (1883) and George Washington (1931) bridges. North of 14th Street the streets are laid out in a grid. There are few open spaces or green parks to provide relief—only one or two squares, such as Union, Washington and Madison, or small pockets of asphalt with benches, statues and fountains. Instead, there is one vast park, Central Park, separating the Upper East Side and the Upper West Side. It functions as the city's playground.

THE GRID AND THE WARREN
Most visitors to New York City quickly grasp the logic of the streetscape north of 14th Street. A series of broad north–south avenues is crossed by east–west streets, numbered logically. Below 14th Street things get more complicated. Here the narrow streets twist and turn, reminiscent of a medieval city, and have names rather than numbers. This came about because the city grew haphazardly and there were only a few long arteries connecting farms and villages. So in 1811 an orderly grid of 12 broad avenues and 155 streets was established, subdivided into lots measuring 25 by 100ft (7.5 by 30m). It was thought that traffic would be heaviest on the east–west routes, so more streets than avenues were planned. This pattern remains.

Clockwise from above *From the top of the Empire State Building even other skyscrapers can look tiny; Central Park provides a haven for recreation and relaxation in the city; commuting on the subway is part of daily life in New York City*

UNDERGROUND CITY

First-time visitors to Manhattan often notice the rooftop water towers, fire hydrants, potholes and, weirdest of all, steam-belching funnels. The last give an inkling of what lies below—a multilevel network of electric and telephone cables, plus steam, water, gas and sewage pipes, all laid above the subway. A large water tunnel under the subway supplies the city's drinking water. The subway alone has 660 miles (1,062km) of track and 490 stations. There's 100 million miles of telephone cable. City water comes from upstate New York reservoirs, and the 1,500 million gallons a day is delivered by more than 6,000 miles (9,654km) of tunnel and water mains. Installed before 1930 and made of cast iron, they can rupture, which causes chaos. When the piped gases build up, they cause manhole explosions. The steam-belching funnels help to relieve the pressure and stop the 60,000 manholes from erupting.

ROBERT MOSES— NEW YORK'S BARON HAUSSMANN

Robert Moses (1888–1981), who served on the Parks and Planning commissions, had a huge impact on the city's overall design, in a similar way to Baron Haussmann in Paris. Between 1924 and 1968, Moses transformed New York City, building 17 parkways, 14 expressways (including the Brooklyn–Queens Expressway), the FDR and Harlem River drives, the Robert F. Kennedy and Verrazano bridges, Lincoln Center and Stuyvesant Town. In the process he destroyed whole neighborhoods, tearing down slums and relocating residents in public housing in Harlem, the Lower East Side, the Bronx and Brooklyn. Not surprisingly, the citizens got angry. And when Moses moved to route cars through Washington Square and put parking lots in Central Park the citizens mobilized in an attempt to preserve the small scale of their neighborhoods. Still, Moses left a gigantic imprint on the city.

WAKING UP TO THE WATERFRONT

For years New York City's 580 miles (930km) of waterfront lay blighted, the site of rusting piers, crumbling warehouses and refuse-strewn lots. Now it's as if the city has woken up to its potential pleasures, as citizens go kayaking, fishing and sailing. A 28-mile (45km) bicycle path now encircles Manhattan, and the waterfront has been converted into a park with a promenade and gardens stretching from the Battery to 58th Street. It's hard to pinpoint when this regeneration began. In the 1980s, South Street Seaport with its retail outlets and museum, Battery Park City and Chelsea piers were important beginnings to the process, followed by Riverbank State Park (1993). The rest has followed, culminating in Stuyvesant Cove Park (2002) and Hudson River Park (2003).

URBAN GARDENS

New York City has one large park and only two major botanical gardens, so resident horticulturists create their own gardens in unlikely corners. If you look up at the residential buildings you might see green fronds peeking out from the roofline. Some of these roof gardens are luxurious indeed, planted with trees and flowers and decorated with urns and statues. In contrast are the hundreds of community gardens, usually created on vacant city-owned lots, which serve as neighborhood social centers. The impetus for such gardens can be traced to 1972 and a garden at Bowery and Houston tended by the Green Guerrillas. Mayor Giuliani sought to destroy such gardens and battled with neighborhood activists, but Mayor Michael Bloomberg has moved quickly to make peace.

New York City is a city of immigrants. Between 1892 and 1924, 12 million immigrants poured through Ellis Island, many heading to the Lower East Side. Today, the gateways are Kennedy and Newark airports, and the immigrants' destinations are often the ethnic mosaics of Brooklyn and Queens, where such high schools as New Town have students who speak 30 different languages, and where the Central Library caters to a population that speaks nearly 40 languages. The Dutch, of course, were the first immigrants. They were interested in talent and enterprise and opened the city to immigrants of all sorts—Huguenots, Jews, Germans, Africans (slave and free) and the English, Scottish, French and Irish. At the turn of the 20th century, large numbers of Jews, Italians and Russians arrived, and after 1965, people from the Caribbean, Central America and Asia. The percentage of foreign-born citizens has always fluctuated. At 43 percent, it is today at its highest. The lowest was in 1970 (18 percent). The total population of New York City is 8.2 million, of which 35 percent are white, 27 percent Latino, 25 percent black and 12 percent Asian.

INTERNATIONAL EXPRESS—THE NUMBER 7 TRAIN

In the census of 2000, Queens had the fastest-growing population, having risen by 11 percent in the preceding decade. Much of that rise can be attributed to the arrival of new immigrants from all over the globe—Indians, Colombians, Ecuadorians and Peruvians in Jackson Heights; Dominicans, Colombians and Mexicans in Corona; Chinese, Koreans and Vietnamese in Flushing. Queens is the city's new melting pot—the new gateway to America. A ride on the number 7 train will confirm this. The first few stations (40th to 61st streets and Queens Boulevard) are in Sunnyside and Woodside, where the most recent influx of Irish immigrants has settled. It then proceeds along Roosevelt Avenue, stopping in Jackson Heights (74th Street), Corona (111th Street) and, finally, Flushing.

Above *New York's Chinatown, with its colorful street signs, is the largest in the United States, and has been home to immigrants from China, Taiwan, Korea and Vietnam for more than 150 years*

HISPANICS—SECOND IN STRENGTH

The 1961 movie *West Side Story* depicted the struggle of Puerto Rican immigrants living in New York, the city's first Hispanic community. Today, joined by nationals from Cuba, Ecuador, Colombia, El Salvador, the Dominican Republic and Mexico, Hispanics are the city's largest minority, representing 27 percent of the population. The Hispanic influence can be seen everywhere, from media and music to politics and cuisine. Turn on the TV and you'll find Telemundo and Univision offering Spanish talk shows and steamy soap operas. Scan a newspaper stand and you will see the Hispanic publications *El Diario/La Prensa, Hoy, El Nacional* and *El Tiempo*. Baseball teams are peppered with Hispanic names; the Latino music craze continues, as more artists cross over in the footsteps of Ricky Martin; and chefs deliver the latest Spanish and Latino cuisine at such hot spots as Pipa and Casa Mono.

BOLLYWOOD ON THE HUDSON

Before 1965 only a few South Asian students lived in the city, but after 1965, the Indian, Pakistani, Bangladeshi, Sri Lankan and Nepalese presence increased noticeably. Gradually Asian cuisine and music registered on the consciousness of New Yorkers. Now fusion is occurring between Asian cultures and those of other national origin. Witness Panjaba MC and Jay-Z's hit *Beware of the Boys*, in which hip-hop meets British *bhangra*. In the 1970s more Asian professionals settled in Queens. Jackson Heights became the principal commercial center, with Sam and Raj's appliance store opening in 1976 on 74th Street. Here are stores selling saris, South Asian DVDs, music and cooking staples. There are also several Hindu temples. And it's not uncommon to walk past venues like Madison Square Garden and see top Bollywood entertainers headlining their marquees.

TRACING AFRICAN-AMERICAN HERITAGE

A scholar interested in researching black history in New York would begin at the Schomburg Center on 125th Street. Documents here chart the growth of the community from 14,000 in 1830 to 1.96 million today, along with the lives of such famous black New Yorkers as abolitionists Henry Highland Garnet and Alexander Crummell, and civil rights leaders Adam Clayton Powell and Malcolm X. A casual visitor might start at the African Burial Ground at Broadway and Duane. Here, from 1712 to 1794, 10,000–20,000 black people were buried as they were excluded from the Trinity Church graveyard. Few traces remain of Manhattan's 19th-century black communities, but much is found in Harlem: the church where Adam Clayton Powell, Sr. and Jr. preached, at 138th Street; the mosque associated with Malcolm X; and many Harlem Renaissance sites.

UNDERSTANDING YIDDISH

Every New Yorker knows what *chutzpah, mensch* and *kvetch* mean, and what the difference is between *shlep, shlemiel* and *schmozzle*. New York has the largest Jewish community outside Israel, but it's not its size so much as its spirit that counts. The greatest number of Jews came in the late 19th century, fleeing pogroms in Russia and Eastern Europe and settling on the Lower East Side. Their story is told in Irving Howe's history, *World of Our Fathers*. A tale of struggle rewarded by success and assimilation, it's a journey seen in the contrast between Woody Allen's Jewish outsider and Jerry Seinfeld's totally assimilated incidental Jew. Successful Jews moved from the Lower East Side and Brooklyn to the Upper West Side and the suburbs. They became financiers, doctors, lawyers, stand-up comedians and schoolteachers, and passed along Yiddish.

Above *Immigrants from all over the world make a home in New York*
Below *The African Burial Ground at Broadway and Duane*

NEW YORK ARCHITECTURE

There are so many great buildings in New York that it can be overwhelming. Many of these have also been lost to redevelopment, and that too is overwhelming, but not surprising, given the city's commercial nature. Skyscrapers dominate the island of Manhattan, a building style made possible by the confluence of several factors—the geological bedrock, the availability of steel, and the techniques of engineering. City governments had always emphasized growth and innovation, which helped create such real-estate moguls as John Jacob Astor, William Zeckendorf, Harry Helmsley and Donald Trump. Zoning laws arrived only in 1916 and conservation came even later. Robert Moses razed whole neighborhoods, and between 1900 and 1965 many architectural gems were replaced with inferior substitutes. New Yorkers finally woke up in 1965, after Penn Station was demolished and replaced with the underground station there today. A Landmarks Preservation Commission was founded, but it still had to be re-affirmed by the Supreme Court in 1978 when the fabric of Grand Central Terminal was threatened with redevelopment.

BEYOND SIGNATURE SKYSCRAPERS
Yes, the Empire State and Chrysler buildings are two stunning skyscrapers, but they're not alone. The Bayard Condict Building (1898) on Bleecker Street is the only example of Louis Sullivan's work in the city. Later skyscrapers often incorporated elements from earlier eras, as did Daniel Burnham's Renaissance Revival Flatiron Building (1902). Raymond Hood's Radiator Building is a beauty—black brick and blue-green tiles with gold ornamentation. The Seagram Building on Park Avenue, by Mies van der Rohe and Philip Johnson, is a good example of 1950s modernism. Architects are still building the skyscrapers of tomorrow—Daniel Libeskind's design was chosen for the new complex to be built at the site of the former World Trade Center.

Clockwise from above *Grand Central Terminal is a magnificent public space and one of the city's finest landmarks; the Woolworth Building, designed by Cass Gilbert, has stunning interior decoration; tenements with their characteristic fire escapes in SoHo*

BROWNSTONES AND TENEMENTS

Besides skyscrapers there are plenty of other building types to appreciate. Brownstones—named after the sandstone from the banks of the Connecticut and Hackensack rivers—line the streets of Greenwich Village, Chelsea and other districts. Today they make elegant residences. In the mid-19th century, cast iron was used for the facades of factories, shops and warehouses, many in SoHo. They seem to be carved in stone, but are in fact some of the first pre-fabs ever made. The most spectacular examples are at Nos. 260–561 Broadway and Mercer Street in SoHo.

Humble tenements with fire escapes are also city trademarks. Built to house the 19th-century immigrants, they were narrow, cramped and unsanitary, but cheap—$2–$3 per month. Examples still line the streets of the Lower East Side and East Village. Today the rent is 500 times more.

MEWS, AND OTHER NOOKS AND CRANNIES

Visitors soon discover Midtown's pocket parks and plazas, but if you wander farther you'll find more charming oddities. Pomander Walk (West 94th and 95th streets), for example, is 16 two-story Tudor-style cottages. Sniffen Court, 150–158 East 36th Street, is a beguiling collection of brick carriage houses now used as residences. The Village has several oddities. The enclaves of Patchin Place (1848), West 10th Street, and Milligan Place (1852), on Sixth Avenue between West 10th and 11th streets, were originally built to house Basque waiters, who worked at the Brevoort House on Fifth Avenue. Later residents were more famous—among them e e cummings. Along Bedford Street, between Morton and Commerce, stands the narrowest house in the city—it's only 9ft (3m) wide and was home to Edna St. Vincent Millay in 1924.

SCULPTORS AND PAINTERS HELP TO GILD THE LILY

Visitors often focus on the number and size of Manhattan skyscrapers, failing to notice the many embellishments created by famous and not so famous stonemasons, sculptors and painters. Daniel Chester French adorned the US Custom House with monumental portraits of Asia, America, Europe and Africa. Reginald Marsh painted the interiors, celebrating the maritime wealth of the city. The lower facades of the art deco Rockefeller Center are encrusted with sculptures and bas-reliefs. Lee Lawrie's *Wisdom* hovers above the entrance to the G. E. Building, while inside José Maria Sert's mural, *Man's Conquests*, covers the walls. Portraits of Mary Pickford and Ethel Barrymore by Alexander Stirling Calder grace the Miller Building at West 46th Street and Seventh Avenue. French artist Marc Chagall adorned the Metropolitan Opera House with two murals.

CASS GILBERT

Cass Gilbert stands out as the designer of some of the city's most beautiful and luxuriant buildings. Venture into the Woolworth Building (1910–1913) at 233 Broadway, for example. Frank W. Woolworth, who paid the $15.5 million price tag in cash, certainly got his money's worth. The exterior soars 792ft (241m) without a setback. The interior decoration is stunning. The vaulted lobby is swathed in veined marble, gold leaf and mosaic, and decorated with humorous sculptures, including one of Cass Gilbert himself holding the building and another of Woolworth counting his dimes. Gilbert's other great building is the Beaux Arts US Custom House (1907) at No. 1 Bowling Green, a suitably grand repository for the wealth of the early city. He also contributed the New York Life Insurance Building (1907) at 51 Madison Avenue, between 26th and 27th streets, and the postmodern curtain wall Federal Courthouse on Foley Square (1936).

Most New Yorkers are not born in the city. They come to it. They come for many reasons, most of which involve dreams of success and the money, power and fame that follow. So the city is full of competitive people trying to make it on stage, in music, in real estate, on Wall Street, Madison Avenue or in any other arena. Even though many citizens seem to be in a constant state of "success overdrive," there are other factors that affect the rhythms of city life. New York is not monolithic. It's a cluster of neighborhoods, each with a different ambience and energy. The West Village wakes up late and operates at a slow pace; the East Village wakes up very late and parties very late; Washington Heights is loud and moves to a Dominican rhythm; Beekman Place is always subdued. The city may stay open 24 hours, but each individual neighborhood plays its own rhythmic variation.

EXERCISE, EXERCISE!
Although a recent study reported that 35 percent of New Yorkers are overweight or obese, you would not know it from the frequent sightings of earnest New Yorkers pumping iron or running on treadmills. Most executives receive a standard gym membership as part of their remuneration package and many have personal trainers, who show them how to work the machines and set their fitness goals. Of course, the Old Guard have their clubs, where they go to swim, exercise or get a massage—the Knickerbocker, the Union, the Colony or the Harmonie are examples. After these come luxury gyms like the Sports Club/ L. A. Average New Yorkers are more likely to join Bally Fitness or Crunch and take aerobics classes. It's all part of the endless regimen of health and beauty.

Clockwise from above *Yellow cabs first hit the streets more than a hundred years ago, in 1907; skateboarding and bicycling are popular ways to keep fit in Central Park; Trinity Church is one of the numerous places of worship in the city*

YELLOW CABS—LOVE OR HATE?

The average New Yorker rides the bus or the subway, but many prefer to hail a cab, one of around 13,000 licensed to roam the city streets. You can't miss the yellow chariots. They have been in business since 1907. Early operators were so corrupt that in 1923 a Taxi and Limousine Commission began issuing licenses. LaGuardia sold the first medallion for $10 in 1937. Today they cost as much as $379,000. Every immigrant group has driven cabs—initially Jewish settlers, Italians and Irish and more recently people from Russia, Africa, Haiti and South Asia. They often receive only 24 hours of instruction. Some cabs perform some wild maneuvers to grab passengers. The bulletproof partitions separating passenger from driver were installed in 1967. Most recently, touch-screen GPS units and credit card machines have been the cause of strikes.

NEW YORK SOLUTIONS TO SINGLEDOM

There are 100 million "singles" in the United States. Several million of them live in New York and many are looking for the perfect mate, supporting a veritable marriage market industry. Even in the 1860s, matrimonial brokers' ads ran in the press. For example, John Johnson and Co. offered services to "ladies wishing agreeable and wealthy husbands," and to men desiring "beautiful, rich and accomplished wives." If you scan the ads in the local media, you'll find little has changed. Now, though, individuals advertise themselves, posting photographs in such publications as *New York Magazine,* revealing their most intimate data online at itsjustlunch.com, or signing up for TV shows such as *Perfect Partner* and *Boy Meets Boy.* There are singles groups of all kinds, from speed-dating specialists to one for tall people only.

CONVENIENCE GREASES THE DAILY WHEELS

To the average New Yorker, speed and convenience take precedence over everything else. Time is, after all, money. So meals on the run are habitual. Workers en route to their offices and exercisers sporting Adidas, stop for an Egg McMuffin at McDonald's or coffee and a danish at Starbucks. At lunch, New Yorkers "order in" a sandwich or salad and soft drink, instead of going out for a leisurely meal. Or if they have a corporate cafeteria they go there. Some of these are extraordinary, the most famous being the Philippe Starck version at Condé Nast. If workers do go out, it will often be to "brown bag it," taking a sandwich to a park.

At night, they may go home and order a take-out from one of the many neighborhood menus that they keep by their phone—Thai, Chinese, Mexican, Indian, Italian or Japanese.

WORSHIP AT YOUR CHOICE OF ALTAR

Many visitors are surprised to learn how religious New Yorkers are and how many people attend religious services. From the city's founding it has offered an array of religious options, when Anglicans, Presbyterians, Quakers, Anabaptists, Jews, Catholics and Lutherans co-existed. Today, Christians, Buddhists, Hindus, Sikhs, members of the Jewish community and Muslims all have a place to worship in the city. If you want to understand a culture, attend one of its religious services. In New York, head to Harlem and hear the gospel choirs raising the roofs of the Baptist churches, or go to West 113th Street to the Mosque of Islamic Brotherhood. Take the train to the Hindu temples or Sikh gurdwaras in Queens, or drop in to one of the Buddhist temples in Chinatown. Or visit St. John the Divine or St. Patrick's.

THE ARTS

New York City leads the nation in arts and entertainment innovation and provision. It's the world's center of contemporary art, and also has a phenomenal collection of performing arts companies in dance, music and theater. The city's cultural groups have also led the way in finding innovative fundraising solutions to finance their endeavors. For years, although they have received some funding from government, city cultural institutions and groups have developed their own funding resources— private donors, bequests, memberships, bookstores and other types of ancillary profit center. The arts scene is constantly evolving. There is an uptown mainstream scene and a downtown more experimental scene, and within each shifts are always occurring—SoHo galleries migrating to Chelsea, for example. Don't worry, whatever excites you in the arts can be found in New York.

CULTURE AND MONEY

Wealthy dynasties have always served as patrons of the arts, and New York's are no different. Mayor Bloomberg donates a large part of his fortune to cultural institutions, as do many in the Social Register. Today, the money is likely to be dispensed by the 525 city-based foundations, which control $82 billion. These cultural donors are copying earlier magnates whose names still resonate throughout the city— Astor, Carnegie, Morgan, Rockefeller, Vanderbilt and Whitney. John D. Rockefeller gave away $1.5 million annually and launched the Rockefeller Foundation in 1913 with $100 million. His son, John, Jr., founded Rockefeller University and donated the Cloisters, Fort Tryon Park and the site for the United Nations building. John Jacob Astor left $400,000 for a library, which Brooke Astor, the wife of John Jacob's great-great grandson, still supports.

Clockwise from above *Visitors interested in contemporary art should head for Chelsea with its plethora of art galleries; the 1903 Lyceum is the oldest theater still in use on Broadway; names up in lights— Broadway shows are advertised in Times Square*

NEW YORK, NEW YORK, IT'S A HELLUVA TOWN

The film industry may have moved from New York to Hollywood after World War I, but it is still a film town, thanks to the renovation of old studios and the encouragement of the Mayor's Office of Film. Film-makers have long conducted a love affair with the city, sometimes using fake studio backdrops, as they did in *King Kong*, and other times filming the reality on location. The directors most associated with New York are Martin Scorsese, Paul Mazursky, Sidney Lumet, John Cassavetes, Spike Lee and Wes Anderson *(The Royal Tenenbaums)*. But the love affair goes back a long way to such films as *Miracle on 34th Street* (1947), *The Naked City* (1948) and *On the Waterfront* (1954).

If you are looking for an architectural tour of New York plus an insight into its collective unconscious, treat yourself to any Woody Allen film.

THEY STILL MAKE STEINWAYS IN NEW YORK

The name Steinway signifies the best pianos in the world, and it has done so since 1853, when Henry Steinweg started the company. The company was so successful that by 1873 the family was able to build a company town in Astoria, Queens, complete with factory, housing, a school and other amenities. At one time, the company made 6,000 grand pianos a year, but the industry collapsed in 1927 with the introduction of radio and the phonograph. The company survived, although the family sold it in 1972. Today it continues to operate with 450 workers, who handcraft about 3,000 grand pianos (and 600 uprights) a year, which cost from $25,000 to $147,000. Even though the year-long process is the same as it was in 1853, each one has a different musical personality, depending on the wood and other subjective factors.

CHELSEA—NEW CENTER OF CONTEMPORARY ART

Although the acclaimed Dia Center for the Arts has closed its Chelsea gallery and is looking for a new home, in the late 1980s and early 1990s it made Chelsea the new vortex for contemporary art, surpassing SoHo and 57th Street.

Since then, the area between 19th and 29th streets and 10th and 11th avenues has grown into a large gallery district with more than 200 spaces. All the former big names in SoHo and Uptown are now represented in the gallery district—Matthew Marks, Larry Gagosian, Mary Boone, Pace Wildenstein, Paula Cooper, Robert Miller, Barbara Gladstone, Holly Solomon and Sonnabend. Some galleries have vast hangar-like spaces, large enough to accommodate massive works produced by such artists as Richard Serra. In some cases entire buildings (529 West 20th Street and 526 West 26th Street, for example) now house multiple galleries.

THE CHALLENGE OF BROADWAY

Every year Broadway is reported to be teetering on the edge of economic disaster and accused of abandoning serious theater for warmed-over revivals. It's tough to make money on Broadway. Back in 1866, *Black Crook,* a musical melodrama, ran for only 475 performances and took in $1.1 million, easily recouping the $24,000 investment. Today a musical costs on average $8 million to produce and stage, and the show has to run for at least 520 performances just to break even.

When producers have to rely on tourists to fill the seats, it gets really tough. Success then depends on low costs, good press, a Tony Award and lots of luck. Few shows meet the test. In fact, about 80 percent of Broadway shows fail to recoup their investments. So producers turn to locations off- and off-off Broadway, where costs are lower and they can afford to nurture new playwrights.

Summarizing New York City politics is difficult. It's a complex city divided into five boroughs—Manhattan, Brooklyn, the Bronx, Queens and Staten Island—populated by around 8 million people of different ethnic origins and religious beliefs, and with diverse socio-economic interests. As a consequence, city politics are often contentious, with ethnic rivalries playing a large part in the political process. The municipal employee unions—police, fire, teachers, sanitation and transit—also play a major role in city politics and can make the city a more, or less, pleasant place in which to live and work. As far as national politics goes, New York City is firmly Democratic, even though it has voted for three Republicans in the last four mayoral elections. Only Staten Island votes pretty solidly Republican. The print media cut across party lines. The *New York Times*, the *Daily News* and *Newsday* lean toward the liberal side while the *Wall Street Journal*, the fledgling *New York Sun* and Rupert Murdoch's *New York Post* take a more conservative tack.

WHO'S IN CHARGE?

It's hard for outsiders to determine who is in charge. Under the federal system, the responsibilities are divided among the federal, state and municipal governments. Although there have been many powerful mayors—LaGuardia, Koch, and Giuliani in particular—their power is limited by the state governor, the state assembly and senate, the borough presidents and the city council, to name the major challengers. In 2009, for example, even though Mayor Bloomberg presided over a city with 38 percent of the state's population, he was battling Governor Patterson over the allocation of federal stimulus funds for health care.

The city lives under a tough set of fiscal rules imposed by the state 30 years ago, with four agencies monitoring city finances. If the city fails to balance the budget or pay its debt, the state will assume financial control.

Clockwise from above The New York Times *is traditionally a liberal newspaper; Madison Avenue is the powerhouse of the US advertising industry; Mayor Michael Bloomberg's 2003 ban on smoking in all public places did not go down well with New Yorkers*

EDUCATION IS THE TOPIC OF THE DAY

From the 1960s to the early 1990s crime and race dominated the headlines, but under Mayor Giuliani crime dropped dramatically and although race continued to play a divisive role, it diminished as a headline issue. Today, education is such a compelling issue that among the wealthy even getting into the "right" nursery school matters. Although there are top-notch schools (Stuyvesant, Bronx Science), the public (state) school system has been in crisis. It educates 1.1 million students in 1,200 schools. Bloomberg has staked his reputation on reforming it by streamlining the bureaucracy and imposing a standard curriculum. Now standardized tests have been implemented. Teachers and students are held accountable for good grades.

THE SMOKING EDICT

Mayor Giuliani disciplined New Yorkers for such "bad behavior" as jaywalking, panhandling, staging scatological art shows, squeegeeing and sleeping on, or occupying, two seats on the subway. Initially, New Yorkers grumbled, but came to appreciate the improvement in the quality of life that followed.

When Mayor Bloomberg tried the same, he ran into resistance, particularly when he banned smoking from all public spaces, including bars. Bar and nightclub owners, libertarians and dedicated smokers were irate. A few years on, everyone has calmed down. In fact smokers even admit to enjoying smoke-free interiors and the camaraderie of smoking outside with others. Business has not been adversely affected.

GOSSIP

Gossip has a high profile in New York City because power, money, sex and celebrity drive society and gossip helps keep score on who's in and who's out. Gossip may have begun with Mrs. William Astor and her 400 and continued on the zebra-striped banquettes at El Morocco and at Walter Winchell's table at the Stork Club, but now it's everywhere. It's not confined to the tabloids, either. They may not be called gossip columns, but that's what they are: the *New York Times* has "Boldface Names"; *New York Magazine* has "The Intelligencer"; The *New Yorker* calls it the "Talk of the Town" and *Town & Country* insists that it's "Parties." Tina Brown leavened *Vanity Fair* with it. Everyone has to read the *New York Post's* Liz Smith, Cindy Adams and Page Six. And it's becoming even more center stage, as the *Star* moves into Manhattan and gossip drives the content of glossies *U.S.* and *People*.

MADISON AVENUE

Madison Avenue may be the Golden Mile of designer retailing, but it is also synonymous with one of the largest and most important city industries. In 2002, a massive $117 billion was spent on advertising, plus $6.8 billion on focus groups alone. With consumer spending accounting for 60 percent of the national economy and 22,000 new packaged products being launched annually, advertising plays a huge marketing role.

New York City remains the advertising capital of the United States, because all the national TV networks and major publishing companies have their headquarters or offices here. Although the advertising companies are not necessarily on or near Madison Avenue anymore—Saatchi & Saatchi is at 375 Hudson in the West Village—they do need to be near media buyers and sellers, so that they can participate in the seasonal media buying frenzy.

In spite of their reputation as indoor-dwellers, vast numbers of New Yorkers have a passion for sunshine, fresh air and healthy outdoor activity. This trend has been growing in recent years, prompting the city to undertake one of its most ambitious projects to date. Although the New York Greenway is only partly completed (the whole project will take years), long stretches exist and are an urban oasis for outdoor lovers. Of course, the ultimate outdoor space in New York—the green heart of the city—is Central Park. On sunny days, New Yorkers flock to the park to stroll along the well-tended paths and enjoy the gardens, woodlands and open meadow-like spaces that offer an oasis away from the concrete canyons of Manhattan. The city has other popular parks too, including Riverside Park, Battery Park and the new elevated High Line park, which opened in 2009. New Yorkers are also rediscovering their love affair with the 500 miles (800km)-plus of scenic city waterfront. Water tours are springing up everywhere, as are boat rental and tour operations that offer a chance to paddle a canoe or kayak along the city's waterfront. And city dwellers have long known that a ferry ride to Staten Island offers a romantic way to see the city from the water.

Clockwise from above *The extensive waterfront offers many opportunities for walking; Conservatory Garden in Central Park is the city's oldest floral garden; the Liberty Island ferry affords tremendous views of the cityscape*

CENTRAL PARK

The Queen of Parks, this remarkable 843 acre (340ha) green space has been the verdant center of the city since it was designed and created by then-farmer Frederic Law Olmsted and architect Calvert Vaux in 1851. Today it entertains young and old alike with 58 miles (95km) of trails and bicycle paths, several lakes, open plazas, restaurants and plenty of quiet green nooks for relaxation. Favorite things to do in the park include visiting the 5 acre (2ha) wildlife center (zoo), renting a rowboat at the Loeb Boat House, attending a performance of Shakespeare in the Park at the Delacorte Theater, or enjoying refreshments in the garden at Tavern on the Green. Kids will love Conservatory Water where the fanciful sculptures based on *Alice in Wonderland* and Hans Christian Andersen stories are a big hit.

ROOFTOPS AND HIGH PLACES

One of the favored ways to get outdoors in New York is to enjoy dining or drinks in a rooftop garden. The quality of these is often expressed by the quality of the view and ambience of the gardens. The long-term champion on both counts may be the elegant Rooftop Restaurant which graces the fifth floor of the Museum of Modern Art and offers spectacular views of the Abby Aldrich Rockefeller Sculpture Garden and the city skyline. Another top contender is the über-chic 230 Fifth, which is the largest rooftop in the city. For a family-friendly venue, head to the Metropolitan Art Museum's Roof Garden Café.

ON THE WATER

One of the best ways to see the city is from the water, and there are many great options available for doing this. One of the best and cheapest ways to enjoy spectacular harbor views of the south end of the city and the Statue of Liberty is aboard the Staten Island Ferry. Best of all, it's free! Easily the most romantic of the many commercial harbor tours is the two-hour cruise aboard the beautiful sailing schooner *Pioneer*, which leaves from South Street Seaport. Do-it-yourselfers will also find numerous kayak rental operations that allow you to explore the city waterways under your own power, or join a guided tour to do the same.

SMALL PARKS AND GREENWAYS

Beyond Central Park, New York offers a wealth of other opportunities to enjoy the outdoors. The most impressive of these is also the newest. The New York Greenway will eventually be a dedicated pedestrian and bicycle route that will encircle the city and provide more than 350 miles (560km) of multi-modal cycling and jogging paths in Manhattan and the other four boroughs. Roughly half finished, many miles of the existing route follow the city's waterfront offering splendid views. The Greenway links several of the city's popular parks which are well worth exploring, including the beautiful and lush Riverside Park on the city's west side and the elegant Battery Park at Manhattan's southernmost tip.

FLORAL GARDENS

With the current passion for all things green, it's easier than ever to find flower-lined paths and fragrant green spaces within the city. One of the city's oldest and best-known gardens is the Conservatory Garden in Central Park which offers 6 acres (2.5ha) of floral abundance. New to the city is the open and airy British Memorial Garden in Lower Manhattan, which commemorates British lives lost on 9/11. Still, the best gardens lie just outside Manhattan. They include the phenomenal New York Botanical Gardens in the Bronx, as well as the lovely themed gardens that make up the Brooklyn Botanical Garden. And if you want to retreat from the world, the best place to do it is in the medieval monastic walled gardens of The Cloisters.

New York City has always been a money-making city. John Jacob Astor made his fortune in real estate, J. P. Morgan in banking, Cornelius Vanderbilt in transportation and John D. Rockefeller in oil. Today wealth is still made in finance, real estate and commodities, but the new money is in technology and communications and less in manufacturing and trade. Manufacturing has moved south or to Mexico and Asia, while the once mighty port business has shifted to New Jersey. New York is still the financial capital of the United States and the center of banking and insurance. The securities industry is vital to the city's economy. When it is booming, the city flourishes and when it declines, the city does too. When the dot-com bubble burst in March 2000 and was followed a year and half later by the tragedy of 9/11, the city suffered and by fall 2002 the city had a projected deficit of $5 billion. Under Mayor Bloomberg the city staged a remarkable economic recovery. However, the city deficit increased again with the economic recession that began in 2008.

SEVENTH AVENUE HANGS ON

From the 1930s to the 1950s, the garment industry was the biggest in the city. Cutters, pattern-makers and sewing-machine operators and button- and zipper-makers jammed the blocks between 36th and 38th streets from Madison to Eighth Avenue. (Seventh Avenue is called Fashion Avenue between 23rd and 42nd streets.) Today the only evidences of the trade are the racks being pushed along the sidewalks and the "seconds" bins. Most manufacturing has gone to low-cost countries like China. What remains is on the Lower East Side, and in Chinatown and Queens, where Chinese, Thai and Dominicans staff sweatshops. The Garment Industry Development Corporation is working to reinvigorate the industry.

THE NYSE, AMEX AND NASDAQ—THE THREE PILLARS

The New York Stock Exchange (NYSE), whose 1,366 seats are for sale by auction, is the most prestigious of the three. The first seats sold in 1868 for $4,000; in 2005 a seat sold for $3.5 million. Only the most carefully scrutinized companies—about 2,800 of them—are listed on the NYSE, which has a global market capitalization of $28 trillion and trades an average 1.6 billion shares every day. Those who could not afford to join the NYSE started the Amex. It was originally called the Curb Market because the brokers did their business at the curbside. It was acquired by NYSE Euronet (NYX) in 2008, and rebranded to NYSE Amex Equities in 2009.

In 1971 the National Association of Securities Dealers Automated Quotation (Nasdaq) was launched as the world's first electronic stock market. It lists 3,800 mostly high-growth companies.

Above *The Broad Street building has housed the New York Stock Exchange since 1903*

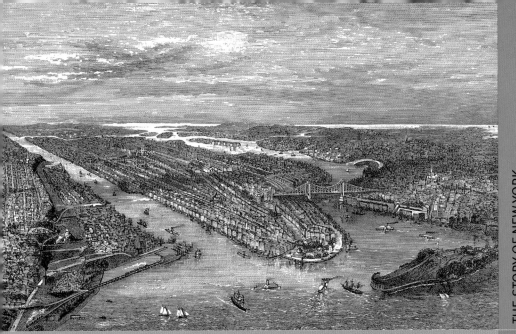

THE STORY OF NEW YORK

t' Fort nieuw Amsterdam op de Manhatans.

In the 16th century the area now known as Manhattan was a land of natural beauty, populated by wild animals and Native American tribes. Early explorers' engravings and vellum maps depict the hilly terrain and early settlements, including the Native American longhouses near Coney Island. In the early 16th century, Giovanni da Verrazano, a Florentine navigator and merchant working for the French, attempted to find the supposed Northwest Passage, a more direct route between Europe and Asia. Instead, he found himself sailing into the wonderful natural harbor that is now New York Harbor on April 17, 1524, and was greeted by the astonished native Algonquians. However, not much exploring went on until the arrival in 1609 of the English navigator Henry Hudson who reported to Europe on the quality of fur. The Dutch, recognizing the potential, went into business and brought traders to settle the area. One farm belonged to Jonas Bronck, whose name has stuck firmly to the area known today as the Bronx. In 1664 the English seized the territory and named it New York.

NATIVE AMERICANS

During the early colonial days, the Algonquians were often at war with each other and with the Iroquois. To protect themselves, the tribes lived in tight-knit groups under strong chiefs.

In the beginning, the Algonquians were a friendly people and showed the Dutch colonists where to hunt, farm and fish. The Native Americans enjoyed trading just as much as the Dutch, but then, as the colonists tried to take land away, fighting broke out. The Dutch attacked two encampments, killing 80 Native Americans, and started a very bloody war. Reports of this fighting got back to Holland, discouraging emigration to the New World.

Clockwise from above *Manhattan was named New Amsterdam after the Dutch took control; a view of Fort George and the early settlement of New York; Peter Stuyvesant's lack of a limb never held him back*

DUTCH COLONY

Peter Minuit bought Manhattan Island in 1626 for a cool $24 worth of kettles, axes and cloth. However, the Native Americans he paid did not share his concept of land ownership and did not understand the sale; furthermore, the transaction was made with the Canarsie tribe, who were merely passing by on that day. Dutch garrisons built a windmill, a fort, a barracks, a jail, a church, a tavern and a governor's house. There were about 120 houses by 1656, and about 300 four years later. Merchants and traders ran the municipal government and everyone was happy until the Dutch governor tried introducing measures to civilize the rowdy populace.

PETER STUYVESANT

The early colonists were a fairly lawless lot, and drunkenness and violence were common. Then, in 1647, the one-legged Peter Stuyvesant stepped in as governor. Under his strict control, law and order were established, along with a school, hospital, prison and post office. But Stuyvesant was not popular, and he eventually surrendered to English attackers, then returned to Holland in 1665 to defend himself against charges of misconduct. In 1667, he came back to his New York farm, the *bouwerij* that has given its name to New York's Bowery. Stuyvesant died in 1672 and was buried on his farm, now the site of St. Mark's Church-in-the-Bowery (▷ 120).

THE ENGLISH

In 1609 English navigator Henry Hudson had first sailed up the river that now bears his name. He drew attention to the abundance of otter, beaver, mink and wildcat and on the possibilities of the fur trade. In 1664, with 8,000 unhappy Dutch colonists living on the island, now known as New Amsterdam, Colonel Richard Nicolls easily seized the territory from the Dutch on the orders of King Charles II of England. The king's brother, the Duke of York, took control and changed the colony's name to New York. The terms of the surrender were generous, and not a single Dutch resident took Nicolls up on his offer to repatriate them. Nicolls became governor and was both efficient and popular. In 1673, when a war between Holland and England broke out, New York returned to Dutch control, but it bounced back to the English in 1674 under the terms of the Treaty of Westminster.

FREEDOM OF THE PRESS

German immigrant John Peter Zenger became the editor of the *New York Weekly Journal* in 1733 and quickly grew unpopular with Governor William Cosby. His opposition to the governor's arbitrary acts gained support from lawyers, merchants and others of independent spirit. In 1734 he was arrested for seditious libel. His lawyer, Andrew Hamilton, refuted the libel charge on the basis that the offensive article was not actually false. The court disagreed, stating that whether or not the publication was true was irrelevant and that merely publishing such wicked words about the government was enough to convict.

However, Hamilton's eloquent appeal to the judge and jury resulted in Zenger's acquittal and a victory for freedom of the press. This set a precedent against judicial tyranny in libel suits and thus led eventually to the First Amendment to the Constitution.

King's College, now Columbia University (▷ 203), was established in 1754 by royal charter of King George II of Britain. As the American colonies grew more independently minded, students such as Alexander Hamilton emerged to become America's patriot leaders. In 1765 a Stamp Act passed by Parliament in London taxed marriage licenses, playing cards, newspapers and 40 other necessities of life, and infuriated the colonists. Leading opposition to the Stamp Act, New York sent a formal protest to the king; 28 delegates from nine colonies attended the Stamp Act Congress in New York. After protests that included suspension of all port activity for nearly two weeks, Parliament repealed the Act in March 1766. New York joined the fight against taxation that led to the American Revolution. Although New York did not see a great deal of action, it was Britain's military headquarters and was the only city occupied by the British throughout the conflict. When the war ended, many loyalists left America for the West Indies or Canada and the population dwindled to 12,000. But within six years of the British departure, New York had become America's most vibrant city.

BRITISH OCCUPATION

The city's Tories, who supported the British Crown, were jubilant when British troops entered New York in June 1776. Patriots surrounded the city, denying the British easy communications with other colonies. Under military occupation, the city suffered terrible fires and loss of life and property. A fire on September 21, 1776 destroyed a quarter of the city, including Trinity Church (▷ 79). On August 3, 1778, 100 houses burned. The guerrilla war between the two opposing sides involved cattle-rustling, abductions and deliberate burning of crops. American prisoners of war were either incarcerated in a crowded, appalling dungeon on Liberty Street or in ships anchored in the harbor. Almost 11,000 soldiers perished in the horrendous conditions.

Above *The impressive entrance to the library of Columbia University*
Opposite *The inauguration of the first president, George Washington, on the balcony of Federal Hall*

DEFEAT ON LONG ISLAND

After forcing the British General William Howe to evacuate Boston in March 1776, General George Washington arrived in Manhattan on April 13. Knowing that he would meet General Howe's army again, forts were built in Brooklyn Heights and Lower Manhattan. On July 2, Howe's force landed on Staten Island. On July 9, the Declaration of Independence was read to Washington's soldiers on Bowling Green. The delighted soldiers and civilians tore down the statue of King George III and melted it down to make bullets—42,088 of them. Meanwhile, Howe's army moved to the south of Brooklyn, where his 20,000 British regulars surprised Washington's 7,000 militiamen. The Battle of Long Island, a terrible defeat for Washington, left 2,000 Americans dead.

BENEDICT ARNOLD

In today's United States, the name Benedict Arnold is synonymous with traitor. After Arnold had fought for General Washington against the British at Lake Champlain and in Connecticut, he was placed in command of Philadelphia in 1778. But he became disillusioned with Congress after he was overlooked for promotion. He knew British General Clinton was bribing Americans to desert and he began a treasonable correspondence with Clinton. He was in the process of making plans to surrender West Point, the military academy then under his command, to the British when the plot was revealed. Arnold managed to escape and became a leader of British troops in New York. After the British surrendered, Arnold and his wife moved to England, where they were deeply unpopular.

FROM GENERAL TO PRESIDENT

On November 25, 1783, General Washington made his ceremonial entry into New York and gave a farewell address to his troops in front of Fraunces Tavern at 54 Pearl Street, then returned to his home at Mount Vernon in Virginia. On February 4, 1789, he was unanimously chosen as president of the new United States at a convention in Philadelphia.

On April 30, 1789, Washington took the oath of office on the balcony of L'Enfant's Federal Hall, on the site of today's Federal Hall National Monument (▷ 67). Thousands of supporters lined Murray's Wharf at the end of Wall Street as Washington arrived by ceremonial barge. The cheering crowds, waving their hats, then followed him on his route through the downtown streets of the city.

THE TEA PARTY

The British Parliament approved the Tea Act in 1773, giving the British East India Company a monopoly on all the tea sold in the colonies. The angry Manhattan Sons of Liberty encouraged the public to repel the tea ships; New Yorkers boycotted all establishments offering East India tea.

On December 16, 1773, the Boston Tea Party, a protest in which a group of men masquerading as Mohawks dumped 342 cases of East India tea into Boston Harbor, further fueled radicalism in New York. Britain passed the Intolerable Acts which closed Boston's port, alarming New Yorkers. On April 22, 1774, New York had its own Tea Party and dumped 18 boxes of tea into the bay. This led to the establishment of the revolutionary government in New York State.

Savings Bank.   *Erie Canal.*   *Opera House.*

The first half of the 19th century brought New York conflict, epidemics and disaster, as well as an explosion of commerce and riches. During the War of 1812 between the United States and Britain, New York's port was blockaded. Ten years later, a yellow fever epidemic broke out in Front Street, and in 1832 a cholera epidemic killed 4,000. The Great Fire of 1835 gutted 700 buildings in a 17-block area below Wall Street; in 1845, another fire destroyed 300 buildings in Lower Manhattan. The achievement that brought growth, prosperity and international commerce to the city was the building of the Erie Canal in 1825, a project of Governor DeWitt Clinton. In following years, powerful men went from rags to riches practically overnight. Cornelius Vanderbilt (1794–1877), an uneducated Staten Island farm boy, became one of the wealthiest men in America when he took control of much of the shipping business in the harbor and along the Hudson River to Albany. The swelling city needed news. William Cullen Bryant, whose name is now associated with Bryant Park, became editor of the *New York Evening Post* in 1829. In 1841 Horace Greeley became the founding editor of the *New York Tribune*, while other newspapers also flourished.

KNICKERBOCKER

The word "knickerbocker" was a literary invention of author Washington Irving (1783–1859) in his *Diedrich Knickerbocker's History of New York* (1809). A satire on pedantry, manners, politics and history told by an imaginary Dutch colonist, Knickerbocker, it won Irving much acclaim in the United States and Europe. New Yorkers of Dutch descent, and by extension the entire city, became known as Knickerbockers. The group of writers including Irving, novelist James Fenimore Cooper and poet William Cullen Bryant was known as the Knickerbocker Group.

Clockwise from above *The Erie Canal gave the farmlands of the Midwest a route to the port of New York; engineer John Randel, Jr. devised the street grid system in 1811; John Jacob Astor bequeathed his library to the city*

ERIE CANAL

The Erie Canal, connecting the Hudson River and the Great Lakes, made New York the only eastern port with a waterway route to the farmlands of the Midwest, and instantly turned the city into America's thriving center of commerce. It was New York governor DeWitt Clinton who oversaw the $7 million project, which skeptics at the time called "Clinton's Folly."

The 10-day canal trip from New York to Buffalo meant that goods from around the world could be transported via New York to the interior of the New World. There was an explosion of new office space and warehouse development along the harbor, and New York began its career as a major world trading center.

ARTIST AND INVENTOR

By 1825, many of the most respected American painters were living in New York—that is, the ones who stayed in the country and did not go to Paris. A significant artist of the Romantic School and a successful portrait painter, Samuel F. B. Morse is best remembered as the inventor of the Morse Code.

He moved permanently to New York in 1824 and became a founder of the National Academy of Design in 1826. *The House of Representatives* (1822–23), one of Morse's most notable paintings, includes more than 80 portraits of politicians. By the early 1830s, he was more interested in electrical experiments than in painting, and in 1844 he tapped out in code the famous message, "What hath God wrought?"

JOHN JACOB ASTOR

By 1808, John Jacob Astor—who emigrated to America from Germany in 1783—had amassed a fortune in the fur trade and was the sole owner of the American Fur Company. When he grew fat and his health deteriorated, he sold the company and took up real estate. After he invested in farmland north of New York City, in what is now the heart of Manhattan, the city's rapid expansion turned his farmland into a goldmine. Astor House, the biggest hotel in the world at the time, stood on what is now City Hall Park (▷ 65) and was the first building to bear the family's name. The Astor Library, which he bequeathed to the city, is now part of the New York Public Library (▷ 159).

GRID SYSTEM

New York City's grid system of streets was devised in 1811, at a time when the population was increasing rapidly. In need of new streets for the undeveloped land north of Washington Square, city officials accepted the plans put forward by engineer and surveyor John Randel, Jr.

The commissioners dismissed the idea of ovals, circles or stars and opted for the economy of straight lines and right angles, while no street was to be less than 50 feet (15m) wide, and no main street less than 60 feet (18m) wide. The Commissioner's Plan called for 2,000 long, narrow blocks, disregarded the contours of the land, and provided for neither parks nor open spaces.

By 1875 more than a million people lived in New York. The poor, many of them recent immigrants, lived in tenements that bred hatred, violence and disease, especially tuberculosis. Jacob Riis published a book of photographs, *How the Other Half Lives* (1890), which called the public's attention to the atrocious living conditions. As a result, reformers like Theodore Roosevelt and Frances Perkins joined a crusade to rid the city of these inhumane dwellings. The enormous task of transportation in the growing city was a major problem. In 1858, about 35 million passengers used horse-drawn trams to move around. In the 1860s, trains were a welcome improvement. Washington Bridge, opened in 1889, made it easier to go from Manhattan to the Bronx. Commissioner George Waring reorganized the sanitation system and, in 1893, New York began chlorinating its drinking water. Progressive reformers brought education to immigrant children and they were offered free medical examinations in 1895.

Clockwise from above *Abraham Lincoln proclaimed the emancipation of slaves in 1863; immigrants poured into the city in the second half of the 19th century; a cartoon satirizing William Marcy "Boss" Tweed (1823–78), the corrupt politician who defrauded New York City of $30 million*

ELIZABETH BLACKWELL

Elizabeth Blackwell came from Bristol, England, to New York in 1832 to train as a doctor. She applied to eight medical schools before being accepted at Geneva Medical School. Graduating in 1847, she was ostracized by the profession because she was a woman. With great determination, she opened a dispensary for the poor in the slums of the Lower East Side. In 1857 she founded the New York Infirmary for Indigent Women and Children (the New York Infirmary). In 1868, after creating a training school for nurses, she founded the Women's Medical College of the New York Infirmary. She died in 1910, in Hastings, England.

SLAVERY

By the middle of the 18th century, New York had the highest concentration of slaves north of Virginia. They were sold at the slave market at the foot of Wall Street until slavery was abolished in New York State in 1827. But slavery was to continue, especially in the South, for another 38 years. New York provided a pivotal stage for its demise. On February 27, 1860, Abraham Lincoln arrived in New York City to give his celebrated antislavery address in the Great Hall of the Cooper Union Foundation Building on East Seventh Street, now a designated historic landmark. His eloquent defense of the Constitution and the call for the freedom of slaves helped him secure the Republican presidential nomination.

TAMMANY HALL

In 1850 William Marcy Tweed organized the formation of a volunteer fire department, a move which made him popular enough to get elected to city and state posts.

In the 1860s and 1870s, under Tweed's direction, corrupt politicians at the Democratic Party headquarters, Tammany Hall, ran the party by a combination of bribery, coercion and vote rigging.

Having swindled the city authorities at every opportunity, Tweed was finally caught after the Tweed Ring reneged on a deal with the sheriff, who went to the press with his story. *The New York Times* revealed the facts, and on November 19, 1873, Tweed was sentenced to 12 years in prison.

DRAFT RIOTS 1863

A dearth of volunteers for the Civil War led to conscription in 1862. In New York, as in other places, the draft met with great opposition and bounty hunters found substitutes for men who could pay. Others with $300 in their pocket could pay to be exempt.

The cost of living in New York had doubled and the mostly Irish dock workers had gone on strike for higher wages; they were furious when African-Americans were brought in to work. Under the circumstances the Irish workers could see no reason why they should be required to fight for black freedom and bitterly resented conscription. Four days of rioting in scorching heat ended on July 17, 1863, but not before 120 men had died, mostly African-Americans killed by Irish immigrant laborers.

JEWISH IMMIGRANTS

The first Jewish people, 27 of them, arrived in New York in 1633. The pogroms in Russia and Eastern Europe caused the great influx of Jewish immigrants at the turn of the 19th century. In 1892, around 81,000 Jewish people arrived at Ellis Island (▷ 72–74) and 258,000 more between 1905 and 1906. They crowded into the tenements on the Lower East Side (▷ 75), alongside the Irish, who had arrived in the country earlier and who resented the newcomers. Given that many of the police officers of the day were Irish, it is hardly surprising that Mayor McClellan's police commissioner claimed that 50 percent of the city's crimes were committed by Jewish people. The outraged Jewish community then forced him to make a full public retraction.

By 1900 Greater New York had a population of 3.5 million and was the world's second-largest city after London. In Manhattan, 42,700 tenements housed the 1.5 million poor in dire conditions. By the 1920s a campaign to restrict immigration resulted in legislation that brought a decline in the number of newcomers from Poland, Russia and Italy. The great metropolis experienced terrible disasters and celebrated remarkable triumphs. In 1901, a heatwave killed nearly 100 New Yorkers in just 24 hours. The first skyscrapers went up, starting with the Flatiron Building in 1902, symbolizing the city's wealth and hopes for the future. Writer John J. Fitz Gerald first coined the city's nickname "Big Apple" in 1921. Meanwhile, Prohibition drove New Yorkers to illegal speakeasies. Many went uptown to Harlem for nights of pleasure. Then, on October 24, 1929, the New York stock market collapsed, bringing the Roaring Twenties to a sudden halt. The resulting Great Depression lasted a decade. After World War II the city experienced an economic boom and became a major political player when the United Nations headquarters was established in the city.

HARLEM

Jazz flourished in Harlem in the 1920s and 1930s as white New Yorkers discovered establishments such as the Cotton Club, famous for its "Colored Revues" and as the home of Duke Ellington, the Great Orchestrator of Jazz. Ellington's band, the Washingtonians, and his arrangements dominated big-band jazz for three decades. In 1932, he wrote a song whose title served as a slogan for the next 10 years: *It Don't Mean a Thing If It Ain't Got That Swing.* Cotton Club owner Owney Madden, a gangster and bootlegger, strictly enforced segregation. The Depression took the swing out of these Harlem nightspots, and the Cotton Club moved downtown to West 48th Street, eventually closing in 1940.

Clockwise from above *New Yorkers got their kicks on Coney Island's Boardwalk, thanks to the subway; since 1904 the subway system has been an important factor in New Yorkers' daily life; Edwardian New York is apparent in the 20-floor Flatiron Building*

TRIANGLE SHIRTWAIST FIRE

Sweatshops in the Lower East Side at the beginning of the 20th century employed immigrant families in dreadful conditions on very low pay. Wages were increased after a series of strikes, but the tragedy of the Triangle Shirtwaist Fire in 1911 was to bring improvements in factory safety standards.

The factory, on the top three floors of a 10-story building at the corner of Washington Place and Greene Street, employed 600 workers, mainly young women. They were ready to go home when the fire broke out. Many doors to the fire escapes were locked, as was common during working hours, and 146 workers perished, some leaping to their deaths. Public outrage brought new legislation for safety in the workplace.

TIN PAN ALLEY

By 1900 New York was the place to be for the young, ambitious songwriter. Theaters were flourishing and music publishers needed as many songs as they could get their hands on. Hundreds of composers and small publishing firms crowded into the abandoned brownstones on 28th Street, between Fifth Avenue and Broadway, and the area became known as Tin Pan Alley because of the cacophony coming from the open windows. Two of the great songwriters of this era were George and Ira Gershwin, sons of Russian immigrants. At 15 years old, George was the youngest song demonstrator. The brothers' many hits included the classics *I Got Rhythm, Embraceable You* and *Somebody Loves Me*. George died of a brain tumor in 1937 at the age of 38.

THE SUBWAY

The elevated railways, financed by Jay Gould, Russell Sage and J. P. Morgan in the 1860s, improved public transportation, but were already inadequate by 1900. It was time to go underground. The Interborough Rapid Transit Company was born. The first line, 22 miles (35km) long, opened in 1904, carrying 600,000 passengers each day. It was a huge success and the profits enabled the city to expand the system. In 1921, New York and New Jersey joined forces to create the Port of New York Authority to develop and operate transportation. Delightful Coney Island, with its family entertainment, vaudeville and exhibitions, became accessible to everyone, thanks to New York's subways, which now total 660 miles (1,062km) in length, across 25 lines.

ORGANIZED CRIME

Just before Mayor William O'Dwyer, first elected as New York's mayor in 1946, began a re-election campaign, the *Brooklyn Eagle* published some extremely damning news about the mayor's connection to organized crime in the city. The newspaper charged that police officers and judges were being paid off in return for protection for 4,000 bookies. The mayor fled to Florida "for health reasons." In the hope of avoiding prosecution, more than 110 police officers resigned.

In August 1950, the mayor also resigned. Subpoenaed and left with little alternative, O'Dwyer had to admit he knew all about the corruption and that he too had associations with mobsters. Yet for a lack of hard evidence of willful wrongdoing, he went unpunished.

The years between 1950 and 2000 swung back and forth between economic booms (1950s, 1980s, 1990s) and financial crisis (1970s), and Wall Street struggled and soared with the times. New York's Abstract Expressionist painters inspired the art world in the late 1940s and 1950s; the Pop Artists shocked and thrilled the public from the late 1950s to the 1970s. Music and theater got a massive boost when the Lincoln Center was built in the 1960s. The number of Asian and Hispanic immigrants swelled, with Hispanics eventually overtaking the African-American population as the city's largest minority group. In 1989 the city elected its first black mayor, David Dinkins, who beat Rudolph Giuliani. Crime soared in the 1970s and 1980s, and vandals defaced landmarks and public buildings with graffiti. After Rudolph Giuliani was elected mayor in 1994, the number of recorded crimes dropped from 430,460 per year in 1993 to 161,956 in 2001, and the city had bright hopes for the future.

GREENWICH VILLAGE

By the 1950s, New York was America's cultural marketplace and Greenwich Village, with its cheap rents and bohemian flair, attracted America's finest artists and writers. Cedar Street Tavern at 24 University Place was the favorite Village hang-out for Abstract Expressionist painters Jackson Pollock, Willem de Kooning and Franz Kline. Regulars at the San Remo bar on the corner of Bleecker and MacDougal streets included writers James Agee, James Baldwin, Allen Ginsberg, Jack Kerouac and William Burroughs. It was here that the word "Beatnik" entered the language. Writers Dylan Thomas and Norman Mailer preferred the White Horse at Hudson and West 11th Street. Mailer's disregard for the Beats produced the Hip Generation.

Above *The Lincoln Center was part of a 12-block urban renewal project in the 1960s, replacing tenement buildings in the Upper West Side*

WOODY ALLEN

Allan Konigsberg changed his name when he started out as a comedian in Greenwich Village comedy clubs. He went on to make about a movie a year after 1965, most of them about New Yorkers. In 1977 for *Annie Hall* the brainy, scrawny actor and director won Oscars for Best Director and Best Screenplay.

He sometimes shows up on Monday night at the Cafe Carlyle (35 East 76th Street at Madison Avenue) to play clarinet with the resident jazz band.

His 1992 affair with and later marriage to the adopted daughter of his then partner, fellow actor Mia Farrow, shook his fans and seriously damaged his subsequent career.

ED KOCH

The Big Apple was in such dire financial straits in the 1970s that it seemed only a miracle could prevent a collapse. In October 1975, for instance, the city was only 53 minutes from defaulting on its almost $477 million debt. After the Federal government proved unwilling to extend a hand, money from teacher pension funds inched the city back from the brink of disaster. When Ed Koch ran for mayor, he vowed to restore prosperity. He kept his promise after winning the 1977 election, and was re-elected by a landslide victory in 1981. His tax cuts, along with changes to investment banking, restored corporate America's confidence in New York.

SWEET SUCCESS

In 1962, astronaut John Glenn, the first American to orbit the earth, arrived in New York and jubilant throngs lined Broadway for a tickertape parade, an honor bestowed only on visiting heads of state, generals, victorious baseball teams, athletes and great politicians. New Yorkers flung 3,474 tons of tickertape, more than anyone had ever seen before, from the windows of office buildings and skyscrapers along the route.

In 1969 the New York Mets rose from ninth place in the National League, defeating the Baltimore Orioles in the World Series and ending up with their first victory pennant. But they received only a tickertape flurry compared to the blizzard that welcomed John Glenn.

ANDY WARHOL

Pop Art changed the art scene when Andy Warhol opened his Factory in 1963. His Coca-Cola bottle, Campbell's Soup cans and multicolor silk-screen images of icons Marilyn Monroe, Elvis Presley and Jackie Kennedy were as astonishing at the time as the openly gay lifestyle he confidently espoused in an era when "homophobic" wasn't even a word. As a movie director he filmed *Kiss* and *Blow Job* in friends' apartments on the Lower East Side and in Greenwich Village. He lived as a recluse for the last 13 years of his life at 57 East 66th Street and died in 1987 rather bizarrely after routine gallbladder surgery.

Above *Woody Allen*
Right *Astronaut John Glenn was greeted with a tickertape parade*

New York City's financial situation was not rosy at the start of the millennium. Mayor Rudolph Giuliani had cut taxes by $3 billion, and the city was heavily in debt. Then came the terrorist attack on September 11, 2001, that killed nearly 3,000 people, destroyed millions of square feet of office space and closed the Stock Exchange for four days. Mayor Giuliani's courage and compassion was admired by all. For plain-speaking Michael Bloomberg, elected in 2002, Giuliani was a hard act to follow. The billionaire businessman won re-election in 2005. Bloomberg turned the $6 billion deficit into a $3 billion surplus. By late 2008 Bloomberg once again trimmed the budget to counteract the effects of the worldwide recession.

Above *Nightlife thrives in a city made safer and healthier by the reforms of its 21st-century mayors*

CRIME

In 2003, New York happily boasted that it was America's safest large city, and given its history of disturbing crime statistics, this is good news. New York was ranked 160th in total crime among 205 American cities. The 15-year trend of crime reduction, with homicides at a 40-year low, is continuing. It was the controversial, aggressive policing during the Giuliani years that helped to cut crime by 62 percent. The mayor beefed up the police force with 4,000 new officers and sent them out to tackle jaywalking, sleeping on subways, defacing property, and other petty crime and quality of life issues. Mayor Bloomberg has continued to fight crime.

SOCIAL REFORMS

Bloomberg's trend-setting social reforms have gained followers in municipalities across the United States and Europe. The smoking ban was extended in 2003 to include all commercial establishments. New York was the first city in the United States to ban trans-fat in all restaurants—the law was implemented in 2008. Bloomberg made education reform a top priority, and achieved an 18 percent increase in the high school graduation rate.

In 2007 he announced an aggressive program to improve the environment by reducing pollution and traffic congestion. Hybrid taxicabs will be one of the early changes, along with planting 1 million trees.

ON THE MOVE

On the Move gives you detailed advice and information about the various options for traveling to New York before explaining the best ways to get around the city once you are there. Handy tips help you with everything from buying tickets to renting a car.

ARRIVING

ARRIVING BY AIR

You can fly direct to New York from most major European, American and other cities around the world. International carriers fly into John F. Kennedy International Airport, 15 miles (24km) from Manhattan, on Jamaica Bay, and Newark Liberty International Airport, 16 miles (26km) west of town. LaGuardia Airport handles mainly domestic flights and is 8 miles (13km) from Manhattan in the borough of Queens.

Above *The city has three major airports*

TRANSPORTATION FROM MAJOR AIRPORTS		
	JOHN F. KENNEDY INTERNATIONAL AIRPORT (JFK)	**LAGUARDIA AIRPORT (LGA)**
Distance from Manhattan:	15 miles (24km).	8 miles (13km).
Journey time to Manhattan:	Taxi 45–60 minutes, subway 60–100 minutes.	Taxi 20–35 minutes, bus 40–50 minutes.
Ground transportation information:	Baggage claim level of all terminals.	Baggage claim level of all terminals.
Transport	**Shuttle/subway** ›› The subway costs $2.25 but you will need to buy a MetroCard (▷ 45). **AirTrain** ›› Buy your ticket ($5 each way) at the station, or from a vending machine in the airport. ›› The AirTrain connects to the LIRR at Jamaica station, subways at Howard Beach/JFK Airport station and Sutphin Blvd.-Archer Ave./Jamaica station, and local bus lines.	**Bus** ›› Follow the "Ground Transportation" signs out of the terminal. You will see the M60 bus stop sign at the curb. ›› The fare is $2.25, but you save on the transfer if you use a MetroCard (▷ 45). ›› Take the M60 to 106th Street at Broadway. ›› Get off at Lexington Avenue to catch the 4, 5 and 6 subway trains; at Malcolm X Boulevard for the 2 and 3 trains; at St. Nicholas Avenue for the A, B, C and D trains; at 116th Street-Columbia University for the 1 train. ›› The bus runs daily between 4am and 1am, leaving every 30 minutes. ›› For current information, visit www.mta.info/nyct/service/airport.htm

John F. Kennedy International Airport (JFK)

JFK has nine passenger terminals. Terminal 7 handles all British Airways flights, jetBlue uses Terminal 5, and Delta Terminal 2. There are information desks, restaurants and concession stands in all terminals. An AirTrain links the airport and the New York subway, local bus lines and the LIRR.

LaGuardia Airport (LGA)

Most domestic flights go through LaGuardia Airport, with United Airlines and Continental Airlines operating the lion's share. If you need assistance, look for the Customer Service Agents in their red jackets or go to the information desk between concourse C and D on the departure level. There are restaurants in the USAir and Delta terminals, which are accessible via a free shuttle service.

Newark Liberty International Airport (EWR)

Major carriers that fly into this airport include Virgin Atlantic, British Airways, Lufthansa and Continental Airlines. All passenger terminals— A, B and C—have restaurants on the concourse level, and the information desk is in Terminal B, lower level. The AirTrain system links the airport with the NJ Transit, Amtrak and Long Island Railroad (LIRR), and is quick and cheap.

LEAVING THE AIRPORT

After collecting your bags and going through Customs, you can get into the city in several ways (▷ below).

TAXIS

Taxi stands are outside all terminals. Dispatchers work peak hours at JFK and LaGuardia, and 24 hours a day at Newark. For more information, ▷ 53.

Tip your drivers 15 to 20 percent.
» At JFK, you are charged a flat rate of $45, plus round-trip tolls and tip.
» At LaGuardia, you pay by the meter ($24–28), plus tolls and tip.
» At Newark, dispatchers ask you where you are going. Give an address and you will be quoted the fare ($40–$75, plus tolls, tip and a $15 surcharge).

TIP

» Avoid airport hustlers offering taxi services. City cabs and car services are a better option from outside terminals in designated areas.

NEWARK LIBERTY INTERNATIONAL AIRPORT (EWR)
16 miles (26km).
Taxi 35–50 minutes, AirTrain 30 minutes.
On the baggage claim level.

AirTrain
» This modern speedy monorail/rail link operated by NJ Transit and Amtrak is comfortable, fast and easy, provided you do not have a lot of baggage.
» Follow signs to the AirTrain from any Newark arrivals terminal.
» Buy your ticket at the station (NJ Transit trains $14/children under 5 free) or from a vending machine in the airport or at the train station.
» The AirTrain takes you to Penn Station at Eighth Avenue and 31st Street in Manhattan.
» Do not get off at Newark's Penn Station if you want to go to Manhattan—stay on board until the next stop to reach New York's Penn Station. From there, you can easily catch a cab, the subway or a bus to your hotel.
» NJ Transit trains run two to three times an hour during peak travel times, once an hour off-peak.
» It is easy to make connections to destinations beyond Manhattan from the Newark International Airport Station. For details, phone NJ Transit 973/275-5555 or visit www.njtransit.com, or phone Amtrak 800/USA-RAIL or visit www.amtrak.com

ADDITIONAL INFORMATION

Telephone contact
The Air-Ride number, 800/247-7433, describing transportation to and from all three airports, is answered by an operator Monday to Friday between 8am and 6pm; at all other times you get recorded information.

NYC and Co.
810 Seventh Ave., New York, NY 10019
212/484-1200
www.nycgo.com

Contact NYC and Co. to order the *Official Visitor Guide* listing hotels, restaurants, theaters, attractions and events. The visitor's kit also includes a map, brochures, a newsletter and information on services.

PRIVATE TRANSPORTATION FROM MAJOR AIRPORTS
New York Airport Service
Express Bus
www.nyairportservice.com

Follow the "Ground Transportation" signs to the pick-up point outside the terminal.

☎ 718/875-8200

From JFK
This service runs between 6.05am and 11pm, and travel time is 45 to 65 minutes, longer during rush hour. The trip to the Port Authority Bus Terminal, at 42nd Street and Eighth Avenue, costs $15 ($27 round trip). The journey to Grand Central Terminal at Vanderbilt Avenue and 42nd Street or to Bryant Park costs $15 ($27 round trip), or $27 round trip to hotels between 31st and 60th streets. The service to New York's Penn Station costs $15 ($27 round trip).

From LaGuardia
This service runs between 7.30am and 11pm, and travel time is 30 to 45 minutes, longer during rush hour. The journey costs $12 ($21 for a round trip) to Port Authority Bus Terminal at 42nd Street and Eighth Avenue or Grand Central Terminal at Vanderbilt Avenue and 42nd Street or Bryant Park, and $21 for a round trip to hotels between 31st and 60th streets. From Grand Central there are onward connections from the 30-minute journeys to Penn Station (also $21 for a round trip from LaGuardia).

Right *A local bus on Madison Avenue*

USEFUL TELEPHONE NUMBERS AND WEBSITES
John F. Kennedy International Airport (JFK)
718/244-4444
www.panynj.gov
LaGuardia Airport
718/533-3400
www.panynj.gov
Newark Liberty International Airport
973/961-6000
www.panynj.gov

SuperShuttle
www.supershuttle.com

Go to the Ground Transportation desk and dial SuperShuttle on the courtesy phone in the baggage claim area of JFK, LaGuardia or Newark airports. Vans run 24 hours a day, throughout all five boroughs of New York City. Reservations are not required. The fares range from $20 to $30.

☎ 800/258-3826 or 212/ 315-3006

Coach USA
www.coachusa.com

Operating only out of Newark Airport, Coach USA takes passengers to Penn Station, at 34th Street and Eighth Avenue; to Grand Central Terminal, at Vanderbilt Avenue and 42nd Street; to the Port Authority Bus Terminal, at Eighth Avenue and 42nd Street; and to Chinatown and Lower Manhattan. The bus leaves every 15 minutes to Midtown and every 30 minutes to Lower Manhattan and costs $15 ($25 round trip); children under 12 ride free.

☎ 877/8-NEWARK (639275)

SECURITY AT CUSTOMS
Since 9/11, security has been stepped up at airports, tunnels, bridges and train stations. To facilitate departure, do cooperate. Do not carry sharp items on your person or in your carry-on bags.

Empty your pockets into the tray provided before walking through the security detection scanner. Be prepared to open your bags to be hand searched or remove your shoes for inspection or to allow a security officer to scan your body with a hand-held scanner.

ARRIVING BY ROAD
Driving into Manhattan is not for the faint-hearted and once you've got into the city, you then have the problem of finding somewhere to park. Always expect lengthy delays on the bridges and tunnels that cross to the island of Manhattan, especially on the bridges that cross the East River (repairs are ongoing). It is best to avoid the morning, lunchtime and evening rush-hour traffic if you can.

ARRIVING BY RAIL
Most commuter trains operating from Connecticut and the suburbs north of the city serve Grand Central Terminal (on 42nd Street at Park Avenue, ▷ 156–157).

Amtrak's long-distance trains from across the United States pull into Penn Station at 31st Street and Seventh Avenue.

For journeys to and from Long Island and New Jersey, the Long Island Railroad and New Jersey Transit are the trains to catch, also operating out of Penn Station.

The best way to see Manhattan is on foot. Streets in most Manhattan neighborhoods are safe both by day and after dark. However, walking takes time, and if you want to visit several museums or neighborhoods, or if the weather is bad, the subways are a better option. They are easy to use, inexpensive, and relatively clean and safe. Buses are more pleasant than subways because you get a chance to see street life as you travel, although you need to pay with correct change, and during rush hour traffic slows your progress—sometimes it's faster to walk.

OPTIONS

If you will be in New York for seven days or more, buy a MetroCard to save money on transit fares. You swipe the card at the subway turnstile or as you get on the bus, and you do not have to worry about having the correct change. Taxis are the quickest way for many to travel but the most expensive. When you take a cab, don't forget to tip the driver 15 percent or more.

Driving your own car in New York is not usually the best option for getting around. Besides the traffic, you will need to park on the street, and garages are expensive. If you do arrive in New York by car, the best course is to leave your car in a garage until you are ready to leave town (head for the eastern or western fringes of Manhattan if saving money matters more to you than convenience).

WALKING IN NEW YORK

>> Always use crosswalks; jaywalking is against the law.
>> Stay to the right as you would when driving.
>> When the light changes and you are about to cross, check the intersection to make sure that no drivers or bicyclists have decided to make a dash through the light. This is not uncommon.

METROCARD

What is it?
A magnetically encoded card that debits the fare when you swipe it through the turnstile in the subway or the fare box on a bus.

What about transfers?
When you use a MetroCard for a trip, transfers between subways and buses within a two-hour period are free.

Where can I buy one?
From staffed subway booths (cash only), special vending machines in most subway stations (cash, credit cards, debit cards), drugstores like Rite Aid, Hudson News at Penn Station and Grand Central Terminal, or at the Times Square Visitors Center at 1560 Broadway between 46th and 47th streets (cash, credit cards, debit cards). Many hotels sell them, too.

What's the cost?
Pay-Per-Ride MetroCard: choose how many rides to buy when you purchase the card. Cards can be swiped four times in succession, so are good for up to four people traveling together. Just swipe, walk through, and hand the card to the person behind you, who swipes, walks through, and hands it to the person behind. You can refill these cards—that is, put more rides on them—in the vending machines located in most subway stations. Just put the card in, indicate how much money you want to spend, and insert your credit card or cash.

Unlimited Ride MetroCard: $8.25 buys a 1-Day Fun Pass, $27 buys a 7-Day Card, $89 buys a 30-Day Card. These can't be used by more than one person—an 18-minute interval must elapse between successful card swipes at the same station. These cards go into effect the first time you use them, not the day you buy them.

Can I get a discount?
Seniors and visitors with disabilities can get reductions; phone 718/243-4999.

How do you use a MetroCard?
When you swipe your card, the turnstile indicator shows how much money is left on the card. If you swipe the card too fast or too slowly, the indicator asks you to swipe it again. If this happens, swipe it again. Do not go to a different turnstile, as you may end up paying twice.

Where can I get more information?
Phone 212/638-7622, from Monday through Friday between 9am and 5pm or visit www.mta.nyc.ny.us/metrocard

THE SUBWAY

The Metropolitan Transit Authority (MTA) runs the subway system. It runs 24 hours a day, seven days a week. Rush hour is roughly between 7.30 and 9.30am and again from 4.30 to 6.30pm Monday through Friday except holidays. The subway is quick, inexpensive, efficient, generally safe, and fairly easy to figure out.

TIP
» New Yorkers refer to subway lines as trains. "Take the A train" means "Take subway line A."

Fares are $2.25 ($1.10 for seniors and people with disabilities); children under 44 inches (1.12m) ride free. The best way to pay is by MetroCard (▷ 45).

A campaign promotes polite behavior: posters ask passengers to give their seats to the elderly and infirm, to move to the center of the train so as not to block the doors, and to walk rather than run.

SUBWAY HELP
» Station clerks are very helpful, and many subway stations are manned.

» For help in English, call 718/330-1234, 24 hours a day.
» For help in other languages, call 718/330-4847, between 7am and 7pm.

FINDING A SUBWAY
» In the station look for the signs with colored circles showing the subway line letter (A, B, C, etc.) or

UNDERSTANDING THE SUBWAY MAP

MTA maps are free and easy to understand. You can get them in any subway station, at information centers and in hotel lobbies.

The map (▷ 47) shows each line as a different color, but it is the number or letter that you need to know. No one refers to trains by color.

Solid black circles on the colored lines indicate stops for local trains, which make more stops than express trains.

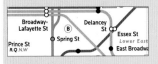

Black and white lines connecting white and black circles indicate free subway transfers.

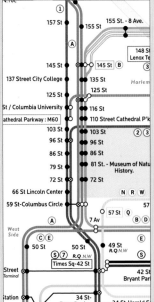

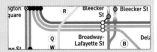

White circles on the colored lines indicate express train stops. Express trains skip about three stops for every one they make.

Below the name of every stop, the letters or numbers of the lines that stop there are indicated. Boldface type, for example **B**, indicates that the line offers a full-time service. Lightface type, for example B, indicates a part-time service. At 72nd Street, you see B, **C**, indicating part-time service on line B and full-time on C.

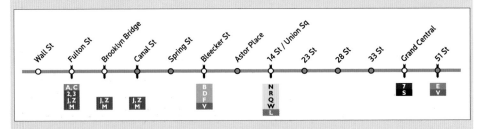

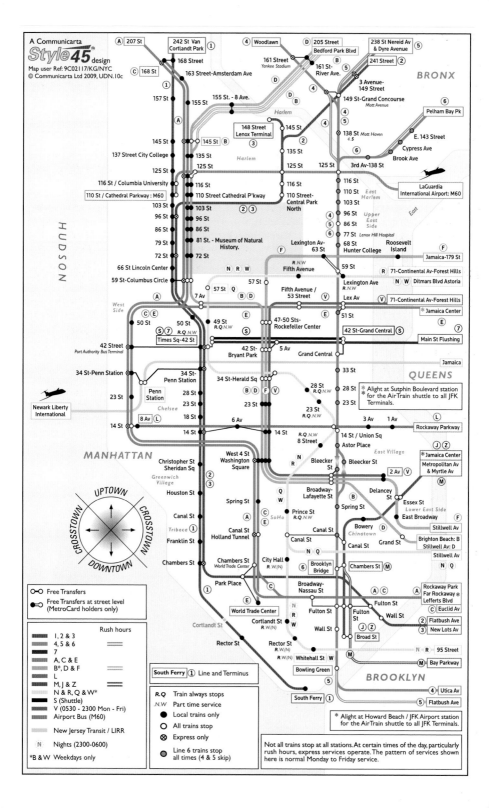

the subway line numbers of the trains that stop there.

» If you need help finding a subway station, ask a policeman or step into a hotel lobby, museum or store to ask. Most people working in such places are used to helping tourists but even regular New Yorkers on the street do so quite happily.

TIP

» The Lower East Side and the East Village are not well served by subways. If you are traveling to or from these areas at night, it is best to take a taxi.

FINDING THE RIGHT SUBWAY LINE

» After you have paid and walked through the turnstile, look for the colored circles. Find the line you want, and follow the signs. Above the platform edge, signs indicate the trains that stop there, their destinations and hours of operation. Changes to the line's service are usually posted, but signs are not very large, so you need to look carefully.

» Uptown or downtown? If you want to go north of where you are, no matter where in the city you happen to be, you want an uptown train. If you want to go south of where you are, you want a downtown train. Some stations are Uptown Only or Downtown Only—clearly marked at street level. If you find the color circle with the number or letter you want and know that you want to go north, for example, do not go into a subway entrance marked Downtown Only—any train you catch there will take you in the opposite direction. Trains headed in the right direction are nearby—the entrance is usually across the street.

» On the front and side of every train, the route number or letter is displayed. Make sure you look for this before getting on the train to be sure it is the one you want.

» If you really want to be sure, stand in the middle of the platform, halfway between the two ends of the train, and when the train

HOW TO USE THE SUBWAY

» Although the New York subway once had a bad reputation for safety, trains are now safer and cleaner. However, pickpockets and beggars are perennial, so keep a close eye on your bags. Keep your money well hidden and do not wear expensive jewelry or even jewelry that looks expensive.

» Do not wait for trains near the edge of the platform; stand back a bit.

» If there are few people on the platform or if you are alone, stand under the yellow sign "During Off Hours Trains

Stop Here." When the train stops, the conductor sticks his or her head out the window from a middle car, which is where he or she rides, and you should, as well.

» Let passengers get off first before getting on.

» Stay out of empty cars.

» After 11pm or midnight, take a taxi until you know your way around in the subway.

» If you find yourself on an express train speeding past your destination, get off at the next stop and either take the same line back to where you got on or ask the station clerk for directions. Be prepared to pay an extra fare to re-enter the platform; at some stations, you may need to exit the station, cross the street, and re-enter the station on the other side to catch the train that's going in the right direction for you.

rolls into the station, look for the conductor leaning out of a window in the center car—he or she can tell you where the train is headed.

KNOWING WHEN TO GET OFF

» Conductors make announcements before each stop. On new trains, these are recorded.

» Every subway car has a map posted on the wall by a door, so you can make sure you are traveling in the right direction and can see how many stops you need to go.

» Look for signs on the station walls as you pull into the station.

LEAVING THE SUBWAY

After you get off the train, go upstairs (usually a stairway, but sometimes an escalator). You have to go through the turnstiles to exit the station, but you do not need to use your MetroCard again. Make sure you choose the right exit for your destination.

DISRUPTIONS

» Subway lines are occasionally closed or re-routed for maintenance or construction work. Weekly service advisories for all lines are posted on the MTA website and alternative route directions are given (www.mta.info/nyct/service/advisory.htm).

» Weekend service is sometimes altered on some lines to allow for maintenance. Announcements are posted in the affected stations.

IN CASE OF EMERGENCY

» Look for a police officer. The Transit Bureau Police patrol the subways.

» Look for a telephone and call 911. This is a free call.

» Go to the station clerk in the booth.

» On the subway train, make your way to the middle of the train to find the conductor or to the front of the first car to find the operator.

TRAVELERS WITH DISABILITIES

Not all subways are wheelchair accessible. You can find information on the 30 or more stations that are by visiting www.mta.nyc.ny.us

Above *An elevated section of the subway*
Left *Using a ticket machine at Times Square subway station*
Opposite *A line 6 train arrives at Grand Central subway station*

TRAINS MOST USEFUL FOR VISITORS	
4, 5 and 6	The trains run up and down the east side of Manhattan, to the Bronx and to Brooklyn.
1, 2, 3, A, B, C, D, E and F	The trains run up and down the west side of Manhattan, to the Bronx and to Brooklyn.
N, R, Q and W	The trains run from Brooklyn and Queens in and out of Manhattan.
S	The train runs between Times Square and Grand Central Terminal, operating as a shuttle.
L	The train runs across 14th Street to Brooklyn.

BUSES

The Metropolitan Transit Authority (MTA) runs the city's buses, and fares are the same as for subways (▷ 46–49). You can use your MetroCard (▷ 45) or exact change to pay for your ride. Bus drivers do not give change, so travel with plenty of quarters if you do not buy the more practical and economical MetroCard. Buses are slower than subways. Buses run 24 hours a day on most routes but less often at night, and on weekends. Drivers are helpful, so if you need advice, don't be afraid to ask.

FINDING A BUS

» Go to a designated bus stop, recognized by the yellow-painted curb and blue-and-white sign.
» Look at the posted Guide-A-Ride boxes, showing the route map and service schedule.
» Most major avenues have their own bus routes, running north or south.
» Stops for crosstown buses, running east and west, are strategically located on major streets across Manhattan.

GETTING ON AND OFF

Board buses at the front. Swipe your MetroCard or pay in exact change. Leave seats in front for the elderly, the infirm and adults with small children. You will notice a tape strip above and beside the windows. To indicate to the driver where you wish to get off, push on this about one block before your stop. Front doors open automatically; to exit by the back, wait for the green light to go on above the doors. Press the yellow tape on the doors to open them.

WHICH BUS TO TAKE

The routes given below are the ones most used by visitors for the main attractions. If you need further guidance, see the Bus Buster Chart (▷ 52), or pick up an MTA bus map from any visitor center (▷ 282), subway station or hotel lobby.

North–South buses

» M1, M2, M3 and M4 basically run north up Madison and south down Fifth. These buses take you to the museums along Fifth Avenue, also

ADDRESS LOCATOR

To locate the cross street of an address on an avenue:

» Drop the last digit of the street number.

» Divide by 2.

» Add or subtract the number given below.

» The answer is approximately the nearest number cross street (for example 54th Street).

Avenues		
A, B, C, D, First, Second add 3		
Third, Eighth	add 10	
Fourth	add 8	
Sixth	subtract 12	
Seventh	add 12	
Ninth	add 13	
Tenth	add 14	
Amsterdam	add 60	
Broadway	(23rd to	
	192nd St)	subtract 30
Fifth	up to 200	add 13
	up to 400	add 16
	up to 600	add 18
	up to 775	add 20
	up to 1286	drop last digit
		and subtract 18
	up to 1500	add 45
	above 2000	add 24
Central Park West		divide by 10
		and add 60
Columbus		add 60
Lexington		add 22
Madison		add 26
Park		add 35

called Museum Mile; M4 travels as far north as The Cloisters in Fort Tryon Park (▷ 260–261).

» **M5** runs from Houston Street north along Sixth Avenue, then up Riverside Drive and Broadway to Washington Heights.

» **M6** runs from Central Park South down Broadway to South Ferry, through Times Square, Union Square, Greenwich Village, SoHo and the Financial District, then back up Sixth Avenue.

» **M7** runs between Union Square and West 146th Street/Malcolm X Boulevard. It runs up Sixth Avenue, over Broadway, up Amsterdam Avenue, and across Central Park North, then up to 146th Street. On the return, it travels south on Columbus, Seventh Avenue and Broadway back to Union Square.

» **M9** runs from Union Square to Battery Park along Manhattan's Lower East Side.

» **M10** runs from West 31st Street/ Seventh Avenue (Penn Station) to West 159th Street/Frederick Douglass Boulevard. It travels up Central Park West, stopping at the American Museum of Natural History.

» **M11** runs along the west side of Manhattan, north on Tenth Avenue/

Amsterdam Avenue right up into Harlem.

» **M15** runs from South Ferry, north along the East Side to Second Avenue/East 126th Street.

» **M60** runs from West 106th Street/ Broadway to LaGuardia Airport.

» **M100** runs from West 220th Street/Broadway to East 127th Street/Second Avenue.

Crosstown buses

» **M8** runs from Avenue D to West Street through the East Village and Greenwich Village.

» **M14A** and **M14D** run from the Chelsea Piers to the Lower East Side.

» **M27** runs between West 41st Street/Eighth Avenue (Port Authority Bus Terminal) and East 42nd Street/ First Avenue.

» **M34** runs from Jacob Javits Convention Center at 11th Avenue/ West 34th Street to the Ferry Terminal at East 34th Street.

» **M42** runs along 42nd Street from Circle Line Pier to the United Nations Headquarters.

» **M72** runs from the Upper West Side to the Upper East Side from West 68th Street/Freedom Place to East 72nd Street/York Avenue.

» **M79** runs from West 79th Street/ Riverside Drive to East 79th Street/ East End Avenue.

SAFETY

Buses are safe throughout the day and the early hours of the night, but after 10pm it is best to take a taxi rather than wait for a bus on a deserted street. If a beggar asks you for money, just shake your head and do not get embroiled in conversation.

TRAVELERS WITH DISABILITIES

Buses are equipped with wheelchair lifts, and drivers can make the buses "kneel" by lowering the front step of the vehicle for people who have difficulty getting on.

Left *A typical bus stop*
Opposite *New York City Port Authority Bus Terminal*

MAIN TOURIST BUS ROUTES

Certain bus routes link key attractions. All routes shown are circular (north to south section of M15 shown only). Start and end stops are given as well as stops near to main attractions.

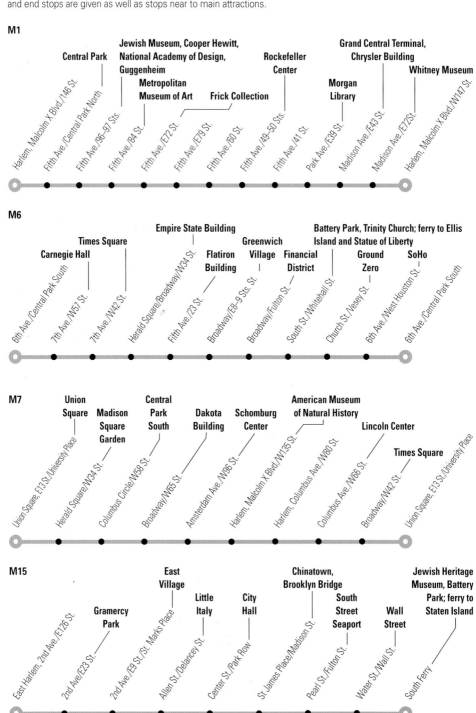

M1

- Central Park
- Jewish Museum, Cooper Hewitt, National Academy of Design, Guggenheim
- Metropolitan Museum of Art
- Frick Collection
- Rockefeller Center
- Morgan Library
- Grand Central Terminal, Chrysler Building
- Whitney Museum

Harlem, Malcolm X Blvd./146 St. · Fifth Ave./Central Park North · Fifth Ave./96–97 Sts. · Fifth Ave./84 St. · Fifth Ave./E72 St. · Fifth Ave./E79 St. · Fifth Ave./60 St. · Fifth Ave./49–50 Sts. · Fifth Ave./41 St. · Park Ave./E39 St. · Madison Ave./E43 St. · Madison Ave./E72 St. · Harlem, Malcolm X Blvd./W147 St.

M6

- Carnegie Hall
- Times Square
- Empire State Building
- Flatiron Building
- Greenwich Village
- Financial District
- Battery Park, Trinity Church; ferry to Ellis Island and Statue of Liberty
- Ground Zero
- SoHo

6th Ave./Central Park South · 7th Ave./W57 St. · 7th Ave./W42 St. · Herald Square/Broadway/W34 St. · Fifth Ave./23 St. · Broadway/E8–9 Sts. St. · Broadway/Fulton St. · South St./Whitehall St. · Church St./Vesey St. · 6th Ave./West Houston St. · 6th Ave./Central Park South

M7

- Union Square
- Madison Square Garden
- Central Park South
- Dakota Building
- Schomburg Center
- American Museum of Natural History
- Lincoln Center
- Times Square

Union Square, E13 St./University Place · Herald Square/W34 St. · Columbus Circle/W58 St. · Broadway/W65 St. · Amsterdam Ave./W96 St. · Harlem, Malcolm X Blvd./W135 St. · Harlem, Columbus Ave./W80 St. · Columbus Ave./W68 St. · Broadway/W42 St. · Union Square, E13 St./University Place

M15

- Gramercy Park
- East Village
- Little Italy
- City Hall
- Chinatown, Brooklyn Bridge
- South Street Seaport
- Wall Street
- Jewish Heritage Museum, Battery Park; ferry to Staten Island

East Harlem, 2nd Ave./E126 St. · 2nd Ave./E23 St. · 2nd Ave./E9 St./St. Marks Place · Allen St./Delancey St. · Center St./Park Row · St. James Place/Madison St. · Pearl St./Fulton St. · Water St./Wall St. · South Ferry

TAXIS AND CAR SERVICES

New York's official taxicabs are licensed by the Taxi and Limousine Commission (TLC). They are easily recognizable; they are always yellow, always display the rates on the door, and always have a light on the roof and a flat bronze medallion on the hood. Do not get into any other taxi; only yellow cabs with the distinctive markings are legally licensed. Car services operated by private companies are available at an hourly rate and must be arranged in advance; they are not allowed to pick up passengers who hail them. Limousines are also available to rent.

HOW TO GET A TAXI

You can hail a taxi on any street by holding out your arm at the curb. When the light on the roof is turned on, the taxi is available, unless the "Off Duty" lights are also turned on. Usually you don't have to wait long before getting one, but it sometimes takes a while—after the theater, in the theater district and just about anywhere with the approach of rush hour time (4pm). Try to hail a taxi in the direction you would like to travel, which saves travel time and money. The best way to direct the driver is by giving the cross street and the avenue—for example, 42nd Street and Fifth Avenue. As you get closer to your destination, you can let the driver know the exact address. Many taxi drivers do not have a great command of the English language, so speak clearly and not too quickly when giving addresses.

HOW MUCH IS THE FARE?

» As soon as you get into the cab, the meter is turned on; this flag-drop fare is $2.50.

» After that, it's 40 cents for every one-fifth mile (0.3km) or 40 cents per minute in stopped or slow traffic.
» Tolls at tunnels and bridges cost extra. The driver may ask you for the toll money as you approach or may pay it himself then charge you at the end of the journey. Tolls range from $8 to $16. For more information on toll charges, visit www.panynj.gov
» Between 8pm and 6am, you pay a night surcharge of 50 cents; during weekday peak hours from 4 to 8pm the surcharge is $1.
» Tip your driver between 15 percent and 20 percent on the fare excluding tolls.
» Note down the taxi driver's four-digit medallion identity number, which is posted on the divider behind the driver's head and ask for a receipt. These will be useful if you accidentally leave one of your possessions in the taxi or if you want to make a complaint.
» There is no extra charge per passenger, but taxis cannot take more than four people. There is also no extra charge for luggage.

KNOW YOUR RIGHTS

Drivers are required by law to:
» Be polite;
» Take passengers anywhere in the five boroughs, to Westchester and Nassau counties, and to Newark Airport;
» Provide air conditioning;
» Turn off the radio if asked;
» Refrain from smoking while a passenger is in the taxi.

For full information on the Taxi Rider's Bill of Rights, call the 24-hour Consumer Hotline 212/NYC-TAXI or visit www.nyc.gov/taxi

TRAVELERS WITH DISABILITIES

Taxis are required to carry passengers with folding wheelchairs, as well as those with guide dogs and therapy dogs.

CAR SERVICES

Most car services have a two-hour minimum rental period and rates start at $42 per hour. Try Allstate Car and Limousine Service (tel 212/741-7440), Carmel (tel 212/666-6666) or Dial 7 (tel 212/777-7777). The Yellow Pages has a complete listing. Alternatively, you can contract with a car service, through a concierge. It might be possible to agree a pre-set rate for a specific trip.

TIP

» Fasten your seatbelt. All taxis are required by law to provide them and passengers in the front seat are required to wear them.

Left *A distinctive yellow New York taxi*

DRIVING

Driving in New York City is not for everyone. Garage parking runs to $40 a day or more, and finding on-street parking is nearly impossible; restrictions are designed to discourage drivers from using their cars. Plus tow trucks are out in force, and to get your car back if it's towed, you have to pay a hefty fine—in cash, often in a neighborhood you would rather not visit. Traffic is taxing during rush hours, between 7.30 and 9.30am and again from 4.30 to 6.30pm. Drivers are aggressive, unpredictable, or both.

DRIVING CUSTOMS AND LAWS

» Most streets in New York are one-way. Newcomers from Britain and Australia need to remember to drive on the right.

» No right turn is permitted on red lights in New York City.

» Drivers must wear seatbelts. By law, front-seat passengers and children aged 4 to 10 in the back seat must also wear them. Children under 4 ride in child safety-seats.

» Passing (overtaking) is permitted on the inside and outside lanes of Interstate Highways.

PARKING

» Check street parking signs carefully. For street cleaning, parking is prohibited on alternate sides of the street on different days.

» For on-street parking you may need to feed the parking meter with change, sometimes on an hourly basis. In Midtown, look for Mini Meters, kiosks that dispense timed parking chits to leave locked inside your car, visible to parking inspectors.

» Do not park within 15ft (4.6m) of a fire hydrant.

» Never leave anything inside a parked vehicle, not even in the trunk (boot). Even an empty shopping bag can provoke a thief's curiosity—and lead to a broken window or locks.

» Parking garages are easy to find but in the range of $15 for the first hour to $40 a day, with special rates if you arrive before 10 or 11am. Midtown is the priciest area; to save money, park closer to the rivers.

CAR RENTALS

Car rental companies are at all three major airports and at various

ROAD SIGNS

Regulatory information appears on signs with a white background.

Warning information appears on signs with a yellow background.

Give way to
other traffic

Intersection
lane control

Left reverse turn
ahead

Sharp curve to
the right

Intersection
within curve

Y intersection
ahead

T intersection
ahead

Give way to other
traffic ahead

High occupancy vehicle
lane ahead

Divided highway

Divided highway
ahead

Stop ahead

Advisory speed
on deceleration
lane for exit

locations around the city. Prices vary, but as a rule, a one-day weekday rental costs between $75 and $100, weekly rates run between $210 and $300, and weekend rates run around $65 for one day to $175 for two days. If you require a specific type of car then make sure the rental company is aware of your needs: generally you will be reserving the rental rate and not an actual car model when you make your booking. When working out costs, remember to consider the 13.63 percent tax in addition to the quoted price and remember that rates are calculated using the 24-hour clock. Most rental companies will offer various insurance packages which may include Collision Damage Waiver (CDW), Loss Damage Waiver (LDW), Physical Damage Waiver (PDW) or Additional Liability Insurance (ALI) in their cover. Another charge to look out for is the "dropping off" charge levied when you want to leave the car in a different place to where you collected it. This charge can be quite high if you journey interstate. Most car rental companies have a stock of childrens' car safety seats but these need to be requested when you make your initial booking.

CAR RENTAL COMPANIES

NAME	TELEPHONE	WEBSITE
Alamo	800/462-5266	www.alamo.com
Avis	800/331-1212	www.avis.com
Budget	800/527-0700	www.budget.com
Dollar	800/800-3665	www.dollar.com
Hertz	800/654-3131	www.hertz.com
National	800/227-7368	www.nationalcar.com

TIPS
To rent a car you must:
» Be 25 years old to rent a car from most companies (and be aware that some companies may have an upper age limit, too);
» Have a valid driver's license bearing your photo;
» Produce a major credit card and, if you're not an American citizen, your passport;
» Have your own insurance or purchase maximum insurance from the rental company;
» Make sure you fill up with a full tank of fuel when you return the car or the company will fill it up and add the cost to your bill.

Above *A traffic police officer*
Left *Exits from expressways and major streets are clearly signed*

SPEED LIMITS

Major streets	30mph (48kph)
Residential areas	25mph (40kph)
Major expressways (in New York City)	50mph (80kph)
Highways in rural areas out of town	55mph (88kph)

ALTERNATIVES

Depending on where you want to go, your trip can be a travel experience.

FERRIES

Ferries offer a comfortable ride with spectacular views. The free Staten Island Ferry has been running since 1905; it gives you a great view of the Statue of Liberty and New York Harbor. Boats depart from Whitehall Terminal 1 (Whitehall Street, tel 718/727-2508, www.nyc.gov) and operate from Staten Island to Manhattan round the clock, except on holidays, roughly every 30 minutes during the day and hourly at night. Vehicles are not allowed on the ferry at the present time. The trip, 5.2 miles (8.4km), takes 25 minutes. Listed below are only some of the ferry commuter services available. For sightseeing cruises, ▷ 270.

NY Waterway (tel 800/53-FERRY, www.nywaterway.com) operates commuter ferries from New Jersey to points in Manhattan and from Manhattan to Yankee Stadium and Citi Field using several piers: Midtown at West 39th Street, Pier 11 at Wall Street, and the World Financial Center. Ferries run between 6am and 9.30pm, depending on location. Harbor sightseeing cruises are also available.

New York Water Taxi (tel 212/742-1969, www.nywatertaxi.com) runs a shuttle between several piers around Manhattan, including Chelsea Piers on West 26th Street and at Pier 45 at Christopher Street.

Circle Line operates sightseeing cruises (▷ 270).

NYC Department of Transportation

(tel 311) can give you information on all New York City ferries.

PEDICABS

On weekends and evenings in Greenwich Village, SoHo, Times Square, Midtown and the East Village, consider a pedicab for a unique view of town. Some drivers are licensed NYC tour guides. Most fares from Manhattan Rickshaw (tel 212/604-4729, www. manhattanrickshaw.com) are from $15–$30 and upwards, depending on the distance. Consult a driver or contact the company by telephone. Pedicabs can be hailed in the street; there are no stands.

CARRIAGES

A good old-fashioned carriage ride around Central Park can be an idyllic experience. Carriages stand at Fifth Avenue and Central Park South. Most charge $40 for 20 minutes. For specific information call Central Park Carriages (547 West 37th Street, tel 212/736-0680, www.central parkcarriages.com).

Below *New York Water Taxi operates a shuttle service between piers*

If you want to sample life away from the metropolis for a day then head out to the boroughs. If you have more time, travel north into the beautiful Hudson Valley, with its pretty towns and historical buildings, or go south to Philadelphia or Washington, D.C. Trains and buses serve all major routes out of town if you decide not to take to the road yourself.

BY RAIL

New York has two train stations: Grand Central Terminal on the east side and Pennsylvania Station on the west.

» Local Metro-North commuter trains run in and out of Grand Central Terminal to the New York and Connecticut suburbs. (For information, tel 212/532-4900 or 800/METRO-INFO; www.mta.info/mnr)

» Long Island Railroad (LIRR) runs commuter trains to and from Long Island. Information: 718/217-5477; www.mta.info

» PATH connects Manhattan to many New Jersey cities. Information: 201/216-6000 or 800/234-7284; www.panynj.gov/path

» Amtrak's high-speed Acela trains serve Penn Station as well as Boston, Philadelphia and Washington, D.C. Amtrak also has a daily service to cities throughout the US. Information: 800/872-7245 or 212/630-6400; www.amtrak.com

BY ROAD

Long-distance and commuter buses, as well as airport buses, operate from the Port Authority Bus Terminal (625 Eighth Avenue, tel 212/564-8484), which is New York's main bus station.

Greyhound® buses (tel 800/231-2222; www.greyhound.com) travel to cities and towns across the United States.

Bolt Bus (www.boltbus.com) and Megabus (www.megabus.com) run between New York City and Boston, Washington D.C. and Philadelphia. Both these companies provide free Wi-Fi on board. The buses are a good alternative to Greyhound, as fares are often cheaper. They leave from around Penn Station.

BUS VERSUS TRAIN

All prices are based on pre-booked one-way tickets. To ensure availability, bookings should be made at least 24 hours in advance. Some train journeys involve transfers; contact Amtrak for information.

ALBANY–HUDSON RIVER VALLEY
Train 2 hours 30 min. $59
Coach 2 hours 49 min. $43.50

HARTFORD
Train 2 hours 45 min. $33
Bus 2 hours 20 min. $29.50

BOSTON
Train Acela Express 3 hours 30 min. $101
Bus 4 hours 20 min. $35

PHILADELPHIA
Train 1 hour 30 min. $43
Bus 2 hours. $21

WASHINGTON, D.C.
Train 3 hours 15 min. $117
Bus 4 hours 20 min. $27

CHICAGO
Train 19 hours, reservations only. $126
Bus 17 hours 15 min, reservations only. $54

ATLANTA
Train 18 hours, reservations only. $186
Bus 18–22 hours. $54

Thanks to the Americans with Disabilities Act, New York City is a fairly accessible place for wheelchair users. Most streets are level with curbs, cut at corners. Buses have lifts for wheelchairs, and taxis are required to pick up those with folding wheelchairs or guide dogs.

GETTING AROUND

All three airports serving New York are wheelchair accessible and have restrooms for travelers with disabilities as well as TDD telephones in all terminals.

Most subway stations provide elevators and ramps, and there are tactile and audio features on ticket vending machines. If you use a wheelchair, alert the station clerk, who will collect your fare and buzz you through the entry gate near the turnstile; customers can enter the subway with a special Autogate MetroCard (▷ 45).

The MTA buses are equipped with wheelchair lifts that are at the rear of most vehicles and are operated by the bus driver. Once on board, the driver makes sure that the wheelchair is secure. The buses are also fitted with a device that lowers the front of the vehicle so that people with impaired mobility are able to board and alight safely.

The car rental companies Avis and Hertz have some hand-operated cars for rent (▷ 55). There are car rental desks at each airport.

Many theaters offer discounts to people with disabilities, and most cultural events are sign-language interpreted. Museums are accessible, but some old buildings have not yet been converted.

USEFUL CONTACTS

If you have accessibility concerns and require information on visiting sights, contact individual venues or any of the following.

Mayor's Office for People with Disabilities (tel 212/788-2830; www.nyc.gov/mopd) will send the free, large-type book *Access New York* to people who phone in a request.

Metropolitan Transit Authority (tel 718/596-8585, TTY 646/252-3050; 877/337-2017 for Access-a-Ride) provides information on New York's public transportation system.

Gray Line Air Shuttle (tel 212/445-0848) provides transportation between the three major airports and area hotels with 24-hour notice.

Travel Information Center for Hearing Impaired Visitors (tel TTY 718/596-8273) can help with advice on purchasing tickets and using the various transportation systems in the city.

Society for Accessible Travel and Hospitality (SATH; tel 212/447-7284; www.sath.org) gives information on travel worldwide.

Big Apple Greeter (tel 212/669-8159, 212/669-3602, TDD 212/669-8273; www.bigapplegreeter.org) provides free tours of New York's neighborhoods with native New Yorkers. If you wish, you may ask for a volunteer guide with a disability. Reserve tours at least six weeks in advance.

Scoot Around (tel 888/441-7575; www.scootaround.com) provides wheelchairs and scooters for rental.

Hospital Audiences (tel 212/575-7676, TTY 212/575-7673; www.hospitalaudiences.org) arranges seats at theaters, concert halls and other venues.

Hands On Sign Interpreted Performances (tel 212/740-3087; www.handson.org) can tell you where you will find sign language interpreters at exhibitions, performances and film screenings citywide.

New York City Sports Commission (tel 877/NYC-SPORTS; www.nyc.gov/sports) gives information on accessible sports leagues and venues.

Sprint Relay Operator (tel voice 800/421-1220, TTY 800/662-1220; www.consumer.att.com/relay). Operators act as interpreter between a TTY user and a voice telephone user. The operator reads the TTY user's typed message back to the other party.

REGIONS

This chapter is divided into four regions of New York (▷ 7). Region names are for the purposes of this book only and places of interest are listed alphabetically in each region.

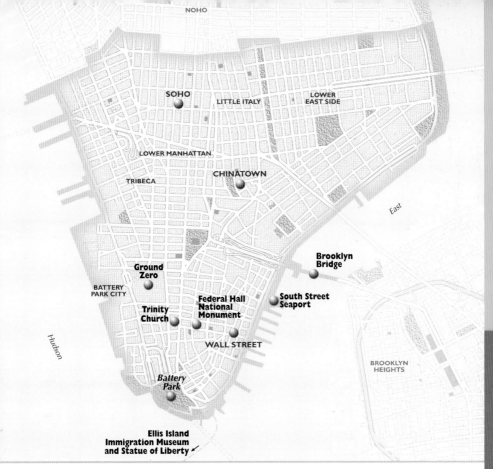

Map labels:
NOHO
SOHO
LITTLE ITALY
LOWER EAST SIDE
LOWER MANHATTAN
TRIBECA
CHINATOWN
East
Ground Zero
BATTERY PARK CITY
Trinity Church
Federal Hall National Monument
South Street Seaport
Brooklyn Bridge
WALL STREET
BROOKLYN HEIGHTS
Hudson
Battery Park
Ellis Island Immigration Museum and Statue of Liberty

LOWER MANHATTAN

If there is one city that represents America's raucous, can-do, anything-is-possible spirit, it is New York. Lower Manhattan was the first area of today's city to be settled, by the Dutch in 1625, and the area known as South Street Seaport thrived in the 17th century by providing dockage for large commercial ships. By the early 1670s the British were firmly in control of the city which they named New York.

Twelve million immigrants arrived at Ellis Island between 1892 and 1954, and today the Ellis Island Immigration Museum tells the powerful story of America's immigrants through photos, exhibits and oral histories. Nearby, the Statue of Liberty provided the first glimpse of America for immigrants and visitors alike, representing freedom, liberty and hope. There are cruises that take visitors to both Ellis Island and the Statue of Liberty, or there is the free Staten Island Ferry that provides views of the Statue of Liberty, New York Harbor and the Manhattan skyline.

The financial district is best known for Wall Street and the New York Stock Exchange, the world's largest securities trader (which is no longer open to the public). Wall Street is surprisingly narrow, for it was originally an 18th-century lane, and is lined with tall neoclassical buildings. Nearby the towers of the new World Trade Center are being built, slowly rising above the National September 11 Memorial and Museum.

Lower Manhattan grew as successive waves of immigrants arrived at Ellis Island and settled in New York, forming the now historic neighborhoods. Chinatown is home to many of New York's most recent Asian immigrants, and offers visitors fabulous ethnic restaurants and shopping, as well as colorful, bustling streets and sidewalks lined with merchants selling all manner of goods to throngs of pedestrians. The SoHo neighborhood was once the center of 19th-century industry, and the cast iron buildings of that era now house trendy loft apartments, shops and popular nightspots. TriBeCa is known for art galleries and boutique shops, while the Lower East Side is in transition with the traditional Jewish neighborhood gradually being modernized by wealthy, hip newcomers.

Charles Street
West 10th Street
Bedford
Great Jones Street
Bond
Lafayette
Broadway

Church of St. Luke-in-the-Fields
House of Oldies Rare Records

Christopher
Barrow
Morton
Hudson Street
Saint Luke's Pl.
Leroy
Commerce
Street
Downing
Minetta Lane
La Guardia Place

Bleecker Street
Macdougal
Sullivan
Thompson
Mercer
Broadway
Bleecker Street

WEST HOUSTON STREET
Broadway-Lafayette Street
Jersey St

Morton
Leroy
Clarkson
HOUSTON STREET
VARICK STREET
AVENUE OF THE AMERICAS (6TH AVENUE)
Houston Street
Prince Street
Jersey St
Prince Street
St Patrick's Old Cathedral

WEST
King
Charlton
Vandam
Greenwich Street
Spring Street
West Broadway
Wooster Street
Greene Street
Mercer Street
Crosby
Singer Building
Spring Street

New York City Fire Museum
Renwick St.
Dominick
Spring
Spring
SOHO
Haughwout Building
Broome

American Numismatic Society
Watts
Grand
Thompson Street
West Broadway
Wooster Street
Greene Street
Mercer Street
Children's Museum of the Arts
Broome

CANAL ST
Washington Street
Hudson Street
Desbrosses
Vestry
Hubert
Watts
Beach St
VARICK STREET
Saint John's
CANAL STREET
Lispenard
Walker
White
Canal Street
Grand
Canal Street
Museum of Chinese in America
Howard Street
Canal Street
Canal Street

HOLLAND TUNNEL

LAIGHT STREET
North Moore
Franklin
Beach St
West Broadway
Franklin Street
Franklin
Leonard
Franklin Place
LOWER MANHATTAN

TRIBECA
Ericsson Place
Harrison
Worth
BROADWAY
Thomas
Duane
Leonard
Thomas Paine Park
US Courthouse
Duane Street

Washington Market Park
Reade St
Chambers Street
CHAMBERS STREET
Greenwich Street
Duane
Reade
CHURCH STREET
Reade
Chambers Street
Chambers Street

Warren Street
Park Place West
Murray Street
Warren
Murray
Chambers Street
Warren
Murray
City Hall
City Hall Park
Brooklyn Bridge City Hall
City Hall

BATTERY PARK CITY
9A
Barclay Street
BARCLAY
Park Place
PARK PLACE
Vesey
VESEY STREET
Woolworth Building
Church of St Peter
PARK ROW
Spruce
Beekman

St Paul's Chapel
World Trade Center
VESEY ST
Fulton St
Ann
Broadway-Nassau Street
Nassau Street
Dutch Street

Ground Zero
Cortlandt Street
CHURCH STREET
Fulton Street
Dey St
Cortlandt Street
John
BROADWAY
Fulton Street
Fulton Street
William Street

Liberty Street
Liberty Street
WEST STREET
Washington
Greenwich
Cortlandt Street
Maiden Lane
Federal Reserve Bank
Liberty St

Albany Street
Cedar
TRINITY PLACE
Trinity Church
Pine
Cedar
Nassau Street
Federal Hall National Monument

Rector
Rector Place
Rector Street
Wall Street
New York Stock Exchange
Exchange Aly
Broad Street
Wall Street
Wall Street
Museum of American Finance

West Thames Street
South End Avenue
GREENWICH STREET
HIGHWAY 9A
Morris Street
Washington
Battery Place
Beaver
Pearl Street

Hudson

Museum of Jewish Heritage
1st
2nd
Battery Place
Little
Robert F Wagner Jr Park
Bowling Green
BROADWAY
Fraunces Tavern Museum
Water
Rectory of the Shrine of Elizabeth Ann Seton
Whitehall Street
STATE STREET
PETER MINUIT PLAZA

0 —— 250 m
0 —— 250 yds

Battery Park

Castle Clinton
Admiral George Dewey Promenade
BROOKLYN BATTERY TUNNEL
HIGHWAY 9A
South Street
Staten Island Ferry Terminal

Ellis Island Immigration Museum,

⑬ ⑭ ⑮ ⑯ ⑰ ⑱

B C D

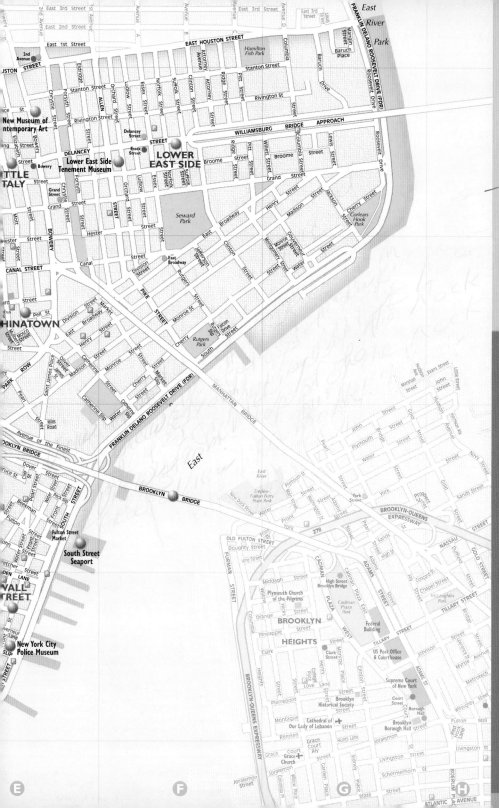

East 3rd Street
East 2nd Street
East 1st Street
2nd Avenue
STREET
JUSTON

EAST HOUSTON STREET
Hamilton Fish Park

New Museum of Contemporary Art

Stanton Street
Rivington Street
Stanton Street
Allen
Forsyth
Eldridge
Orchard Street
Ludlow Street
Essex Street
Norfolk Street
Suffolk Street
Clinton Street
Attorney
Ridge Street
Pitt Street
Willett Street
Columbia Street
Baruch Drive
Mangin Street
Baruch Place

East River Park

FRANKLIN DELANO ROOSEVELT DRIVE (FDR)

Roosevelt Drive

Chrystie
Forsyth
Elizabeth
Street
Bowery
LITTLE ITALY

DELANCEY
Lower East Side Tenement Museum

Delancey Street
STREET
Essex Street

LOWER EAST SIDE
Broome
Grand Street

WILLIAMSBURG BRIDGE APPROACH

Rivington St

Stanton Street

Columbia Street
Lewis Street

Broome Street
Grand Street

Delancey Street

Street

Street

Roosevelt Drive

Grand Street
Bowery
Chrystie Street
Grand Street
Hester Street

Orchard
Ludlow
Essex
Norfolk Street
Suffolk Street
Clinton Street

East Broadway
Henry
Madison
Monroe Street
Gouverneur Street
Jackson Street
Cherry Street
Corlears Hook Park

CANAL STREET
Hester Street
Canal Street

Seward Park

Broadway
East Broadway
Jefferson Street
Clinton Street
Montgomery Street
Street
Water Street

CHINATOWN
Mott
Hester
Pell St
Bowery
Division Street
East Broadway
Market
Division Street
Rutgers
PIKE STREET
Monroe Street
Madison Street
Cherry Street
Market Street

ROW
PARK
Saint James Place
James
Catherine Street
Monroe Street
Jefferson Street
Cherry
St Falcon Drive
Rutgers Park
South

MANHATTAN BRIDGE

Mills Road
Avenue of the Finest

FRANKLIN DELANO ROOSEVELT DRIVE (FDR)

East River

BROOKLYN BRIDGE

Dover Street
Cliff St
Pearl Street
South Street
Water Street
Peck Slip
Front Street
Beekman
Fulton
Front Street
Water Street

Brooklyn Bridge

Fulton Street Market

South Street Seaport

BROOKLYN BRIDGE

East
BROOKLYN BRIDGE

New Dock Street
Empire-Fulton Ferry State Park
Water Street
Front Street
York Street
York Street

Plymouth Street
Water Street
Adams Street
York Street
Pearl Street
Gold Street

Hudson Avenue
Evans Street
John Street
Little Street
Marshall Street
Bridge Street
Jay Street
Navy Street

BROOKLYN-QUEENS EXPRESSWAY

278

Sands Street
High Street

NASSAU STREET
GOLD STREET
Concord Street
Chapel Street
Duffield Street

TILLARY STREET

WALL STREET

John Street
Gold Street
Front Street
Water Street
Pearl Street

New York City Police Museum

OLD FULTON STREET
Doughty Street
Vine Street

Middagh Street

FURMAN STREET

Willow Street
Columbia Heights
Hicks Street
Henry Street
Orange Street
Pineapple Street

BROOKLYN HEIGHTS

Clark Street

High Street-Brooklyn Bridge

Plymouth Church of the Pilgrims

Cadman Plaza Park

CADMAN PLAZA WEST

ADAMS STREET

Federal Building

US Post Office & Courthouse

McLaughlin Park

Johnson Street
Myrtle Avenue
Metrotech

BROOKLYN-QUEENS EXPRESSWAY

Clark Street
Monroe Place
Henry Street
Love Lane

Pierrepont Street

Brooklyn Historical Society

Montague Street
Cathedral of Our Lady of Lebanon

Remsen Street

Clinton Street
Court Street

Supreme Court of New York

Borough Hall

Brooklyn Borough Hall

Johnson Street

Lawrence Street

Willoughby Street

Fulton Mall

Grace Court Aly
Grace Court
Grace Church

Hunts Lane
Joralemon Street

Sidney Place
Garden Place

Livingston Street

Schermerhorn St

Joralemon Street
Court Street
State Street

Boerum Place

ATLANTIC AVENUE

E   F   G   H

63

AMERICAN NUMISMATIC SOCIETY AT THE FEDERAL RESERVE BANK OF NEW YORK

www.numismatics.org

This society has a huge collection of coins, estimated at around 800,000 items, as well as maps and photographs. The society's library, educational and research facilities are open to the public. Exhibitions documenting the heritage of US coins and medals and the history of money are held nearby at The Federal Reserve Bank of New York, 33 Liberty Street.

✚ 62 D14 ✉ 75 Varick Street, 11th Floor, 10013 ☎ 212/571-4470 🕐 Mon–Fri 9.30–4.30 👣 Free 🚇 1, A, C, E 🚌 M1, M6, M20

BATTERY PARK

▷ 66.

BATTERY PARK CITY

www.batteryparkcity.org

From Pier A to Chambers Street, the $4-billion Battery Park City was created in the 1970s. It's a great place for a stroll along the waterfront, or for watching the boats on the Hudson River. Cesar Pelli's World Financial Center (1987) sits amid residential towers, plazas and parks. The Gardens of Remembrance were planted here two months after 9/11.

✚ 62 C16 ✉ Southwest tip of Manhattan 🚇 1, 2, 3, N, R 🚌 M1, M6, M9, M15, M20

BROOKLYN BRIDGE

▷ 68–69.

CHINATOWN

▷ 70–71.

CITY HALL AND CIVIC CENTER

Built between 1802 and 1812 in the Federal style with French influence, City Hall is one of New York's most elegant buildings. It is where the City Council meets and where the mayor has his office. Tours are available on weekdays free of charge, by reservation only. The surrounding Civic Center area includes City Hall Park and Foley Square, several city, state and federal government offices and police headquarters, including the New York State Supreme Court, the US Courthouse and the New York City Criminal Courts Building.

✚ 62 D16 ✉ Broadway and Chambers Street, 10007 ☎ 212/788-3000 🚇 2, 3, 4, 6, N, R 🚌 M1, M6, M15 📷 Tours by appointment ☎ 212/788-2656

ELLIS ISLAND IMMIGRATION MUSEUM

▷ 72–74.

FEDERAL HALL NATIONAL MONUMENT

▷ 67.

FRAUNCES TAVERN MUSEUM

www.frauncestavernmuseum.org

The 18th-century Queen's Head Tavern on this site, run by Samuel Fraunces, was visited in 1783 by George Washington himself. Here, in the Long Room, now reproduced in the style of a dining room of the period, he met with fellow officers and gave his famous farewell address at the end of the American Revolution. The current structure is a 1907 reconstruction sponsored by the Sons of the Revolution and now, together with adjacent 19th-century buildings, contains a museum of early American history and culture. Children can dress up in costume and try writing with quills. Separate from the museum is a restaurant busy all day serving all-American dishes to downtown workers.

✚ 62 E17 ✉ 54 Pearl Street, 10004 ☎ 212/425-1778; restaurant 212/968-1776 🕐 Mon–Sat 12–5 👣 Adult $10, child (6–18) $5 🚇 4, 5 🚌 M6, M15 🍴 ♿

Opposite *Elegant City Hall.* **Below** *Fraunces Tavern contains a museum of American history*

INFORMATION

www.thebattery.org

✚ 62 D17 ✉ Southwest tip of Manhattan on the Hudson River 🚇 1, 4, 5, N, R 🚌 M9, M15, M20, M22

TIP

» If you enter the park from Bowling Green subway station, you will pass the damaged 22-ton bronze *Sphere*, which once stood between the twin towers of the World Trade Center. The sculpture was recovered and placed temporarily in the park as a memorial to the victims of the 9/11 attack.

Above *Spectacular views take in New York Bay to the south and the Financial District skyscrapers rising to the north*

BATTERY PARK

These 21 acres (8.5ha), at the southern tip of Manhattan, are the site of Castle Clinton, a national monument, where you can buy tickets for the ferries to Liberty Island (▷ 84–85) and Ellis Island (▷ 72–74). The park's meandering paths are scattered with large, poignant memorials to more than 200 years of war dead. With its terrific view of the harbor, it is a pleasant place to get away from the busy, skyscraper-packed Financial District. Once a rocky ledge, Battery Park was created with landfill to protect the island from British attack in 1811, and it was named for the cannons that stood here.

CASTLE CLINTON

Castle Clinton was built between 1807 and 1809 for defense. In 1823 the US government ceded it to the city, and it became a center for theatrical and musical entertainment, hosting such events as the triumphal 1850 appearance of the Swedish soprano Jenny Lind. From 1855 to 1890 almost 8 million newly landed immigrants passed through Castle Clinton, when it was the immigration processing center, recalled by the statue in front of the castle, *The Immigrants* by Luis Sanguino. In 1892 immigration processing moved to Ellis Island. From 1896 to 1911, Castle Clinton was home to New York's first aquarium, now at Coney Island. Dioramas in the small museum depict Castle Clinton's history.

THE HARBOR

At the south end of Battery Park is the terminal for the Staten Island Ferry. From here, looking out across the city's harbor, you have a magnificent view of the Statue of Liberty, Ellis Island, Governors Island, and the Verrazano Narrows Bridge with the Atlantic Ocean beyond. Just past Slip 6 is a sculpture by Marisol, the *American Merchant Mariners Memorial*, dedicated to all merchant mariners who have served the United States since the Revolutionary War. Throughout the park vendors sell everything from T-shirts to ice cream.

FEDERAL HALL NATIONAL MONUMENT

As you approach the Federal Hall National Monument there's no escaping the massive bronze John Quincy Adams Ward statue of George Washington on the front steps. This Doric-columned, Greek Revival building resembles a simplified Parthenon, and looks a bit out of place among Wall Street's massive structures. Inside, the rotunda has 16 marble Corinthian columns, a domed ceiling and ornate bronze railings. One exhibit explores the Constitution. Another showcases the Bible used to administer the solemn oath to Washington.

A HISTORIC SITE

New York's first City Hall was built on this site in 1699 and petty offenders were flogged in front of the building. In 1789 it was reconstructed by Pierre Enfant, who later designed Washington, D.C., and the First Continental Congress met here to draft the Bill of Rights, guaranteeing the rights to freedom of worship, speech, press, assembly, keeping and bearing arms, trial by jury, and the right against unreasonable searches and seizures. April 30, 1789, the day Washington took the oath of office, was an occasion for massive celebrations. The building remained the nation's first capitol until 1790, when the "famed deal" between Thomas Jefferson and Alexander Hamilton moved the seat of government along the Potomac River.

Many other important historic events took place on this site. Newspaper publisher John Peter Zenger was imprisoned here for seditious libel in 1734; a brilliant defense by lawyer Andrew Hamilton secured him victory in court and was an important step towards freedom of the press (▷ 29). In 1765, the Stamp Act Congress assembled here to protest taxation without representation. In 1787, after the colonies won their independence, the First Continental Congress met here to establish procedures for the creation of new states. The state, war and treasury departments were established here, as was the Supreme Court. Customs stayed for 20 years before moving to Wall Street. The building became a National Historic Site on May 26, 1939, and a National Memorial to George Washington on August 11, 1955.

INFORMATION

www.nps.gov/feha

✚ 62 D17 ✉ 26 Wall Street, 10005
☎ 212/825-6990 🕐 Mon–Fri 9–5
✋ Free 🚇 4, 5 🚌 M9 🎫 Free guided tours at 10, 11, 1, 2 and 3

Above *On the site of the nation's first capitol, the first president of the newly created United States, George Washington, took the oath of office*

INFORMATION

➕ 63 F16 ✉ From southern Manhattan over the East River to Brooklyn ✋ Free
🚇 2, 3, 4, 5, 6, N, R 🚌 M9, M15, M103

Above *The bridge has been described as the crowning glory of an age memorable for great industrial achievements*

INTRODUCTION

This remarkable feat of 19th-century engineering, designed by John Roebling and built between 1867 and 1883, was the world's first steel suspension bridge. It spans a mile (1.6km) across the East River, roughly between Cadman Plaza in Brooklyn and Park Row in Manhattan.

The construction of the bridge cost several lives, including that of the chief engineer. While doing the final survey for the bridge, John Roebling suffered a severe injury to his foot. He survived the amputation of his toes, but died on July 22, 1869, of the resulting tetanus infection. His son, Washington Roebling, an engineer with the Union Army during the Civil War, took over as chief engineer. Working underwater on the caissons one day in 1872, Washington surfaced too quickly and was partially paralyzed by the resulting attack of the bends, also known as decompression sickness. He carried on, directing construction from his window in Brooklyn Heights with the aid of a telescope, while his wife Emily marched back and forth delivering his instructions to workers. Of the 600 laborers who worked on this project, 20 lost their lives in construction accidents.

When the bridge opened in May 1883, the public marveled at the Gothic-inspired span with its stone pylons and web of steel cables. Roebling's understanding of aerodynamic stability was very advanced for the time and he was the first to introduce radiating stays extending from the tops of the towers to the lower end of the suspender cables. It is estimated that 150,000 people walked across Brooklyn Bridge on opening day—but not Roebling, who refused to come after a bitter dispute with the company that financed the project. Disaster struck days later. A woman stumbled and fell while walking across. As people tried to see what was happening, there was much pushing and shoving. It was Memorial Day, a national holiday commemorating American servicemen killed in action, so there were great crowds on the bridge. A rumor started that the bridge was about to collapse, and everyone panicked and rushed toward land. Twelve people were trampled to death in the stampede and many were injured. On a cheerier note, in 1884 the great circus entertainer P. T. Barnum led 21 elephants across the bridge, which bore the weight without incident.

WHAT TO SEE

THE BRIDGE TODAY

As you walk along the wooden pedestrian walkway, you will come to a viewing spot where a bronze plaque gives information about the Roeblings. Take a look at the map etched in metal alloy, so that you know which skyscrapers are which among the towers looming ahead.

American poet Walt Whitman described the bridge and the views as the best medicine his soul had ever experienced. He might balk at the number of skyscrapers, and probably at the number of bicycle-riders, roller skaters and joggers racing across it today, but they have their own lane so pedestrians can stroll at their own pace and in safety.

The twin Gothic arches tower 277ft (84m) above the East River. The bridge was repainted in 1973, in its original beige and light brown. The walkway was reconstructed in 1983. In 2009, work started to paint the bridge and strengthen the approaches at a cost of $500 million.

TIP

» Walk across the bridge at dusk on a summer evening as the sun slowly sets behind Liberty Island and the city lights begin to twinkle.

REGIONS LOWER MANHATTAN • SIGHTS

Left *The Manhattan skyline, framed by Brooklyn Bridge*
Below *The pedestrian walkway is a mile (1.6km) long*

INFORMATION

www.explorechinatown.com

✚ 63 E15 ✉ Between Little Italy and the Lower East Side, bounded by Canal and Worth streets between Broadway and Bowery 🚇 J, M, N, Q, R, W, Z, 6 🚌 M1, M6, M103 🍴 Hundreds of restaurants ☕ Ten Ren Tea Time, 79 Mott Street 10013 ☎ 212/732-7178 ℹ Kiosk at Canal Street and Baxter Street ⏰ Daily 10–6 🛍 Dozens of souvenir shops; a few concentrate in the mini-mall at 15 Elizabeth Street

Above *Signs are in Cantonese and English along Chinatown's busy shopping streets*

INTRODUCTION

Chinatown, northeast of City Hall and below Canal Street, has been home to generations of immigrants from China, Hong Kong, Taiwan, Korea, Vietnam and other Asian countries for more than 150 years. Now covering 3 square miles (8sq km), it has all but crowded out its neighbors, Little Italy and the Lower East Side. For cheap restaurants, bargain clothing, souvenirs, and exotic herbs and spices, no other Manhattan neighborhood compares.

The district occupied by today's densely populated Chinatown was dominated by the hog and cattle industry in the 17th and early 18th centuries; many streets were named for prominent local butchers (including Joshua Pell and John Mott). During the 1800s, the area was populated by Irish and German immigrants; some of New York's dirtiest and most crowded tenements were around the intersection of today's Mosco, Worth and Baxter streets, then known as the Five Points—the setting for Martin Scorsese's 2002 movie *Gangs of New York*. Chinese immigrants arrived in the late 1870s.

WHAT TO SEE

MUSEUM OF CHINESE IN THE AMERICAS

The popular Museum of Chinese in the Americas (▷ 76) reopened in 2009 with additional exhibits in a new, and much larger, Chinatown location. Exhibits are captivating, drawing visitors into the experience of Chinese culture as well as displaying ancient artifacts. History and culture are not only preserved, but the new *Archeology of Change* exhibit captures the changing landscape of Chinatown through five landmarks.

SHOPPING

Chinatown's most popular streets for shoppers are Canal Street and Mott Street. The variety of shops ranges from chic boutiques to ancient antiques, souvenirs and food markets. Look for exotic Chinese vegetables, herbs, spices, ducks' feet and neat rows of fish on shaved ice. The ornate storefront at 32 Mott Street dates to 1891, the oldest storefront in Chinatown; the store is now home to Good Fortune Gifts (tel 212/791-9989) offering feng shui products, snuff bottles and teapots.

EASTERN STATES BUDDHIST TEMPLE
Visit this small temple, a place of prayer, compassion and community, to admire the statues of Buddha and three altars adorned with flowers and fruit frequented by local Buddhists who light incense and pray. The temple is known for its collection of 100 golden Buddhas.
✉ 64 Mott Street ☎ 212/966-6229

COLUMBUS PARK
From 8am to 9pm residents of Chinatown gather in Columbus Park (67 Mulberry Street, near Bayard Street, tel 212/408-0100). T'ai chi practice begins early in the morning, and by early afternoon the park is filled with neighbors playing mah-jong, Chinese chess, betting on dominoes, sitting in the shade socializing, or playing basketball. Fortune-tellers will read palms, and artists offer their paintings for sale.

MORE TO SEE
CONFUCIUS SQUARE
The statue of Confucius, located in Confucius Square on Bowery Street, was sculpted by Liu Shih and has been a Chinatown landmark since 1976. The great teacher is dressed in a long toga and stands atop a pedestal of green marble inscribed with his teachings.

CHINATOWN ICE CREAM FACTORY
For 30 years this family business, one of Chinatown's oldest, has created and served homemade American-style ice cream with a delicious Chinese twist to visitors from all over the world. The Asian flavors are excellent, with options like green tea, almond cookie, ginger and Zen butter.

KIM LAU CHINESE MEMORIAL ARCH
Located in Chatham Square, also known as Kimlau Square, at Bowery and East Broadway, this arch commemorates the Chinese-Americans who died in World War II. A statue of imperial commissioner Lieutenant B. R. Kim Lau, who fought against the opium smuggling that led to the Opium Wars, stands facing the arch.

TIPS
» Go to Chinatown to enjoy the colorful, crowded, noisy and exotic atmosphere, which is very different to the rest of Manhattan.
» Eat at a Chinese restaurant, where entrees are usually served family style. Choose a restaurant where lots of Chinese are eating for the probability of good food, and then be adventurous when you order. But you may want to skip dessert and head over to the ice cream shop at the Chinatown Ice Cream Factory.

Below *Columbus Park is a popular meeting place for Chinatown's residents*

INFORMATION

www.nps.gov/ellis
www.ellisisland.org
✚ Off map 62 E18 ✉ Ellis Island,
New York 10004 ☎ Information
212/363-3200, ferry 877/523-9849;
audiotours, café and gift shop 212/344-
0996 🕐 Daily 9.30–5, last outbound
ferry departs 3.30. Extended hours in
summer 🏛 Museum free, including
film. Ferry ticket: adult $12, child (4–12)
$5. Audiotours $8 🎫 Buy tickets in
Castle Clinton, Battery Park. Ferry
runs approximately every 30 min daily
9–3.30, depending on season 🚇 1,
4, 5 🚌 M1, M6, M9, M15 🌳 Park
rangers periodically conduct tours; check
schedules on arrival 🍴 Ellis Island
Café serves burgers, pizza, sandwiches,
soft drinks and beer and wine. Outdoor
seating 🏛

INTRODUCTION

Ellis Island is a deeply moving memorial to the 12 million immigrants who
arrived from distant lands between 1892 and 1954. Permanent exhibits include
passports, clothing, baggage and family heirlooms donated by immigrants and
their families. Dutch settlers named this 3-acre (1.2ha) island Oyster Island
because of the abundance of oyster beds in the area. In the 1760s, after the
execution of pirates on the island, it was known as Gibbet Island. It then came
under the ownership of Samuel Ellis, and when the city of New York bought it
after his death in 1807, it was renamed again. Expanded by landfill to 272 acres
(110ha), it became home to Fort Gibson and housed munitions. The original
wooden fort burned down in 1897.

IMMIGRATION

From 1892 Ellis Island replaced Castle Clinton as the inspection center for
newly landed immigrants. The architectural firm Boring & Tilton designed its
current Beaux Arts buildings. Until 1924, while the island was active,
70 percent of the immigrants to the US passed through the receiving facility;
it served as a hospital, detention facility and transportation station. First- and
second-class passengers were processed on board ship in more comfortable
quarters, but steerage passengers were herded onto the island. Because
it was assumed that these huddled masses came from countries with
substandard hygiene, no one was allowed to sleep on a bed provided by Uncle
Sam without first having a bath. Public Health Service doctors examined every
person and if they detected signs of heart problems, mental problems or
moral degradation, they would return the individual to their homeland. Eyes
were examined for signs of trachoma, a highly contagious eye disease that
led to blindness and even death; doctors, who came to be called "buttonhook
men," used their fingers or a button-hook to turn eyelids inside out in search
of redness caused by inflammation. Via translators, immigrants had to answer
questions about their finances, their intended residence, and any waiting
relatives. They had to prove they were strong, intelligent and able to find
work. Fearful, many immigrants gave contradictory answers and corrupt
immigration officers took advantage of many by accepting bribes when they
gave a "wrong" answer. Inspectors questioned 400 to 500 individuals each
day, spending only a few minutes with each. The bureaucracy was daunting,

Above The museum building seen from
the water

and Ellis Island became known as the Island of Tears, although most new arrivals received the landing card that allowed them to enter the US. Despite this, immigrants were often overcharged for their first train tickets in their new homeland so that many began their new lives in the poverty and squalor of New York City tenements.

AFTER WORLD WAR I

During World War I, the island came under US Army control and was used as a hospital. In 1924, after changes in legislation, prospective immigrants were checked in US consulates abroad and Ellis Island became a deportation center for illegal aliens. A new immigration building, a ferry house and a recreation building were added between 1934 and 1936 under the Public Works Administration. During World War II, the US Army used the island to detain enemy aliens. Between 1945 and 1954, the buildings were abandoned and deteriorated. In 1952, despite a proposal to convert the main building into a museum, it remained unused and was closed in 1954. In 1965, President Lyndon Baines Johnson designated the island part of the Statue of Liberty National Monument. In the 1980s, architects Beyer Blinder Belle led a massive restoration project. The museum opened in 1990.

GETTING THERE

To reach Ellis Island, buy a ferry ticket at Castle Clinton in Battery Park (▷ 66). Boarding is on a first-come, first-served basis, so in spring and summer, catch the ferry early to avoid long lines. From Battery Park, take the Circle Line-Statue of Liberty ferry; en route you can stop at Liberty Island (▷ 84–85). Upon arrival at Ellis Island, walk under the glass-and-metal canopy from the ferry slip to the museum, an ornate Beaux Arts building with fanciful copper-domed turrets. The magnificent arched portals must have been both imposing and intimidating to the arriving immigrants. There are three floors with permanent and changing exhibits about the immigration process, the living conditions of the detainees, memorabilia and displays on the building itself and its restoration. Upon entering, collect your free ticket for the 30-minute film *Island of Hope, Island of Tears*. The audiotour is also well worth getting.

WHAT TO SEE

FIRST FLOOR

The Peopling of America Exhibit, in the old railroad ticket office, provides information on the history of immigration to the US from as early as the 17th century. Trace migration patterns on the 6ft (180cm) globe.
The American Family Immigration History Center helps anyone to research their ancestors using high-tech facilities. Visit the website at www.ellisislandrecords.org

SECOND FLOOR

The Registry Room is reached by climbing the stairs to the Great Hall, as every immigrant did, with doctors scrutinizing their walk for physical impairment. The voices of thousands of people speaking in many different languages filled this hall as inspectors and their interpreters questioned each adult and asked any child who looked old enough to give his or her name. The inspectors asked each immigrant up to 29 questions he or she had already answered on the ship's manifest. If the immigrants' answers did not match their previous answers, they were detained and questioned further. It was a harrowing experience for people who had traveled far, leaving family and possessions behind and enduring a long and difficult journey across the Atlantic. The railings that were here to keep the immigrants in orderly lines were removed in 1911 and replaced with benches. Today visitors pay tribute to the immigrants in this quiet space.

TIPS

» Allow at least three hours; the museum alone usually takes two to three hours. Add extra time to visit the gift shop if you are interested in immigration or genealogy.
» Stop by the Information Booth to check the times of the daily free tours given by park rangers.

IN THE GROUNDS

The American Immigrant Wall of Honor displays the names of more than 700,000 immigrants whose descendants made donations to the Ellis Island Restoration Project. It serves as a memorial to all those who passed through here as they fled persecution and disease, poverty and hopelessness.

MUSEUM GUIDE
KEY TO MAIN ROOMS

THIRD FLOOR

17: *Restoring a Landmark:* photographs of the restoration
16: *Silent Voices:* large photographs of the abandoned building before restoration
15: *Treasures from Home:* immigrants' memorabilia
14: *Ellis Island Chronicles:* detailed models depicting the island's history 1897–1940
13: Dormitory Room: early 20th-century furnished room showing cramped conditions
12: Changing exhibits

SECOND FLOOR

11: *Peak Immigration Years:* photographs, memorabilia and recorded commentaries on immigration 1880–1924
10: Theater 2: shows *Island of Hope, Island of Tears* film, where immigrants tell their stories
9: Registry Room: the now empty great hall where immigrants were processed
8: *Through America's Gate:* 14 rooms with exhibits on the inspection process and the "Stairs of Separation"

FIRST FLOOR

7: Shop
6: Ellis Island Café
5: Theater 1: shows *Island of Hope, Island of Tears* film, where immigrants tell their stories
4: *The Peopling of America:* immigration patterns from 17th century to the present, and a Word Tree explaining the origins of words
3: Baggage Room: immigrants' suitcases and bags
2: Learning Center
1: American Family Immigration History Center

In 1916 the spectacular arched ceiling with Guastavino tiles and the red Ludowici tiled floor were added. During the 1980s restoration, only 17 of the 28,000 tiles needed replacing.

In the West Wing is an exhibit re-creating the step-by-step immigration process. In the East Wing, photographs and memorabilia explore the immigrants' hopes and expectations, fears and hardships. You can also listen to first-hand accounts of the process.

THIRD FLOOR

Treasures from Home displays more than 1,000 objects, including clothing, jewelry, family heirlooms and photographs donated by immigrants and their descendants. There are touching reminders of the life each person left behind and of the bright future they were hoping to find. A wedding dress, a grandmother's bracelet, a child's teddy bear—all testify to the heartbreaking sacrifices made by people desperate to find freedom and hoping for prosperity.

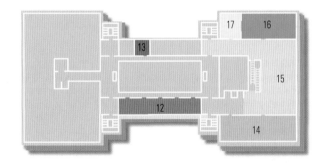

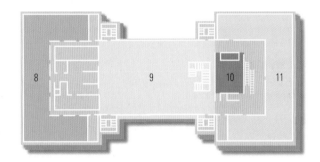

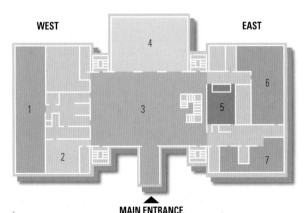

WEST   EAST

MAIN ENTRANCE

LITTLE ITALY

Once the overcrowded destination of Italian immigrants coming from Ellis Island, Little Italy is shrinking under pressure from New York's burgeoning Chinatown (▷ 70–71). A few blocks along Mulberry Street recall the friendly, festive area chock-a-block with Italian restaurants and grocery stores, where lavish displays of cheese, olives and salami entice visitors. Descendants of the initial immigrants still gather for family occasions. In mid-September the Feast of San Gennaro, patron saint of Naples, fills Mulberry Street, the main artery, from Canal Street to Spring Street. With gaudy lights and carnival booths, it's a scene to see if you don't mind crowds.

✚ 63 E14 ✉ Between Canal, Lafayette, and Houston streets and the Bowery 🚇 6 🚌 M1, M103

LOWER EAST SIDE

A slum tenement here was the next stop for most 19th-century immigrants after the ordeal of Ellis Island. The squalor, stench and disease in these overcrowded apartments during the area's heyday—from the mid-19th century until the 1920s—can barely be imagined today. Few of the original town houses survived the frenzied 19th-century building of tenement blocks, but most of these survived later rebuilding.

Today, although there is little to admire in the architecture, the area is thick with history. It is also one of New York shoppers' best bargain-hunting destinations, particularly on Sundays. Almost every day except Saturday (when stores are closed), the discount garment stores in the streets off Delancey and Orchard streets are crowded. Ethnic food shops in the area are wonderful; Essex Street Market (Mon–Sat) is a great place to appreciate the changes in the ethnic mix of residents.

✚ 63 F14 ✉ East of the Bowery, south of East Houston to the East River 🚇 F, J, M, V, Z 🚌 M9, M14A

LOWER EAST SIDE TENEMENT MUSEUM

www.tenement.org

Four re-created apartments in a typical, five-story tenement dating from 1863 give a disturbing insight into how the other half lived, or at least managed to exist, in the overcrowded, unsanitary conditions common on the Lower East Side between the 1870s and 1920s.

Some 10,000 seekers of the American Dream and refugees from violent pogroms passed through this building over 70 years, as you learn on a guided tour. Fewer people go on each of these—never more than 15—than lived in a typical apartment. None of this is really for kids. For them, take in the interactive living history program, where they can try on period clothes and talk to "Victoria Confino," a Jewish teenager who lived here in 1916.

✚ 63 F14 ✉ 90 and 97 Orchard Street, between Broome and Delancey streets ☎ 212/431-0233 🕐 Guided tours only; available from the Visitor Center. Times vary but normally every 30 or 40 min daily 11–5 💵 Adult $17, under 5 free. Advance tickets (advisable) ☎ 212/982-8420 🚇 F, J, M, V, Z 🚌 M9, M14A, M15 ♿ 🎧 Guided tours

MUSEUM OF AMERICAN FINANCE

www.moaf.org

On the site of Alexander Hamilton's law office, once the headquarters of multimillionaire John D. Rockefeller's Standard Oil Company, this four-room, Smithsonian Museum affiliate celebrates America's spirit of entrepreneurship with exhibits of coins, tickertape from the Wall Street Crash of 1929, curiously interesting photographs and murals of Wall Street and other documents and artifacts. Interactive financial news terminals help children understand the stock market. Special exhibitions have included informative displays about the history of the Dow Jones Industrial Average, banknote engraving and counterfeiting. The shop has interesting gifts for that person who has everything.

✚ 62 E17 ✉ 48 Wall Street, 10005 ☎ 212/908-4110 🕐 Tue–Sat 10–4 🚇 2, 3 💵 Adult $8, child 6 and under free ♿

Left *Go to Little Italy to experience the flavors and colors of the Mediterranean*

MUSEUM OF CHINESE IN AMERICA

www.mocanyc.org

MoCA's new 14,000 square-foot (1,300sq m) space in a former machine shop was designed by architect Maya Lin. The walls of the building's central skylit courtyard have been left untouched to reveal the original brick; the courtyard opens into the exhibition galleries and the auditorium. The galleries present the stories and artifacts of Chinese immigrants spanning a 200-year period. The artifacts, photographs, historical documents, musical instruments and clothing reflect the hardships, triumphs and daily life of the immigrants. Videos and photographs are projected onto screens accompanied by narrated oral histories which present the real-life stories of Chinese immigrants.

Changing exhibits of contemporary Chinese artists are featured in one of the main exhibition galleries.

➕ 62 E14 ✉ 211–215 Center Street, 10013 ☎ 212/619-4785 🕓 Mon and Fri 11–5, Thu 11–9, Sat–Sun 10–5 👋 Adult $7, under 12 free Ⓡ N, Q, R X Y 🚍 M103

MUSEUM OF JEWISH HERITAGE

www.mjhnyc.org

This museum, opened in 1996 and designed by Kevin Roche and John Dinkeloo in a hexagonal shape to represent the Star of David, houses an exhibition of 20th-century Jewish history and culture. Presenting the story of Jewish suffering, survival and renewal, the museum has three main sections: Jewish Life a Century Ago, The War Against the Jews, and Jewish Renewal.

Displays take you back to the now-vanished worlds of a century ago, through the horror of industrialized mass murder, to the resurgence of hope in a world not yet free of hatred and intolerance. Film clips, interspersed with displays of physical objects, include testimonies from Spielberg's *Survivors of the Shoah* project and also footage from the museum's own archives.

Above *Architects from Tokyo designed the building for the New Museum of Contemporary Art, opened in 2007*

➕ 62 D17 ✉ 36 Battery Place, 10280 ☎ 646/437-4200 🕓 Sun–Tue, Thu 10–5.45, Wed 10–8, Fri 10–5, eve of Jewish holidays 10–3; closed Jewish holidays and Thanksgiving 👋 Adult $12, under 12 free Ⓡ 4, 5 🚍 M1, M6, M9, M15, M20 🛒 🖥 🏛

NEW MUSEUM OF CONTEMPORARY ART

www.newmuseum.org

The museum has been inviting international contemporary artists to mount shows of experimental work since 1977. It presents several major exhibitions each year as well as shows in a space dedicated to digital art, experimental video and sound works.

In late 2007 the museum moved into its new home in this stunning building designed by Tokyo-based architects SANAA. In addition to purpose-built galleries it contains a theater, education floor, café, shop and a top-floor events space with roof terraces.

➕ 63 E14 ✉ 235 Bowery at Prince Street ☎ 212/219-1222 🕓 Wed–Sun 12–6 (Thu–Fri to 9pm) 👋 Adult $12, free Thu evenings, under 18 free Ⓡ J, M 🚍 M103 🖥 🏛

NEW YORK CITY FIRE MUSEUM

www.nycfiremuseum.org

A former firehouse of Rescue Company No.1, built in 1904, this museum packs three floors with firefighting paraphernalia, the most comprehensive collection in the United States.

Equipment from the 1700s to the present includes buckets, pumps, horse-drawn fire engines, a fire hydrant and more equipment and there's an exhibit on fire safety. Firefighters are usually around to share stories.

This is one of the best places in the city to pay tribute to the 343 firefighters who lost their lives on September 11, 2001. You can also see exhibits relating to the disaster.
✚ 62 D14 ✉ 278 Spring Street at Hudson/Varick, 10013 ☎ 212/691-1303 🕐 Tue–Sat 10–5, Sun 10–4 ✋ Contribution requested (adult $5, child $1) 🚇 C, E 🚌 M10, M21 ☛ Tours by appointment 🏛

NEW YORK CITY POLICE MUSEUM

www.nycpolicemuseum.org

This small museum exhibits a collection of uniforms, ceremonial batons, New York Police Department (NYPD) shields, handguns, and even the machine gun used by Al Capone's gang to assassinate Frankie Yale, the first homicide in New York by such a weapon. Visit a prison cell and see the display on vintage weapons and notorious criminals, which includes arrest records. Learn about fingerprinting and forensics, then view the NYPD Hall of Heroes, which now has a memorial to the 23 policemen and women who died in the attack on the World Trade Center. "Policing a Changed City" covers the way New York has become one of the world's safest cities.
✚ 63 E17 ✉ 100 Old Slip, 10005 ☎ 212/480-3100 🕐 Mon–Sat 10–5 (also Jul–end Aug Sun 12–5) ✋ Suggested donation adult $5, child (6–18) $2 🚇 2, 3, N, R 🚌 M15 🏛

RECTORY OF THE SHRINE OF ELIZABETH ANN SETON

From 1801 to 1803, this red-brick town house was the home of the New York socialite and mother of five, Elizabeth Ann Seton, the first American-born woman to be canonized by the Roman Catholic Church. Born in 1774, she converted to Catholicism as an adult and became a spiritual leader and educator. She founded the first order of nuns in the US, the Sisters of Charity. Her legacy includes six religious communities with more than 5,000 members, schools, and social service centers and hospitals across the world. Pope Paul VI declared her a saint in 1975.
✚ 62 D17 ✉ 7 State Street ☎ 212/ 269-6865 🕐 Mon–Fri, ring bell for admission

ST. PATRICK'S OLD CATHEDRAL

www.oldcathedral.org

French architect Joseph François Mangin had been busy with the building of City Hall until 1809, when he began work on this Gothic structure, the first Roman Catholic cathedral of New York. At 120ft long (36m) and 80ft (24m) wide, it opened in 1815, when the area was populated by Irish immigrants. The work of enlarging the cathedral was well under way in 1866, when a fire destroyed it. Restored and completed by 1868, the cathedral remained the seat of the archdiocese until the dedication of the new St. Patrick's in 1879, when the old cathedral was demoted to parish church. Now restored, the interior is grand and gloomy, the timber roof is supported on iron columns and the organ is one of only a few good organs in the city.
✚ 62 E14 ✉ 260–264 Mulberry Street, 10013 ☎ 212/226-8075 🕐 N, Q, R V 🚌 M15, M103

Below *Displays in the New York City Fire Museum*

ST. PAUL'S CHAPEL
www.saintpaulschapel.org
Modeled on London's St. Martin-in-the-Fields, this church was built of local stone between 1764 and 1768, with the spire added in 1796. In 1789 the inaugural prayer service for George Washington, the first president, was held here. Pierre I'Enfant, the soldier-architect who designed the Federal Hall, is credited with the altar. After his inauguration, Washington worshiped here regularly and his pew, together with Governor Clinton's, is preserved. On Mondays at 1pm there is an hour of classical music—and it's free.

🔠 62 D16 ✉ 209 Broadway, between Fulton and Vesey streets, 10007 ☎ 212/233-4164 🕐 Mon–Sat 10–6, Sun 8–4. Classical music Mon 1–2pm; free 🚇 4, 5 🚌 M1, M22 ☞

SOHO
▷ 80–81.

SOUTH STREET SEAPORT
▷ 82–83.

STATEN ISLAND FERRY
www.nyc.gov/dot
These commuter craft, which shuttle Staten Islanders to and from jobs in Manhattan, are—for tourists—a free, hour-long, round-trip excursion in the harbor—past the Statue of Liberty (▷ 84–85), Ellis Island (▷ 72–74) and Governors Island, with the Verrazano Narrows Bridge in the distance. In good weather, try for one of the old orange and green boats. The white boats are newer and have no outside deck. To get the best view, sit on the right side. Avoid rush hours, and disembark at Staten Island. On your right as you get off, look for the boat-loading sign, which directs you to the next loading dock.

🔠 62 E18 ✉ Whitehall Terminal, 1 Whitehall Street, 10004 ☎ Dial 311 for ferry information 🕐 Daily 6am–1am both ways, less frequently on weekends, holidays and off-peak 🅿 Free 🚇 1, 4, 5, N, R 🚌 M1, M6, M9, M15

STATUE OF LIBERTY
▷ 84–85.

Above *Cass Gilbert's neo-Gothic Woolworth Building was the tallest in the world in 1913*

TRIBECA
TriBeCa (pronounced *try-beck-a*), the *Tri*angle *Be*low *Ca*nal Street, is where artists went in the late 1970s after SoHo (▷ 80–81) became unaffordable to all but the very rich. They converted cast-iron warehouses into loft apartments, and now a wealthy group has moved in along with antiques shops, design shops and some fine restaurants.

There are some notable buildings, especially 2 White Street, dating from 1809; the Fleming Smith warehouse at 451 Washington Street, home of long-established Capsouto Frères bistro; and the Corinthian-columned, cast-iron 47 Worth Street. The area was greatly damaged on 9/11, but returned to full swing remarkably quickly.

🔠 62 D15 ✉ Between Hudson River and Broadway, Chambers and Canal streets 🚇 1, 2, 3, A, C, E 🚌 M20

TRINITY CHURCH
▷ 79.

WALL STREET
▷ 86.

WOOLWORTH BUILDING
F. W. Woolworth, the department store mogul, hired fashionable architect Cass Gilbert to build the tallest building in the world in 1913. At 792ft (241m), this terracotta-faced, neo-Gothic masterpiece held the record until the Chrysler Building was completed in 1929 (▷ 148–149). Inside, the lobby is a marvel of Skyros marble, with murals of *Labor and Commerce* and plaster depictions of some of the builders, including Gilbert, with a model of the building and Woolworth himself counting his cash.

🔠 62 D16 ✉ 233 Broadway, 10007 🚇 2, 3, 4, 5, 6, N, R 🚌 M1, M6, M15

TRINITY CHURCH

As you walk up Broadway, north of Bowling Green, you come to Trinity Church. Now dwarfed by the surrounding skyscrapers, Richard Upjohn's 1846 rose-pink sandstone masterpiece, with beautiful stained-glass windows and an eight-sided, 280ft (85m) spire, was once the tallest building in New York. The church bell was presented to the church in 1704 by the Bishop of London.

As you enter, notice the biblical scenes on the bronze doors, designed by Richard Morris Hunt and donated in memory of John Jacob Astor III. Look for the white marble altar, the wooden vault and the screen of the Chapel of All Saints. To the left, at the back of the church, is a small museum (Mon–Fri 9–5, Sat 9–3, Sun 1–3.45) selling postcards, pamphlets outlining the church's history, books and videos, and gifts. The 30-minute guided tours of the church start from this museum. Check the website for details of classical music concerts and other events which take place regularly. Men must remove their hats as a sign of respect, even in the dead of winter, or they will be reminded to do so by one of the church wardens.

THE FIRST CHURCH

In 1697, by royal charter, the Anglican parish of Trinity became one of the largest landholders in Manhattan, and the first church was put up the next year, only to burn in the great fire of 1776, when the British army occupied New York. You will find the original royal charter for the church on display in the museum. During the struggle for independence, Trinity Church was a Loyalist bastion, but when the revolution ended, so did the Loyalists' hold on the city. A second building on the same spot was structurally flawed and was torn down in 1839. British architect Richard Upjohn, together with James Renwick, Jr., were commissioned to build the third Trinity Church. In the process, Upjohn made his reputation and went on to design many more churches around the country.

Before you leave the church, stroll around the small churchyard, a green oasis that is now estimated to be worth several million dollars for its prime location. Here are the graves of steamboat inventor Robert Fulton, statesman Alexander Hamilton, killed in a duel with Aaron Burr, and Francis Lewis, a signatory to the Declaration of Independence. The large cross in the churchyard is dedicated to Caroline Webster Schermerhorn Astor, the queen of high society in the 1800s.

INFORMATION

www.trinitywallstreet.org

✚ 62 D17 ✉ Broadway at Wall Street, 10006 ☎ 212/602-0800 🕐 Mon–Fri 7–6, Sat 8–4, Sun 7–4 🚇 4, 5, 2, 3 🚌 M1, M6 ☛ Free guided tours daily 2pm

Above *A historic church tucked away among Lower Manhattan's skyscrapers, Trinity Church is the final resting place of a handful of great Americans*

INFORMATION

✚ 62 D14 ✉ Canal Street to Houston Street, between Sixth Avenue and Lafayette Street ⓢ C, E, N, R, 6 🚌 M1, M6 🍴 Rocky's, 45 Spring Street ☎ 212/ 274-9756 ☕ Le Pain Quotidien, 100 Grand Street ☎ 212/625-9009 🎁

INTRODUCTION

This area *South* of *Hou*ston (pronounced *how-stun*)—which actually extends as far south as Canal Street, and runs from Sixth Avenue on the west to Lafayette Street on the east—started out in the 19th century as an industrial zone. Architects kept catalogs of cast-iron window frames, balustrades and columns, then pieced together what they liked; an Italian Renaissance motif was very popular. Fashion moved uptown in the early 20th century, taking industry and business out of the area. Development stalled; nothing went up—but nothing came down, either. Rents plummeted, opening up opportunities for artists and sculptors in need of cheap accommodations and studio space. Preservationists caught wind of the phenomenon and soon all New York was singing the praises of SoHo.

Today, there are 50 cast-iron structures on Greene Street alone. The most admired include the Haughwout Building at the corner of Broome Street and Broadway, the Little Singer Building at 561 Broadway, and the St. Nicholas Hotel, where Mark Twain met his future wife, at 521–523 Broadway. Across the street at 504 Broadway, Harry Houdini worked as a tie-cutter before his career as an escape artist took off. It was in the Haughwout Building that Elisha Graves Otis installed his first passenger elevator; unfortunately it is no longer in the building. (▷ 88–89 for a walk around this neighborhood.)

WHAT TO SEE

GALLERIES

By the 1970s, SoHo was one of the most desirable addresses in town, rents shot up and struggling artists left. But many dealers and galleries thrived, like the Leo Castelli Gallery, which exhibited Andy Warhol, Frank Stella and Roy Lichtenstein in the 1960s, at 420 Broadway.

By the end of the 20th century there were about 200 other art galleries, as well as more photography galleries than anywhere else in New York. Today many of the galleries have moved to Chelsea (▷ 113) and, to a lesser extent, to TriBeCa (▷ 78), but some remain. The Peter Blum Gallery at 99 Wooster Street (tel 212/343-0441) exhibits artists working in a variety of media, including photographs, drawings, sculpture and cartoons. Nearby, at 461 Broome Street, the Animazing Gallery (tel 212/226-7374) specializes in original animation, illustration and distinctive fine art.

Above *Stylish boutiques and stores, fashionable restaurants, fascinating architecture and plenty of art galleries make up the SoHo scene*

Two tiny art museums offer very different and unique works of art for anyone looking for an original SoHo experience. The innovative New York Earth Room (tel 212/473-8072; Wed–Sun) at 141 Wooster Street, displays 14 tons of soil in a second-floor apartment in a residential building. The innovative earth sculpture was created by Walter De Maria in 1977. Expect an unusual, earthy, peaceful and sensory encounter with urban nature. The Museum of Comic and Cartoon Art (tel 212/254-3511; www.moccany.org; Tue–Sun 12–5; adult $5) at 594 Broadway, Suite 401 (between Houston and Prince) displays every genre of this art form. Special exhibits feature works by some of the world's finest illustrators, focusing on the craft with respect to historical time and place. Displays can include animation, comic books, caricature, graphic novels, and computer-generated art.

SHOPPING

Stores followed the galleries, pushing out both galleries and artists. But in the interim, many well-to-do New Yorkers moved into the loft spaces on the buildings' upper floors, attracting still other high-end retailers to SoHo, along with chic cafés and lots of bars and music venues. Rents for apartments here can rise to $15,000 per month.

No matter what the season, SoHo's streets offer the ultimate New York retail experience.

Left *A SoHo designer boutique*
Below *SoHo loft spaces are sought-after apartments*

INFORMATION

www.southstreetseaport.com
www.southstreetseaportmuseum.org
🚇 63 E16 ✉ South of Brooklyn
Bridge at Fulton Street ☎ Museum:
212/748-8786 🕐 Most shops Mon–Sat
10–7, Sun 11–6. Museum: Apr–end Dec
Tue–Sun 10–6; Jan–end Mar Fri–Sun
10–5 (ships open 12–4), shops 12–5, Mon
10–5 Schermerhorn Row galleries only
💰 Museum: adult $10, child (5–12) $5
🚇 12 Fulton Street ☎ 212/732-7678
or 212/748-8600 🕐 Apr–end Oct daily
10–6; rest of year daily 10–5 🚇 2, 3, 4,
5 🚌 M15 🚶 Guided walking tours:
ask at the ticket booth across from Pier
17 🍴 15 restaurants and food outlets
☕ Seaport Café on Pier 17 ☎ 212/964-
1120; Skipper's Pierside Café, Pier 16
☎ 212/349-1188

Above *Historic ships are berthed between
piers 15 and 17*

INTRODUCTION

The South Street Seaport Museum, at 207 Front Street, opened in 1967 and was the original draw to this then-neglected area, leading to a complete restoration project. Schermerhorn Row is the most significant historical landmark in the South Street Seaport complex. Nos. 191 and 193 Front Street were built in the 1790s by Peter Schermerhorn, a leading merchant from a prominent New York family. He built further groups of four-story Georgian and Federal-style warehouses and counting houses on Fulton Street in 1812. The stone warehouse at 167–171 John Street was built in 1849 for A. A. Low & Brothers. By the 1860s, the South Street area was no longer the hub of commercial port activity and only the Fulton Fish Market remained. In the 1980s the Rouse Company moved in to start restoring.

This "museum without walls" is a 12-square-block landmark district at the eastern edge of downtown Manhattan on the East River. Buildings include the Pier 17 Pavilion, the South Street Seaport Museum and retail outlets on the surrounding blocks. Begin your visit at Pier 17, where the eateries and shops are concentrated. Pick up a visitors' leaflet from one of the many display racks at the entrance to the pier. The clear, well-labeled map and listing of the stores and restaurants will enable you to decide the route that appeals to you most.

A four-year historic renovation coupled with a pedestrian friendly expansion of the Seaport is scheduled to begin in 2010. The historic Tin Building will be restored, the shopping mall will be reconfigured, neighborhood markets and boutique shops added and additional space for year-round events.

WHAT TO SEE

PIER 17
From this impressive three-story glass-and-steel pier, transformed into a shopping center with dozens of restaurants and eateries, you can enjoy the magnificent views of the East River from the outdoor terrace.

SOUTH STREET SEAPORT MUSEUM
Historic Ships
Berthed between piers 15 and 17, the collection of ships includes the 1911 *Peking*, a four-masted cargo vessel built by Blohm and Voss in Hamburg, Germany, which made several trips around Cape Horn. After numerous voyages between Europe and South America, then serving as a stationary school ship for the British, it came to New York in 1975. The *Pioneer*, an 1885 schooner, takes visitors on a 2.5-hour harbor cruise, including close-up views of the Statue of Liberty and Governors Island (call for hours and reservations, tel 212/748-8786).

World Port New York
The museum's core exhibition, with 24 galleries on the upper floors of the renovated Schermerhorn Row and the A. A. Low Building, explores the history of the port from colonial times to the present.

THE TITANIC MEMORIAL LIGHTHOUSE
At the Water Street entrance to the seaport, this monument to the victims of the *Titanic*, which sank on April 15, 1912, on its maiden voyage from Southampton, England, to New York, was put up in 1913 overlooking the East River. It was moved to its present site in 1968. John Jacob Astor, owner of the Astoria Hotel, which stood on the site of the Empire State Building, was one of the 1,513 people who died.

TIP
» If you plan to take a harbor cruise, reserve in advance to avoid disappointment.

Below *A landmark district of historic buildings, a maritime museum, and more than 100 shops, cafés and restaurants occupies the waterfront*

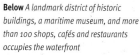

STATUE OF LIBERTY

INFORMATION

www.nps.gov/stli

✚ Off map 62 D18 ✉ Liberty Island in New York Harbor ☎ General information 212/363-3200, ferry tickets 212/269-5755 🕐 Daily 9.30–5, extended hours in peak season 🎟 Ferry tickets (good for a round trip that includes a stop at Ellis Island) adult $12, child (4–12) $5. Free admission to Liberty Island and the Statue of Liberty. Crown tickets are $3, sold with ferry tickets—advance reservations required 🚇 1, 4, 5 🚌 M1, M6, M15 🍴 Refreshments on ferries; café on Liberty Island 🎫 On ferries

Above *The Statue of Liberty is the city's most important landmark*

INTRODUCTION

A symbol of freedom and democracy, the Statue of Liberty was the first sight for millions of immigrants as they approached their new homeland. As you sail toward her today, it's easy to imagine how they felt.

When the Statue of Liberty was unveiled on October 28, 1886, thousands of spectators were filled with awe. Nearly three times the height of the Colossus of Rhodes, one of the Seven Wonders of the World, this gift from the people of France was in recognition of the friendship established between the two countries during the American Revolution. The French statesman Edouard de Laboulay proposed that the statue be made in France, but that the pedestal be made by the Americans. Alexandre-Gustave Eiffel, who designed the Eiffel Tower in Paris, came up with the concept of a revolutionary support system of interlocking angle irons for the enormous statue, which was designed by Frédéric-Auguste Bartholdi.

Paying for the project was a problem for both nations and great effort was put into fundraising events, such as theatrical performances, art exhibitions, auctions and prize-fights. But the public showed little interest. Joseph Pulitzer, who established the Pulitzer Prize, criticized the rich in his newspaper *The World* for failing to help finance the pedestal construction. He also criticized the middle classes for expecting the rich to provide all the money. Donations then came pouring in and the pedestal was completed in 1886. The French shipped the statue to New York in June 1885; it took four months to assemble.

WHAT TO SEE
VITAL STATISTICS

Lady Liberty, as she is often affectionately called, was installed on Bedloe's Island, renamed Liberty Island in 1956. By presidential proclamation the Statue of Liberty became a National Monument in 1924; the United Nations designated her a World Heritage Site in 1984. After almost 100 years, the statue needed some attention; an $87-million restoration project ended with fireworks to celebrate the statue's centennial, coinciding with Independence Day, on July 4, 1986. Her measurements are impressive. She weighs 225 tons and measures 151ft 1in (46.05m) from the top of the base to the torch. Her hands measure a whopping 16ft 5in (5m) and even her nose is 4ft 6in (1.37m). Richard Morris Hunt's magnificent pedestal measures 154ft (46.9m).

VISITING LADY LIBERTY

She can be fully appreciated only up close, and many consider the strenuous climb up 354 narrow steps into the statue's crown for views of the harbor to be the high point of a visit. Access to the crown is limited to just 10 visitors per hour, only 240 each day, and advance tickets are mandatory. Early morning is the best time for the climb as the staircase is cramped and hot in the summer with no air conditioning.

It is still worth taking the trip across the harbor to peer up at this impressive monument to liberty and freedom, even if crown tickets are not available. For a panoramic view of the harbor, you can climb to an observation deck on the 16th floor at the top of the pedestal.

The museum displays the original Statue of Liberty Torch, numerous models of the statue including a full size replica of the Lady's face, and a collection of historic posters and postcards.

To visit Liberty Island, take the Statue of Liberty & Ellis Island Ferry from Battery Park. In advance, buy tickets online, by telephone or at the ticket office. In person, use the CityPass (▷ 274) or get your ticket from Castle Clinton ticket office (▷ 66). Lines are long during peak season so, as there are no reservations, arrive early. Everyone must clear security, including x-ray inspection of baggage and metal detectors, before boarding the ferry and again before entering the statue. There is a Time Pass system (free) for visiting the museum and pedestal observation deck. During peak periods it's best to order tickets in advance and request a time pass from the ferry company (tel 1-877/523-9849, www.statuecruises.com).

Above *Ferries ply the water between Battery Park and Liberty Island, giving their passengers a close-up view of the famous statue*

INFORMATION

www.downtownny.com

➕ 63 E17 ✉ Financial District 🚊 2, 3, 4, 5 🚌 M1, M6, M15, M22 🎫 Free 90-min Wall Street walking tour every Thu, Sat noon; meet on the steps of the US Customs House at 1 Bowling Green ☎ 212/606-4064 🍴 John Street Bar & Grill, 17 John Street ☎ 212/349-3278 🕐 Daily 11am–2am 🍴 Mangia, 40 Wall Street ☎ 212/425-4040 🕐 Mon–Fri 7am–4pm

TIP

» As the Financial District is deserted on weekends, visit on a weekday when this little street becomes a superhighway for stockbrokers in dark suits.

WALL STREET

The heart of New York's financial center and the historic site of George Washington's inauguration, this symbol of wealth is in fact a narrow 18th-century lane running from Broadway to South Street. The New York Stock Exchange (closed to the public since 9/11) stands on the corner of Broad Street and Wall Street. At the west end of the street on Broadway, framed between towering office buildings, is the Gothic Revival Trinity Church (▷ 79)—an impressive sight, and a great photo opportunity, with the many US flags waving from their perches on the buildings along the street. Stop in front of Federal Hall National Monument (▷ 67); a statue of George Washington marks the spot where the first president took the oath of office. The two skyscrapers at Nos. 40 and 55 Wall Street rise up 930ft (283m) and 951ft (290m) respectively. This is an area steeped in history, evidenced by the many historical plaques, cornerstones, markers and notices. Take a look at the J. P. Morgan Bank headquarters at No. 60. Its bold arcade vies for attention as one of the tallest skyscrapers in the Financial District. Visit the white marble lobby.

Wall Street was named for the northern wall erected in 1653 to defend New Amsterdam from Native Americans. North of this wall were the *bouwerijs* (farms). After the English defeated the Dutch, and New Amsterdam was renamed New York, the wall started to crumble and in 1699 it was torn down. The bastion stones from the Dutch wall were carted off and used in the foundation of City Hall (▷ 65).

THE FIRST TRANSACTION

In 1792, 22 brokers and merchants stood in front of a buttonwood tree on Wall Street and made their first trading agreement. They were actively trading government securities, seeking to establish fixed commissions on transactions and favoring brokers who were signatories. This "Buttonwood Agreement," as it was called, eventually gave birth to the New York Stock Exchange. Their open-air trading activities moved indoors, probably to taverns, until premises on William Street were acquired in the 1860s.

The telegraphic ticker, new in 1867, has been replaced by today's latest market information display technology. The adrenaline rushes as hundreds of brokers on the trading floor, the size of a football field, trade billions of shares in about 3,000 companies. Sadly, this frenetic trading cannot be viewed live, because the Stock Exchange is closed indefinitely to visitors. Call 212/656-3000 for further information.

Below *This world-famous financial district has been trading since 1792*

WORLD TRADE CENTER SITE (GROUND ZERO)

Ground Zero looks like nothing so much as a construction site, but seeing this corner of Lower Manhattan brings home vividly the horrors of 9/11. The World Trade Center once filled seven buildings on the 16 acres (6.5ha) bordered by Church Street, Liberty Street, Park Place and West Street. The center's twin towers became the tallest buildings in the world in 1973, and for the next 28 years more than a million visitors visited every year, thrilling to the views from the open-air rooftop observation level. Then, on the morning of September 11, 2001, New Yorkers and the rest of the world watched with horror on their televisions as two hijacked commercial jets slammed into the towers. A total of 2,752 people were killed, 343 of them firefighters. When the towers collapsed, six buildings were destroyed and about 100,000 jobs were lost. Streets like Church and Vesey were completely enshrouded in thick white dust, people were in shock, and emergency crews and firemen rushed to the scene, hoping to find survivors, but there were very few. When the fires were eventually extinguished, Ground Zero was all that was left.

LOOKING TO THE FUTURE

Within a year, clean-up crews had completed their gruesome task and workers had started rebuilding subway stations. The Lower Manhattan Development Corporation (LMDC) staged a design competition, inviting top architects to create plans for the site. Six were unveiled in July 2002; all were rejected. Calling for more plans, the LMDC got responses from 406 teams of architects, and in March 2003 the governor and the mayor announced the winner: Daniel Libeskind, a Polish immigrant who had arrived in the US in 1960, aged 13.

Construction began in 2006 on the National September 11 Memorial and Museum, which is planned to be a pavilion and gateway to the subterranean memorial. The underground museum will have interactive exhibits, display artifacts and provide contemplative areas. An 8-acre (3.24ha) plaza will be the centerpiece of the new complex.

Formerly known as the Freedom Tower, the One World Trade Center building is under construction, and will be a symbolic 1,776ft (541m) high, representing the year that the Declaration of Independence was signed. Completion of the office tower, observation deck and restaurant is scheduled for 2013. Three additional high-rise office towers are planned for the site, and two of the three are currently under construction.

INFORMATION

www.national911memorial.org
www.tributewtc.org
www.projectrebirth.org
✚ 62 D16 ✉ Church to West streets, Liberty to Vesey streets 🚇 1, E, N, R
🚌 M6, M9, M20

TIP

» The National September 11 Memorial and Museum and the Downtown Alliance have an information kiosk open seven days a week. The kiosk is located on Vesey Street across from the entrance to the World Trade Center PATH station.
» You can take a walking tour of the World Trade Center Site with a guide who has personal experience of the 9/11 tragedy. Go to the Tribute WTC Visitor Center, 120 Liberty Street.

Above *A patriotic and poignant memorial to 9/11 adorns fences in Greenwich Village*

SOHO'S PUCK BUILDING TO THE SOHO GRAND HOTEL

If you enjoy gallery-hopping or architecture, put this walk at the top of your list. SoHo, *So*uth of *Ho*uston (pronounced *how-stun*), a landmark district famous for the prefabricated cast-iron facades of its buildings, is full of galleries where some of the city's most interesting contemporary artists show their work.

THE WALK
Distance: 2 miles (3.2km)
Time: 1.5 to 2 hours
Start at: Broadway/Lafayette subway station
End at: Canal Street subway station

HOW TO GET THERE
Subway F and downtown 6; bus M6.

★Leave the Broadway/Lafayette Street subway and turn right (south) on Lafayette.

❶ The restored Puck Building is at 295 Lafayette Street. Don't miss the statue of Puck, decorated with gold leaf, above the door. Here the satirical magazine *Puck* was published, in German (1876–96) and in English (1877–1918). A plaque on the Houston Street side of the building relates its history. With its complex brickwork, the building was instantly revered as a prime example of classic New York commercial design.

Continue south along Lafayette, and turn right on Prince Street, then left on Broadway.

❷ The Little Singer Building at 561 Broadway was designed by Ernest Flagg. It was very avant-garde in 1904 with its curled steel, recessed glass and textured terracotta. It suggested the next great architectural step: replacing cast-iron floor supports with steel—the basis of the modern skyscraper.

Walk two blocks south to the corner of Broadway and Broome. Look across Broadway to the northeast corner of Broome and Broadway.

❸ The 1857 Haughwout Building is SoHo's oldest cast-iron beauty. Cast-iron facades were stylish, cheap, easy to assemble and recyclable. The Haughwout Building architect based the facade on a window arch from a Venice library, repeating it 92 times. The first Otis elevator was installed here, inaugurating an era of ever-higher buildings.

Turn right onto Broome Street and right again onto Mercer Street. Go north on Mercer.

❹ Stop for drinks at Bar 89, two doors down—and make sure you check out the now-you-see-through-them-now-you-don't doors on the toilet facilities on the mezzanine.

Continue to Prince Street and turn left (west), then go left again onto

Opposite The Little Singer Building was a forerunner of modern skyscrapers

Greene Street, where there are more cast-iron buildings.

❺ Many of these structures started out as warehouses. By 1962, a lot of them had been abandoned, and there were plans to raze the neighborhood in order to accommodate a new highway, but the area was saved from demolition when residents protested. Rents were low here at the time so many artists, attracted to the huge, light-filled spaces, set up their homes and studios here; by the 1970s, artists had almost completely taken over the neighborhood. Landmark designation for the neighborhood came in 1973. As you walk south on Greene Street, watch for Nos. 72–76, known as the King of Greene Street, with cast-iron Corinthian columns, and Nos. 28–30, the Queen of Greene Street, with a Second Empire roof.

Return along Greene to Grand Street and turn right. Walk one block west to Wooster Street and turn right. On the corner of Broome and Wooster streets, a shop called Vintage New York has more than 200 wines for you to sample, all from wineries in New York State.

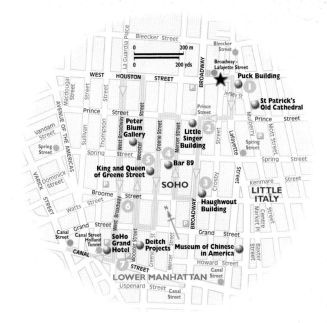

❻ On Wooster Street, the Peter Blum Gallery at No. 99 is worth a visit. Exhibiting artists here work in a variety of media, with paintings, drawings, sculptures, photographs and cartoons on display. Nearby at No. 18 is the fashionable Deitch Projects in a huge loft. At No. 141, the innovative New York Earth Room exhibits great mounds of earth.

When you reach West Houston Street, turn left and walk one block west to West Broadway, where you turn left again and walk south all the way down to Canal Street.

❼ Just north of Canal Street is the SoHo Grand Hotel. Have a look at the postmodern industrial interiors, then join the hip crowds at the bar.

Continue south on West Broadway, and turn right at Canal Street. You'll see the Canal Street station for A, C and E subway lines two blocks down the street and, two blocks beyond that, the 1 and 2 subway stations.

WHEN TO GO
To make the most of this walk, go when the art galleries are open, generally Tuesday to Sunday from 10 to 6.

WHERE TO EAT
BAR 89
✉ 89 Mercer Street ☎ 212/274-0989

PLACE TO VISIT
NEW YORK EARTH ROOM
✉ 141 Wooster Street ☎ 212/473-8072
🕐 Wed–Sun 12–3, 3.30–6 🎫 Free

Left The gold Puck statue outside the building of the same name

BOWLING GREEN TO SCHERMERHORN ROW

New York City began as a settlement here in the 17th century, so if you are interested in the city's history, this is the walk for you. From Bowling Green to South Street Seaport, this area encompasses some of the city's greatest treasures.

THE WALK
Distance: 2.5 miles (4km)
Time: 2 to 2.5 hours
Start at: Bowling Green subway station
End at: Fulton Street subway station (A, 2, 3)

HOW TO GET THERE
Subway 4, 5; bus M6.

★ Leave Bowling Green station, and you'll see Battery Park ahead of you. Taking the path to the right, walk toward Castle Clinton.

❶ Castle Clinton (tel 212/ 344-7220; Mon–Sun 8.30–5) was the immigrant clearing center before Ellis Island. You'll pass a temporary memorial to the victims of the World Trade Center, *The Sphere*, a sculpture which once stood between the towers as a symbol of world peace and is now a symbol of

hope. In 1850, P. T. Barnum brought Europe's greatest soprano, Jenny Lind, to Castle Clinton, securing international stardom for both "the Swedish nightingale" and for himself as her promoter. Inside the gate to your right, a small museum displays dioramas depicting the castle's various uses from fort and entertainment center to ticket office for boat trips to Liberty Island and the Statue of Liberty (▷ 84–85) and Ellis Island Immigration Museum (▷ 72–74).

Leave through the gate straight ahead and walk to your right, keeping to the path as it veers left past Slip 6.

❷ In the water, just beyond Slip 6, is the site of the *American Merchant Mariners Memorial*, a sculpture of

a sinking ship by Marisol, dedicated to all merchant mariners who have served the United States from the Revolutionary War to the present.

Turn back and walk east past the ferries to Slip 3. Walk up the steps to your left.

❸ Albino Manca's sculpture of a bronze eagle with a funeral wreath, the *East Coast Memorial*, honors the memory of all the people who died in American waters during World War II.

Take the path west back toward Castle Clinton and turn right at the east gate. Walk past the Hope Garden to the point where Battery Place, Broadway and State Street meet. This small park is Bowling Green, where a statue of King

George III was torn down by fervent nationalists in 1776.

❹ The imposing neoclassical US Custom House on the right of the park houses the National Museum of the American Indian. The impressive rotunda inside the Great Hall is well worth viewing.

Pass Bowling Green and walk north on Broadway, passing Arturo Di Modica's bronze *Charging Bull* on your right. Continue past this symbol of stockmarket prosperity to Trinity Church, on your left.

❺ Trinity Church is historic (▷ 79). Many famous people are buried in the churchyard, including statesman Alexander Hamilton, steamboat inventor Robert Fulton and Captain James Lawrence, whose last words ("Don't give up the ship") are now legendary.

As you leave the churchyard, cross to the east side of Broadway and continue east on famous Wall Street, straight ahead.

❻ Wall Street (▷ 86) is where you will find the New York Stock Exchange, now closed to the public, halfway down the street on your right. No. 40 is the Trump Building. The Museum of American Finance is at No. 48.

Walk east on Wall Street to William Street and go left, then left again onto Pine Street.

❼ On Pine Street, steps lead up to the Chase Manhattan Plaza, where sculptor Jean Dubuffet's *Group of Trees* takes center stage. Below the plaza is Isamu Noguchi's *Sunken Garden* sculpture.

Return to William Street by descending the steps to the right of the *Group of Trees*. Turn left to view the four abstract metal sculptures in

Louise Nevelson Plaza. Across the street from the largest sculpture is the Federal Reserve Bank, designed to look like a Florentine palazzo. Just past the bank is Maiden Lane. Here turn left onto Maiden Lane, then right onto Nassau Street, and then right again onto John Street. At No. 44 is the United Methodist Church, with a fine Palladian front window. Continue east on John Street for five blocks, then left onto Water Street.

❽ The South Street Seaport Historic District (▷ 82–83) is full of boutiques and restaurants, more shopping mall than historic, but the atmosphere is festive and it's fun to be on the water; you have fine views of the East River, Brooklyn Bridge and the river craft. At the northern end of Water Street is Manhattan's oldest saloon, the Bridge Café, dating from 1847, where you can have a drink and a meal.

Turn right (east) onto Dover Street, then right again onto Front Street. When you get to Beekman Street, turn left to the city's former fish market, Fulton Street Market. Go across South Street and walk to the end of Pier 17, and go up the steps for a spectacular view of Brooklyn

Bridge (▷ 68–69). Then head toward South Street, cross over and continue straight ahead along Fulton Street.

❾ Schermerhorn Row, the Federal-style buildings along this street, were built as warehouses or counting houses in the early 1800s and named for the developer.

Continue west on Fulton Street to William Street and the subway station.

WHEN TO GO
To fully appreciate the bustle of Wall Street it is best to do this walk on weekdays.

WHERE TO EAT
Any of the eateries at South Street Seaport.

BRIDGE CAFÉ
✉ 279 Water Street ☎ 212/227-3344

PLACE TO VISIT
NATIONAL MUSEUM OF THE
AMERICAN INDIAN
www.nmai.si.edu
✉ 1 Bowling Green ☎ 212/514-3700
🕐 Mon–Wed, Fri–Sun 10–5, Thu 10–8
✋ Free

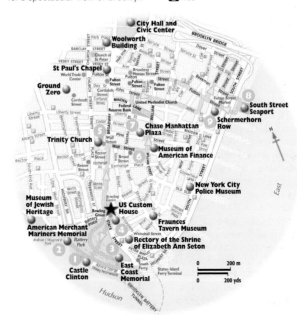

CITY HALL PARK TO WASHINGTON SQUARE PARK

Starting out from City Hall Park, you'll walk past the famous Woolworth Building, the world's tallest building until 1930 when the Chrysler Building spired even higher. Beyond lies Ground Zero, the site of the World Trade Center. You'll continue to SoHo and what remains of once-bustling Little Italy.

THE WALK
Distance: 3 miles (4.8km)
Time: 2 to 2.5 hours
Start at: Park Place subway station
End at: West 4th Street/Washington Square

HOW TO GET THERE
Subway 2, 3; bus M6.

★When you leave Park Place subway station, City Hall and its park are on your left at the northern end of City Hall Park.

❶ The principal designer of City Hall (▷ 65) was a Frenchman, Joseph François Mangin, who also worked on the place de la Concorde in Paris. This mini-palace is where the mayor and city council have their offices. A wrought-iron fence keeps the rest of us out. In the park in front of City Hall is a statue of Nathan Hale, a spy for Washington's army, hanged by the English in 1776. Just before his execution he uttered his famous last words of regret that he had "but one life to lose for my country." The same area was the site of the 1863 Draft Riots (▷ 35). Behind City Hall facing Chambers Street is the old Tweed Courthouse, now the Department of Education. In 1872, when Boss Tweed (▷ 35) ran the city and milked taxpayers of millions of dollars, the estimated cost of constructing the courthouse was $250,000. But by the time Tweed paid off friends and lined his own pockets to the tune of some $10 million, the tab was $14 million. Tweed died penniless in jail in 1878. Across Broadway is Cass Gilbert's Woolworth Building (▷ 78), between Park Place and Barclay Street, a skyscraper with lavish Gothic ornamentation and an amazingly rich lobby.

Continue south down Broadway.

❷ St. Paul's Chapel (▷ 78), on Broadway between Fulton and Vesey streets, is Manhattan's only remaining pre-Revolution building. George Washington worshiped here when New York was the nation's capital; his pew is inside.

Turn right on Fulton Street and continue west.

❸ Along the fence protecting the site of the World Trade Center

92

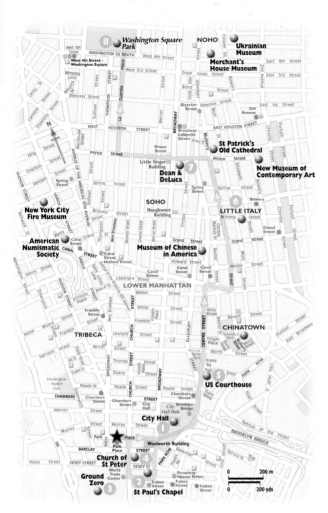

Opposite *Washington Memorial Arch in Washington Square Park*

A little farther north are the criminal courts. As you approach Canal Street, the proximity to Chinatown becomes obvious: open-fronted shops sell everything from Chinese lanterns to refrigerator magnets and made-in-China trinkets. When you reach the corner of Centre Street and Canal Street, turn right. Walk two blocks east, then turn left on Mulberry Street and walk north.

❻ You are now in the heart of Little Italy (▷ 75), with a handful of Italian restaurants and cafés. Two blocks north, at 195 Grand Street, is Ferrara Café, founded in 1892, with strong coffee and sweet pastries.

Continue north on Mulberry Street to Prince Street, and turn left.

❼ On the southeast corner of Prince Street and Broadway is Dean & DeLuca, a temple to food and cuisine offering beautiful displays of the finest pastries, meats, fish and produce, plus good coffee at the front counter. Cross Broadway and continue along Prince Street and turn right on West Broadway toward Houston Street.

As you cross Houston Street, West Broadway becomes LaGuardia Place.

❽ Three blocks north is Washington Square Park. Once a hanging ground and a burial site for more than 10,000 unidentified paupers, this space became a public park in 1828.

After a rest in the park, you can catch a downtown train from West 4th Street/Washington Square back to Chambers Street near City Hall.

WHEN TO GO
The area around City Hall Park is at its liveliest on weekdays.

WHERE TO EAT
FERRARA CAFÉ
✉ 195 Grand Street, between Mulberry and Mott streets ☎ 212/226-6150

(also known as Ground Zero, ▷ 87) at the end of Fulton Street, on Church Street, photos, flags, candles, flowers, teddy bears and other poignant memorials to the victims of the 9/11 tragedy can still be seen. Alongside the memorial, people sell T-shirts, photographs and hats to anyone willing to buy such reminders of the disaster. Reconstruction on this site is well underway. If you wish to have a closer look, cross Church Street to the viewing wall.

Turn right on Church Street.

❹ At the corner of Church and Barclay streets is the Church of St. Peter, founded in 1785, and New York's oldest Catholic parish church.

Turn right on Park Place and you'll see City Hall Park ahead. Walk east through the park to get a good view of Brooklyn Bridge. Take Park Row to Centre Street and walk north to the US Courthouse.

❺ The US Courthouse, designed by architect Cass Gilbert, stands on the corner of Centre Street and Foley Square.

SHOPPING

37=1
www.jeanyu.com
Jean Yu makes dresses, lingerie and separates of rich silks. The garter belts are to die for. Prices are up there.

🪧 106 E14 ✉ 37 Crosby Street, between Grand and Broome streets ☎ 212/226-0067 🕐 Tue–Fri 1–6 (appointment only) 🚇 Canal Street (N, R) 🚌 M1, M6

ALIFE RIVINGTON CLUB (SHOES)
The unmarked steel door opens onto a space paneled in cherry wood, where sneakers are treated as high fashion, and you can find limited-edition American, European and Japanese lines in fantastic colors.

🪧 107 F14 ✉ 158 Rivington Street, between Clinton and Suffolk streets ☎ 212/375-8128 🕐 Mon–Sat 11–7, Sun 12–6 🚇 Delancey/Essex (F, J, M, Z) 🚌 M9

APC
Atelier Production and Creation doesn't immediately suggest what you'll find here—good-looking, well-constructed Parisian-style basics. You can buy entire outfits, including cotton T's, turtlenecks, sweatshirts, dress shirts, leather jackets and very stylish jeans.

🪧 106 D14 ✉ 131 Mercer Street, between Prince and Spring streets ☎ 212/966-9685 🕐 Mon–Sat 11–7, Sun 12–6 🚇 Prince Street (N, R, W) 🚌 M1, M6

BCBG BY MAX AZRIA
www.bcbg.com
Bon Chic, Bon Genre brings you great style and fine quality from designer Max Azria. The women's fashions are stylish and sexy, suitable for day or night. Eye-catching accessories too, all at fair prices. Also at 770 Madison Avenue.

🪧 106 D14 ✉ #1B, 120 Wooster Street, between Prince and Spring streets ☎ 212/625-2723 🕐 Mon–Sat 11–7, Sun 12–6 🚇 Prince Street (N, R, W) 🚌 M1, M6

CENTURY 21
www.c21stores.com
Customers do their trying on in the aisles at this resource for discounted designer fashions. Look for Prada, Armani and Jil Sander among other designers at 40 to 75 percent off or more.

🪧 106 D16 ✉ 22 Cortlandt Street, between Broadway and Church Street ☎ 212/227-9092 🕐 Mon–Wed 7.45am–9pm, Thu–Fri 7.45am–9.30pm, Sat 10–9, Sun 11–8 🚇 Fulton Street (4, 5) 🚌 M1, M6

Above *SoHo has some of the hippest stores in the city*

DEAN & DELUCA

www.deandeluca.com

A wonderful place to browse. Absolutely everything here is top quality—pastries, cheeses, meats, fishes, chocolates and packaged products, plus the baskets of hand-picked fruits and vegetables. There's also a coffee bar. There are two other branches in Manhattan.

➕ 106 E14 ✉ 560 Broadway at Prince Street ☎ 212/226-6800 🕐 Mon–Fri 7am–8pm, Sat–Sun 8–8 🚇 Prince Street (N, R, W) 🚌 M1, M5, M6

DOLCE VITA

http://shopdolcevita.com

High prices needn't freeze you out of fashionable footwear. This acclaimed brand has all the coolest styles in boots, flats, heels, pumps, platforms and wedges at good prices.

➕ 107 F14 ✉ 159 Ludlow Street at Stanton Street ☎ 212/529-2111 🕐 Mon–Sat 12–8, Sun 12–7 🚇 Essex Street-Delancey Street (F, J, M, Z) 🚌 M9, M14a, M15, B39

DOYLE AND DOYLE

Doyle and Doyle offers some very alluring, historic estate jewelry in prime condition.

➕ 107 F13 ✉ 189 Orchard Street, between Houston and Stanton streets ☎ 212/677-9991 🕐 Tue–Fri 1–7 (Thu until 8), Sat–Sun 12–7 🚇 Lower East Side/ Second Avenue (F, V) 🚌 M9, M15

EDITH MACHINIST

Everything from boots to ballet shoes, military-style jackets to furs, evening wear and jewelry comes through this Lower East Side shop, including designer names minus the high prices.

➕ 107 F14 ✉ 104 Rivington Street, between Ludlow and Essex streets ☎ 212/979-9992 🕐 Mon–Fri 1–8, Sat 12–8, Sun 12–7 🚇 Delancey St (F), Essex St (J, M, Z) 🚌 M9, M14a, B39

EILEEN FISHER

www.eileenfisher.com

New Yorkers love these easy-to-wear clothes—they are versatile enough to take a woman right through the day with minimal changes.

This is the flagship store featuring Eileen Fisher's entire line, all made of natural fabrics. March and August sales are a big draw. Other stores are on Madison Avenue (at 53rd and 79th Streets) and Fifth Avenue (at 22nd).

➕ 106 D14 ✉ 395 West Broadway, between Spring and Broome streets ☎ 212/431-4567 🕐 Mon–Thu 11–7, Fri–Sat 11–8, Sun 12–6 🚇 Spring Street (C, E) 🚌 M1, M6

EMPORIO ARMANI

www.emporioarmani.com

At this flagship of Giorgio Armani's less expensive line, you get the same great design at a fraction of the price.

➕ 106 D14 ✉ 410 West Broadway at Spring Street ☎ 646/613-8099 🕐 Mon–Sat 11–7, Sun 12–6 🚇 Spring Street (C, E), Prince Street (N, R, W) 🚌 M1, M6

ERES

www.eresparis.com

In 1968 Eres opened in Paris on chic place de la Madeleine, selling the ultimate swimwear—bikinis, suits and other one-pieces. Today the company issues a cruise collection in November and a summer collection in January each year. Some equally beautiful and flattering ranges of lingerie are offered in addition to the swimwear.

➕ 106 D14 ✉ 98 Wooster Street, between Spring and Prince streets ☎ 212/431-7300 🕐 Mon–Sat 11–7, Sun 12–6 🚇 Prince Street (N, R) 🚌 M1, M6

FOLEY & CORINNA

www.foleyandcorinna.com

Fashionistas and celebrities flock here to see the famous silk and vintage lace butterfly blouses, mohair and cashmere knit coats and other romantic hippie-chic fashions created by Dana Foley, who began her career at a city flea market. Partner Anna Corinna selects the vintage clothing and accessories.

➕ 107 E13 ✉ 114 Stanton Street, between Ludlow and Essex streets ☎ 212/529-2338 🕐 Sun–Mon 12–7, Tue–Sat 12–8 🚇 Delancey/Essex (F, J, M, Z) 🚌 M15, M21

GAS BIJOUX

This outpost of the St. Tropez and Paris jeweler has lovely inspirational handmade jewelry featuring semi-precious stones.

➕ 107 E14 ✉ 238 Mott Street, between Prince and Spring streets ☎ 212/334-7290 🕐 Mon–Sat 11–7, Sun 12–6 🚇 Broadway-Lafayette (F, S, V) 🚌 M1, M103

INA

www.inanyc.com

The designer resale stock, discounted by 30 to 50 percent, changes daily, as models turn in their cast-offs. Look for Diane Von Furstenberg and Anna Sui. There's usually a fantastic array of Manolos, Pradas and Sigerson Morrisons, too.

Below Dean & Deluca is a magnet for New York's gourmets

✚ 106 D14 ✉ 101 Thompson Street, between Spring and Prince streets ☎ 212/941-4757 🕐 Sun–Thu 12–7, Fri–Sat 12–8 🚇 Spring Street (C, E), Prince Street (N, R, W) 🚌 M5, M6, M21

ISSEY MIYAKE
www.isseymiyake.com
This TriBeCa store, designed by Frank Gehry and his protégé Gordon Kipping, stocks all of Miyake's lines including the A-POC ("a piece of cloth"), each item created from a seamless cloth.
✚ 106 D15 ✉ 119 Hudson Street at North Moore Street ☎ 212/226-0100 🕐 Mon–Sat 11–7, Sun 12–6 🚇 Franklin Street (1, 9) 🚌 M20

J & R MUSIC AND COMPUTER WORLD
www.jr.com
This store, opened in 1971, stocks every conceivable brand of audio, video, computer, camera and cell phone, plus software and household appliances. Prices are excellent, and the staff are knowledgeable and helpful. The Music Store has separate stores for jazz, classical and pop.
✚ 106 D16 ✉ 23 Park Row (across from City Hall Park) ☎ 212/238-9000 🕐 Mon–Sat 9–7.30, Sun 10.30–6.30 🚇 Park Place (2, 3), City Hall (N, R, W), Brooklyn Bridge/City Hall (4, 5, 6) 🚌 M9, M15

KAM MAN FOODS
This large Chinese food hall overflows with exotic products, from live fish and edible birds' nests to ginseng priced at hundreds of dollars. It also sells inexpensive Asian cookware.
✚ 107 E15 ✉ 200 Canal Street at Mott Street ☎ 212/571-0330 🕐 Daily 8.30am–8.45pm 🚇 Canal Street (J, M, Z) 🚌 M1, M103

KATE SPADE
www.katespade.com
The former *Mademoiselle* accessories editor, Kate started out in 1993, making handbags that emphasized utility, color and fabric. She opened her first store in 1996, and now sells a full line of exquisite nylon, leather and fabric bags, plus wallets, luggage, stationery, eyeglasses, fragrance and beauty products.
✚ 106 D14 ✉ 454 Broome Street at Mercer Street ☎ 212/274-1991 🕐 Mon–Sat 11–7, Sun 12–6 🚇 Prince Street (N, R, W) 🚌 M1, M6

KATE'S PAPERIE
www.katespaperie.com
Expensive but beautiful gifts can be found at this elegant store. Gorgeous stationery, handsome journals and date books, photo frames, alluring and exquisite wrapping papers and ribbons, a variety of writing tools, and all kinds of ingenious paper items are attractively displayed.
✚ 106 E14 ✉ 72 Spring Street between Crosby and Lafayette streets ☎ 212/941-9816 🕐 Mon–Sat 10–8, Sun 11–7 🚇 Spring Street (N, R) 🚌 M1, M6

KELLY CHRISTY
www.kellychristyhats.com
Kelly Christy makes eye-catching hats for men and women in all kinds of fabrics and in every conceivable style, from fedora to beret. Every hat is named to reflect a mood or character—recent examples are "Miss Marple" and "Let's skate". Prices vary according to complexity and exclusivity of style and fabric, and start at about $200.
✚ 106 D14 ✉ 453 Broome Street at Mercer Street ☎ 212/965-0686 🕐 Tue–Fri 12–6, Sat 12–5 🚇 Spring Street (6, A, C, E), Prince Street (N, R) 🚌 M21, M103

KIRNA ZABETE
www.kirnazabete.com
Beth Buccini and Sarah Easley assemble their choice of the avant-garde designers at this pretty store. You might find knitwear by Giambattista Valli, sunglasses and bags by Balenciaga, Ts by Alexander Wang, leather jackets by Rick Owens, plus exciting ranges by other renowned designers such as Stella McCartney, Azzedine Alaïa, Balmain and Proenza Schouler.
✚ 106 D14 ✉ 96 Greene Street, between Prince and Spring streets ☎ 212/941-9656 🕐 Mon–Sat 11–7, Sun 12–6 🚇 Prince Street (N, R, W) 🚌 M1, M6

MARC JACOBS
www.marcjacobs.com
Marc Jacobs is one of the hottest designers, turning out luxurious, updated vintage designs in soft, feminine colors. He also has two stores on Bleecker Street, one selling accessories (retro flats plus), the other his less expensive Marc by Marc Jacobs line, which includes his must-have cargo pants.
✚ 106 D14 ✉ 163 Mercer Street, between Houston and Prince streets ☎ 212/343-1490 🕐 Mon–Sat 11–7, Sun 12–6 🚇 Prince Street (N, R, W) 🚌 M1, M6

ME & RO
www.meandrojewelry.com
The collection of Michelle Quan and Robin Renzi uses precious and semi-precious stones in stackable rings, bangles, necklaces and other pieces with a lotus petal motif or Sanskrit and Tibetan calligraphy.
✚ 107 E14 ✉ 241 Elizabeth Street, between Houston and Prince streets ☎ 917/237-9215 🕐 Mon–Sat 11–7, Sun 12–6 🚇 Broadway-Lafayette (F, S, V) 🚌 M21, M103

MODELL'S
www.modells.com
Savvy New Yorkers come here to get the best deal on their running and athletic shoes (Adidas, New Balance, Reebok). The chain also stocks sports attire and equipment, from treadmills and trampolines to baseball and yoga gear. Sports fans appreciate the reasonable prices on NFL, NBA and MLB team souvenirs and memorabilia.
✚ 106 D15 ✉ 55 Chambers Street ☎ 212/732-8484 🕐 Mon–Fri 8.30–8, Sat 10–7, Sun 11–6 🚇 Chambers Street (E), City Hall (R), Park Place (1, 2, 3) 🚌 M1, M6

THE MYSTERIOUS BOOKSHOP
www.mysteriousbookshop.com
An essential stop for the compulsive mystery reader as well as the collector of first editions and rare volumes. Sherlock Holmes,

Raymond Chandler, P. D. James and Patricia Highsmith are all here. Recommendations from owner Otto Penzler are sure-fire winners.

✚ 106 D16 ✉ 58 Warren Street at Church Street, TriBeCa ☎ 212/587-1011 🕓 Mon–Sun 11–7 🚇 Chambers Street (1, 2, 3, A, C, E) 🚌 M20, M22

PATRICIA FIELD

www.patriciafield.com

Patricia Field's latest and largest shop sells camp fashions made of rubber, PVC, leather, spandex, plastic and feathers. Styles range from bustiers and garter belts to micro minis. Not for the faint of heart, accessories, wigs and cosmetics are equally outrageous.

✚ 107 E13 ✉ 302 Bowery, between Bleecker and Houston streets ☎ 212/966-4066 🕓 Mon–Thu 11–8, Fri–Sat 11–9, Sun 11–7 🚇 2nd Avenue (V, F), Bleecker Street (4, 5, 6) 🚌 M21, M103

PEARL PAINT

www.pearlpaint.com

You won't find a better place for fine arts supplies at discounted

prices than this multilevel store. The selection of oils, acrylics and other mediums, brushes, easels, markers, pens, pastels, sketchbooks, photo frames and sculpting tools is superb.

✚ 106 D15 ✉ 308 Canal Street, between Mercer Street and Broadway ☎ 212/431-7932 🕓 Mon–Fri 9–7, Sat 10–7, Sun 10–6 🚇 Canal Street (N, R) 🚌 M1, M6

PEARL RIVER

www.pearlriver.com

New Yorkers who have moved out of town often return here to browse the bargains–Asian-style robes, embroidered silk slippers, good-looking ceramics, Asian cuisine ingredients, paper lanterns, and many other appealing objects.

✚ 106 D14 ✉ 477 Broadway, between Broome and Grand streets ☎ 212/431-4770 🕓 Daily 10–7 🚇 Canal Street (N, R) 🚌 M1, M6

THE PUMA STORE

www.puma.com

Puma has made a dramatic return to the fashion scene, with shoes in olive and beige, as well as hot,

vibrant colors like canary yellow and lime green.

✚ 106 D14 ✉ 521 Broadway, between Spring and Broome streets ☎ 212/334-7861 🕓 Mon–Sat 10–8, Sun 11–7 🚇 Prince Street (N, R, W)

RESURRECTION VINTAGE

www.resurrectionvintage.com

This store has great vintage designer clothes—Pucci slips, pieces by Miyake and Vivienne Westwood, and 80s-style skateboard clothes from Alva, Thrasher and others. The owners sell their own lines.

✚ 107 E14 ✉ 217 Mott Street, between Spring and Prince streets ☎ 212/625-1374 🕓 Mon–Sat 11–7, Sun 12–7 🚇 Broadway-Lafayette (F, S, V) or Spring Street (6) 🚌 M1, M21, M103

SIGERSON MORRISON

www.sigersonmorrison.com

The shoes from this exciting designer are not as pricey as Manolos but are stunning nonetheless. Colors range across

Above *Kirna Zabete stocks designer ranges*

the spectrum from red to lavender, and materials include pony skin, suede, satin and metallic leather. Styles range from slingback stilettos to flats and boots.

🚇 107 E14 ✉ 28 Prince Street, between Mott and Elizabeth streets ☎ 212/625-1641 🕐 Mon–Sat 11–7, Sun 12–6 🚇 Broadway-Lafayette (F, S, V), Prince Street (N, R, W) 🚌 M21, M103

SPACE.NK
www.spacenk.com

SoHo is the perfect location for the Stateside opening of British founder Nicky Kinnaird's must-have brand of beauty products. This spacious boutique is a temple of temptation, stocked with her lines in skin care and hair products, carefully sourced from specialists around the world. You'll find all the top names and latest innovations in moisturizers, masks, make-up, fragrances, bath products and much more on the well-stocked shelves. You can also book facials and other treatments.

🚇 106 D14 ✉ 99 Greene Street, between Spring and Prince streets ☎ 212/941-4200 🕐 Mon–Sat 11–7, Sun 12–7 🚇 Spring Street (6), Broadway-Lafayette (B, D, F, V) 🚌 M1, M5, M6, M21

LE SPORTSAC
www.lesportsac.com

Fold-in-a-pouch bags made of rip-stop parachute nylon made this name famous after they were introduced in 1974. Today the brand continues to deliver practical, affordable totes, messenger bags and backpacks, now in fun prints and patterns including batik. A couture line features such materials as sheared mink and fox.

🚇 106 D14 ✉ 118 Greene Street at Prince Street ☎ 212/625-2626 🕐 Mon–Sat 11–7, Sun 12–6 🚇 Broadway/Prince Street (R, W) 🚌 M5, M21

STEVEN ALAN
www.stevenalan.com

Radical fashions for daring fashionistas. The store stocks the very latest international designers such as Vanessa Bruno, Alice Roi and Kateyone Adeli.

Above *Designer clothes from yesteryear can be found at Resurrection Vintage*

🚇 106 D15 ✉ 103 Franklin Street, between West Broadway and Church Street ☎ 212/343-0692 🕐 Mon–Sat 11.30–7 (Thu until 8), Sun 12–6 🚇 Franklin Street (1) 🚌 M1, M6

YOHJI YAMAMOTO
www.YohjiYamamoto.co.jp

Impeccable design and classical draping informs the fashions, often in striking black and white, of this designer. The store itself is an aesthetic gem.

🚇 106 D14 ✉ 103 Grand Street at Mercer Street ☎ 212/966-9066 🕐 Mon–Sat 11–7, Sun 12–6 🚇 Canal Street (A, C, E, J, M, N, Q, R, W, Z, 6) 🚌 M1, M6

ENTERTAINMENT AND NIGHTLIFE

ARLENE'S GROCERY
www.arlenesgrocery.net

This former bodega is one of the best rock clubs in the city. The bar is pleasant, and the back room casually comfortable. It's the place to hear up-and-comers.

🚇 107 F14 ✉ 95 Stanton Street, between Ludlow and Orchard streets ☎ 212/995-1652 🕐 Daily 6pm–4am 🎫 Varies 🚇 Lower East Side/Second Avenue (F, V) 🚌 M15, M21

BARRAMUNDI

Manhattanites enjoy the odd woodsy Adirondack accents at this funky bar. The martinis and caipirhinas taste fine, and the crowd is friendly.

🚇 107 F14 ✉ 67 Clinton Street, between Rivington and Stanton streets ☎ 212/529-6900 🕐 Daily 6pm–4am 🚇 Delancey/Essex (F, J, M, Z)

BOWERY BALLROOM
www.boweryballroom.com

When Patti Smith came out of retirement, it was to this rollicking tri-level venue in a 1929 Beaux Arts building that she returned. The club opened in 1997 and has comfortable lounges, good sound systems, a large stage and excellent sight lines. Beth Orton, Soul Asylum, Chris Robinson, David Byrne and Counting Crows have played here.

🚇 107 E14 ✉ 6 Delancey Street, between Bowery and Chrystie streets ☎ 212/533-2111 🎫 $13–$35 🚇 Delancey/Essex (F, J, M, Z) 🚌 M103

BRIDGE CAFÉ
www.eatgoodinny.com

In New York they don't come much older than the Bridge Café, a tavern that was first opened in 1794 and still has the feel of the 18th century. The bright red wood-framed building stands in the shadow of Brooklyn Bridge. With a colorful history as a brothel and a speakeasy, today the tavern has a fine bar menu and is terrific for a Sunday brunch.

⊹ 107 E16 ✉ 279 Water Street, between Dover Street and Peck Slip ☎ 212/227-3344 🕐 Tue–Thu 11.45am–11pm, Fri 11.45am–midnight, Sat 5pm–midnight, Sun–Mon 11.45am–10pm 🚇 Fulton St.-Broadway/ Nassau (2, 3, 4, 5, A, C, J, M, Z)

THE BUBBLE LOUNGE
www.bubblelounge.com

This 1930s-style lounge celebrates champagne by serving more than 24 types by the glass and 350 by the bottle, amid luxurious red sofas, marble tables and light orbs.

⊹ 106 D15 ✉ 228 West Broadway, between Franklin and White streets ☎ 212/431-3433 🕐 Mon–Thu 5pm–2am, Fri–Sat 5pm–4am 🚇 Franklin Street (1)

EAR INN
http://earinn.com

This 1817 bar near the Hudson River used to cater to sailors and stevedores and now attracts writers and artists.

⊹ 106 C14 ✉ 326 Spring Street, between Greenwich and Washington streets ☎ 212/226-9060 🕐 Daily noon–3am 🚇 Spring Street (C, E), Canal Street (1)

ELEMENT
www.elementny.com

Opened in 2006 in a former bank building (and once the studio of artist Jasper Johns), by 2007 Element was already being acclaimed as one of the city's best dance clubs in an online poll. Attractions include a powerful sound system and a huge hardwood dance floor.

⊹ 107 F13 ✉ 225 East Houston Street at Essex ☎ 212/254-2200 🕐 Thu–Sun 10pm–4am 🚇 Lower East Side-Second Avenue (F, V)

FANELLI CAFE
www.fanellicafe.com

Open the etched-glass doors and step through, and you could be in

London. A few artists still gather here, and you can get pub food in the back room.

⊹ 106 D14 ✉ 94 Prince Street at Mercer Street ☎ 212/226-9412 🕐 Mon–Thu 10am–1am, Fri–Sat 10am–2am, Sun 11.30am–1am 🚇 Prince Street (N, R)

FILM FORUM
www.filmforum.com

The leading cinema for independent films, Film Forum also shows domestic and foreign documentaries, as well as revivals of classics.

⊹ 106 D14 ✉ 209 West Houston Street, between Sixth Avenue and Varick Street (Seventh Avenue) ☎ 212/727-8110 or 212/727-8112 ✋ $10.50 🚇 Houston Street (1) 🚌 M5, M6, M20, M21

FLEA THEATER
www.theflea.org

Interestingly named, Flea Theater is home to the Bat Theater Company, which presents works by playwrights who are breaking boundaries—society's or their own.

⊹ 106 D15 ✉ 41 White Street, between Broadway and Church Street ☎ 212/226-2407 🚇 Canal Street (A, C, E) 🚌 M1, M6

HAPPY ENDING

This duplex lounge still reveals traces of its former life as a massage parlor, from the bellybutton-level showerheads to the tiled sauna alcoves and the circular booths (which used to be tubs). Innovative drinks are served.

⊹ 107 E14 ✉ 302 Broome Street, between Eldridge and Forsythe streets ☎ 212/334-9676 🕐 Tue 10pm–4am, Wed–Sat 7pm–4am 🚇 Delancey/Essex (F, J, M, Z)

HOUSING WORKS USED BOOK CAFÉ
www.housingworks.org

This bookstore with a gallery has become a major literary hub for readings, parties and events. Every third Friday of the month, there's an acoustic music concert. All monies go to support homeless people.

⊹ 106 E14 ✉ 126 Crosby Street at Jersey Street ☎ 212/334-3324 🕐 Mon–Fri

10–9, Sat–Sun 12–7 (readings/events vary) ✋ Free–$20 🚇 Prince Street (N, R), Broadway-Lafayette (F, S, V), Bleecker Street (6) 🚌 M1

JAZZ GALLERY
www.jazzgallery.org

The Jazz Gallery opened in 1995. This exhibition and performance space is used for jazz-oriented and jazz-influenced art, literature, drama and music.

⊹ 106 C14 ✉ 290 Hudson Street, between Dominick and Spring streets ☎ 212-242-1063 🕐 Times vary, check program ✋ $12–$65 🚇 Spring Street (C, E), Houston Street (1) 🚌 M20, M21

JOYCE SOHO
www.joyce.org

This theater offers cutting-edge dance, often with an alternative perspective. Rehearsals are open to the public.

⊹ 106 D14 ✉ 155 Mercer Street, between Houston and Prince streets ☎ 212/431-9233 or 212/334-7479 ✋ $19–$40 🚇 Prince Street (N, R, W) 🚌 M1, M6, M21

KUSH
www.thekushnyc.com

Exotic Moroccan-inspired decor sets the stage for the hip crowd at this seductive lounge, with its private alcoves and sunken hookah lounge. Global music spins on the turntable most nights.

⊹ 107 E14 ✉ 191 Chrystie Street, between Stanton and Rivington streets ☎ 212/677-7328 🕐 Wed–Sun 7pm–4am 🚇 Lower East Side/2nd Avenue (F, V), Bowery (J, M, Z)

LANDMARK SUNSHINE CINEMA
www.landmarktheatres.com

This five-screener offers a medley of movies, from challenging documentaries such as *Bowling for Columbine*, foreign films and oldies, to first-run movies. Seating is raked and more comfortable than at other similar movie houses.

⊹ 107 E13 ✉ 143 East Houston Street, between First and Second avenues ☎ 212/330-8182 ✋ $12.50 🚇 Second Avenue (F, V) 🚌 M15, M21

MANHATTAN ENSEMBLE THEATER

www.met.com

Home to the Manhattan Ensemble, which was founded by David Fishelson, this theater presents new plays that may well be by well-known playwrights.

⊞ 106 D14 ✉ 55 Mercer Street, between Broome and Grand streets ☎ 212/925-1900 🚇 Canal Street (J, M, N, Q), Spring Street (C, E) 🚌 M1, M6

MERC BAR

www.mercbar.com

The ultra-hip have moved on, but this bar has comfortable seating, seductive lighting and groovy music. The front banquettes are great places for people-watching in the summer months.

⊞ 106 D14 ✉ 151 Mercer Street, between Houston and Prince streets ☎ 212/966-2727 ⊙ Sun–Thu 5pm–1am, Fri–Sat 5pm–3.30am 🚇 Broadway/ Lafayette (F, S, V), Bleecker Street (6)

Below *Cocktail bars and lounges abound in Lower Manhattan*

MERCURY LOUNGE

www.mercuryloungenyc.com

This is a regular stop for sampling the downtown music scene. Bands—both local and international—perform back to back in one amazing, raucous room. You might find Holly Go Lightly, who sang with punk Brit Billy Childish, doing garage rock, for example. The adjacent lounge is slightly more serene.

⊞ 107 F13 ✉ 217 East Houston Street, between First Avenue and Avenue A ☎ 212/260-4700 ⊙ Daily 8pm–3am 🖐 $8–$20 🚇 Lower East Side/Second Avenue (F, V) 🚌 M14, M21

Ñ

A tiny narrow bar, Ñ serves sangria with tasty tapas. There is a good selection of sherry and excellent Spanish wines.

⊞ 106 E14 ✉ 33 Crosby Street, between Broome and Grand streets ☎ 212/219-8856 ⊙ Sun–Thu 5pm–2am, Fri–Sat 5pm–4am 🚇 Spring Street (6)

PERFORMING GARAGE

www.thewoostergroup.org

Home to the Wooster Group, an Obie-winning troupe founded in 1975 by Jim Clayburgh, Willem Dafoe, Spalding Gray and others. The group produces and develops experimental entertainment and theater.

⊞ 106 D14 ✉ 33 Wooster Street at Grand Street ☎ 212/966-9796 🚇 Canal Street (A, C, E) 🚌 M6

PIANOS

www.pianosnyc.com

Don't expect piano entertainment at this bi-level bar—the name is a relic of a previous occupant. Go for the alternative music on Friday, Sunday and Monday.

⊞ 107 F14 ✉ 158 Ludlow Street, between Stanton and Rivington streets ☎ 212/505-3733 ⊙ Daily 3pm–4am 🖐 $8–$10 🚇 DeLancey/Essex Street (F, J, M, Z)

POETS HOUSE

www.poetshouse.org

Poet's House is a 45,000-volume poetry library and meeting place with panoramic views of the Hudson River and Statue of Liberty. It has regular readings and lectures, and offers poetry workshops run by established poets.

⊞ 106 C16 ✉ 10 River Terrace at Battery Park City ☎ 212/431-7920 🖐 Free–$7 🚇 Chambers Street (1, 2, 3), World Trade Center (E) 🚌 M1

PRAVDA

Caviar and other Russian snacks accompany the vodka at this classy lounge. An amazing 65 different vodkas are available, many infused with a variety of exotic ingredients like ginger, mango or horseradish.

⊞ 106 E14 ✉ 281 Lafayette Street, between Houston and Prince streets ☎ 212/226-4944 ⊙ Mon–Wed 5pm–1am, Thu–Sat 5pm–4am, Sun 6pm–1am (closed Sun, Jul–Aug) 🚇 Broadway/ Lafayette (F, S, V), Bleecker Street (6)

SLIPPER ROOM

www.slipperroom.com

The name Slipper Room captures the mood of this lounge, which claims to be "New York's True Home of Burlesque." Shows feature aspiring cabaret artists, stand-up comedy and live music. Try the cocktails while being entertained.

⊞ 107 F14 ✉ 167 Orchard Street at Stanton Street ☎ 212/253-7246 ⊙ Daily 8pm–4am 🚇 Lower East Side/Second Avenue (F, V)

SOB'S

www.sobs.com

Since 1982 this club (Sounds of Brazil) has been at the forefront of Afro-Latino music. The featured band might play hip-hop and rap or driving Latin salsa with Haitian, reggae and Bhangra music, too.

⊞ 106 C14 ✉ 204 Varick Street at Houston Street ☎ 212/243-4940 ⊙ Show times and opening hours vary; call for details 🖐 $20 minimum 🚇 Houston Street (1) 🚌 M20, M21

Opposite *Ride the Staten Island Ferry for great, free, views of the harbor*

SPORTS AND ACTIVITIES
NEW YORK KAYAK COMPANY
www.nykayak.com

This company offers classes and guided tours by kayak. The tours last two or three hours.

✚ 106 C14 ✉ Pier 40 at Houston Street, ☎ 212/924-1327 🕓 Tours early May to mid-Oct ✋ Classes: $50 per hr; tours: $100–$150 🚇 Houston Street (1) 🚌 M21

PATRIOT TOURS
▷ 270.

HEALTH AND BEAUTY
SOHO SANCTUARY
www.sohosanctuary.com

This spa and yoga studio achieved a well-deserved reputation when actor Julia Roberts made frequent visits. It offers a full range of facials, therapeutic body wraps and massage.

✚ 106 D14 ✉ 119 Mercer Street near Prince Street ☎ 212/334-5550 🕓 Tue–Fri 10–9, Sat 10–8, Sun 12–6, Mon 3–9 ✋ Facial $125–$250, massage $125–$210 🚇 Prince Street (N, R, W) 🚌 M1, M6

FOR CHILDREN
CHILDREN'S MUSEUM OF THE ARTS
www.cmany.org

Children aged from 1 to 11 are welcome at this playground-cum-museum, which offers all kinds of hands-on art projects.

✚ 106 E14 ✉ 182 Lafayette Street, between Broome and Grand streets ☎ 212/274-0986 🕓 Wed, Fri–Sun 12–5, Thu 12–6 ✋ $10, child (under 1) free 🚇 Spring Street (6), Prince Street (N, R) 🚌 M1

ELLIS ISLAND
▷ 72–74.

MUSEUM OF COMIC AND CARTOON ART
www.moccany.org

Adults seeking to relive their childhoods and older kids who love their super heroes enjoy coming here. The museum aims to promote the art of telling stories through pictures. Exhibits are dedicated to the works of such seminal figures as Harvey Kurtzman, founder of *MAD*

magazine, or are theme-oriented like the recent Infinite Canvas exhibit, which explored the world of web-based comics.

✚ 106 D14 ✉ 594 Broadway (4th floor), between Houston and Prince ☎ 212/254-3511 🕓 Tue–Sun 12–5 ✋ $5, under 12 free 🚇 Broadway-Lafayette (B, D, F, V, 6), Prince Street (N, R, W) 🚌 M1, M6

SOUTH STREET SEAPORT MUSEUM AND MARKETPLACE
▷ 82–83.

STATEN ISLAND FERRY
www.siferry.com

The view from the decks of the harbor, the Statue of Liberty and the Lower Manhattan skyline is stunning—and free.

✚ 106 E18 ✉ Whitehall Terminal, 1 Whitehall Street ☎ 718/727-2508 or 718/815-2628 🕓 Daily ✋ Free 🚇 South Ferry (1), Whitehall Street (N, R, W) 🚌 M1, M6, M15

STATUE OF LIBERTY
▷ 84–85.

PRICES AND SYMBOLS

The prices given are the average for a two-course lunch (L) and a three-course dinner (D) for one person, without drinks. The wine price is for the least expensive bottle.

For a key to the symbols, ▷ 2.

AQUAGRILL

www.aquagrill.com

The day's fresh selection of seafood—cod, halibut, grouper, monkfish, tuna—can be prepared to your specifications, roasted, poached or grilled, or served in such dishes as sea bass with smoked pepper and crispy bacon in thyme vinaigrette. The oyster bar offers about 24 varieties.

✚ 106 D14 ✉ 210 Spring Street at Sixth Avenue ☎ 212/274-0505 🕓 Mon–Thu 12–3, 6–10.45, Fri 12–3, 6–11.45, Sat 12–3.45, 6–11.45, Sun 12–3.45, 6–10.30 ✋ L $30, D $50, Wine $27 🚇 Spring Street (C, E) 🚌 M6

BALTHAZAR

www.balthazarny.com

Keith McNally has cloned a classic Paris brasserie. Bistro fare includes the seafood platter piled high with oysters, clams, shrimp and scallops; chicken paprika; and skate in brown butter. The place is crowded and vibrant and loaded with celebrity cachet. Bread and pastries come from the adjacent bakery. The wine list features a selection of totally French varieties.

✚ 106 E14 ✉ 80 Spring Street, between Broadway and Lafayette Street ☎ 212/965-1414 🕓 Mon–Thu 7.30–11.30, 12–5, 5.45–12, Fri 7.30–11.30, 12–5, 5.45–1, Sat 8–4, 5.45–1, Sun 8–4, 5.30–12 ✋ L $30, D $45, Wine $26 🚇 Prince Street (N, R), Spring Street (6) 🚌 M1, M5

BAR PITTI

Actors, writers, fashion designers and Village residents gather at this European-style *boîte*. In summer, the sidewalk dining affords great people-watching and the chance to observe the comings and goings at celebrity hot spot Da Silvano. Your best bet is to select one of the reliable meat, fish or pasta chalkboard specials. Otherwise, choose one of the typical pastas, perhaps spaghetti with clam sauce. Credit cards are not accepted.

✚ 106 D13 ✉ 268 Sixth Avenue, between Bleecker and Houston streets ☎ 212/982-3300 🕓 Daily 12–12 ✋ L $25, D $38, Wine $30 🚇 West 4th (A, C, F, S, V), Houston Street (1) 🚌 M5, M6

BIG WONG KING

At this Manhattan restaurant you're guaranteed a cheap, tasty meal. Don't expect tablecloth or efficient service. You're here for noodles (with duck, chicken, shrimp), congee and other standard Cantonese dishes. Credit cards are not accepted.

✚ 107 E15 ✉ 67 Mott Street, between Bayard and Canal streets ☎ 212/964-0540 🕓 Daily 8.30am–9pm ✋ L $15, D $20 🚇 Canal Street (J, M, N, Q, R, W, Z, 6) 🚌 M1

BLUE RIBBON BAKERY

www.blueribbonrestaurants.com

Sandwiches made with house-baked breads and tasty small plates—mushroom ravioli, sweet *sopressata*, smoked red trout—draw crowds at lunch, while such dinner entrées as New Orleans barbecue shrimp and filet mignon with tomato, onion and watercress salad and potato cake draw night-time customers. There is a wide choice of cheese and an extensive wine list. The restaurant's hundred-year-old brick oven produces the tantalizing varieties of fresh-baked lunch sandwich and dinner breads. The extensive dessert menu features crème brûlée, bread puddings and sundaes.

Opposite *Fresh flavors on a plate*

✚ 106 C13 ✉ 35 Downing Street
at Bedford Street ☎ 212/337-0404
🕐 Mon–Thu 12–12, Fri 12pm–2am, Sat
11.30am–2am, Sun 11.30am–midnight
✋ L $25, D $50, Wine $28 🚇 Houston
Street (1)

BOULEY
www.davidbouley.com
The new Bouley is down the street
from the old restaurant. David
Bouley has created a romantic
candle-lit atmosphere, with vaulted
ceiling, fireplace and Impressionist
paintings. Entrées include chicken
with black truffle and fresh almond
purée, or cod with black onion crust.
The desserts are the real show here:
try the caramelized Anjou pear with
biscuit, chocolate and a scoop of
vanilla-flavored ice cream, or the
complex chocolate frivolous with
multiple components and textures.
✚ 106 D15 ✉ 163 Duane Street at
Hudson ☎ 212/964-2525 🕐 Daily
11.30–3, 5–11.30 ✋ L $55, D $75, Wine
$45 🚇 Chambers Street (A, C, E, 1, 2, 3)
🚌 M6, M20

BREAD
This small casual café makes
delicious paninis, soups, salads and
daily plates. Try the gazpacho in
summer and the prosciutto di Parma
with truffle oil, bruschetta, spicy
shrimp salad, and delicious bread
and tomato soup in winter. There is a
choice of wines with 12 wines sold
by the glass.
✚ 107 E14 ✉ 20 Spring Street, between
Elizabeth and Mott streets ☎ 212/334-
1015 🕐 Sun–Thu 10.30–midnight, Fri–Sat
10.30–1am ✋ L $15, D $25 🚇 Spring
Street (6), Bowery (J, M, Z), Grand Street
(S) 🚌 M1

CHANTERELLE
www.chanterellenyc.com
The presentation of the superb
food is simply exquisite at this
ultra-spacious classic restaurant.
The menu changes monthly, but
the cuisine is always full-flavored
and of a consistently high standard.
Conclude with one of the luscious

desserts—molten vanilla cake with
spring strawberries, for example.
✚ 106 D15 ✉ 2 Harrison Street
at Hudson Street ☎ 212/966-6960
🕐 Thu–Sat 12–2.30, 5.30–11, Sun–Wed
5.30–11 ✋ L $35, 3-course prix fixe $42,
D 3-course prix fixe $98, tasting $128, Wine
$30 🚇 Franklin Street (1) 🚌 M20

DIM SUM GO GO
At this small, modernist restaurant
you can find the latest in Chinese
cuisine: dim sum, presented in
bamboo steamers or on pupu
platters. Expect jicama and lotus
root dumplings, crabmeat stuffed
in green spinach dough, wood
mushrooms and carrot dumplings.
✚ 107 E15 ✉ 5 East Broadway, between
Catherine and Oliver streets ☎ 212/732-
0797 🕐 Daily 10am–11pm ✋ L $23,
D $32 🚇 East Broadway (F), Canal Street
(J, M, N, R, Q, W, Z, 6) 🚌 M9, M15, M22

HAMPTON CHUTNEY
www.hamptonchutney.com
South Indian dosas and uttapas
are the specialties of this counter-
style eatery. The classic dosa is
filled with spiced potato here, but
many Western-inspired variations
are offered, from avocado, tomato,
arugula and jack cheese, to tuna
with cilantro-chutney dressing. Good
sandwiches on black, sourdough and
other breads, too. Chai and lassi are
the choice drinks.
✚ 106 E14 ✉ 68 Prince Street, between
Crosby and Lafayette streets ☎ 212/226-
9996 🕐 Daily 11–9 ✋ $15 🚇 Prince
Street (N, R), Broadway/Lafayette (F, S, V),
Spring Street (6) 🚌 M1, M6

THE HARRISON
www.theharrison.com
With its tufted leather banquettes
and weathered wood paneling, this
friendly, inviting restaurant is the
kind of neighborhood spot where
people drop in regularly. The food
is brimming with flavor; the skillet
calf's liver comes with bacon,
onion and potato strudel in a rich
sherry sauce, while sautéed skate
is redolent of treviso, pancetta and
preserved lemon. The spicy French
fries are superb.

✚ 106 D15 ✉ 355 Greenwich Street
at Harrison Street ☎ 212/274-9310
🕐 Mon–Thu 5.30–10.30, Fri–Sat 5.30–11,
Sun 5–10 ✋ D $55, Wine $36 🚇 Franklin
Street (1) 🚌 M20

KATZ'S DELI
www.katzdeli.com
The site of the hilarious climactic
scene in *When Harry Met Sally*
is the last remaining deli in what
was once a thriving Jewish
neighborhood. Opened in 1888, it
upholds deli traditions: nondescript
surroundings and immense knishes
and pastrami sandwiches. They
make their own salami, the corned
beef takes 30 days to cure, and the
sandwiches, platters and meats are
served in large portions. Always
bustling, this popular deli serves
presidents, foreign dignitaries,
movie stars and hungry visitors from
around the world as well as locals.
Credit cards are accepted on bills of
$20 and more only.
✚ 107 F13 ✉ 205 East Houston Street,
between Ludlow and Orchard streets
☎ 212/254-2246 🕐 Sun, Wed–Thu
8am–10.45pm, Mon–Tue 8am–9.45pm,
Fri–Sat 8am–2.45am ✋ L $11, D $22
🚇 Lower East Side/Second Avenue (F, V)
🚌 M14, M15, M21

LUPA
www.luparestaurant.com
Lupa, the moderately priced
restaurant owned by beloved Food
Channel host Mario Batali and two
partners, has the feel of a casual
Roman trattoria. The cuisine starts
with ultra-fresh staples, many of
which are made on the premises,
notably the pasta, sausages and
cheeses featured as appetizers.
The simple, intense main dishes
range from a classic saltimbocca to
bucatini all'amatriciana, made with
bacon, onions and cilantro. Side
dishes such as braised escarole and
cauliflower with capers are worthy
additions to the menu.
✚ 106 D13 ✉ 170 Thompson Street,
between Bleecker and Houston streets
☎ 212/982-5089 🕐 Daily 12–12
✋ L $32, D $45, Wine $21 🚇 West 4th
Street (A, C, E, F, S, V) 🚌 M5, M6, M21

MARK JOSEPH STEAKHOUSE
www.markjosephsteakhouse.com
Those who have had enough of Peter Luger's sawdust-on-the-floor style claim that this sleek and more modern meat specialist is the city's best steakhouse. The porterhouse is the choice cut. Finish with the apple galette or a slice of pecan pie.
🏠 107 E16 ✉ 261 Water Street at Peck Slip ☎ 212/277-0020 🕐 Mon–Fri 11.30–10, Fri 11.30–11, Sat 5–11 ✋ L $30, D $60, Wine $40 🚇 Broadway-Nassau (A, C), Fulton Street (J, M, Z, 2, 3, 4, 5) 🚌 M9, M15

NAM
www.namnyc.com
Nam stands out for its style and its authentic and unique dishes. Particularly alluring are appetizers. *Banh xeo*, for example, is a crêpe filled with mushrooms, bean sprouts, coconut-flavored rice, shrimp and chicken; *ca tim nuong* consists of grilled Asian eggplant (aubergine) with ginger, lime, garlic and a little chili. Among the many main dishes, crisp red snapper and chicken with chile lemongrass sauce make excellent dinner choices.
🏠 106 D15 ✉ 110 Reade Street at West Broadway ☎ 212/267-1777 🕐 Mon–Fri 12–2pm, Sun–Thu 5.30–10, Fri–Sat 5.30–11 ✋ L $25, D $39, Wine $28 🚇 Chambers Street (1) 🚌 M20

NOBU
www.noburestaurants.com
Celebrities flock to Drew Nieporent's TriBeCa hotspot for the artistic sushi and sashimi fashioned by chef Nobu Matsuhisa. The *omakase* menu will deliver the chef's inspirations for the day. Or choose from baby abalone, live scallop or sashimi drizzled with garlic and ginger-flavored olive oil. Masu sake is served in small cedar cups with salted rims; finish with green tea crème caramel. Reservations are hard to come by; the next best thing is to drop in to Next Door Nobu.
🏠 106 D15 ✉ 105 Hudson Street, between Franklin and North Moore streets ☎ 212/219-0500 🕐 Mon–Fri 11.45–2.15, 5.45–10.15, Sat–Sun 5.45–10.15 ✋ L $30,

D $60, *omakase* $100, $120 or $150, Wine $34 🚇 Franklin Street (1) 🚌 M20

NYONYA
You can sample some of Malaysia's appealing, sometimes spicy dishes at this plain favorite. You have a wide choice of rice, noodle, casserole and other dishes; start with a roti (Indian pancake) or the satays, and follow with a fiery sambal or a curry made with lemongrass, chili and coconut milk. Credit cards are not accepted.
🏠 107 E14 ✉ 194 Grand Street, between Mott and Mulberry streets ☎ 212/334-3669 🕐 Sun–Thu 11am–11.30pm, Fri–Sat 11am–midnight ✋ L $20, D $25 🚇 Grand Street (S) 🚌 M1

ODEON
www.theodeonrestaurant.com
In the early 1980s this cafeteria-turned-hip-bistro was the incubator of the downtown scene. Odeon still has Venetian blinds on the windows and chrome stools at the bar, but nowadays it caters to neighborhood residents as well as downtown celebrities, with a typical bistro menu of onion soup gratinée, moules and steak frites. This is a great late-night stop.
🏠 106 D15 ✉ 145 West Broadway, between Thomas and Duane streets ☎ 212/233-0507 🕐 Mon–Fri 11.45–3, 5.30–midnight, Sat–Sun 10am–2am (also Mon–Wed midnight–1am, Thu–Sat midnight–2am) ✋ L $32, D $45, Wine $32 🚇 Chambers Street (A, C, E), Chambers Street (1, 2, 3) 🚌 M6, M20

PEASANT
www.peasantnyc.com
This cozy storefront has become a popular chef's hang-out. As the name suggests, it produces bold rustic Italian cuisine from its wood-fired ovens. Wood-roasted sardines, roasted clams and really fine pizzas are carefully prepared. The grilled fishes are flavored with the best olive oil, lemon and herbs.
🏠 107 E14 ✉ 194 Elizabeth Street, between Prince and Spring streets ☎ 212/965-9511 🕐 Tue–Sat 6–11, Sun 6–10 ✋ D $40, Wine $20 🚇 Bowery (J, M, Z), Spring Street (6) 🚌 M1, M6

TOMOE SUSHI
Around the corner from New York University, this plain sushi parlor does a brisk trade among students and other sushi aficionados, drawn by its reasonable prices. About 30 different sushi choices and 30 varieties of *maki* rolls are available, along with hot dishes and noodles.
🏠 106 D13 ✉ 172 Thompson Street, between Bleecker and Houston streets ☎ 212/777-9346 🕐 Mon 5–11, Tue–Sat 1–3, 5–11, Sun 5–10 ✋ L $28, D $44 🚇 West 4th Street (A, C, E, F, S, V) 🚌 M5, M6, M21

WD-50
www.wd-50.com
Wylie Dufresne made the Lower East Side a dining destination when he cooked at 71 Clinton Street. Now he has his own place, a sleek postmodern dining room where he mixes exciting but harmonious flavor combinations—octopus with celery pesto, pineapple and almonds, striped bass with passion fruit. Desserts are also creative.
🏠 107 F14 ✉ 50 Clinton Street, between Stanton and Rivington streets (east side of the street) ☎ 212/477-2900 🕐 Wed–Sat 6–11, Sun 6–10 ✋ D $55, Wine $44 🚇 Delancey (F), Essex (J, M, Z) 🚌 M9, M21

WOO LAE OAK
www.woolaeoaksoho.com
Here, you'll find a stylized American version of Korean cuisine. Start with the hot Dungeness crab wrapped in spinach crêpes, or tuna tartare served over Korean pear. Among the selections for the on-the-table barbecue there are 17 meats, fishes and vegetables, including ostrich, squid and tripe. Among other dishes, short ribs are swathed in sweet soy sauce, and then there are soups, casseroles and rice dishes. Don't forget the kimchi—pickle dishes that are always on the Korean table.
🏠 106 D14 ✉ 148 Mercer Street, between Houston and Prince streets ☎ 212/925-8200 🕐 Sun–Thu 12–10.30, Fri–Sat 12–11.30 ✋ L $15, D $45, Wine $34 🚇 Broadway/Lafayette (F, S, V), Prince Street (N, R), Bleecker Street (6) 🚌 M1, M5

PRICES AND SYMBOLS

Prices are the lowest and highest for a double room for one night. Breakfast is included unless noted otherwise. All the hotels listed accept credit cards unless otherwise stated. Note that rates vary widely throughout the year.

For a key to the symbols, ▷ 2.

COSMOPOLITAN HOTEL–TRIBECA
www.cosmohotel.com
This hotel has a great downtown location and good-looking rooms. They're all furnished with Scandinavian-style pieces, and they have private bath, TV and telephone.
✚ 106 D15 ✉ 95 West Broadway at Chambers Street, 10007 ☎ 212/566-1900 ✋ $270–$275 ℹ 125 Ⓒ Chambers Street (1, 2, 3), Chambers Street (A, C) 🚌 M20

HOTEL AZURE
www.hotelazure.com
The Azure is a compact boutique hotel in SoHo, which is smoke-free. Room rates include a newspaper and bottled water. Rooms are simple but bright and modern, with lots of blue and white, and all have free high-speed internet, direct-dial phones with voice mail and 32-inch flat-screen TVs with cable.
✚ 106 E15 ✉ 120 Lafayette Street at Canal Street, 10013 ☎ 212/925-4378 ✋ $303–$400 ℹ 28 Ⓒ Canal Street (4, 5, 6)

MERCER
www.mercerhotel.com
The Hollywood crowd loves this East Coast version of Andre Balaz's Château Marmont. The SoHo location is ultra-hip, but the place is discreet, comfortable and tranquil. The loft-style rooms are spacious and minimalist. Christian Liaigre used neutral colors, glass, fabrics like linen, and rich woods from Africa. Spacious bathrooms are standard, and most offer marble tubs for two. If that's not enough,

Above *Lower Manhattan has some lovely boutique hotels*

then the Mercer Kitchen under star chef Jean Georges Vongerichten is the clincher. Access to a nearby fitness center is provided.
✚ 106 D14 ✉ 147 Mercer Street, between Prince and Spring streets, 10012 ☎ 212/966-6060 ✋ $600–$820, suite from $1,500 ℹ 75 rooms and suites Ⓒ Prince St (N, R, W) 🚌 M1, M6

OFF-SOHO SUITES
www.offsoho.com
These suites, which have bedroom and living/dining areas, are on the Lower East Side, the last of Manhattan's gentrified neighborhoods. Savvy travelers will appreciate the low prices. Ideal for two couples traveling together, as each suite shares a kitchen and bath, they are well equipped with cable TV, telephone, modular jack and minibar.
✚ 107 E14 ✉ 11 Rivington Street, between Chrystie and Bowery streets, 10002 ☎ 212/979-9815 ✋ $199–$459, quads $289–$379 ℹ 38 suites 🍴 Ⓒ Bowery (J, M, Z) 🚌 M103

SOHO GRAND
www.sohogrand.com
Since the CEO of Hartz pet food owns this stylish downtown hotel, it puts out a welcome mat for animals. It was a pioneer, too, when it opened in art-oriented SoHo. A cast-iron staircase studded with

coke-bottle glass leads up to the vibrant lobby. Cool tones create the ambience in the rooms, but there are plenty of guest comforts— bathrobes, Frette linens, velvet drapes, plus DVD, WiFi, restaurant, and two bars.
✚ 106 D14 ✉ 310 West Broadway, between Canal and Grand streets, 10013 ☎ 212/965-3000 ✋ From $399, suite $3,500 ℹ 363 rooms and suites 🍴 Ⓒ Canal Street (A, C, E) 🚌 M5

TRIBECA GRAND
www.tribecagrand.com
With its luxurious 98-seat private screening room, this hotel, close to SoHo and the Village, caters to the independent film crowd. The lobby opens to a dramatic atrium lounge/ restaurant. The rooms are modern and come with such gadgets as wireless keyboards, a bathroom TV with waterproof remote, Bose radio and fax/printer. Bliss and Kiehl products in the bathroom and the Dean & DeLuca snacks are alluring extras. The business center is well equipped, and the workstations have flat-panel screens. Hartz owns the place, so pets are welcome.
✚ 106 D15 ✉ 2 Avenue of the Americas at White Street, 10013 ☎ 212/519-6600 ✋ Doubles from $450, suite from $699 ℹ 203 rooms 🍴 Ⓒ Franklin Street (1) 🚌 M6

Hudson

Charles Street
West 10th Street
Christopher Street
Barrow
Morton Street
Bedford St
Church of St Luke-in-the-Fields
House of Oldies Rare Records
Minetta Lane
La Guardia Place
Great Jones Street
Bond Street
Lafayette Street

Bar Pitti
Blue Ribbon Bakery
Bleecker Street
Lupa
Tomoe Sushi
Bleecker Street

Saint Luke's Place
11 Walker Park
Leroy Street
Downing Street
Carmine Street
WEST HOUSTON
Thompson
Sullivan
MacDougal
Broadway
Mercer

Woo Lae Oak
St Patrick's Old Cathedral
Prince Street
Jersey St

Clarkson Street
Washington
Greenwich
HOUSTON
VARICK
Houston Street
King Street
Charlton Street
Vandam Street
West HOUSTON
Prince Street
West Broadway
Wooster Street
Greene Street
Mercer
Singer Building
Hamp Chutn
Spring Street

WEST
Aquagrill
Spring Street
Spring Street
Mercer
Balthazar

New York City Fire Museum
Dominick
Broome Street
SOHO
Haughwout Building

AVENUE OF THE AMERICAS (6TH AVENUE)
Watts Street
Grand
Children's Museum of the Arts
Grand

American Numismatic Society
CANAL
Canal Street
Grand
Thompson
SoHo Grand
Museum of Chinese in America
Crosby
Broom

Renwick
Spring Street
Watts
Desbrosses
Vestry
HOLLAND TUNNEL
CANAL ST
Saint John's Lane
Canal Street
Howard Street
Hotel Azure
Canal Street

VARICK
Beach St
Lispenard
White Street
LOWER MANHATTA
Walker Street

LAIGHT STREET
Hubert
HUDSON STREET
Ericsson Place
Franklin Street
Tribeca Grand
Franklin
CHURCH STREET
LAFAYETTE STREET
CENTRE STREET

Beach Street
North Moore
Nobu
Franklin St
TRIBECA
Leonard
Street
Thomas Paine Park

WEST STREET
The Harrison
Greenwich St
Chanterelle
Worth
Street

Harrison
Jay St
Staple St
Duane
Bouley
Odeon
Thomas
Trimble
Duane
US Courthouse
Diane

Washington Market Park
Reade St
Chambers Street
Nam
Reade Street
BROADWAY
Reade
Chambers Street

CHAMBERS
Cosmopolitan Hotel-Tribeca
Chambers Street
City Hall
Brooklyn Bridge
City Hall Park
City Hall

Warren Street
Park Place West
Murray Street
Barclay Street
Warren
Greenwich
WEST
CHURCH STREET
Murray Street
Warren
Park Place
City Hall

9A
Park Place
Woolworth Building
PARK ROW
Spruce
Beekman

BATTERY PARK CITY
Vesey Street
BARCLAY
Park Place
Church of St Peter
VESEY ST
Ann
Beekman
WILLIAM STREET

VESEY STREET
St Paul's Chapel
World Trade Center
Fulton St
Fulton Street
Dey St
Fulton Street
Broadway-Nassau St
Dutch Street
Fulton Street

Ground Zero
Cortlandt Street
John
Maiden Lane
Platt St

Cortlandt Street
Cortlandt Street
BROADWAY
Federal Reserve Bank

Liberty Street
Liberty Street
Cedar
MAIDEN LANE
Liberty St
WEST STREET
Washington
Greenwich

Albany Street
TRINITY PLACE
Trinity Church
Pine
Federal Hall National Monument
Wall Street

Rector Street
Wall Street
Rector Street
Rector Street
New York Stock Exchange
Exchange Aly
Broad
Museum of American Finance
Wall Stre

South End Avenue
West Thames Street
GREENWICH STREET
Morris Street
Beaver
Broadway
South William St

Little West Street
Morris Street
Battery Place
Bowling Green
Fraunces Tavern Museum
Water

Hudson

Museum of Jewish Heritage
HIGHWAY 9A
1st Place
Battery Place
Whitehall Street
Rectory of the Shrine of Elizabeth Ann Seton
PETER MINUIT PLAZA

Robert F Wagner Jr Park
Battery Park
STATE STREET

Castle Clinton
Admiral George Dewey Promenade
BROOKLYN BATTERY TUNNEL
Staten Island Ferry Term
South Ferry

0   250 m
0   250 yds

B   C   D

Ellis Island Immigration Museum,

East 3rd Street
East 2nd Street
East 1st Street

2nd Avenue
STREET

New Museum of Contemporary Art

asant

Bread

TTLE
ALY

yonya

are

BOWERY

CANAL STREET

Big Wong King

INATOWN

treet

EAST HOUSTON STREET

Katz's Deli

WD-50

Off-SoHo Suites

Eldridge   Forsyth   Chrystie   ALLEN   Orchard   Ludlow   Essex   Norfolk   Suffolk   Clinton   Attorney

Stanton Street
Rivington Street
Hamilton Fish Park

Columbia   Baruch   Mangin   Louis   Baruch Place

EAST RIVER PARK

Attorney Avenue

Stanton Street
Rivington St

DELANCEY

Lower East Side Tenement Museum

Delancey Street

Essex Street

STREET

LOWER EAST SIDE

WILLIAMSBURG BRIDGE APPROACH

Ridge   Pitt   Willett   Columbia   Lewis   Street

Broome   Broome Street
Grand   Street

Seward Park

Jefferson   Clinton   Monroe   Madison   Jackson   Henry   Street

Cherry   Corlears Hook Park

Grand Street

Hester
Canal

East Broadway

Division Street

Broadway

PIKE STREET

MARKET

Rutgers Park

Dim Sum Go Go

Pell St

Division   East Broadway

Henry   Oliver   Madison   Catherine   Monroe   Cherry   Water   Market   South   Falcon Drive   Jefferson   Clinton   Rutgers

MANHATTAN BRIDGE

FRANKLIN DELANO ROOSEVELT DRIVE (FDR)

Mills Road

Avenue of the Finest

OKLYN BRIDGE

ark Joseph teakhouse

Fulton Street Market

South Street Seaport

New York City Police Museum

SOUTH STREET
Dover   Cliff   Pearl   Water   Front   South   Peck Slip

Beekman   Fulton

LANE

ALL
REET

BROOKLYN BRIDGE

East

East River

Empire-Fulton Ferry State Park

New Dock Street

OLD FULTON STREET

Doughty Street
Vine Street

Middagh   Street

Willow   Columbia   Orange   Pineapple   Clark   Heights

Plymouth Church of the Pilgrims

BROOKLYN HEIGHTS

Cadman Plaza West

278

Pearl   Water   Front   York   Main   Plymouth   Hudson   John   Adams   Washington

York Street

BROOKLYN-QUEENS EXPRESSWAY

High Street Brooklyn Bridge

High Street Brooklyn Bridge

CADMAN PLAZA

Federal Building

US Post Office & Courthouse

Supreme Court of New York

Brooklyn Historical Society

Montague   Street

Cathedral of Our Lady of Lebanon

Remsen

Grace Church

Grace Court Aly

Joralemon   Street

BROOKLYN-QUEENS EXPRESSWAY

Pierrepont   Street
Love Lane
Clark Street

Monroe Place   Clinton   Henry   Hicks   Willow   Columbia Heights

College Place

Court Street

Brooklyn Borough Hall

Borough Hall

Johnson   Tillary   Adams   Jay   Bridge   Duffield   Gold   STREET

NASSAU

TILLARY STREET

Metrotech

Myrtle   Avenue

Willoughby Street

Fulton   Mall

Livingston   St

Schermerhorn   Street

Joralemon

Columbia Pl   State   Street

BOERUM PL   AVENUE   ATLANTIC

Garden Place   Sidney Place   Clinton   Court   Boerum Pl

John Street
Marshall   Evans Street
Hudson Ave
Little Street

Navy Street   Gold   Prospect   Sands Street

Concord Street
Chapel Street
St. Laughlin Park

TILLARY STREET
Adams   Bridge   Jay   Pearl   Gold

GOLD STREET

Concord   High St   Sands   Prospect

E   F   G   H

107

CHELSEA

GRAMERCY PARK
HISTORIC DISTRICT

Union
Square

UNION SQUARE

GREENWICH
VILLAGE

EAST VILLAGE

NOHO

Hudson

East

SOHO

LITTLE
ITALY

LOWER
EASTSIDE

LOWER MANHATTAN

DOWNTOWN AND CHELSEA

Don't let the Downtown moniker fool you, for this section of Manhattan is all about unique neighborhoods brimming with one-of-a-kind coffeeshops, cafés, bars and boutiques. The museums here are smaller, the buildings only mid-rise, and young, hip professionals and students mingle with the established residents.

The East Village was settled in the 1800s, first by the Irish, then Germans followed by the Ukrainians whose influence has been the most lasting. The Ukrainian Museum commemorates the Ukrainian history of the neighborhood through folk art, crafts, costumes and art works. Musicians and artists took up residence in the 1950s and 1960s, and the area reached its artistic heyday in the 1980s. New York University has expanded into this neighborhood of brownstones and historic residences.

Now a chic neighborhood with a large population of celebrities, Greenwich Village was the bohemian district of New York from the late 1800s through the mid-1900s when it attracted colorful, artistic personalities and alternative lifestyles. Cherry Lane Theatre, the oldest continuously running off-Broadway theater, opened here in 1924. The performing arts scene is still vibrant, with many off-Broadway and off-off-Broadway theaters. Washington Square is the heart of the neighborhood, where street musicians, students and chess players gather in warm weather. The Washington Memorial Arch was built in 1889, and many artists have painted it over the years. Nearby, Washington Mews is a pretty cobblestone street lined with the former stables and servants' quarters for the town houses along the north side of the park, known as The Row.

Union Square is a popular, centrally located gathering place in Manhattan. Numerous subway lines intersect in the bustling 14th Street/Union Square station, and many fine, expensive restaurants and bars surround the square. New York's premier Greenmarket is held here four days a week, drawing crowds who come to shop for fresh produce.

West 36th Street
West 35th Street
West 34th Street
West 33rd Street
West 31st Street
West 30th Street
West 29th Street
West 28th Street
West 27th Street
West 26th Street
West 25th Street
West 24th Street
West 23rd Street
West 22nd Street
West 21st Street
West 20th Street
West 19th Street
West 18th Street
West 17th Street
West 16th Street
West 15th Street
WEST 14TH STREET

FASHION AVENUE
Macy's
34th Street Penn Station
34th Street Herald Square
Empire State Building
Madison Square Garden
Pennsylvania Station

Little Church Around the Corner
Flatiron Building
Madison Square Park
UNION SQUARE
Forbes Magazine Galleries

12TH AVENUE
11TH AVENUE
10TH AVENUE
9TH AVENUE
8TH AVENUE
7TH AVENUE
AVENUE OF THE AMERICAS (6TH AVENUE)
5TH AVENUE

Chelsea Park
Chelsea Waterside Park
CHELSEA

28th Street
23rd Street
18th Street
14th Street
8th Avenue
6th Avenue

11TH AVENUE
9A
WEST STREET
10TH AVENUE

Bloomfield Street
Cansevoort Street

West 13th Street
Little West 12th Street
West 12th Street
West 11th Street
West 10th Street
West 9th Street
West 8th Street

Jefferson Market Library

GREENWICH VILLAGE
Christopher Street
Sheridan Square
Christopher Park
McNulty's Rare Teas and Choice Coffee Shop
Church of St Luke-in-the-Fields

Horatio Street
Jane Street
Bethune Street
Bank Street
West 11th Street
Perry Street
Charles Lane
Charles Street
West 10th Street
Christopher Street
Barrow Street
Morton Street
Leroy Street
Clarkson Street

Greenwich Street
Washington Street
Hudson Street
Bleecker Street
Perry Street
Grove Street
Bedford Street
Commerce St
Barrow St
Morton St

8TH AVENUE
Waverly
Bank St
West 4th St
Charles St
West 10th St
7TH AVENUE SOUTH
Cornelia St
Jones St
Leroy St
Carmine

WASHINGTON SQUARE NORTH
WASHINGTON SQUARE WEST
Washington Square Park
Mac Dougal Alley
Washington Mews
Waverly Place
West 4th Street – Washington Square
Minetta Lane
Minetta Street
Bleecker Street
Macdougal Street
Sullivan Street
Thompson Street
La Guardia Place

House of Oldies Rare Records
11 Walker Park
Saint Luke's Pl

Hudson

HOUSTON STREET
Houston Street
WEST HOUSTON
King Street
Charlton Street
Vandam Street
Spring Street

New York City Fire Museum
Dominick Street
American Numismatic Society
Broome Street
Watts Street

VARICK STREET
AVENUE OF THE AMERICAS (6TH AVENUE)
Prince Street
Spring Street
Thompson Street
Sullivan Street
Macdougal Street

CANAL ST
Canal Street
Grand Street

0   250 m
0   250 yds

GRAMERCY PARK HISTORIC DISTRICT

Gramercy Park North
Gramercy Park South

Theodore Roosevelt Birthplace

Block Beautiful

Metropolitan Life Insurance Tower

PARK AVENUE SOUTH

Grace Church

St Mark's Church-in-the-Bowery

Ukrainian Museum

NOHO

Merchant's House Museum

EAST VILLAGE

Tompkins Square Park

Stuyvesant Oval

Waterside Plaza

FRANKLIN DELANO ROOSEVELT DRIVE (FDR)

East River Park

FDR DRIVE SERVICE ROAD

East River

St Patrick's Old Cathedral

New Museum of Contemporary Art

LITTLE ITALY

Children's Museum of the Arts

Museum of Chinese in America

Lower East Side Tenement Museum

LOWER EAST SIDE

Seward Park

Hamilton Fish Park

Baruch Place

WILLIAMSBURG BRIDGE APPROACH

Corlears Hook Park

111

CHELSEA

Galleries, studios and dance and media centers add the artsy edge to this now-stylish district. Before World War I the US movie industry developed in disused warehouses and theaters here before moving to California. The Kitchen, at 512 West 19th Street, has film, music and dance. Among the many galleries worth visiting are the Gagosian (555 West 24th Street, tel 212/741-1111) and Cheim & Read (547 West 25th Street, tel 212/242-7727).

West of the West Side Highway, a series of piers on the Hudson, known as Chelsea Piers, forms a sports and entertainment complex with ice skating, roller skating, swimming and restaurants.

➕ 110 C11 ✉ Seventh to Eleventh avenues, between 14th and 28th streets
🚇 C, E 🚌 M20 🍴 🛍 🏧

EAST VILLAGE AND NOHO
▷ 114–115.

FLATIRON BUILDING AND DISTRICT

Squeezed into the angle where Broadway crosses Fifth Avenue, the Flatiron Building, at a mere 285ft (87m), never competed for New York's tallest-building status. Originally known as the Fuller Building, it was built to designs by architect Daniel Burnham in 1902. The unusual proportions and elaborate architecture have attracted the interest of photographers and the amazement of tourists for more than a century. Below 23rd Street, Fifth and Sixth avenues and Broadway were once the swankiest shopping district of New York, and this stretch of Sixth Avenue was called Ladies' Mile. Large department stores brought commercialism, a new style of architecture, and prestige to the area. Just northeast of the Flatiron Building is Madison Square Park.

Above *Publishing magnate Malcolm Forbes' fascinating collections are on display here*
Opposite *Chelsea is a chic, artsy district in a former warehousing area*

➕ 110 D11 ✉ 175 Fifth Avenue at Broadway, 10017 🚇 N, R 🚌 M2, M3, M5, M6

FORBES MAGAZINE GALLERIES

www.forbesgalleries.com
Publishing magnate and adventurer Malcolm Forbes (1919–90) had a passion for collecting, and the former home of the Macmillan publishing house, now the offices of *Forbes* magazine, includes a gallery that displays the result: old Monopoly games, model boats, whole battlefields with model soldiers, about 3,000 historical documents (including Abraham Lincoln's *Emancipation Proclamation*) and, among a display of objets d'art, a dozen of the fabled, bejeweled Easter eggs crafted for Russian czars by the house of Fabergé.

Children enjoy the antique toy collection, the model boats and other watercraft.

➕ 110 D12 ✉ 60–62 Fifth Avenue, 10011 ☎ 212/206-5548 🕐 Tue–Wed, Fri–Sat 10–4; call to confirm hours on day of visit ✋ Free 🚇 1, 4, 5, 6, N, R, A, C, E, B, D 🚌 M1, M2, M3, M6

GRACE CHURCH

www.gracechurchnyc.org
By the time James Renwick, Jr. began building churches, the Gothic Revival was in full swing. Renwick, like Richard Upjohn, who designed Trinity Church (▷ 79) on Lower Broadway—once the tallest building in New York City—took up the style with enthusiasm. Grace Church, completed in 1846, was one result, another was the massive, Gothic Revival St. Patrick's Cathedral (▷ 160), on Fifth Avenue at 50th Street.

Grace Church's original wood steeple was replaced by marble in 1888. It stands on the first bend of Broadway, so that it anchors the view along Broadway from downtown. The complex that surrounds the church includes Renwick's Grace House (1881) and the Rectory, and, on Fourth Avenue South, Renwick's fine Grace Memorial House.

➕ 111 E12 ✉ 800 Broadway at 10th Street, 10004 ☎ 212/254-2000 🕐 Mon–Fri 10–4, Sun for services only 🚇 N, R, W, 6 🚌 M1, M7

INFORMATION

⊞ 111 E13 ✉ South of 14th Street, east of Bowery 🚇 4, 5, 6 🚌 M8, M15

Above *Alternative culture thrives in the East Village*

INTRODUCTION

This is a funky area of vintage-clothing shops, ethnic diners, innovative restaurants and trendy clubs, with numerous historic sites. The East Village and NoHo (*North of Ho*uston) extend between 14th Street and Houston Street, between Broadway and Avenue B. Once farmland owned by Dutch governor Peter Stuyvesant, this area was home to Irish, German, Jewish, Ukrainian and Italian immigrants in the 1800s and 1900s. Today you can visit the Ukrainian Museum (▷ 120) to appreciate the culture of immigrants from the Ukraine.

New York's second-oldest church, St. Mark's-in-the-Bowery (▷ 120), on Second Avenue at 10th Street, is on land that was once part of the Stuyvesant farm; the old governor is buried in the churchyard. Poet W. H. Auden, who lived at 77 St. Mark's Place from 1953 to 1972, was a parishioner at the church.

In the 1830s the richest of the rich lived at 428–434 Lafayette Street, south of Astor Place, known as Colonnade Row. Among them were John Jacob Astor, some of the Vanderbilts, and the Delano family. Today only four of the original nine houses remain. Cooper Union, at 51 Astor Place, was founded by one of America's great engineering geniuses, Peter Cooper. Now a designated New York landmark, the building was completed in 1859 and was where Abraham Lincoln made the antislavery speech that helped earn him the Republican Party's presidential nomination. In the 1870s, wealthy New York women attended services at Grace Church (▷ 113), designed by architect James Renwick, Jr., one of the finest examples of Gothic Revival architecture in the United States.

WHAT TO SEE

JEWISH, RUSSIAN AND TURKISH HERITAGE

At the beginning of the 20th century, Second Avenue between Houston Street and 14th Street became a center of Yiddish culture and came to be known as the Jewish Rialto. Edward G. Robinson and Walter Matthau got their start in the Yiddish theater here. Although the much-loved Second Avenue Deli has been driven out by rent rises, plaques in the sidewalk outside its old location at No. 156 honor Yiddish theater stars. The Christadora House, on the corner of 9th Street and Avenue B, was where George Gershwin gave his first public recital. On 10th Street, between First Avenue and Avenue A, the Russian and Turkish Baths (tel 212/674-9250) opened in 1892; unlike many similar establishments, it has survived to become a New York institution. Inside, the baths are not glamorous but poignantly evoke 19th-century New York.

A BOHEMIAN DISTRICT

In the 1960s and 1970s, the East Village was a focal point of the American hippie culture. Anarchist Abbie Hoffman lived on St. Mark's Place and Allen Ginsberg, Timothy Leary, Andy Warhol and a motley collection of Hell's Angels, Hare Krishnas and political rebels frequented the area, often meeting for protest rallies and rock concerts in Tompkins Square Park. For years, until a 1990s restoration, the area attracted the homeless and drug-users. Today it is lovely by day, but still best avoided after dark.

The Joseph Papp Public Theater on Lafayette Street is one of the city's most famous off-Broadway theaters. Impresario Joseph Papp rescued the old Astor Library from demolition, and his theater opened in 1967 with the original production of the musical *Hair*.

The mix of ethnic restaurants in the East Village gives visitors a choice of great food at budget prices. For more stylish dining at higher prices, head for NoHo, the area around Lafayette Street and Broadway between Bleecker and Fourth streets.

The farthest area east, known unofficially as Alphabet City because the streets are designated by letters not numbers, is less accessible by subway, so it's best to arrive and leave by taxi. The area has some chic shops and fashionable bistros.

TIPS

» Skip the area east of Avenue B— it's not really worth visiting and can be intimidating.

» Check local listings to find out what's on at theaters.

» Visit in late afternoon or early evening for a stroll and an inexpensive dinner.

Left and below There is a wealth of places to eat in the East Village, from ethnic restaurants to stylish bistros

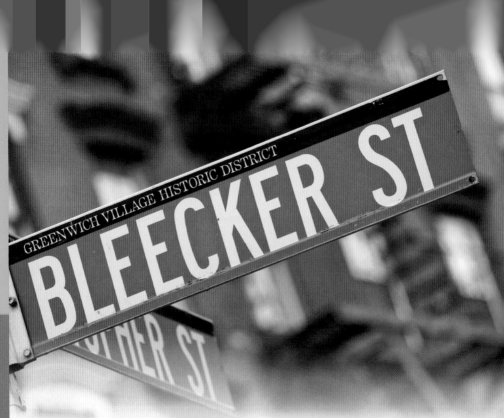

INFORMATION

✚ 110 C13 ✉ From Broadway west to the Hudson River, between Houston Street to the south and 14th Street to the north 🚇 A, C, E, F, N, R, V 1, 2, 3 🚌 M1, M2, M3, M5–8, M20 🍴 A huge number of restaurants on Bleecker Street, Greenwich Avenue and streets in between provide a choice of international cuisines 🍕 John's Pizzeria (▷ 137) 🛍 Shops on Bleecker Street and Greenwich Avenue and many others 🛈 Information centers at Sixth Avenue and Christopher Street and at Astor Place Triangle, both Jul 1–Labor Day daily 12–6

Above *Lively Bleecker Street has great shops and cafés*

INTRODUCTION

In this fascinating, once bohemian, now celebrity-studded area, bursting with funky shops, unique bookstores, sidewalk cafés and cool clubs, famous artists, writers and radical thinkers lived and hung out.

Broadway divides Greenwich Village into the East Village (▷ 114–115) and the West Village. Bleecker Street is the main thoroughfare of the West Village and is full of cafés, restaurants and shops. Coffeehouses, music and poetry still thrive, and this is definitely a lively place for a late night out, whether you take in the bars and clubs, or just go for a stroll.

By 1700 Greenwich Village, named after Greenwich in London, England, had become a small village of wood-framed houses and tree-lined, mud streets north of the city. A single grand estate, Richmond Hill, built by a British paymaster-general at what is today the intersection of Varick and Charleston streets, was George Washington's headquarters during the attempt to defend New York in 1776 and was later home to vice-presidents John Adams (1767–1848) and Aaron Burr (1756–1836). Burr sold much of the land to John Jacob Astor, who divided it up into 456 lots, which he leased for a tidy little profit.

The streets grew up, sometimes along former cowpaths, before the grid street plan was introduced in 1811. When yellow fever struck in the 1820s, half the population fled the city, and prominent families looking for fresh air settled in Greenwich Village, tearing down most of the original frame houses and rebuilding in brick. The Village was a fashionable residential area by July 4, 1826, when Washington Military Parade Ground (Washington Square) was officially opened to celebrate the 50th anniversary of the signing of the Declaration of Independence. African-Americans moved in after the Draft Riots in 1863 and soon Italian immigrants from Little Italy were spilling over into the neighborhood. Tenements and factories were built, and wealthy New Yorkers moved to northern districts.

In the early 1900s, social changes and new zoning laws created cheap housing, attracting artists looking for studio space and low rents. Intellectuals, writers and rebels took up residence, creating a bohemian enclave. Social critics, including suffragists, anarchists and Communist sympathizers, turned the Village into a hotbed of disaffection. Writers such as Henry James, O. Henry, Mark Twain, Edgar Allen Poe and Stephen Crane all lived here. The Village's artist-residents, including Edward Hopper, Jackson Pollock, Franz Kline and Willem de Kooning, created a new American style. Today, the Village is one of the liveliest parts of the city, and maintains its artsy overtones, despite being a very expensive place to live and popular with wealthy professionals.

WHAT TO SEE

CHRISTOPHER PARK
Bordered by Christopher Street, West Fourth Street and Seventh Avenue, Christopher Park is home to George Segal's life-size sculpture *Gay Liberation*, which depicts a gay couple standing in front of a bench where two lesbians sit. Behind them is the Stonewall Bar & Grill, where riots in 1969 sparked the nation's Gay Liberation movement. Christopher Street is a focal point of gay life in New York City.

CHUMLEY'S
At 86 Bedford Street, near Grove Street, this former speakeasy is not easy to find—it has no sign outside and the number does not appear on the front of the building. Over time many New York writers, including John Steinbeck (1902–68), have found solace in a drop or two here. Photos of famous patrons decorate the interior walls. The bar has appeared in movies, including Woody Allen's *Sweet and Lowdown*. Chumley's is currently closed for renovation.

JEFFERSON MARKET LIBRARY
In 1885, a survey of architects found this Gothic building (originally the Jefferson Market Courthouse) at 425 Sixth Avenue, designed by Calvert Vaux and Frederick Clarke Withers between 1874 and 1877, to be the fifth most beautiful building in the United States. The richly ornamented facades include a pediment depicting the trial scene from Shakespeare's *The Merchant of*

TIPS
» Enjoy the outrageous costumes and partying up and down Sixth Avenue at the Village Halloween Parade.
» Stop at the Village Chess Shop at 230 Thompson Street, between Bleecker and West 3rd streets, for a friendly game of chess (www.chess-shop.com).
» Chumley's has been closed since a chimney collapsed in 2007. Repairs are underway, but no date has been set for its reopening.

Below *George Segal's sculpture* Gay Liberation *was installed in Christopher Park in 1992*

ADDRESS GUIDE
ARTISTS
24 University Place: The site of the Cedar Street Tavern, where Jackson Pollock, Franz Kline and Willem de Kooning shared ideas, along with Beat writers Allen Ginsberg and Jack Kerouac.

8 West 8th Street: The first address of the Whitney Museum of American Art (▷ 222–225).

Garrick Theater, Bleecker Street: Crowds flocked here for seven months to see Andy Warhol's movie *Flesh*, which premiered in October 1968.

WRITERS
145 Bleecker Street: Home to James Fenimore Cooper, author of *The Last of the Mohicans*, in 1833.

172 Bleecker Street: Where James Agee wrote the screenplay for *The African Queen*.

130–132 MacDougal Street: Louisa May Alcott stayed in this house and, it is believed, wrote *Little Women* here.

137 MacDougal Street: Home to the Liberal Club. Writers such as Upton Sinclair, Jack London, Theodore Dreiser and Sinclair Lewis regularly met in the house that once stood here.

85 West 3rd Street: Edgar Allen Poe lived on the third floor in 1845 (his was the last window on the right).

11 Commerce Street: Washington Irving wrote *The Legend of Sleepy Hollow* while living here.

14 West 10th Street: Home of Mark Twain when he moved to New York at the age of 65.

RADICALS
12 Charles Street: Home of suffragette Crystal Eastman and a suffragist gathering place.

91 Greenwich Avenue: Where *The Masses* was published. This left-wing publication backed the Communist Party and was a precursor to the counter-culture of the 1960s.

147 West 4th Street: John Reed rented a room in this house while he wrote *Ten Days That Shook the World*.

Venice. The building's tower was originally used by firewatchers, who had an uninterrupted view of the village from the balcony. The original bell used to summon volunteer firefighters still hangs in the tower. After years of neglect, the building was about to be demolished when local activists saved it and it became a branch of the New York Public Library in 1967, housing a special collection of books on New York and Greenwich Village history. The Adult Reading Room was once a civil court, the Children's Room was originally a police court, and the brick-arched basement that was once a holding area for prisoners is now the Reference Room.

SHERIDAN SQUARE
Sheridan Square is at the point where Seventh Avenue, West Fourth Street and Barrow Street intersect. Named for the Civil War general Philip Henry Sheridan, it is the site of the first protests that culminated in the Draft Riots of 1863 when 120 were killed, mostly African-Americans, by Irish immigrants (▷ 35). You can see the statue of General Sheridan in Christopher Park.

WASHINGTON MEMORIAL ARCH IN WASHINGTON SQUARE
Built in 1889 as the entrance to the park at the base of Fifth Avenue, the original triumphal arch commemorated the centenary of George Washington's inauguration. Architect Stanford White designed the first arch, which was made of wood, plaster and papier mâché. It was so successful that a fund to erect a permanent stone arch of the same design soon raised $134,000. The arch you see today, 30ft (9m) across and 77ft (23m) high, became the gateway to fashionable Fifth Avenue in the 1950s, when cars passed directly underneath it and the avenue cut through the park, and remains a treasured city icon.

Many artists have painted or drawn the arch, including Childe Hassam in his 1894 *Washington Arch, Spring*. Many New Yorkers feel that New York University's 12-story Helen and Martin Kimmel Center on Fifth Avenue at Washington Square North detracts from the magnificence of the arch.

WASHINGTON MEWS
As you approach Memorial Arch from Fifth Avenue, on your left is a lovely little cobblestone street called Washington Mews. Originally the houses here were the stables and servants' quarters for the elite town houses on Washington Square North, known as "The Row," a street lined with fashionable homes built in 1833 by John Jacob Astor and Cornelius Vanderbilt.

The delightful old houses lining Washington Mews have long been sought as residences by artists and painters, including Gertrude Vanderbilt Whitney, founder of the Whitney Museum of American Art (▷ 222–225). Members of the faculty of New York University have more recently taken up residence here.

WASHINGTON SQUARE PARK
Washington Square is the heart of Greenwich Village. In warm weather the park is alive with street musicians, students, skateboarders, rollerbladers, the occasional film crew and chess players (bring your own set), so this lively little park is great for people-watching.

Originally the site was marshland and a hunting ground; until the 1820s, criminals were hanged from the large elm in the northwest corner, and from 1797 until 1926 it was a potters' field, where paupers were buried. The remains of about 10,000 people rest here in peace, if not quiet. Washington Square was eventually acquired by the city, cleared, and laid out as a military parade ground. The Common Council then purchased more land, and the 9 acres (3.5ha) became the city's largest park in the 1840s. In 1963 the city closed the park to traffic, making it even more attractive to the students in the area. By the 1970s, alcohol and drug abusers had taken over. A clean-up over the past decade has left it the mellow, genial place you see today.

GRAMERCY PARK HISTORIC DISTRICT

Copied from elegant London squares by the developer Samuel Ruggles in 1831, Gramercy Park is the only private park in New York City and is still surrounded by the original high iron railings. The elegant area, full of attractive buildings, has long been favored by well-to-do citizens. At No. 16 Gramercy Park South the actor Edwin Booth, brother of Lincoln's assassin, lived in a superb brownstone. Booth's statue is inside the park. At No. 15, Samuel Tilden, Governor of New York from 1875 to 1877, installed steel doors and a tunnel to 19th Street in fear of the mob.

✚ 111 E11 ✉ Between Park Avenue South and Third Avenue from 18th to 21st streets 🚇 N, Q, R, 6 🚌 M1, M2, M3, M6, M7

GREENWICH VILLAGE

▷ 116–118.

LITTLE CHURCH AROUND THE CORNER

www.littlechurch.org
The Episcopal Church of the Transfiguration is affectionately called the Little Church Around the Corner. Nothing could better demonstrate changed attitudes to all things theatrical than the way in which this charming little church acquired its nickname. In 1870, a nearby church declined to conduct funeral rites for actors, and directed one such request to "the little church around the corner." It has been favored by theater folk ever since.

An English-style lychgate leads to the church, set back from the street in a quiet garden. The interior maintains the intimate, modest atmosphere with carved wooden pillars and beams.

✚ 110 D10 ✉ East 29th Street, between Fifth and Madison avenues ☎ 212/684-6770 🕐 Daily 9–5 🚇 1, 6, N, R, W 🚌 M2, M3, M4

MERCHANT'S HOUSE MUSEUM

www.merchantshouse.com
This museum is an 1832 time capsule, one of six Federal-style row houses with a charmingly gracious Greek Revival doorway. Bought by wealthy merchant Thomas Tredwell in 1835, the house was lived in by his daughter for 93 years. Renovated after her death in 1933, it was opened to the public as a museum in 1936 with the original furnishings intact, including personal family possessions. It is the only 19th-century house in Manhattan to be so completely preserved. Seven rooms on three floors and a secret garden are on view. Miss Tredwell is thought to have been the model for a character in Henry James' *Washington Square*.

✚ 111 E13 ✉ 29 East 4th Street, 10003 ☎ 212/777-1089 🕐 Thu–Mon 12–5 💵 Adult $8, under 12 free 🚇 6, N, R 🚌 M1, M5, M6, M102 📷 Tours every half hour Sat–Sun ♿

METROPOLITAN LIFE INSURANCE TOWER

Met Life's 1893 main building on 23rd Street stands on the site of the Madison Square Presbyterian Church, whose minister savagely attacked the corrupt politicians who ran the city in 1892. This 54-story tower, built in 1909, was their revenge. Planned as the tallest building in the world and a proud symbol of Met Life's prominence, it was soon overtaken by the Woolworth Building (▷ 78). The Met's campanile was 700ft (213m); in 1913, the Woolworth surpassed it by 92ft (28m). In 1962, the tower was stripped of its original ornamentation, leaving the gold dome and the huge clock faces.

✚ 111 D11 ✉ 1 Madison Avenue 🚇 4, 5, 6 🚌 M1, M3

Above *An avenue in Gramercy Park*

Left St. Mark's Church-in-the-Bowery

hunting and outdoor memorabilia. Roosevelt was sickly as a child, and a small gym that was intended to build up his health adjoins the nursery. There is also an exhibition about his eventful life.

⊞ 111 D11 ✉ 28 East 20th Street, 10003 ☎ 212/260-1616 ⊗ Guided tour only (30 min) Tue–Sat at 10, 11, 1, 2, 3, 4 ✋ Adult $3, under 17 free 🚇 6, N, R 🚌 M1, M6, M23

UKRAINIAN MUSEUM

www.ukrainianmuseum.org

Ukrainian immigrants came to America in the 19th century and many stayed in New York and lived in the tenements on the Lower East Side, not far from this museum. Committed to preserving the cultural heritage of Ukrainians, this museum displays folk art items, including traditional costumes, decorative brass and silver jewelry, decorated Easter eggs, ceramics and woven and embroidered ritual cloths used as talismans at important events. It also curates shows of works by important Ukrainian artists.

⊞ 111 E13 ✉ 222 East Sixth Street, between Second and Third Avenues, 10003 ☎ 212/228-0110 ⊗ Wed–Sun 11.30–5 ✋ Adult $8, under 12 free 🚇 6 🚌 M101, M102, M103

Below *Theodore Roosevelt Birthplace is a replica of the original house*

ST. MARK'S CHURCH-IN-THE-BOWERY

http://smhlf.org/TheSite.htm

Peter Stuyvesant, New Amsterdam's last Dutch governor, had a *bouwerij* (farm) in the quiet countryside north of the bustling settlement. As the city expanded and land values soared, Stuyvesant's grandson sold off plots for development. In 1779, a year after the Stuyvesant mansion was destroyed by fire, his great-grandson sold the site of Stuyvesant's private chapel to the Episcopal Church for a nominal dollar. And so it was that St. Mark's Church-in-the-Bowery was built and named. The original church was Federal-style; in keeping with the area's increasing affluence it later acquired a cast-iron portico. Stuyvesant and six generations of his descendants are buried in the graveyard.

⊞ 111 E12 ✉ East 10th Street, 10004 ☎ 212/674-6377 ⊗ Events only 🚇 6, N, R 🚌 M8, M15

THEODORE ROOSEVELT BIRTHPLACE

www.nps.gov/thrb

Theodore (Teddy) Roosevelt, the great outdoorsman and 26th president of the United States, was born in New York in 1858 and spent his first 14 years in a fashionable brownstone just off Broadway. The house was demolished just before his death in 1919, but the lot where the house stood was acquired in 1923 by the Women's Roosevelt Memorial Association, which commissioned a female architect to reconstruct it as it had been in Roosevelt's youth.

Rooms are furnished with objects preserved from the original house. The "lion's room" is filled with

UNION SQUARE

On a sunny day, the park is a pleasant place to people-watch and relax. There are also sculptures of Washington (1856) and Lincoln (1866), both by Henry Kirke Brown, and Lafayette by Statue of Liberty sculptor Frédéric-Auguste Bartholdi. Nearby are the Center for Jewish History at 15 West 16th Street; the eclectic Forbes Magazine Galleries at 62 Fifth Avenue at 12th Street (▷ 113); and Theodore Roosevelt's reconstructed birthplace at 28 East 20th Street.

At last count there were some 100 restaurants in the Union Square area, including some of the city's top tables. In September, at a fundraiser called Harvest in the Square, you can sample signature dishes of top neighborhood chefs. Also in September, the free outdoor Manhattan Short Film Festival screens 14 of the world's best short films and gives new film-makers a chance to compete for prizes.

A VARIED HISTORY

Run down and with a threatening atmosphere in the 1970s, Union Square is thriving and proud today. Every Monday, Wednesday, Friday and Saturday, a green market—one of the best farmers' markets in the United States—draws New Yorkers from all over the city and inspires local chefs. The bright idea of Barry Benepe (director of the green market)—who saw it as a way to simultaneously help Hudson Valley farmers and improve the neighborhood—it encouraged other communities to set up similar markets.

Union Square went residential in the 1840s, and America's greatest concentration of theaters, nightclubs, restaurants, hotels and luxury shopping followed. Union Square Park was laid out for the wealthy residents. In the 1800s, Ladies' Mile—Broadway and Sixth Avenue between 15th and 24th streets—was the height of fashionable shopping, until the turn of the 20th century when wealth moved uptown and the area deteriorated. In the late 1800s, Union Square was the center for demonstrations and political protests. In the early 1930s the editorial offices of The New Masses and the offices of the Communist Party's Yiddish-language paper moved here. A renovation of the square in 1936 discouraged further demonstrations.

INFORMATION

www.unionsquarenyc.org

✚ 111 D12 ✉ From East 12th Street to East 20th Street, between Third and Fifth avenues 🚇 4, 5, 6, L, N, Q, R 🚌 M2, M3, M6, M7 👣 Free walking tour Sat 2pm, meet at the Lincoln statue near the Pavilion Building in Union Square Park 🍴 Old Town Bar & Restaurant, 45 East 18th Street between Broadway and Park Avenue ☎ 212/529-6732

Below *Relax in the shade of the trees in Union Square's gardens*

GREENWICH VILLAGE: IFC CENTER TO WASHINGTON SQUARE

Some of the country's finest literature and most radical ideas have developed in the area covered by this stroll. From the revolutionary Thomas Paine, who decried taxation without representation in colonial times, to the Stonewall rioters, whose protests sparked the gay liberation movement beginning in 1969, Village people have long been at the forefront of liberalism in America.

THE WALK
Distance: 1.9 miles (3km)
Time: 2 hours
Start/End at: West 4th Street/Washington Square subway station

HOW TO GET THERE
Subway A, C, E, F; bus M5, M6.

★ Leave the subway on Avenue of the Americas (Sixth Avenue), cross the avenue at West Fourth Street and position yourself in front of the IFC Center. Turn to your left (as you face the theater) and head along the avenue to Carmine Street. Turn right.

❶ Along Carmine Street you pass first the Unoppressive, Non-Imperialist Bargain Books store on the left and then the House of Oldies Rare Records (on the right), both worth a browse.

Continue to Seventh Avenue South, cross it, and turn right. At St. Luke's Place (also called Leroy Street), go left. On your left you will pass J. J. Walker Park, once a graveyard, which locals claim is the resting place of the lost son of Louis XVI and Marie Antoinette. The brick and brownstone houses along this street date from the 1850s. Theodore Dreiser wrote *An American Tragedy* while he was living at No. 16. At Hudson Street, turn right, and walk two blocks to Barrow Street where you turn left.

❷ On Barrow Street, take a look at the pretty garden behind the Church of St. Luke-in-the-Fields, built in 1822. The gate is on your right just before you reach Greenwich Street. Backtrack along Barrow Street to Hudson Street, and stop for a snack or light lunch at the popular

Belgian café, Petite Abeille. Go across Hudson Street to 81 Barrow Street, where a plaque gives some architectural history of the area. Continue heading east on Barrow, then turn right onto Commerce Street. To the right at the bend in Commerce Street is the Cherry Lane Theatre.

❸ Cherry Lane Theatre, an off-Broadway venue, was founded in 1924 by the Pulitzer Prize-winning poet Edna St. Vincent Millay. Samuel Beckett's *Waiting for Godot* and *Endgame* both premiered here, as have plays by Edward Albee, David Mamet and many other distinguished writers.

Continue east on Commerce Street for one block and then turn right on Bedford Street. Notice the first two houses on your right.

Opposite *Christopher Park is the site of George Segal's* Gay Liberation *sculpture*

4 The Isaacs-Hendricks House, 77 Bedford Street, is the oldest in the West Village. The narrowest house in the city is at No. 75, which was home to Edna St. Vincent Millay in 1923–24. The actor Cary Grant also lived here when he was young.

Return along Bedford Street, past Chumley's, a famous speakeasy, which put in an appearance in Warren Beatty's *Reds* and Woody Allen's *Sweet and Lowdown*. John Steinbeck, Eugene O'Neill, e e cummings and F. Scott Fitzgerald are among past patrons. As of 2009 the building is closed for renovation. When you reach Grove Street, turn left.

5 The pretty, leafy Grove Court, 10–12 Grove Street, was once dubbed "Ale Alley" because of the original Irish tenants' fondness for a brew.

Return to the corner of Grove and Bedford streets. The oldest wooden house in the Village stands at 17 Grove Street. Continue one block roughly north on Bedford Street to Christopher Street, and turn right.

6 The long-established McNulty's Rare Teas and Choice Coffee Shop is at 109 Christopher Street, and from its looks it hasn't changed much since it opened in 1895. Go in and enjoy the aroma.

Continue east on Christopher Street and cross Seventh Avenue South.

7 Tiny Christopher Park, which was part of a tobacco farm from 1633 to 1638, is to your right. Stop for a rest on the bench next to George Segal's sculpture *Gay Liberation*, then look behind you at the Stonewall Bar and Club, where gay resistance to police arrests provoked the Stonewall Riot in 1969, the start of the gay rights movement. There's a modest plaque on the building. Christopher Street is

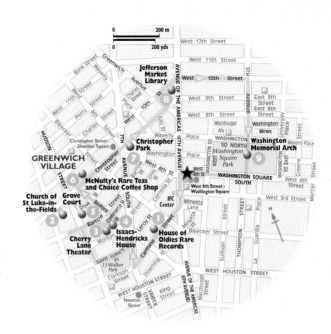

also called Stonewall Place from the park up to Greenwich Avenue.

Walk along the Stonewall side of Christopher Street to Greenwich Avenue, and turn left. Go north one block, turn right onto West 10th Street and you'll come to Patchin Place; No. 4 was famously the home of e e cummings. Continue on West 10th Street one block east.

8 The ornate landmark Jefferson Market Library, at 425 Sixth Avenue, is a former courthouse built in 1877. The tower originally served as a fire-watching lookout.

Continue on West 10th Street, crossing Avenue of the Americas, until you come to Fifth Avenue. Turn right and walk four blocks south on Fifth Avenue, through Washington Memorial Arch.

9 The original wooden arch was erected in 1889, in honor of George Washington 100 years after his inauguration. The marble Stanford White arch you see now was erected in 1895. The residential

Washington Mews, on the east side of Fifth Avenue just north of the arch, were originally built as carriage houses for the wealthy residents of the fine town houses on Washington Square Park south of the arch. In the mews, John Dos Passos lived at No. 14A and Sherwood Anderson at No. 54. Washington Square Park, the focus of Greenwich Village, was once a potter's field and was the site of public executions until the early 19th century.

Walk straight through the park to Washington Square South and turn right. This becomes West Fourth Street, and ahead are the entrances to the subway on Avenue of the Americas.

WHEN TO GO
If you want to visit shops along the way, it is best to do this walk between 10 and 5 Monday to Saturday.

WHERE TO EAT
PETITE ABEILLE
✉ 466 Hudson Street ☎ 212/741-6479
🕐 24 hours

SHOPPING

ABC CARPET AND HOME
www.abchome.com
Fabrics, furnishings and artifacts from around the world are artfully displayed on 10 floors. Provençal armoires, Venetian chandeliers and Kashmiri silks keep company with rugs from India, Nepal and China.
🔢 142 D11 ✉ 888 Broadway, between 19th and 20th streets ☎ 212/473-3000 🕐 Mon–Sat 10–7, Sun 11–6.30 🚇 23rd Street (N, R, W) 🚌 M6, M7

ALEXANDER MCQUEEN
www.alexandermcqueen.com
The late British fashion shock jock, who died just before this book went to press, made his name at Givenchy and went on to design at Gucci, began his career on Savile Row and at theatrical costumer Angels and Bermans.
🔢 142 B12 ✉ 417 West 14th Street, between Ninth Avenue and Washington Street ☎ 212/645-1797 🕐 Mon–Sat 11–7, Sun 12.30–6 🚇 14th Street (A, C, E), Eighth Avenue (L) 🚌 M11, M14

ANNA
www.annanyc.com
Designer Kathy Kemp named her label after her grandmother, who taught her how to sew. Everyone from punk rock babes to uptown trendies makes a beeline for her East Village boutique to check out her latest offbeat designs.
🔢 143 F13 ✉ 150 East 3rd Street at Avenue A ☎ 212/358-0195 🕐 Mon–Sat 1–8, Sun 1–7 🚇 2nd Avenue (F), Essex Street (J, M, Z) 🚌 M15, M14a

AN REN
A small, colorful boutique featuring coats, jackets and tops finely crafted from top-of-the-line fabrics, An Ren sells modern styles with carefully detailed craftsmanship. Many pieces skilfully combine several fabrics and textures. Look for interesting designs, varied color combinations and details such as large buttons and contrasting stitching.
🔢 143 E13 ✉ 315 East Ninth Street, between First and Second avenues ☎ 212/388-9486 🕐 Mon–Fri 1–8, Sat 12–8, Sun 12–7 🚇 Astor Place (6) 🚌 M1, M8, M103

AVIREX/COCKPIT
www.avirex.com
Lusting for the bomber jacket worn by Tom Cruise in *Top Gun*? Head for Avirex, official supplier of the US Air Force's A-2 leather flight jacket. It sells unisex military fashions, biker gear and varsity styles.
🔢 143 E13 ✉ 652 Broadway, between Bleecker and Bond streets ☎ 212/254-4000 🕐 Mon–Sat 11–7.30, Sun 12–6.30 🚇 Broadway-Lafayette (F, S, V) 🚌 M1, M5, M6

BARNES & NOBLE
www.barnesandnoble.com
Although not the original of this megachain, this is the flagship store. Like most branches, this store has a café and comfortable chairs for reading, and sells music, software and magazines as well as books. The main college bookstore is at Fifth Avenue and 18th Street.
🔢 143 D12 ✉ Union Square North at 33 East 17th Street, between Broadway and Park Avenue South ☎ 212/253-0810 🕐 Daily 10–10 🚇 14th Street/Union Square (4, 5, 6, L, N, Q, R, W) 🚌 M1, M2, M3, M6, M7

BROADWAY PANHANDLER
www.broadwaypanhandler.com
Originally selling to professional kitchens, Broadway Panhandler now offers the very best cookware, tools, appliances and gadgets to domestic cooks at decent prices. There are hundreds of different types of pots,

pans and skillets—about 10,000 items in all. Special weekend demonstrations bring in the likes of Jean-Georges Vongerichten, Eric Ripert and Jacques Pépin.
✚ 143 D13 ✉ 65 East 8th Street, between Broadway and University ☎ 212/966-3434 🕐 Mon–Sat 11–7, Sun 11–6 🚇 8th Street (N, R, W) 🚌 M1, M6

CHELSEA MARKET
www.chelseamarket.com
On the first floor of this building, you can put together an entire meal, including table decorations. You'll find bakers, fishmongers, florists, wine merchants and Buon Italia, which sells cheeses, sausages, oils, sauces and other Italian products.
✚ 142 C12 ✉ 75 Ninth Avenue, between 15th and 16th streets ☎ 212/243-6005 🕐 Mon–Sat 7am–10pm, Sun 8–8 🚇 14th Street (A, C, E) 🚌 M11, M14

DARLING
www.darlingnyc.com
Former Broadway costume designer Ann French Emonts offers traffic-stopping silk dresses, formal gowns, sexy and business dresses.
✚ 142 C12 ✉ 1 Horatio Street ☎ 212/367-3750 🕐 Mon–Sat 11–8 (Thu until 10), Sun 12–6 🚇 8th Avenue/14th Street (A, C, E, L 🚌 M20

DIANE VON FURSTENBERG
www.dvf.com
Famous for her signature Wrap dresses, Diane von Furstenberg encouraged women to "feel like a woman, wear a dress." Her DVF label includes sports and swimwear, accessories and cosmetics.
✚ 142 B12 ✉ 874 Washington Street at 14th Street ☎ 646/486-4800 🕐 Mon–Sat 11–7 (Thu until 8), Sun 12–6 🚇 14th Street (A, C, E) 🚌 M20, M14a, M14d

DIESEL
www.diesel.com
This Italian clothes house always keeps one step ahead of the latest trends. Diesel jeans are de rigueur and so, too, are the shoes and bags. Also at 770 Lexington Avenue.

✚ 143 D12 ✉ 1 Union Square West at University Place ☎ 646/336-8552 🕐 Mon–Sat 11–9, Sun 11–8 🚇 14th Street/Union Square (L, N, Q, R, W, 4, 5, 6) 🚌 M2, M3, M5, M14

DISC-O-RAMA
http://discorama.com
From vinyl LPs to the latest CD by top pop artists, you'll find it here at a saving. Rock, pop, R&B, hip-hop, country, jazz, classical, reggae and more, as well as DVDs, books and used CDs and records.
✚ 142 D13 ✉ 44 West 8th Street ☎ 212/206-8417 🕐 Mon–Thu 10am–11pm, Fri–Sat 10–midnight, Sun 12–8 🚇 W. 4th St-Washington Square (A, B, C, D, E, V) 🚌 M4, M5, M6

EYE CANDY
www.eyecandystore.com
The bags, costume jewelry and sunglasses here are the stuff of whimsical dreams.
✚ 143 E13 ✉ 329 Lafayette Street, between Bleecker and Houston streets ☎ 212/343-4275 🕐 Daily 12–8 🚇 Broadway-Lafayette (F, V, S) 🚌 M1, M5, M6, M21

JAZZ RECORD CENTER
www.jazzrecordcenter.com
This store stocks all the great jazz names and labels, plus books, videos and ephemera. It specializes in rare and out-of-print recordings.
✚ 142 C11 ✉ 236 West 26th Street, between Seventh and Eighth avenues (8th floor, room 804) ☎ 212/675-4480 🕐 Mon–Sat 10–6 🚇 28th Street (1) 🚌 M20

JEFFREY
It took courage for former Barneys shoe buyer Jeffrey Kalinsky to open this giant boutique in the blighted Meatpacking District before it became hip. Naturally, the shoe department is stellar, chock full of Manolos and other designer names. You will also find fashions by such leaders as Fendi, Jil Sander, Celine, Prada, Gucci and Dolce & Gabbana.
✚ 142 B12 ✉ 449 West 14th Street, between Ninth and Tenth avenues ☎ 212/206-1272 🕐 Mon–Fri 10–8 (Thu until 9),

Sat 10–7, Sun 12.30–6 🚇 14th Street (A, C, E), Eighth Avenue (L) 🚌 M11, M14

JUSSARA LEE
This Korean-Brazilian designer's clothes have an edge but are eminently wearable. Coats, dresses, tops, pants, skirts and bathing suits are elegantly displayed here.
✚ 142 B12 ✉ 11 Little West 12th Street, between Washington Street and Ninth Avenue ☎ 212/242-4128 🕐 Mon–Sat 11–7, Sun by appointment 12–6 🚇 14th Street (A, C, E) 🚌 M11, M14

KIEHL'S
www.kiehls.com
Kiehl's is now owned by cosmetics giant L'Oréal. It has been selling homeopathic remedies and natural cosmetics and treatment products since its inception in 1851.
✚ 143 E12 ✉ 109 Third Avenue, between East 13th and 14th streets ☎ 212/677-3171 🕐 Mon–Sat 10–8, Sun 11–6 🚇 14th Street/Union Square (L, N, Q, R, W, 4, 5, 6), Third Avenue (L) 🚌 M101, M102, M103

LOEHMANN'S
www.loehmanns.com
This place has been a name on the discount shopping scene ever since Frieda Mueller Loehmann began selling well-priced skirts and blouses out of her Brooklyn home in 1920. This flagship store has five floors.
✚ 142 C12 ✉ 101 Seventh Avenue at 16th Street ☎ 212/352-0856 🕐 Mon–Sat 9–9, Sun 11–7 🚇 14th Street (1, 2, 3) 🚌 M14, M20

OLD NAVY
This huge store features affordable basics for men, women, boys, girls and infants, as well as a complete line of accessories. There is even clothing for pets.
✚ 142 D12 ✉ 610 Sixth Avenue at 18th Street ☎ 212/645-0663 🕐 Mon–Sat 9am–9.30pm, Sun 10–8 🚇 6th Avenue/14th Street (F, L, V) 🚌 M5, M6, M7

PARAGON SPORTING GOODS
www.paragonsports.com
New Yorkers come to this store to buy clothes and equipment for every conceivable type of sport

or pastime. It stocks camping and hiking gear, binoculars, golfing gear, skis, snow and surfboards, tennis racquets and brand clothing.

✚ 142 D12 ✉ 867 Broadway at 18th Street ☎ 212/255-8036 🕐 Mon–Sat 10–8, Sun 11.30–7 🚇 14th Street/Union Square (L, N, Q, R, W, 4, 5, 6) 🚌 M6, M7

LA PETITE COQUETTE
www.thelittleflirt.com

This may well be the best lingerie store in the city. In a boudoir setting, it sells swimwear and sexy top-of-the-line, multi-hued lingerie.

✚ 142 D13 ✉ 51 University Place, between 9th and 10th streets ☎ 212/473-2478 🕐 Mon–Sat 11–7 (Thu until 8), Sun 12–6 🚇 8th Street (N, R, W) 🚌 M1, M3, M6

ST. MARK'S BOOKSHOP
www.stmarksbookshop.com

This counterculture bookstore offers political and alternative titles plus general books.

✚ 143 E13 ✉ 31 Third Avenue, between St Mark's Place and 9th Street on east side ☎ 212/260-7853 🕐 Mon–Sat 10am–midnight, Sun 11am–midnight 🚇 Astor Place (4, 5, 6) 🚌 M101, M102, M103

SCREAMING MIMI'S
www.screamingmimis.com

The stock at this old-timer ranges from 1940s to 1980s. It's well displayed and in good condition. Cool and hip still, even though *Sex and the City* made it famous.

✚ 143 E13 ✉ 382 Lafayette Street, between Great Jones and West 4th streets ☎ 212/677-6464 🕐 Mon–Sat 12–8, Sun 1–7 🚇 Broadway-Lafayette (F, S, V) 🚌 M1, M103

SHAKESPEARE & CO
www.shakeandco.com

One of the city's few surviving small independent book chains. As the name suggests, it leans toward literary and small press titles.

✚ 143 D13 ✉ 716 Broadway, between West 4th Street and Washington Place ☎ 212/529-1330 🕐 Mon–Fri 10am–11pm, Sat–Sun 12–9 🚇 Astor Place (4, 5, 6), 8th Street (N, R, W), West 4th Street (A, C, E, F, S, V) 🚌 M1, M5, M6

SHELLY STEFFEE
www.shellysteffee.com

The sign outside reads "Design Studio" and the clothes are displayed, in a museum-like fashion. The designs are sexy and fun.

✚ 142 C12 ✉ 34 Gansevoort Street between Hudson Street and Ninth Avenue ☎ 917/408-0408 🕐 Sun–Tue 11.30–7, Wed–Sat 11.30–9 🚇 14th Street (A, C, E) 🚌 M11, M14

STELLA McCARTNEY
www.stellamccartney.com

Stella McCartney began her rise to stardom at Chloe and continues in partnership with Gucci. In this store, fitting rooms are lined with marquetry or hand-printed fabric. Her full line of well-tailored but nicely draped fashions is for sale.

✚ 142 B12 ✉ 429 West 14th Street, between Ninth and Tenth avenues ☎ 212/255-1556 🕐 Mon–Sat 11–7, Sun 12.30–6 🚇 14th Street (A, C, E), Eighth Avenue (L) 🚌 M11, M14

STRAND BOOKSTORE
www.strandbooks.com

Here you can pore over the stacks and tables of publishers' review copies, sold at half price. The management claims to shelve 18 miles (29km) of books.

✚ 143 E12 ✉ 828 Broadway at 12th Street ☎ 212/473-1452 🕐 Mon–Sat 9.30am–10.30pm, Sun 11–10.30 🚇 14th Street/Union Square (L, N, Q, R, W, 4, 5, 6) 🚌 M1, M5, M6

THREE LIVES
www.threelives.com

The proprietor of this store stocks an amazing variety of titles given the size of the place. A real neighborhood store, and one of the last personal bookstores in the city.

✚ 142 C13 ✉ 154 West 10th Street at Waverly Place (southwest corner) ☎ 212/741-2069 🕐 Wed–Sat 11–8.30, Sun 12–7, Mon–Tue 12–8 🚇 Christopher Street (1), West 4th Street (A, C, E, F, V, S) 🚌 M5, M6, M8, M20

UNION SQUARE GREEN MARKET

Drop by this busy market to get a sense of the agricultural scene

outside the city and to participate in a city happening.

✚ 143 D12 ✉ Union Square 🕐 Mon, Wed, Fri, Sat from 8am 🚇 14th Street/Union Square (L, N, Q, R, W, 4, 5, 6) 🚌 M2, M3, M5, M7

ZERO

In this store you'll see capes, jackets and coats with an avant-garde look which Maria Cornejo sews in the back of the store.

✚ 143 E13 ✉ 33 Bleecker Street, between Lafayette and Bowery streets ☎ 212/925-3849 🕐 Mon–Fri 12.30–7.30, Sat–Sun 12.30–6.30 🚇 Prince Street (N, R) 🚌 M1, M6

ENTERTAINMENT AND NIGHTLIFE
49 GROVE

In the deep-purple lounge you'll find comfortable couches to sink right into while bottles or cocktails are brought to your table as the city's fashion crowd mingle. The music is hip-hop, house, funk, and garage and the prices are seriously high, even by New York club standards.

✚ 142 C13 ✉ 49 Grove Street at Bleecker Street ☎ 212/727-1100 🕐 Thu–Sat 10pm–4am 🚇 Christopher Street-Sheridan Square (1), 4th Street-Washington Square (A, B, C, D, E, F, V)

ACTOR'S PLAYHOUSE

This small downstairs venue, which has been around for 40 years, presents musical revues, often with a gay theme.

✚ 142 C13 ✉ 100 Seventh Avenue South, between Bleecker and West 4th streets ☎ 212/463-0060 or 212/239-6200 🚇 Christopher Street/Sheridan Square (1) 🚌 M20

ANGELIKA FILM CENTER
www.angelikafilmcenter.com

This multiplex principally shows foreign films with English subtitles, plus films by such artists as Atom Egoyan and other independent moviemakers.

✚ 143 D13 ✉ Mercer and Houston streets ☎ 212/995-2000 ✋ $10–$11 🚇 Broadway-Lafayette (F, S, V), Bleecker Street (6) 🚌 M1, M5, M6, M21

ANGEL'S SHARE

Tucked away upstairs in a Japanese restaurant, this tiny bar is named for the alcohol that evaporates while whiskey is aging. The lychee daiquiri is delicious.

✚ 143 E12 ✉ 8 Stuyvesant Street (2nd floor), between 9th Street and Third Avenue ☎ 212/777-5415 🕓 Mon–Thu 6pm–1.30am, Fri–Sat 6pm–2.30am 🚇 Astor Place (6)

ANTHOLOGY FILM ARCHIVES

www.anthologyfilmarchives.org
Shows new film-makers along with old and rare vintage pieces and occasional tributes to directors.

✚ 143 E13 ✉ 32 Second Avenue at East 2nd Street ☎ 212/505-5181 ✋ $8 🚇 Astor Place (6), Lower East Side/Second Avenue (F, V) 🚌 M15, M21

APT

www.aptnyc.com
You must be on the A-list to snag one of the sofas in the upstairs apartment-style lounge (with a big bed as well as coffee tables). The sleek basement lounge is more accessible, but you still need to look good at this designer nightlife spot.

✚ 142 B12 ✉ 419 West 13th Street, between Ninth Avenue and Washington Street ☎ 212/414-4245 🕓 Daily 7pm–4am ✋ Free–$20 🚇 14th Street (A, C, E), Eighth Avenue (L)

ARTHUR'S TAVERN

www.arthurstavernnyc.com
This funky down-home bar has jazz, Dixieland or blues most nights of the week.

✚ 142 C13 ✉ 57 Grove Street between Seventh Avenue South and Bleecker Street ☎ 212/675-6879 🕓 Mon–Sat 7pm–3am, Sun 8pm–3am ✋ Free 🚇 Christopher Street/Sheridan Square (1) 🚌 M8, M20

AUTOMATIC SLIM'S

An outpost of the original Automatic Slim's in Memphis, the kid brother in the Meatpacking District brings a soulful Southern feel, with a fun atmosphere and good music.

✚ 142 C13 ✉ 733 Washington Street at Bank Street ☎ 212/645-8660 🕓 Tue–Wed 5.30pm–2am, Thu–Sat 5.30pm–4am

🚇 Christopher Street-Sheridan Square (1), 14th Street (A, C, E)

B BAR

www.bbarandgrill.com
B Bar has cooled as a hot spot, but its Tuesday night extravaganza, Beige, still draws gay society and other beauties. Large outdoor summer patio.

✚ 143 E13 ✉ 40 East 4th Street at Bowery ☎ 212/475-2220 🕓 Mon 11am–2am, Tue, Thu–Fri 11am–4am, Wed 11.30am–3am, Sat 10am–4am, Sun 10am–2am 🚇 Broadway/ Lafayette (F, S, V), Bleecker Street (6)

BITTER END

www.bitterend.com
The cradle of the antiwar folk music scene in the 1960s, the Bitter End is much more rock-oriented today. Performances every night.

✚ 142 D13 ✉ 147 Bleecker Street at Thompson Street ☎ 212/673-7030 🕓 Mon–Thu, Sun 7.30pm–2am, Fri–Sat 7.30pm–4am ✋ $5–$15 🚇 West 4th Street (A, C, E, F, V, S) 🚌 M5, M6, M21

BLEECKER STREET THEATRE

Home of the Culture Project, which produces eclectic works by contemporary playwrights.

✚ 143 E13 ✉ 45 Bleecker Street, between Bowery and Lafayette Street ☎ 212/253-9983 or 212/307-4100 🚇 Bleecker Street (6), Broadway/Lafayette (F, S, V) 🚌 M1, M21, M103

BLUE NOTE

www.bluenotejazz.com
Tiny and ultra-expensive, the Blue Note is jammed with fans grooving to the sounds of contemporary leaders in jazz, blues, Latin and R & B. Monday night showcases up-and-coming local musicians.

✚ 142 D13 ✉ 131 West 3rd Street at Sixth Avenue ☎ 212/475-8592 🕓 Daily at 8pm and 10.30pm (and 12.30am weekends) ✋ $20–$65 at tables, $40–45 at bar, plus $5 minimum 🚇 West 4th Street (A, C, E, F, S, V) 🚌 M5, M6

BOUWERIE LANE

The Jean Cocteau Repertory Company (1971) presents five to

seven masterworks from Euripides to Samuel Beckett year round at this beautiful old bank building.

✚ 143 E13 ✉ 330 Bowery at Bond Street ☎ 212/677-0060 🚇 Broadway-Lafayette (F, V, S) 🚌 M21, M103

BOWERY POETRY CLUB

www.bowerypoetry.com
All kinds of poets and performance artists play here. There are shows almost every night, and weekend lunchtime performances, too.

✚ 143 E13 ✉ 308 Bowery, between Bleecker and Houston streets ☎ 212/614-0505 or 212/206-1515 ✋ $5–$15 🚇 Bleecker Street (6), Broadway/Lafayette (F, S, V) 🚌 M21, M103

BUNGALOW 8

The challenge at Bungalow 8 is to get through the doors, as you either have to be a celebrity or be able to drop the right name. Inside it's surprisingly small, which is another reason they keep people out, but it's definitely kudos to say you've been to Bungalow 8.

✚ 142 B11 ✉ 515 West 27th Street, between 10th and 11th avenues ☎ 212/629-3333 🕓 Daily 11pm–4am 🚇 28th Street (1), 23rd Street (C, E)

CAIN

www.cainnyc.com
If you can get through the door of this exclusive Chelsea nightspot, it's like being out in Africa with zebra-skin decor and the occasional drummer who accompanies the DJ. Wednesdays and Saturdays are the best nights: they like people to buy a bottle and chill out.

✚ 142 B11 ✉ 544 West 27th Street, between 10th and 11th avenues ☎ 212/947-8000 🕓 Wed–Sat 10.30pm–4am 🚇 23rd Street (C, E)

CENTER STAGE/NY

www.labtheater.org
Thirteen actors founded the Labyrinth Repertory Company in 1992 to enable members to write, direct and act. Now it has 60 international members, who produce annual plays at Center Stage/NY.

✝ 142 D11 ✉ 48 West 21st Street, between Fifth and Sixth avenues, fourth floor ☎ 212/513-1080 🚇 23rd Street (N, R, W), 23rd Street (F, V) 🚌 M2, M3, M5, M6, M7

CHERRY LANE
www.cherrylanetheatre.org
In 1924 Edna St. Vincent Millay and others turned a warehouse into a theater. Today the Cherry Lane Alternative continues the theater's tradition of producing emerging playwrights.
✝ 142 C13 ✉ 38 Commerce Street, between Hudson and Bedford streets ☎ 212/989-2020 🚇 Christopher Street/ Sheridan Square (1) 🚌 M20, M21

CINEMA VILLAGE
www.cinemavillage.com
Renovated in 2000, this independent cinema, housed in a former fire station, now has three screens. Documentaries and old movies are the staples.
✝ 142 D12 ✉ 22 East 12th Street, between University Place and Fifth Avenue ☎ 212/924-3363 ✋ $10 🚇 14th Street/ Union Square (L, N, Q, R, W, 4, 5, 6) 🚌 M1, M2, M14, M101, M103

COMEDY CELLAR
www.comedycellar.com
A cave-like venue that features nationally known comedians— Seinfeld, Stewart, Williams et al.
✝ 142 D13 ✉ 117 MacDougal Street, between West 3rd and Bleecker streets ☎ 212/254-3480 🕐 Nightly, check program ✋ $10–$18, plus 2-drink minimum 🚇 West 4th Street (A, C, E, F, S, V) 🚌 M5, M6

COMMON GROUND
www.commongroundnyc.com
A few blocks north of Tompkins Square Park is this bar that looks like a bar should, with shelves filled with books, and even chandeliers giving it a hint of Victorian London. Nothing Victorian about the patrons, though, a mix of office workers and locals, enjoying either the bar snacks or the extremely tasty main plates on offer. Wednesday is trivia night, and there's an open-mic night on Sunday.

✝ 143 F12 ✉ 206 Avenue A, between 12th and 13th streets ☎ 212/228-6231 🕐 Mon–Thu 4pm–2am, Thu–Fri 4–4, Sat noon–4am, Sun noon–2am (kitchen closes midnight) 🚇 1st Avenue (L)

COOPER UNION GREAT HALL
www.cooper.edu/ce
Everything from fado (Portuguese folk music) and contemporary classical music to Afro-Brazilian drum groups and samba bands can be heard at a private tuition-free college for the Advancement of Science and Art. Abraham Lincoln spoke here in 1860.
✝ 143 E13 ✉ Seventh Street at Third Avenue ☎ 212/353-4195 ✋ Free–$25 🚇 Astor Place (6), 8th Street (N, R, W) 🚌 M8, M101, M102, M103

CORNELIA STREET CAFÉ
www.corneliastreetcafe.com
This subterranean space hosts everything from structured free jazz and cabaret to poetry and performance art.
✝ 142 C13 ✉ 29 Cornelia Street, between Bleecker and West 3rd streets ☎ 212/989-9319 🕐 Daily 10am–10.45pm ✋ Free–$15, plus 1-drink minimum 🚇 West 4th Street (A, C, E, F, S, V) 🚌 M5, M6, M21

DANCE THEATER WORKSHOP
www.dtw.org
In 1965 Jeff Duncan, Art Bauman and Jack Moore founded this choreographers' collective, and it still promises innovative performances here and at other city venues. Many famous dancers have begun careers here—Bill T. Jones, Mark Morris, Ann Carlson, Eiko and Koma—plus such theatrical talents as Bill Irwin, Whoopi Goldberg and Paul Zaloom.
✝ 142 C11 ✉ 219 West 19th Street at Seventh Avenue ☎ 212/691-6500 🚇 18th Street (1) 🚌 M14, M20

DARYL ROTH THEATER
www.darylroththeater.com
Pulitzer Prize-winning Daryl Roth owns this theater in an old bank building. The space is dramatic.
✝ 143 D12 ✉ 101 East 15th Street at Union Square ☎ 212/375-1110 🚇 14th

Street/Union Square (L, N, Q, R, W, 4, 5, 6) 🚌 M1, M2, M3, M6, M7, M14

D.B.A.
Serious drinkers appreciate the massive selection of single malts (90) and beers (16 on tap and 260 in bottles) at this friendly bar. The backyard garden is great in summer.
✝ 143 E13 ✉ 41 First Avenue, between East 2nd and 3rd streets ☎ 212/475-5097 🕐 Daily 1pm–4am 🚇 Lower East Side/ Second Avenue (F, V)

DECIBEL
www.sakebardecibel.com
Subterranean, funky and cramped, this Japanese bar has a huge selection of sake.
✝ 143 E13 ✉ 240 East 9th Street, between Second and Third avenues ☎ 212/979-2733 🕐 Mon–Sat 8pm–2.50am, Sun 8pm–12.50am 🚇 Astor Place (6)

THE DUPLEX
www.theduplex.com
A launching pad for Woody Allen, Joan Rivers and Rodney Dangerfield, the tradition continues in the upstairs cabaret room. There is a piano bar downstairs.
✝ 142 C13 ✉ 61 Christopher Street at Seventh Avenue South ☎ 212/255-5438 🕐 Nightly, check program ✋ Cover varies, plus 2-drink minimum 🚇 Christopher Street/Sheridan Square (1) 🚌 M8, M20

ENOTECA I TRULLI
This light and airy wine bar offers some 50 wines by the glass at the marble bar. Accompany them with first-class cured meats, cheeses and olives from I Trulli next door.
✝ 143 E11 ✉ 122 East 27th Street between Park Avenue South and Lexington Avenue ☎ 212/481-7372 🕐 Mon–Sat 5–12, Sun 5–10 🚇 28th Street (6)

FAT CAT BILLIARDS
http://fatcatmusic.org/
For a New York experience it's hard to beat going into a basement bar and playing pool. The Fat Cat has 10 tables, along with 10 ping-pong tables, 10 shuffleboard tables and three foosball (table football)

machines. A good range of beers too, from around the world, and live music including jazz and salsa every night of the week.

✚ 142 C13 ✉ 75 Christopher Street at 7th Avenue ☎ 212/675-6056 ◷ Mon–Thu 2pm–5am, Fri–Sun noon–5am ✋ Pool $5 per hour, $3 cover on music nights ⊜ Christopher Street–Sheridan Square (1), 4th Street–Washington Square (A, B, C, D, E, F, V)

FLANNERY'S BAR
www.flannerysny.com
Flannery's has been one of New York's best Irish bars for more than 20 years, with a winning mix of drink, music and conversation. There are DJs twice a week, darts tournaments Wednesday and Saturday, and a rock and blues jam with the house band on Sundays.

✚ 142 C12 ✉ 205 West 14th Street at 7th Avenue ☎ 212/229-2122 ◷ Mon–Sat 8pm–4am, Sun noon–4am ✋ $5 cover on darts nights ⊜ 14th Street (1, 2, 3, A, C, E), 8th Avenue (L)

GLASS
This sleek modernist space is fun and futuristic—worthy of the arty neighborhood. Check out the two-way mirrors in the bathrooms, and other visual tricks.

✚ 142 B11 ✉ 287 Tenth Avenue, between West 26th and 27th streets ☎ 212/904-1580 ◷ Thu–Sat 10pm–4am ⊜ 28th Street (1)

GOTHAM COMEDY CLUB
www.gothamcomedyclub.com
Old and new hands on the comedy scene play this elegant club in the Flatiron District.

✚ 142 C11 ✉ 208 West 23rd Street, between 7th and 8th avenues ☎ 212/367-9000 ⊜ 23rd Street (1) 🚌 M14, M20

HOME
www.homeguesthouse.com
Long banquettes run the length of some of the walls of this Chelsea nightclub, which oozes style and atmosphere with its low lights, red wood floors, candles and couches. If rock and pop music is too staid, try the Guest House down the street.

✚ 142 B11 ✉ 532 West 27th Street, between 10th and 11th avenues ☎ 212/273-3700 ◷ Wed–Mon 10pm–4am ⊜ 28th Street (1), 23rd Street (C, E)

JAZZ STANDARD
www.jazzstandard.com
The Union Square Café's Danny Myers established this popular downstairs venue with food from his ground-floor restaurant Blue Smoke. It's a sleek, comfortable place for music and a meal.

✚ 143 E11 ✉ 116 East 27th Street between Park Avenue South and Lexington Avenue ☎ 212/576-2232 ◷ Daily 6.30pm–3am (show times vary) ✋ $20–$30 ⊜ 28th Street (6) 🚌 M1, M101, M102, M103

JOE'S PUB
www.joespub.com
A favorite cabaret club of many New Yorkers, named after Public Theater founder Joe Papp. It's comfortable the way a club should be, with couches and tables. DJs spin during Late Night at Joe's.

✚ 143 E13 ✉ Public Theater, 425 Lafayette Street, between Astor Place and East 4th Street ☎ 212/967-7555 or 212/539-8778 ◷ Daily 6pm–4am (show times vary) ✋ From $10, plus 2-drink minimum ⊜ Astor Place (6) 🚌 M1, M8

THE JOYCE THEATER
www.joyce.org
The city's premier dance venue hosts top international and domestic dance companies and showcases such important dance series as Altogether Different. Expect to see the Eliot Feld Ballet, Pilobolus Dance Theater and many others.

✚ 142 C12 ✉ 175 Eighth Avenue, southwest corner of 19th Street ☎ 212/691-9740 or 212/242-0800 ⊜ 23rd Street (C, E) 🚌 M20, M23

THE JUDSON MEMORIAL CHURCH
www.judson.org
For many decades this Baptist Church has nurtured avant-garde artists. It's most famous for hosting the late Judson Poets Theater, but the Memorial Church still

hosts experimental dance series. Movement Research performs a regular series here.

✚ 142 D13 ✉ 55 Washington Square South ☎ 212/477-0351 ◷ West 4th Street (A, C, E, F, S, V) 🚌 M5, M6, M8

THE KITCHEN
www.thekitchen.org
At this fixture of the downtown scene established in 1971, the careers of such artists as Philip Glass, Laurie Anderson, Eric Bogosian, Robert Mapplethorpe and Cindy Sherman were nurtured. It's still going strong.

✚ 142 B12 ✉ 512 West 19th Street, between Tenth and Eleventh avenues ☎ 212/255-5793 ✋ $10–$20 ⊜ 23rd Street (C, E) 🚌 M11, M23

LEVEL V
This basement lounge at Vento is the latest hotspot in the Meatpacking District. Black leather couches, glass tables and dramatic lighting set the scene for a chic and coiffed young crowd. VIPs are ushered into the private vaulted brick stalls. To be sure of a table, reservations are recommended.

✚ 142 C12 ✉ 675 Hudson Street at 14th Street ☎ 212/699-2410 ◷ Wed–Sun 9pm–4am, Tue 6pm–4am ⊜ 14th Street (A, C, E), Eighth Avenue (L)

LOTUS
www.lotusnewyork.com
European jet-setters flock to this chic supper club with attitude, attracted by the international DJs and the luxe balcony lounge and basement dance club. It's tough to get past the fu dogs at the door. Make a dinner reservation and bring the platinum.

✚ 142 B12 ✉ 409 West 14th Street, between Ninth and Tenth avenues ☎ 212/243-4420 ◷ Dinner Tue–Sat 7–11; club Tue–Sat 10–4 ✋ $20 ⊜ 14th Street (A, C, E)

LOUNGE
http://crimescenebar.com
If you like a bar with character then Lounge fits the bill with a hip atmosphere and a gritty party buzz. This trendy lounge attracts an

up-and-coming clientele. Weeknights offer DJs in a relaxing atmosphere. Weekends are party nights.
✚ 143 E13 ✉ 310 Bowery at Bleecker Street ☎ 212/477-1166 ◷ Mon–Fri 3pm–4am, Sat 3pm–5am ⊕ Bleecker Street (6), Lower East Side-2nd Avenue (F, V)

MCSORLEY'S OLD ALE HOUSE
McSorley's, established in 1854, refused to admit women until 1970. The walls are plastered with old newspaper clippings. Students are the principal patrons today.
✚ 143 E13 ✉ 15 East 7th Street, between Second and Third avenues ☎ 212/473-9148 ◷ Mon–Sat 11am–1am, Sun 1–1 ⊕ Astor Place (6), 8th Street (N, R)

LA MAMA EXPERIMENTAL THEATRE CLUB
www.lamama.org
One of the most famous off-off-Broadway theaters was founded in 1961 by Ellen Stewart to nurture new playwrights. It has three theaters: the Annex, the First Floor and the Club, a cabaret space.
✚ 143 E13 ✉ 74A East 4th Street, between Second Avenue and Bowery ☎ 212/475-7710 ⊕ Astor Place (6) 🚌 M8, M15

MANNAHATTA PARTY AT CRIME
www.mannahatta.us/
A swanky, chic and laid-back bar and lounge, this is a great place to relax and have a party with hip friends. The upscale lounge features changing events and DJs weeknights, and Happy Hour prices are from 4pm–8pm featuring some of the best prices in the city. Weekends are crazy party nights with DJs spinning an eclectic mix of music. Reservations are recommended for weekends.
✚ 143 E13 ✉ 310 Bowery at Bleecker Street ☎ 212/477-1979 ◷ Mon–Sat 4pm–4am ⊕ Bleecker Street (6) 🚌 M21, M103

MARIE'S CRISIS
A mixed crowd of gays and straights gather around the upright piano and sing along to Broadway show tunes at this downstairs bar.

✚ 142 C13 ✉ 59 Grove Street ☎ 212/243-9323 ◷ Daily 4–4 ⊕ Christopher Street/ Sheridan Square (1)

MARQUEE
www.marqueeny.com
This club has a lot of buzz and attracts a celebrity crowd who appreciate its plush comforts, French elegance and cabaret room. Baby Tuesday caters to the fashion industry. The crowd is mainly straight, but there's a smattering of fashion-conscious gays too. Hip hop, house, funk and soul are the main musical themes.
✚ 142 B11 ✉ 289 Tenth Avenue, between 26th and 27th streets ☎ 646/473-0202 ◷ Tue–Sat 10pm–4am ✋ Cover $20 ⊕ 23rd Street (C, E)

MERCE CUNNINGHAM STUDIO
www.merce.org
The Studio Performance Series for Emerging Choreographers uses this large studio space from September to July. It seats 99. Cunningham, now in his 90s, still teaches here.
✚ 142 C13 ✉ 55 Bethune Street at Washington Street (11th floor) ☎ 212/255-8240 ✋ $15 ⊕ 14th Street (A, C, E), 14th Street (1, 2, 3) 🚌 M8, M11, M20

MINETTA LANE
This Greenwich Village theater is a major off-Broadway player.
✚ 142 D13 ✉ 18 Minetta Lane ☎ 212/420-8000 ⊕ West 4th Street (A, C, E, F, S, V) 🚌 M5, M6, M8

NEW SCHOOL
www.nsu.newschool.edu
The prestigious university stages concerts, lectures and readings by writers such as Edmund White, poetry, film shows and discussions.
✚ 142 D12 ✉ Tishman Hall, 66 West 12th Street, between Fifth and Sixth avenues ☎ 212/229-5488 ⊕ 14th Street (F, V) 🚌 M5, M6, M7, M14

NEW YORK THEATRE WORKSHOP
www.nytw.org
A main player on the Manhattan theater scene. *Rent* began life here, and the workshop has staged Caryl Churchill and Athol Fugard.

✚ 143 E13 ✉ 79 East 4th Street, between Second Avenue and Bowery ☎ 212/780-9037 or 212/460-5475 ⊕ Broadway-Lafayette (F, S, V), Bleecker Street (6) 🚌 M1, M21

NUYORICAN POETS CAFÉ
www.nuyorican.org
Originally a platform for Puerto Rican poets and artists, the café is still famous for its Wednesday and Friday night poetry slams. Expect to see theater, screenplay readings and even Latin jazz. Take a cab.
✚ 143 F13 ✉ 236 East 3rd Street, between Avenues B and C ☎ 212/780-9386 ◷ Tue–Sat 7–12, Sun 4–12 ⊕ Lower East Side/Second Avenue (F, V) 🚌 M9, M21

OLD TOWN BAR
www.oldtownbar.com
At this authentic hang-out, dating from 1892, look for the private booths. Tiled floors, a long mirrored bar, pressed-tin ceiling and original gas lamps complete the look. No jukebox, conversation reigns.
✚ 143 D12 ✉ 45 East 18th Street, between Broadway and Park Avenue ☎ 212/529-6732 ◷ Mon–Fri 11.30am–1am, Sat–Sun noon–1am ⊕ 14th Street/Union Square (L, N, Q, R, W, 4, 5, 6)

ONTOLOGICAL-HYSTERIC THEATER
www.ontological.com
The theater is an important home for the avant-garde. The founder Richard Foreman presented his 40th-anniversary production here in 2008.
✚ 143 E12 ✉ St. Mark's Church, 131 East 10th Street, between Second and Third avenues ☎ 212/420-1916 ⊕ Astor Place (6), Eighth Street (N, R, W) 🚌 M8, M15

THE PARK
www.theparknyc.com
This gargantuan complex features a glass-enclosed atrium with a fireplace. The main dining room has windows onto the outdoor garden dining area.
✚ 142 B12 ✉ 118 Tenth Avenue between West 17th and 18th streets ☎ 212/352-3313 ◷ Sun–Thu 10am–1am, Fri–Sat 11am–4am ⊕ 14th Street (A, C, E), Eighth Avenue (L)

PEOPLE'S IMPROV THEATER

www.thepit-nyc.com

Improvisation at this theater comes with the addition of caustic social commentary. Audience participation is encouraged.

🚏 142 D10 ✉ 154 West 29th Street, between Sixth and Seventh avenues ☎ 212/563-7488 🚇 28th Street (1) 🚌 M5, M6, M7, M20

PETE'S TAVERN

www.petestavern.com

The writer O. Henry supposedly wrote *The Gift of the Magi* in a beer-stained booth here. In summer, snag a sidewalk table if you can, for some great people-watching.

🚏 143 E12 ✉ 129 East 18th Street at Irving Place ☎ 212/473-7676 🚇 Mon–Fri 10.30am–3am, Sat–Sun 11am–3am 🚇 14th Street/Union Square (L, N, Q, R, W, 4, 5, 6)

THE POETRY PROJECT

www.poetryproject.org

This legendary outpost in the East Village, which hosted W. H. Auden, Allen Ginsberg and many others, has readings most Mondays, Wednesdays and Fridays.

🚏 143 E12 ✉ St. Mark's Church-in-the-Bowery, 131 East 10th Street at Second Avenue ☎ 212/674-0910 🚇 Astor Place (6), First Avenue (L) 🚌 M8, M15

IL POSTO ACCANTO

This is a friendly and welcoming wine bar. Order appetizers to go with one of 30 Italian wines sold by the glass.

🚏 143 F13 ✉ 190 East 2nd Street, between Avenues A and B ☎ 212/228-3562 🚇 Tue–Sun 6pm–2am 🚇 Lower East Side/Second Avenue (F, V)

QUAD CINEMA

www.quadcinema.com

This four-screen art house shows foreign and independent films and works by new directors.

🚏 142 D12 ✉ 34 West 13th Street, between Fifth and Sixth avenues ☎ 212/255-8800 or 212/255-2243 💷 $10 🚇 14th Street (F, V), 14th Street/Union Square (L, N, Q, R, W, 4, 5, 6) 🚌 M2, M3, M5, M6

RF LOUNGE

Couches and antique chairs are clustered around the fireplace in the upstairs bar, which attracts an over-35 crowd. There is a convivial restaurant downstairs.

🚏 142 C13 ✉ 531 Hudson Street, between Charles and West 10th streets ☎ 212/929-3343 🚇 Daily 3pm–4am 🚇 Christopher Street (1)

RODEO BAR

www.rodeobar.com

This Southern-style roadhouse serves Tex-Mex food and margaritas, along with nightly live bluegrass, country, rockabilly or alt-country.

🚏 143 E11 ✉ 375 Third Avenue at East 27th Street ☎ 212/683-6500 🚇 Daily 11.30am–2am (music Mon–Tue 9–12, Wed 10–12, Thu 10–1, Fri–Sat 10.30–1.30) 💷 Free 🚇 28th Street (6) 🚌 M101, M102, M103

STAR LOUNGE

www.starloungechelsea.com

In the basement of the Hotel Chelsea, the Star Lounge is the new cool bar in Downtown. The two rooms are dark and small, with regular DJ sessions.

🚏 142 C11 ✉ Hotel Chelsea, 222 West 23rd Street, between Seventh and Eighth avenues ☎ 212/255-4646 🚇 Tue–Sat 6pm–4am 🚇 23rd Street (1)

STONEWALL INN

www.stonewall-place.com

It's nondescript, but this place has acquired near-mythic status for the gay movement. Here in 1969 some transvestites, using their stilettos, took a stand against the police.

🚏 142 C13 ✉ 53 Christopher Street between Seventh Avenue South and Waverly Place ☎ 212/488-2705 🚇 Mon–Sat 3pm–4am, Sun noon–4am 🚇 Christopher Street/Sheridan Square (1)

SUGARCANE

The gimmick at this Latino lounge is the "Cocktail Tree," a sampler holding the entire drinks menu. The DJ spins funky Brazilian-Caribbean sounds.

🚏 143 D11 ✉ 245 Park Avenue South, between 19th and 20th streets ☎ 212

475-9377 🚇 Mon–Wed 5.45–1, Thu–Sat 5.45–2, Sun 5.45–midnight 🚇 23rd Street (6), 23rd Street (N, R, W)

SULLIVAN HALL

www.sullivanhallnyc.com

An eclectic variety of music styles is performed here, but don't expect to hear hard core or heavy metal.

🚏 142 D13 ✉ 214 Sullivan Street, between Bleecker and West 3rd streets ☎ 212/477-2782 🚇 Nightly 💷 $10–$20 🚇 West 4th Street (A, C, E, F, S, V), Bleecker Street (6) 🚌 M5, M6, M21

SWEET RHYTHM

www.sweetrhythmny.com

The late Gil Evans played here when the place was called Sweet Basil. It's a casual spot where mainstream jazz artists play sets nightly.

🚏 142 C13 ✉ 88 Seventh Avenue South, between Grove and Bleecker streets ☎ 212/255-3626 💷 $12–$25, plus $10 minimum 🚇 Christopher Street/Sheridan Square (1), West 4th Street (A, C, E, F, S, V) 🚌 M8, M20

SWIFT HIBERNIAN LOUNGE

Numerous brews are on tap at this slice of Dublin named for satirist Jonathan Swift.

🚏 143 E13 ✉ 34 East 4th Street, between Bowery and Lafayette Street ☎ 212/260-3600 🚇 Daily noon–4am 🚇 Broadway/Lafayette (F, S, V), Bleecker Street (6)

TEMPLE BAR

This ultra-expensive bar attracts models and their coterie.

🚏 143 E13 ✉ 332 Lafayette Street, between Houston and Bleecker streets ☎ 212/925-4242 🚇 Mon–Thu 5–1, Fri–Sat 5–2 🚇 Broadway/Lafayette (F, S, V), Bleecker Street (6)

TERRA BLUES

www.terrablues.com

At this second-floor club, acoustic acts warm up the crowd for the nightly blues show.

🚏 142 D13 ✉ 149 Bleecker Street between LaGuardia Place and Thompson Street ☎ 212/777-7776 🚇 Nightly at 7pm, blues show 10pm 💷 From $5, plus 2-drink minimum 🚇 West 4th Street (A, C, E, F, S, V) 🚌 M5, M6

THEATER FOR THE NEW CITY

www.theaterforthenewcity.net

Thought-provoking, often politically inspired dramas are the repertory of this community-oriented company, founded in 1970.

✚ 143 E13 ✉ 155 First Avenue, between 9th and 10th streets ☎ 212/254-1109 🚇 Astor Place (6) 🚌 M8, M15

VILLAGE UNDERGROUND

www.thevillageunderground.com

A subterranean club with a good line-up of artists ranging from salsa bands to blues artists.

✚ 142 D13 ✉ 130 West 3rd Street, between Sixth Avenue and MacDougal Street ☎ 212/777-7745 🚇 West 4th Street (A, C, E, F, S, V) 🚌 M5, M6

VILLAGE VANGUARD

www.villagevanguard.com

Founded by Max Gordon in 1935, it's still the premier jazz club in the city, presided over by Lorraine Gordon since her husband died in 1989. The Vanguard is intimate, has terrific acoustics and features top-flight artists—Lester Young, Thelonious Monk, John Coltrane, Keith Jarrett and Miles Davis have played here. Nowadays evenings often morph into a vibrant jam session.

✚ 142 C12 ✉ 178 Seventh Avenue at West 11th Street ☎ 212/255-4037 🕐 Daily from 8pm (sets Sun–Fri 9 and 11, Sat 9, 11 and sometimes 12.30) 👆 Cover varies, plus $10 minimum 🚇 14th Street (1, 2, 3) 🚌 M14, M20

VINEYARD THEATRE

www.vineyardtheatre.org

Located in a residential tower, this off-Broadway theater has staged Pulitzer Prize-winning plays before they went to Broadway. The auditorium seats 120.

✚ 143 E12 ✉ 108 East 15th Street, between Union Square and Irving Place ☎ 212/353-3366, 212/353-0303 🚇 14th Street/Union Square (L, N, Q, R, W, 4, 5, 6) 🚌 M14, M101, M102, M103

WHITE HORSE TAVERN

Dylan Thomas, Brendan Behan and Jack Kerouac all slaked their thirst here. In summer, the benches and picnic tables make perfect perches for Village people-watching.

✚ 142 C13 ✉ 567 Hudson Street at 11th Street ☎ 212/989-3956 🕐 Sun–Thu 11am–1.30am, Fri–Sat 11am–3.30am 🚇 Christopher Street/Sheridan Square (1), 14th Street (A, C, E)

XUNTA

On Thursdays flamenco and guitar music provide the atmosphere for sangria and tapas at this lively bar.

✚ 143 E12 ✉ 174 First Avenue, between East 10th and 11th streets ☎ 212/614-0620 🕐 Sun–Thu 5–midnight, Fri–Sat 5–2 🚇 14 Street (L), Lower East Side/Second Avenue (F, V)

ZINC BAR

www.zincbar.com

Music-lovers and musicians come to this casual, tiny bar to hear newcomers and established names such as George Benson and Max Roach. There's usually Brazilian music on Saturdays and Sundays.

✚ 142 D13 ✉ 82 West 3rd Street near Thompson Street ☎ 212/477-9462 🕐 Daily 6pm–3.30am (show times vary) 👆 Cover varies 🚇 West 4th Street (A, B, C, D, E, F, V), Houston Street (1), Bleecker Street (6) 🚌 M5, M6

SPORTS AND ACTIVITIES

BOWLMOR LANES

www.bowlmor.com

This funky bowling alley has 42 lanes with automatic scoring. At Monday's Night Strike (10pm–2am), DJs spin music as you bowl.

✚ 143 D12 ✉ 110 University Place, between 12th and 13th streets ☎ 212/255-8188 🕐 Sun 11am–midnight, Tue–Wed noon–1am, Mon, Thu noon–2am, Fri–Sat 11am–3.30am 👆 $8.45–$9.95 per game (shoe rental $5.50). Night Strike $24 🚇 14th Street/Union Square (L, N, Q, R, W, 4, 5, 6) 🚌 M3

MANHATTAN KAYAK COMPANY

www.manhattankayak.com

This company offers instruction and more than 30 local tours for all abilities. Longer tours go to the Verrazano Bridge and farther.

✚ 142 A11 ✉ Pier 66, 26th Street and 12th Avenue ☎ 212/924-1788 🕐 Mid-Apr to end Oct 👆 Tours $40–$250 🚇 8th Avenue (C, E) then M23 bus 🚌 M23

NEW YORK GALLERY TOURS

▷ 270.

PRESSURE

This bubble on the roof of Bowlmor Lanes (▷ this page) is the ultimate pool hall/multimedia lounge. It has 21 tables, plus a huge bar/lounge and one 21ft (6.5m) and three 16ft (5m) movie screens.

✚ 143 D12 ✉ 110 University Place, between 12th and 13th streets ☎ 212/352-1161 🕐 Fri–Sat 9pm–3am 👆 $26 per hr 🚇 14th Street/Union Square (L, N, Q, R, W, 4, 5, 6) 🚌 M3

SLATE

www.slate-ny.com

This is one of the city's best billiard-pool halls, with 31 tables.

✚ 142 D11 ✉ 54 West 21st Street, between Fifth and Sixth avenues ☎ 212/989-0096 🕐 Mon–Sat noon–4am, Sun 12–12 👆 $15–$17 per hour 🚇 23rd Street (N, R, W), 23rd Street (F, V) 🚌 M2, M3, M5, M6, M7

HEALTH AND BEAUTY

ACQUA BEAUTY BAR

www.acquabeautybar.com

Treatments include an Indonesian "ritual of beauty," an Adlay (Asian wheat) body scrub and an indulgent Garden of Eastern Delights, combining a mist facial with a shiatsu massage. You can still get a Swedish massage and French manicure or pedicure, though.

✚ 142 D12 ✉ 7 East 14th Street near Fifth Avenue ☎ 212/620-4329 🕐 Mon, Thu 10–9, Tue–Wed, Fri 10–8, Sat–Sun 10–7 👆 Facial $135–$250, manicure $12–$22, massage $100–$110 🚇 Union Square-14th Street (L, N, Q, R, W)

BALLY TOTAL FITNESS

www.ballyfitness.com

This national chain has several facilities in Manhattan. The Sixth Avenue club has more than 70 pieces of cardiovascular equipment, 73 pieces of resistance-training equipment, personal trainers and classes in yoga and Pilates.

✚ 142 D12 ✉ 641 Avenue of the Americas at 19th Street ☎ 212/645-4565 🕐 Mon–Thu 5.30–11, Fri 5.30–10, Sat 9–8, Sun 9–7 ✋ Day pass $15 🚇 18th Strreet (1) 🚌 M5, M6, M7

CHELSEA PIERS
www.chelseapiers.com
The city's ultimate sports complex is built on four Hudson River piers. In summer, the beach, sundecks, large pool and kayaking layout are inviting. There's a climbing wall as well as 200-meter and quarter-mile tracks, an ice rink, and rows of cardiovascular, circuit and strength-training equipment. There are courts for basketball, indoor sand volleyball and touch football, plus a boxing ring, golf driving range and batting cages. Some 125 classes a week offer everything from aerobics to yoga. Other facilities include a sports medicine clinic, café and spa.
✚ 142 A11 ✉ Piers 59–62 at 23rd Street and the Hudson River ☎ 212/336-6000 🕐 Daily 6am–midnight ✋ Day passes available 🚇 23rd Street (C, E) 🚌 M23

CLAY
www.insideclay.com
Sleek, serene and minimal, Clay combines bodywork therapies with exercise (weights, cardio-boxing, yoga). The fireside lounge and rooftop deck are bonuses.
✚ 142 D12 ✉ 25 West 14th Street, between Fifth and Sixth avenues ☎ 212/206-9200 🕐 Mon–Thu 5.30am–11pm, Fri 5.30am–10pm, Sat–Sun 8–9 ✋ Massage $110–$145 🚇 14th Street/Union Square (L, N, Q, R, W, 4, 5, 6) 🚌 M2, M3, M5, M14

CRUNCH FITNESS
www.crunch.com
Crunch, which has 12 locations in the city, is the premier brand of Bally Fitness. The instructors are first rate, and the studio is known for its innovative classes, from street stomp to cycle karaoke.
✚ 143 E12 ✉ 113 4th Avenue at 12th Street ☎ 212/533-0001 🕐 Mon–Fri 5am–11pm, Sat–Sun 8am–9pm ✋ Day pass $16 🚇 14th Street/Union Square (L, N, Q, R, W, 4, 5, 6) 🚌 M1, M2, M3, M5

GREAT JONES SPA
www.greatjonesspa.com
The Great Jones Spa blends organic principles (a raw food café) with unashamed indulgence. They provide a kind of feng shui for the body, and the facilities are as impressive as the ambience is relaxing. There are water cures, acupuncture, detoxifying and spa treatments.
✚ 143 E13 ✉ 29 Great Jones Street at Lafayette ☎ 212/505-3185 🕐 Mon 4–10pm, Tue–Sun 9am–10pm ✋ Manicure $25–$40, facial $130–$295, massage $140–$210 🚇 Bleecker Street (6)

JENIETTE
www.jeniette.com
Since 1979 this East Village salon has been providing good manicures, pedicures, facials and massage at much lower prices than uptown. It uses Dinur products.
✚ 143 D12 ✉ 58 East 13th Street, between University Place and Broadway ☎ 212/529-1616 🕐 Mon, Wed, Sat 10–7, Tue, Thu, Fri 10–8, Sun 11–6 ✋ Manicure $12–$20, facial $68, massage $75–$170 🚇 14th Street/Union Square (L, N, Q, R, W, 4, 5, 6) 🚌 M1, M5, M6, M14

NEW YORK HEALTH AND RACQUET CLUB
www.nyhrc.com
The ten Manhattan branches of this chain offer sports and classes from t'ai chi to aqua-cise. Each branch has a pool. Members have access to a beach and tennis club in New Rochelle, and a yacht docked at 23rd Street.
✚ 142 D12 ✉ 24 East 13th Street, between Fifth Avenue and University Place ☎ 212/924-4600 🕐 Mon–Fri 6am–11pm, Sat–Sun 8am–9pm ✋ Day pass $20 🚇 14th Street/Union Square (L, N, Q, R, W, 4, 5, 6) 🚌 M1, M2, M3, M5

NEW YORK SPORT CLUBS
www.mysportsclubs.com
This chain has close to 100 locations around town, mostly aerobic studios with cardio-fitness machines and free weights, plus a full program of exercise classes—cardio-kick-boxing, step, abs, Pilates and yoga. Massage treatments are available.

✚ 142 C12 ✉ 128 Eighth Avenue at 16th Street ☎ 212/627-0065 🕐 Mon–Thu 6am–11pm, Fri 6am–10pm, Sat–Sun 8am–9pm ✋ Day pass $25 🚇 18th Street (1) 🚌 M20

OASIS DAY SPA
www.nydayspa.com
Candlelight and soft music enhance this popular spa, which offers 15 massage treatments. There is also a hair and nail salon.
✚ 143 D10 ✉ 1 Park Avenue, between 32nd and 33rd streets ☎ 212/254-2722 🕐 Mon–Fri 10–10, Sat–Sun 9–9 ✋ Facial $65–$200, massage $65–$185 🚇 33rd Street (6) 🚌 M1, M2, M3

RESCUE BEAUTY LOUNGE
www.rescuebeauty.com
Rescue takes a medical approach to pampering, maintaining hospital standards of cleanliness. This is the place to get the ultimate manicure.
✚ 142 C12 ✉ 34 Gansevoort Street, between Hudson and Greenwich streets, second floor ☎ 212/206-6409 🕐 Tue–Fri 11–8, Sat–Sun 10–6 ✋ Manicure $30–$70, pedicure $50–$125, facial $85–$225 🚇 14th Street (A, C, E), Eighth Avenue (L) 🚌 M11, M20

FOR CHILDREN
FORBES MAGAZINE GALLERIES
▷ 113.

TADA THEATER AND DANCE ALLIANCE
www.tadatheater.com
Young professionals aged 8 to 17 put on entertaining shows and revues at this theater company-and-school.
✚ 142 D11 ✉ 15 West 28th Street at Sixth Avenue ☎ 212/252-1619 ✋ Adult $25, child $8 🚇 23rd Street (F, V) 🚌 M5, M6, M7

THEATREWORKS USA
www.theatreworksusa.org
Plays and musicals for children are based on such favorites as *The Lion, the Witch and the Wardrobe*.
✚ 142 C13 ✉ Lucille Lortel Theatre, 121 Christopher Street, between Hudson and Bleecker ☎ 212/647-1100 🕐 Call for details ✋ $25 🚇 Christopher St–Sheridan Square (1) 🚌 M8, M20

PRICES AND SYMBOLS

The prices given are the average for a two-course lunch (L) and a three-course dinner (D) for one person, without drinks. The wine price is for the least expensive bottle.

For a key to the symbols, ▷ 2.

ANGELICA KITCHEN

www.aangelicakitchen.com
This ecological restaurant proves that vegetarian cuisine does not have to be bland. Go for the hearty soups, chili or tasty noodle dishes and sandwiches. There is no alcohol, and credit cards are not accepted.
✚ 143 E12 ✉ 300 East 12th Street, between First and Second avenues ☎ 212/228-2909 🕔 Daily 11.30–10.30 🖐 L $18, D $26 🚇 14th Street/Union Square (4, 5, 6, L, N, Q, R, W) 🚌 M14, M15

ANNISA

www.annisarestaurant.com
At this minimalist restaurant chef Anita Lo cooks fusion cuisine. For appetizers, oysters might arrive with three root vegetables, while roasted kabocha squash and maiiake mushrooms could be combined with bitter chocolate. Smoked lamb hominy is enriched with chili and lime. Credit cards are not accepted.

✚ 142 C13 ✉ 13 Barrow Street, between Bleecker and West 4th streets ☎ 212/741-6699 🕔 Mon–Sat 5.30–10, Sun 5.30–9.30 🖐 D $60, 5-course tasting $75, 9 courses $95, Wine $27 🚇 West 4th Street (A, C, E, F), Christopher Street/Sheridan Square (1) 🚌 M20, M21

BABBO

www.babbonyc.com
Mario Batali has a lust for life that's infectious and an originality that is breathtaking. He has authored numerous cookery books and has a prime-time PBS series. At Babbo, his flagship restaurant, the welcome is warm and the food some of the freshest and lustiest anywhere. Try the handmade beef cheek ravioli or the prosciutto with spicy fig jam. The all-Italian wine list is a revelation.
✚ 142 D13 ✉ 110 Waverly Place, between MacDougal Street and Sixth Avenue ☎ 212/777-0303 🕔 Mon–Sat 5.30–11, Sun 5–11 🖐 D $70, Wine $25 🚇 West 4th Street (A, C, E, F, S, V) 🚌 M5, M6

BANJARA

Sixth Street is lined with Indian restaurants, but Banjara is the best of the lot. Northern Indian cuisine is the specialty. The tandoori dishes

are particularly good with their fine smoky flavor. Also appealing are the pasanda lamb, cooked in a yogurt-based curry sauce, and the palak ghost—lamb in a purée of spinach, tomatoes, ginger and cumin seeds.
✚ 143 E13 ✉ 97 First Avenue at 6th Street ☎ 212/477-5956 🕔 Daily 12–12 🖐 L $20, D $30, Wine $19 🚇 Astor Place (6) 🚌 M8, M15

BLUE HILL

www.bluehillnyc.com
Candlelight and bouquets set the inviting tone of this below-ground dining room. It's named for a farm in Massachusetts where the chef finds his seasonal, locally grown ingredients. Expect corn shoots in June, squash and apples in fall. The menu offers six appetizers and seven entrées—say, fall mushrooms braised and steamed with fingerling potato tart, followed by roasted trout with a pistou of vegetables with puréed basil, or poached duck with a stew of organic carrots with toasted spices. Desserts are enticing.
✚ 142 D13 ✉ 75 Washington Place, between MacDougal and Sixth Avenue ☎ 212/539-1776 🕔 Mon–Sat 5.30–11, Sun 5.30–10 🖐 D $65, Wine $35 🚇 W 4th Street (A, C, E, F, S, V) 🚌 M5, M6

Opposite *The vegetarian Angelica Kitchen*

BLUE SMOKE
www.bluesmoke.com
The secret of barbecue is slow cooking and well-blended spices. Danny Meyer studied it for three years and traveled 62,000 miles before opening this rustic red-hot restaurant. Barbecue addicts drool over the rib sampler. Eight beers are on tap, while the bourbon whiskey and wine list pairs well with the food. A good jazz room downstairs shares the upstairs menu.
✚ 143 E11 ✉ 116 East 27th Street, between Park Avenue South and Lexington Avenue ☎ 212/447-7733 🕐 Sun–Mon 11.30–10, Tue–Thu 11.30–11, Fri–Sat 11.30am–1am ✋ L $25, D $36, Wine $32 🚇 23rd Street (6) 🚌 M1, M101, M102, M103

BOND ST
www.bondstrestaurant.com
The buzz has lessened at this sleek Japanese spot in a SoHo brownstone, but the glistening sushi and sashimi are as beautiful as ever. Among the appetizers, expect seared duck with shitake and truffle glaze, or monkfish filet with spicy-and-sour salsa. Desserts are innovative Japanese. Traditional tatami rooms are upstairs; downstairs there's a fashionable lounge serving exotic *saketinis*.
✚ 143 E13 ✉ 6 Bond Street, between Broadway and Lafayette Street ☎ 212/777-2500 🕐 Tue–Sat 6–11.30, Sun–Mon 6–10.30 ✋ D $50, *omakase* $60–$100, Wine $35 🚇 Broadway/Lafayette (F, S, V) 🚌 M1, M5, M6

CASA MONO
www.casamononyc.com
Mario Batali has turned to Spain for inspiration at this small tapas bar reminiscent of those found in Barcelona and Madrid. It's crowded and noisy and the dishes invite experimentation. There might be bacalao croquettes with orange flavored aioli, cockles with scrambled eggs and Serrano ham, or oxtails with *piquillo* peppers along with more substantial dishes and

great artisanal cheeses. Affordable wine and sherry selection.
✚ 143 E12 ✉ 52 Irving Place at 17th Street ☎ 212/253-2773 🕐 Daily 12–12 ✋ L $25, D $42, Wine $30 🚇 14th Street/ Union Square L, N, Q, R, W 🚌 M1, M2, M3, M6, M7, M101, M102, M103

I COPPI
www.icoppinyc.com
This restaurant is like a piece of Tuscany in Manhattan. Wood tables and rush-seated chairs create a rustic charm accompanied by music from the opera. Tuna carpaccio is paper-thin and spiked with green peppercorn sauce; sliced pears with Gorgonzola and stracchino cheese make for a perfect salad. Among the *secondi,* there might be grilled wild boar, or wild striped bass with caper and black olives.
✚ 143 F13 ✉ 432 East 9th Street, between First Avenue and Avenue A ☎ 212/254-2263 🕐 Sun–Thu 5.30–10, Fri–Sat 5–11 (also brunch Sat–Sun 11.30–3) ✋ Brunch $15, D $50, Wine $25 🚇 Astor Place (6) 🚌 M8, M14, M15

CORNER BISTRO
www.cornerbistro.ypguides.net
The graffiti-covered tables and booths at this plain West Village bar remain the best place in town to grab burgers. Made with 8oz (225g) ground chuck, they come plain or topped with bacon or blue cheese. Other sandwiches and chili are also available. The jukebox has great sounds and the beer is good. Credit cards are not accepted.
✚ 142 C12 ✉ 331 West 4th Street, between Jane Street and Eighth Avenue ☎ 212/242-9502 🕐 Mon–Sat 11.30am–4am, Sun noon–4am ✋ L $10, D $16 🚇 14th Street (A, C, E) 🚌 M14, M20

CRAFT AND CRAFTBAR
www.craftrestaurant.com
When Tom Colicchio conceived Craft he wanted diners to create their own dishes from a menu that was just a list of ingredients. This is still the focus, but the chef now supplies more direction. Most dishes are roasted (striped bass, quail) or braised (red snapper, short ribs).

Desserts can be fresh fruits, intense sorbets or decadent confections like the toffee steamed pudding. The cheeses are stunning. The leather, copper and steel, and plain wood furnishings and fittings recall the Arts and Crafts movement. Craftbar serves sandwiches and oysters.
✚ 143 D11 ✉ 43 East 19th Street, between Broadway and Park Avenue South ☎ 212/780-0880 🕐 Mon–Fri noon–2, Mon–Thu 5.30–10, Fri–Sat 5.30–11, Sun 5–9 ✋ L $50, D $75, Wine $28 🚇 23rd Street (N, R, W), 23rd Street (6) 🚌 M1, M2, M3, M6, M7

CREMA RESTAURANTE
www.cremarestaurante.com
Julieta Ballasteros has been voted among the top two Mexican chefs in New York six years in a row, by Zagat. Her Chelsea restaurant combines the zingy flavors of Mexico with the subtlety of fine French cuisine, with dishes such as a casserole of cheese and Mexican chorizo served with corn tortillas. Leave room for unusual desserts like the pumpkin cheesecake.
✚ 142 D12 ✉ 111 West 17th Street, between 6th and 7th avenues ☎ 212/ 691-4477 🕐 Tue–Wed, Sun 12–11, Thu–Sat 12–12 ✋ L $25, D $45, Wine $22 🚇 18th Street (1), 14th Street (F, V) 🚌 M5, M6, M7, M20

CRU
www.cru-nyc.com
The 3,000-selection wine list (50 by the glass) is a gift to wine lovers to be accompanied by some carefully prepared contemporary European cuisine in elegant surroundings. Start with *crudo* or appetizers, which will supply such delights as fluke with mango and caviar or tuna with caper espresso and olives praline. Entrees are equally exciting, even revelatory—just try the silky poussin baked in buttermilk and finished with orange paprika carrots and chanterelles and parsley root.
✚ 142 D13 ✉ 24 Fifth Avenue at Ninth Street ☎ 212/529-1700 🕐 Mon–Sat 5.30–11 (closed Mon in Aug) ✋ D $78, Wine $36 🚇 8th Street (N, R, W) 🚌 M2, M3, M5, M8

DEVI

www.devinyc.com

The decor and food will transport you to India in a minute. Dishes draw inspiration from street food and regional cuisine. Goan shrimp are cooked with *balchao*, a vinegar based sauce; fishes are baked in banana leaf; Manchurian cauliflower is a mixture of tomato sauce with scallions and chilies. All are redolent with cilantro (coriander), mint, tamarind and coconut.

✚ 142 D12 ✉ 8 East 18th Street, between Fifth Avenue and Broadway ☎ 212/691-1300 🕐 Mon–Sat 5.30–11, Sun 5–10 🖐 D $45, $55 7-course tasting menu, chef's tasting menu $85, Wine $35 🚇 14th Street/Union Square (L, N, Q, R, W, 4, 5, 6) 🚌 M2, M3, M5, M6, M7

DOS CAMINOS

www.brguestrestaurants.com

The space is celebratory, the bar stocks 150 tequilas, and the fare covers all Mexican bases— guacamole made tableside; shrimp, scallop and tuna ceviche; chicken mole; and pan-roasted snapper with pineapple-passion fruit sauce. Desserts are ice creams and sorbets such as guava-mango sorbet.

✚ 143 E11 ✉ 373 Park Avenue South, between 26th and 27th streets ☎ 212/294-1000 🕐 Daily 11.30–4, Sun–Mon 5–10, Tue–Thu 5–11, Fri–Sat 5–midnight 🖐 L $28, D $46, Wine $32 🚇 28th Street (6) 🚌 M1

ELEVEN MADISON PARK

www.elevenmadisonpark.com

This dramatic dining space, once the brokers' hall of the Metropolitan Life insurance company, is worthy of the cuisine. The fish dishes are fragrant and moist (seared Arctic char in black truffle vinaigrette), and meat dishes robust (grilled hanger steak in shallot sauce). Appetizers include seared foie gras in a sauternes coulis. The international wine list leans to the French.

✚ 143 D11 ✉ 11 Madison Avenue at 24th Street ☎ 212/889-0905 🕐 Daily 11.30–2, Sun–Thu 5.30–10, Fri–Sat 5.30–10.30 🖐 L $60, D $92, Wine $45 🚇 23rd Street (6) 🚌 M1, M2, M3

FLEUR DE SEL

www.fleurdeselnyc.com

The place may look unassuming but the food is not at this French gem. Many dishes have surprising elements. Imagine venison in a beet licorice sauce, sea bass with Malbec wine sauce or rack of lamb with horseradish crème and rosemary jus. Desserts are equally inspired.

✚ 142 D11 ✉ 5 East 20th Street, between Broadway and Fifth Avenue ☎ 212/460-9100 🕐 Daily noon–2, Mon–Sat 5.30–10.30, Sun 5–9 🖐 L prix fixe $29, D prix fixe $76, 6-course $89, Wine $48 🚇 23rd Street (N, R, W) 🚌 M2, M3, M5, M6, M7

GNOCCO

www.gnocco.com

No prizes for guessing the house specialty here—delicious home-made gnocco which are fried and served with either a sauce or a cold meat plate and not to be confused with gnocchi. Either way these, and the other fresh pasta dishes, are Italian cooking at its best. The intimate dining room conceals a lovely garden dining area out back, and the service is relaxed and amiable Italian-style.

✚ 143 F12 ✉ 337 East 10th Street, between A and B avenues ☎ 212/677-1913 🕐 Mon–Fri 5pm–midnight, Sat–Sun 12–12 🖐 L $20, D $45, Wine $28 🚇 Astor Place (6), First Avenue (L) 🚌 M8, M9, M14a

GONZO

Gonzo may be moderately priced, but the rustic food is very good, made with ultra-fresh ingredients and served to a hip lively crowd in a comfortable setting. Start your meal with a plate of sliced meats and cheeses or *cicchetti*, such as beet and Gorgonzola salad, or chickpea and sun-dried tomato spread. The pastas and pizzas are inventive. Among entrées, the Venetian calf's liver is superb.

✚ 142 C12 ✉ 140 West 13th Street, between Sixth and Seventh avenues ☎ 212/645-4606 🕐 Mon–Thu 5.30–11, Fri 5.30–midnight, Sat 5–midnight, Sun 5–10.30 🖐 D $44, Wine $28 🚇 14th Street 🚌 M5, M6, M20

GOTHAM BAR & GRILL

www.gothambarandgrill.com

Unique among Manhattan celebrity chefs, Alfred Portale has not yet created his own mini-chain. This may be why his fresh-tasting, dramatically presented contemporary cuisine continues to excite even after more than 20 years. Rack of lamb is Portale's signature dish, but you can't go wrong with the truffle-crusted halibut with verjus sauce or the Snake River Farms pork with caramelized *cipollini* onions. The warm apple and mango tartes Tatin and the warm Gotham chocolate cake are sublime. There are extra-special tea selections.

✚ 142 D12 ✉ 12 East 12th Street, between Fifth Avenue and University Place ☎ 212/620-4020 🕐 Mon–Fri noon–2.15, Mon–Thu 5.30–10, Fri 5.30–11, Sat 5–11, Sun 5–10 🖐 L $40, D $80, Wine $45 🚇 14th Street/Union Square (L, N, Q, R, W, 4, 5, 6) 🚌 M2, M3, M5

GRAMERCY TAVERN

www.gramercytavern.com

Danny Meyer's stellar restaurant, under Executive Chef Michael Anthony, still shines. Both the main dining room (made up from a warren of several cozy rooms) and the more casual tavern in the front of the building are both striking and comfortable. The truly warm hospitality and the seamless service make this one of the city's top tables. You can't go wrong on this menu, which offers a seared foie gras paired with a rhubarb tart, arugula (rocket) and sherry vinegar, and a roasted monkfish wrapped with pancetta. Twenty-five wines from the superb list are available by the glass. Desserts are just as delightful as the main dishes.

✚ 142 D11 ✉ 42 East 20th Street, between Broadway and Park Avenue South ☎ 212/477-0777 🕐 Dining room: Mon–Fri noon–2, Sun–Thu 5.30–10, Fri–Sat 5.30–11; Tavern: Sun–Thu noon–11, Fri–Sat 12–12 🖐 L $45, tasting menu $55, D 3-course prix fixe $86, tasting menu $112; Tavern L $30, D $40, Wine $24 🚇 23rd Street (N, R, W) 🚌 M1, M2, M3, M6, M7

HOLY BASIL

www.holybasilrestaurant.com

This is one of the city's best Thai restaurants. Here, the kitchen balances the flavors of sweet and salt associated with the cuisine. The stars are the fish dishes, such as the whole crisp fish, which you can order in red chili sauce or a delicious tamarind sauce. Wine selections pair well with the food.

➕ 143 E13 ✉ 149 Second Avenue, between East 9th and 10th streets ☎ 212/460-5557 🕐 Mon–Thu 5–11.30, Fri 5–midnight, Sat 4–midnight, Sun 4–11 ✋ D $32, Wine $23 🚇 Astor Place (6) 🚌 M15

JOHN'S PIZZERIA

www.johnspizzerianyc.com

The pizza served at this John's Pizzeria is frequently touted as the best in the city, and it is extraordinarily good indeed. Note that this is not a pizza parlor; slices are not available. Instead, take a booth and order a whole pie loaded with toppings—more than 50 are available. Credit cards are not accepted here.

➕ 142 C13 ✉ 278 Bleecker Street, between Sixth and Seventh avenues ☎ 212/243-1680 🕐 Mon–Sat 11.30–11.30, Sun noon–11.30 ✋ L $20, D $30, Wine $21 🚇 West 4th Street (A, C, E, F, S, V), Christopher Street/Sheridan Square (1) 🚌 M5, M20

MERMAID INN

www.themermaidnyc.com

This is the closest that Manhattan can come to a seafood shack, complete with ocean paraphernalia and navigational charts. The menu opens with a small selection of raw shellfish and follows with everything from chowder and spaghetti *fra diavolo* to *zaruela* brimming with lobster tail, cod and squid. No desserts are available, except whatever the house provides as complimentary.

➕ 143 E13 ✉ 96 Second Avenue, between 5th and 6th streets ☎ 212/674-5870 🕐 Mon–Sat 6–1 ✋ D $42, Wine $28 🚇 Astor Place (6), Eighth Street (N, R, W) 🚌 M15, M103

MESA GRILL

www.mesagrill.com

When Bobby Flay opened this restaurant in 1991, he introduced New Yorkers to the spices of the Southwest, and the place continues to excite. The red walls recall Sedona rock, the shrimp and fresh corn with black pepper tamale is hot off the grill, and the cactus pear margaritas cool the heat. Follow the cornmeal-crusted oysters and mango *habanero* sauce with 16-spice chicken in cilantro (coriander)-pumpkin seed sauce. Brunches are distinctive as well—it's not everywhere you'll find tequila-smoked-salmon quesadilla.

➕ 142 D12 ✉ 102 Fifth Avenue, between 15th and 16th streets ☎ 212/807-7400 🕐 Mon–Thu 12–2.30, 5.30–10.30, Fri 12–2.30, 5.30–11, Sat 11.30–2.30, 5–11, Sun 11.30–2.30, 5.30–10.30 ✋ L $30, D $57, Wine $28 🚇 14th Street/Union Square (L, N, Q, R, W, 4, 5, 6) 🚌 M2, M3, M5, M14

NEGRIL VILLAGE

www.negrilvillage.com

The neo-Caribbean dishes sit wonderfully on the tongue at this sultry restaurant. It's hard to choose between the succulent curried goat, and such specialties as the ackee and the saltfish. Tropical desserts include key lime cheesecake with mango coulis. The downstairs rum lounge pours an amazing 50 different rums.

➕ 142 D13 ✉ 70 West 3rd Street, between La Guardia Place and Thompson Street ☎ 212/477-2804 🕐 Mon–Thu 12–12, Fri–Sat noon–3am, Sun 11.30–11 ✋ L $22, D $40, Wine $20 🚇 West 4th Street (A, C, E, F, S, V) 🚌 M5, M21

OTTO ENOTECA PIZZERIA

www.ottopizzeria.com

Mario Batali continues to apply his genius to educating the average American palate to real Italian cuisine and wine. Here, the arena is pizza, which you can have with marinara, or—a better idea—in one of the combinations dreamed up by Mario, such as topped with porcini and taleggio or with tomato, fennel,

bottarga (silver mullet roe), pecorino and mozzarella. The wine card is extraordinary, and the gelati are the best in the city, period.

➕ 142 D13 ✉ 1 Fifth Avenue at 8th Street ☎ 212/995-9559 🕐 Daily 11.30am–midnight ✋ L $24, D $39, Wine $32 🚇 West 4th Street (A, C, E, F, S, V) 🚌 M2, M3, M5

LA PALAPA

www.lapalapa.com

At this dark and sultry Mexican, the cooking reveals the complex flavors of *epazote,* cactus pads, avocado leaves and numerous chilies. The balance is always right, whether in the shrimp with red mole sauce, or the baked cod with *guajillo,* garlic and achiote barbecue sauce. Meat dishes are also well spiced. Then there are the extras—pinto beans with smoked bacon and chayotes in spicy cream.

➕ 143 E13 ✉ 77 St. Mark's Place, between First and Second avenues ☎ 212/777-2537 🕐 Mon–Fri 12–12, Sat–Sun 11am–midnight ✋ L $20, D $35, Wine $26 🚇 Astor Place (6) 🚌 M8, M15

PARADOU

www.paradounyc.com

A taste of Provence in the Meatpacking District, Paradou is equally popular with workers, shoppers and in the evening with lovers of good hearty French cooking. The garden gives a country feel right in the heart of the city, and with dishes such as cassoulet, duck *magret* and venison pot-au-feu on the menu, you could almost be in Provence.

➕ 142 B12 ✉ 8 Little West 12th Street, between 9th Avenue and Washington Street ☎ 212/463-8345 🕐 Mon–Wed 6–12, Thu–Fri 6–1, Sat noon–1am, Sun 12–10 ✋ D $45, Wine $32 🚇 14th Street (A, C, E), 8th Avenue (L) 🚌 M11, M14a

PASTIS

www.pastisny.com

At Pastis, you could just as easily be on rue St Denis in Paris, around the corner from Les Halles. Every detail rings true: the zinc bar, the smoky mirrors, the tiles and the

French ads. Then there are the *plats* (dishes)—onion soup gratinée, croque-monsieur, skate *au beurre noir*, steak and moules frites, and, at breakfast, wonderful brioche and egg dishes. Owner Keith McNally's heritage shows through, though, in the fish and chips and the beans on toast. Wine is served in tumblers. Expect to have to wait for a table.

✚ 142 C12 ✉ 9 Ninth Avenue at Little 12th Street ☎ 212/929-4844 🕐 Mon–Wed 8–11.30, noon–1am, Thu 8–11.30, noon–2am, Fri 8–11.30, noon–3am, Sat 10–4.30, 6–3, Sun 10–4.30, 6–1 🖑 L $35, D $48, Wine $18 🚇 14th Street (A, C, E) 🚌 M11, M14

PEARL OYSTER BAR
www.pearloysterbar.com

The fiercely loyal patrons of this spot with a marble bar don't mind lining up for New England favorites such as oysters, creamy chowder and the fried oyster sandwiches doused in rémoulade sauce. La pièce de résistance is the delicious lobster roll encased in a toasted bun.

✚ 142 D13 ✉ 18 Cornelia Street ☎ 212/691-8211 🕐 Mon–Fri noon–2.30, Mon–Sat 6–11 🖑 L $32, D $44, Wine $28 🚇 West 4th Street (A, C, E, F, S, V) 🚌 M5, M6, M20

PERIYALI
www.periyali.com

This was the first authentic Greek restaurant to open in Manhattan, and it has remained a premier Greek destination. The ambience is warm and appealing (white plaster, dark wood beams and attractive displays of appetizers). Everything is carefully prepared, from the fragrant *avgolemono* soup to the grilled lamb chops with fresh rosemary.

✚ 142 D11 ✉ 35 West 20th Street, between Fifth and Sixth avenues ☎ 212/463-7890 🕐 Mon–Fri noon–3, Mon–Thu 5.30–11, Fri–Sat 5.30–11.30 🖑 L $35, D $50, Wine $40 🚇 23rd Street (N, R, W) 🚌 M2, M3, M5, M6, M7

PIPA
www.abchome.com

Nuevo Latin king Douglas Rodriguez does Spanish at this lively

restaurant, whose name means "great time." You can make a meal of the tapas—succulent fried oysters with banana-and-lentil salad, horseradish aioli and crispy bacon; shrimp with garlic oil and chilies; or sautéed chorizo. Follow up with a rice, meat or fish dish, or perhaps a paella. The white or red sangria are perfect accompaniments, or go for one of the rum drinks.

✚ 143 D12 ✉ ABC Carpet and Home, 38 East 19th Street, between Broadway and Park Avenue South ☎ 212/677-2233 🕐 Mon–Thu noon–11, Fri 12–12, Sat 11am–midnight, Sun 11–10.30 🖑 L $24, D $44, Wine $32 🚇 4th Street/Union Square (L, N, Q, R, W, 4, 5, 6) 🚌 M1, M2, M3, M6, M7

PRUNE
www.prunerestaurant.com

Everything is meticulously prepared at this small, idiosyncratic restaurant. Dinner entrées might include roast duck with green olives, or whole grilled fish with fennel oil and salt. Order one of the carefully prepared vegetable accompaniments. Choose, perhaps, between the roast beets or the bitter greens salad with oil and lemon juice to complement the beautifully presented dishes.

✚ 143 E13 ✉ 54 East 1st Street, between First and Second avenues ☎ 212/677-6221 🕐 Mon–Thu 11.30–3.30, 5.30–11, Fri 11.30–3.30, 5.30–12, Sat 10–3.30, 5.30–12, Sun 10–3.30, 5–11 🖑 L $24, D $55, Wine $27 🚇 Lower East Side/Second Avenue (F, V) 🚌 M15, M21

THE RED CAT
www.theredcat.com

A downtown art crowd packs this vivacious, inviting bistro in a narrow crimson room illuminated by large Moroccan lanterns. The contemporary kitchen puts plenty of flavor into its creations—take, for example, the crisp skate wing in caper brown butter or the calves' liver au poivre. Tasty Parmesan fries spiked with mustard aioli are one of the most popular side orders. Desserts are eclectic but equally delicious. The wine list is carefully

chosen, and 17 selections are available by the glass.

✚ 142 B11 ✉ 227 Tenth Avenue, between West 23rd and 24th streets ☎ 212/242-1122 🕐 Mon–Thu 5–11, Fri–Sat 5–midnight, Sun 4.30–10.30 🖑 D $45, Wine $32 🚇 23rd Street (C, E) 🚌 M11, M23

SPICE MARKET
www.jean-georges.com

Expect a sensual experience. Beguiling and theatrical are the only words to describe this Southeast Asian space swathed in teak lit by silk lanterns, and dotted with palm trees. It's Jean-Georges Vongerichten's stage for exciting spicy street food. Roll the spring rolls in lettuce with fresh mint and cilantro (coriander) and dip them in sweet lime and rice vinegar broth, sample the fiery pork vindaloo or the black pepper shrimp with pineapple.

✚ 142 C12 ✉ 403 West 13th Street at Ninth Avenue ☎ 212/675-2322 🕐 Sun–Wed 12–12, Thu–Sat noon–1am 🖑 L $30, D $45, Wine $35 🚇 14th Street (A, C, E, L) 🚌 M11

THE SPOTTED PIG
www.thespottedpig.com

It may have Ken Friedman as part owner, but it is the chef April Bloomfeld who is drawing crowds at this small "gastro pub." She comes most recently from London's River Café and delivers some gutsy cuisine—veal kidneys, lamb with salsa verde, roast cod with parsley sauce and her beloved *gnudi* (gnocchi with sheep's milk ricotta and brown butter and sage).

✚ 142 C13 ✉ 314 West 11th Street at Greenwich Street ☎ 212/620-0393 🕐 Mon–Fri noon–2am, Sat–Sun 11am–2am 🖑 L $25, D $50, Wine $32 🚇 Christopher Street (1), 14th Street (A, C, E, L) 🚌 M11, M20

STRIP HOUSE
www.theglaziergroup.com

Recalling a 19th-century bordello with its tufted leather banquettes and swathe of velvet, this place serves up juicy succulent beef, notably the New York strip. Other cuts are available along with a couple of fish dishes, wild striped bass with artichokes, pancetta and basil sauce, for example.

✚ 142 D12 ✉ 13 East 12th Street, between Fifth Avenue and University Place ☎ 212/328-0000 🕐 Mon–Sat 5–11.30, Sun 5–10.30 🍴 D $65, Wine $35 🚇 14th Street/Union Square (L, N, Q, R, W, 4, 5, 6) 🚌 M2, M3, M5

SUEÑOS

www.suenosnyc.com

Traditional Mexican cooking with a contemporary twist is served here, and the New York Times said it is the most exciting Mexican food in the city. The menu does feature familiar dishes like tortillas, quesadillas and guacamole, but re-invented and served alongside entrées such as tamarind-glazed steak.

✚ 142 C12 ✉ 311 West 17th Street, between 8th and 9th avenues ☎ 212/243-1333 🕐 Tue–Thu 5–11, Fri–Sat 5–midnight, Sun 5–10 🍴 D $40, 3-course prix fixe $30, Wine $26 🚇 14th Street (A, C, E), 8th Avenue (L) 🚌 M11, M14d, M20

TABLA

www.tablany.com

Danny Meyer's Tabla delivers a superb dining experience with its gracious service and fragrant cuisine. In the coral and jade jewel box of a room upstairs, the menu offers Bombay native Floyd Cardoz's dishes, which use the spices of South India—tamarind, kokum, clove, cinnamon and black pepper. Goan-spiced crab cake, rice-flaked black bass, and duck samosa, set off by shaved fennel, almonds and dried fruit chutney, are just a few favorites. The sorbets are packed with flavor. The wine selections pair beautifully with the food (16 by the glass). On the ground floor, Bread Bar serves a selection of tandoori dishes and small plates of superb Indian breads.

✚ 143 D11 ✉ 11 Madison Avenue at 25th Street ☎ 212/889-0667 🕐 Mon–Fri 12–2, Sun–Wed 5.30–10, Thu–Sat 5.30–10.30 🍴 L $35, 3-course prix fixe $32, D 3-course prix fixe $64, tasting menu $92, Wine $35 🚇 23rd Street (N, R, W), 23rd Street (6) 🚌 M2, M3

TAMARIND

www.tamarinde22.com

The dining room of this Indian restaurant is sleek and comfortable (although noisy), and the wine list is expansive. The flavor of tamarind infuses many dishes, such as shrimp cooked in coconut sauce flavored with curry leaves and smoked tamarind, but there are other flavors as well—the she-crab soup with sweet spices, ginger and saffron is another winner. The lamb vindaloo is authentically spiced, as are many of the vegetarian dishes. Some are refreshingly new—bhindi do piazza, which is okra-flavored with brown onions and dried mango, for example. Even the desserts shine.

✚ 143 D11 ✉ 41–43 East 22nd Street, between Broadway and Park Avenue South ☎ 212/674-7400 🕐 Daily 11.30–3, Sun–Thu 5.30–11.30, Fri–Sat 11.30–midnight 🍴 L $24, D $40, Wine $30 🚇 23rd Street (N, R), 23rd Street (6) 🚌 M1, M2, M3, M6, M7

UNION SQUARE CAFÉ

www.unionsquarecafe.com

Led by chefs Michael Romano and Carmen Quagliata, the menu features a fusion of American and Italian cuisine. The compositions include spaghettini with flaked halibut in a garlic, chili and wine sauce, or pan roasted chicken

with asparagus bread pudding and mushrooms. Weekly classics may include filet mignon of tuna or pan-roasted quail. For dessert there is warm rustic apple crostata with sour cream ice cream, or the signature warm banana tart with vanilla ice cream and macadamia brittle.

✚ 142 D12 ✉ 21 East 16th Street, between Fifth Avenue and Union Square West ☎ 212/243-4020 🕐 Daily noon–2, Sun–Thu 5.30–10, Fri–Sat 5.30–11 🍴 L $42, D $62, Wine $35 🚇 14th Street/Union Square (L, N, Q, R, W, 4, 5, 6) 🚌 M2, M3, M5, M7

VERITAS

www.veritas-nyc.com

With 3,200 selections, Veritas has the most comprehensive wine list in the city. And the kitchen offers some gutsy cuisine to go with the wines. Expect pepper-crusted venison with Armagnac or juniper, or braised veal in Barolo reduction. Even a dish like red snapper brings a surprise—here it arrives in Thai red curry nage. Hot chocolate and doughnuts is the signature dessert.

✚ 143 D11 ✉ 43 East 20th Street, between Broadway and Park Avenue South ☎ 212/353-3700 🕐 Mon–Sat 5.30–10.30, Sun 5–10 🍴 D 3-course prix fixe $82, Wine $20 🚇 23rd Street (N, R), 23rd Street (6) 🚌 M1, M2, M3, M6, M7

Below A burger bar in Downtown

PRICES AND SYMBOLS

Prices are the lowest and highest for a double room for one night. Breakfast is included unless noted otherwise. All the hotels listed accept credit cards unless otherwise stated. Note that rates vary widely throughout the year.

For a key to the symbols, ▷ 2.

ABINGDON GUEST HOUSE

www.abingdonguesthouse.com
Located in two historic three-story red-brick town houses above a coffee shop in Greenwich Village, the guest house is unmarked. The nine rooms are individually decorated and well furnished with antiques. Amenities include private bath (with hairdryer), cable TV and free WiFi internet access. The patio garden is a bonus.

✚ 142 C12 ✉ 13 Eighth Avenue at West 12th Street, 10014 ☎ 212/243-5384 ✋ $209–$279 (minimum stay 2 nights weekdays, 3 nights weekends) ❶ 9 ⓠ 14th Street (A, C, E), Christopher Street/ Sheridan Square (1) 🚌 M20, M14

CHELSEA

www.hotelchelsea.com
Many artists and bohemians have stayed or lived here since it opened in 1884, including Mark Twain and Dylan Thomas. The rooms vary in size and decor. Serena's, the bar opened by Serena Bass, attracts a Brit-pack crowd.

✚ 142 C11 ✉ 222 West 23rd Street, between Seventh and Eighth avenues, 10011 ☎ 212/243-3700 ✋ From $279, suites from $399 ❶ 375 rooms (250 permanent residents) ⓠ 23rd Street (C, E), 23rd Street (1) 🚌 M20, M23

CHELSEA LODGE

www.chelsealodge.com
In very fashionable Chelsea, this small hotel occupies a handsome red-brick town house, which has been lovingly restored by the owners. The rooms are decorated in plain American country style with patterned wallpaper and eclectic furnishings. Most have hardwood floors and small TVs, plus sink and shower. The toilet is in the hall.

✚ 142 C11 ✉ 318 West 20th Street, between Eighth and Ninth avenues, 10001 ☎ 212/243-4499 ✋ $129 ❶ 22 ⓠ 23rd Street (C, E) 🚌 M11, M20

GERSHWIN

www.gershwinhotel.com
The Gershwin attracts young budget travelers, who stay in plain doubles or dormitory-style rooms with 10

Opposite The striking Gershwin hotel provides budget accommodations

beds. Rooms have cable TV and phone. On weekends, live bands play in the Gallery Lounge.
142 D11 ✉ 7 East 27th Street, between Fifth and Madison avenues, 10016 ☎ 212/545-8000 💷 $119, suite from $249, dorm for two $53, women only dorm $43, coed dorm $39 ⬆ 130 rooms, 6 suites 🚇 28th Street (N, R, W) 🚌 M2, M3

GIRAFFE
www.hotelgiraffe.com
A small boutique hotel in the Flatiron neighborhood evokes the 1920s and 1930s. Each floor has only seven rooms, decorated in glamorous colors and materials. Many have balconies. There is an on-premises restaurant, plus access to a nearby health club.
143 E11 ✉ 365 Park Avenue South, between 26th and 27th streets, 10016 ☎ 212/685-7700 💷 $409–$559, suite from $650, including wine and cheese (weekday evenings) ⬆ 52 rooms, 21 suites 🚇 23rd Street (6) 🚌 M1

HOTEL GANSEVOORT
www.hotelgansevoort.com
This Meatpacking District hotel adopts South Beach style with such dramatic features as heated rooftop pool, kaleidoscopic illuminated glass columns that change color and mood, and a Japanese restaurant with a fetching outdoor courtyard bar-dining area. Rooms are decorated in minimalist style and hues, and feature the latest amenities—plasma TVs and complimentary WiFi. A spa and fitness center occupy a lower level.
142 C12 ✉ 18 Ninth Avenue at 13th Street, 10014 ☎ 212/206-6700 💷 Doubles from $435, suite from $675 ⬆ 167 rooms, 20 suites 🚇 14th Street (A, C, E) 🚌 M11

INN AT IRVING PLACE
www.innatirving.com
These two 1834 town houses have plenty of ersatz atmosphere. Rooms have fireplaces and four-poster beds dressed with Frette linens, plus antique reproductions. Amenities include two-line telephones with data port, VCRs and CD players. Guests sit on tufted chairs around the fireplaces in Lady Mendl's at afternoon tea. There is a lounge, too.
142 E12 ✉ 56 Irving Place, between East 17th and 18th streets, 10003 ☎ 212/533-4600 💷 $415–$625 ⬆ 12 rooms and suites 🚇 14th Street/Union Square (L, N, Q, R, W, 4, 5, 6) 🚌 M1, M2, M3, M14

THE INN ON 23RD
www.innon23rd.com
If you prefer a bed-and-breakfast, then this inn in a 19th-century town house (with an elevator!) has much to offer. The Fisherman family has furnished it with family heirlooms and eclectic pieces. The rooms have such modern amenities as dual-line phone (local calls are free). Bathrooms are small. Guest amenities include an inviting second-floor library and an honor bar with liquor, wine and beer, plus a microwave.
142 C11 ✉ 131 West 23rd Street, between Sixth and Seventh avenues, 10011 ☎ 212/463-0330 💷 $219–$269, suite from $329 ⬆ 14 🚇 23rd Street (F, V), 23rd Street (1) 🚌 M5, M6, M7, M20, M23

LARCHMONT
www.larchmonthotel.com
This is a great buy on an extra-quiet side street in Greenwich Village. It has plenty of character and appeals to European travelers who don't mind shared bathrooms (bathrobe and slippers provided). The rooms are attractively decorated, ultra clean and well equipped with air conditioning, cable TV and telephone.
142 D12 ✉ 27 West 11th Street, between Fifth and Sixth avenues, 10011 ☎ 212/989-9333 💷 $130–$165 ⬆ 58 🚇 14th Street (F, V), Sixth Avenue (L) 🚌 M2, M3, M5, M6

MARCEL
www.nychotels.com
Modern and chic, the recent transformation of the Marcel presents a hip,

style throughout. Graphic prints and animal patterns set off the comfortable, ultramodern guest rooms that feature custom designed beds with down comforters and Frette linens, marble bathrooms, LCD flat-screen TVs and iPod docking stations. Restaurant Inoteca features Northern Italian cuisine and a European-style breakfast buffet is available daily.
143 E11 ✉ 201 East 24th Street, between Second and Third avenues, 10011 ☎ 212/696-3800 💷 $375–$650 ⬆ 135 rooms and suites 🚇 23rd Street (6) 🚌 M15, M23, M101, M102, M103

MARITIME HOTEL
www.themaritimehotel.com
In Chelsea and close to nightlife central, the Meatpacking District, this hotel was formerly the headquarters of the Maritime Union. The rooms are small and cabin-like with teak paneling and porthole windows. Furnishings are modern and the rooms feature the latest technology—flat panel TVs and high-speed internet access. It has two attention-grabbing restaurants. Matsura is a dramatic basement supper-club style Japanese restaurant; there's also a Mediterranean café with a large outdoor terrace garden landscaped with magnolia trees and lily pond.
142 C12 ✉ 363 West 16th Street at Ninth Avenue, 10011 ☎ 212/242-4300 💷 $280–$400 ⬆ 120 rooms, 4 suites 🚇 14th Street (A, C, E) 🚌 M11

WASHINGTON SQUARE
www.washingtonsquarehotel.com
On the northwest corner of Washington Square Park, this small hotel has a casual bohemian air. The rooms are small, basic and unimaginative, but the price is right. They do have cable TV and telephone with data port. Facilities include an attractive restaurant-lounge (with occasional jazz).
142 D13 ✉ 103 Waverly Place, between Fifth and Sixth avenues, 10011 ☎ 212/777-9515 💷 $150–$260 ⬆ 160 🍴 🚇 West 4th Street (A, C, E, F, S, V) 🚌 M5, M6, M8

West 36th Street
West 35th Street
WEST 34th STREET
West 33rd Street
West 32nd Street
West 31st Street
West 30th Street
West 29th Street
West 28th Street
West 27th Street
West 26th Street
West 25th Street
West 24th Street
West 23rd Street
West 22nd Street
West 21st Street
West 20th Street
West 19th Street
West 18th Street
West 17th Street
West 16th Street
West 15th Street
WEST 14TH STREET
West 13th Street
Little West 12th Street

10TH AVENUE
11TH AVENUE
12TH AVENUE
9TH AVENUE
8TH AVENUE
7TH AVENUE
AVENUE OF THE AMERICAS (6th Avenue)
9A

FASHION AVENUE
Macy's
34th Street Penn Station
34th Street Penn Station
34th Street Herald Square
Empire State Building
Madison Square Garden
Pennsylvania Station

Chelsea Park
Chelsea Waterside Park

10

11

12

13

14

28th Street
23rd Street
18th Street
14th Street
8th Avenue
14th Street
6th Avenue
13th Street
5th Avenue

Little Ch...
Around the Co...
Gershwin
Metropolita
Insurance
Flatiron Building
Fleur de Sel
Periyali
Gramercy Tave...
Devi
Union Square Café
Mesa Grill
UNION SQU...
EAS

Red Cat
Inn on 23rd Street
Chelsea
CHELSEA
Chelsea Lodge
Sueños
Crema Restaurante
Maritime Hotel

Spice Market
Hotel Gansevoort
Paradou
Pastis
Corner Bistro
Gonzo
Forbes Magazine Galleries
Strip House
Larchmont
Gotham Ba... & Gr...
Abingdon Guest House
Cru
Spotted Pig
GREENWICH VILLAGE
Otto Enoteca Pizzeria
Washington Square
Jefferson Market Library
Christopher Street / Sheridan Square
Christopher Park
Babbo
Blue Hill
Washington Square Park
Tangerine
Annisa
WASHINGTON SQUARE N...
WASHINGTON SQUARE NO...
WASHINGTON SQUARE S...
John's Pizzeria
Pearl Oyster Bar
Ne...
Vill...
Church of St Luke-in-the-Fields
House of Oldies & Rare Records

Hudson

Bloomfield Street
Cansevoort Street
Gansevoort Street
Horatio Street
Jane Street
Bethune Street
Bank Street
Perry Street
Charles Street
West 11th Street
West 10th Street
Washington Street
West Street

Christopher Street
Barrow Street
Morton Street
Leroy Street
Clarkson Street
Hudson Street
Service Road

Greenwich Street
Greenwich Avenue
Waverly Place
Mac Dougal Alley
Gay Street
SOUTH
West 4th Street
Jones Street
Cornelia Street
Bedford Street
Bleecker Street
Commerce Street
Grove Street
St Luke's Pl
Carmine Street
Downing Street
Bedford Street
Leroy St

St Walker Park

New York City Fire Museum

American Numismatic Society

HOUSTON
West Houston Street
WEST HOUSTON

Prince Street
Spring Street
Broome Street
Grand Street
Watts Street
Dominick Street
Canal Street
CANAL ST

VARICK Street
Mac Dougal Street
Sullivan Street
Thompson Street
Guardia
King Street
Charlton Street
Vandam Street
Hancock St
West Broadway
Avenue of the Americas (6th Avenue)
Renwick St

0   250 m
0   250 yds

A   B   C   D

Morgan
Library

PARK AVENUE
Union
33rd
Street

EAST 36th Street
East 35th Street
EAST 34TH STREET
East 33rd Street

East

East 30th Street

East 29th Street

28th
Street

Blue
Smoke
Giraffe   Dos Caminos

Marcel

Tabla
Eleven
Madison Park
Tamarind

GRAMERCY PARK
HISTORIC DISTRICT

Gramercy Park North
Gramercy
Park
Gramercy Park South

itas

Craft and
Craftbar
Pipa

Block Beautiful

Casa Mono   Inn at
Irving Place

Union
Square

3rd
Avenue

EET 14th Street
Union Square

Mt. Carmel
Place

East 28th Street
East 27th
Street

East 26th Street
Waterside
Plaza

East 25th Street

East 24th Street
East 24th St
East 23rd Street

East 22nd Street
East 21st Street
East 20th Street
East 19th Street
East 18th Street
East 17th Street
East 16th
Street
East 15th Street

EAST 14TH STREET

Peter Cooper Road

Asser Levy
Place

FRANKLIN DELANO ROOSEVELT DRIVE (FDR)

FDR DRIVE SERVICE ROAD

Anew
Street

20th Street Loop

Avenue C Loop
Stuyvesant
Oval
Stuyvesant
Walk

14th Street Loop

EAST 14TH STREET SERVICE DRIVE

East 16th
Street
East 15th Street

EAST 14TH STREET

East

East
River
Park

East 13th Street
East 12th Street
Grace
Church
St Mark's Church
-in-the-Bowery
Holy Basil
8th Street
NYU
Astor
Place

NOHO

Wanamaker
Place
Astor Place

Ukrainian
Museum
Mermaid
Inn
Merchant's
House Museum

Bond St
Bleecker
Street

EAST HOUSTON STREET
Broadway -
Lafayette
Street

St Patrick's
Old Cathedral
New Museum of
Contemporary Art

SOHO   Haughwout
Building

LITTLE ITALY

Children's Museum
of the Arts
Museum of Chinese
in America

Angelica Kitchen
East 11th Street
Gnocco
East 10th Street
I Coppi
La
Palapa   Saint Marks Place
EAST VILLAGE

Banjara

Prune

East 13th Street
East 12th Street
East 11th Street
East 10th Street
East 9th Street
East 8th Street
East 7th Street

Tompkins
Square Park

East 6th Street
East 5th Street
East 4th Street
East 3rd Street
East 2nd Street
East 1st Street

EAST HOUSTON STREET

Eldridge
Street

Stanton Street
Rivington St
Delancey
Street

WILLIAMSBURG BRIDGE APPROACH

LOWER
EAST SIDE

Lower East Side
Tenement Museum

DELANCEY
Grand
Street

Seward
Park

East 13th Street
East 12th Street
East 11th Street
East 10th Street
East 9th Street
East 8th Street
East 7th Street
East 6th Street
East 5th Street   East 5th Walk
East 4th Street   East 4th Walk
East 3rd
Street

Hamilton
Fish Park
Columbia

Baruch
Place

FRANKLIN DELANO ROOSEVELT DRIVE (FDR)

Mangin
Street

Corlears
Hook
Park

E   F   G   143

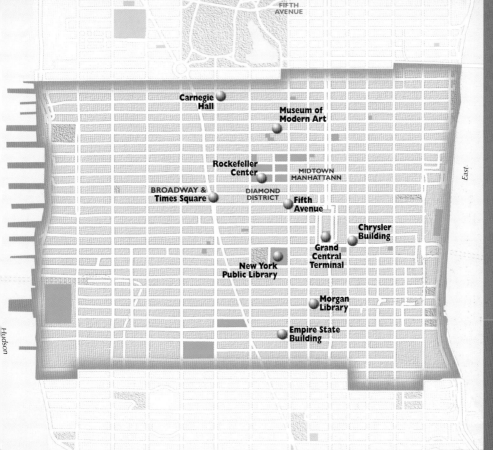

MIDTOWN

The Midtown skyline boasts many of New York City's finest towers and spires. Spectacular modern skyscrapers, ranging from the Citigroup Center wedge to the tall Trump Tower and the gleaming United Nations Building are accompanied by the art deco spires of the Empire State Building and the Chrysler Building.

New York's famous entertainment intersection, Times Square, is well known for the crystal ball that drops at midnight every New Year's Eve. And for the nightly drama as throngs of theatergoers and visitors move beneath the blazing neon billboards and electronic advertisements.

The Empire State Building is New York's most famous skyscraper, and a visit to the 86th-floor observation deck presents amazing views of Manhattan. At night the tower is bathed in light, and on some nights colored lights denote special dates, including red for Valentine's Day and green for St. Patrick's Day.

Fifth Avenue from the Empire State Building north is a paradise for shoppers of luxury merchandise. Tiffany & Co and Cartier for jewelry, department stores Saks Fifth Avenue and Bergdorf Goodman, and the wonderful FAO Schwarz toy store are just a few examples of the many big name offerings.

Lovers of art and architecture have many choices in Midtown, beginning with Grand Central Terminal, the city's magnificent Beaux Arts train station. Here high arched windows flood the main concourse with natural light and, overhead, the vaulted ceiling is decorated with a mural of constellations. Another Beaux Arts building, the marble New York Library, has a vast, richly paneled cathedral-like reading room that is almost two blocks long. For modern art from the late 19th century to the present, the Museum of Modern Art displays famous paintings by noted artists, including Van Gogh, Cézanne and Picasso, and sculpture in the delightful Abby Aldrich Rockefeller Sculpture Garden.

⑦

⑧

⑨

⑩

⑪

HIGHWAY 9A

12th Av

12th Avenue

12TH AVENUE

12th Avenue

11th Avenue

11th Avenue

Avenue

10TH AVENUE

10TH AVENUE

10TH AVENUE

9th Avenue

9th Avenue

9TH AVENUE

8th Avenue

8th Avenue

8TH AVENUE

8TH AVENUE

BROADWAY

Broadway

7th Avenue

7TH AVENUE

FASHION AVENUE

DYER AVENUE

West 63rd Street

West 62nd Street

West End Drive

West 61st Street

West 60th Street

West 59th Street

West 58th Street

WEST 57TH STREET

West 56th Street

West 55th Street

West 54th Street

West 53rd Street

West 52nd Street

West 51st Street

West 50th Street

West 49th Street

West 48th Street

West 47th Street

West 46th Street

West 45th Street

West 44th Street

West 43rd Street

WEST 42ND STREET

West 41st Street

West 40th Street

West 39th Street

West 38th Street

West 37th Street

West 36th Street

West 35th Street

West 34th Street

West 33rd Street

West 31st Street

West 30th Street

West 29th Street

West 28th Street

West 27th Street

West 26th Street

West 62nd Street

West 61st Street

West 63rd Street

Lincoln Center

Museum of Biblical Art

Central Park West

59th Street Columbus Circle

COLUMBUS CIRCLE

Central

57th Street

Carne Hall

De Witt Clinton Park

50th Street

50th Street

49th Street

BROADWAY

West 46th Street

Intrepid Sea, Air and Space Museum

Hudson

9A

Times Square

Holy Cross Church

Reuters Building

Times Sc 42nd Str

42nd Street Port Authority Bus Terminal

New Amsterdam Theater

Times Sc 42nd Stre

HIGHWAY 495

Jacob K Javits Convention Center

34th Street Penn Station

34th Street Penn Station

Madison Square Garden

Pennsylvania Station

28th Street

0 — 250 m

0 — 250 yds

Chelsea Park

Ⓐ

Ⓑ

Ⓒ

CHRYSLER BUILDING

The Chrysler Building's diamond-honed Enduro KA-2 steel is as incandescent today as it was in 1929. From the street, look up at the spire with its pattern of 30 radiating triangular windows. Note the 9ft (3m) pineapples on the spire and the mighty, gargoyle-like eagle heads at the corners of the building. Around the 30th floor, a brick frieze depicts hubcaps. Go inside to view the lobby's sumptuous walls of African marble and steel and the Parisian-style elevators. The elaborate ceiling was painted by Edward Trumbull.

Walter Chrysler, the third-biggest automobile manufacturer in America, spent $2 million of his own money to buy the skyscraper's site. Chrysler had been an automobile mechanic for most of his life and had very little formal education, but when it came to machines he was a genius. After saving General Motors a fortune with his new techniques, he moved to New York from Chicago at the age of 45. Already earning a million dollars a year, he produced his first line of Chryslers in January 1924. They appealed to the rich and were a symbol of wealth and luxury—they were the right product for the booming 1920s. For Chrysler, building a skyscraper more fantastic than anything anyone had ever seen was a challenge he could not resist.

THE TALLEST BUILDING IN THE WORLD

In late 1929, architect William Van Alen watched anxiously as the spire was raised above the 77-story structure to make it, at 1,048ft (320m), the world's tallest building, beating the Bank of the Manhattan Company Building at 40 Wall Street. It held the title for only a short time. Opened on May 1, 1931, the 1,250ft (381m) Empire State Building surpassed it. Securing an object at such a height had never been done before, and the job had been kept so secret that no reporters were around when it actually happened—probably on October 24, 1929, the day before the Wall Street Crash. The spire was as daring as it was ingenious and took the city by surprise. Many thought the building a crass piece of architectural advertising; today it is a symbol of an age when anything was possible.

In 1978, the Chrysler Building was designated a New York City Landmark. In 1997, Tishman Speyer Properties took it over and restored the art deco lobby. The lancet crown was first switched on in 1981.

INFORMATION

✚ 147 E9 ✉ 405 Lexington Avenue at 42nd Street ☎ 212/682-3070
🚇 Mon–Fri 8–6 🚇 4, 5, 6, 7, S
🚌 M98, M101, M102, M103

Above *New York's most stunning art deco skyscraper has a magnificent lobby with walls of African marble and steel*
Opposite *With its shining stainless-steel spire, the Chrysler Building is an icon*

INFORMATION

www.carnegiehall.org

✚ 146 C8 ✉ 154 West 57th Street at Seventh Avenue, 10019 ☎ 212/247-7800 ◈ For performance schedule, check website or phone 212/903-9765 ✋ Check website or phone 212/247-7800 ☛ One-hour tours Mon–Fri 11.30am, 2pm, 3pm, Sat 11.30, 12.30, Sun 12.30 when concert schedule permits; adult $10, child (under 12) $3 🚇 N, Q, R, W 🚌 M5, M6, M7, M10, M30, M57 🍴🎁

CARNEGIE HALL

This superb Italian-Renaissance-inspired concert hall took seven years to build, opening in 1891. With 2,804 seats and excellent acoustics, it remains one of New York's most highly prized music centers. The Rose Museum on the second floor (mid-Sep to end Jun daily 11–4.30 and available to concert patrons in the evenings; free) has archival treasures relating to the history of the building and famous figures who have performed here.

EARLY HISTORY

Late 19th-century New York was an important place but it did not have a concert hall. When the steel magnate Andrew Carnegie heard this, he put up the $2 million needed to construct the building, on the condition that the city provide the land on which to build it: at that time New York was a stretch of vacant lots, coal yards and row houses. Chief architect William B. Tuthill was a gifted amateur cellist, so was determined to get the acoustics right. Tchaikovsky opened the hall, making his American conducting debut in 1891. In the years since, the world's greatest musicians, including Rachmaninov, Horowitz, Stravinsky, Ravel and George Gershwin, have all performed here. The New York Philharmonic orchestra made this its home until moving to the Lincoln Center (▷ 218–219) on the Upper West Side in 1962.

The second building, added in 1894, housed famous musicians, architects, dancing classes and agencies. In 1894 the green mansard roof of the main building was removed to build the studio floor. There is a small recital hall within the original building and an elegant auditorium, which was a movie theater until 1997.

THE HALL TODAY

In the 1960s, Carnegie Hall was saved from demolition largely by violinist Isaac Stern. So it is for good reason that the main auditorium is named after him. The Weill Recital Hall features singers and chamber groups; Zankel Hall offers contemporary innovative programming. Between 1981 and 1990, Carnegie Hall underwent a $50-million renovation. The modern 60-story office tower next door, sensitively designed by César Pelli, was built in 1990.

Below *The outstanding acoustics of this famous concert hall attract the world's most gifted musicians*

INTREPID SEA, AIR AND SPACE MUSEUM
www.intrepidmuseum.org

The veteran aircraft carrier *Intrepid*, built in 1943, makes a fascinating museum. It is 898ft (274m) long, weighs 42,000 tons, and had a crew of 3,500. On the Flight Deck you can inspect aircraft, including a Lockheed A-12 Blackbird, a Russian MIG and a Cobra helicopter. You can tour the destroyer *Edson* and the submarine *Growler*; take a seven-minute SR-2 flight simulator ride; and rent a two-hour audiotour. The museum reopened in 2008 following restoration and painting of *Intrepid*, refurbishment of the 16 aircraft onboard, rebuilding of Pier 86 and completion of the Intrepid Sea, Air & Space Museum. The Hangar Deck exhibits have been redesigned and new exhibits have been added, including an interactive wind tunnel.
✚ 146 A9 ✉ Hudson River Pier 86, west end of 46th Street, 10036 ☎ 212/245-0072 🕐 Apr–end Sep Mon–Fri 10–5, Sat–Sun 10–6; Oct–end Mar Tue–Sun 10–5 🤚 Adult $19.50, child (6–17) $14.50, child (2–5) $7.50, under 2/those on active duty with ID free 🚇 A, C, E 🚌 M16, M42, M50 👆 Free tours

Above *Exterior of the Daily News Building*
Below *Intrepid Sea, Air and Space Museum*

CHRYSLER BUILDING
▷ 148–149.

DAILY NEWS BUILDING
Founder of the *Daily News*, James Patterson commissioned this modernist steel-and-concrete song of praise to popular journalism in 1925. It was one of the first skyscrapers in New York not built in Gothic style. On the ground floor, outside and in, abstract art deco ornamentation contrasts with the modernist strips on the upper facade. Inside, the lobby is still mostly original. Note the revolving globe, 12ft (3.5m) in diameter; the frieze representing the early days of the paper; and the clock that gives the time in 17 different time zones. The floor is laid out like a giant compass. In 1995, the *Daily News* moved out and the building was renamed the News Building.
✚ 147 E9 ✉ 220 East 42nd Street, 10036 🕐 Daily 9–5, lobby only 🚇 4, 5, 6, 7 🚌 M42, M104

EMPIRE STATE BUILDING
▷ 152–154.

GRAND CENTRAL TERMINAL
▷ 156–157.

INTERNATIONAL CENTER OF PHOTOGRAPHY
www.icp.org

In the heart of Midtown Manhattan, the ICP is both a school and a museum. The permanent collection has 60,000 photographs ranging from old daguerreotypes to iris prints, mainly from American and European reportage and documentation from the 1930s to the present. There are photographs by Henri Cartier-Bresson, Elliott Erwitt and Harold Edgerton, along with 13,000 original prints by Weegee, who photographed crime scenes and New York nightlife in the 1930s and 1940s.
✚ 147 D9 ✉ 1133 Avenue of the Americas at 43rd Street, 10036 ☎ 212/857-0000 🕐 Tue–Thu 10–6, Fri 10–8, Sat–Sun

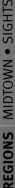

INTRODUCTION

In 1827, William B. Astor bought the farm where the Empire State Building now stands for $20,500, and in 1897 the first Waldorf-Astoria hotel was constructed. In 1928 the hotel was sold for $20 million and demolished to make way for the present structure. Excavation began in 1930. The developer was General Motors' vice-president, John Jacob Raskob, who wanted to create the world's tallest structure as quickly as possible. As a result, designs to decorate the limestone facade and the chromium-steel windows were machine-stamped. Completed in 1931, and $5 million under budget, the Empire State Building replaced the Chrysler Building as the world's tallest building and held this title until surpassed by the World Trade Center in 1971. Since 9/11 it has again become the tallest building in New York City, although the new One World Trade Center building (▷ 87), currently under construction, will be taller.

The Depression and then World War II put an end to the city's prosperity and much of its office space stood vacant. The Empire State Building was dubbed the Empty State Building. However, the Observation Deck was so popular that the income from admission charges paid the taxes on the building. In 1933 the thriller *King Kong* was released and the Empire State Building became a movie star for the first time. Concerns about the stability of the building were put to rest on July 28, 1945, when a US Army B-25 bomber crashed into the 78th and 79th floors, killing 13 people and causing extensive damage.

The main entrance is on Fifth Avenue. You pass through a security checkpoint similar to those at airports. There is no coat check (cloakroom), so you must carry your belongings. If you have not purchased a ticket in advance, take the escalator or elevator to the Concourse level and the Observatory ticket office. Signs indicate the waiting time and visibility. After buying your tickets, go back up the escalator to the main floor and follow the signs to the Observatory elevators on the second floor. Elevators let you out on the 80th floor, where staff direct you to the Tower elevator to the 86th floor. Viewing areas are indoors and outdoors.

INFORMATION

www.esbnyc.com

✚ 147 D10   ✉ 350 Fifth Avenue, 10118
☎ 212/736-3100   ◷ Daily 8am–2am, last elevator ascends at 1.15am
💲 Adult $20, child (12–17) $18, child (6–11) $14, under 5s free, military in uniform free. 102nd floor observatory $15 extra   Ⓢ 6 to 33rd Street or B, D, F to 34th Street/Herald Square   🚍 M1, M2, M3, M4, M6, M7   🎧 Observatory audiotour $8, corresponds to signs on the Observation Deck so you know exactly what buildings you are seeing   🍴 📷

Above *Millions of visitors a year go up to the 86th-floor Observation Deck for spectacular panoramas of the great metropolis*
Opposite *This New York City icon is the most famous skyscraper in the world*

TIPS

» To avoid waiting in line for tickets, buy them online, or in advance at the NYC & Company Visitor Center (tel 212/484-1200) at 810 Seventh Avenue between 52nd and 53rd streets.

» Come on a clear day and bring some quarters for the binoculars outside.

» The elevators carry only 16 people at a time, so be patient.

» Dusk is a popular time, so buy a ticket in advance if you can. Starry nights are magical and you can stay until closing time. There is no time limit on your visit.

» The Express Pass ($45) puts you first in each of the lines for security, tickets and elevators.

STATISTICS

» The Empire State Building weighs 365,000 tons; took 7 million man-hours to build; and is made up of 60,000 tons of steel, 2.5 million ft (760,000m) of electrical wire, 10 million bricks, 62 miles (100km) of water pipes, 6,500 windows, 72 elevators, 7 miles (11km) of elevator shafts, 1,860 steps, and a foundation that extends 55ft (17m) below street level.

» The purchase price for the land, the site of the old Waldorf-Astoria Hotel, was an $15 million; construction costs were $25 million. Construction time was an amazing 14 months. The building opened on May 1, 1931.

» With 102 stories, the Empire State Building stands 1,454ft (449m) tall, including the pinnacle. Eighty-six stories are usable office space. The Observation Tower is 16 stories.

» The TV antenna, installed in 1985, is 22 stories high.

» More than 3.8 million visitors ascend annually. The stupendous 360-degree view extends for around 80 miles (130km) on a clear day.

» The Fleet Empire State Building Run-Up Race, a New York Road Runners Club event, was first run in 1978 and is now held annually in February. Competitors run up 1,567 steps. The current record is 9 minutes 33 seconds.

WHAT TO SEE

FIFTH AVENUE LOBBY

Interesting exhibits show off memorabilia from New York's museums, galleries and artists. The art deco lobby is exceptional, with floor-to-ceiling marble walls obtained from quarries in France, Germany, Italy and Belgium, and a dazzling metal relief sculpture of the building.

34TH-STREET LOBBY

Eight huge color panels by artists Roy Sparkia and Renee Nemerov depict the Seven Wonders of the Ancient World and the eighth wonder from the modern world. The tallest Wonder of the Ancient World is the 600ft (183m) Lighthouse of Pharos.

CONCOURSE LEVEL

In addition to the Observatory ticket office, there is a collection of photographs of famous people who have visited the Empire State Building, including Queen Elizabeth II and Fidel Castro.

SECOND FLOOR

Special exhibits about New York City and its museums, cultural institutions and tourist attractions are on this floor. NY SKYRIDE (tel 212/279-9777; www.skyride.com; daily 8am–10pm; adult $36, child (6–11) $18, under 6s free) gives a thrilling simulated tour of the city via the same simulator hardware that is used to train 747 commercial pilots.

86TH-FLOOR OBSERVATION DECK

The most popular observation deck, the 86th floor has an outdoor deck without glass walls. Here the wind blows and the view on a clear day encompasses an 80-mile (130km) sweep with a magnificent panoramic view of the city. On the outside deck you can get close-up views of the surrounding buildings and area using the high-powered binoculars. There is also an indoor, enclosed deck, which is useful if it's raining.

102ND FLOOR OBSERVATORY

The highest observation deck on the 102nd floor reopened in November 2005. Separate admission tickets must be bought at the Observatory ticket office on the second floor, at an additional cost. The view is much the same as from the 86th-floor deck, and although this deck is smaller the vantage point is much higher and the glass windows offer shelter from the wind.

FLOODLIGHTS

Powerful floodlights illuminate the upper 30 floors between 9pm and midnight every night. Significant colors are used for special occasions—red, white and blue for Independence Day (July 4); green on St. Patrick's Day (Mar 17); red, black and green on Martin Luther King Day (third Mon in Jan); yellow and white for Easter; lavender and white on Gay Pride Day (Jun); red and green for Christmas. The stainless-steel window frames glimmer by day and night. In spring and fall during the bird migration season, the lights are turned off on foggy nights because the light shining through the fog confuses them.

THE TOWER

Broadcast cameras and microwave antennae on the east and west sides of the building monitor city traffic conditions for major TV and radio stations. The National Broadcasting Company (NBC) sent out the United States' first experimental transmission from the TV station here on December 22, 1931. Since 1965, FM radio has been transmitting from the tower, as has the New York Telephone Company.

FIFTH AVENUE

The Empire State Building was completed in 1931, on Fifth Avenue at 34th Street. From its 86th-floor Observation Deck all of Fifth Avenue stretches out below you. The avenue begins downtown in Washington Square Park. Nearby, at No. 47, the Salmagundi Club, in an elegant Italianate brownstone, is America's oldest club for artists, founded in 1871. At No. 62 are the Forbes Magazine Galleries (▷ 113). At 23rd Street is Manhattan's first skyscraper, the triangular Flatiron Building (▷ 113).

St. Patrick's Cathedral (▷ 160) is between 50th and 51st streets. At No. 645 is the Olympic Tower, the headquarters of the late Aristotle Onassis's empire, with shops, offices, apartments and a restaurant. These two landmarks are at the heart of a section famous for its luxury shopping, between 49th and 59th streets. Tiffany & Co., founded in 1837, is now at 57th Street. Along with Saks Fifth Avenue, between 50th and 51st, and Bergdorf Goodman, also at 57th Street, are the Disney Store and many other retailers. Beyond the Trump Tower (▷ 171), Central Park (▷ 208–213) spreads out on the west side.

MANSIONS AND MUSEUMS

In the 19th century, Fifth Avenue was the fashionable address for the very wealthy, such as coke-and-steel tycoon Henry Clay Frick, tobacco magnate James Duke and railroad baron Jay Gould, who built increasingly large mansions. Some of them were demolished in the 1920s to make way for luxury apartments, but many remain. The first one, at No. 998, built in 1912, was such a success that it became the model that hundreds copied in form and detail. The starched doormen are an indication of the wealth of the residents, who enjoy spectacular views of Central Park. Henry Clay Frick's mansion at 70th Street is now open to the public, displaying the outstanding Frick Collection (▷ 215) of European art in a residential setting. Andrew Carnegie's 64-room home at 91st Street is now the Cooper-Hewitt National Design Museum (▷ 203). The Jewish Museum, at 92nd Street, occupies another fine old home. The stretch between 79th and 104th streets is also punctuated by museums and has become known as Museum Mile, with the Metropolitan Museum of Art, the Guggenheim Museum (▷ 216–217) and the Museum of the City of New York (▷ 220).

INFORMATION

✚ 147 D9 ✉ From Washington Square north to the Harlem River 🚇 4, 5, 6 🚌 M1, M2, M3, M4

TIP

» Be sure to catch a parade on Fifth. The St. Patrick's Day Parade on March 17 is the biggest, but there are others. Check the NYC & Company events calendar for details. Crowds are so thick on the sidewalks during parades that you will not be able to shop or sightsee.

Above *Fifth Avenue is one of New York's most fashionable streets, with luxury shopping, excellent museums and a few landmark skyscrapers*

INFORMATION

www.grandcentralterminal.com
✚ 147 D9 ✉ East 42nd Street at Park Avenue, 10017 ☎ 212/532-4900; for travel information 718/330-1234, or tours 212/340-2345 🕐 Daily 5.30am–1.30am 🚇 Free 🚆 4, 5, 6, 7, S 🚌 M1, M2, M3, M4, M101, M102 🎫 Excellent free tour by the Municipal Arts Society on Wed at 12.30. Meet at the information desk, under the clock, in the main concourse 🍴 Grand Central Oyster Bar & Restaurant on the lower level; Mon–Sat ☎ 212/490-6650, www. oysterbarny.com. Michael Jordan's The Steak House N.Y.C. serves just that ☎ 212/328-0000, www.theglaziergroup. com. Métrazur serves Charlie Palmer's progressive American cuisine along with seafood and pasta ☎ 212/687-4600, www.charliepalmer.com/properties/metrazur 🛍 68 specialist shops on the mezzanine and lower levels

INTRODUCTION

New York's most magnificent public space and one of the city's finest landmarks, Grand Central is full of sophisticated shops and interesting places for a quick bite. Every day, trains running on 48 pairs of railroad tracks bring in half a million commuters from the northern suburbs. New York Central Railroad magnate Cornelius Vanderbilt ordered the construction of Grand Central Terminal. Built between 1903 and 1913, it replaced the 42nd Street Terminal, an iron and glass train shed dating from 1871. At the turn of the 20th century, this area was the northern edge of the city, but as the new station flourished, stores, hotels, restaurants and offices grew up around it. By the 1920s it had become a fine boulevard graced with luxury apartment buildings.

Grand Central is an outstanding example of Beaux Arts design, with triumphal arches filled with glass and steel, a grand waiting room, sumptuous concourse, superb vaulted ceiling and imposing sculptures of Roman deities. The innovative design, by engineer William Wilgus and architects Reed & Stem, included extensive tunnels, a ramp system instead of stairs to keep people moving, and upper and lower level concourses. Architect Whitney Warren, a Vanderbilt cousin, was responsible for the outstanding facades and interior. The public was delighted with this marvel, but by the 1970s, the station had acquired layers of grime and was not a place to linger. The steel was rusty, the asbestos was falling out and the stairways stank: it had become a symbol of urban decay.

In 1978, a New York City developer proposed building a 55-story office tower on top of the station, obliterating the facade. After a series of legal challenges, a US Supreme Court decision sided with the New York City Landmarks law and saved it from this fate. Jacqueline Kennedy Onassis was a prime force in the battle against the tower. Restoration was completed in 1998 under architects Beyer Blinder Belle, who examined 4,500 of Warren's original drawings and blueprints. Over a period of four years, 80-year-old wiring and plumbing were replaced, air conditioning was installed and new entrances were built. All of this was done while the station continued to operate, and not a single train was late or delayed owing to construction.

Enter Grand Central on 42nd Street at Park Avenue in order to experience the full impact and grandeur of the main concourse. As you enter, the feeling of space, sophistication and city bustle creates an awesome introduction to Manhattan. The careful $200-million renovation project that has restored its grandeur fills even cynical New Yorkers with civic pride. Notice the 75ft (23m) windows, the Tennessee marble floor, the brass clock over the central kiosk, and the gold-and-nickel chandeliers. Stroll around the arcades leading to Lexington Avenue and the lower level where you'll find restaurants and shops, including The Children's General Store, The Discovery Channel Store, Banana Republic and Godiva Chocolatier. Off the main concourse is the Grand Central Market, packed with fresh produce. The New York Transit Museum Annex & Store is worth visiting if you've got time. A maze of underground walkways links the terminal to surrounding streets; you can stay underground as far north as 48th and Park streets.

WHAT TO SEE

THE MAIN CONCOURSE CEILING
With 59 electric stars replicating the zodiac constellations, in reverse, the design is based on an illustration from a medieval manuscript. It is not known whether the ceiling's French creator, Paul Helleu, was aware that depicting the heavens in reverse, or from God's point of view, was a common practice of medieval illustrators. The main concourse itself is 375ft long (114m) and 120ft wide (36m).

JULES ALEXIS COUTAN'S SCULPTURE
Mercury, the Roman god of travel and commerce, is the central figure of this 1935 sculpture over the south entrance. He is supported by Minerva and Hercules, representing mental and physical strength.

GRAND CENTRAL OYSTER BAR AND RESTAURANT
This restaurant, with its low-vaulted ceiling, is worth seeing. The tiles are by Guastavino. Order a bowl of clam chowder—either Manhattan (tomato-based) or New England (cream-based) style (▷ 188).

THE CAMPBELL APARTMENT
This elegant (if pricey) cocktail bar was built by John Campbell as an office and pied-à-terre in the 1920s in the style of a 13th-century Florentine palazzo, with its stained-glass windows by Louis Comfort Tiffany and elegant dark paneling. Follow signs to the small staircase across from Michael Jordan's The Steak House off the west balcony.

NEW YORK TRANSIT MUSEUM GALLERY & STORE
This gallery annex has changing exhibits on the history, impact and future of public transportation (tel 212/878-0106, http://mta.info/mta/museum).

SPECIAL EVENTS
Exhibitions, food tastings, treasure hunts and concerts take place regularly. The Christmas Market in Vanderbilt Halt showcases the work of dozens of innovative regional craftspeople and retailers.

TIPS

» Take one of the free area tours sponsored by Grand Central Partnership (GCP), one of the largest business improvement districts, every Friday at 12.30, rain or shine. Meet inside the Whitney Museum Annex at the Philip Morris Building at 42nd Street and Park Avenue.

» For lunch in New York, the food concourse on the lower level is fun, with its many interesting options from Cajun pizza to Vietnamese sandwiches. But go early—after 12.30 it's next to impossible to find a seat.

» Don't rush, take your time to enjoy the shopping, restaurants and most of all the architecture. This is not just a train station, it's a New York experience.

» When you leave the building, walk a couple of blocks south to 40th Street, then turn around and look back at Coutan's neoclassical sculpture over the south entrance.

Opposite *The main concourse is a fine example of Beaux Arts style*
Below *The brass four-faced clock tells the time from all angles*

MTA METRO-NORTH
TRAIN INFORMATION

INFORMATION

www.themorgan.org

✚ 147 D10 ✉ 225 Madison Avenue
at 36th Street, 10016 ☎ 212/685-0008
🕐 Tue–Thu 10.30–5, Fri 10.30–9,
Sat 10–6, Sun 11–6 ✋ Suggested
admission: adult $12, under 12 with
adult free 🚇 4, 5, 6, 7 🚌 M2, M3, M4
🍴 Morgan Court Café serves lunch and
afternoon tea 📖 Bookshop closes
15 min before galleries

MORGAN LIBRARY

The Morgan Library reopened in spring 2006 with twice the gallery space,
an enlarged auditorium, a café, a bigger shop and more open public spaces,
following three years of improvement work. The Reading Room is now better
equipped and the storage areas are much improved.

By the end of the 19th century, John Pierpont Morgan was one of New
York's wealthiest financiers. To fulfill his desire to match Europe's greatest
libraries, he began his opulent private library of European cultural treasures:
illuminated and literary manuscripts, paintings, prints and furniture. His travels
abroad resulted in this priceless collection of nearly 10,000 drawings and
prints, including some by Leonardo da Vinci and Albrecht Dürer. In 1902, he
commissioned Charles McKim to design the magnificent Renaissance-style
building. Later additions include those by Benjamin Morris in 1928, the annex,
which was Morgan's private residence, at 231 Madison Avenue, and the garden
courtyard in the 1990s.

MORGAN'S STUDY

The West Room of the library remains as Morgan left it when he died in 1913.
He used it as a study and his huge wooden desk is still here, along with the
Italian Renaissance paintings lining the walls. From the study you pass green-
veined marble columns as you proceed toward the rotunda and the East Room.
The beautiful three-tiered, walnut and bronze bookcases are almost as amazing
as the ceiling covered with frescoes and the signs of the zodiac. Notice the
16th-century Flemish tapestry above the fireplace. But it is the collection of
letters and manuscripts that most intrigues.

Morgan acquired nearly 600 medieval and Renaissance manuscripts,
including the 9th-century Lindau Gospels, a rare vellum copy of the Gutenberg
Bible, and the medieval Dutch masterpiece *The Hours of Catherine of Cleves*.
He also purchased handwritten scores by such composers as Beethoven,
Mozart and Puccini, which are protected under glass. The collection also
includes manuscripts by authors of the calibre of Jane Austen, Charles
Dickens, Henry David Thoreau and Mark Twain.

Below The Adoration of the Magi, *from a choirbook executed in around 1540*

NEW YORK PUBLIC LIBRARY

Some things in New York are surprises, and this amazing research library is one of them. The massive white marble building, one of the first major commissions of the firm Carrère & Hastings in 1911, is absolutely gorgeous. Half of its $9-million cost was donated by steel magnate and philanthropist Andrew Carnegie (1835–1919). The two lions at the foot of the staircase fronting the museum are New York icons affectionately named Patience and Fortitude by New York's 1930s mayor, Fiorello LaGuardia; in the gift shop they adorn tote bags, spoons, charm bracelets, bookends, paperweights and more.

Up the imposing staircase and through the triple-arched portico is beautiful Astor Hall, named after John Jacob Astor (1763–1848), whose private library, along with that of James Lenox, was the foundation of this great collection. (Former New York governor Samuel J. Tilden bequeathed the $2.4 million to combine the libraries and erect the building.)

WHAT TO SEE, AND WHERE

Upon entering, pick up a floor plan at the information desk and ask about free tours around the library. Gottesman Hall, straight ahead, displays temporary exhibits. The DeWitt Wallace Periodical Room, to the left, is embellished with Richard Haas murals of New York magazine and newspaper offices. At the top of the marble stairs is the McGraw Rotunda. The stupendous Main Reading Room, restored in 1998 so that the oak and brass gleam, is to your right. Across the hall is the Edna Barnes Salomon Room, where recent popular exhibitions have included *New York Eats Out*, *Baseball at the Library*, *Prints of James McNeill Whistler (1834–1903)* and *The Charles Addams Mother Goose*.

This is not a lending library, but there are more than 80 branches in Manhattan and the outer boroughs. Occasionally, you can see important items here from the vast collection, which include a Gutenberg Bible, a 1493 folio edition of a letter written by Christopher Columbus describing his discoveries in the New World, a first folio edition of Shakespeare's works from 1623, an early draft of Thomas Jefferson's Declaration of Independence, and much more.

INFORMATION

www.nypl.org

147 D9 Fifth Avenue and 42nd Street, 10018 917/275-6975 Mon, Thu–Sat 11–6, Tue–Wed 11–7.30, Sun 1–5 Free B, D, F M1, M2, M3, M4 Free tours Mon–Sat 11 and 2, Sun 2 from Astor Hall

Above *The Main Reading Room in the grand and beautifully restored Beaux Arts New York Public Library*

MUNICIPAL ART SOCIETY

www.mas.org

Founded in 1893, MAS is a non-profit, private, membership society aiming to promote a "more livable city." It advocates excellence in architecture, design and planning, public art and the preservation of historic buildings, and believes sensible development is critical to the city's economic health and social well-being. The MAS also organizes exhibitions and walking tours. The guides on these informative tours are highly qualified and give insights into the history and significance of the urban scene. Exhibitions are held at the headquarters on the 16th floor of the Steinway Building, and are open to the public free of charge.

✚ 147 D8 ✉ 111 West 57th Street, 16th floor, 10022 ☎ 212/935-3960 reservations; 212/439-1049 for tours and meeting places ◷ Mon–Sat 10–6 (Wed to 8), Sun 11–5 ✋ Guided walking tours $15; some walking and bus tours are more expensive

MUSEUM OF MODERN ART

▷ 162–163.

NEW YORK PUBLIC LIBRARY

▷ 159.

PALEY CENTER FOR MEDIA

www.paleycenter.org

Formerly called the Museum of Television and Radio, the new name reflects the growing range of media in modern times. William S. Paley (1901–90), former chairman of CBS, donated the land for this 17-story building, erected in 1989, to a design by architects Philip Johnson and John Burgee. Theaters, screening rooms, three public galleries and individual viewing and listening consoles are your access to the museum's collection of tapes of 100,000 programs and commercials celebrating nearly 100 years. Thousands of new programs are added every year. When you arrive, make a reservation to use the computer catalog on the fourth floor to locate what interests you, then reserve it and watch it in one of the museum's consoles. Or take in a show or two at one of the screening rooms or theaters.

✚ 147 D8 ✉ 25 West 52nd Street, 10019 ☎ 212/621-6800 ◷ Tue–Sun noon–6, Thu until 8, Fri theater programs until 9 ✋ Adult $10, under 14 $5 ⓔ E, V 🚌 M1, M2, M3, M4 🛒 🍴 ♿

ROCKEFELLER CENTER

▷ 164–167.

ST. PATRICK'S CATHEDRAL

www.saintpatrickscathedral.org

Each year the largest Roman Catholic cathedral in the United States, seating about 2,200, welcomes more than 3 million visitors. Designed by James Renwick, Jr., this Gothic Revival cathedral was inspired by European originals, most notably Cologne Cathedral in Germany. The spires are 330ft (100m) above street level. The pietà inside is three times the size of the one in St. Peter's in Rome. Tiffany & Co. designed the beautiful St. Michael and St. Louis altar. Work began on the church in 1853 and it was consecrated in 1879. The cathedral's arrival encouraged the rich and powerful to move north and contributed to the development of Fifth Avenue's many sumptuous mansions.

✚ 147 D8 ✉ Fifth Avenue (between 50th and 51st streets), 10022 ☎ 212/753-2261 ◷ Daily 6.30am–8.45pm ⓔ 6, B, D, E, F, V 🚌 M1, M2, M3, M4

Opposite *A neoclassical entrance for the 1989 17-story building designed to house the Paley Center for Media*

Below *The striking Gothic Revival interior of St. Patrick's Cathedral*

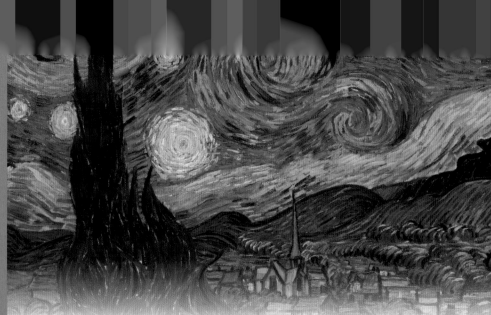

INFORMATION

www.moma.org

147 D8 ✉ 11 West 53rd Street, 10019 ☎ 212/708-9400 ⏰ Sat–Mon 10.30–5.30, Wed–Thu 10.30–5.30, Fri 10.30–8; closed Tue 🖐 Adult $20, under 16 with adult free, free Fri 4–8; audioguide $5 Ⓜ Fifth Avenue/53rd Street (E, V), 47th–50th St/Rockefeller Center (B, D, F) 🚌 M1, M2, M3, M4, M5 🎧 Audio programs free 🖥 1 restaurant, 2 cafés 🏛 MoMA Design and Book Store at museum ☎ 212/708-9700; MoMA Design Store, 44 West 53rd Street ☎ 212/767-1050; MoMA Design Store SoHo, 81 Spring Street ☎ 646/613-1367

INTRODUCTION

When MoMA opened in 1929 it occupied six rooms on 57th Street. Today, after a dramatic $425 million renovation by architect Yoshio Taniguchi, it offers an unparalleled collection of modern and contemporary art. The new MoMA opened in November 2004 to much acclaim. Taniguchi's redesign doubled the institution's space, allowing it to display much more of its superb collection. Visitors can now enter from 53rd or 54th streets to view the galleries, which are clustered around a 110ft tall (34m) atrium, which diffuses light throughout the building and gives great views of the sculpture garden, which features Aristide Maillol's *The River*, Henry Moore's *Family Group* and other works in an inviting outdoor setting.

WHAT TO SEE

FOURTH AND FIFTH FLOORS

The permanent collection, spanning art from the late 19th century to the late 1960s, is displayed on the fourth and fifth floors. The works are presented in chronological sequence to create a comprehensive history of modern art. The 12 galleries on the fifth floor cover Postimpressionism, Cubism, Italian Futurism, Austrian and German Expressionism, Social Realism and Surrealism. Each boasts a string of masterpieces; Vincent Van Gogh's *The Starry Night* and Salvador Dalí's *The Persistence of Memory* are just two of the most celebrated examples. One gallery is devoted entirely to Matisse. Fourth-floor galleries present works from the late 1940s to the late 1960s and include works by such major artists as Willem de Kooning, Jasper Johns, Francis Bacon and Andy Warhol, as well as some splendid holdings of Jackson Pollock's work.

SECOND AND THIRD FLOORS

Contemporary works created since 1970 are shown in the second-floor galleries, which also include a dedicated media gallery. The collections of drawings, photography, architecture and design are found on the third floor. The drawing collection contains 7,000 works from 1880 onward and the photography collection 25,000 works, which document the development of photography from the 1840s. The photograph collection ranges from Henri Cartier-Bresson to Diane Arbus, highlighted by William Fox Talbot's *Lace* and

Above *Among many fine works in the Museum of Modern Art is Van Gogh's* The Starry Night *(1889)*

Paul Strand's *Fifth Avenue, New York*. With 19,000 films and four million film stills, the Film and Media Department is also impressive. The sixth floor is reserved for special exhibits.

MARC CHAGALL, OIL ON CANVAS: *I AND THE VILLAGE*
Painted in 1911, a year after Chagall (1887–1985) arrived in Paris, *I and the Village* portrays his memories of his native community outside Vitebsk. Here Chagall's personalized version of Cubism used a disjunctive geometric structure to evoke the rural and magical. Objects jumble together, representing the peasants and animals living side by side with a mutual dependence. The peasant's flowering sprig symbolizes the tree of life, the reward of a harmonious relationship between man and animal.

PAUL GAUGUIN, OIL ON BURLAP: *THE SEED OF THE AREOI*
In this 1892 portrait of a Polynesian goddess siting on a blue-and-white cloth, Gauguin (1848–1903) combines elements from multiple cultures to portray the island in sharp contrast to the European world. The pose derives from ancient Egypt, with Javanese style used for the arm position based on a relief from the Temple of Borobudur. The eclectic use of color is pure Gauguin, and not reflective of the island's visual reality.

AUGUSTE RODIN, BRONZE: *MONUMENT TO BALZAC*
This 1898 cast Bronze by Rodin (1840–1917) was commissioned in honor of France's great novelist, Honoré de Balzac (1799–1850). Rodin strived to capture the spirit of the man rather than his physical appearance, although he clothed him in a robe similar to the one he often wore while writing.

Left *The world's greatest collection of painting and sculpture from the late 19th century to the present is on display in this modern space*

ROCKEFELLER CENTER

INTRODUCTION

The land on which Rockefeller Center stands belonged to Columbia University at the beginning of the 20th century. The university rented the land to farmers, but eventually developers came along and put up brownstones. By the late 1920s, the area was noisy and unpleasant, with elevated trains rumbling down Sixth Avenue and many residents too poor to spend money on the upkeep of the buildings. During Prohibition, the area was known as the "speakeasy belt," and along 52nd Street police raids were common. When liquor regained its legal status, the area became a popular setting for jazz clubs, where great musicians like Count Basie and Harry James entertained.

In 1928, John D. Rockefeller leased 12 acres (5ha) from Columbia University in order to build a colossal new opera house for the Metropolitan Opera. Rockefeller had a 24-year lease, but the project was dropped when the stock market crashed in 1929. But the rent still had to be paid, so Rockefeller decided to build a commercial center. In all, 228 buildings were demolished to make way for 12 new buildings to be designed by Associated Architects, a group directed by Raymond Hood. Between 1932 and 1940, this "city within a city," to use Rockefeller's words, was built. The central tower, the former RCA Building (now the G. E. Building), was planned with dense concentration of facilities for the creation and broadcasting of sound, with a vision of television's bright future. Today NBC occupies 11 floors.

Building Rockefeller Center was the largest privately sponsored real-estate venture in New York City's history. The complex was an instant success, and seven more buildings were added between 1947 and 1973. Today, 19 buildings

INFORMATION

www.rockefellercenter.com

✚ 147 D8 ✉ West 48th to West 51st streets, between Fifth and Sixth avenues ☎ 212/332-6868 or 632-3975; Radio City Music Hall 212/247-4777 👤 Free 🚇 B, D, F, Q 🚌 M1, M2, M27, M50 📖 Free walking-tour brochure from the main information desk in the lobby of the G. E. Building 🍴 Many eateries and restaurants including Cucina & Co., Mendy's Kosher Deli, Hale and Hearty, Ben & Jerry's. The Rainbow Room, 65th floor of the G. E. Building is famous for its art deco revolving dance floor ☎ 212/632-5000 🍽 Rock Center Café, 20 West 50th Street ☎ 212/332-7620 🎟 Rockefeller Center tour Mon–Sat 11, 12, 1, 3, 4, 5, Sun 11, 12, 1, 3, 4; adult $12, departs from NBC Experience Store (☎ 212/664-7174)

Above *Top of the Rock observation deck*
Opposite *The centerpiece G. E. Building*

» If you're in town between early December and early January don't miss Rockefeller Center. An enormous Christmas tree is put up and decked with 20,000 tiny lights—a favorite New York tradition.

» Go early if you plan to ice-skate on the rink in the Lower Plaza. The rink can hold only 150 skaters at a time and it gets busy, especially at lunchtime. Skate rentals and rink fees are cash only—and not cheap.

» NBC Experience store, 49th Street and Rockefeller Plaza, offers one-hour tours of news and entertainment studios. See the "Saturday Night Live" set: arrive before noon in the busy holiday and summer period to get tickets, which are on a first-come, first-served basis.

cover 22 acres (9ha), about 65,000 people work in the offices here, and many more visit daily.

To get a good sense of the place begin at Channel Gardens, on Fifth Avenue between 49th and 50th streets, which are six pools surrounded by pretty flower boxes running between the Maison Française and the British Empire Building (hence the name). Straight ahead as you face the Channel Gardens, with your back to Fifth Avenue, is Rockefeller Plaza, with its sunken garden, which is turned into an ice-skating rink in winter and a restaurant in summer. The gilded *Prometheus*, stealing the sacred fire from the Greek gods to give to man, rises ahead, while flags flutter around the plaza's perimeter. At the top of the steps down to the Lower Plaza a bronze plaque from multimillionaire and philanthropist John D. Rockefeller, whose fortune built Rockefeller Center, praises the virtues of hard work. On the southeast corner of the Lower Plaza is a branch of the Metropolitan Museum of Art Store, full of elegant souvenirs and gifts. As the complex is large, it is best to pick up a walking-tour guide from the information desk in the lobby of the G. E. Building to help you decide what to see and do.

WHAT TO SEE

THE G. E. BUILDING

Over the east entrance of this prominent tower, the former RCA Building, is Lee Lawrie's limestone-and-glass frieze, *Wisdom*, inspired by William Blake's painting of the same name. The beautiful granite and marble east lobby is worth visiting; it houses José Maria Sert's sepia mural *Man's Conquests*, commissioned to replace one by Diego Rivera, which was rejected because it included an image of Joseph Stalin. The anticommunist Rockefellers had insisted that Rivera remove the offending portrait, but Rivera refused and his mural was destroyed. The signature clock on the 51st Street corner has

Right *Detail of* Friendship Between America and France *(1934) above the entrance to La Maison Française at 610 Fifth Avenue*
Below *Looking down at the sunken garden and* Prometheus *statue*

projecting arms grasping electric bolts (RCA was a subsidiary of General Electric). The stylized figures at the building's crown have haloes of electric rays. The viewing platform is open to patrons of the elegant Rainbow Room restaurant on the 65th floor; for a drink and a view, stop in at the adjacent Rainbow Grill.

CHANNEL GARDENS AND PROMENADE
Named after the English Channel and located between the French and British Empire Buildings, the Channel Gardens provide a lush urban oasis of greenery, plants and seasonal blooms. The fountainhead figures on the theme of "Qualities that Spurred Mankind," cast bronze sculptures by Rene Paul Chambellan, are found at the east end of the six pools. For Christmas, 12 charming, glowing aluminum and brass *Christmas Angels* by English sculptor Valerie Clarebout are displayed along the promenade with a view of the famous Christmas tree at the west end.

ICE-SKATING RINK
When this ice rink in the Lower Plaza opened on Christmas Day 1933, it was a novelty made possible by new refrigeration technology. Today, a quarter of a million skaters test their blades here every year. The rink is small—only 122ft long (37m) and 59ft (18m) wide.

☎ 212/332-7654 ⊘ Mid-Oct to mid-Apr Mon–Thu 9am–10.30pm, Fri–Sat 8.30am–midnight, Sun 8.30am–10pm ⊌ Adult $12 weekdays/$16 weekends, child $7.50 weekdays/$8.50 weekends, skate rental $8

Above *Radio City Music Hall is used for live concerts and film premieres*

RADIO CITY MUSIC HALL
With about 6,000 seats, Radio City was the world's largest theater when it opened in 1932. Impresario Samuel (Roxy) Rothafel's original plans were for live entertainment, but movies soon became the main fare, with the high-kicking Roxyettes, later called the Rockettes, performing before each feature film. Donald Deskey was the interior design coordinator. The great arched proscenium in the form of a setting sun is an art deco masterpiece. The Grand Foyer's 24-carat gold-leaf ceiling, sweeping staircase and elegant chandeliers are breathtaking. Radio City was designated a New York City Landmark in 1979 and a National Historic Landmark in 1987. Intensive renovation in the late 1990s then won it a National Preservation Award in 2000.

⊂ Guided tours daily 11–5

TOP OF THE ROCK
www.topoftherocknyc.com
Sky shuttles whiz you to the top of 30 Rockefeller Plaza for a fabulous 360-degree view of New York from the three-tiered observation deck on the 67th, 69th and 70th floors. The view of Central Park from above is unparalleled. There are enclosed and open terraces.

☎ 212/698-2000 ⊘ Daily 8am-midnight (last shuttle 11pm) ⊌ Adult $18, child 6–12 $13

NBC STUDIO SHOWS
To get standby tickets to join the studio audience of "Late Night with Jimmy Fallon," line up at 9am on the day of taping outside 30 Rockefeller Plaza on 49th Street under the NBC Studios awning. Or reserve tickets by calling 212/664-3056. You must be aged at least 16. Every weekday between 7 and 9am, hundreds of people crowd the blue police barricades at the corner of West 49th Street and Rockefeller Plaza, just outside the ground-level NBC studio of the long-running morning "Today Show." The lure is a glimpse of the anchors or national exposure for a greeting for the folks back home scrawled on a piece of cardboard. In good weather a segment or two may be presented outdoors on the street.

INFORMATION

www.timessquarenyc.org
146 C9 Times Square Information Center, 1560 Broadway, between 46th and 47th streets Mon–Fri 9–7, Sat–Sun 8–8 (on Seventh Avenue)
Times Square Information Center 212/869-1890 1, 2, 3, N, R M6, M7, M27, M42, M104 Free walking tour every Friday at noon from the Times Square Information Center
Broadway Joe's Steakhouse, 315 West 46th Street—steaks and seafood
212/246-6513 Planet Hollywood, 1540 Broadway at 45th Street, serves burgers and other American favorites, but movie memorabilia and giant screens are the real stars 212/333-7827

INTRODUCTION

Called Heere Straat (Main Street) by Dutch settlers, Broadway is New York's longest and oldest street. As the city's population grew, seedy bars, brothels and gambling dens opened on both sides. By the early 1800s, it bustled with pedestrians and horse-drawn carriages; there were even traffic jams. In the 1860s a row of minstrel halls opened along Broadway, and by 1900 the area on and off Broadway around Union Square had become the city's theater district. In 1880, the advent of electricity began to turn Broadway between 14th and 34th streets into the Great White Way. In the 1890s, when Oscar Hammerstein built the Olympia Theater on Broadway between 44th and 45th streets, the city's theatrical entertainment moved to the area that is now Times Square; it was then known as Longacre Square and was renamed only in 1904, when The *New York Times* moved into Times Tower on 42nd Street. In 1928, 14,900 electrical lights were added to the four sides of the Times Tower, creating the first moving electrical sign.

After the subway came to the Theater District, beginning in 1900, the crowds poured in. By the 1920s, movies had taken over many theaters. After this, the theaters started showing pornography and the crowd turned seedy.

Sex joints drove out reputable business, and by the 1970s the district was crawling with hookers, pimps and other dubious characters.

During the 1990s, an aggressive clean-up operation—which included legislation against noise, gambling and prostitution, as well as new zoning laws—transformed the area. There's no question that the current state of the square and surrounding area has been an amazing show of effective planning, and a great triumph for the city.

Begin your visit at the Times Square Information Center, originally the attractive landmark Embassy Theater and now dominated by a branch of McDonald's. Even if you don't need information, take a look at the grand foyer. Over time, many of the old theaters have been renovated and now have landmark status. A special security force patrols the streets, and the area is as safe as any crowded urban neighborhood can be. If your visit to New York happens to coincide with New Year's Eve and you don't mind dense crowds, join the throngs in Times Square to see the glass ball drop at midnight to ring in the New Year. It's a great New York tradition.

WHAT TO SEE

ED SULLIVAN THEATER
Built by Arthur Hammerstein as a memorial to his father, Oscar Hammerstein I, this theater was formerly called the Hammerstein Theater. The neo-Gothic vestibules, lobbies and auditorium are unique on Broadway. Used as a dance hall for many years, it made history when it became a television studio. "The Ed Sullivan Show," the longest-running TV show in history, was broadcast from here during the 1950s and 1960s. Today it is perhaps even more famous as the home of the "Late Show with David Letterman."

✉ 1697–1699 Broadway, between West 53rd and West 54th streets

Opposite and below *Times Square is New York at its flashiest: neon signs, huge billboards, live TV broadcasts, enormous stores and gigantic family-friendly theme restaurants, not to mention theaters*

TIPS

» Broadway extends from Lower Manhattan to beyond Manhattan's northern tip, but Broadway as most visitors understand it refers to the area north–south between West 53rd and West 40th streets and east–west from Sixth to Eighth avenues. Most theaters are not on Broadway but on side streets.

» The TKTS booth is located at Times Square "under the Red Steps" in Father Duffy Square on Broadway and 47th Street (www.tdf.org; open Mon, Wed–Sat 3–8, Tue 2–8, Sun 3–half an hour before curtain time, 10–2 for Wed and Sat matinées, 11–3 for Sun matinées; only cash or traveler's checks). It sells day-of-show tickets for on and off-Broadway performances at 20–50 percent off face value. By 6pm the line is short.

» Times Square Information Center has a Metropolitan Transit Authority desk for transit maps and MetroCards; a Broadway Ticket Center selling full-price tickets; an HSBC Bank Center with ATMs and currency-exchange machines; computers with free internet access; free brochures and leaflets—some with discount.

LYCEUM THEATRE

The oldest New York theater, saved from demolition in 1939, it is Broadway's most imposing structure with its magnificent Beaux Arts facade and powerful neo-Baroque columns. Inside are marble walls with murals by James Wall Finn. Many of Broadway's highly acclaimed comedies and dramas have been performed here, as well as classics by the National Actors Theatre. Such famous names as Ethel Barrymore, Bette Davis, Joseph Cotton, Melvyn Douglas, Alan Bates and Lauren Bacall have all performed at the Lyceum.
✉ 149 West 45th Street ☎ 212/239-6200

NEW VICTORY THEATER

www.newvictory.org
Built by Oscar Hammerstein I in 1899 and once known as Minsky's, the New Victory was restored and remodeled in 1995 and is the city's first full-time family-oriented performing arts center.
✉ 209 West 42nd Street

PARAMOUNT THEATRE BUILDING

The tallest building in Times Square when it was completed in 1927, the Paramount is crowned by a four-faced clock with a glass globe, a focal point of the area that is visible for miles when it's illuminated. The World Wrestling Entertainment's 2,000-seat theme restaurant, WWE New York, whose sign boasts the latest in fiber-optic technology, is in the old theater space; a 30ft (9m) video screen and 110 monitors ensure that every diner can watch live broadcasts of shows like "Raw" and "Smackdown!", and appearances by WWE stars. Other entertainments vary from concerts to magic shows.
✉ 1501 Broadway

TV SHOW TICKETS GUIDE

Tickets for live tapings of TV shows are free but usually hard to obtain because of the high demand, especially the immensely popular "Late Show with David Letterman." If you are seriously addicted to a show and you know six months in advance that you'll be in New York, you can always register your preferred dates online.

Many studios hand out stand-by tickets on the day of taping, but you have to get up early and stand in line. In the dead of winter, you stand a better chance, as snow and cold winds put some people off. For more information call NYCVB on 212/484-1222. You can also phone or check show websites for information on ticket availability, waiting lists and stand-by tickets. When you attend a show, take photo ID, as it may be required.

"Late Show with David Letterman"

Register at www.cbs.com/latenight/lateshow or telephone 212/247-6497 for stand-by tickets on the day of taping at 11am sharp. You must be 18 or over to attend. You can request two tickets (maximum) in advance by filling out the request form online, or in person at the theater. Tapings are held at the Ed Sullivan Theater (▷ 169).

"Good Morning, America"

Visit www.abcnews.go.com/GMA and you may be lucky and get to join Diane Sawyer and Charlie Gibson in their street-facing studio on Broadway at 44th Street. The show runs Monday to Friday from 7am to 9am. Tickets can only be reserved online for individuals.

Left *Broadway is by far New York's longest street*

SEAGRAM BUILDING

Erected in 1958 with interiors by Philip Johnson, this is New York City's only Mies van der Rohe building and one of the finest International-style skyscrapers in the world. The decision to set it toward the back of the granite-paved plaza was daring at the time, especially given real-estate values, but it ignited a taste for pedestrian plazas that lingers in Manhattan to this day.

The building is also notable as the site of the esteemed Four Seasons restaurant, famed venue for power lunches, and of the bustling Brasserie restaurant.

🕂 147 E8 ✉ 375 Park Avenue, 10022 ☎ 212/572-7000 🕐 Mon–Fri 9–5

TIMES SQUARE AND BROADWAY

▷ 168–170.

TRUMP TOWER

Not to be confused with the older Trump Building, originally the Manhattan Company Building, or with other Trump structures about town, this one rose in the 1980s as a glass monument to affluent lifestyles. Upper floors contain 263 plush apartments. (Trump himself was one of the first to move in.) Below them, the interior is a six-story atrium with escalators, waterfalls and glittering boutiques surrounded by pink marble, mirrors and shrubbery. It's ridiculously ostentatious but still quite a sight.

🕂 147 D8 ✉ 725 Fifth Avenue, 10022 ☎ 212/832-2000 🕐 8am–10pm 🚇 E, N, R, V 🚌 M1, M2, M3, M4 📇

UNITED NATIONS HEADQUARTERS

www.un.org

At the end of World War II John D. Rockefeller, Jr. donated $8.5 million to purchase this site for the United Nations complex. The 544ft (166m) Secretariat building that dominates the site opened in 1950. Alongside are the General Assembly building, the Conference building (fronting the river) and the Dag Hammarskjöld Library. Fittingly, architects from many countries contributed to the designs. A 45-minute guided tour covers the General Assembly Hall and Security Council Chamber. You can see donated exhibits such as stained glass by Marc Chagall, a replica sputnik, and, in the park, sculptures by Barbara Hepworth and Henry Moore. Visit the landscaped grounds, with beautiful views. Arrive early at peak times.

🕂 147 F9 ✉ United Nations Plaza, 10017 ☎ 212/963-8687 🕐 Daily 9.30–4.45; closed Sat, Sun in Jan and Feb ✋ Adult $13, child (6–14) $7, under 5 not admitted 🚇 4, 5, 6, 7 🚌 M15, M27, M42 🚢 Tours every half-hour Mon–Fri 9.30–4.45, Sat and Sun 10–4.30 🍴 📇

Below *The United Nations headquarters (foreground) is a symbol of peace and unity*

42ND STREET TO THE UN HEADQUARTERS

This walk along 42nd Street is architecturally fascinating, taking you past some of the finest buildings in the city, including nine designated landmarks. It's a great stroll for families. Times Square is exciting, surprising and lots of fun, with its flashing billboards, electronic news and stock tickers, theater marquees and posters. The walk ends at the United Nations complex in a quiet, peaceful spot alongside the East River.

THE WALK

Distance: 1.5 miles (2.4km)
Time: 2 hours
Start at: 42nd Street/Port Authority subway
End at: United Nations Building, 46th Street and First Avenue

HOW TO GET THERE

Subway A; bus M27, M42, M50, M104.

★Leave the 42nd Street/Port Authority subway station and turn right, then proceed to the intersection of West 42nd Street and Eighth Avenue.

❶ Times Square and 42nd Street are famous today for their theaters, giant neon advertisements and megastores. Look back toward Ninth Avenue and you will catch a glimpse of an older side of the area: Holy Cross Church, one of its oldest buildings, dates from 1887.

Face east toward Seventh Avenue and you'll see the gleaming spire of the Chrysler Building in the distance. Walk east toward it, passing the AMC 25-screen multiplex, formerly the Empire Theater, on your right. Next door is Madame Tussaud's and next to that the Candler Building.

❷ The Candler Building was named for a salesman for the Coca-Cola Company, which built this white terracotta tower in 1914. Two doors farther east is the New Amsterdam Theater, lavishly restored by the Walt Disney Company with an outstanding art nouveau foyer.

To see the building directly opposite, the New Victory Theater, you will need to cross this very busy street, so continue east to the traffic lights and use the crosswalk. The New Victory Theater, once known as Minsky's, was built in 1899 by

Oscar Hammerstein I. Restoration in 1995 has retained the beautiful old-fashioned interior. Continue east along West 42nd Street on this side of the street. Two doors east of the New Victory is the Reuters Building, and just east of that, Times Square (▷ 168–169), the triangle created by 42nd Street, Seventh Avenue and Broadway.

❸ The 25-story tower at No. 1 Times Square became the home of the *New York Times* on December 31, 1904; the inaugural fireworks display was almost outshone by the illuminated globe lowered from the roof to herald the New Year. Almost 100 years later, the globe is still lowered every New Year's Eve, and for many New Yorkers and visitors Times Square is still the place to celebrate the holiday. The tower now functions as an office block. On the southeast corner of West 42nd

Street and Broadway, on the right, is the former Knickerbocker Hotel, commissioned by Colonel John Jacob Astor. The songwriter George M. Cohan lived here for a time. The building now houses studios and showrooms.

Continue east along 42nd Street, crossing Broadway and Sixth Avenue (now officially known as Avenue of the Americas).

4 The flashy glass building leaning away from traffic on the north side of 42nd Street, 41 West 42nd Street, is the W. R. Grace Building, built in 1974 by architects Skidmore, Owings and Merrill.

Cross to the south side of the street and Bryant Park. Bryant Park sits on top of the subterranean stacks of the New York Public Library. During the World's Fair of 1853, the first to be held on United States soil, the park was the site of the Crystal Palace. To reach the library, continue east along 42nd Street to Fifth Avenue. The library rises ahead of you on the southwest corner of 42nd Street and Fifth Avenue.

5 The majestic Beaux Arts New York Public Library (▷ 159) is guarded by two stone lions, Patience and Fortitude, who sit at the base of an imposing front stairway. Inside the building, the marble entrance

area on the ground floor and the usually packed second-floor Main Reading Room are well worth a look.

Return to 42nd Street and continue along east, crossing Madison Avenue. On your left at Park Avenue is Grand Central Terminal. Cross the street and plunge in.

6 Inside Grand Central Terminal (▷ 156–157), look at the ceiling in the main concourse, decorated with the constellations of the zodiac, and the dining concourse downstairs.

Back on 42nd Street, continue east to Lexington Avenue and the Chanin Building (on the southwest corner). Named for the brothers who developed the Times Square Theater District, the building has an art deco bas-relief, the work of Edward Trumbull. Continue to the northwest corner for the Chrysler Building.

7 The Chrysler Building (▷ 148–149) is one of the world's great 20th-century buildings—completed in 1929. Around the 30th floor a brick frieze depicts hubcaps and there are 9ft (3m)-high pineapples and giant stainless-steel radiator caps. The art deco foyer is made of African marble and steel.

Continue to 220 East 42nd Street and you'll come to the Daily News Building.

8 The Daily News Building (▷ 151) was until 1995 the home of America's first tabloid newspaper.

Cross Second Avenue and continue on 42nd Street until you come to an area with steps on both sides of the street. These lead to the charming Tudor City apartments. From the top of the steps there is a splendid view of the United Nations Building, the East River and, beyond it, the borough of Queens. Turn left onto Tudor City Place, then right onto 43rd Street. Here, steps lead down to Ralph Bunche Park. Cross United Nations Plaza (as First Avenue is called here) and turn left.

9 At the United Nations Headquarters (▷ 171), view the General Assembly lobby (foyer) and stroll through the gardens. The entrance to the complex is on 46th Street. John D. Rockefeller, Jr. donated the $8.5 million needed for the site.

WHEN TO GO
Crowds will not be out in full force if you begin your walk on a weekday morning before 10. If you wish to visit the United Nations Building at the end of the walk, arrive early—the last tour begins at 4.45pm.

WHERE TO EAT
The dining concourse at Grand Central Terminal, 42nd Street at Park Avenue, is just the place to refuel; for variety at affordable prices, it can't be beaten. The Oyster Bar & Restaurant (tel 212/490-6650), on the same level, offers excellent seafood, but at higher prices.

PLACE TO VISIT
MADAME TUSSAUD'S WAX MUSEUM
✉ 234 West 42nd Street ☎ 212/512-9600 or 800/246-8872 🕐 Sun–Thu 10–8, Fri–Sat 10–10 🖐 Adult $35, child (4–12) $28

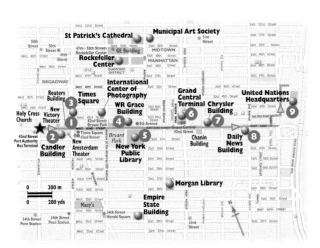

Opposite *The Paramount Building in Times Square*

MACY'S TO ROCKEFELLER CENTER

Some of New York's most striking sights are along this route—the Empire State Building, the Diamond District and Rockefeller Plaza, where you may be tempted to stop in at the NBC Experience Store to pick up a "Will & Grace," "Friends" or "Law & Order" T-shirt.

THE WALK
Distance: 3 miles (4.8km)
Time: 2.5 hours
Start at: 34th Street/Penn Station subway station
End at: 34th Street/Herald Square

HOW TO GET THERE
Subway 1, 2, 3; bus M10.

★Leave the 34th Street/Penn Station subway so you come out onto West 34th Street at Seventh Avenue (also known as Fashion Avenue).

❶ You are standing in front of Macy's, arguably New York's most famous department store. Encompassing two entire city blocks, this store is so big you could spend days here.

Head east on West 34th Street. Continue to Broadway, cross it and turn left onto Sixth Avenue (Avenue of the Americas), keeping to the right as you go through the

intersection. Six blocks north on Sixth, past lots of shops and banks, is Bryant Park on your right, where you can rest or get a coffee in the park. Continue north past the park. At the corner of 43rd Street is the International Center of Photography (▷ 151).

❷ The Diamond District is concentrated on 47th Street between Fifth and Sixth avenues. Notice the diamond-motif street lights illuminating the corners. Millions of dollars worth of gems are traded daily in the businesses here.

Continue north on Sixth Avenue.

❸ At 49th Street you'll see the 70-story G. E. Building tower to the right at 30 Rockefeller Plaza. This building is the headquarters of General Electric and NBC (National Broadcasting Corporation) and is part of the Rockefeller Center (▷ 164–167), a city landmark. The ground floor of the building is worth visiting;

note José Maria Sert's sepia murals depicting the progress of man. From Top of the Rock observation decks, on floors 67–70 of the G. E. Building, there are spectacular views.

Continue on Avenue of the Americas (Sixth Avenue) to 50th Street.

❹ Stop to admire the landmark art deco Radio City Music Hall (▷ 167), another city landmark and important element of the Rockefeller Center. Most famous for its Rockettes Christmas spectacular, it also hosts other music shows throughout the year. This was the world's largest indoor theater when it opened in 1932. Hour-long guided tours are worth the time and the money. The block-long entry, with its 24-carat-gold ceiling and two-ton glass chandeliers, is spectacular. Just past Radio City, at 1290 Avenue of the Americas, is the AXA Financial Center. Stop in to view the foyer's magnificent multi-panel murals by Thomas Hart Benton depicting the

Opposite *Entrance to Macy's department store, decorated for Christmas*
Below *Rockefeller Center*

nation's economic and social life on the eve of the Depression.

Back on Avenue of the Americas, go north a block to 52nd Street and turn right. The CBS Building, constructed in a dark granite in 1965, is on the corner of Avenue of the Americas and 52nd Street, a part of which is also known as Swing Street because of the many jazz clubs that flourished along here after the repeal of Prohibition.

5 At 25 West 52nd Street is the Paley Center for Media (▷ 160). Next door at No. 21 is the 21 Club, a still-fashionable hang-out, now a fine restaurant. Note the jockeys above the door.

At the corner of 52nd Street and Fifth Avenue, turn right and walk south a block.

6 At St. Patrick's Cathedral (▷ 160), the largest Catholic cathedral in America, the flying buttresses and 330ft (100m) twin spires vie for your attention.

Turn left on 51st Street, and walk east past the cathedral toward Madison Avenue. Cross Madison Avenue.

7 On the southeast corner of 51st and Madison is the New York Palace Hotel, which rises out of the Villard Houses, twin brownstone mansions built in 1884 by the Bavarian-born journalist, financier and railroad tycoon Henry Villard.

Continue walking east on 51st as far as Park Avenue. Turn left and walk one block north.

8 The bronze-glass tower at 375 Park Avenue is the Seagram Building (▷ 171), a lively place in summer and a delight at Christmas with a tree and lights. Diagonally across

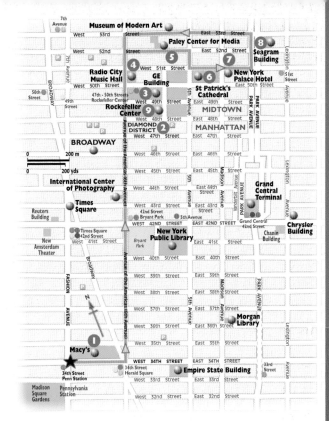

the avenue is Lever House, built in 1952 with an avant-garde metal-and glass-curtain wall that reflects everything around.

Go left on East 53rd Street, walk west to Sixth Avenue and turn left again. Walk four blocks south.

9 The Rockefeller Center is a great place to shop, stop for a snack or just wander around.

From here you can take the subway to Herald Square.

WHEN TO GO
Avoid this walk on Sunday if you want to shop and visit St. Patrick's Cathedral. Monday to Saturday from 10 to 6 is best.

WHERE TO EAT
Rainbow Room in the Rockefeller Center (212/632-5000) or Rock Center Café, 20 West 50th Street (212/332-7620)

PLACES TO VISIT
PALEY CENTER FOR MEDIA
✉ 25 West 52nd Street ☎ 212/621-6800
🕐 Tue–Sun 12–6, Thu until 8

RADIO CITY MUSIC HALL
✉ 1260 Sixth Avenue ☎ 212/247-4777
🕐 Daily 11–3 🎫 Hour-long behind-the-scenes tours every 30 min

SHOPPING

B & H PHOTO

www.bhphotovideo.com

Even if you're not in the market for a new camera, you might want to make a detour to this vast store to pick up inexpensive supplies. You'll find every conceivable brand and type of camera, plus darkroom equipment and other accessories. Don't expect service—come knowing what you want to buy.

✚ 196 C10 ✉ 420 Ninth Avenue, between West 33rd and 34th streets ☎ 212/444-5000 🕐 Mon–Thu 9–7, Fri 9–2, Sun 10–6. Closed Sat 🚇 34th Street/Penn Station (A, C, E) 🚌 M11

BERGDORF GOODMAN

www.bergdorfgoodman.com

Some shoppers actually dress up to visit this luxurious store, which showcases classics and new talent. The store is beautifully laid out, the shoe department marvelous and the designer boutiques extraordinary. The men's store is just across the street.

✚ 197 D7 ✉ 754 Fifth Avenue, between 57th and 58th streets ☎ 212/753-7300 🕐 Mon–Fri 10–8, Sat 10–7, Sun 12–6 🚇 Fifth Avenue/59th Street (N, R, W) 🚌 M5, M30, M57

CARTIER

www.cartier.com

Cartier opened in Paris in 1847 and has been famous for beautiful design ever since, creating such signature pieces as the three-band ring and the Portico Mystery Clock. Richard Burton went to Cartier for the diamond for Elizabeth Taylor. Today, it sells jewelry and watches, leather goods and other luxuries.

✚ 197 D8 ✉ 653 Fifth Avenue, between 51st and 52nd streets ☎ 212/753-0111 🕐 Mon–Fri 10–6, Sat 10–5.30, Sun 12–5 🚇 Fifth Avenue/53rd Street (E, V) 🚌 M1, M2, M3, M4, M50

CASWELL-MASSEY

www.caswell-massey.com

This apothecary, founded in 1752, provided perfume to George Washington and Dolly Madison and continues to produce a range of delicious floral scents such as freesia, lilac, rose, geranium and lily of the valley. You can find rosewater and glycerin soap, sandalwood massage oil and appealing gift sets.

✚ 197 E8 ✉ 518 Lexington Avenue at East 48th Street ☎ 212/755-2254 🕐 Mon–Fri 8–7, Sat 10–6, Sun 10–5 🚇 51st Street (6) 🚌 M98, M101, M102, M103

CHANEL

www.chanel.com

Coco Chanel created the little black dress and slacks for women. Now Karl Lagerfeld designs the styles and the accessories, shoes and scents to go with them. Two stores on Madison Avenue sell accessories and jewelry only.

✚ 197 D7 ✉ 15 East 57th Street, between Madison and Fifth avenues ☎ 212/355-5050 🕐 Mon–Fri 10–6.30, Sat 10–6, Sun 12–5 🚇 Lexington Avenue/59th Street (N, R, W, 4, 5, 6) 🚌 M1, M2, M3, M4, M57

COACH

www.coach.com

This successful leather purveyor has a line of classics as well as seasonal collections. There are nine other branches in the city.

✚ 197 D7 ✉ 595 Madison Avenue, between East 57th and 58th streets ☎ 212/754-0041 🕐 Mon–Sat 10–8, Sun 11–6 🚇 Fifth Avenue/59th Street (N, R, W), 59th Street (4, 5, 6) 🚌 M1, M2, M3, M4, M57

COLE HAAN

www.colehaan.com

Nike now owns this maker of traditional, good-quality shoes and is jazzing it up with new ideas, colors and styles.

➕ 197 D8 ✉ 620 Fifth Avenue at 50th Street ☎ 212/765-9747 🕐 Mon–Fri 10–8, Sat 10–7, Sun 12–6 🚇 47th–50th streets/ Rockefeller Center (B, D, F, V) 🚌 M1, M2, M3, M4

EUGENIA KIM
www.eugeniakim.com
Former *Allure* editor Kim fell into her career when she fashioned a hand-feathered cloche for herself, went shopping, and attracted attention from shop owners. Her hats are dashing, flamboyant, beautifully crafted, and expensive, made of straw and cotton, and trimmed with feathers, leather and ribbons.

➕ 196 C10 ✉ 347 West 36th Street, between 8th and 9th avenues ☎ 212/674-1345 🕐 By appointment only 🚇 34th Street-Penn Station (1, 2, 3, A, C, E) 🚌 M11, M16, M20

FAO SCHWARZ
www.fao.com
This famous store has been in Manhattan since 1876. It stocks action figures, stuffed toys, books, games, dolls, educational toys, electronics, furniture and fashions.

➕ 197 D7 ✉ 767 Fifth Avenue, between 58th and 59th streets ☎ 212/644-9400 🕐 Mon–Wed 10–6, Thu–Sat 10–8, Sun 11–6 🚇 59th Street/Fifth Avenue (N, R, W) 🚌 M1, M2, M3, M4

FENDI
www.fendi.com
The Fendi label conveys money and glitz, and women wear Fendi for that reason. This flagship store sells the full line: handbags, shoes, accessories and furs.

➕ 197 D8 ✉ 677 Fifth Avenue, between 53rd and 54th streets ☎ 212/759-4646 🕐 Mon–Sat 10–7, Sun 12–6 🚇 Fifth Avenue/53rd Street (E, V) 🚌 M1, M2, M3, M4, M57

GUCCI
www.gucci.com
Tom Ford left Gucci in 2004 and now Frida Giannini has become creative

director of womenswear and John Ray at menswear. Shop here for ultra-glamorous fashions.

➕ 197 D8 ✉ 725 Fifth Avenue at East 54th Street ☎ 212/826-2600. Also at 840 Madison Avenue, between 69th and 70th streets ☎ 212/717-2619 🕐 Mon–Sat 10–7, Sun 12–6; Madison Avenue: Mon–Sat 10–6 (Thu until 7), Sun 12–5 🚇 Fifth Avenue/53rd Street (E, V), 68th Street (6) 🚌 M1, M2, M3, M4

HAMMACHER SCHLEMMER
www.hammacher.com
Ingenuity meets the future. At this longtime innovator, which started as a hardware store on the Bowery in 1848, you will find such items as the upside-down tomato garden and the Roomba, a robotic cleaning device that navigates whole rooms removing dust from carpet and floor.

➕ 197 E7 ✉ 147 East 57th Street, between Lexington and Third avenues ☎ 212/421-9000 🕐 Mon–Sat 10–6 🚇 59th Street (4, 5, 6) 🚌 M57, M98, M101, M102, M103

HENRI BENDEL
www.henribendel.com
Henri Bendel is synonymous with sophistication and elegance. The inventory is similar to Bergdorf's, but the displays reveal the store's élan. If you want to see works by the hottest new designers, check out the New Creators boutique, which features such names as Michael Soheil, Peter Som, Alice Roi, Zac Posen and Behnaz Sarafpour.

➕ 197 D8 ✉ 712 Fifth Avenue at 56th Street ☎ 212/247-1100 🕐 Mon–Sat 10–8, Sun 12–7 🚇 Fifth Avenue/59th Street (N, R, W), Fifth Avenue/53rd Street (E, V) 🚌 M5, M30, M57

LACOSTE
www.lacoste.com
The alligator has been around since French tennis champion René Lacoste, nicknamed "alligator," sold his first polo shirt in 1933. Today, Christophe Lemaire is re-energizing the company, adding fragrance, home fabrics, eyewear, underwear and footwear to the selection of golf, tennis and yachting sportswear.

➕ 197 D8 ✉ 575 Madison Avenue, between East 54th and 55th streets ☎ 212/750-8115 🕐 Mon–Sat 10–7 (Thu until 8), Sun 12–5 🚇 Fifth Avenue/53rd Street (E, V), 51st Street/Lexington (6) 🚌 M1, M2, M3, M4

LORD & TAYLOR
www.lordandtaylor.com
This classic, established in 1826, targets traditional shoppers, from Greenwich matrons to young working women. The Christmas windows are a must-see.

➕ 197 D9 ✉ 424 Fifth Avenue, between 38th and 39th streets ☎ 212/391-3344 🕐 Mon–Sat 10–9, Sun 11–7 🚇 42nd Street (B, D, F, V) 🚌 M2, M3, M5

MACY'S
www.macys.com
Macy's calls itself the "world's largest department store." The Cellar stocks housewares and culinary delights, and clothing, generally mainstream, comes from a range of well-known names. The store has good seasonal sales, and sponsors the Thanksgiving Day parade and the July 4th fireworks.

➕ 197 D10 ✉ Herald Square at 34th Street and Broadway ☎ 212/695-4400 🕐 Mon–Sat 10–9.30, Sun 11–8.30 🚇 34th Street/Herald Square (B, D, F, N, Q, R, V, W) 🚌 M6, M7, M34

MANOLO BLAHNIK
www.manoloblahnik.com
The sexy, strappy sandals, plain stiletto pumps, slingbacks and mules are beloved of the fashion and celebrity crowd, who pay $450 and up for these most glamorous accessories. They're fashioned from pony skin and other elegant materials in a brilliant palette.

➕ 197 D8 ✉ 31 West 54th Street, between Fifth and Sixth avenues ☎ 212/582-3007 🕐 Mon–Fri 10.30–6, Sat 10.30–5.30, closed Sun 🚇 Fifth Avenue/53rd Street (E, V) 🚌 M5, M6, M7

MORRELL & COMPANY
www.morrellwine.com
Morrell, in business since 1947, is the other great wine shop in Manhattan after Sherry-Lehmann

(▷ 232). It has its own wine bar and café next door.

✚ 197 D8 ✉ 1 Rockefeller Plaza
☎ 212/688-9370 🕐 Mon–Sat 10–7
🚇 47th–50th streets/Rockefeller Center (B, D, F, V) 🚌 M1, M2, M3, M4, M50

PAUL STUART
www.paulstuart.com
This pricey haberdashery opened in 1938. It sells fine-quality suits, Italian dress shirts, Irish argyles and other good-looking traditional fashions for men. Women will find similar—silk cashmere turtlenecks, pinstripe pantsuits and leather jackets.
✚ 197 D9 ✉ Madison Avenue at East 45th Street ☎ 212/682-0320 🕐 Mon–Wed, Fri 8–6.30, Thu 8–7, Sat 9–6, Sun 12–5 🚇 42nd Street (B, D, F, V), 42nd Street/Grand Central (4, 5, 6, 7, S) 🚌 M1, M2, M3, M4, M5

POSMAN BOOKSELLERS
www.posmanbooks.com
A general bookstore which offers a good selection of journals and sharp insightful staff recommendations.
✚ 197 D9 ✉ 9 Grand Central Terminal (Vanderbilt Avenue and 42nd Street) ☎ 212/983-1111 🕐 Mon–Fri 8am–9pm, Sat 10–7, Sun 10–6 🚇 42nd Street (4, 5, 6) 🚌 M1, M2, M3, M4, M42

RIZZOLI
www.rizzoliusa.com
This store has an excellent stock of art, design, and fashion books.
✚ 197 D7 ✉ 31 West 57th Street, between Fifth and Sixth avenues (north side) ☎ 212/759-2424 🕐 Mon–Fri 10–7.30, Sat 10.30–7, Sun 11–7 🚇 Fifth Avenue 59th Street (N, R, W), 57th Street (F) 🚌 M1, M2, M3, M4, M5, M6, M7, M57

SAKS FIFTH AVENUE
www.saksfifthavenue.com
Saks offers a very fine selection of clothing by an excellent range of established and up-and-coming designers for men and women.
✚ 197 D8 ✉ 611 Fifth Avenue, between 49th and 50th streets ☎ 212/753-4000 🕐 Mon–Sat 10–7 (Thu until 8), Sun 12–7 🚇 Fifth Avenue/53rd Street (E, V), 47th–50th streets/Rockefeller Center (B, D, F, V) 🚌 M1, M2, M3, M4, M50

SEPHORA
www.sephora.com
This European chain has an efficient self-service orientation and sells more than 200 brands of beauty products, from Adrienne Vittadini to Philosophy. There's a scent-testing bar, and treatments by skin type.
✚ 196 C9 ✉ 1500 Broadway, between 43rd and 44th streets ☎ 212/944-6789 🕐 Mon–Fri 9am–midnight, Sat–Sun 10am–midnight 🚇 Times Square (N, Q, R, W, 1, 2, 3) 🚌 M6, M7, M10, M20

SHANGHAI TANG
www.shanghaitang.com
Asian styling informs fashions at this store. Chinese frog closures detail women's jackets and blouses fashioned from pagoda prints. Kung fu and Fuji jackets with mandarin collars are favorites for men.
✚ 197 D7 ✉ 600 Madison Avenue, between East 57th and 58th streets ☎ 212/888-0111 🕐 Mon–Sat 10–6, Sun 12–6 🚇 59th Street (4, 5, 6), Lexington Avenue/53rd Street (F) 🚌 M1, M2, M3, M4

SUAREZ HANDBAGS
Here are copies of designer handbags for a fraction of the price.
✚ 197 D8 ✉ 450 Park Avenue at East 56th Street ☎ 212/753-3758 🕐 Mon–Sat 10–6 🚇 59th Street (4, 5, 6) 🚌 M1, M2, M3, M4

TAKASHIMAYA
www.takashimaya-ny.com
Step into this beautiful branch of Japan's largest department store even if you're not a shopper. Look for gold-leaf cups, lacquer saucers and silk pillows.
✚ 197 D8 ✉ 693 Fifth Avenue, between 54th and 55th streets ☎ 212/350-0100 🕐 Mon–Sat 10–7, Sun 12–5 🚇 Fifth Avenue/53rd Street (E, V) 🚌 M1, M2, M3, M4, M5

THOMAS PINK
www.thomaspink.com
This British store sells formal, business and casual shirts for men and women in strikingly beautiful colors and patterns.
✚ 197 D8 ✉ 520 Madison Avenue, between East 53rd and 54th streets

☎ 212/838-1928 🕐 Mon–Fri 10–7 (Thu until 8), Sat 10–6, Sun 12–6 🚇 Fifth Avenue/53rd Street (E, V), 51st Street (6) 🚌 M1, M2, M3, M4

TIFFANY
www.tiffany.com
Tiffany is famous for its silver and crystal and beautiful design. Some items are astronomically priced, but it also displays more moderately priced luxury gifts—embossed note cards ($40 for 15) and singular silver pieces. All are packaged in the signature duck-egg blue box tied with red or white ribbon, introduced when the store opened in 1837.
✚ 197 D8 ✉ Fifth Avenue at 57th Street ☎ 212/755-8000 🕐 Mon–Fri 10–7, Sat 10–6, Sun 12–5 🚇 Fifth Avenue/59th Street (N, R, W), 57th Street (F) 🚌 M1, M2, M3, M4

ENTERTAINMENT AND NIGHTLIFE

ALVIN AILEY AMERICAN DANCE THEATER
www.alvinailey.org
In 2005 this black modern dance company opened a permanent home with a 285-seat theater and 12 studios. Even if you don't go to a performance, stop by to see them working out in the first-floor studios.
✚ 196 C8 ✉ 405 West 55th Street at Ninth Avenue ☎ 212/405-9000 ✋ $25–$110 🚇 Columbus Circle (1, A, B, C, D), 57th Street/Seventh Avenue (N, R, Q, W) 🚌 M11

AMBASSADOR THEATRE
www.shubertorganization.com
Opened in 1921, this 1,125-seat auditorium is wider than it is deep, so viewing is good but with a mezzanine overhang.
✚ 196 C8 ✉ 219 West 49th Street, between Broadway and Eighth Avenue ☎ 212/239-6200 🕐 Wed–Sat 8, Sun 7.30, Mon 8, Tue 7, matinees Sat–Sun 2 🚇 50th Street/Seventh Avenue (1), 49th Street (N, R) 🚌 M6, M7, M10, M27, M50, M104

AMERICAN AIRLINES THEATRE
www.roundabouttheatre.org
This restored 1918 theater is now the home of the Roundabout Theatre

Company, founded in 1965 to perform the classics and new plays at affordable prices.
🏠 196 C9 ✉ 227 West 42nd Street, between Seventh and Eighth avenues ☎ 212/719-1300 🕐 Tue–Sat 8, matinees Wed, Sat–Sun 2 🚇 42nd Street/Times Square (N, Q, R, S, W, 1, 2, 3, 7) 🚌 M6, M7, M10, M42, M104

AUGUST WILSON THEATRE
The Theater Guild commissioned this striking theater with its Tuscan-style facade, and it opened in 1925.
🏠 196 C8 ✉ 245 West 52nd Street, between Broadway and Eighth Avenue ☎ 212/239-6200 🕐 Tue 7, Wed–Sat 8, matinees Wed, Sat 2, Sun 3 🚇 50th Street (1), 50th Street (C, E) 🚌 M6, M7, M10, M27, M50, M104

B. B. KING BLUES CLUB AND GRILL
www.bbkingblues.com
Little Richard and Roberta Flack, among others, have entertained at this large bi-level club. On Sunday a gospel choir shakes up the Sunday brunch from 12.30 to 2.30.
🏠 196 C9 ✉ 237 West 42nd Street ☎ 212/997-4144 🕐 Daily 11am–1am; shows at 8pm and 10.30pm 🚇 42nd Street/Times Square (N, Q, R, S, W, 1, 2, 3, 7) 🚌 M10, M20, M42, M104

BELASCO
www.shubertorganization.com
Named after the bishop of Broadway David Belasco, this gem of a theater with 1,018 seats has some gorgeous Tiffany lamps and murals by Everett Shinn. Avoid the side orchestra.
🏠 197 D9 ✉ 111 West 44th Street, between Broadway and Sixth Avenue ☎ 212/239-6200 🕐 Tue–Sat 8, matinees Wed, Sat 2, Sun 3 🚇 42nd Street/Times Square (N, R, S, W, 1, 2, 3, 7), 42nd Street/Sixth Avenue (B, D, F) 🚌 M5, M6, M7, M10, M42, M104

BERNARD B. JACOBS THEATRE
www.shubertorganization.com
Laurence Olivier starred in The Entertainer on this stage, which opened in 1927.
🏠 196 C9 ✉ 242 West 45th Street, between Broadway and Eighth Avenue

☎ 212/239-6200 🕐 Tue–Sat 8, matinees Wed 2, Sun 3 🚇 42nd Street/Times Square (N, Q, R, S, W, 1, 2, 3, 7), 42nd Street/Eighth Avenue (A, C, E) 🚌 M6, M7, M10, M42, M104

BIRDLAND
www.birdlandjazz.com
Charlie Parker inspired the original Birdland, which opened in 1949, and he was its first headliner. This is perhaps the most elegant jazz club in town. Expect to hear everyone from Kurt Elling to Diana Krall.
🏠 196 C9 ✉ 315 West 44th Street, between Eighth and Ninth avenues ☎ 212/581-3080 🕐 Shows daily, times vary ✋ $20–$50 plus $10 minimum 🚇 42nd Street (A, C, E) 🚌 M10, M11, M20, M42

BOOTH THEATRE
www.shubertorganization.com
Numerous hits have played at this Italianate theater dating to 1913 and named after actor Edwin Booth.
🏠 196 C9 ✉ 222 West 45th Street, between Broadway and Eighth Avenue ☎ 212/239-6200 🕐 Mon, Wed, Fri–Sat 8, Tue 7, matinees Wed and Sat 2, Sun 3 🚇 42nd Street/Times Square (N, R, S, W, 1, 2, 3, 7) 🚌 M6, M7, M10, M42, M104

BROADHURST THEATRE
www.shubertorganization.com
Named after Anglo-American playwright George Broadhurst, this theater was built by the Shuberts and has welcomed star-studded casts since opening in 1918.
🏠 196 C9 ✉ 235 West 44th Street, between Broadway and Eighth Avenue ☎ 212/639-6200 🕐 Tue–Sat 8, matinees Wed, Sat 2, Sun 3 🚇 42nd Street/Times Square (N, R, S, W, 1, 2, 3, 7) 🚌 M6, M7, M10, M42, M104

BROADWAY THEATRE
www.shubertorganization.com
This 1,752-seat theater was built as a movie house in 1924. Avoid the back of the house if you can.
🏠 196 C8 ✉ 1681 Broadway, between 52nd and 53rd streets ☎ 212/239-6200 🕐 Tue–Sat 8, matinees Wed, Sat 2, Sun 3 🚇 50th Street/Eighth Avenue (C, E), 50th Street/Seventh Avenue (1) 🚌 M6, M7, M10, M27, M50, M104

BROOKS ATKINSON THEATRE
www.brooksatkinsontheater.com
Built in 1926, this ornate theater is named for longtime New York Times theater critic Brooks Atkinson. With 1,086 seats, you may feel you're too far from the stage if you sit in the rear mezzanine.
🏠 196 C9 ✉ 256 West 47th Street, between Broadway and Eighth Avenue ☎ 212/307-4100 🕐 Tue–Sat 8, matinees Wed, Sat 2, Sun 3 🚇 50th Street/Eighth Avenue (C, E), 50th Street/Seventh Avenue (1) 🚌 M10, M27, M50, M104

CAMPBELL APARTMENT
It's worth seeking out this quintessential New York bar. Originally designed as an office for wealthy businessman John W. Campbell, it's dark and richly decorated in a Renaissance style. Today it caters to suburbanites en route to their homes in Connecticut and Westchester County.
🏠 197 D9 ✉ 15 Vanderbilt Avenue in Grand Central Terminal (southwest corner) ☎ 212/953-0409 🕐 Mon–Thu noon–1am, Fri noon–2am, Sat 3pm–2am, Sun 3pm–11pm 🚇 42nd Street/Grand Central (4, 5, 6, S)

CARNEGIE HALL
www.carnegiehall.org
"Practice, practice, practice" is the answer to the old chestnut of a question, "How do you get to Carnegie Hall?" Many well-practiced conductors and artists have played in this famous hall, which was built with Carnegie money in 1891, from Tchaikovsky and Mahler to the Beatles and the Rolling Stones. Programming includes the great orchestras of the world, top-class instrumentalists, the New York Pops under Skitch Henderson, and performers of jazz, folk, pop and comedy. A small free museum on the second floor (tel 212/903-9629) displays associated memorabilia.
🏠 196 C8 ✉ Seventh Avenue at West 57th Street ☎ 212/247-7800 🕐 Museum: daily 11–4.30; tours (tel 212/903-9765) Mon–Fri 11.30, 2 and 3, Sat 11.30, 12.30, Sun 12.30 ✋ $10–$102 🚇 57th Street (N, Q, R, W) 🚌 M6, M7, M57

CAROLINE'S ON BROADWAY
www.carolines.com
First opened by Caroline Hirsch as a cabaret in Chelsea in 1981, the club gained a name throughout the 1980s and 1990s for comedy. Now in its glitzy Times Square venue, it presents live entertainment 365 nights a year.
✚ 196 C8 ✉ 1626 Broadway, between 49th and 50th streets ☎ 212/757-4100 🕐 Nightly, check program 💵 $20–$50, plus 2-drink minimum 🚇 50th Street (1) 🚌 M10, M20, M50

CENTRAL SYNAGOGUE
www.centralsynagogue.org
Concerts at the synagogue often feature well-known or overlooked Jewish composers.
✚ 197 E8 ✉ 123 East 55th Street at Lexington Avenue ☎ 212/415-5500 or 212/838-5122 🚇 51st Street (6) 🚌 M98, M101, M102, M103

CHICAGO CITY LIMITS
www.chicagocitylimits.com
This comedy revue company relocated from Chicago in 1979. The resident troupe puts on improv shows. Don't sit in the front row if you're worried about being heckled.
✚ 196 C8 ✉ 318 West 53rd Street at Eighth Avenue ☎ 212/888-5233 🕐 Fri–Sat 💵 $15 (plus 2-drink minimum) 🚇 50th Street (C, E) 🚌 M11

CHINA CLUB
www.chinaclubnyc.com
This glitzy spot has been attracting celebrities for 25 years. Today, sports figures and music heavies still head to its VIP lounge, especially on Monday nights. Other nights have house, salsa, merengue and R & B.
✚ 196 C9 ✉ 268 West 47th Street, between Broadway and Eighth Avenue ☎ 212/258-2547 🕐 Mon, Thu–Sat 10pm–3am 💵 $20–$25 🚇 49th Street (N, R, W), 50th Street (1)

CIRCLE IN THE SQUARE (UPTOWN)
Opened in 1972, this theater is in the same building as the Gershwin theater. All 681 seats have good sight lines.

✚ 196 C8 ✉ 1633 Broadway at 50th Street ☎ 212/239-6200 🕐 Tue 7, Wed–Sat 8, matinees Wed 2, Sat 11.30, 3.30 🚇 50th Street/Eighth Avenue (C, E), 50th Street/Seventh Avenue (1) 🚌 M6, M7, M10, M27, M50, M104

CORT THEATRE
www.shubertorganization.com
Named for producer John Cort, this 1,084-seat theater was modeled on the Petit Trianon, Versailles, and built in 1912. All seats have good views.
✚ 196 C8 ✉ 138 West 48th Street, between Sixth and Seventh avenues ☎ 212/239-6200 🕐 Tue–Sat 8, matinees Wed, Sat 2, Sun 3 🚇 47th–50th streets/Rockefeller Center (B, D, F, V) 🚌 M6, M7, M10, M27, M50, M104

DIVINE BAR WEST
A young professional singles crowd turns this long tapas bar into late-night Madrid. Flights of the 60 wines are available and 40 different beers.
✚ 196 C8 ✉ 236 West 54th Street ☎ 212/265-9463 🕐 Mon–Fri 4.30–1.30, Sat 7–3, Sun 6–10 🚇 59th Street (1), Seventh Avenue (B, D, E)

DON'T TELL MAMA
www.donttellmamanyc.com
Diverse singers and cabaret artists perform here nightly.
✚ 196 C9 ✉ 343 West 46th Street between Eighth and Ninth avenues ☎ 212/757-0788 💵 Cover, drink minimum 🚇 42nd Street (A, C, E) 🚌 M11, M20

ETHEL BARRYMORE THEATRE
www.shubertorganization.com
Ethel Barrymore starred in *The Kingdom of God* to open this theater in 1928. Fred Astaire gave his last stage performance here in *The Gay Divorcée* in the 1930s.
✚ 196 C9 ✉ 243 West 47th Street, between Seventh and Eighth avenues ☎ 212/239-6200 🕐 Tue–Sat 8, matinees Wed, Sat–Sun 2 🚇 50th Street (C, E), 50th Street (1), 49th Street (N, R, W) 🚌 M10, M20, M104

EUGENE O'NEILL
Opened in 1926, this theater was named for the great playwright in 1959.

✚ 196 C8 ✉ 230 West 49th Street, between Broadway and Eighth Avenue ☎ 212/239-6200 🕐 Tue–Sat 8, matinees Wed, Sat 2, Sun 3 🚇 50th Street/Eighth Avenue (C, E), 50th Street/Seventh Avenue (1) 🚌 M6, M7, M10, M27, M50, M104

FLUTE
www.flutebar.com
Perfect, if pricey, for an after-theater celebration, this gilt-and-mirror subterranean bar serves 20 champagnes by the glass. Snag one of the private curtained alcoves.
✚ 196 C8 ✉ 205 West 54th Street, between Seventh Avenue and Broadway ☎ 212/265-5169 🕐 Sun–Wed 4–2, Thu 4–3, Fri–Sat 4–4 🚇 Seventh Avenue (B, D, E)

GERALD SCHOENFELD THEATRE
www.shubertorganization.com
Drama and comedy from Noël Coward's *Present Laughter* to the Royal Shakespeare Company's *Nicholas Nickleby* have played at this 1918 theater.
✚ 196 C9 ✉ 236 West 45th Street, between Broadway and Eighth Avenue ☎ 212/239-6200 🕐 Wed–Sat 8, Mon 8, Tue 7, matinees Wed, Sat 2, Sun 3 🚇 42nd Street/Times Square (N, Q, R, S, W, 1, 2, 3, 7), 42nd Street/Eighth Avenue (A, C, E) 🚌 M6, M7, M10, M42, M104

GERSHWIN
www.gershwin-theater.com
Owned by the Broadway producers the Nederlanders, the Gershwin opened in 1972. The auditorium is on the second floor. It was renamed in 1983 after George and Ira.
✚ 196 C8 ✉ 222 West 51st Street, between Broadway and Eighth Avenue ☎ 212/307-4100 🕐 Tue 7, Wed–Sat 8, matinees Wed, Sat 2, Sun 3 🚇 50th Street/Eighth Avenue (C, E), 50th Street/Seventh Avenue (1) 🚌 M6, M7, M10, M27, M50, M104

HELEN HAYES THEATRE
This small Colonial Revival-style theater was built in 1912 to house new and experimental productions.
✚ 196 C9 ✉ 240 West 44th Street, between Seventh and Eighth avenues ☎ 212/944-9450 or 212/239-6200

Tue–Sat 8, matinees Wed, Sat 2, Sun 3
42nd Street/Times Square (N, Q, R, S, W, 1, 2, 3, 7), 42nd Street/Eighth Avenue (A, C, E) M6, M7, M10, M42, M104

HILTON THEATER
The Lyric (1903) and the Apollo (1920) were renovated and combined to create this 1,839-seat house ideal for spectacular musicals. Most seats have good sight lines.
196 C9 213 West 42nd Street, between Seventh and Eighth avenues 212/556-4750 or 212/307-4100
Tue–Sat 8, matinees Wed, Sat 2, Sun 3 42nd Street/Times Square (N, Q, R, S, W, 1, 2, 3, 7), 42nd Street/Eighth Avenue (A, C, E) M6, M7, M10, M42, M104

IMPERIAL THEATRE
www.shubertorganization.com
Gypsy, *Fiddler on the Roof* and *Les Misérables* played here.
196 C9 249 West 45th Street, between Broadway and Eighth Avenue 212/239-6200 Mon–Sat 8, matinees Wed, Sat 2 42nd Street/Times Square (N, Q, R, S, W, 1, 2, 3, 7), 42nd Street/Eighth Avenue (A, C, E) M6, M7, M10, M42, M104

IRIDIUM
www.iridiumjazzclub.com
At this chic club, top R&B and jazz names appear, plus there are Cuban jazz nights twice a month.
196 C8 1650 Broadway at 51st Street 212/582-2121 Mon–Thu 5–midnight (sets at 8 and 10), Wed–Sun 7pm–2am (sets at 8, 10 and 11.30) $25–$95 ($5 minimum at bar, $10 at table) 49th Street (N, R, W), 50th Street (1) M6, M7, M50

IRISH ARTS CENTER
www.irishartscenter.org
Comedy, theater, film and music with a Celtic-Gaelic flavor are performed here all week.
196 B8 553 West 51st Street, between Tenth and Eleventh avenues 212/757-3318 50th Street (C, E) M11, M50

JAPAN SOCIETY
www.japansociety.org
Japanese music concerts, dance, theater and cultural events are held in the Lila Acheson Wallace Auditorium.
197 E9 333 East 47th Street, between First and Second avenues 212/832-1155 51st Street (6) M15, M27, M50

JOE ALLEN
www.joeallenrestaurant.com
It's really a restaurant, but the bar is ideal for a pre- or post-theater drink.
196 C9 326 West 46th Street, between Eighth and Ninth avenues 212/581-6464 Mon–Tue, Thu 12–11.45, Wed, Sun 11.30am–11.45pm, Fri 12–12, Sat 11.30am–midnight 42nd Street (A, C, E)

JULIA MILES THEATER
www.womensproject.org
Founded in 1978 by Julia Miles, the Women's Project Theatre is the nation's pre-eminent women's theater company.
196 B8 424 West 55th Street 212/765-1706, tickets 212/757-3900 59th Street (A, B, C, D, 1) M11, M57

KING COLE BAR
Named for the 1906 Maxfield Parrish mural *Old King Cole*, this bar claims to have invented the Bloody Mary. It serves excellent cognacs, grappas and single malts.
197 D8 St. Regis Hotel, 2 East 55th Street, between Fifth and Madison avenues 212/753-4500 Mon–Thu 11.30–1, Fri–Sat 11.30am–2am, Sun 12–12 Fifth Avenue/53rd Street (E, V)

LANDMARK TAVERN
www.thelandmarktavern.org
The Landmark Tavern is worthy of its name, since it opened in 1868. The mahogany bar, antique mirrors and tile floor provide a historic patina. The traditional pub fare is good.
196 B9 626 Eleventh Avenue at the southeast corner of 46th Street 212/247-2562 Daily 11.30am–3am (kitchen closes at 11pm) 42nd Street (A, C, E), 50th Street (C, E)

LONGACRE THEATRE
www.shubertorganization.com
Named for Longacre Square, today's Times Square, this 1,095-seat

theater opened in 1913. Orchestra seats have the best sight lines.
196 C8 220 West 48th Street, between Broadway and Eighth Avenue 212/239-6200 Tue–Fri 8, Sat 5 and 9, Sun 3 and 7 50th Street/Seventh Avenue (1), 49th Street (N, R), 47th–50th streets/Rockefeller Center (B, D, F, Q) M6, M10, M27, M42, M50, M104

LUNT-FONTANNE THEATRE
http://luntfontannetheatre.com
Designed by Carrère and Hastings in 1910, the theater was gutted in 1958. It was the New York home of *The Sound of Music*.
196 C9 205 West 46th Street, between Broadway and Eighth Avenue 212/575-9200 or 212/307-4747
Tue–Wed 7, Thu–Sat 8, Sun 6.30, matinees Wed, Sat 2, Sun 1 42nd Street/Times Square (N, Q, R, S, W, 1, 2, 3, 7), 50th Street/Seventh Avenue (1, 9), 50th Street/Eighth Avenue (C, E) M6, M10, M27, M42, M50, M104

LYCEUM THEATRE
www.shubertorganization.com
Built in 1903 in Beaux Arts style, this is the oldest theater still in use on Broadway.
196 C9 149 West 45th Street, between Broadway and Sixth Avenue 212/239-6200 Tue–Sat 8, matinees Wed, Sat 2, Sun 3 49th Street (N, R), 47th–50th streets/Rockefeller Center (B, D, F) M5, M6, M7, M10, M42, M104

MADISON SQUARE GARDEN
www.thegarden.com
Located on top of Penn Station, this arena hosts sports events, concerts and other entertainment. Bob Dylan, Madonna, the Rolling Stones, Elton John and other star tours stop here.
196 C10 4 Penn Plaza 212/465-6741 34th Street/Penn Station (A, C, E, 1, 2, 3) M10, M16, M20, M34

MAJESTIC THEATRE
www.shubertorganization.com
This theater opened in 1927 and has hosted hits from *Carousel* to *Phantom of the Opera*, currently the longest-running show on Broadway.
196 C9 245 West 44th Street, between Broadway and Eighth Avenue

☎ 212/239-6200 🕐 Mon–Sat 8, matinees Wed, Sat 2 🚇 42nd Street/Times Square (N, Q, R, S, W, 1, 2, 3, 7), 42nd Street/Eighth Avenue (A, C, E) 🚌 M6, M7, M10, M42, M104

MINSKOFF THEATRE

www.minskofftheatre.com
This Nederlander theater, built in 1973, is rather impersonal. An escalator takes you to the fourth-floor orchestra.
✚ 196 C9 ✉ 200 West 45th Street, between Seventh and Eighth avenues ☎ 212/ 307-4100 🕐 Tue 7, Wed–Sat 8, matinees Wed, Sat 2, Sun 3 🚇 42nd Street/Times Square (N, Q, R, S, W, 1, 2, 3, 7) 🚌 M6, M7, M10, M42, M104

THE MINT SPACE

www.minttheater.org
Home of the Mint Theater, one of the most recognized companies off-off-Broadway, it performs plays often drawn from foreign traditions.
✚ 196 C9 ✉ 311 West 43rd Street, between Eighth and Ninth avenues ☎ 212/315-9434 or 212/315-0231 🚇 42nd Street (A, C, E) 🚌 M11, M20, M42

MOMA FILM

www.moma.org
MoMA offers an ambitious film program of documentaries, historic retrospectives and director tributes.
✚ 197 D8 ✉ 11 West 53rd Street ☎ 212/708-9480 🖐 $10 🚇 Rockefeller Center (B, D, F, V), 53rd Street/Fifth Avenue (E) 🚌 M1, M2, M3, M4, M5, M6, M7

MORGANS BAR

www.morganshotel.com
This basement hideaway draws celebrities. Sink into the leather chairs and enjoy the candlelight and well-made cocktails. Go after 10 to catch the place at its best.
✚ 197 D10 ✉ Morgans Hotel, 237 Madison Avenue, between East 37th and 38th streets ☎ 212/726-7755 🕐 Mon–Thu 5–1, Fri 5–2, Sat 6–2 🚇 33rd Street (6)

MUSIC BOX THEATRE

www.shubertorganization.com
Note the plaque, just inside the lobby, commemorating Irving Berlin,

who built this theater in 1921 with producer Sam Harris to house his Music Box Revues.
✚ 196 C9 ✉ 239 West 45th Street, between Broadway and Eighth Avenue ☎ 212/239-6200 🕐 Tue–Sat 8, matinees Sat 2, Sun 3 🚇 42nd Street/Times Square (N, Q, R, S, W, 1, 2, 3, 7), 42nd Street/Eighth Avenue (A, C, E) 🚌 M6, M7, M10, M42, M104

NEDERLANDER THEATRE

www.nederlandertheatre.org
When *Rent* moved from the East Village, it came to this theatre, and *Who's Afraid of Virginia Woolf?* opened here. Avoid the side seats.
✚ 196 C9 ✉ 208 West 41st Street, between Seventh and Eighth avenues ☎ 212/921-8000 or 212/307-4100 🕐 Mon–Tue, Thu–Sat 8, matinees Sat, Sun 2 🚇 42nd Street/Times Square (N, Q, R, S, W, 1, 2, 3, 7) 🚌 M6, M7, M10, M27, M42, M50, M104

THE NEGRO ENSEMBLE COMPANY

www.necinc.org
Founded in 1967, this group holds workshops for playwrights and actors; it also mounts productions.
✚ 196 C9 ✉ 303 West 42nd Street at Eighth Avenue ☎ 212/582-5860 🚇 42nd Street (A, C, E) 🚌 M10, M20, M42

NEIL SIMON THEATRE

www.neilsimontheatre.com
This ornate theater, opened in 1927, has been home to many musicals, including *Porgy and Bess*, *Funny Face* and *Hairspray*. It seats 1,334.
✚ 196 C8 ✉ 250 West 52nd Street, between Broadway and Eighth Avenue ☎ 212/757-8646 or 212/307-4100 🕐 Tue 7, Wed–Sat 8, matinees Wed, Sat 2, Sun 3 🚇 50th Street/Eighth Avenue (C, E), 50th Street/Seventh Avenue (1) 🚌 M6, M7, M10, M27, M50, M104

NEW AMSTERDAM THEATRE

http://disney.go.com
Florence Ziegfeld commissioned this art nouveau beauty in 1903. In 1997 the Walt Disney Company restored it with its murals, stucco, tiles and woodwork, and installed *The Lion King* for a run. Avoid the side seats.

✚ 196 C9 ✉ 214 West 42nd Street, between Seventh and Eighth avenues ☎ 212/282-2900 or 212/307-4747 or 212/282-2907 for tours 🕐 Wed–Sat 8, Sun 6.30, matinees Wed, Sat 2, Sun 1. Tours Mon 9.30–5.30, Tue, Thu–Sat 9.30–11.30 🚇 42nd Street/Times Square (N, Q, R, S, W, 1, 2, 3, 7), 42nd Street/Eighth Avenue (A, C, E) 🚌 M6, M7, M10, M42, M104

NEW YORK CITY CENTER

www.nycitycenter.org
The exotic Moorish-style building dating from 1922–24 is famous for dance productions. The Dance Theater of Harlem, Alvin Ailey American Dance Theater, Paul Taylor Dance Company, American Ballet Theatre and the San Francisco Ballet have performed here. The Gilbert and Sullivan Players are residents. Originally a Shriner's temple, the building was converted into a "people's theater" in 1943.
✚ 196 C8 ✉ 131 West 55th Street, between Sixth and Seventh avenues ☎ 212/247-0430 or 212/581-1212 🖐 $15–$100 🚇 57th Street (N, Q, R, W) 🚌 M5, M6, M7, M57

NEW YORK PUBLIC LIBRARY

Foreign films, shorts and documentaries are shown here.
✚ 197 D9 ✉ Donnell Media Center, 20 West 53rd Street, between Fifth and Sixth avenues ☎ 212/621-0609 🖐 Free 🚇 53rd Street/Fifth Avenue (E, V) 🚌 M1, M2, M3, M4, M5, M6, M7

OAK ROOM

www.algonquinhotel.com
By nurturing such artists as Steve Ross, Michael Feinstein, Harry Connick, Jr. and Diana Krall, this room led a revival of cabaret. Dinner is available before the first show.
✚ 197 D9 ✉ Algonquin Hotel, 59 West 44th Street, between Fifth and Sixth avenues ☎ 212/419-9331 🕐 Tue–Sat 9pm, Sat only 11.30pm, Sun 1pm 🖐 $60–75, plus 2-drink minumum, dinner packages. Reservations required 🚇 42nd Street (B, D, F, V) 🚌 M1, M2, M3, M4, M5, M6, M7

PADDY REILLY'S MUSIC BAR

The Celtic house band plays excellent Irish music on a small

stage in this friendly bar with Guinness on tap. Wednesday and Saturday nights are open mic.
🕀 197 E10 ✉ 519 Second Avenue at 29th Street ☎ 212/686-1210 ⏰ Daily 11am–4am 🖐 $5–$15 🚇 28th Street (6) 🚌 M15

PALACE THEATRE

www.palacetheatreonbroadway.com
The Palace opened as a vaudeville house in 1913, and such legends as Bob Hope, Sophie Tucker, Jimmy Durante and the Marx Brothers all entertained here. The Nederlanders restored it in 1965.
🕀 196 C9 ✉ 1564 Broadway, between 46th and 47th streets ☎ 212/730-8200 or 212/307-4747 ⏰ Tue–Sat 8, matinees Wed, Sat 2, Sun 3 🚇 50th Street (1), 49th Street (N, R) 🚌 M7, M10, M27, M50, M104

PARIS THEATRE

www.theparistheatre.com
The films that play here are mostly foreign.
🕀 197 D7 ✉ 4 West 58th Street, between Fifth and Sixth avenues ☎ 212/688-3800 🖐 $10–11 🚇 Fifth Avenue/59th Street (N, R, W) 🚌 M1, M2, M3, M4, M57

P. J. CLARKE'S

www.pjclarkes.com
The tiny building which houses P. J. Clarke's is overshadowed by skyscrapers. The bar played a major role in Billy Wilder's 1945 film The Lost Weekend.
🕀 197 E8 ✉ 915 Third Avenue at 55th Street ☎ 212/317-1616 ⏰ Daily 11.30am–4am 🚇 59th Street (4, 5, 6)

PLAYWRIGHTS HORIZONS THEATER

www.playwrightshorizons.org
This company is dedicated to the production of new American plays and musicals. In its 37 years it has produced the work of more than 350 writers. The main stage seats 198 and the studio 96.
🕀 196 B9 ✉ 416 West 42nd Street between Ninth and Tenth avenues ☎ 212/564-1235 🚇 42nd Street (A, C, E) 🚌 M11, M42

RADIO CITY MUSIC HALL

www.radiocity.com
This theater with plenty of art deco paraphernalia was refurbished in 1999 to the tune of $70 million.
🕀 197 D8 ✉ 1260 Sixth Avenue at 50th Street ☎ 212/247-4777 ⏰ One-hour tours daily 11–3 🖐 Tours: adult $18.50, child (under 12) $10 🚇 47th-50th streets/ Rockefeller Center (B, D, F, V) 🚌 M5, M6, M7

RAINBOW GRILL BAR

www.rainbowroom.com
You can spend a fortune dining and dancing at the Rainbow Room—or head to this bar for cocktails. Jackets are required.
🕀 197 D8 ✉ 30 Rockefeller Plaza at 49th Street, between Fifth and Sixth avenues ☎ 212/632-5000 ⏰ Sun–Thu 5–midnight, Fri–Sat 5–1, dining and dancing selected Fri–Sat 🚇 47th–50th Streets (B, D, F, V)

ROSELAND BALLROOM

www.roselandballroom.com
The original Roseland opened at 51st Street in 1919, but moved here in 1956. Once a legendary ballroom featuring the bands of Fletcher Henderson and Tommy Dorsey, today it hosts rock concerts and occasional sporting events.
🕀 196 C8 ✉ 239 West 52nd Street, between Broadway and Eighth Avenue ☎ 212/247-0200 🖐 $25–$60 🚇 50th Street (1), 50th Street (C, E) 🚌 M6, M7, M10, M20, M50

RUSSIAN VODKA ROOM

http://russianvodkaroom.com
A huge selection of flavored vodkas, apple-cinnamon and horseradish, for example, are poured into martinis or drunk straight, the preference of the Russians who gather at this old-fashioned basement bar. The menu is inexpensive.
🕀 196 C8 ✉ 265 West 52nd Street, between Broadway and Eighth Avenue ☎ 212/307-5835 ⏰ Tue–Thu 4–2, Fri–Sat 4–3, Sun–Mon 4–1 🚇 50th Street (C, E)

ST. ANDREW'S

www.standrewsnyc.com
Scotch-lovers crowd the bar at this traditional pub-style restaurant. Here

they select their favorites from about 175 or so single malts. Go early or late to avoid the crush.
🕀 196 C9 ✉ 140 West 46th Street, between Broadway and Sixth Avenue ☎ 212/840-8413 ⏰ Daily 11.30am–4am 🚇 42nd Street (B, D, F, V)

ST. JAMES THEATRE

Oklahoma!, The King and I, Hello Dolly and The Producers have all played in this Beaux Arts theater. Its mezzanine hangs over the orchestra.
🕀 196 C9 ✉ 246 West 44th Street, between Seventh and Eighth avenues ☎ 212/239-5800 ⏰ Tue 7, Wed–Sat 8, matinees Wed, Sat 2, Sun 3 🚇 42nd Street/Times Square (N, Q, R, S, W, 1, 2, 3, 7), 42nd Street/Eighth Avenue (A, C, E) 🚌 M6, M7, M10, M42, M104

SAKAGURA

www.sakagura.com
In the basement of a high-rise building, this bar seems lifted from Japan. Shelves are lined with 200 different types of sake, and you can order flights of four selections.
🕀 197 E9 ✉ 211 East 43rd Street, between Second and Third avenues ☎ 212/953-7253 ⏰ Mon–Fri noon–11.30, Sat 6–11.30, Sun 6–11 🚇 42nd Street/ Grand Central (4, 5, 6)

SALON DE NING

Who can resist an invitation to a well-dressed outdoor rooftop bar in the heart of Manhattan? You'll pay for the privilege, but that's what makes memories.
🕀 197 D8 ✉ Peninsula Hotel, 700 Fifth Avenue at 55th Street ☎ 212/903-3097 ⏰ Mon–Thu 4–midnight, Fri–Sat 4–1, Sat 3–10 🚇 59th Street/Fifth Avenue (E, V) 🚌 M1, M2, M3, M4, M5

SAMUEL J. FRIEDMAN THEATRE

This landmark theater opened in 1925 and hosted such winners as Hair and Neil Simon's Barefoot in the Park. It is the Broadway home of the Manhattan Theatre Club.
🕀 196 C9 ✉ 261 West 47th Street, between Broadway and Eighth Avenue ☎ 212/239-6200 ⏰ Tue–Sat 8, Sun 7, Sat, Sun 2 🚇 50th Street (C, E), 50th Street (1) 🚌 M10, M20

SCANDINAVIA HOUSE

www.scandinaviahouse.org

Scandinavia House shows films by directors and actors from Denmark, Finland, Iceland, Norway and Sweden.

✚ 197 D10 ✉ Victor Borge Hall, 58 Park Avenue, between East 37th and 38th streets ☎ 212/879-9779 ✋ $8 🚇 42nd Street/ Grand Central (4, 5, 6) 🚌 M1

SECOND STAGE THEATER

www.2st.com

Dutch architect Rem Koolhaas helped revamp the old bank building that is home to this company, which stages modern American plays.

✚ 196 C9 ✉ 307 West 43rd Street, between Eighth and Ninth avenues ☎ 212/246-4422 🚇 79th Street (1) 🚌 M79, M104

SHUBERT THEATRE

www.shubertorganization.com

This theater, opened in 1913, is the cornerstone of the Shubert empire.

✚ 196 C9 ✉ 225 West 44th Street, between Seventh and Eighth avenues ☎ 212/239-6200 🕐 Mon–Tue, Thu–Sat 8, Sun 7, matinees Sat, Sun 2 🚇 42nd Street/ Times Square (N, Q, R, S, W, 1, 2, 3, 7), 42nd Street/Eighth Avenue (A, C, E) 🚌 M6, M7, M10, M42, M104

STUDIO 54

This former discotheque is now a theater. The musical *Cabaret* has played here.

✚ 196 C8 ✉ 254 West 54th Street, between Broadway and Eighth Avenue ☎ 212/239-6200 🕐 Tue–Sat 8, matinees Sat, Sun, Wed 2 🚇 Seventh Avenue (B, D, E), 57th Street (N, R, Q) 🚌 M6, M7, M27, M50, M57

SWING 46

www.swing46.com

At this 1940s-style jazz club, you can lindy and jitterbug to top-notch live bands. Friday and Saturday is always swing. The management provides lessons to neophytes.

✚ 196 C9 ✉ 349 West 46th Street, between Eighth and Ninth avenues ☎ 212/262-9554 🕐 Sun–Thu 5–12, Fri–Sat 9–1 ✋ $12–$15 🚇 42nd Street (A, C, E)

TAO

www.taorestaurant.com

A large golden Buddha presides over this loft space, so crowded with singles after work that it made it into an episode of *Sex and the City*.

✚ 197 D7 ✉ 42 East 58th Street, between Madison and Park avenues ☎ 212/888-2288 🕐 Wed–Fri 11.30am–1am, Sat 5–1, Sun 5–12, Mon–Tue 11.30am–midnight, 🚇 Fifth Avenue/59th Street (N, R, W), 59th Street (4, 5, 6)

THEATRE AT ST. CLEMENTS

Playwrights such as David Mamet and Terrance McNally have premiered works here. The plays often focus on contemporary issues.

✚ 196 B9 ✉ 423 West 46th Street, between Ninth and Tenth avenues ☎ 212/246-7277 or 212/279-4200 🕐 Varies 🚇 42nd Street (A, C, E) 🚌 M11, M42

TOP OF THE TOWER

This 26th-floor cocktail lounge is neither overhyped nor overpriced—a miracle for such a romantic the place with bewitching views.

✚ 197 E8 ✉ Beekman Tower, 3 Mitchell Place on First Avenue at 49th Street ☎ 212/980-4796 🕐 Sun–Thu 5–1, Fri–Sat 5–2 🚇 51st Street (6), 53rd Street/ Lexington (E, V)

THE TOWN HALL

www.the-townhall-nyc.org

Founded in 1921 by the suffragist League for Political Education, this theater offers eclectic programming with Broadway songs, cabaret, opera, pop and world music as well as lectures and readings.

✚ 196 C9 ✉ 123 West 43rd Street, between Sixth Avenue and Broadway ☎ 212/840-2824 (recording) and 212/997-6661 (Mon–Sat 12–6) ✋ Free–$75 🚇 42nd Street/Times Square (N, Q, R, S, W, 1, 2, 3, 7), 42nd Street (B, D, F, V) 🚌 M5, M6, M7, M42

THE TOWNHOUSE

www.townhouseny.com

Upscale gay professionals gather around the piano here.

✚ 197 E7 ✉ 236 East 58th Street at Second Avenue ☎ 212/754-4649

🕐 Sun–Wed 4–3, Thu–Sat 4–4 🚇 59th Street (4, 5, 6)

WALTER KERR

Named after the famous *New York Times* critic, this is an ideal house for serious drama and classic comedy. Seats 947.

✚ 196 C8 ✉ 219 West 48th Street, between Broadway and Eighth Avenue ☎ 212/239-6200 🕐 Tue 7, Wed–Sat 8, matinees Wed, Sat 2, Sun 3 🚇 50th Street/ Eighth Avenue (C, E), 50th Street/Seventh Avenue (1) 🚌 M7, M10, M27, M50, M104

YORK THEATRE

www.yorktheatre.org

The material presented at the modern space in St. Peter's church at Citicorp Center is often experimental and challenging.

✚ 197 E8 ✉ 619 Lexington Avenue at 54th Street ☎ 212/935-5824 🚇 51st Street (6), Fifth Avenue/53rd Street (E, V) 🚌 M98, M101, M102, M103

SPORTS AND ACTIVITIES

DOWNTOWN BOATHOUSE

www.downtownboathouse.org

This organization offers free kayaking trips and instruction on the Hudson River from several locations.

✚ 196 A8 ✉ Pier 96, Clinton Cove Park at 56th Steeet 🕐 Mid-May to mid-Oct ✋ Free 🚇 Columbus Circle (1) 🚌 M20

GRAND CENTRAL PARTNERSHIP TOURS

▷ 270.

NEW YORK KNICKS

www.nba.com/knicks

The Knicks are the city's hottest ticket. This team and the Boston Celtics are the only remaining charter members of the NBA. Walt Frazier, Bill Bradley and Willis Reed made them golden in the 1970s, and Patrick Ewing helped them to the play-offs in 1994 and 1999.

✚ 196 C10 ✉ Madison Square Garden, 2 Pennsylvania Plaza, Seventh Avenue, between West 31st and 33rd streets ☎ 212/465-5867 or 212/465-6741 (Madison Square Garden), 212/307-7171 for tickets, 212/465-5802 for tours

$15–$3,000 🤚 34th Street/Penn Station (A, C, E, 1, 2, 3) 🚌 M20, M34

NEW YORK LIBERTY
www.wnba.com/liberty
The team has become a star in the Women's National Basketball Association (WNBA) and has played in WNBA finals.
➕ 196 C10 ✉ Madison Square Garden, 2 Pennsylvania Plaza, Seventh Avenue, between West 31st and 33rd streets
☎ 212/564-9622 🤚 $10–$88 🚇 34th Street/Penn Station (A, C, E, 1, 2, 3) 🚌 M20, M34

ROCKEFELLER CENTER ICE RINK
www.therinkatrockcenter.com
It's dreamlike to glide on this legendary rink under the golden statue of Prometheus. There is a live DJ on Thursday from 7pm till 11pm.
➕ 197 D8 ✉ 1 Rockefeller Center Plaza, Fifth Avenue, between 49th and 50th streets
☎ 212/332-7654 🕐 Oct–late Apr several sessions daily, phone or visit website for timings 🤚 Mon–Thu $5 lunch, $10 otherwise Fri–Sun and holidays $19; under 11 and seniors Mon–Thu $7.50, Fri–Sun and holidays $8.50, skate rental $7
🚇 47th–50th streets/Rockefeller Center (B, D, F, V) 🚌 M1, M2, M3, M4, M50

HEALTH AND BEAUTY
CORNELIA DAY RESORT
www.cornelia.com
You can have rooftop massages here and underwater shiatsu massage in the *watsu* pool. This resort offers a full range of spa services.
➕ 197 D8 ✉ 663 Fifth Avenue, between 52nd and 53rd streets ☎ 212/871-3050
🕐 Mon–Sat 9am–10pm, Sun 9–9
🤚 Facial $195, massage from $190
🚇 5th Avenue/53rd Street (E, V)
🚌 M1, M2, M3, M4

EQUINOX FITNESS CLUB
www.equinoxfitness.com
All 19 Equinox clubs in Manhattan are sleek and sophisticated and almost invariably offer spinning, Pilates, yoga, cardio-boxing and cardio machines.
➕ 197 D9 ✉ 521 Fifth Avenue at 44th Street ☎ 212/972-8000 🕐 Mon–Thu 5.30am–10pm, Fri 5.30am–8pm 🤚 Day

pass $35 🚇 42nd Street/Grand Central (4, 5, 6) 🚌 M1, M2, M3, M4, M5

MARIO BADESCU
www.mariobadescu.com
You might expect Mario Badescu, whose clients include Sharon Stone, Kate Moss and P Diddy, to charge an arm and a leg to treat your hands and your feet, but his prices are very reasonable and if you want one spa session in New York, book it here.
➕ 197 E8 ✉ 320 East 52nd Street, between 1st and 2nd avenues ☎ 212/758-1065 🕐 Mon–Tue, Fri 8.30–6, Wed–Thu 8.30–8.30, Fri 8.30–6, Sat 9–5, Sun 10–5.30
🤚 Facial $65, manicure $15, pedicure $25, massage $70 🚇 51st Street (6), Lexington Avenue-53rd Street (E, V)

FOR CHILDREN
CIRCLE LINE CRUISES
www.circleline42.com
Circling around Manhattan in a boat is the best way to grasp the contours of the island and the extraordinary city piled high upon it. Depending on the attention span of your kids, you can opt for the two-hour afternoon trip or the three-hour version. The narration can be great or mediocre, but the fresh air, the passing craft and the sights make it fun. The same company also runs day-long tours up the Hudson River.
➕ 196 A9 ✉ Pier 83, West 42nd Street and Hudson River ☎ 212/563-3200 🕐 Call for departure times and schedules. Operates Thu–Mon only in winter 🤚 $19–$34 plus $1 fuel surcharge 🚇 42nd Street (A, C, E) then M42 🚌 M42, M50

FAO SCHWARZ
▷ 177.

LIBERTY HELICOPTERS
www.libertyhelicopters.com
Helicopters take off from the heliport on tours from 2 to 17 minutes hovering above the city and the Hudson River. If you can afford it, why not?
➕ 196 A10 ✉ West 30th Street and Twelfth Avenue ☎ 212/967-6464
🤚 $135 (6–8 min), $165 (12–15 min), $230 (16–20 min) 🚇 34th Street (A, C, E) 🚌 M11, M34

MADAME TUSSAUD'S
www.madame-tussauds.com
The New York version of this world-famous London waxworks museum opened in 2000. It contains the usual collection of lifelike figures—here, geared to a New York audience, you'll see realistic replicas of such luminaries as comedian Joan Rivers, actor and director Woody Allen and basketball star Michael Jordan).
➕ 196 C9 ✉ 234 West 42nd Street, between Eighth and Seventh avenues
☎ 800/246-8872 🕐 Sun–Thu 10–8, Fri–Sat 10–10 🤚 Adult $35, child (4–12) $28, under 4 free 🚇 42nd Street (A, C, E), 42nd Street/Times Square (N, Q, R, S, W, 1, 2, 3, 7) 🚌 M5, M6, M7, M42

NBC STUDIO TOUR
www.nbc.com
Take one of the 70-minute tours of the NBC (National Broadcasting Company) network's studios where *The Today Show* and *Saturday Night Live* are produced. Visitors peek into studios and also see how shows are made.
➕ 197 D8 ✉ 30 Rockefeller Plaza, 49th Street, between Fifth and Sixth avenues
☎ 212/664-7174 🕐 Mon–Thu 8.30–4.30, Fri–Sat 9.30–5.30, Sun 9.30–4.30. Reservations recommended 🤚 Adult $19.25, child (6–12) $16.25 (under 6 not admitted) 🚇 47th–50th streets/Rockefeller Center (B, D, F, V) 🚌 M1, M2, M3, M4, M5, M6, M7

SONY WONDER TECHNOLOGY LAB
www.sonywondertechlab.com
Interactive exhibits fill four floors here, demonstrating the latest developments in communications, robotics, medical technology and entertainment. It is not as much of a hard sell as you might expect. Reservations are needed and can be made one week to three months in advance.
➕ 197 D8 ✉ Sony Plaza, 550 Madison Avenue at East 56th Street ☎ 212/833-8100 🕐 Tue–Sat 10–5, Sun 12–5 🤚 Free 🚇 Fifth Avenue/53rd Street (E, V), Fifth Avenue/59th Street (N, R, W) 🚌 M1, M2, M3, M4

PRICES AND SYMBOLS

The prices given are the average for a two-course lunch (L) and a three-course dinner (D) for one person, without drinks. The wine price is for the least expensive bottle.

For a key to the symbols, ▷ 2.

'21' CLUB

www.21club.com

The hamburger makes headlines for its price ($30 and climbing), but this storied locale is about so much more than the sandwich. Two college students opened it as a speakeasy in Greenwich Village in 1920; it was frequented by Humphrey Bogart, F. Scott Fitzgerald and Joe Di Maggio after relocating to this town house in 1929. Old-fashioned and masculine, it purveys fist-size medallions of beef flambéed with cognac and Dijon, chicken hash and Dover sole, along with newer, lighter dishes like black sea bass in champagne sauce. The daily special ice creams, gussied up or plain, are the choice desserts, and the wine cellar is renowned. Jacket and tie required.

✚ 197 D8 ✉ 21 West 52nd Street, between Fifth and Sixth avenues ☎ 212/582-7200 ⏲ Mon–Fri 12–2.30, Mon–Thu 5.30–10, Fri–Sat 5.30–11

🍴 L $60, D $80, Wine $30 🚇 47th–50th streets (B, D, F, V) 🚌 M1, M2, M3, M4, M5, M6, M7

AQUAVIT

www.aquavit.org

In a sleek modern space, Chef Marcus Samuelsson creates contemporary interpretations of Swedish–Scandinavian cuisine: Oysters come with a mango-curry sorbet; mushroom broth is poured over delicately smoked arctic char. There's a wide selection of aquavits, plus 250 wines (15 by the glass). Jackets are required in the dining room, but the front café is more casual and offers more traditional Scandinavian fare.

✚ 197 D8 ✉ 65 East 55th Street, between Madison and Park avenues ☎ 212/307-7311 ⏲ Mon–Thu 12–2.30, 5.30–10.30, Fri–Sat 12–2.30, 5.30–10.45, Sun 5.30–10.30 🍴 L $35, D $84, Wine $45 🚇 Fifth Avenue (E, V) 🚌 M1, M2, M3, M4, M5, M6, M7

ARTISANAL

www.artisanalbistro.com

This gem is all about cheese, and the quality of the 250 varieties in the walk-in cheese vault is astonishing, ranging from *cabecou de*

Rocamadour to *callu de cabreddu.* Savor them straight or in a fondue. Not to worry if you don't eat cheese: escargots, moules and main dishes such as crisp skate wing with blood orange *Grenobloise* and steak frites complete the menu.

✚ 197 D10 ✉ 2 Park Avenue at 32nd Street ☎ 212/725-8585 ⏲ Mon–Thu 11.45–11, Fri–Sat 11.45am–midnight, Sun 11–10 🍴 L $40, D $54, Wine $32 🚇 33rd Street (6) 🚌 M1

LE BERNARDIN

www.le-bernardin.com

Le Bernardin is the best seafood restaurant in the city. The teak-paneled room is spacious and comfortable, the service discreet and precise, and the food exquisite. Chef Eric Ripert's dishes are designed to show off the flavor and texture of the specific type of fish. Cod is served in a sage and garlic broth, halibut poached in lemongrass and coconut, and monkfish oven roasted and served with lemon-paprika sauce. Signature appetizers—tuna carpaccio; a scallop wrapped in a cabbage leaf with foie gras and truffles and steamed; and black bass ceviche topped with coriander, mint, jalapeños and tomatoes—are all gems. Desserts are equally inspirational.

➕ 196 C8 ✉ 155 West 51st Street, between Sixth and Seventh avenues ☎ 212/489-1515 🕐 Mon–Fri 12–2.30, Mon–Thu 5.30–10.30, Fri–Sat 5.30–11 ✋ L prix fixe $68, D 3-course prix fixe $109, Wine $50 🚇 47th–50th streets/Rockefeller Center (B, D, F, V), 49th Street (N, R, W) 🚌 M5, M6, M7

BLUE FIN
www.brguestrestaurants.com
The vast, theatrical Blue Fin offers the freshest fish, prepared simply in such dishes as salmon in a warm bacon sherry vinaigrette, or poached halibut in ancho-chili-and-vegetable broth. Sushi is available on the first floor of the two-story space, which has a floating staircase that looks out over a school of black fish suspended from the ceiling against an undulating wall. There are 600 wines on the list, 30 by the glass.
➕ 196 C9 ✉ W Hotel Times Square, 1567 Broadway at 47th Street ☎ 212/918-1400 🕐 Daily 7–11.30, 11.30–4, Sun–Mon 5–11, Tue–Thu 5–11.30, Fri–Sat 5–12 ✋ L $36, D $60, Wine $28 🚇 49th Street (N, R, W), 50th Street (1) 🚌 M10, M20, M27, M104

BRASSERIE
www.patinagroup.com
From its theatrical entrance ramp to its buzzing bar, Brasserie is one very cool room and so very New York. The French-Mediterranean menu is satisfying, ranging as it does from salad Niçoise and burgers (with oyster mushrooms, bacon and roasted onions) to duck cassoulet and rice-crusted black sea bass in lemongrass and lime broth. Great sushi and a raw bar, too.
➕ 197 E8 ✉ 100 East 53rd Street, between Park and Lexington avenues ☎ 212/751-4840 🕐 Mon–Fri 7–10, 11.30–11, Sat 11–3.30, 4.30–11, Sun 11–3.30, 4.30–10 ✋ L $40, D $50, Wine $30 🚇 53rd Street/Lexington Avenue (E, V), 51st Street (6) 🚌 M1, M2, M3, M4, M98, M101, M102, M103

CHO DANG GOL
www.chodanggolny.com
This popular Korean place makes its own tofu daily, but it's not a vegetarian restaurant. The tasty tofu can be mixed with pork, squid and octopus, among other things, with a casserole being the house specialty. Korean wine is served, but most people opt for sake. Sweet-lovers should note there are no desserts.
➕ 197 D10 ✉ 55 West 35th Street, between 5th and 6th avenues ☎ 212/695-8222 🕐 Daily 11.30–10.30 ✋ L $30, D $30, Wine $14 🚇 34th St. Herald Square (B, D, F, N, Q, R, V, W), 34th St. Penn Station (1, 2, 3) 🚌 M5, M6, M7, M16, M34

LE COLONIAL
www.lecolonialnyc.com
The French colonial ambience is a perfect backdrop for the Vietnamese cuisine at this striking spot. Start with *chao tom* (grilled shrimp wrapped around sugarcane with angel-hair noodles, lettuce, mint and peanut dipping sauce) or the steamed ravioli with chicken and mushrooms. The steamed sea bass dishes are outstanding.
➕ 197 E7 ✉ 149 East 57th Street, between Lexington and Third avenues ☎ 212/752-0808 🕐 Mon–Fri 12–2, Sun–Mon 5.30–10.30, Tue–Thu 5.30–11, Fri–Sat 5.30–11.30 ✋ L $35, D $50, Wine $38 🚇 59th Street (4, 5, 6), 59th Street/Lexington Avenue (N, R, W) 🚌 M57, M98, M101, M102, M103

DAWAT
www.restaurant.com/dawat
Cookbook author Madhur Jaffrey consults at this comfortable Indian. The spices are skillfully blended to subtle effect in such dishes as shrimp in coconut sauce flavored with curry leaves and smoked tamarind; chicken tikka; and baby goat in cardamom sauce. There are rice and vegetarian specialties.
➕ 197 E7 ✉ 210 East 58th Street, between Second and Third avenues ☎ 212/355-7555 🕐 Mon–Sat 11.30–3, 5.30–11, Sun 5.30–11 ✋ L $60, D $65, tasting menus $50–$80, Wine $19 🚇 59th Street/Lexington Avenue (6) 🚌 M15, M57, M98, M101, M102, M103

DB BISTRO MODERNE
www.danielnyc.com
This most casual and contemporary of Daniel Boulud's restaurants is a great Theater District choice. It's famous for its $32 sirloin burger—a fistful of ground sirloin wrapped around red wine-braised short ribs with truffle and foie gras, served with tomato confit and fresh horseradish. Other delights include roast salmon with honeyed eggplant (aubergine) and stuffed zucchini (courgette) flowers, and Muscovy duck breast with blood orange jus.
➕ 197 D9 ✉ 55 West 44th Street, between Fifth and Sixth avenues ☎ 212/391-2400 🕐 Mon–Fri 7–10, 12–2.30, Mon 5–10, Tue 5–11, Wed–Thu 5.15–11, Fri 5–11.30, Sat 8–11, 12–2.30, 5–11.30, Sun 8–11, 5–10 ✋ L $45, D $65, Wine $25 🚇 42nd Street/Grand Central (S, 4, 5, 6, 7), 42nd Street (B, D, F, V) 🚌 M1, M2, M3, M4, M42

ESCA
www.esca-nyc.com
Esca, another star in Mario Batali's firmament, prepares fish southern Italian style. The menu changes daily, but you might find Mediterranean sea bass in sea salt or Amalfi-style fritto misto, with crispy scrod, skate, calamari, steamers, oysters and shrimp. Appetizers run to crispy Neapolitan-style eel and juicy morsels from a serious raw bar.
➕ 196 C9 ✉ 402 West 43rd Street at Ninth Avenue ☎ 212/564-7272 🕐 Mon–Sat 12–2.30, Mon 5–10.30, Tue–Sat 5–11.30, Sun 4.30–10.30 ✋ L $40, D $70, Wine $35 🚇 42nd Street (A, C, E) 🚌 M11

FELIDIA
www.lidiasitaly.com
Felidia is a top Italian restaurant. The Istrian wedding pillows, stuffed with rum, raisins and three cheeses, are a signature dish, but chef Fortunato Nicotra has added regional dishes, such as roasted goose ravioli.
➕ 197 E7 ✉ 243 East 58th Street between Second and Third avenues ☎ 212/758-1479 🕐 Mon–Thu 12–2.30, 5–11, Fri 12–2, 5–11.30, Sat 5–11.30 ✋ L $50, 3-course prix fixe $29.50, D $75,

Wine $44 🚇 59th Street (4, 5, 6) 🚌 M15, M57, M98, M101, M102, M103

FOUR SEASONS
www.fourseasonsrestaurant.com
This modernist power restaurant was designed by Philip Johnson and Mies van der Rohe. When it opened in 1959, it helped launch the city's food revolution. The square bar at the center of the Grill Room is a great cocktail spot. The pièce de résistance is the Pool Room, with a large fountain as centerpiece. Chef Christian Albin's signature dish is roast duck, which is carved tableside. The soufflés are famous.
✚ 197 E8 ✉ 99 East 52nd Street, between Park and Lexington avenues ☎ 212/754-9494 🕐 Mon–Fri 12–2.15, 5–9.30, Sat 5–11 🖐 L $70, D $100, Wine $45 🚇 51st Street (6), Fifth Avenue/53rd Street (E, V) 🚌 M50, M98, M101, M102, M103

GORDON RAMSAY AT THE LONDON
www.gordonramsay.com
In 2007 Ramsay won two Michelin stars. You'll need to book two months ahead—exactly two months ahead, as tables go as soon as they're available, with diners longing to try Ramsay's supreme ability to combine flavors and let every single one shine through in dishes like his baked fluke with almond bread, celery hearts, Concord grapes and champagne velouté.
✚ 196 C8 ✉ The London NYC Hotel, 151 West 54th Street between 6th and 7th avenues ☎ 212/468-8888 🕐 Daily 12–2.30, 5.30–11 🖐 L 3-course prix fixe $50, D $110, 7-course menu prestige $150, Wine $43 🚇 7th Avenue (B, D, E), 57th Street (N, Q, R, W) 🚌 M6, M7

GRAND CENTRAL OYSTER BAR
www.oysterbarny.com
You don't have to love oysters to love this legendary room in the lower level of Grand Central. Since it opened in 1913 it has starred in many a movie. Today, it's jammed at lunch and busy in the early evening with people sampling the fresh fish choices, or slurping down oysters, all flown in daily from around the world. Choose from some 30 varieties of fresh oysters: East Coast, West Coast, Kumamoto, Wellfleet and many more. Or try the steamed mussels, lobsters, broiled scallops, grouper, sole, trout, bass or even fish and chips. You might like the renowned chowder-like panroasts. The extensive wine list includes more than 50 varieties by the glass, and there is also a large beer list.
✚ 197 D9 ✉ Grand Central Terminal, 42nd Street and Park Avenue ☎ 212/490-6650 🕐 Mon–Fri 11.30–9.30, Sat 12–9.30 🖐 L $35, D $45, Wine $26 🚇 42nd Street/Grand Central (4, 5, 6) 🚌 M1, M2, M3

HELL'S KITCHEN
www.hellskitchen-nyc.com
Here, a contemporary interpretation of Mexican cuisine uses prime American ingredients. Start with calamari in smoked chipotle broth, or chayote and portobello mushroom roll with chipotle pepper sauce. The strong exotic drinks from the bar match the robust flavors.
✚ 196 C9 ✉ 679 Ninth Avenue, between West 46th and 47th streets ☎ 212/977-1588 🕐 Tue–Fri 11.30–3, Sun–Wed 5–11, Thu–Sat 5–midnight 🖐 L $22, D $45, Wine $24 🚇 42nd Street (A, C, E) 🚌 M11

MOLYVOS
www.molyvos.com
This large space with a café, a bar and two dining rooms, brings Greece to Manhattan. The dips and spreads are irresistible, including the garlicky roasted eggplant (aubergine) purée and the tzatziki, a blend of yogurt, cucumber, garlic, mint, dill and lemon. Outstanding are the cold meze such as grilled baby octopus with olives, fennel, lemon and oregano, and fava beans mashed with olive oil. Marinated lamb shanks, whole grilled fish and rabbit stew are traditional main courses.
✚ 196 C8 ✉ 871 Seventh Avenue, between West 55th and 56th streets ☎ 212/582-7500 🕐 Mon–Fri 12–3, 5.30–11.30, Sat 12–3, 5–12, Sun 12–11 🖐 L $38, D $60, Wine $32 🚇 Seventh Avenue (B, D, E), 57th Street (N, R, Q, W) 🚌 M10, M20

NAPLES 45
www.patinagroup.com
Authentic Neapolitan pizzas emerge piping hot from the wood-fired ovens, as do the fish of the day. The menu showcases southern Italian cooking with a good range of fish, chicken and steak dishes—and vegetarians won't leave unsatisfied, either. The *piccoli piatti,* or small plates, are popular appetizers, especially the steamed mussels and veal meatballs.
✚ 197 D9 ✉ Met Life Building, 200 Park Avenue at East 45th Street (entrance on 45th) ☎ 212/972-7000 🕐 Mon–Fri 7.30am–10pm 🖐 L $30, D $40, Wine $22 🚇 Grand Central-42nd Street (4, 5, 6, 7, S) 🚌 M1, M2, M3, M4, M101, M102, M103, M98

PAMPANO
www.modernmexican.com
Placido Domingo helped open this restaurant where chef Richard Sandoval, who hails from Mexico City, via California, produces great contemporary Mexican using such ingredients as *huitlacoche, epazote,* pomegranate, *queso blanco* and every conceivable kind of pepper. The *chile rellenos* are roasted not fried and stuffed with seafood and tart manchego. Start with any one of the ceviches and continue with a seafood dish. Meat lovers are out of luck although the lamb in adobo orange sauce is tasty. The outdoor terrace is as close to the beach as you can get in midtown Manhattan.
✚ 197 E8 ✉ 209 East 49th Street, between 2nd and 3rd avenues ☎ 212/751-4545 🕐 Mon–Fri 11.30–2.30, Mon–Wed 5–10, Thu–Sat 5–10.30, Sun 5–9.30 🖐 L $30, D $60, Wine $32 🚇 51st Street (6) 🚌 M15, M27, M50, M101, M102, M103

PAM REAL THAI
At this authentic Thai, none of the sweet, sour and salt dishes have been compromised to suit a more timid palate. The traditional favorites are all available: superb hot and milder curries, fiery salads made with green papaya, ground pork with lime dressing, noodle dishes and, best of all, duck with chili sauce and

lime leaves. Bring your own bottle. Credit cards are not accepted.
✚ 196 B8 ✉ 404 West 49th Street, between Ninth and Tenth avenues ☎ 212/333-7500 🕐 Sun–Thu 11.30–11, Fri–Sat 11.30–11.30 🍴 L $16, D $24 🚇 50th Street (C, E, 1, 9) 🚌 M11, M50

SHUN LEE PALACE
www.shunleepalace.com
It's still the best Chinese restaurant in the city, even though it's been around since 1972. It may be expensive, but the dining rooms are comfortable and elegant and the Shanghai, Szechuan and Cantonese cuisine is beautifully presented. Besides such traditional dishes as crispy sea bass Hunan style and lobster in black bean sauce, you will find such extraordinary specialties as Grand Marnier prawns and red cooked short ribs Hang Chow style. There's a branch near the Lincoln Center at 43 West 65th Street between Central Park West and Columbus Avenue (tel 212/595-8895)—a good bet for a leisurely meal or a pre-concert snack.
✚ 197 E8 ✉ 155 East 55th Street, between Lexington and Third avenues ☎ 212/371-8844 🕐 Mon–Sat noon–11.30, Sun noon–11 🍴 L $40, D $56, Wine $40 🚇 Lexington Avenue/53rd Street (E, V), 51st Street (6) 🚌 M57, M98, M101, M102, M103

SUGIYAMA
www.sugiyama-nyc.com
Here, the seasons inform chef Nao Sugiyama's Kaiseki cuisine. You have a choice of various 5-, 6-, or 8-course dinners and post- or pre-theater. Each includes an appetizer, sashimi, soup, a sizzling dish on hot stone and dessert. The sashimi is exceptionally fresh, featuring uni (sea urchin), octopus, tuna, red snapper and more. The excellently prepared dishes are attractively presented, and offer a variety of flavors and textures, with soup, appetizers, vegetable creations and main dishes of seafood or meat. There is an extensive selection of sake, available by the glass and by the bottle.

✚ 196 C8 ✉ 251 West 55th Street, between Broadway and Eighth Avenue ☎ 212/956-0670 🕐 Tue–Sat 5.30–11.45 🍴 D $58–$192, $32 pre-theater, Wine $28 🚇 59th Street/Columbus Circle (A, B, C, D, 1)

SUSHI YASUDA
www.sushiyasuda.com
Here owner Naomichi Yasuda displays his artistry, selecting the best fish, evaluating its texture, masterfully cutting it to release the best flavor, and cooking and seasoning the rice to perfection. Then he crafts a meal for the individuals who sit down at his sushi bar, according to their tastes and experience, and to the size of their mouths. It's custom-made perfection, but naturally it comes at a high price. For a delightful meal request one of his eight tuna specialties or one of the eel pieces for which he is renowned.
✚ 197 E9 ✉ 204 East 43rd Street, between Second and Third avenues ☎ 212/972-1001 🕐 Mon–Fri 12–2.15, 6–10.15, Sat 6–10.15, closed Sun 🍴 L $80, D $100, Wine $18 (sake) 🚇 42nd Street/Grand Central (S, 4, 5, 6, 7)

TOWN
www.townnyc.com
Strands of crystal beads suspended in the two-story loft space in this stylish subterranean dining room swathed in suede and blond wood sparkle magically. Chef Geoffrey Zakarian's fusion cuisine sparkles, too. Start with the fragrant octopus fricassée in lemongrass broth, or the lobster bisque, zapped with ginger, coconut and wood sorrel. Zakarian poaches or roasts his fish to retain moisture, glazing swordfish with mushroom tapenade and serving with smoked tomato and marjoram coulis, for instance; the venison is simply slow-roasted to exquisite tenderness. Desserts are fabulous show-stoppers.
✚ 197 D8 ✉ Chambers Hotel 15 West 56th Street, between Fifth and Sixth avenues ☎ 212/582-4445 🕐 Mon–Sat 7–10.30am, 12–2.30, 5.30–10.30, Sun 7–10.30, 11–2.30, 5.30–10.30 🍴 L $40, D 5-course prix fixe

$85, Wine $36 🚇 53rd Street/Fifth Avenue (E, V) 🚌 M1, M2, M3, M4, M57

UNCLE VANYA CAFÉ
Russian home cooking starts at this plain storefront restaurant: hearty borscht, beef dumplings with sour cream, stuffed cabbage rolls and beef Stroganoff with kasha. It's all good and filling and costs very little. Try one of the Georgian wines, if you dare.
✚ 196 C8 ✉ 315 West 54th Street, between Eighth and Ninth avenues ☎ 212/262-0542 🕐 Mon–Sat noon–11, Sun 2–11 🍴 L $20, D $25, Wine $25 🚇 50th Street (C, E) 🚌 M10, M11, M20

VIRGIL'S REAL BARBECUE
www.virgilsbbq.com
The aroma of hickory wood smoke alone is enough to draw you into Virgil's vast barbecue emporium. Here, the enormous platters of Memphis-style barbecue or fried chicken arrive with grits or mashed potatoes and biscuits and gravy. Po'boys, also known as hero sandwiches, round out the Southern-style menu.
✚ 196 C9 ✉ 152 West 44th Street between Sixth Avenue and Broadway ☎ 212/921-9494 🕐 Sun–Mon 11–11, Tue–Fri 11.30am–midnight, Sat 11am–midnight 🍴 L $26, D $36 🚇 42nd Street/Times Square (N, Q, R, S, W, 1, 2, 3, 7), 42nd Street (B, D, F, V) 🚌 M5, M6, M7

ZARELA
www.zarela.com
Don't be fooled by the festive ambience of this restaurant, for it offers some of the most authentic regional Mexican cuisine in the city. Whether or not you are looking for northern fajitas and flautas, or Oaxacan moles and coastal Veracruz-style dishes, you will find it here along with some rare seasonal specialties.
✚ 196 E8 ✉ 953 Second Avenue, between 50th and 51st streets ☎ 212/644-6740 🕐 Mon–Fri noon–3, Mon–Thu 5–11, Fri–Sat 5–11.30, Sun 5–10 🍴 L $23, prix fixe $29.95, D $40, prix fixe $42, Wine $21 🚇 Lexington/53rd Street (E, V), 51st Street (6) 🚌 M15

PRICES AND SYMBOLS

Prices are the lowest and highest for a double room for one night. Breakfast is included unless noted otherwise. All the hotels listed accept credit cards unless otherwise stated. Note that rates vary widely throughout the year.

For a key to the symbols, ▷ 2.

70 PARK AVENUE

www.70parkave.com

In quiet Murray Hill, Kimpton's first property in New York City has been designed in contemporary style, but with comfort in mind, even though the rooms are on the small side. Guest rooms are decorated in a gracious style, with at-home comfort. Deep soaking tubs invite tranquil repose in the well-appointed bathrooms. Yoga mats and a 24-hour yoga channel are also available. Technical equipment includes 42-inch flat panel TVs, DVD/CD players, and wireless and wired high-speed internet access. Pets are welcome. The Silverleaf Tavern offers contemporary American fare.

➕ 197 D10 ✉ 70 Park Avenue at 38th Street, 10016 ☎ 212/973-2400 ✋ Doubles from $325, suites from $1,000 ⓘ 205 rooms and suites ⓠ Grand Central/42nd Street (4, 5, 6, 7) 🚌 M1, M2, M3, M4, M42

ALGONQUIN

www.algonquinhotel.com

It's famous for being the place where in the 1920s Robert Benchley, Dorothy Parker and the rest of the *Vanity Fair/New Yorker* crowd gathered regularly for lunch at the Round Table. The rooms are moderate in size and furnished with reproductions of American antiques. The wood-paneled Oak Room (▷ 182) is the city's best cabaret.

➕ 196 C9 ✉ 59 West 44th Street, between Fifth and Sixth avenues, 10036 ☎ 212/840-6800 ✋ $300–$499, suite from $349 ⓘ 150 rooms, 24 suites 🍴 ⓠ 42nd Street (B, D, F, V) 🚌 M5, M7, M42

AMERICANA INN

www.theamericanainn.com

Rooms here are bright, modern and comfortable, if plainly decorated. They are equipped with cable TV and telephone. All rooms share a bath, and each floor has a kitchenette.

➕ 197 D9 ✉ 69 West 38th Street, between Fifth and Sixth avenues, 10018 ☎ 212/840-6700 ✋ $110–$150 ⓘ 54 ⓠ 42nd Street (B, D, F, V) 🚌 M5, M6, M7

AVALON

www.theavalonny.com

This small hotel is near the Empire State Building and has traditionally furnished rooms. Executive suites have fax, Bose radio and cordless phone. Complimentary breakfast and morning newspaper are set out in the mahogany-paneled library off the lobby.

➕ 197 D10 ✉ 16 East 32nd Street at Madison Avenue, 10016 ☎ 212/299-7000 ✋ Double from $269, suite from $315 ⓘ 70 rooms, 30 suites ⓠ 33rd Street (6) 🚌 M1, M2, M3, M4, M34

BEEKMAN TOWER

www.thebeekmanhotel.com

This all-suite hotel, in a 1928 art deco building near the UN, has accommodations that include bedroom, sitting room and fully equipped kitchen. The deluxe suites have such extras as VCRs and two-line phones. The bar/ restaurant on the top floor is one of the most romantic aeries in the city. There is a fitness center on-premises.

➕ 197 E8 ✉ 3 Mitchell Place (East 49th Street and First Avenue), 10017 ☎ 212/355-7300 ✋ From $220, 2-bedroom suite from $350 ⓘ 174 suites 🍴 ⓠ 51st Street (6) 🚌 M15

Opposite *The Peninsula hotel occupies a fine Beaux Arts building on Fifth Avenue*

BELVEDERE
www.belvederehotelnyc.com
The most expensive hotel in the Empire Hotel group, the Belvedere has handsome sizable rooms with kitchenettes fitted with microwave, refrigerator and coffeemaker. Executive rooms are also available. On the premises is the Churrascaria Plataforma, a Brazilian steakhouse.
✚ 196 C8 ✉ 319 West 48th Street, between Eighth and Ninth avenues, 10036 ☎ 212/245-7000 ✋ $264–$369 ⓘ 335 rooms and suites ⓠ 50th Street (C, E) ⓔ M11, M20, M50

BENJAMIN
www.thebenjamin.com
Conveniently situated in Midtown, this Manhattan Suites hotel offers good-looking rooms and excellent facilities in a handsome 1927 building. The rooms are furnished with mahogany pieces. Guests can select from a ten-type pillow menu. The Affinia Spa and Wellness Center is a bonus. There is a restaurant and bar.
✚ 197 E8 ✉ 125 East 50th Street at Lexington Avenue, 10022 ☎ 212/715-2500 ✋ Doubles from $459, suites from $559 ⓘ 209 ⓠ 51st Street (6) ⓔ M50, M98, M101, M102, M103

BLAKELY
www.blakelyny.com
The rooms are handsome with a traditional English flavor conveyed in foxhunt prints and cherry furnishings. Amenities include full kitchenettes with microwave and mini-fridge plus the latest in tech—flat-screen TVs, DVD/CD players, cordless phones and complimentary WiFi. Comforts run to Frette bathrobes and Penhaligon toiletries. There is a restaurant-bar and fitness center.
✚ 196 C8 ✉ 136 West 55th Street, between Sixth and Seventh avenues, 10019 ☎ 212/245-1800 ✋ $260–$365, suite from $585 ⓘ 58 rooms, 55 suites ⓥ ⓠ 57th Street (N, Q, R, W), 57th Street (F) ⓔ M5, M6, M7, M57

CASABLANCA
www.casablancahotel.com
Close to the Theater District, the boutique-style Casablanca is small and personal and offers stylish, modern, well-equipped guest rooms. The public areas have a distinctly Moroccan feel complete with tiles and rattan chairs.
✚ 196 C9 ✉ 147 West 43rd Street, between Sixth and Seventh avenues, 10036 ☎ 212/869-1212 ✋ Doubles from $299, suites from £399 ⓘ 40 rooms, 8 suites ⓠ 42nd Street/Times Square (N, Q, R, S, W, 1, 2, 3, 7, 9), 42nd Street (B, D, F, V) ⓔ M6, M7, M10, M20

DREAM HOTEL
www.dreamny.com
From the minute you enter the stylish lobby you know that this hotel is all about design. Sculptures, dramatic lighting and modern styling dominate the lobby. The rooms are dramatically furnished with blue satin headboards and lit blue too. Bathrooms are hip-minimalist. The rooms have the latest tech amenities—plasma TV, iPod with Bose speakers. Lounges are found in the lobby, on the rooftop and underground. Plus Deepak Chopra has located an Ayurvedic center in this hotel.
✚ 196 C8 ✉ 210 West 55th Street, between Broadway and Seventh Avenue, 10019 ☎ 212/247-2000 ✋ Doubles from $259, suite from $519 ⓘ 204 rooms and 16 suites ⓠ 7th Avenue (B, D, E), 57th Street/7th Avenue (N, Q, R, W) ⓔ M10, M20

EDISON
www.edisonhotelnyc.com
Theater patrons appreciate this art deco 1931 hotel in the center of the Theater District. The entrance lobby is somewhat bland, but it is functional. The rooms are moderately priced and have cable TV and telephone. There is a restaurant and bar too.
✚ 196 C9 ✉ 228 West 47th Street, between Broadway and Eighth Avenue, 10036 ☎ 212/840-5000. ✋ Doubles from $195, suites from $255 ⓘ 900 rooms and suites ⓠ 50th Street (C, E), 50th Street (1) ⓔ M6, M7, M20, M27, M104

ELYSÉE
www.elyseehotel.com
This little gem of a hotel, built in 1926, has comfortable rooms decorated with fine French antique reproductions and luxurious fabrics. Bathrooms are marble and brass. The Monkey Bar, named for its murals, was once home to such regulars as actress Tallulah Bankhead. Guests have use of a nearby sports club.
✚ 197 D8 ✉ 60 East 54th Street, 10022 ☎ 212/753-1066 ✋ Doubles from $320, suites from $450, including Continental breakfast and wine and cheese (weekday evenings) ⓘ 86 rooms, 15 suites ⓠ 53rd Street/Fifth Avenue (E, V), 51st Street (6)

FOUR SEASONS
www.fourseasons.com
The service at this hotel is legendary; staff are trained to cater to a guest's every whim. I. M. Pei designed the 53-story building, which opened in 1993. The rooms, averaging 600sq feet (55sq m), are the largest in the city and include a dressing area. The suites have walk-in closets and balconies with grand city views. The large fitness center contains a full spa, and the restaurant and bar are both top-of-the-line.
✚ 197 D7 ✉ 57 East 57th Street, between Madison and Park avenues, 10022 ☎ 212/758-5700 ✋ From $725, suite from $1,550 ⓘ 305 rooms, 63 suites ⓠ 59th Street (4, 5, 6) ⓔ M1, M2, M3, M4

GRAND UNION
www.hotelgrandunion.com
This old-fashioned hotel in the trend-setting Flatiron neighborhood has clean basic rooms that are equipped with small refrigerators and phones with data ports. Coffee shop.
✚ 197 D10 ✉ 34 East 32nd Street, between Madison and Park avenues, 10016 ☎ 212/683-5890 ✋ $175–$375 ⓘ 95 ⓠ 33rd Street (6) ⓔ M1, M2, M3, M34

HOTEL CHANDLER
www.hotelchandler.com
This 14-floor boutique hotel in the Murray Hill neighborhood occupies a 1903 Beaux Arts building, which

has been carefully renovated and decorated in retro style. Rooms are small but chic, with CD and DVD, free high-speed internet, personal phone number and flat-screen TV. The 12:31 bar attracts a hip after-work crowd. There is a fitness room with sauna.

✚ 197 D10 ✉ 12 East 31st Street, between Fifth and Madison avenues, 10016 ☎ 212/889-6363 ✋ $345–$510, suite from $595 ⬆ 120 rooms, 8 suites Ⓜ 33rd Street (6) 🚌 M2, M3, M5

HOTEL ROGER WILLIAMS
www.rogerwilliamshotel.com
In 1997 Unique Hotels Group renovated this fine old hotel (1928). The good-sized rooms have been decorated in bright, bold colors. Stylish and spacious with modern furnishings, the rooms are stimulating and relaxing. Amenities include flat-screen plasma TV, ergonomic desk chair and high-speed internet. Bathrooms have hairdryers, Frette robes and Aveda toiletries. Cappuccino and espresso are available 24 hours. There's also a fitness studio.

✚ 197 D10 ✉ 131 Madison Avenue at 31st Street, 10016 ☎ 212/448-7000 ✋ $345–$615, suite from $500 ⬆ 183 rooms, 2 suites 🍽 Ⓜ 33rd Street (6) 🚌 M1, M2, M3

HUDSON
www.hudsonhotel.com
The Hudson is Ian Schrager's and Philippe Starck's latest "hotel as on-going party". Guests arrive in the ivy-draped lobby via escalators encased in a chartreuse-green tube. Starck trademarks include oversized chairs and other objects like the 500-gallon (1,890-litre) watering can in the garden courtyard. The rooms are small and furnished with minimalist stainless-steel pieces, plus the latest technical amenities. The Library lounge has plenty of leather, a hearth and a dramatically lit antique billiard table. A long gilded table serves as a bar in the lounge, which converts into a dance club at night. The landscaped roof terrace is a bonus.

✚ 196 C7 ✉ 356 West 58th Street, between Eighth and Ninth avenues, 10019 ☎ 212/554-6000 ✋ Doubles from $259, suites from $389 ⬆ 1,000 rooms, 11 suites Ⓜ 59th Street/Columbus Circle (A, B, C, D, 1) 🚌 M1, M20, M57

KIMBERLY
www.kimberlyhotel.com
This small personal hotel in Midtown has a European flavor. Originally built in 1985 as an apartment house, it has large rooms with fully equipped kitchens. Some rooms have balconies; they all have three dual-line phones and high-speed internet access. Guests also have membership at the New York Health and Racquet Clubs.

✚ 197 E8 ✉ 145 East 50th Street, between Third and Lexington avenues, 10022 ☎ 212/702-1600 ✋ Doubles from $359, suites from $479 ⬆ 26 rooms, 158 suites Ⓜ 51st Street (6) 🚌 M50, M98, M101, M102, M103

LIBRARY
www.libraryhotel.com
It's not just the design concept that book lovers appreciate at this boutique property, it's also the service. Each floor of the hotel is dedicated to a subject category from the Dewey Decimal system and each room has a collection of art and books related to a sub-category. The decor is modern and minimalist. Amenities include multi-line phones and free WiFi. Refreshments are served in the second-floor, book-lined Reading Room. There's also an American Bistro and Wine Bar and complimentary passes to a nearby fitness center.

✚ 197 D9 ✉ 299 Madison Avenue at 41st Street, 10017 ☎ 212/983-4500 ✋ $345–$435, suite from $525, including breakfast and afternoon wine and cheese ⬆ 52 rooms, 8 suites Ⓜ Grand Central/42nd Street (S, 4, 5, 6, 7) 🚌 M1, M2, M3, M4, M42

MANSFIELD
www.mansfieldhotel.com
Occupying a 1904 Beaux Arts building with many original features, this hotel is convenient for the theater and Midtown shopping. The elegantly furnished rooms have sleigh beds with steel mesh headboards, metal and fabric armoires, plus free WiFi. There is a nearby health club.

✚ 197 D9 ✉ 12 West 44th Street, between Fifth and Sixth avenues, 10036 ☎ 212/277-8700 ✋ Doubles from $319, suites from $419 ⬆ 100 rooms, 24 suites Ⓜ 42nd Street (B, D, F, V) 🚌 M1, M2, M3, M4, M5, M42

METRO
www.hotelmetronyc.com
This has to be one of the best-value hotels in the city. It has a good Midtown location and plenty of art deco style. The rooms are classic, with earth-toned decor, nightstands and chairs, and are equipped with cable TV, and phone with data port. The marble bathrooms have hairdryers. Guests can relax in the library, which actually has books, or on the rooftop garden terrace. The sleek Metro Grill provides room service.

✚ 197 D10 ✉ 45 West 35th Street, between Fifth and Sixth avenues, 10001 ☎ 212/947-2500 ✋ $295–$450, suite from $375 ⬆ 179 rooms and suites Ⓜ 34th Street (B, D, F, N, Q, R, V, W) 🚌 M2, M3, M5, M6, M7

THE MICHELANGELO
www.michelangelohotel.com
The boutique Michelangelo hotel is in Midtown Manhattan, a block west of Radio City Music Hall and convenient for Broadway's theater district. It's the only US property of an Italian hotel chain, and the Italian influences are everywhere: the friendliness of the staff, the Italian marble in the reception and in guest bathrooms, and in the Limoncello restaurant. All the rooms are very spacious by New York standards and feature high-speed internet, CD players, voice mail and large whirlpool bathtubs.

✚ 196 C8 ✉ 152 West 51st Street, between 6th and 7th avenues, 10019 ☎ 212/765-0505 ✋ $495, suites from $695 ⬆ 178 rooms and suites Ⓜ 49th Street (N, R) 🚌 M1, M2

MODERNE

www.nychotels.com

This small retro-style hotel in a fine location near Carnegie Hall is reliable. The rooms are sleekly decorated (padded high back bed, built-in nightstands, op art) and equipped with the latest gadgetry—VCR, CD player and telephone with data port—plus hairdryer and an extra phone in the bathroom.

✚ 196 C8 ✉ 243 West 55th Street, between Broadway and Eighth Avenue, 10019 ☎ 212/397-6767 ✋ Doubles from $225 ⓘ 37 ⓟ Seventh Avenue (B, D, E), 59th Street/Columbus Circle (A, B, C, D, 1) 🚌 M10, M20, M104

MORGANS

www.morganshotel.com

In 1984 Ian Schrager opened this hotel, his first in New York City. The 2008 renovation created a smart, chic boutique hotel with an emphasis on clean lines and decor in white, gray and black tones. Lighting elements add an artistic flair throughout. Sophisticated and understated, the guest rooms are elegant, modern and comfortable. Crafted furnishings include stylish lighting, inlaid Corian table and wood-upholstered chair with fine linen bedding and down comforter. Bathrooms have whirlpool tubs

and stainless-steel fixtures, striking granite floors and eye-catching black and white tiles. The rooms also have the latest amenities. The dramatic cellar bar and the restaurant Asia de Cuba attract a fashion-conscious crowd. Residents have complimentary access to a nearby fitness club.

✚ 197 D10 ✉ 237 Madison Avenue, between East 37th and 38th streets, 10016 ☎ 212/686-0300 ✋ Doubles from $329, suites from $489 ⓘ 113 rooms and suites ⓟ 33rd Street (6), 42nd Street/Grand Central (S, 4, 5, 6, 7) 🚌 M1, M2, M3, M4, M42, M34

THE MUSE

www.themusehotel.com

Close to the Broadway theater district, the Muse pays homage to New York's performing arts with specially commissioned artworks in rooms and public areas. It's close by the Rockefeller Center too. The rooms and bathrooms are spacious and smartly decorated in contemporary style, with such amenities as in-room spa treatments, on-demand movies, high-speed internet. Some rooms have balconies with city views. The Muse has a complimentary 24-hour fitness center, daily paper delivery and evening wine receptions.

✚ 196 C9 ✉ 130 West 46th Street, between 6th and 7th avenues, 10036 ☎ 212/485-2400 ✋ $439, suites from $629 ⓘ 181 rooms, 19 suites ⓨ ⓟ 42nd Street (B, D, F, V) 🚌 M6, M7, M20, M27, M104

NEW YORK PALACE

www.newyorkpalace.com

Six landmark brownstones designed by McKim, Mead and White make up the core of this luxury hotel. Owner Sultan of Brunei has spent lavishly on the decor of the public areas and the guest rooms. Several gorgeous Louis Comfort Tiffany windows and alabaster sculptures by Saint-Gaudens grace the interiors. The accommodations are located in a 55-story tower. Business travelers appreciate the executive amenities: fax, three phones and spacious desk. The restaurant Istana serves elegant, creative takes on American classics for breakfast, lunch and dinner. A fitness center is available.

✚ 197 D8 ✉ 455 Madison Avenue, between 50th and 51st streets, 10022 ☎ 212/888-7000 ✋ $430–$680, suite from $1,000 ⓘ 813 rooms, 86 suites ⓟ 51st Street (6) 🚌 M1, M2, M3, M4, M50

LE PARKER MERIDIEN

www.parkermeridien.com

The rooms in this French hotel are furnished with sleek modernist pieces and contain the latest amenities—32-inch TV, ergonomic chairs, fax, DVD, CD player and free high-speed internet access. There are several places to eat. Hip bistro-style Seppi's serves Mediterranean fare, while Norma's luxury all-day breakfast is famous. Burger Joint serves one of the best burgers in town. There is an excellent 42nd-floor fitness center with a rooftop jogging track.

✚ 197 D8 ✉ 119 West 56th Street, between Sixth and Seventh avenues, 10019 ☎ 212/245-5000 ✋ $350–$800, suite from $780 ⓘ 600 rooms, 100 suites ⓨ ⓟ 57th Street (N, Q, R, W) 🚌 M6, M7, M57

Left *The New York Palace hotel*

PENINSULA

www.peninsula.com

This small hotel in a beautiful 23-story 1902 Beaux Arts building has a premier Fifth Avenue location. To complement the address, there are luxurious interiors and superb service. The rooms contain the latest amenities: fax, hands-free telephone, TV in the bathroom, free WiFi, free "Water Bar," and bedside electronic control of all the electrical systems. The furnishings are sumptuous and made even more so by the mood lighting. The Salon De Ning bar and terrace (▷ 183) is ideal for summertime trysts and Fives is an inviting bar/restaurant overlooking Fifth Avenue. A large, outstanding fitness center is also available for guests; there is an indoor pool, sundeck and spa.

✚ 197 D8 ✉ 700 Fifth Avenue at 55th Street, 10019 ☎ 212/956-2888 👜 $775–$1,125, suites from $1,275 ❶ 185 rooms, 54 suites ☲ Indoor 🔽 🚇 59th Street/Fifth Avenue (E, V) 🚌 M1, M2, M3, M4, M5

THE POD HOTEL

www.thepodhotel.com

If space is not a factor, then the new Pod Hotel (previously the Pickwick Arms) is New York's version of the increasing world trend for providing simple but small rooms for travelers on a budget or in a hurry. Designed like ships' cabins to maximize storage space, they still manage to provide bathrooms, safes, TVs, free WiFi and iPod docking stations. Some single rooms have shared bathrooms.

✚ 197 E8 ✉ 230 East 51st Street, between Second and Third avenues, 10022 ☎ 212/355-0300 👜 $169 twin bunk room, $269 double ❶ 348 🚇 51st Street (6) 🚌 M15, M50, M98, M101, M102, M103

RENAISSANCE NEW YORK HOTEL 57

www.hotel57.com

Little wonder that travelers love this place. It has a great location, and the contemporary rooms are clean, comfortable and attractively decorated after a makeover. All guest rooms have cable TV and telephone with data port.

✚ 197 E8 ✉ 130 East 57th Street at Lexington, 10022 ☎ 212/753-8841 👜 From $295, suites from $465 ❶ 205 rooms and suites 🚇 59th Street (4, 5, 6) 🚌 M59, M98, M101, M102, M103

ROYALTON

www.royaltonhotel.com

The first hotel conceived by Ian Schrager, the late Steve Rubell and Philippe Starck became an instant sensation and a magnet for the city's movers and shakers. The Royalton has a sexy, modern, sophisticated look. The lobby is decorated in wood, metal and glass, softened by suede-covered furnishings. Guest rooms are designed for comfort with luxurious bedding and either soaking tubs or slate and glass showers. Rooms have workspaces and flat-screen HD TVs. Bar 44 is a pleasant place for a drink. The fitness center is open 24 hours.

Above *The 1904 luxury St. Regis*

✚ 197 D9 ✉ 44 West 44th Street, between Fifth and Sixth avenues, 10036 ☎ 212/869-4400 🖐 Doubles from $289, suites from $499 ⓘ 165 rooms, 3 suites 🍽 🖥 42nd Street (B, D, F, V) 🚌 M1, M2, M3, M4

ST. REGIS

www.stregis.com

Colonel John Jacob Astor IV conceived this beautiful 1904 Beaux Arts-style hotel. The hallmarks of luxury, marble, gold leaf, tapestries and Louis XVI furniture, are joined by the latest in technical wizardry. The service—each floor has 24-hour butler service—is also extraordinary. Suites have CD player/stereo, flat-screen TV, MP3 player, and high-speed internet. The King Cole Bar is famous for the 1932 murals painted by Maxfield Parrish and for the creation of the first Bloody Mary in 1934 (originally called the "Red Snapper"). Tea in the Astor Court is one of the city's best. There is a spa.
✚ 197 D8 ✉ 2 East 55th Street at Fifth Avenue, 10022 ☎ 212/753-4500 🖐 $695–$995, suites from $1,200 ⓘ 182 rooms, 74 suites 🍽 🖥 Fifth Avenue/53rd Street (E, V) 🚌 M1, M2, M3, M4

SHOREHAM

www.shorehamhotel.com

This mid-size Midtown hotel, right behind the Museum of Modern Art, has been imaginatively updated and now boasts the latest looks and the most up-to-date technology and amenities in the rooms. Mesh headboards shimmer above the beds. The decor includes plenty of aluminum, plus entertainment musts such as plasma TVs and DVDs. Choice rooms are in the back. A restaurant and bar is available.
✚ 197 D8 ✉ 33 West 55th Street, between Fifth and Sixth avenues, 10019 ☎ 212/247-6700 🖐 Doubles from $359, suites from $569 ⓘ 143 rooms, 31 suites 🖥 53rd Street/Fifth Avenue (E, V) 🚌 M1, M2, M3, M4, M5, M6, M7

THIRTY THIRTY

www.thirtythirty-nyc.com

On the edge of the burgeoning Flatiron District in a refurbished 1902 building, this hotel is decent value. The rooms sport the latest minimal look, but they are small with European-style solutions—TVs suspended on walls and limited furnishings. They do have telephone with data port and hairdryer. Superior rooms have 27-inch TVs.
✚ 197 D10 ✉ 30 East 30th Street, between Madison and Park avenues, 10016 ☎ 212/689-1900 🖐 $249–$399 ⓘ 235 rooms and suites 🖥 33rd Street (6) 🚌 M1, M101, M103

TRAVEL INN

www.newyorkhotel.com

The benefits of this Manhattan hotel are the outdoor pool and the free parking. The rooms are simple but comfortable, with data port.
✚ 196 B9 ✉ 515 West 42nd Street, between Tenth and Eleventh avenues, 10036 ☎ 212/695-7171 🖐 $105–$400 ⓘ 160 🏊 Outdoor 🖥 42nd Street (A, C, E) 🚌 M42, M11

W NEW YORK – TIMES SQUARE

www.whotels.com

W is the hip Starwood Hotels chain. Here, as elsewhere in the group, the lobby is a living room space, where you can relax on ottomans or play board games. Natural elements are always evident, too: pots of grass, waterfalls, polished chunks of tree trunk as coffee tables and bouquets of grasses and seedpods, for example. Rooms are modern and equipped with Web TV, two-line phones, VCRs and CD players. Good food and beverage outlets polish the image—Rande Gerber's Whiskey Blue and Drew Nieporent's Heartbeat Restaurant. The spa and fitness center is a standout.
✚ 197 E8 ✉ 541 Lexington Avenue, between East 49th and 50th streets, 10022 ☎ 212/755-1200 🖐 $239–$550, suites from $1,000 ⓘ 647 rooms, 67 suites 🍽 🖥 51st Street (6) 🚌 M50, M101, M102, M103

WALDORF-ASTORIA HOTEL AND TOWERS

www.waldorfastoria.com

The Waldorf opened in 1931 to rave reviews. The largest hotel in the world at the time, it remains monumental—some would say overwhelming. The Towers, which occupy the 28th to 42nd floors, have a separate entrance and the most luxurious rooms. The clubby Bull and Bear is popular for steaks, while Peacock Alley is famous for its afternoon tea. Oscar's is a very chic coffeeshop and Inagiku is authentically Japanese. Large fitness center; excellent business center.
✚ 197 D8 ✉ 301 Park Avenue, between 49th and 50th streets, 10022 ☎ 212/355-3000 🖐 Waldorf $239–$629, suites from $549; Waldorf Towers $399–$799, suites from $599 ⓘ 1,049 rooms, 197 suites (Waldorf), 79 rooms, 101 suites (Towers) 🍽 🖥 51st Street (6) 🚌 M1, M2, M3, M4, M50

WARWICK

www.warwickhotelny.com

William Randolph Hearst built this hotel in 1927 as his East Coast hideaway. Many a movie celebrity settled into residence here, including Cary Grant. The large rooms have such rare amenities as walk-in closets and extra-large marble bathrooms, plus modern ones such as high-speed internet and two dual-line phones. Facilities include a restaurant, bar and fitness center.
✚ 197 D8 ✉ 65 West 54th Street at Sixth Avenue, 10019 ☎ 212/247-2700 🖐 $220–$500, suites from $485 ⓘ 359 rooms, 67 suites 🍽 🖥 57th Street (F) 🚌 M5, M6, M7, M57

WOLCOTT

www.wolcott.com

Close to the Empire State Building, this hotel has comfortable rooms decorated in an old-fashioned style (candy-stripe wallpaper, wing chair). The amenities you can expect in the rooms include cable TV, telephone with data port, hairdryer and air conditioning. There is a fitness room.
✚ 197 D10 ✉ 4 West 31st Street, between Fifth Avenue and Broadway, 10001 ☎ 212/268-2900 🖐 Doubles from $200, suites add $20 ⓘ 144 rooms, 23 suites 🖥 28th Street (N, R, W), 34th Street/Herald Square (B, D, F, N, Q, R, V, W) 🚌 M2, M3, M5, M6, M7

7

8

9

10

11

A

B

C

West 63rd Street
West 63rd Street

Lincoln Center

BROADWAY

Central Park West

West End Drive

West 62nd Street

West 62nd Street

Amsterdam Avenue

Museum of Biblical Art

West 61st Street

West 61st Street

Columbus Avenue

West 60th Street

West 59th Street

12th Av

59th Street Columbus Circle

COLUMBUS CIRCLE

Central

West 58th Street

WEST 57TH STREET

Hudson

57th Street

12th AVENUE

11th Avenue

10TH AVENUE

West 56th Street

BROADWAY

Carnegie Hall

9th Avenue

Moderne

Molyvos

7th Avenue

West 55th Street

Uncle Vanya Café

Sugiyama

Blake

De Witt Clinton Park

West 54th Street

8th Avenue

Dream Hotel

7th Avenue

Gordon Ramsay at the London

West 53rd Street

West 52nd Street

Le Bernardin

West 51st Street

West 50th Street

The Michaelangelo

50th Street

50th Street

49th Street

West 49th Street

Pam Real Thai

Belvedere

12th

West 48th Street

Blue Fin

West 47th Street

Edison

Hell's Kitchen

BROADWAY

The Muse

Hudson

West 46th Street

Intrepid Sea, Air and Space Museum

West 46th Street

9A

West 45th Street

10TH AVENUE

9th Avenue

Algonquin

11th Avenue

West 44th Street

8th Avenue

Virgil's Real Barbecue

West 43rd Street

Times Square

Casablan

Esca

WEST 42ND STREET

Holy Cross Church

Reuters Building

Times Squa 42nd Street

Travel Inn

West 41st Street

42nd Street Port Authority Bus Terminal

New Amsterdam Theater

BROADWAY

West 40th Street

West 39th Street

DYER AVENUE

FASHION AVENUE

HIGHWAY 495

West 38th Street

8TH AVENUE

Jacob K Javits Convention Center

West 37th Street

West 36th Street

West 35th Street

West 34th Street

West 33rd Street

34th Street Penn Station

34th Street Penn Station

0   250 m
0   250 yds

West 31st Street

Madison Square Garden

Pennsylvania Station

Mar

West 30th Street

10TH AVENUE

9TH AVENUE

8TH AVENUE

7TH AVENUE

West 29th Street

West 28th Street

28th Street

11th AVENUE

12TH AVENUE

Chelsea Park

West 27th Street

West 26th Street

196

Park Drive North

The Pond

East 63rd Street
East 62nd Street
East 61st Street
East 60th Street
Lexington Avenue 63rd Street

P York Avenue

PARK AVENUE

Lexington Avenue

East 63rd Street
East 62nd Street
East 61st St
East 60th Street

1st Avenue
2nd Avenue
3rd Avenue

5th Avenue

59th Street

South

HIGHWAY 25

East 59th Street

Felida

East 58th Street

Four Seasons

Le Colonial

Dawat

WEST 57TH STREET   EAST 57TH STREET

Le Parker Meridien

Trump Tower

Renaissance New York Hotel 57

East 57th Street

West 56th Street   East 56th

Shoreham   Town

Aquavit

Warwick   St Regis

West 55th Street

Peninsula

Shun Lee Palace

Lipstick Building

East 55th Street

East 54th Street

West 54th Street

Museum of Modern Art

Elysée

5th Avenue / 53rd Street

Lexington Avenue

East 53rd Street

West 53rd Street

Brasserie

'21' Club

West 52nd St

Four Seasons

Seagram Building

East 52nd Street

St Patrick's Cathedral

Municipal Art Society

The Pod Hotel

East 51st Street

West 51st Street

Radio City Music Hall

New York Palace

51st Street

Benjamin

Kimberly

Zarela

West 50th Street   East 50th Street

G.E. Building

MIDTOWN

W-New York

Pampano

Mitchell Place

West 49th Street   East 49th Street

Rockefeller Center

MANHATTAN

Waldorf Astoria Hotel & Towers

Beekman Tower

West 48th Street   East 48th Street

DIAMOND DISTRICT

West 47th Street   East 47th Street

West 46th Street   East 46th Street

West 45th Street   East 45th Street

Naples 45

United Nations Headquarters

DB Bistro Moderne

West 44th Street   East 44th Street

Royalton

International Center of Photography

Mansfield

Grand Central Oyster Bar

Sushi Yasuda

Madison Avenue

Vanderbilt Avenue

West 43rd Street   East 43rd Street

5th Avenue

42nd Street - Bryant Park

Grand Central Terminal

Grand Central 42nd Street

Chrysler Building

United Nations Plaza

WEST 42ND STREET   EAST 42ND STREET   EAST 42ND STREET

Bryant Park

New York Public Library

Library

Chanin Building

Daily News Building

City Place

495 QUEENS MIDTOWN TUNNEL

West 41st Street   East 41st Street

West 40th Street   East 40th Street

West 39th Street   East 39th Street

Americana Inn

West 38th Street   East 38th Street

Morgans

70 Park Avenue

West 37th Street   East 37th Street

Morgan Library

West 36th Street   East 36th Street

Gol

Metro

East 35th Street

West 35th Street

ho Dang

WEST 34TH STREET   EAST 34TH STREET   EAST 34TH STREET

Empire State Building

33rd Street

West 33rd Street   East 33rd Street

4th Street Herald Square

Grand Union

Artisanal

West 32nd Street   East 32nd Street

Avalon

Hotel Chandler

Hotel Roger Williams

West 31st Street   East 31st St

Wolcott

Thirty Thirty

West 30th Street   East 30th Street

Little Church Around the Corner

West 29th Street   East 29th Street

28th Street

West 28th St   East 28th Street

28th Street

West 27th Street   East 27th Street

Mt Carmel Place

East 27th Street

West 26th Street   East 26th Street

FRANKLIN DELANO ROOSEVELT DRIVE (FDR)

Sutton Place

FDR DRIVE SERVICE ROAD

East

Waterside

D   E   F

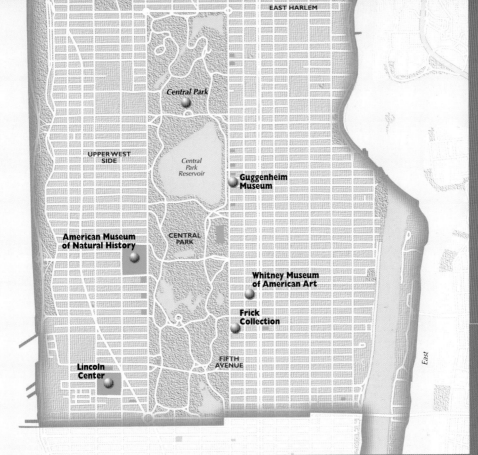

CENTRAL PARK AND AROUND

New York's Central Park, a magnificent 843-acre (341ha) oasis of green, was designed by Frederick Law Olmsted and Calvert Vaux in 1858. Wealthy New Yorkers soon moved north and settled along the east and west sides of Central Park. Today Central Park East is best known for Museum Mile, where many fabulous museums are located along Fifth Avenue, while Central Park West is home to the Lincoln Center, trendy clubs and restaurants.

A daytime stroll through Central Park is the perfect way to see the highlights, and to escape the noise, congestion and frantic pace characteristic of Manhattan. The park offers vast expanses of grass, lakes and ponds, paths through the wooded Ramble as well as Belevedere Castle, Bethesda Fountain and the Victorian Gothic Dairy Building which houses the visitor center.

Of the many museums in Central Park East, the Guggenheim Museum displays an exceptional collection of modern and contemporary art in Frank Lloyd Wright's stunning spiral-ramped building. The Whitney Museum of American Art presents the entire range of American modern and contemporary art, while the Frick Collection showcases the wealthy lifestyle and mansion of steel magnate Henry Clay Frick, as well as his opulent furnishings and fine art collection.

The Lincoln Center performing arts complex houses the Metropolitan Opera, New York Philharmonic and the Juilliard School of Music, and provides more than a dozen venues for a broad variety of theater, music and children's performances. Nearby, the American Museum of Natural History is one of the largest in the world, with more than 30 million artifacts and specimens. The Rose Center for Earth and Space with its planetarium, the Hall of the Universe and Big Bang Theater is one of the highlights here, closely followed by the dinosaur exhibits in the five-story Theodore Roosevelt Rotunda.

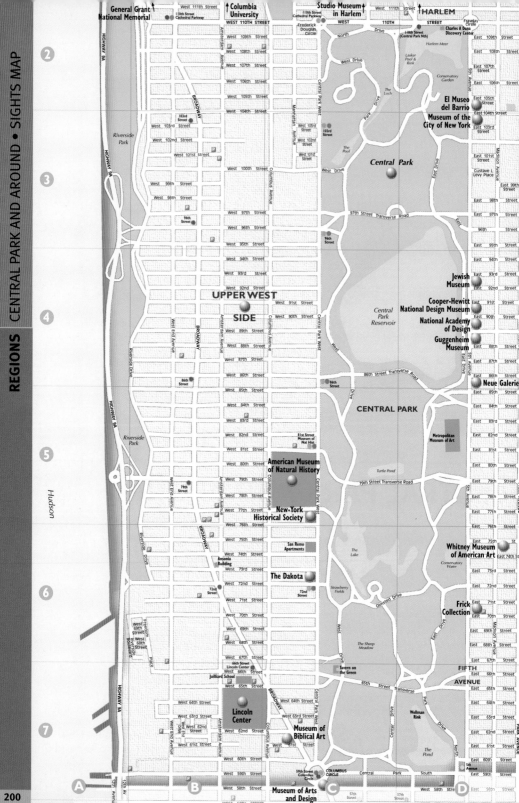

General Grant
National Memorial

110th Street
Cathedral Parkway

Columbia
University

WEST 110TH STREET

Studio Museum
in Harlem

WEST 111th Street

HARLEM

Fraway
Circle

West 109th Street

110th Street
Cathedral Parkway

Frederick
Douglass
Circle

110th
STREET

110th Street
(Central Park Nth)

Charles A Dana
Discovery Center

North

Drive

East 109th Street

West 108th Street

Amsterdam Avenue

West 107th Street

WEST

Lasker
Pool &
Rink

Harlem Meer

East 108th Street

West 106th Street

East 107th
Street

West 105th Street

Manhattan Avenue

Conservatory
Garden

East 106th Street

West 104th Street

El Museo
del Barrio

East 105th Street

East 104th Street

West 103rd
Street

103rd
Street

Museum of the
City of New York

East 103rd
Street

Riverside
Park

West 103rd Street

West 102nd Street

West 102nd
Street

The Pool

5th Avenue

East 101st
Street

West 101st Street

West 100th Street

Columbus Avenue

Central Park

West 99th Street

103rd
Street

Gustave L
Levy Place

East 98th Street

West 98th Street

Madison Avenue

West 97th Street

97th Street Transverse Road

East 97th Street

West 96th Street

96th
Street

96th
Street

East 96th Street

West 95th Street

East 95th Street

West 94th Street

East 94th Street

West 93rd Street

Jewish
Museum

East 93rd Street

West 92nd Street

East 92nd Street

UPPER WEST
SIDE

West 91st Street

Central
Park
Reservoir

Cooper-Hewitt
National Design Museum

East 91st Street

West 90th Street

Central Park West

National Academy
of Design

East 90th Street

West 89th Street

Broadway

Guggenheim
Museum

East 89th Street

West 88th Street

East 88th Street

West 87th Street

West

East 87th Street

86th
Street

86th Street transverse Road

Neue Galerie

East 86th Street

West 85th Street

86th
Street

East 85th Street

West 84th Street

CENTRAL PARK

East 84th Street

West 83rd Street

East 83rd Street

West 82nd Street

81st Street
Museum
of Nat Hist

Metropolitan
Museum of Art

East 82nd Street

West 81st Street

East 81st Street

West 80th Street

Turtle Pond

East 80th Street

79th
Street

American Museum
of Natural History

79th Street Transverse Road

East 79th Street

West 78th Street

East 78th Street

West 77th Street

New-York
Historical Society

East 77th Street

West 76th Street

East 76th Street

West 75th Street

San Remo
Apartments

The
Lake

Whitney Museum
of American Art

East 75th
Street

Ansonia
Building

West 74th Street

Conservatory
Water

East 74th St

West 73rd Street

The Dakota

East 73rd Street

Broadway

West 72nd Street

72nd
Street

72nd
Street

Strawberry
Fields

East 72nd Street

West 71st Street

Olmsted Drive

Frick
Collection

East 71st Street

West 70th Street

East 70th Street

Riverside Drive

West 69th Street

The Sheep
Meadow

East 69th Street

West 68th Street

East 68th Street

Freedom
Place

West 67th Street

West

East 67th Street

64th Street
Lincoln Center

West 66th Street

Tavern on
the Green

FIFTH

West 65th Street

65th

Street

Transverse

AVENUE

Juilliard School

West 64th Street

East 64th Street

Lincoln
Center

West 63rd Street

Broadway

West 63rd Street

Central Park West

East 63rd Street

Wollman
Rink

East 62nd Street

West 62nd Street

Columbus Avenue

East 61st Street

Museum of
Biblical Art

Drive

West 61st Street

The
Pond

East 60th Street

Highway 9A

West 60th Street

59th Street
Columbus
Circle

COLUMBUS
CIRCLE

Central

Park

South

5th
Avenue

East 59th Street

12th Avenue

West 59th Street

Museum of Arts
and Design

57th
Street

West 58th Stre

WEST 57TH STREET

EAST

Hudson

Riverside
Park

Highway 9A

12th Av

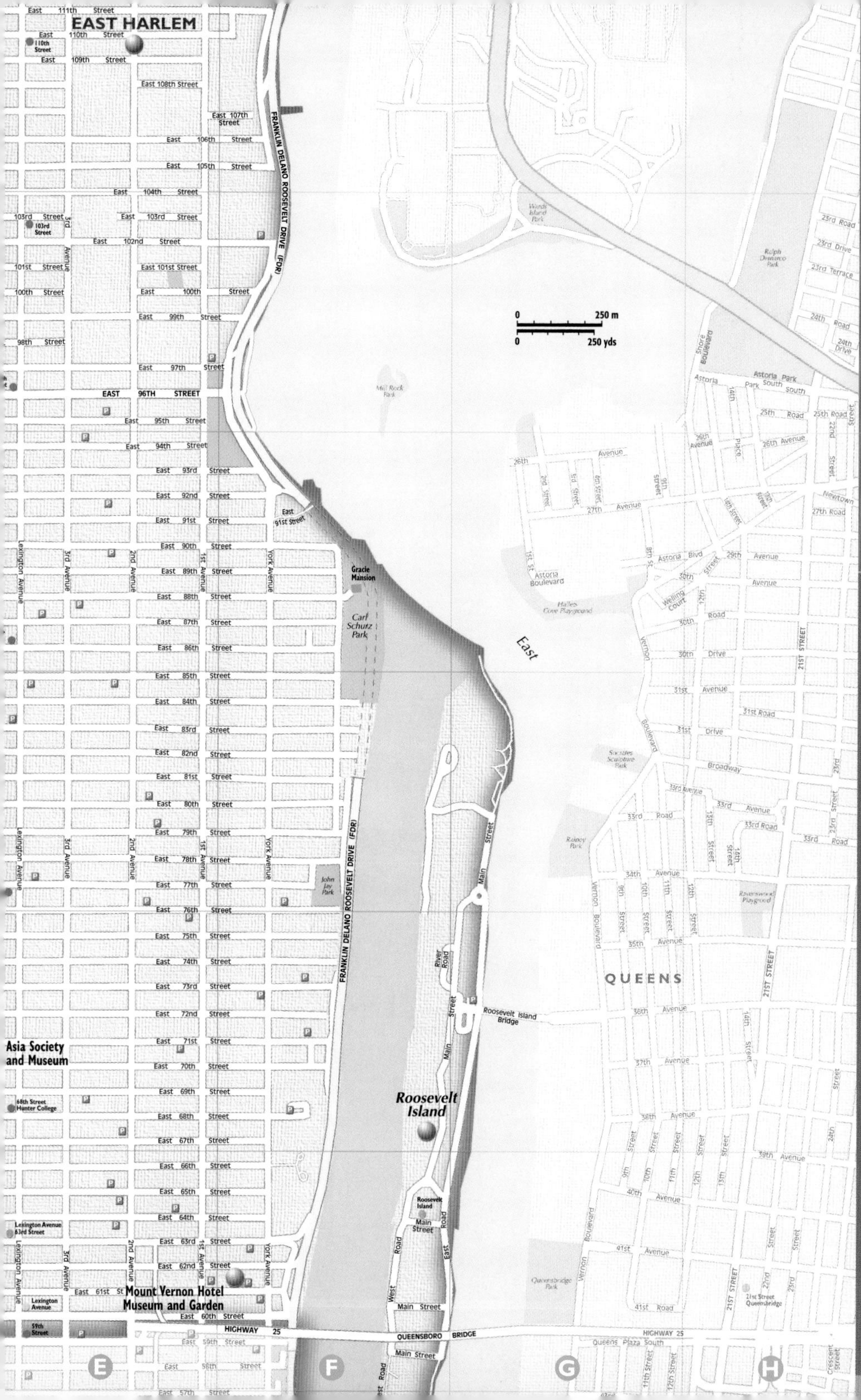

EAST HARLEM

East 111th Street
East 110th Street
East 109th Street
East 108th Street
East 107th Street
East 106th Street
East 105th Street
East 104th Street
103rd Street 3rd Street
103rd Street
East 103rd Street
East 102nd Street
101st Avenue
East 101st Street
100th Street
East 100th Street
98th Street
East 99th Street
East 97th Street
EAST 96TH STREET
East 95th Street
East 94th Street
East 93rd Street
East 92nd Street
East 91st Street
East 91st Street
East 90th Street
East 89th Street
East 88th Street
East 87th Street
East 86th Street
East 85th Street
East 84th Street
East 83rd Street
East 82nd Street
East 81st Street
East 80th Street
East 79th Street
East 78th Street
East 77th Street
East 76th Street
East 75th Street
East 74th Street
East 73rd Street
East 72nd Street
East 71st Street
East 70th Street
East 69th Street
East 68th Street
East 67th Street
East 66th Street
East 65th Street
East 64th Street
East 63rd Street
East 62nd Street
East 61st St
East 60th Street
East 59th Street
East 57th Street

Lexington Avenue
3rd Avenue
2nd Avenue
1st Avenue
York Avenue

FRANKLIN DELANO ROOSEVELT DRIVE (FDR)

Gracie Mansion
Carl Schurz Park
John Jay Park

Mill Rock Park

East River

QUEENS

Wards Island Park
Ralph Demarco Park
Astoria Park
23rd Drive
23rd Terrace
23rd Road
24th Road
24th Drive
Astoria Park South
25th Road
25th Avenue
Astoria Blvd
26th Avenue
27th Avenue
27th Road
Welling Court
28th Avenue
29th Avenue
30th Drive
30th Road
31st Avenue
31st Road
31st Drive
Broadway
33rd Avenue
33rd Road
34th Avenue
35th Avenue
36th Avenue
37th Avenue
38th Avenue
39th Avenue
40th Avenue
41st Avenue
41st Road

Hallets Cove Playground
Socrates Sculpture Park
Rainey Park
Riverside Playground
Queensbridge Park
21st Street Queensbridge

Roosevelt Island Bridge
Roosevelt Island
River Road
Main Street
East Road
West Road
Main Street

Asia Society and Museum
68th Street Hunter College
Lexington Avenue 63rd Street
Lexington Avenue 59th Street
Mount Vernon Hotel Museum and Garden

HIGHWAY 25
QUEENSBORO BRIDGE
Queens Plaza South
HIGHWAY 25

0   250 m
0   250 yds

E   F   G   H

201

ALMA MATER

AMERICAN MUSEUM OF NATURAL HISTORY
▷ 204–207.

ASIA SOCIETY AND MUSEUM
www.asiasociety.org
Founded by John D. Rockefeller III in 1956 to promote relations between America and Asian countries, the society mounts exhibitions, lectures, conferences, concerts and workshops. A $30-million renovation of the 1981 building completed in 2001 doubled the exhibition space. The collection is based on Rockefeller's donation of acquisitions from all over Asia, and ranges from 11th-century BC Chinese ceramics to Japanese prints and Cambodian sculptures to 19th-century objects.
⊹ 201 E6 ✉ 725 Park Avenue at 70th Street, 10021 ☎ 212/288-6400 🕓 Tue–Sun 11–6, Fri 11–9 (except July 4–Labor Day) 🖐 Adult $10, under 16s and members free, Fri 6pm–9pm free for all (except July 4–Labor Day) 🚇 6 🚌 M1, M2, M3, M4, M30, M66, M101, M102 🎁 🏛

CENTRAL PARK
▷ 208–213.

COLUMBIA UNIVERSITY
www.columbia.edu
Founded as King's College in 1754 as a rival to the by then well-established Harvard and Yale, this was New York's first college and the fifth-oldest in the nation, and is among the Ivy League's wealthiest universities. Originally located in the schoolhouse of Trinity Church (▷ 79), the college has occupied several Manhattan locations. It moved to the current 36-acre (15ha) campus, originally the site of Bloomingdale's Insane Asylum, in 1897. The heart of the campus is the magnificent Low Library, inspired by the Pantheon in Rome; academic buildings are arranged around it. In 1934 the Low became the university's administrative center, and the library was moved.
⊹ Off map 200 B2 ✉ West 114th to 120th streets, 10027 ☎ 212/854-4900 🚌 M4, M5, M11, M60, M104 🍴 🎁 🏛 🚹 Free guided tours weekdays

COOPER-HEWITT NATIONAL DESIGN MUSEUM
www.si.edu/ndm
This elegant, 64-room, wood-paneled Georgian mansion, built from 1899 to 1902, was the home of the industrialist and philanthropist Andrew Carnegie. It was the first private residence in New York to have an Otis elevator.

Today it houses one of the largest design collections in the world, with more than 250,000 items. The collection, originally from the Cooper Union School for the Advancement of Science, was donated in 1967 to the Smithsonian, which moved it here. It includes a drawing by Michelangelo, furniture designs by Frank Lloyd Wright and industrial design drawings by Donald Deskey and Henry Dreyfuss.
⊹ 200 D4 ✉ 2 East 91st Street, 10128 ☎ 212/849-8400 🕓 Mon–Fri 10–5, Sat 10–6, Sun 12–6 🖐 Adult $15, under 12 free 🚇 4, 5, 6 🚌 M1, M2, M3, M4 🍴 🏛

THE DAKOTA
A vaguely Germanic Upper West Side landmark, this marble-floored, mahogany-paneled structure was the first luxury apartment block on Central Park. Far beyond the city's bright lights, or even the power supply, it seemed as distant from the city as the Dakotas when it opened; the name was a joke on its remoteness. It wasn't long before the city moved uptown, however. Prices soared, and the rich and famous moved in—among them musician Leonard Bernstein and actress Lauren Bacall. John Lennon was tragically shot dead on the sidewalk outside the door, and his widow, Yoko Ono, still lives here.
⊹ 200 C6 ✉ 1 West 72nd Street, 10023 🚌 M7, M10, M11 🚇 B, C

Opposite Alma Mater *statue outside the Low Library at Columbia University*
Below *The Asia Society was founded by John D. Rockefeller in 1956*

INFORMATION

www.amnh.org

➕ 200 C5 ✉ Central Park West at 79th Street, 10024-5912 ☎ 212/769-5100 🕐 Daily 10–5.45. Space shows Mon, Tue, Thu, Fri 10.30–4.30, Wed 11–4.30, Sat–Sun 10.30–5 every half hour (tickets can sell out, so buy in advance online or phone 212/769-5200) ✋ Museum and Rose Center suggested donation: adult $15, child $8.50. Admission and Space Show suggested donation: adult $24, child $14. Additional charge for IMAX and some special exhibitions 🚇 B, C 🚌 M7, M10, M11 ◀ Rose Center audiotours at desk near the Planetarium shop on the lower level, free. Hour-long guided Highlights Tour on the hour 10.15–3.15, free. Free thematic Spotlight Tours change each month 🍴 Museum Food Court on the lower level (daily 11–4.45); Café on 4 on the fourth floor (Sat–Sun 11–4.45); Café on One on the first floor (daily 11–4.45); Starlight Café (Sat–Sun 11–4.45) ♿

Above *The Rose Center glass cube is made up of 736 panes of glass*

INTRODUCTION

Increasing interest in natural history and the discovery of fossils, particularly of dinosaurs, across the United States provided the inspiration for this great museum, founded in 1869 by Albert S. Bickmore. Originally the museum was in the Arsenal building in Central Park. Construction on this site began in 1874, to plans conceived by Calvert Vaux and J. Wrey Mould. President Ulysses S. Grant laid the cornerstone, and President Rutherford B. Hayes formally opened the museum in 1877. Additions in many architectural styles have expanded the museum since. The Theodore Roosevelt Memorial Hall, finished in 1936, was designed by John Russell Pope. Roosevelt, a keen hunter and collector, donated specimens from his many expeditions, including a bat and the skull of a red squirrel. The museum also includes a research center with numerous laboratories, teaching and other facilities, and a library that has the largest collection of natural history books in the Western hemisphere. The collection of dinosaurs and other fossils is the largest in the world, and many of those on view are real, not cast reproductions.

There are three entrances to the museum: the main entrance on Central Park West, where you will see the impressive bronze statue of President Theodore Roosevelt on horseback; the Columbus Avenue entrance onto West 77th Street; and an entrance on West 81st Street into the Rose Center for Earth and Space, a planetarium with a narrated history of the universe. The museum has grown over the years and now has 40 grand exhibition halls, so you will have to decide what interests you most and save the rest for other visits. A good way to start a visit is to join one of the free Highlights Tours; you will hear about some of the museum's prized treasures and get orientation on the layout of the exhibits. Ask at the information desk inside the main entrance, where the tour begins. The tour guides are friendly, well informed, usually very entertaining and easy to spot: they hold up a yellow flag as they proceed through the museum. You can join in along the way.

WHAT TO SEE

ROTUNDA

Inside the main entrance is the Rotunda, a city landmark, where colorful murals depict great accomplishments of Theodore Roosevelt, the first New Yorker to become president of the United States. The *Barosaurus* in the middle of the Rotunda is the tallest mounted dinosaur in the world at 50ft (15m). The real bones are stored elsewhere; the ones you see here are casts.

ROSE CENTER FOR EARTH AND SPACE
Hayden Sphere

Part of the four-story, $210-million Rose Center for Earth and Space, opened in 2000, which occupies a glass cube designed by James Polshek, the great Sphere contains the planetarium (access from first floor only). Take a 30-minute virtual ride through the Milky Way and find out about distant planets and superclusters through the fascinating commentary and stellar special effects. The spiral Cosmic Pathway winds down around the course of the Sphere.

FIRST FLOOR
Dzanga-Sangha Rainforest (Hall of Biodiversity)

The full-size rainforest diorama, 90ft (27m) long, 26ft (8m) wide and 18ft (5.5m) high, re-creates a forest in the Central African Republic. Visitors can go behind the glass into a world where high-resolution imagery, video, sound and smell take you into a rainforest experience. On the forest floor, insects, reptiles and small mammals scuttle through the saplings, shrubs, herbs, ferns and leaf litter; a stream runs past, and in the distance you may catch glimpses of elephants moving about, while birds and primates hang around in the tangle of overhead vines, branches and trunks.

Below *The dinosaur and fossil collection is the largest of its kind in the world*

Above *A huge model blue whale hangs above the Hall of Ocean Life*

TIPS
» Go on a free Highlights Tour.
» On the first Friday of every month top jazz musicians entertain for free at 5.30 and 7.15. Tapas and drinks are available.
» Purchase a CityPass (▷ 274), good for nine days, to save money and avoid standing in line for tickets.
» The gift shop has a wide range of jewelry, pottery, metalwork and glasswork from all over the world.

Blue Whale (Hall of Ocean Life)
One of the museum's favorite exhibits, the 94ft (29m) model of a blue whale dominates the state-of-the-art Hall of Ocean Life. Video projection screens and interactive computer stations help you to understand marine environments.

Discovery Room
Designed to interest children between the ages of 5 and 12, the Discovery Room has puzzles, games, scientific challenges and investigations to explore.

SECOND FLOOR
Elephant Diorama (Akeley Hall of African Mammals)
This venerable diorama, constructed in the 1930s, set the standard for natural history museum displays. The group of elephants is set amid vegetation typical of their natural habitat. Other dioramas in the hall show more of Africa's stunning wildlife.

THIRD FLOOR
Passenger pigeon (Hall of New York City Birds)
Two centuries ago, the passenger pigeon was one of the most abundant birds in North America. Now extinct, the bird's life is traced through vivid displays.

FOURTH FLOOR
Stegosaurus* and *Triceratops (Hall of Ornithischian Dinosaurs)
These two huge dinosaurs were vegetarians, protected from rapacious attacks by massive bony jaw plates. Begin with a visit to the Wallach Orientation Center for an overview of the six fossil halls. Did you know that the word dinosaur means "terrible lizard"?

Tyrannosaurus* and *Apatosaurus (Hall of Saurischian Dinosaurs)
You may feel very small when you enter the Hall of Saurischian Dinosaurs and meet the giants displayed here. *Tyrannosaurus rex* is an awesome sight, with the horrendous teeth of a meat-eater.

Above *A huge model blue whale hangs above the Hall of Ocean Life*

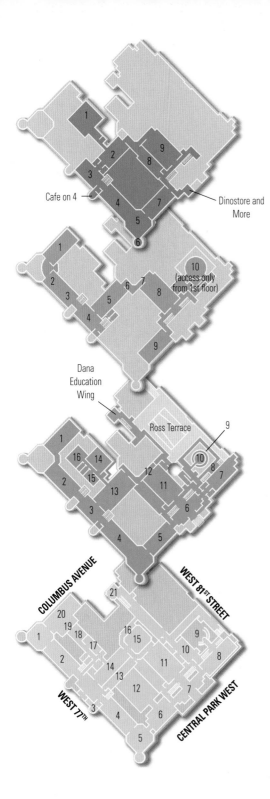

Cafe on 4

Dinostore and More

Dana Education Wing

Ross Terrace

COLUMBUS AVENUE

WEST 81ST STREET

WEST 77TH

CENTRAL PARK WEST

GALLERY GUIDE
KEY TO MAIN ROOMS

FOURTH FLOOR
1: Research library
2: Vertebrate origins
4: Advanced mammals
5: Primitive mammals
7: Ornithischian dinosaurs (Stegosaurus and Triceratops)
9: Saurischian dinosaurs (Tyrannosaurus and Apatosaurus)

THIRD FLOOR
1: Pacific peoples
2, 3: Plains and Woodlands Indians
4: Primates
5: North American birds
6: New York State mammals
7: New York City birds
8: African mammals
9: Reptiles and amphibians (including the world's largest lizard, the 10ft/3m Komodo dragon)
10: Hayden Planetarium Space Theater

SECOND FLOOR
1: South American peoples
2: Mexico and Central America
3: Birds of the world
4: Asian peoples
5: Asian mammals
6: Main entrance and Rotunda
7: Oceanic birds
8: Scales of the universe
9: Cosmic pathway
10: Big Bang
11: African mammals
13: African peoples

FIRST FLOOR
1: Ross Hall of Meteorites
2: Spitzer Hall of Human Origins
3: Discovery Room
4: New York state environment
5: North American forests
6: Hall of Biodiversity
7: Theodore Roosevelt Memorial Hall
8: Hall of Planet Earth
9: Cosmic pathway
10: Rose Gallery (space show boarding)
11: North American mammals
12: Hall of Ocean Life
14: Northwest Coast Indians
15: IMAX theater
19, 20: Gems and minerals (Star of India sapphire)

INFORMATION

www.centralparknyc.org
✚ 200 C3 ✉ Central Manhattan from 59th to 110th streets, between Fifth and Eighth avenues ☎ 212/310-6600 or 212/628-1036 🕐 6am–1am 🚇 A, B, C, D, 1 to Columbus Circle (southwest corner) 🚌 M1, M2, M3, M4 to Fifth Avenue (East Side) and M10 (West Side) ℹ Look for park lamp posts to find out where you are in relation to city streets. The first two digits on the lamp post are those of the nearest street. There are direct-line emergency phones throughout the park and a 24-hour Park Line (☎ 212/570-4820) you can call from mobile phones 🍴 The lavish Tavern on the Green (▷ 241) ☕ The open-air Boathouse Café serves contemporary American cuisine from early spring to late October. Other cafés and food stalls throughout the park 🚲 Guided Central Park Conservancy Walking Tours (☎ 212/360-2726) and Central Park Bicycle Tours (☎ 212/541-8759); horse-drawn hansom cabs (☎ 212/736-0680)

INTRODUCTION

New York's "great green lung" was designed by Frederick Law Olmsted and Calvert Vaux in 1858—843 acres (341ha) of green space with woods, gardens, playing fields and a zoo. It's a great place for birdwatching, cycling, rowing, ice skating, rollerblading, strolling or jogging along 58 miles (93km) of paths.

In the 1850s, many New Yorkers felt that their growing city needed a park. A large central site was chosen, and a competition in 1858 attracted 33 entries. A farmer, Frederick Law Olmsted, and an architect, Calvert Vaux, won the $2,000 commission. Olmsted was appointed superintendent of Central Park. Jacob Wrey Mould took on the ornamental side and designed the bridges, the Belvedere and the terrace. Construction took 16 years and cost more than $14 million. Three thousand workers, mostly unemployed Irish immigrants, and 400 horses moved stone and earth and planted 500,000 trees, shrubs and vines. The park got its own police force to discourage lawlessness. In 1925, the first of 19 playgrounds, the Heckscher Playground at 61st Street and 7th Avenue, was constructed.

Between 1913 and 1919, decay took its toll on some of the fine designs. By 1934 Vaux's Marble Bridge was beyond repair and had to be demolished. In 1934, when parks commissioner Robert Moses moved the sheep from Sheep Meadow to Brooklyn's Prospect Park, the sheepfold, designed by Mould, was turned into the restaurant that's now the Tavern on the Green. The addition of the Wollman Skating Rink came in 1951 and the Delacorte Theater in 1963. Many statues were added along the way. The 1970s brought another period of neglect and lawlessness and the park was for a while not a safe place to visit. But that changed after the Central Park Conservancy, headed by Elizabeth Barlow Rogers, took the initiative in the 1970s and 1980s to clean up the park and raise funds to establish a safer and cleaner space. The Sheep Meadow, the first area to be restored by the conservancy, was reopened in 1981 and remains one of the safest, most pleasant areas of the park.

Several entrances lead into Central Park from Central Park South (59th Street) at the southern edge and 110th Street at the northern edge. The most popular entrance is at Grand Army Plaza, at 59th Street and Fifth Avenue. From Fifth Avenue on the east side, you can enter at 66th, 72nd, 79th, 85th, 97th and 102nd streets. On the west side, from Central Park West, you can enter at 66th, 72nd, 81st, 86th, 96th and 100th streets. North of 96th Street, the park is more rugged and less suitable for visitors with disabilities. Because there are so many different access points, study the map before entering, read about the highlights, then decide on a route through the park. Many roads that cut through the park are closed to vehicular traffic on weekends in summer, which makes it perfect for joggers, bikers, rollerbladers and baby-strollers. There are bronze statues throughout the park, including monuments to Beethoven, Christopher Columbus, William Shakespeare and Mother Goose in the south end. At the entrance to the Delacorte Theater are lovely statues of Romeo and Juliet, and from Shakespeare's *The Tempest*, Prospero with his daughter, Miranda. Bring binoculars, especially in the Ramble or on the lake.

WHAT TO SEE
SOUTH QUADRANT

The Pond is a lovely first impression of Central Park for visitors who come in at Grand Army Plaza. The gilded bronze statue of Civil War Union General William Tecumseh Sherman by sculptor Augustus Saint-Gaudens is one of the most distinguished equestrian groupings in Western art. Along Central Park South, drivers of horse-drawn carriages wait for passengers. Nearby, the wooded Hallett Nature Sanctuary juts into the Pond, which has an island inhabited by turtles and birds and a lovely waterfall.

The Metropolitan Museum of Art (1000 Fifth Avenue at East 82nd Street, tel 212/535-7710; www.metmuseum.org; Tue–Thu, Sun 9.30–5.15, Fri–Sat 9.30–8.45; suggested donation adult $20, under 12 with adult free) was founded in 1870. The first donation was a Roman sarcophagus, but when multimillionaire J. P. Morgan was elected president of the Board of Trustees, world masterpieces became the main acquisitions. Significant donations of works by Old Masters, Louis Comfort Tiffany and Henri Matisse have been added to the museum's collection over the years. The grand main entrance has an impressive neoclassical facade. As you enter the Great Hall, pick up a museum plan at the information desk, and ask about the day's activities. Allow plenty of time—there is much to see. The collections number more than 2 million items, with around 100,000 on display at any given time, and it can be confusing if you simply wander around. You may wish to rent an audioguide or join a free guided tour; sign up at an information desk in the Great Hall.

With more than 35,000 works ranging from the Neolithic period to AD312, the Greek and Roman Art collection is one of the most comprehensive in North America. In the center of the Steinhardt Gallery is the marble statue of a *kouros* (youth), one of the earliest of such statues of boys to survive complete. Carved in Naxian marble in Attica, it is believed to have marked the grave of a young Athenian aristocrat. In the Belfer Court is a collection of terracotta pots, gemstones, figures and sculptures from the Neolithic period to the fifth century BC. There are interesting pieces from the Minoan Palace of Knossos in Crete and Roman copies of Hellenistic sculptures from classical Greece. Upstairs are bronze mirrors from the sixth century BC, painted amphoras from the fifth century BC, Corinthian and Hellenistic pottery, and bronze reliefs from the Etrusco-Roman period.

European Sculpture and Decorative Arts is one of the largest departments in the museum. In the Northern Renaissance and Florence galleries is *Bacchanal:*

Above *There is plenty to see and do in Central Park*

Opposite *The Sherman Monument (1903) at Grand Army Plaza*

Above *The entrance to the Metropolitan Museum of Art is imposing from any angle*
Below Diana *by Augustus Saint-Gaudens in the Metropolitan Museum of Art's American Wing*

A Faun Teased by Children, a sculpture by Rome's Gian Lorenzo Bernini (1598–1680), which he created when he was only 18. In the Louis XIV Gallery, the little oak, pine and walnut veneered desk, engraved with tortoiseshell, brass, ebony and rosewood, is one of a pair made in France for Louis XIV's small study in the Palace of Versailles by cabinetmaker Alexandre-Jean Oppenordt (1639–1715). In the English galleries are a rococo-style dining room from Kirtlington Park, Oxfordshire, and a lavish dining room from Lansdowne House, London. The French galleries include a Paris shopfront from 1775, a daybed made for Marie Antoinette in the boudoir of the Hôtel de Crillon, and in the Louis XVI Gallery, the king's desk from his study at Versailles. Not to be missed is the beautiful Petrie European Sculpture Court. Fountains and greenery and a splendid view of Central Park and Cleopatra's Needle provide a peaceful setting for fine Italian and French sculptures. Cleopatra's Needle was a gift from the Pasha of Egypt.

One of the Met's most popular areas, the American Wing has three floors and centers on the splendid Charles Englehard Court. Focusing on the development of art and design in America, the collection fills 25 rooms with period furniture and furnishings, more than 1,000 paintings by American artists, 600 sculptures, 2,500 drawings and numerous examples of the decorative arts. The Louis Comfort Tiffany vase, one of the first pieces of American glass in the collection, is a beautiful example of his Favrile glass peacock vases—the fan shaped like a peacock's outspread plumage, the eyes of sliced glass millefiori canes, and the graceful lines depicting each individual feather. *Washington Crossing the Delaware,* painted in 1851 by the German-born painter Emmanuel Gottlieb Leutze (1816–68), ia an American icon depicting General George Washington's surprise attack on the Hessians at Trenton, New Jersey, on Christmas night 1776. The earliest interior in the American Wing, the Hart Room is from the home of Thomas Hart of Ipswich, Massachusetts. Built sometime between 1639 and 1674, this is a typical example of homes of the early New England settlers. In the airy Charles Englehard Court, linger to study Tiffany's *Garden Landscape and Fountain* and the beautiful stained-glass *Autumn Landscape.* The former was inspired by the Byzantine churches Tiffany saw while traveling in Europe. Turn to the right to see Tiffany's extravagant loggia from Laurelton Hall. The sculptures in this glass-enclosed garden are by American artists Augustus Saint-Gaudens, Frederick MacMonnies and Daniel Chester French. In Gallery 127 is the work of the world-famous architect Frank Lloyd Wright. *Living Room from the Little House,* a very modern design in 1912, was designed for Francis Little. Paintings and sculptures by American artists on this floor include John Singleton Copely's *Midshipman August Brine, The Falls of Niagara* by S. F. B. Morse, James McNeill Whistler's *Arrangement in Flesh, Color and Black,* John Singer Sargent's *Madame X* (1884), Mary Cassatt's *Lady at the Tea Table* (1885), and from the Hudson River School Frederic Church's *Heart of the Andes.*

Highlights of the European paintings collection include *Virgin and Child with St. Anne* by Albrecht Dürer (1471–1528), *Cypresses* painted in 1889 by Vincent Van Gogh (1853–90), and *Terrace at Sainte-Adresse* (1867) by Claude Monet (1840–1926). Among the many Italian masters' works are Raphael's *Madonna Enthroned with Child and Saints* (1505), Titian's *Venus and the Lute Player* (c1560), Tintoretto's *Finding of Moses* (c1550), Botticelli's *Last Communion of St. Jerome* (c1450) and Caravaggio's *Musicians* (1504). Early Dutch painters include a Rembrandt *Self-Portrait* (1660), Vermeer's *Woman with a Water Jug* (1664) and works by de Hooch, van Goyen and others. French paintings include Poussin's *Rape of the Sabine Women* (c1635) and Jean Clouet's *Guillaume Budé.* Spanish works include El Greco's *View of Toledo* and *Grand Inquisitor Cardinal Don Fernando Niño de Guevara.* The English collection is represented by William Hogarth, Joshua Reynolds and Thomas Gainsborough. European paintings of the 19th century include Millet's *Autumn Landscape with a Flock*

TIPS

» Don't stroll alone in deserted areas, and stay out of the park at night unless you are going to a play or concert. The park is now generally safe by day and after dark when there are crowds on hand. Police and park rangers patrol in vehicles, on skates and on horseback.

» Count on spending a half day or more here, depending on what you want to see.

» On the roads, watch out for bicycle traffic, and always look carefully when crossing.

» The park has 21 children's playgrounds. Many are state of the art and no two are alike.

of Turkeys (1872–73) and many Impressionist and Postimpressionist paintings. Besides 100 works by Degas, there are paintings by Manet, Renoir, Seurat, Toulouse-Lautrec, Cézanne and Gauguin. One of Cézanne's best still lifes, *Still Life with Apples and a Pot of Primroses* (1895), is also worth seeing.

The Wildlife Center fills 5.5 acres (2ha) just north of Grand Army Plaza. This state-of-the-art zoo (tel 212/439-6500; Apr–end Oct Mon–Fri 10–5, Sat–Sun 10–5.30; rest of year daily 10–4.30; adult $10, child (3–12) $5) is home to more than 130 species from three climate zones: monkeys, crocodiles and snakes in the Rain Forest, Asian and North American animals in the Temperate Territory, and polar bears, penguins and polar foxes in the Polar Circle. The sea lion pool in the central courtyard is very popular, especially at feeding times (daily 11.30, 2 and 4). Young children can feed goats, sheep and a cow in the Children's Zoo. There are also daily animal shows in the Acorn Theater. North of the zoo, the George Delacorte Clock plays a nursery rhyme every hour on the hour as miniature animals glide around playing musical instruments. There is a café.

Wollman Memorial Rink (tel 212/439-6900, www.wollmanskatingrink.com; Mon–Tue 10–2.30, Wed–Thu 10–10, Fri–Sat 10am–11pm, Sun 10–9; Mon–Thu adult $10, child $5.25, Fri–Sun $14, $5.50, respectively, skate rental $6) is filled with ice skaters in winter. With its classic New York views of the Midtown skyline and its terrace overlooking the rink, this is one of the park's gems. Lessons are available and there's a snack shop.

The Dairy (tel 212/794-6564; Tue–Sun 10–5 year-round), a 19th-century building overlooking the Wollman Rink, has an exhibit about the history and design of the park. There's a 12ft (3.6m) model of the park.

Friedsam Memorial Carousel (tel 212/879-0244; Apr–Oct Mon–Fri 10–6, Sat–Sun 10–7; Jan–Mar Sat–Sun 10–dusk; Nov–Dec daily 10–dusk), in the middle of the park at 64th Street, is one of the largest carousels in the US, with 58 handcarved, painted horses. Every year about 250,000 people mount a steed for a magical ride.

Above *The park's famous pond, Conservatory Water, is popular with model boat enthusiasts*

PARK GUIDE
SOUTH QUADRANT

The Arsenal (Mon–Fri 9–5), originally the New York State National Guard's munitions supply depot, was built between 1847 and 1851. Now a New York City Landmark, the Arsenal houses Olmsted and Vaux's original blueprint for Central Park, called the Greensward Plan. You can see it in a glass case on the third floor.

The Dairy, a Gothic Revival cottage, was once a place where children could go for a glass of fresh milk. It now houses a visitor center (tel 212/794-6564; Tue–Sun 10–5) with video information terminals and a permanent exhibit on the history of the park.

To the west of the Dairy is the octagonal Chess and Checkers (draughts) House, where you can test your skills at one of the 24 chess tables.

RESERVOIR QUADRANT

As you walk, or run, around the reservoir, note the three pedestrian wrought-iron bridges, called 24, 27 and 28. New Yorkers call Bridge 28 the Gothic Arch because of its lace-like quality.

NORTH QUADRANT

The Charles A. Dana Discovery Center, opened in 1993 on the northern shore of the Harlem Meer, is a visitor and community center with free educational exhibits relating to Central Park (tel 212/860-1370; Tue–Sun 10–5).

Above *Conservatory Garden is a formal garden with a rustic atmosphere*

The Sheep Meadow is 15 acres (6ha) of grass where you can have a picnic, fly kites and sunbathe. Some 300 sprinkler heads keep the grass green and lush throughout the year. A flock of sheep grazed here until 1934; their sheepfold is now a restaurant, the Tavern on the Green. On the east side of the meadow is a patch of pavement where you can watch talented roller skaters practice their moves.

Bethesda Terrace, in Olmsted and Vaux's original design, was "the heart of the park." By the 1980s it had fallen into disrepair and was rebuilt. Stand on the Upper Terrace for a splendid view of the lake and the wooded area known as the Ramble. The fountain, *Angel of the Waters* (1870), was the work of sculptor Emma Stebbins.

Strawberry Fields was created in 1981 with funds provided by Yoko Ono, widow of musician John Lennon, after his murder in 1980 outside The Dakota (▷ 203), and named after his song *Strawberry Fields Forever*. Italian craftsmen made the black-and-white mosaic embedded in the path near the entrance at West 72nd Street, directly across the street from The Dakota apartment building where he was killed. It is centered around the word "Imagine," recalling another of Lennon's most popular songs. Yoko Ono provides $1 million annually to the Central Park Conservancy for the upkeep of these 2.5 acres (1ha). Fans often stop to pay their respects and leave flowers or candles, and a huge crowd gathers every year on the singer's birthday (October 9) to sing, pray and celebrate his life and work.

Loeb Boathouse rents out rowboats and bicycles (mid-Apr to end Oct daily 10–5.30). Rowboats cost $10 for the first hour, $5 for each extra half hour; each boat takes up to four people. A $30 cash deposit is required. Renting a bicycle costs between $9 and $20 per hour, and you must leave a credit card, driver's license or a passport as a deposit. In June and August (weather permitting) another option is a gondola ride—not cheap at $30 per half hour, but memorable. A fast-food restaurant in the Boathouse offers cold drinks and

snacks. The Boathouse Restaurant is a lovely spot, serving brunch and lunch year round, and dinner from April to November (reservations are a must, tel 212/517-2233). Birdwatchers record their observations in the Bird Register, inside the Boathouse, and other visitors' sightings also make for some interesting reading.

Conservatory Water is the park's famous pond. On Saturdays at 10am from spring through fall, the Model Yacht Club races its radio-powered craft. You can rent miniature boats. North of the pond is the delightful *Alice in Wonderland* sculpture, designed by José de Creeft in 1959, and to the west is the Hans Christian Andersen sculpture; children climb up on it to sit on his lap, and there are story hours on summer Saturdays at 11am.

Belvedere Castle (tel 212/772-0210; Tue–Sun 10–5) was Olmsted and Vaux's folly, an open-air flight of fancy that served as an elaborate scenic lookout across the lake. But during an extensive restoration in the early 1980s windows and doors were put in and it is now the Henry Luce Nature Observatory. Here you will find interesting displays—telescopes, microscopes, skeletons, feathers—intended to help children understand how naturalists observe the world. The US Weather Bureau has been operating from here since 1919, and you can get up-to-the-minute weather reports on the second floor. Also on this floor is a tree loft with a wonderful collection of papier-mâché models of bird species found in the park.

Above *The memorial to John Lennon in Strawberry Fields*
Below *Belvedere Castle is a lakeside folly in the South Quadrant*

The Delacorte Theater, built in 1962, is where Shakespeare in the Park performances delight large audiences in summer. Waiting in line for a free ticket is part of the experience. New Yorkers bring picnic baskets and books when they line up (starting around 10am) and make a day of it. The box office begins distributing tickets at 1pm. Tickets are also handed out at the Public Theater at 425 Lafayette Street on the day of the performance from 1 to 3pm.

RESERVOIR QUADRANT
The Jacqueline Kennedy Onassis Reservoir, named for the widow of President John F. Kennedy because of her fondness for the place and her contributions to the city, is noted for the 1.58-mile (2.54km) track around it. Joggers and walkers come here by the thousands every day. This 106-acre (43ha) body of water no longer supplies Manhattanites with fresh water, but it still feeds the other ponds in the park. In spring glorious ornamental cherry trees blossom on the slopes.

NORTH QUADRANT
The Conservatory Garden is 6 acres (2.5ha) of formal gardens with lovely fountains in an area that has been landscaped in a more rustic, naturalistic style than the southern part of the park. If you enter from Fifth Avenue at East 104th Street, you will pass through giant Parisian wrought-iron gates from the mansion of Cornelius Vanderbilt II.

Harlem Meer, Dutch for "little sea," is a pretty pond, well stocked with about 50,000 fish. Catch-and-release fishing (Apr–end Oct Tue–Sun 11–5) is great entertainment for kids, big and small. Fishing rods can be rented at the Charles A. Dana Discovery Center.

Lasker Memorial Rink and Pool (skating: tel 917/492-3856; pool: 212/534-7639; Jul–Labor Day daily 11–3, 4–7; free), built in the 1960s, is an ice-skating rink from November through March and a roller-skating rink for the rest of the year. Skate rental is available. Very popular in summer, the swimming pool opens on July 1 and closes after Labor Day.

EAST HARLEM

Above the Upper East Side is East Harlem, once known as Spanish Harlem and now as El Barrio (the neighborhood). Unlike Central Harlem, this area developed in the 1870s and 1880s. Its poor-quality working-class dwellings were home to immigrants—first the Irish and then, from the 1890s, Italians. As the Puerto Ricans moved on up the social and employment ladder, they began to move in and soon made the area their own.

The city's Puerto Rican population numbered 45,000 by the 1930s and 600,000 by the 1960s; today more than a million Puerto Ricans live in New York, and Spanish is a second language. El Barrio has a vibrant Hispanic flavor, with family-owned stores and restaurants.

➕ 201 E2 ✉ Fifth to First avenues, East 97th to East 125th streets 🚇 4, 5, 6 🚌 M15, M101, M102, M103

EL MUSEO DEL BARRIO

www.elmuseo.org

Opened in 1969, this is one of the few museums in the United States dedicated to Puerto Rican, Latin American and Caribbean culture and art. There is a permanent display of hand-carved religious statuettes known as *santos de palo*, and another of artifacts from Caribbean cultures that welcomed Christopher Columbus to the New World in the 15th century. An interior and exterior renovation of the building was completed in 2009, unveiling a glass facade and new galleries.

➕ 200 D2 ✉ 1230 Fifth Avenue, between 104th and 105th streets, 10029 ☎ 212/831-7272 🕐 Wed–Sun 11–5 💵 Suggested donation: adult $6 (senior free on Thu), under 12 free. Special exhibition rates apply 🚇 6 🚌 M1, M2, M3, M4 🏛

FRICK COLLECTION

▷ 215.

GENERAL GRANT NATIONAL MEMORIAL

www.nps.gov/gegr

Known as Grant's Tomb, this may be the nation's largest and most impressive sepulcher. Rising dramatically 150ft (46m) next to the Hudson River, the squat, dome-topped granite building fronted by six Doric columns proclaims the importance of the wildly popular Civil War general, and later president, Ulysses S. Grant (1822–85).

The design, chosen after a competition, was copied from the fourth-century BC tomb of Mausolus at Halicarnassus. Work began soon after Grant's death, with contributions from more than 90,000 people, many of them African-Americans, for whom Grant's achievements at the head of the Union army outweighed his less successful efforts as president.

Inside the massive bronze doors, below the domed rotunda and set off by the gleaming white marble, two 9-ton polished black sarcophagi hold the remains of Grant and his wife, Julia.

➕ Off map 200 B2 ✉ Riverside Drive at West 122nd Street, 10027 ☎ 212/666-1640 🕐 Daily 9–5 🚇 A, 1 🚌 M4, M5, M104

Above *Ulysses S. Grant's tomb was completed in 1897*

GUGGENHEIM MUSEUM

▷ 216–217.

HARLEM

Harlem is forever linked with the speakeasies and jazz of the Prohibition era. The area declined in the middle of the last century into the bleak landscape that saw the departure of middle-class families in the 1960s. Today this has given way to housing renovation and a growing, upbeat population. There is much of architectural interest, and nightlife, jazz clubs and cultural attractions, including Manhattan's oldest residence, the Morris-Jumel Mansion Museum (65 Jumel Terrace, tel 212/923-8008, Wed–Sun 10–4, adult $4). After his second term as president, Bill Clinton opened an office in Harlem.

➕ Off map 200 D2 ✉ Fifth Avenue to Morningside Avenue, north of 110th Street 🚇 2, 3, A, B, C, D 🚌 M2, M3, M7, M10, M102 🏛 Harlem Tourist Center and Gift Shop, 2224 Frederick Douglass Boulevard

FRICK COLLECTION

Henry Clay Frick (1849–1919) has gone down in history as a ruthless businessman, staunchly anti-union, obsessed with acquiring wealth—in other words, a master entrepreneur. Frick had his own successful business, the Frick Coke Company in Pittsburgh, when Andrew Carnegie made him his partner in the Carnegie Steel Company. Together they made the Carnegie steel empire one of the most important businesses in the country, and both men became multimillionaires. Frick's sole interest outside the world of steel and coke was art. He collected works painted by many of the world's masters dating from the 14th to the 19th centuries. At the age of 64 he had a palatial residence on Fifth Avenue built as his private home and gallery, to plans drawn up by Carrère & Hastings. Frick and his wife lived in the home until their deaths—his in 1919, hers in 1931. Frick, in a generous move, bequeathed the house and paintings to the public.

After Frick's wife's death, the house was enlarged and became a museum in 1935. There is a reference library, the Frick Art Reference Library, next door on East 71st Street, designed by John Russell Pope, the architect of the National Gallery in Washington, D.C. The house is set back from Fifth Avenue behind an elevated garden designed by Russell Page. As part of multimillion dollar improvements, the stone wall surrounding the site was replaced in 2002 and the wrought-iron fence was restored.

ARTISTIC HIGHLIGHTS

Through the 16 galleries, the paintings are not arranged by period or national origin, but in the way Frick would have had them displayed in his home. The Fragonard Room shows the large Fragonard paintings depicting *The Progress of Love* and contains 18th-century French furniture and porcelain. In the Living Room are paintings by Holbein, El Greco, Titian and Bellini. Through the Library, past Italian bronzes and Chinese vases, is the West Gallery, where there are landscapes by John Constable and portraits by Rembrandt and Velázquez. Especially delightful is the East Gallery, with works by David, El Greco, Goya, Hogarth and Manet. After your visit, pause in the peaceful Garden Court (the enclosed Palm Court is the perfect oasis on a cold New York day), which occasionally hosts special exhibitions.

INFORMATION

www.frick.org

⊞ 200 D6 ✉ 1 East 70th Street at Fifth Avenue, 10021 ☎ 212/288-0700 🕓 Tue–Sat 10–6, Sun 11–5; closed Mon; limited hours, 1–6, on Presidents' Day, Election Day and Veterans' Day ✋ Adult $18, no children under 10. Sun pay what you wish 11–1; ArtPhone audio guide free 🚇 4, 5, 6 🚌 M1, M2, M3, M4 🏪 Books, cards, CDs, videos and museum-inspired gifts

TIP

» Try to come for a chamber music concert (year round on occasional Sundays at 5pm). Check website for details.

Below The Purification of the Temple (c1600), an oil on canvas by El Greco (1541–1614) from the collection

INFORMATION

www.guggenheim.org

🚇 200 D4 ✉ 1071 Fifth Avenue at 89th Street, 10028 ☎ 212/423-3500 🕐 Sat–Wed 10–5.45, Fri 10–7.45 🖐 Adult $18, under 12 free, some Fri 5.45–8 pay-as-you-wish 🚇 4, 5, 6 🚌 M1, M2, M3, M4 📖 Free Guggenheim Guide containing listing of exhibits and programs, available at admission desk 🛍 Sat–Wed 9.30–5.30, Thu 9.30–3, Fri 9.30–8 🍴 Sat–Wed 9.30–5.30, Thu 11–6, Fri 9.30–8 👣 Free tours daily. Reservations are taken at the information desk from 1.30. Audio tours free

Above *A masterpiece of modern architecture designed by Frank Lloyd Wright, the Guggenheim exhibits one of the world's finest collections of modern and contemporary art*

INTRODUCTION

The Solomon R. Guggenheim Museum, designed by Frank Lloyd Wright, opened on October 21, 1959. The inverted-ziggurat design, with its ramp encircling the walls, is as surprising today as it was when it was created. Solomon R. Guggenheim, a wealthy New Yorker whose father was a prominent 19th-century mining and smelting capitalist, used some of his wealth to buy works of art. He was content with Old Masters until 1927, when at the age of 66 he met baroness Hilla Rebay von Ehrenwiesen. The baroness favored European abstract art and introduced Guggenheim to such artists as Wassily Kandinsky, Fernand Léger and Robert Delaunay. It was she who suggested that Wright design a museum to house the great collection Guggenheim was amassing. Guggenheim died in 1949 and never saw the wondrous building, but Wright took on the job with enthusiasm and later pronounced it his "Pantheon."

As you enter, to your right is the admission desk, where you can pick up a free exhibitions program with a floor plan. As you look up at the five levels above the low white walls bordering the ramp you will see a tall, empty atrium-like space so dramatic that it is easy to forget that you came here primarily to see the modern art. Frank Lloyd Wright designed this building with the belief that the eye should not be confronted with angles and sudden changes of form when viewing works of art. From a logistical point of view, the best way to view the works hung here is to take the elevator up to the skylit top of the building and meander down the spiral ramp. However, the exhibits are often hung with the opposite path in mind.

WHAT TO SEE

PAUL CÉZANNE, *STILL LIFE: FLASK, GLASS AND JUG*
In this 1877 still life, Cézanne (1839–1906) perceived objects in space as being interrelated. He created an illusion of objects resting and flowing simultaneously, calling attention to the two-dimensional canvas. This painting, and others, made Cézanne the foremost precursor of Cubism.

PABLO PICASSO, *WOMAN IRONING*
Painted in 1904 at the end of his Blue Period, *Woman Ironing* is Picasso's (1881–1973) quintessential work of labor and fatigue, reminiscent of the years he spent among the Paris working class. His expressionist style, with angular contours and attenuated proportions, expresses the woman's movement poetically, making her the metaphor for the pathos of the working poor.

MAX ERNST, *ATTIREMENT OF THE BRIDE*
This 1940s Surrealist painting by Max Ernst (1891–1976) evokes late 19th-century Symbolist painting, while the sleek, round-bellied figures recall motifs of 16th-century German art. The background architecture indicates the strong influence of the Italian painter Giorgio De Chirico. Ernst's invented alter-ego, the bird-man on the left, depicts the artist with a symbolic phallic spear. The picture-within-a-picture shows the same bride walking amid overgrown Classical ruins, indicating the role of the bride throughout history. Garish colors and beastly figures suggest something violent is about to happen.

Below *Under the rotunda, the ramp spirals downward*

LINCOLN CENTER

INFORMATION

www.lincolncenter.org

✚ 200 B7 ✉ 70 Lincoln Center Plaza, 10023-6583 ☎ 212/546-2656 for main Lincoln Center 🚇 1 🚌 M5, M7, M10, M11, M66, M104 🎫 Guided tours of the Lincoln Center start from the tour desk in the lobby of Avery Fisher Hall, daily 10.30, 12.30, 2.30, 4.30, adult $15 (reservations ☎ 212/875-5350); Metropolitan Opera House backstage tours weekdays at 3.30 Oct–May only, Sun 10.30, adult $15 (reservations ☎ 212/865-5350) 🍽 Avery Fisher Hall: Center Room ☎ 212/874-7000 🕐 Tue–Sat for dinner, lunch on matinée days 🍹 Avery Fisher Hall: Espresso Bar, 5pm–intermission nightly, opens at noon for matinées 🛍 Metropolitan Opera Shop ☎ 212/580-4090; Avery Fisher Hall Shop ☎ 212/875-5017; The Gallery at Lincoln Center ☎ 212/546-2656

Above *The Metropolitan Opera House and Lincoln Center Plaza*

INTRODUCTION

The Lincoln Center is the Upper West Side's performing arts center for the best in opera, classical music, chamber music, jazz, ballet and theater. With 14 venues offering everything from classical music to performances for children, the Lincoln Center is New York's premier center for performing arts. In the 1960s, a block of old tenements on the Upper West Side, where some of *West Side Story* was filmed, was demolished in a 12-block urban renewal project, and the Lincoln Center for the Performing Arts was built on the site. The initial investment for the Lincoln Center was more than $165 million. The state contributed the site and the remainder of the money came from private contributions and donations.

In 1962 the New York Philharmonic moved here from Carnegie Hall (▷ 150), which at the time was threatened with demolition. But the acoustics were never good, so in 1973 Avery Fisher donated $10 million to improve them. The hall closed for a time to undergo this work, but musicians and music-lovers were still not satisfied, so in 1992 the hall underwent further renovation.

WHAT TO SEE

OPERA, BALLET, THEATER, JAZZ

The David H. Koch Theater is home to the New York City Opera and the New York City Ballet. The theater seats 2,700.

The Metropolitan Opera House, affectionately known as the Met, is home to both the opera company and the American Ballet Theater and seats 3,800. General manager Joe Volpe started as an apprentice carpenter and has worked his way up; he knows what attracts crowds and what doesn't.

The Guggenheim Bandshell in Damrosch Park, on 62nd Street near Amsterdam Avenue, hosts open-air concerts in summer.

The Lincoln Center Theater consists of the Vivian Beaumont Theater, with seating for 1,140, and the Mitzi E. Newhouse Theater, an established off-Broadway venue.

Jazz, led by trumpeter and composer Wynton Marsalis, has moved to the massive new Time Warner headquarters at nearby Columbus Circle, after receiving a $10 million gift from the Coca-Cola Company. The $128-million jazz venue is the focal point of the building, with three main performance spaces (tel 212/258-9800).

THE JUILLIARD SCHOOL OF MUSIC
The Juilliard School of Music is the top music school in the United States. The campus includes the Alice Tully Hall, a wonderful venue for chamber music and solo recitals, and the Walter Reade Film Theater, where the New York Film Festival sends up sparks every fall.

CURRENT RENOVATION
West 65th Street is being turned into a broad boulevard, much like a central artery of the Lincoln Center. This is a major portion of the $150-million redesign of the public areas and the center's buildings and grounds. The avant-garde design team of Diller and Scofidio, who are described as "artist architects," and specialize in experimental installations, have been selected for the project. Other features of the plan include technologically sophisticated signs with information about events, a sweeping staircase into the plaza, and a new look to several buildings. This phase is scheduled for completion in late 2010.

Renovations and redevelopment of the Juilliard School of Music, the Alice Tully Hall, the David H. Koch Theater and the Avery Fisher Hall have been completed.

TIPS
» There is a vast underground parking area, if you dare drive in New York.
» Special events take place all year, from summer's Mostly Mozart concert series and swing dancing to live jazz under the stars and the annual run of the Big Apple Circus, which pitches its tent in Damrosch Park at the beginning of November.

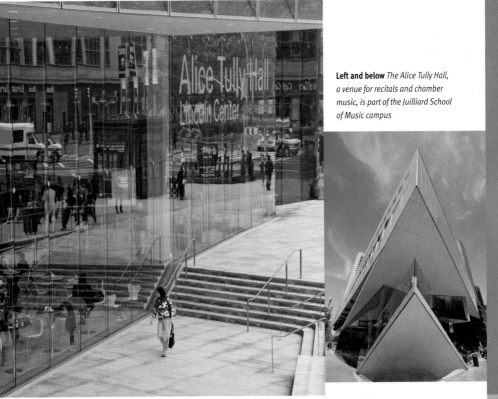

Left and below *The Alice Tully Hall, a venue for recitals and chamber music, is part of the Juilliard School of Music campus*

JEWISH MUSEUM

www.thejewishmuseum.org

A faux Loire Valley chateau, this greystone mansion dating from 1908 contains the Jewish Museum's collection of Jewish ceremonial objects and works of art.

Generous philanthropist Felix Warburg died in 1938 and his widow left the house to the museum in 1944. The permanent exhibit, entitled *Culture and Continuity: The Jewish Journey,* is based on Warburg's personal collection.

In a re-created 1900s café, oral histories reveal Jewish life in Europe at that time and explore the immigrant experience in the US. Family workshops and other events celebrate Jewish culture, holidays and traditions.

✚ 200 D4 ✉ 1109 Fifth Avenue at 92nd Street, 10128 ☎ 212/423-3200 ⏰ Sat–Wed 11–5.45, Thu 11–8, Sat 11–3, Sun 10–5.45. Closed Fri ✋ Adult $12, under 12 free 🚇 4, 5, 6 🚌 M1, M2, M3, M4 ♿ ▯

LINCOLN CENTER

▷ 218–219.

MOUNT VERNON HOTEL MUSEUM AND GARDEN

www.mvhm.org

In this splendid hotel, eight of the rooms were filled with Federal period furnishings by the Colonial Dames of America when they bought the structure in 1924. In the Gentlemen's Tavern Room, you're welcome to sit down and read a newspaper from 1828, and don't miss the museum's delightful 18th-century gardens.

The museum was a house that belonged to Abigail Adams, daughter of US president John Adams and the wife of George Washington's aide, William Stephens Smith. The Smiths had to sell the property in 1798 before all the buildings were complete and so never lived here. In 1826 the building underwent conversion into a hotel. There are regularly scheduled events.

✚ 201 F7 ✉ 421 East 61st Street at York Avenue ☎ 212/838-6878 ⏰ Tue–Sun 11–4 (also Tue from 6pm in Jun and Jul); closed Aug ✋ Adult $8, under 12 free 🚇 4, 6, N, R 🚌 M15, M31, M57

MUSEUM OF ARTS AND DESIGN

www.madmuseum.org

In this museum the American Craft Council displays the nation's biggest exhibition of 20th- and 21st-century American and international crafts. From jewelry to baskets, furniture to teapots, everything is selected to represent the finest in form and function. Stimulating special exhibitions are chosen from the wide-ranging collections, augmented by loans from other collections, to illustrate contemporary trends in technique and design. It's all shown to great advantage in the museum's newly renovated building in Columbus Circle. The building design provides additional space for exhibitions, educational programing and the rapidly expanding permanent collection. The façade features terracotta panels and fritted glass materials to highlight the museum's craft traditions.

✚ 200 C7 ✉ 2 Columbus Circle ☎ 212/299-7777 ⏰ Wed–Sun 11–6, Thu 11–9 ✋ Adult $15, under 12 free (pay-as-you-wish Thu 6pm–9pm) 🚇 59th Street/Columbus Circle (A, B, C, D, 1); 57th Street /7th Avenue (N, R, Q, W); 57th Street/6th Avenue (F) 🚌 M5, M7, M10, M20, M30, M104 to Columbus Circle at 59th Street

MUSEUM OF BIBLICAL ART

www.mobia.org

This museum aims to foster an understanding and appreciation of art inspired by the Bible. It opened its new building in 2005 with an inaugural exhibition of works by self-taught Southern folk artists. The museum evolved out of the American Bible Society (1816), which had amassed a huge collection of scripture, now on view behind a glass curtain wall in the main gallery. Exhibitions focus on the collection's highlights, such as the recent *For Glory and for Beauty,* which displayed 29 rare scriptures.

✚ 200 C7 ✉ 1865 Broadway at 61st Street, 10023 ☎ 212/408-1500 ⏰ Tue–Sun 10–6 (Thu until 8) ✋ Adult $7, under 12 free 🚇 59th Street/Columbus Circle (A, B, C, D, 1) 🚌 M5, M7, M11, M104

MUSEUM OF THE CITY OF NEW YORK

www.mcny.org

A neo-Georgian, colonial-style villa built in 1929 houses this museum devoted to New York's history and life. The collections here hold more than 1.5 million objects relating to the social and economic life of the city—paintings, photographs, costumes, toys, decorative arts and other artifacts. Some are world-class, like the silver collection and the collection on American theater; the photography, marine and costume collections are also outstanding. The museum has sometimes been criticized for taking a dull approach to display, but lively exhibitions such as *Glamor, New York Style* and *El Barrio: Puerto Rican New York* have helped to change that reputation.

✚ 200 D3 ✉ 1220 Fifth Avenue, 10029 ☎ 212/534-1672 ⏰ Tue–Sun 10–5 ✋ Suggested admission: adult $9, under 12 free, family $20 🚇 6 🚌 M1, M2, M3, M4, M106 📷 Highlights tour Sat noon ♿

NATIONAL ACADEMY OF DESIGN

www.nationalacademy.org

The National Academy of Design was founded in 1825 by a group of accomplished artists, architects, sculptors and engravers, including Thomas Cole and artist/inventor Samuel Morse. It is both a museum and a school of fine art, and also owns the largest collection of 19th- and 20th-century American art in the country—an astonishing collection with more than 5,000 works ranging from portraiture of the Federalist period, landscapes of the Hudson River School, gritty realism of the Ashcan Movement, and paintings representing movements from Fauvism to photo-realism.

The building was the home of Archer Milton Huntington and his wife, the sculptor Anna Hyatt Huntington. In 1913, they expanded and remodeled the house and lived here until 1939, when they gave it to the National Academy of Design, who moved in three years later.

Tours covering the collection's highlights and Edith Wharton's New York are available.

✚ 200 D4 ✉ 1083 Fifth Avenue, 10128 ☎ 212/369-4880 🕐 Wed–Thu 12–5, Fri–Sun 11–6 👆 Adult $10, under 12 free 🚇 4, 5, 6 🚌 M1, M2, M3, M4 ▶ Docent tours Fri 2pm, $5 🎫 Tue, Wed–Thu 10–5, Fri 10–6, Sat–Sun 11–6

NEUE GALERIE

www.neuegalerie.org

This museum, dedicated to early 20th-century German and Austrian art and design, has a marvelous collection of fine paintings, decorative arts and other media, including works by Gustav Klimt, Paul Klee, Egon Schiele, Josef Hoffmann and Adolf Loos.

On Friday nights there are cabarets in Café Sabarsky, which serves Austrian fare, including delicious pastries.

Some of the furniture is by Adolf Loos, and lighting fixtures are by Josef Hoffmann. The 1914 Carrère & Hastings mansion housing the museum was built for Mrs. Cornelius Vanderbilt III, and is every bit as remarkable as the collection.

✚ 200 D4 ✉ 1048 Fifth Avenue at 86th Street, 10028 ☎ 212/628-6200 🕐 Thu–Mon 11–6 👆 Adult $15, no children 🚇 4, 5, 6 🚌 M1, M2, M3, M4 🍴 🎫

NEW-YORK HISTORICAL SOCIETY

www.nyhistory.org

At Central Park West, this Upper West Side museum is fascinating. For nearly 200 years, the Society has been collecting, preserving and interpreting books, paintings, sculpture, photographs and newspapers. The Henry Luce III Center on the fourth floor displays lamps by Louis Comfort Tiffany, Hudson River School landscapes, a complete set of watercolors by John James Audubon for *The Birds of America*, George Washington's inaugural chair, and much more. The library is the oldest research library in the country.

✚ 200 C5 ✉ 170 Central Park West at 77th Street, 10024 ☎ 212/873-3400 🕐 Museum: Tue–Sat 10–6 (Fri to 8), Sun 11–5.45. Library: Tue–Sat 10–5. Print Room by appointment only 👆 Adult $10, Fri 6–8 free, under 12 free 🚇 B, C 🚌 M10, M79 🎧 Audiotours 🎫

ROOSEVELT ISLAND

You can take the subway to Roosevelt Island, but the East 60th Street Heliport Aerial Tramway is a much more fun way to travel the 300 yards (274m) over the East River. Today there are 8,000 residents on the island, which is 2 miles (3.2km) long and only 800ft (244m) wide; this is a much sought-after area. in which to live.

Up to the 19th century it was farmed by the Blackwell family, then it housed a prison, a mental health facility, the Octagon Building (1842), as well as the Smallpox Hospital (1854) and, at the northern tip, a lighthouse (1872), both designed by James Renwick, Jr.

✚ 201 F6 ✉ In the East River, between Manhattan and Queens ☎ 212/832-4555 👆 Tram fare $2 🚇 F 🚌 Q102

STUDIO MUSEUM IN HARLEM

www.studiomuseum.org

Specializing in 19th- and 20th-century African-American art, and 20th-century African and Caribbean art and artifacts, this small museum has a lot to offer. Exhibitions have included *Challenge of the Modern: African-American Artists 1925–1945*, which examined the modernist concepts adopted by black artists in the US and the Caribbean; and *Harlem Postcards 2007*. The small sculpture garden is charming. The tempting gift shop offers a good selection of books, postcards and other items.

✚ Off map 200 C2 ✉ 144 West 125th Street between Lenox and 7th Avenue, 10027 ☎ 212/864-4500 🕐 Wed–Fri, Sun 12–6, Sat 10–6 👆 Adult $7, child $3, under 12 free; free Sun 12–6 🚇 2, 3 🚌 M2, M7, M10, M100 🛒 🎫

UPPER WEST SIDE

The Upper West Side is a lively residential area with numerous historic districts, sumptuous landmark buildings, affordable hotels and excellent restaurants, and an affluent crowd that includes many actors, actresses, directors and musicians. The popular American Museum of Natural History (▷ 204–207) is here, as are the city's premier performing arts complex, the Lincoln Center (▷ 218–219), and the Cathedral Church of St. John the Divine. While you stroll, note the San Remo Apartment Building at 145–146 Central Park West, and the Trump International Hotel/Tower on Columbus Circle.

✚ 200 B4 ✉ Between 59th and 125th streets, west of Central Park 🚇 1, 2, 3, A, B, C, D 🚌 M7, M10, M11, M104 🍴 🛒 🎫

Below *Part of the huge collection of scripture at the Museum of Biblical Art*

INFORMATION

www.whitney.org

http://artport.whitney.org/

200 D6 ✉ 945 Madison Avenue at 75th Street, 10021 ☎ 212/570-3600 Wed–Thu 11–6, Fri 1–9, Sat–Sun 11–6 Adult $15, under 12 free ($2 per ticket service charge online), pay-what-you-wish Fri 6pm–9pm 6 M1, M2, M3, M4 Free exhibition tours start at the lobby information desk ☎ 212/570-3676. Select Saturday family programs free with museum admission for children aged under 12 ☎ 212/671-5300 for info (reservations required for some programs) Sarabeth's café (☎ 212/570-3670) serves lunch Tue 11–3.30, Wed–Fri 11–4.30 and weekend brunch Sat–Sun 10–4.30

Above *The Whitney Museum of American Art, established in 1931, has occupied its present building since 1966*

INTRODUCTION

More than 18,000 works by 1,700 prominent 20th- and 21st-century American artists, including Georgia O'Keeffe, Jasper Johns, Edward Hopper, Mark Rothko and Jackson Pollock are on display here. The collection also includes provocative works by innovative and often controversial American independent film-makers, video artists, multimedia artists and photographers.

Gertrude Vanderbilt Whitney (1875–1942), the daughter of Cornelius Vanderbilt II (1843–99), studied sculpture at the Art Students League of New York and went on to become one of the country's most generous patrons of the arts. In 1914, she launched the Whitney Studio Club, at 8 West 8th Street in the West Village, next to her MacDougal Alley studio, to exhibit works of young, avant-garde American artists. She was particularly fond of revolutionary artists such as John Sloan, Everett Shin and George Luks, realist painters Edward Hopper and Thomas Hart Benton, and early modernist painters such as Max Weber and Stuart Davis.

In 1929, after years of collecting, Whitney offered her personal collection to the Metropolitan Museum of Art. When the Met refused it, she established the Whitney Museum of American Art in 1931 with 700 objects, many from her personal collection. Thus the museum became one of the few museums anywhere in the world to be founded by an artist. The Whitney moved to its present building in 1966.

Before entering the museum on Madison Avenue, take a few minutes to look at the striking granite, modernist building by Marcel Breuer and Hamilton Smith. In a neighborhood of traditional brownstone, limestone and brick row houses, this Brutalist architecture attracts attention, and when it was completed in 1966, many people thought it too heavy and dreary. Today, it is generally esteemed as daring and innovative as it rises in a series of inverted stairs above a sunken sculpture garden. As you enter, the ticket desk is to your left. At the ticket desk and checkout counter there are free museum guides with the current exhibition schedule and leaflets about the current and upcoming temporary exhibitions.

Start your visit with rotating selections from the permanent collection, either on the second floor, or on the fifth floor. New exhibitions are also staged (in the past these have featured individual artists and themed shows).

WHAT TO SEE

ROBERT HENRI, *GERTRUDE VANDERBILT WHITNEY*

Henri (1865–1929) captures the founder of the Whitney Museum, Gertrude Vanderbilt Whitney, in this 1916 portrait. Her granddaughter Flora Whitney Miller donated the painting to the museum, and has remarked that the woman of leisure depicted here is surprising to her, as she remembers her grandmother as an energetic woman always on the go.

WILLIAM J. GLACKENS, *HAMMERSTEIN'S ROOF GARDEN*

Glackens (1870–1938) depicts wealthy New Yorkers at the beginning of the 20th century enjoying watching tightrope walkers, acrobats and jugglers on a hot summer's evening at Hammerstein's on the corner of Seventh Avenue and 42nd Street. This 1901 oil on canvas captures the mood of the roof gardens, where New Yorkers sought relief from the heat as well as entertainment.

GEORGIA O'KEEFFE

O'Keeffe (1887–1986) is well represented in the Whitney Collection, which features several of her dazzling flower paintings and *Summer Days* (1936), one of her many cow-skull paintings. The collection also includes her gorgeous *Music Pink and Blue II* (1919) and *Black and White* (1930).

TIPS

» On Fridays from 6pm to 9pm, admission is pay-what-you-wish and there are live musical performances.

» For a good cross section of the latest in American art and to see works by unknown but promising artists, visit when the Whitney Biennial is on (even-numbered years).

» The fifth-floor galleries change from time to time, presenting different aspects of the Whitney's vast collection in themes. Some of the works highlighted on these pages may not be on view when you visit.

Below Dempsey and Firpo *(1924) by George Bellows (left)*; Laughing Child *(1907) by Robert Henri (center)*; Head *(1926) by Gaston Lachaise (right)*

EDWARD HOPPER

The Whitney Museum holds more than 2,500 works by Hopper (1882–1967), the largest collection in the world. This superb collection includes favorites such as *7am* (1948), the earlier *Small Town Station* (1918–20) and *Italian Quarter From Gloucester* (1912), as well as his particularly haunting painting, *Early Spring Morning* (1930). Notice the curtains and blinds in the windows above the storefronts in this picture. By making each window different, some with yellow blinds and some with white curtains, he gives a sense that people live in each of these dwellings, and that something different is going on inside each one. Hold up your hands to block your view of the barber's pole and the fire hydrant, and notice how they give focus and balance to the painting.

THOMAS HART BENTON, *POKER NIGHT*

Benton (1889–1975) created this commissioned painting in 1948 to represent a scene from Tennessee Williams' Pulitzer Prize-winning Broadway play *A Streetcar Named Desire,* which later became a movie.

LOUISE BOURGEOIS, *QUARANTANIA*

This 1941 sculpture, *Quarantania,* was created by artist Bourgeois (born 1911) when she was feeling homesick for her native France while she studied in the United States. One of her earliest works, the seven stylized wood figures in this sculpture represent the loved ones she left behind in France and still missed deeply.

Opposite Road and House, South Truro *(1930–33)*, Study for Railroad Sunset, *(1929)* and Cape Cod Sunset *(1934)*, all by Edward Hopper
Below Large Trademark with Eight Spotlights *(1962) by Ed Ruscha (left)*; New Hoover Convertibles, Green, Blue; New Hoover Convertibles, Green, Blue; Double-Decker *(1981–87) by Jeff Koons (right)*

JACKSON POLLOCK, *NUMBER 27*

Pollock (1912–56) was one of the innovators, producing abstracts like *Number 27* (1950) by placing the canvas on the floor and drizzling paint on it in a controlled and deliberate manner. Created gradually, with layer upon layer of paint, his expression of movement and emotion are revealed.

JASPER JOHNS, *THREE FLAGS*

This classic Johns (born 1930) painting, *Three Flags* (1958), captures an everyday object in an unusual composition.

REGINALD MARSH

The Whitney Museum's collection of almost 200 Marsh (1898–1954) artworks includes some of his best-known paintings. *Why Not Use the "L"?* (1930) and *Twenty Cent Movie* (1936) capture details of modern life in the city.

ROY LICHTENSTEIN, *LITTLE BIG PAINTING*

In the Pop Gallery, *Little Big Painting* (1965) is a celebration of mass media and popular culture. The red, white and yellow with harsh black lines resemble an image of an abstract painting. With no trace of the artist's hand, no visible brushstroke, and the dot screen in the background, Lichtenstein (1923–97) evokes mechanical printing, the culture of mass reproduction.

ALEXANDER CALDER, *CIRCUS*

The fascination of Calder (1898–1976) with the circus and his training as a mechanical engineer inspired him to create *Circus* (1926–31) and to breathe life into the tiny wire tightrope walkers, acrobats, weight-lifters and dancers in this mixed-media, miniature reproduction of an actual circus. The sculpture is accompanied by a continuous screening of a film of the affable ringmaster, Calder, in his studio with his wife, winding up the gramophone, as they performed for the Paris avant-garde in the 1920s.

WHITNEY BIENNIAL

Held every second year (even-numbered years) in the spring, this exhibition's focus is on presenting and showcasing the latest in American contemporary art. Typically, works by more than 75 modern artists are on display, boldly capturing the artistic present in a multi-faceted portrayal of contemporary art in a multitude of media and styles.

GALLERY GUIDE

Floors 1, 2, 3 and 4: Temporary exhibits encompass a broad variety of styles and disciplines. Often these exhibits feature a single artist, or a particular style. Some of the exhibitions present works from the Whitney Museum permanent collection.

Floor 5: Displaying works from the Whitney Museum's permanent collection, the current exhibition was installed in 2008 and showcases Whitney artworks in five themes:

"Form Building, Form Breaking": The early 1900s gave rise to a group of innovative American artists, including Max Weber and Georgia O'Keeffe, whose paintings portrayed recognizable subjects in a fragmented manner.

"The Figure and Its Realities": The representational style was used by artists including Edward Hopper and Paul Cadmus who often portrayed cultural and social issues.

"City and Machine": The Precisionism artists celebrated the city and urban experience in a precise style, capturing speed, movement and mechanical precision. Works by Charles Sheeler, Louis Lozowick and others are displayed here.

"Mind, Body, Gesture": In the 1940s and 1950s Abstract Expressionists came to prominence, and artists including Jackson Pollock and Willem de Kooning introduced feelings into their work.

Changing temporary exhibit: Selected from the Whitney Collection.

NORTHEAST CORNER OF CENTRAL PARK TO GRANT'S TOMB

This northeast corner of Central Park boasts beautiful gardens, commissioned by parks commissioner Robert Moses in 1936. You will also find a pretty pond, meandering paths, woods and picturesque waterfalls. Just outside the park is the largest church in the United States, the Cathedral Church of St. John the Divine. Nearby is Grant's Tomb, where the great Civil War general Ulysses S. Grant lies in rest.

THE WALK

Distance: 2 miles (3.2km)
Time: 2 hours
Start at: Fifth Avenue and 105th Street
End at: 122nd Street and Riverside Drive

HOW TO GET THERE

Take bus M4 to Madison Avenue and 104th Street; walk one block west to Fifth Avenue.

★ Leave Madison Avenue by turning left onto East 105th Street, and walk one block west to the entrance gate of the Conservatory Garden, across the street from El Museo del Barrio (▷ 214) on Fifth Avenue.

❶ The Conservatory Garden—actually a complex of gardens—is at its best in July and August. As you enter, go toward the Classical fountain in the area known as the Italian Garden. Walk to your left to tour the maze-like English Garden. To the right of the Italian Garden is the French Garden, with the charming Untermeyer Fountain (also called "Three Dancing Maidens"). Pass this fountain and walk through the gate toward the pond on your right, whose Dutch name, Harlem Meer, means "little sea."

Skirt around the pond, keeping to the right, with the pond on your left.

❷ The Charles A. Dana Discovery Center, halfway around the pond, displays natural history exhibits in a Victorian-style building.

Continue around the pond and keep to the right of the Lasker Pool and ice-skating rink. Take the path up some steps, then down a few steps, then to the right and walk under the Huddlestone Arch. Still keeping right, with a pretty little waterfall on your left, walk about 300 yards (274m), and you'll come to a very small rustic wooden bridge on your left. Cross the bridge, keeping to the right, and you'll come to the Glenspan Arch. There's a small waterfall beyond the arch and a small pool is just beyond that. Ahead of you, a couple of paths lead to Central Park West, which you can see. The path to the right takes you out to 103rd Street and Central Park West.

On Central Park West, leave the park, turn right and follow the busy street, past Strangers Gate on the right, to Frederick Douglass Circle.

Opposite The Burnett Fountain in the English Garden, Conservatory Garden
Right *Peace Fountain, St. John the Divine*

Cross Central Park West at 110th Street and continue left around the circle until you come to the traffic lights. Cross 110th Street and immediately turn left. You are now in Harlem. Continue west on 110th Street for two blocks to Amsterdam Avenue, passing Morningside Park. Turn right and walk north to 111th Street and the Cathedral Church of St. John the Divine.

❸ The enormous Cathedral Church of St. John the Divine is well worth exploring. The Peace Fountain in the Children's Sculpture Garden depicts a bronze Michael the Archangel slaying the devil.

Leaving the cathedral, cross to the west side of Amsterdam Avenue and follow 112th Street west one block to Broadway. Tom's Restaurant, familiar to fans of the TV show *Seinfeld,* is on the right. If you find that you are tired and feel that you do not want to continue, you can catch a bus on the west side of Broadway or take the M4 to Midtown East or the M104 to Midtown West.

To continue the walk, go north up Broadway to 122nd Street, passing Columbia University (▷ 203), New York City's oldest institution of higher learning, on your right. Turn left onto 122nd Street and then walk two blocks west, passing the Manhattan School of Music on your left, to Riverside Drive. Riverside Church is on your left.

❹ From its 392ft (119m) tower, Riverside Church offers a magnificent view across the Hudson River.

❺ Nearby is the General Grant National Memorial (▷ 214), where Grant and his wife, Julia, rest side by side in two black sarcophagi. The Gaudí-style mosaic benches and tables surrounding the tombs are a good spot for a picnic.

From here you can walk back to Broadway and get the M4 or M104 bus downtown.

WHEN TO GO
Do this walk when the weather is pleasant and you want to have a quiet stroll away from crowds. Although the park is generally safe by day and is patroled, this is not a walk to do alone. Pack a picnic to enjoy along the way.

WHERE TO EAT
Tom's Restaurant, 2880 Broadway at 112th Street (212/ 864-6137).

PLACES TO VISIT
CATHEDRAL CHURCH OF ST. JOHN THE DIVINE
✉ 1047 Amsterdam Avenue at 112th Street
☎ 212/316-7540 🕐 Daily 7–6

RIVERSIDE CHURCH
✉ 490 Riverside Drive ☎ 212/870-6700
🕐 Daily 7am–10pm, Claremont Avenue entrance

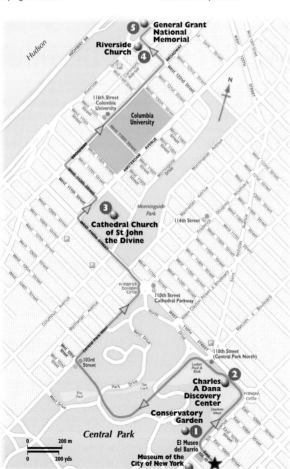

CENTRAL PARK WEST HISTORIC DISTRICT

This walk begins with a quick look at the Dakota building, where former Beatle John Lennon was shot in 1980, then stops at his memorial across the street in Central Park. In the 1960s, with private contributions of about $165 million, Upper West Side tenements were razed and the Lincoln Center was built in their stead, a very pleasant complex of pedestrian open spaces, theaters, concert halls, cinemas and museums. Many actors, actresses and movie directors work and live in the neighborhood—it's fun to see if you can spot any.

THE WALK

Distance: 1.5 miles (2.4km)
Time: 1.5 to 2 hours
Start/End at: 72nd Street subway station

HOW TO GET THERE

Subway B or C; bus M10.

★ Leave the 72nd Street subway at the corner of 72nd Street and Central Park West.

❶ The Dakota (▷ 203) is on the northwest corner of Central Park West and 72nd Street. Look at the front of the building on 72nd Street, where John Lennon was shot. His wife, Yoko Ono, still lives in an apartment in the building.

Walk east across Central Park West and follow the path straight ahead to Strawberry Fields.

❷ Here there is a memorial to Lennon, a black-and-white mosaic called *Imagine*.

Back on Central Park West, turn left, and walk south. Note the residential streets lined with 19th-century brownstones to your right. Turn left into the park at West 67th Street.

❸ Here, at Tavern on the Green, celebrities show up for gala events and film premieres and tourists come (and pay the price) to enjoy the seating on the leafy patio in summer. The Sheep Meadow, straight ahead, is a 15-acre (6ha) expanse created as part of the Olmsted and Vaux design for Central Park; at the time it reminded many city-dwellers of the rural landscapes they had left behind when they emigrated to the United States.

Return to Central Park West and go south for two blocks. Turn right on 65th Street to Columbus Avenue. Cross Broadway and Columbus Avenue. On the west of Broadway is the Lincoln Center.

❹ The Lincoln Center (▷ 218–219) includes the Alice Tully Hall (on the northwest corner of 65th Street) and Avery Fisher Hall (on the southwest corner). Much of the movie *West Side Story* was shot in the tenements that once stood on this spot. Walk south from Avery Fisher about 300 yards (274m) to the Lincoln Center central plaza, with its fountain. On the south side of the plaza is the home of the New York City Ballet, the David H. Koch Theater; rising over the plaza on the west is the Metropolitan Opera House with Austrian chandeliers

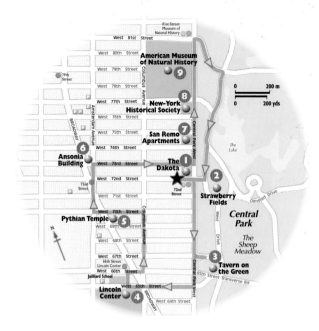

7 Designed in 1930 by architect Emery Roth, the towers of the San Remo Apartments at 145–146 Central Park West grace the skyline. Residents have included Paul Simon and Dustin Hoffman.

Continue north on Central Park West to 77th Street.

8 The New-York Historical Society (▷ 221) is on the corner of 77th and Central Park West. The fascinating collections and unusual variety of gifts in the shop make this worth a stop.

Cross West 77th Street.

9 The enormous American Museum of Natural History (▷ 204–207) is on your left. Go to the main entrance to admire the bronze statue of President Theodore Roosevelt seated upon a horse, then step inside to look at William Mackay's beautiful murals depicting events from Roosevelt's life in the Roosevelt Memorial Hall.

After leaving the museum, walk up Central Park West, and at the 81st Street traffic lights take the entrance to the park straight ahead of you. As soon as you enter, take the path immediately to your right and walk south along this path to West 72nd Street and back again to the 72nd Street subway station.

WHEN TO GO
This walk is very pleasant on Sunday afternoons. Most shops and restaurants are open then.

WHERE TO EAT
CAFÉ LUXEMBOURG
✉ 200 West 70th Street ☎ 212/595-9797

and Marc Chagall murals visible through the glass facade. To the south of the Met is a pleasant open area where open-air concerts are held in summer and the Big Apple Circus holds forth over the year-end holidays. The pond sculpture, Henry Moore's *Reclining Figure*, and the Vivian Beaumont Theater lie to the north of the Met.

Walk up the steps to the Juilliard School to the north, turn right then left down the steps to Broadway. Cross 66th Street, then cross Broadway to your right. Walk east on 66th to Columbus Avenue and turn left. On the right stands the contemporary ABC Building at No. 147 Columbus. Continue along Columbus to West 70th Street and turn left.

5 At 135 West 70th, near the corner of 70th and Broadway is the Pythian Temple, now a condominium; designed by Thomas W. Lamb, and built in 1926, it was dedicated to Pythianism, the cult of the oracle at Delphi, and Assyrian sages still guard the entrance. Bill Haley and the Comets recorded

"Rock Around the Clock" here in 1954. Farther along, at the corner of Amsterdam Avenue, Café Luxembourg is a popular bistro.

Turn right onto Amsterdam Avenue. As you approach West 72nd Street, you'll see one of the few remaining old subway buildings from the early 1900s on your left and a pleasingly harmonious new structure, an expansion of the venerable subway station, across 72nd on the north side of the street. Cross West 72nd Street.

6 The magnificent Beaux Arts Ansonia Building rises at 2109 Broadway between West 73rd and West 74th streets. Caruso, Stravinsky and Toscanini all lived at the Ansonia, and the excellent soundproofing between apartments and floors continues to attract distinguished musicians, singers and conductors.

Turn right on West 73rd Street; 18 row houses, between Nos. 248 and 272, are the earliest houses in the neighborhood, dating from 1885. Turn left on Central Park West.

Opposite *The memorial to John Lennon in Strawberry Fields, Central Park*

WHAT TO DO

SHOPPING

ARGOSY BOOKS
www.argosybooks.com
This store, which has been operating since 1925, is one of the few remaining bookstores in the city for out-of-print and rare books. On its seven floors, it has an extensive stock of books, with strengths in Americana, contemporary first editions, and the history of science and medicine. It also sells prints, autographs and antique maps.
✚ 245 E7 ✉ 116 East 59th Street, between Park and Lexington avenues ☎ 212/753-4455 🕐 Sep–end Apr Mon–Sat 10–6; rest of year Mon–Fri 10–6 🚇 59th Street (4, 5, 6) 🚌 M1, M2, M3, M4, M98, M101, M102, M103

BARNEYS
www.barneys.com
Barneys stocks only what's newest and hippest, so you'll find designers whose names everyone knows, as well as those known only to fashion cognoscenti—say, Proenza Schouler, Behnaz Sarafpour and Tess Giberson. The windows always make a statement, and people flock to the sales at the warehouse on 17th Street, between Seventh and Eighth avenues.

✚ 244 D7 ✉ 660 Madison Avenue, between East 60th and 61st streets ☎ 212/826-8900, warehouse 212/450-8400 🕐 Mon–Fri 10–8, Sat 10–7, Sun 11–6 🚇 Fifth Avenue/59th Street (N, R, W), 59th Street (4, 5, 6) 🚌 M30

BLOOMINGDALE'S
www.bloomingdales.com
Bloomingdale's, opened in 1879, is one of the most venerable names in Manhattan yet keeps up with every trend. It's an icon among its fans, and tourists and locals alike buy logo items emblazoned with the store's name or its sobriquet, "Bloomie's." On weekends locals come along to schmooze.
✚ 245 E7 ☎ 212/705-2000 🕐 Mon–Fri 10–8.30, Sat 10–7, Sun 11–7 🚇 59th Street/Lexington (4, 5, 6) 🚌 M98, M101, M102, M103

BORRELLI
www.luigiborrelli.com
The ultimate Italian tailor favored by many a male film star offers exquisite shirts as well as beautiful suits, coats and sweaters, custom-made and off the rack.
✚ 244 D7 ✉ 16 East 60th Street, between Madison and Fifth avenues ☎ 212/644-9610 🕐 Mon–Sat 10–6, Sun

11–5; closed Sun Jul–end Aug 🚇 Fifth Avenue/59th Street (N, R, W) 🚌 M1, M2, M3, M4, M30

CALVIN KLEIN
www.calvinkleininc.com
The beloved Bronx-born American designer who re-made the American fashion industry in the 1970s has expanded beyond refined sportswear into shoes, accessories and home furnishings. He knows how to cut and he knows how to advertise. The boutique is a paragon of minimalism by British architect John Pawson, worth seeing in its own right.
✚ 244 D7 ✉ 654 Madison Avenue at East 60th Street ☎ 212/292-9000 🕐 Mon–Sat 10–6 (Thu until 7), Sun 12–6 🚇 Lexington Avenue/59th Street (N, R, W, 4, 5, 6) 🚌 M1, M2, M3, M4

CRATE AND BARREL
www.crateandbarrel.com
This chain sells affordable, good-looking designs for your home. The focus is on tableware (from linens to glasses). It also sells attractive outdoor dining stuff.
✚ 244 D7 ✉ 650 Madison Avenue at East 59th Street ☎ 212/308-0011 🕐 Mon–Fri 10–8, Sat 10–7, Sun 12–6

Opposite Bloomingdale's bags are a shopper's "must-have"

🚇 59th Street/Fifth Avenue (N, R, W)
🚌 M1, M2, M3, M4, M5

DKNY
www.dkny.com
Donna Karan delivers what New York women want—comfortable clothes that coordinate easily. Black used to be her favorite color, but the current inventory offers plenty of colorful blouses, dresses, miniskirts, combat jackets and accessories. This striking glass-wrapped boutique opened in 1998. Also at 420 West Broadway and Spring Street.
➕ 244 D7 ✉ 655 Madison Avenue, between East 60th and 61st streets
☎ 212/223-3569 🕐 Mon–Sat 11–8, Sun 11–7 🚇 Fifth Avenue/59th Street (N, R, W) 🚌 M1, M2, M3, M4, M30

DOLCE & GABBANA
www.dolcegabbana.it
Domenico Dolce and Stefano Gabbana have dressed virtually every Hollywood and Broadway star in fashions that exude heat (distressed torn pants and shirts, lots of corset lacing). This spacious and beautiful store is their flagship.
➕ 244 D6 ✉ 825 Madison Avenue, between East 68th and 69th streets
☎ 212/249-4100 🕐 Mon–Sat 10–6 (Thu until 7), Sun 12–5 🚇 68th Street (6) 🚌 M1, M2, M3, M4

DONNA KARAN
www.donnakaran.com
In the elegant and dramatic flagship of this very popular American designer, the floating staircase is worthy of Fred Astaire and Ginger Rogers.
➕ 244 D6 ✉ 819 Madison Avenue, between East 68th and 69th streets
☎ 212/861-1001 🕐 Mon–Sat 10–6 (Thu until 7), Sun 12–5 🚇 68th Street (6) 🚌 M1, M2, M3, M4

GIORGIO ARMANI
www.giorgioarmani.com
The ultimate designer for men and women makes suits in understated fabrics with superb detailing.

➕ 244 D7 ✉ 760 Madison Avenue at 65th Street ☎ 212/988-9191 🕐 Mon–Sat 10–6 (Thu until 7) 🚇 68th Street (6) 🚌 M1, M2, M3, M4

HUE-MAN BOOKSTORE
www.huemanbookstore.com
This bookstore stocks classic and contemporary African-American fiction and non-fiction, and holds author readings.
➕ Off map 244 C2 ✉ 2319 Frederick Douglass Boulevard, between 124th and 125th streets ☎ 212/665-7400 🕐 Mon–Fri 10–8, Sat 10–7, Sun 11–7 🚇 125th Street (A, B, C, D) 🚌 M10

JIMMY CHOO
www.jimmychoo.com
Velvet sofas and satin chairs set the tone at this flagship store selling the exquisite shoes and purses by this legendary Malaysian designer. His line offers a variety of styles from pony boots and evening slides to kitten heels, stilettos and sandals made in all kinds of materials and fabrics, which are decorated with beads, crystals or embroidery, or just beautifully colored.
➕ 244 D7 ✉ 716 Madison Avenue, between 63rd and 64th streets (west side) ☎ 212/759-7078. Also at 645 Fifth Avenue between 5th and Madison ☎ 212/593-0800 🕐 Mon–Sat 10–6 (Thu until 7), Sun 12–5 🚇 59th Street (4, 5, 6) or 68th Street (6) 🚌 M1, M2, M3, M4

KENNETH COLE
www.kennethcole.com
Good, clean styling and quality for the money have made Kenneth Cole a major fashion player. He started with urban shoes, but has expanded to include such fashionable footwear as satin pumps with ankle straps, plus sportswear, handbags, fragrance and other accessories.
➕ 244 C5 ✉ 353 Columbus Avenue, between West 76th and 77th streets ☎ 212/873-2061 🕐 Mon–Sat 10–8, Sun 11–7 🚇 79th Street (1) 🚌 M7, M11

KITCHEN ARTS AND LETTERS
www.kitchenartsandletters.com
You can find all of the classic cookery writers here—Julia Child,

James Beard and M. F. K. Fisher—plus a host of others organized by category. This store is wonderful for rare and historic culinary volumes, too.
➕ 245 E4 ✉ 1435 Lexington Avenue, between 93rd and 94th streets ☎ 212/876-5550 🕐 Mon 1–6, Tue–Fri 10–6.30, Sat 11–6 🚇 96th Street (6) 🚌 M98, M101, M102, M103

NICOLE MILLER
www.nicolemiller.com
Nicole Miller's innovative, sexy and very wearable fashions attract a number of celebrity clients. She makes cowl-neck halter tops, distressed jersey tunics, bags and shoes, and simple but elegant evening gowns.
➕ 244 D7 ✉ 780 Madison Avenue, between 66th and 67th streets ☎ 212/288-9779 🕐 Mon–Fri 10–7, Sat 10–6, Sun 12–5 🚇 68th Street (6) 🚌 M2, M3, M4

PRADA
www.prada.com
Excellent design, luxury and fine leather are the components that moved the Italian Prada house to fashion prominence. Opulent, high quality men's and women's fashions and a complete line of leather accessories, shoes, luggage and hats are on display here.
➕ 244 D6 ✉ 841 Madison Avenue at East 70th Street ☎ 212/334-8888 🕐 Mon–Sat 11–7, Sun 12–6 🚇 68th Street Hunter College (6) 🚌 M2, M3, M4

RALPH LAUREN
www.ralphlauren.com
Bronx native Ralph Lauren sells his distinguished cowboy and English country heritage looks in the Rhinelander Mansion, one of a handful of such turn-of-the-20th-century houses in Manhattan, renovated to gleaming splendor from its amazing hand-carved staircase to its Baccarat chandeliers and 19th-century oil paintings.
➕ 244 D6 ✉ 867 Madison Avenue, between East 71st and 72nd streets ☎ 212/606-2100 🕐 Mon–Wed 10–7, Thu 10–8, Fri–Sat 10–6, Sun 12–6 🚇 68th Street (6) 🚌 M1, M2, M3, M4

SHERRY-LEHMANN
www.sherry-lehmann.com

Even if you don't buy, this is a shop to browse. In business since 1934, it has a $10 million inventory of wines from every corner of the world, a spacious new flagship store, and a friendly, knowledgeable staff. Besides the premier cru Bordeaux and Burgundies, you'll find ice wines from Canada, Swiss and Lebanese varieties, and selections of sake, port and Madeira. Prices are reasonable, too. Try to stop by for the Wednesday tasting session from 3 to 6.

🚻 244 D7 ✉ 505 Park Avenue at East 59th Street ☎ 212/838-7500 🕐 Mon–Sat 9–8 🚇 Fifth Avenue/59 Street (N, R, W), 59th Street/Lexington Avenue (4, 5, 6) 🚌 M1, M2, M3, M4, M30

TIME WARNER CENTER
www.shopsatcolumbuscircle.com

This, the first luxury shopping mall in Manhattan, will be familiar to suburbanites. Here under one roof are such big-name stores as Coach, Cole Haan, Davidoff, Godiva, L'Occitane, Hugo Boss, Thomas Pink and Williams-Sonoma.

🚻 244 C7 ✉ 10 Columbus Circle ☎ 212/823-6000 🕐 Mon–Sat 10–9, Sun 12–6 🚇 59th Street/Columbus Circle (A, C, B, D, 1) 🚌 M7, M10

TOD'S
www.tods.com

This Italian designer makes ultra-comfortable shoes, plus boots with classic equestrian styling and detail. They are relatively expensive, but long-lasting.

🚻 244 D7 ✉ 650 Madison Avenue, between East 59th and 60th streets ☎ 212/644-5945 🕐 Mon–Sat 10–6 (Thu until 7), Sun 12–5 🚇 59th Street/Fifth Avenue (N, R, W) 🚌 M1, M2, M3, M4

ZABAR'S
www.zabars.com

The countermen who wield the knives at this culinary landmark are legendary for their skills and their attitude. Look for the exquisite smoked salmon and other kinds of smoked fish, terrific cheeses, and,

upstairs, top-quality cookware and tableware at great prices.

🚻 244 B5 ✉ 2245 Broadway, between West 80th and 81st streets ☎ 212/787-2000 🕐 Mon–Fri 8–7.30, Sat 8–8, Sun 9–6 🚇 79th Street (1) 🚌 M104

ENTERTAINMENT AND NIGHTLIFE

92ND STREET Y
www.92Y.org

The 92nd Street Y offers some of the city's most varied programs. It hosts music recitals (Guarneri and Tokyo string quartets, Janos Starker), jazz, pop and folk, poetry and literature readings (Thomas Keneally, V. S. Naipaul), and lectures on every conceivable subject by cultural leaders. The 92nd Street Y is a Jewish cultural organization.

🚻 245 E4 ✉ Kauffman Concert Hall, 1395 Lexington Avenue at 92nd Street ☎ 212/415-5500, 212/415-5440 🚇 96th Street (6) 🚌 M96, M98, M101, M102, M103

AARON DAVIS HALL/ HARLEM STAGE
www.harlemstage.org

Harlem's principal center for the performing arts presents established and emerging artists of color in music, dance, theater and multimedia performances.

The Harlem Stage is across the street from the three-theater Aaron Davis Hall.

🚻 Off map 244 C2 ✉ City College of New York, West 135th Street and Convent Avenue ☎ 212/281-9240 🚇 137th Street/Broadway (1) 🚌 M4, M5

ALICE TULLY HALL
www.lincolncenter.org

Redesigned in 2009, the 1,100-seat hall is chic and lively with great acoustics for chamber music, vocal recitals, jazz and other outstanding musical events.

The Chamber Music Society (tel 212/875-5788) resides here.

🚻 244 B7 ✉ 1941 Broadway on 65th Street, between Broadway and Amsterdam Avenue ☎ 212/875-5050 or 212/721-6500 ✋ $27.50–$52 🚇 66th Street (1) 🚌 M5, M7, M66, M104

APOLLO THEATER
www.apollotheater.com

Originally a vaudeville theater, the Apollo has been a venue for black entertainers since 1934. Everyone from Duke Ellington and Billie Holiday to Aretha Franklin and Stevie Wonder has performed here. The Wednesday Amateur Night Competition is famous, drawing crowds who register their approval or disapproval with gusto. Today the entertainment ranges from musicians and singers to musicals, starring many of the biggest names in music.

🚻 Off map 244 C2 ✉ 253 West 125th Street, between Frederick Douglass Boulevard and St. Nicholas Avenue ☎ 212/531-5300 🚇 125th Street (A, B, C, D), Lenox (1, 2, 3) 🚌 M104

ASIA SOCIETY
www.asiasociety.org

The downstairs auditorium showcases arts and culture—dance, film, lectures and music—from Asia. Ravi Shankar made his American debut at the Asia Society.

🚻 244 D6 ✉ 725 Park Avenue at East 70th Street ☎ 212/288-6400 🚇 68th Street (6) 🚌 M1, M2, M3, M4, M72

THE AUCTION HOUSE
Sotheby's meets New Orleans bordello at this wood-paneled, split-level lounge. Patrons sip cocktails on velvet sofas beneath gilt-framed portraits.

🚻 245 E4 ✉ 300 East 89th Street, between First and Second avenues ☎ 212/427-4458 🕐 Daily 7.30pm–4am 🚇 86th Street (4, 5, 6)

AVERY FISHER HALL
www.lincolncenter.org
www.nyphil.org

Home to the New York Philharmonic, this hall seats 2,700. Many other groups perform here, including the American Symphony Orchestra, under Leon Botstein, and the summer Mostly Mozart Festival. During its season, the Philharmonic opens its morning rehearsals to the public (usually on Thursdays at 9.45 for $15).

➕ 244 B7 ✉ 10 Lincoln Center Plaza (Columbus Avenue at 65th Street) ☎ 212/875-5030 or 212/721-6500 ✋ $25–$98 🚇 66th Street (1) 🚌 M5, M7, M66, M104

BEACON THEATRE
www.beacontheatre.com
Many different artists perform here, from the likes of Sinead O'Connor and David Gray to modern ballet.
➕ 244 B6 ✉ 2124 Broadway at 74th Street ☎ 212/465-6500 ✋ $33–$90 🚇 72nd Street (1, 2, 3) 🚌 M72, M104

BEMELMANS BAR
Named for the illustrator of the beloved Madeleine books, Ludwig Bemelmans, this intimate bar attracts the city's most upscale tipplers with first-class cocktails and perfect piano music from Tony De Sare or the Chris Gillespie Trio most evenings (9.30–1.30).
➕ 244 D5 ✉ Carlyle Hotel, 35 East 76th Street, between Park and Madison avenues ☎ 212/744-1600 🕐 Mon–Sat 11am–1am, Sun 9pm–midnight ✋ Fri–Sat $20–$25 ($10 at bar) 🚇 77th Street (6)

BRUNO WALTER AUDITORIUM
Lectures, seminars, concerts and films are the regular fare at this 212-seat hall. The library is a superb performing arts archive.
➕ 244 B7 ✉ The New York Public Library for the Performing Arts, 111 Amsterdam Avenue, between West 64th and 65th streets ☎ 212/870-1630, 212/642-0142 (programs) ✋ Free 🚇 66th Street (1) 🚌 M5, M7, M66, M104

CATHEDRAL CHURCH OF ST. JOHN THE DIVINE
www.stjohndivine.org
Stop by to admire the incomplete edifice, begun in 1892, and you may hear one of the sanctuary's five organs. The repertoire during arts events ranges from choirs singing Bach cantatas or chanting Tibetan monks to music made famous by Duke Ellington and Judy Collins.
➕ 244 B2 ✉ 1047 Amsterdam Avenue at 112th Street ☎ 212/316-7540 🚇 Cathedral Parkway/110th Street (1) 🚌 M4, M11

CLASSICAL THEATRE OF HARLEM
www.classicaltheatreofharlem.org
This company, founded in 1988, has been recognized outside Harlem only recently. It has garnered acclaim for recent productions of Genet's *The Blacks* and Euripides' *The Trojan Women*.
➕ Off map 244 C2 ✉ Harlem School of the Arts Theater, 645 St. Nicholas Avenue, near 141st Street ☎ 212/926-4100 or 212/564-9983 🚇 145th Street (A, B, C)

COTTON CLUB
www.cottonclub-newyork.com
Although its heyday was from 1923 to 1935 (then on 142nd Street), this famous Harlem landmark still has blues, jazz and gospel acts that seem straight out of the 1920s. Monday night is swing night.
➕ Off map 244 B2 ✉ 656 West 125th Street, between Broadway and Riverside Drive ☎ 212/663-7980 🕐 Mon, Thu–Fri 8–midnight, Sat–Sun noon and 2.30pm seating ✋ $15–$40 🚇 125th Street (1) 🚌 M104, Bx 15

DANGERFIELD'S
www.dangerfields.com
Rodney Dangerfield is no longer a regular presence, but this classic seedy club, established in 1969, has hosted many legends, from Jay Leno and Jim Carrey to Jackie Mason and Tim Allen.
➕ 245 E7 ✉ 1118 First Avenue, between East 61st and 62nd streets ☎ 212/593-1650 🕐 Shows Sun–Thu 8.45, Fri 8.30, 10.30, Sat. 8, 10.30, 12.30am ✋ $15–$20, plus 2-drink minimum 🚇 59th Street (4, 5, 6) 🚌 M15, M57

DAVID H. KOCH THEATER
www.nycballet.com
www.nycopera.com
This 2,755-seat auditorium is home to the New York City Opera and the New York City Ballet. The New York City Opera is famous for its emphasis on the ensemble rather than soloists, and many prefer its stimulating productions over those of the Met. The New York City Ballet began in 1933, and is still going strong under artistic director Peter Martins. The company performs for

23 weeks in the State Theater and then moves upstate to Saratoga.
➕ 244 B7 ✉ 20 Lincoln Center Plaza at 63rd Street ☎ 212/870-5570 ✋ City Opera $32–$110 (standing room only $12), NYC Ballet $30–$105 🚇 50th Street (1, 9) 🚌 M5, M7, M11, M66, M104

ELAINE'S
This Italian restaurant offers a full and well-stocked bar, great food and a fun vibe. It's a great place for celebrity spotting.
➕ 245 E4 ✉ 1703 Second Avenue between East 88th and 89th streets ☎ 212/534-8103 🕐 Daily 6–2 🚇 86th Street (4, 5, 6)

FEINSTEIN'S AT LOEWS REGENCY
www.feinsteinsattheregency.com
Feinstein's at Loews Regency is a lush, elegant and exclusive club. Michael Feinstein plays on occasion. Dinner is available.
➕ 244 D7 ✉ Regency Hotel, 540 Park Avenue at East 61st Street ☎ 212/339-4095 🕐 Shows Tue–Sat, usually at 8, and 10.30 on Sat ✋ $50–$110, plus $40 minimum 🚇 Lexington/63rd Street (F), 59th Street (4, 5, 6), 59th Street (N, R, W) 🚌 M1, M2, M3, M4, M57

FILM SOCIETY OF LINCOLN CENTER
www.filmlinc.com
This society hosts many different festivals—the New York Jewish Festival, Spanish Cinema Now, and Women in Film, for example.
➕ 244 B7 ✉ Walter Reade Theater, 165 West 65th Street ☎ 212/875-5600 ✋ $11 🚇 66th Street (1) 🚌 M5, M7, M66, M104

FLORENCE GOULD HALL
www.fiaf.org (click on "Rental")
Chamber groups, opera singers, pop and jazz artists, dance companies, and actors reading all entertain in this 400-seat auditorium associated with the Alliance Française.
➕ 244 D7 ✉ 55 East 59th Street, between Park and Madison avenues ☎ 212/355-6100 ✋ $30–$35 🚇 Fifth Avenue/59th Street (N, R, W) 🚌 M1, M2, M3, M4, M5, M57

FRICK COLLECTION
www.frick.org
The classical music concerts and recitals in this exquisite museum are a must.
✚ 244 D6 ✉ 1 East 70th Street ☎ 212/288-0700 🚇 68th Street (6) 🚌 M1, M2, M3, M4, M72

GRACE RAINEY ROGERS AUDITORIUM
www.metmuseum.org
Small musical groups and individuals entertain in this mid-size, 700-seat auditorium. And the Met always has chamber music in the Great Hall Balcony on Friday and Saturday evenings.
✚ 244 D5 ✉ The Metropolitan Museum of Art, Fifth Avenue at 82nd Street ☎ 212/535-7710 or 212/570-3949 ✋ $35–$55 🚇 77th Street (6) 🚌 M1, M2, M3, M4, M79

HUDSON BARS
The two bars are central to this hipster hotel. In the Hudson, a long ornate table serves as the bar. Late at night, the backlit floor becomes a dance floor. In the Library, there are leather chairs, ottomans and a fireplace, providing a luxurious backdrop to a relaxing drink.
✚ 244 C7 ✉ Hudson Hotel, 356 West 58th Street, between Eighth and Ninth avenues ☎ 212/554-6000 🕐 Hudson Sun–Wed 4–1.30, Thu–Sat 4–3; Library Sun–Wed noon–1am, Thu–Sat noon–2.30am 🚇 59th Street/Columbus Circle (A, B, C, D, 1)

JAZZ AT LINCOLN CENTER
www.jalc.org
Top-drawer jazz artists give stunning performances in the 1,230-seat Rose Theater, the 300- to 600-seat Allen Room (whose 50-foot-high (15m) glass wall overlooks Columbus Circle) and in the more intimate Dizzy's Club Coca-Cola, commemorating the great Dizzy Gillespie.
✚ 244 B7 ✉ Time Warner Center at Broadway and 60th Street ☎ 212/258-9800 or 212/721-6500 ✋ $30–$150; club has cover and minimum 🚇 59th Street (1) 🚌 M5, M104

JUILLIARD SCHOOL
www.juilliard.edu
This world-famous performing arts school is especially well known for music. The young artists who train here can be seen in stimulating programs in two auditoriums. Juilliard also incorporates the School for American Ballet, which is the training ground for the New York City Ballet. Dance aficionados run to secure tickets for the school's annual workshop production in early summer (tel 212/769-6600).
✚ 244 B7 ✉ 60 Lincoln Plaza ☎ 212/799-5000 ✋ Most are free except for opera programs and dance workshops 🚇 66th Street (1) 🚌 M5, M7, M66, M104

KOSCIUSZKO FOUNDATION
www.kosciuszkofoundation.org
Programs at the Kosciuszko Foundation are varied. Events feature works by Polish composers or artists.
✚ 244 D7 ✉ 15 East 65th Street ☎ 212/734-2130 🚇 68th Street (6) 🚌 M1, M2, M3, M4

LENOX LOUNGE
www.lenoxlounge.com
This long-time Harlem hang-out for musicians has jazz every night except Tuesday.
✚ Off map 244 D2 ✉ 288 Lenox Avenue, between 124th and 125th streets ☎ 212/427-0253 🕐 Restaurant Sun–Thu 4.30pm–midnight, Fri–Sat 4.30pm–2am; shows daily, times vary ✋ Free–$25, plus $16 drinks minimum on Fri and Sat 🚇 125th Street (2, 3) 🚌 M7, M102

LINCOLN CENTER FOR THE PERFORMING ARTS
www.lincolncenter.org
This huge complex is home to the Metropolitan Opera House, the David H. Koch Theater, Avery Fisher Hall, the Vivian Beaumont and Mitzi E. Newhouse theaters, the New York Public Library of the Performing Arts, the Walter Reade movie theater and the Juilliard School. In summer there is dancing under the stars on the plaza as well as the Lincoln Center Festival, a free event which presents hundreds of performing artists and

companies of all kinds. For tours of the first three halls mentioned above call 212/875-5350 to make a reservation.
✚ 244 B7 ✉ Columbus Avenue, between 62nd and 66th streets ☎ 212/875-5000 or 212/875-5456 🚇 66th Street (1) 🚌 M7, M11, M66, M104

LINCOLN PLAZA CINEMA
www.lincolnplazacinema.com
A six-screener showing a select group of critically successful first-run movies and foreign films. For example, Gurinder Chadha's Bend it Like Beckham and Almodóvar's Talk to Her both played here.
✚ 244 C7 ✉ 1886 Broadway at 63rd Street ☎ 212/757-2280 ✋ $11 🚇 66th Street (1) 🚌 M5, M7, M66, M104

LUKE'S BAR AND GRILL
www.lukesbarandgrill.com
The bar and grill are equal partners at Luke's, which opened in 1990 and is the kind of respectable bar that appeals to families as well as young professionals. They serve typical bar food, with great burgers, and there's a wide stock of good beers, which becomes more evident when the restaurant closes about midnight/1am.
✚ 245 E5 ✉ 1394 Third Avenue, between 79th and 80th streets ☎ 212/249-7070 🕐 Mon–Fri 11.30am–4am, Sat–Sun 10am–4am 🚇 77th Street (6)

MAKOR
www.92Y.org
This club, part of a Jewish community center, hosts mainly documentaries and oldies. A new branch of the club (92YTribeca) opened in 2008 at 200 Hudson Street, between Vestry and Desbrosses streets (the telephone number is the same as below).
✚ 245 E4 ✉ 1395 Lexington Avenue at 92nd Street ☎ 212/601-1000 ✋ $9 🚇 86th Street (4, 5, 6) 🚌 M1, M2, M86, M96, M101, M102

MANHATTAN SCHOOL OF MUSIC
www.msmnyc.edu
This institution with a world-class reputation has a large concert hall as

well as several smaller venues. The programming is diverse—orchestras, chamber ensembles, recitals—and ticket prices are reasonable. Vocal and orchestral master classes take place on a regular basis.

➕ Off map 244 B2 ✉ 120 Claremont Avenue, Broadway at 122nd Street ☎ 212/749-2802 or 917/493-4428 🚇 125th Street (1) 🚌 M4, M104

MERKIN CONCERT HALL

http://kaufman-center.org/merkin-concert-hall

Part of the Kaufman Center, national and international chamber groups perform here. You might find traditional classical, new music or even a group from Japan.

➕ 244 B6 ✉ 129 West 67th Street ☎ 212/501-3330 💵 $15–$45 🚇 66th Street (1) 🚌 M5, M7, M104

METROPOLITAN MUSEUM ROOF GARDEN

This venue is classy all the way. What better accompaniment to a drink than a view of the sun setting over Central Park? The balcony bar is chic with its chamber music and jazz groups.

➕ 244 D5 ✉ Metropolitan Museum of Art, 1000 Fifth Avenue at 82nd Street ☎ 212/277-8888 🕐 Roof Garden May–Oct Tue–Thu, Sun 10–4.30, Fri–Sat 10–8; Balcony Bar Fri–Sat 4–8 🚇 86th Street (4, 5, 6), 77th Street (6)

METROPOLITAN OPERA HOUSE

www.metopera.org

The Metropolitan Opera, which had its first season in 1883–84, moved to this building on the western side of Lincoln Center Plaza in 1966. Although modern, it is glamorous with its Chagall paintings, plush crimson carpeting, chandeliers and gold leaf. The back of each of the theater's 3,800-seats has a screen that shows subtitles during performances. Most productions are spectacular, with the best international stars. Season-ticket holders snap up most of the best seats (and the best-priced seats) but individual tickets are usually

available. Beginning in May the American Ballet Theatre performs a traditional repertory and modern pieces by such choreographers as James Kudelka and Twyla Tharp.

➕ 244 B7 ✉ 30 Lincoln Center Plaza, between 63rd and 64th streets ☎ 212/362-6000 💵 $15–$295, standing room $15–$20 🚇 66th Street (1) 🚌 M5, M7, M11, M66, M104

MILLER THEATRE

www.millertheatre.com

Many cutting-edge classical groups and composers are presented here at Miller Theatre. Among the most notable are John Zorn, Julia Wolfe and John King.

➕ Off map 244 B2 ✉ Columbia University, 2960 Broadway at 116th Street ☎ 212/854-7799 🚇 116th Street (1) 🚌 M104

MITZI E. NEWHOUSE THEATER

www.lct.org

Spalding Gray performed *Swimming to Cambodia* (1996) at this Lincoln Center theater. Its 299 seats are steeply raked.

➕ 244 B7 ✉ 150 West 65th Street ☎ 212/362-7600 🕐 Tue–Sat 8, matinees Wed, Sat 2, Sun 3 🚇 66th Street (1) 🚌 M5, M7, M66, M104

NEW YORK SOCIETY FOR ETHICAL CULTURE

www.nysec.org

All kinds of cultural events are held here. A program of lectures and discussions often complements the performances.

➕ 244 C7 ✉ 2 West 64th Street at Central Park West ☎ 212/874-5210 or 866/468-7619 🚇 66th Street (1) 🚌 M10

SCHOMBURG CENTER FOR RESEARCH IN BLACK CULTURE

www.nypl.org

This African-American cultural archive sponsors an annual Women's Jazz Festival and a performance of Langston Hughes' *Nativity* in December.

➕ Off map 244 D2 ✉ 515 Malcolm X Boulevard at 135th Street ☎ 212/491-2200 🚇 135th Street (B, C) 🚌 M7

SHAKESPEARE IN THE PARK

www.publictheater.org

The Public Theater sponsors this summer Shakespeare festival in Central Park at the Delacorte Theater. Line up for free tickets from noon onwards.

➕ 244 C5 ✉ Delacorte Theater, 81st Street (West Side), 79th Street (East Side) ☎ 212/539-8500 🕐 Summer only Tue–Sun 🚇 79th Street (1) 🚌 M1, M2, M3, M4, M79, M104

SHOWMAN'S JAZZ CLUB

In the 1940s and 1950s, musicians often dropped into the Showman's Jazz Club after hours to jam or just hang out. Today musicians still frequent the establishment and you might be fortunate enough to find Grady Tate, George Benson or Ed Bradley, for example, whiling away the hours.

➕ Off map 244 C2 ✉ 375 West 125th Street, between St. Nicholas and Morningside avenues ☎ 212/864-8941 🕐 Mon–Thu 8.30pm–12.30am, Fri–Sat 10.30pm–3.30am 💵 $5, 2-drink minimum 🚇 125th Street (A, B, C, D) 🚌 M3

SMOKE

www.smokejazz.com

Intimate and comfortable with excellent acoustics, this club was opened in 1999. Over the years it has headlined great jazz artists including organist Dr. Lonnie Smith and trombonist Slide Hampton, but it is also a good place to see local artists. The food is fresh and seasonal.

➕ 244 B2 ✉ 2751 Broadway, between 105th and 106th streets ☎ 212/864-6662 🕐 Daily 5pm–2am 💵 Varies, but there is a cover minimum 🚇 103 Street (1) 🚌 M104

STAND-UP NEW YORK

www.standupny.com

Audiences here can be hard, but comics at this typical comedy club may emerge as the stars of tomorrow.

➕ 244 B5 ✉ 236 West 78th Street at Broadway ☎ 212/595-0850 💵 Cover varies, 2-drink minimum 🚇 79th Street (1) 🚌 M79, M104

VIVIAN BEAUMONT THEATER

This is categorized as a Broadway theater despite its address. Its deep-thrust stage allows for innovative directing.

✚ 244 B7 ✉ 150 West 65th Street ☎ 212/362-7600 ◉ Tue 7, Wed–Sat 8, matinees Wed, Sat 2, Sun 3 ◉ 66th Street (1) 🚌 M5, M7, M66, M104

SPORTS AND ACTIVITIES
BLADES

www.blades.com

This is the most convenient of these stores to Central Park, where you can rent in-line skates. There's also a branch at Chelsea Piers.

✚ 244 C6 ✉ 156 West 72nd Street at Columbus Street ☎ 212/787-3911 ◉ Mon–Sat 10–8, Sun 10–7 ⚡ Rentals $21.65 for 24 hr ◉ 72nd Street (1, 2, 3) 🚌 M7, M11, M72

CENTRAL PARK BICYCLE TOURS
▷ 270.

CENTRAL PARK RESERVOIR

This 1.6-mile (2.6km) gravel path is the favorite track for Upper West Siders and Upper East Siders.

✚ 244 D4 ⚡ Free ◉ 86th Street (4, 5, 6), 86th Street (B, C) 🚌 M1, M2, M3, M4, M10, M86

CHARLES A. DANA DISCOVERY CENTER

www.centralparknyc.org
www.centralpark.com

Exhibits at the Discovery Center relate to the natural life in the park, and the center sponsors related activities such as birdwatching. For ranger-led activities call 1-866-NYCHAWK.

✚ 244 D2 ✉ Central Park, 110th Street, between Fifth and Lenox avenues ☎ 212/860-1370 ◉ Tue–Sun 10–5 ⚡ Free ◉ Central Park North (2, 3) 🚌 M4

DEPARTMENT OF PARKS AND RECREATION

www.centralparknyc.org

The best tennis courts are: Central Park and 93rd Street (tel 212/280-0205), 30 hard courts; Riverside Drive and 96th Street (tel 212/

496-2006), eight clay courts; Riverside Drive and 119th Street (tel 212/496-2006), eight hard courts.

✚ 244 D7 ✉ 830 Fifth Avenue at 64th Street ☎ 212/360-8111 or 212/408-0243 for court reservations ◉ Tennis courts: early Apr–late Nov daily 6.30am–dusk ⚡ Tennis $7 pass for one hour of play obtainable at office above or at Central Park courts ◉ Fifth Avenue/59th Street (N, R, W) 🚌 M1, M2, M3, M4

EMPIRE SKATE CLUB

www.empireskate.org

The Empire Skate Club sponsors group skates, a variety of skating events and tours. Year-round skates include the Sunday morning roll from Columbus Circle at 11am and the Tuesday night skate from Blades at 120 West 72nd Street, starting at 8pm.

✚ 244 C7 ☎ 212/774-1774 ◉ Daily 6.30am–dusk ⚡ Club membership $25 (you don't have to be a member to join group skates)

LARRY & JEFF'S

www.bicyclesnyc.com

This store rents road and mountain bikes and is conveniently close to Central Park.

✚ 245 E5 ✉ 1400 3rd Avenue, between 79th and 80th streets ☎ 212/794-2929 ◉ Daily 10–7 (until 8 during daylight savings) ⚡ $30 day (3hrs 30mins or more) ◉ 86th Street (4, 5, 6) 🚌 M15, M86

LOEB BOATHOUSE

www.thecentralparkboathouse.com

Weather permitting, you can rent bicycles to ride through the park and rowboats for use on the lake March through October.

✚ 244 D6 ✉ Central Park, near East 72nd Street and Park Drive North ☎ 212/517-2233 ◉ Daily 10am–dusk ⚡ Bicycles $9–$20 per hr, rowboats $10 per hr ◉ 68th Street (6), 72nd Street (B, C) 🚌 M1, M2, M3, M4, M10

NEW YORK CITY AUDUBON SOCIETY

www.nycaudubon.org

The New York City Audubon Society allows visitors to the city to join its birdwatching walks in Central Park

for a small fee. Call the society for further details.

☎ 212/691-7483

NEW YORK MARATHON

www.nyrr.org

Thirty thousand athletes compete in this marathon, watched by 2.5 million spectators. The finish line is in Central Park.

✚ 244 D4 ✉ New York Road Runners Club, 9 East 89th Street at Fifth Avenue ☎ 212/860-4455 ◉ First Sun in Nov

WOLLMAN RINK

www.wollmanskatingrink.com

You can skate against the backdrop of the Manhattan skyline at this romantic outdoor rink—or, in summer, roller skate or blade.

✚ 244 D7 ✉ Central Park at 62nd Street ☎ 212/439-6900 ◉ Mon–Tue 10–2.30, Wed–Thu 10–10, Fri–Sat 10am–11pm, Sun 10–9 ⚡ Adult $10–$14, skate rental $6 ◉ 59th Street/Fifth Avenue (N, R, W) 🚌 M5

HEALTH AND BEAUTY
ASPHALT GREEN

www.asphaltgreen.org

This 5.5-acre (2.25ha) sports complex has Manhattan's only Olympic-size pool. It also has indoor and outdoor running tracks, fields for team sports, a large rooftop terrace with views of the East River, and a multi-level fitness center with 50-plus exercise classes.

✚ 245 F4 ✉ 555 East 90th Street, between York and East End avenues ☎ 212/369-8890 ◉ Mon–Fri 5.30am–10pm, Sat–Sun 8–8 ⚡ Day pass $35 ◉ 96th Street (6) 🚌 M15, M31, M86

PAUL LABRECQUE SALON AND SPA

www.paullabrecque.com

London-trained Labrecque has coiffed the rich and famous for decades. The ultimate facial at this attractive salon provides five levels of hydration. It also offers sensual body treatments and massage treatments (Thai, Reiki, rolfing, phyto-essence and acupuncture).

✚ 245 E7 ✉ 171 East 65th Street, between Lexington and Third avenues

☎ 212/988-7816 🌐 Mon–Fri 8am–9pm, Sat 9–8, Sun 10–8 ✋ Facial $85–$185+, massage $80–$165 🚇 68th Street (6) 🚌 M98, M101, M102, M103

LA PRAIRIE SPA
www.ritzcarlton.com
A wide range of treatments include detoxification, shiatsu massage and exfoliation. There are also men's and women's steam rooms.
🔲 244 D7 ✉ Ritz-Carlton, 50 Central Park South at Sixth Avenue ☎ 212/521-6135

SPORTS CLUB/LA
www.thesportsclubla.com
The spectacular 61st Street location of this urban country club occupies 150,000 square feet (13,935sq m) and offers 50 fitness classes, five squash courts, two basketball courts, a climbing wall, weights, and a cardio deck with more than 200 machines. There's even rooftop tennis and golf.
🔲 245 E7 ✉ 330 East 61st Street, between First and Second avenues ☎ 212/355-5100. Also at 45 Rockefeller Plaza ☎ 212/218-8600 🌐 Mon–Fri 5am–11pm, Sat–Sun 8–8 ✋ Day pass $35 with member only 🚇 59th Street (4, 5, 6) 🚌 M15

FOR CHILDREN

AMERICAN MUSEUM OF NATURAL HISTORY
▷ 204–207.

CENTRAL PARK
▷ 208–213.

CENTRAL PARK ZOO
www.centralparkzoo.com
A perfectly sized zoo for kids, this Manhattan classic is populated by many of the regular youngsters' favorites—sea lions, polar bears, monkeys, pandas, penguins and tropical birds. The Tisch Children's Zoo has fish, birds and llamas, pigs and other domestic animals.
🔲 244 D7 ✉ Fifth Avenue and 64th Street ☎ 212/439-6500 🌐 Daily 10–5 (Sat, Sun and holidays until 5.30) ✋ Adult $10, child (3–12) $5, under 3 free 🚇 Fifth Avenue (N, R), 68th Street (6) 🚌 M1, M2, M3, M4

CHILDREN'S MUSEUM OF MANHATTAN
www.cmom.org
The Children's Museum of Manhattan was designed to be a first museum experience for kids from 10 months to 10 years old. It has plenty of sensory exhibits, plus a regular schedule of sing-alongs and other wonderful programs.
🔲 244 B5 ✉ 212 West 83rd Street, between Broadway and Amsterdam Avenue ☎ 212-721-1223 🌐 Tue–Sun 10–5 ✋ Adults and children $10 🚇 86th Street (1), 81st Street (B, C) 🚌 M7, M11, M79, M104

GUIDED TOUR OF LINCOLN CENTER
www.lincolncenter.org
These one-hour tours take you through the theaters that make up the Lincoln Center. The tour guides tell fascinating stories and you may see a rehearsal in progress.
🔲 244 B7 ☎ 212/875-5350 🌐 Daily at 10.30, 12.30, 2.30, 4.30. Reservations recommended ✋ Adult $15, child (under 12) $8 🚇 66th Street (1) 🚌 M5, M7, M104

GUGGENHEIM MUSEUM
▷ 216–217.

LITTLE ORCHESTRA SOCIETY
www.littleorchestra.org
This company organizes two family concert series: Happy Concerts (children aged 6 to 12) and the Lollipops (tots aged 3 to 5). Performances are held at the Kaye Playhouse at Hunter College.
🔲 244 B7 ✉ Avery Fisher Hall, Lincoln Center, Broadway and West 65th Street ☎ 212/971-9500 ✋ $40–$99 🚇 66th Street (1, 9) 🚌 M5, M7, M104

LOEWS IMAX THEATER
For some kids, the 3-D IMAX experience is too intense; those who tolerate it are usually enthralled. The screen is eight stories high. Programming changes roughly every two months.
🔲 244 B6 ✉ 1998 Broadway and 68th Street ☎ 212/336-5020 🚇 66th Street (1, 9) 🚌 M5, M7, M104

PAPER BAG PLAYERS
www.paperbagplayers.org
The members of this beloved troupe make their costumes and sets out of cardboard and paper bags and perform offbeat plays and revues at five venues in the city.
🔲 244 B3 ✉ Office at 185 East Broadway ☎ 212/353-2332 🌐 Phone for details, as they tour regularly ✋ $10–$30 🚇 68th Street (6) 🚌 M1, M2, M3, M4, M98, M101, M102, M103

YOUNG PEOPLE'S CONCERTS
www.nyphil.org
www.lincolncenter.org
Sponsored by the New York Philharmonic, these concerts introduce kids to great artists and great music. Children can attend demonstrations and workshops given by members of the orchestra. There's also a program for teens.
🔲 244 B7 ✉ Lincoln Center ☎ 212/875-5656 or 212/721-6500 🌐 Four Saturdays during the year ✋ $10–$30 🚇 66th Street (1) 🚌 M5, M7, M104

Below New York's public parks are ideal places for sports activities or relaxation

PRICES AND SYMBOLS

The prices given are the average for a two-course lunch (L) and a three-course dinner (D) for one person, without drinks. The wine price is for the least expensive bottle.

For a key to the symbols, ▷ 2.

AMY RUTH'S

www.amyruthsharlem.com
It's named for the owner's grandmother, who taught her Southern-style cooking. Most items on the menu are named for someone, such as the Reverend Al Sharpton (chicken and waffles). At dinner, look for lusty Southern fried chicken, oxtail stew and fried or baked catfish. No alcohol is served.
✚ Off map 244 D2 ✉ 113 West 116th Street, between Malcolm X Boulevard and Adam Clayton Powell Jr. Boulevard ☎ 212/280-8779 🕐 Mon 11.30–11, Tue–Thu 8.30am–11pm, Fri 8.30am–5.30am, Sat 7.30am–5.30am, Sun 7.30am–11pm 🖐 L $18, D $24 🚇 116th Street (2, 3, B, C) 🚌 M3, M7, M116

ASIATE

www.mandarinoriental.com
Stunning floor-to-ceiling views of Central Park form the backdrop for fine dining in this stylishly decorated tranquil haven. The seasonal menu features Asian and international contemporary cuisine supported by an excellent wine cellar. Specialties include butter poached lobster with white polenta, *hon shimeji* mushrooms and kaffir emulsion, and *étuvée* of bay scallops, langoustine, littleneck clams and hearts of palm in a coconut herb broth.
✚ 244 C7 ✉ 80 Columbus Circle in the Mandarin Oriental Hotel ☎ 212/805-8881 🕐 Mon–Fri 7–10.30, 12–2, 6–10, Sat 7–10.30, 11.30–2, 6–10, Sun 7–10.30, 11.30–2, 6–9 🖐 L $24, D $45, 3-course prix fixe $85, tasting menu $125, Wine $35 🚇 59th Street (A, B, C, D, 1, 9) 🚌 M5, M7, M10, M104

AUREOLE

www.charliepalmer.com
Aureole's chef/owner Charlie Palmer is one of the most highly regarded talents on the American culinary scene. This elegant Upper East Side town house with a grand staircase and towers of wine, liquor and flowers, is made for special occasions. Palmer uses ultra-fresh ingredients in such signature dishes as slow-poached Maine lobster with heirloom tomatoes, which is served with lemon-verbena-infused consommé, and seared Hudson Valley foie gras. The wine list features 600 selections, 25 by the glass.
✚ 244 D7 ✉ 34 East 61st Street, between Madison and Park avenues ☎ 212/319-1660 🕐 Mon–Fri 12–2.30, 5.30–11, Sat 5–11 🖐 L $46, D $95, Wine $45 🚇 59th Street (4, 5, 6), 59th Street/Fifth Avenue (N, R, W) 🚌 M1, M2, M3, M4

BARNEY GREENGRASS

www.barneygreengrass.com
An Upper West Side tradition since 1929, Barney Greengrass is frantic on weekends, when locals come to feast on huge platters of smoked fish—whitefish, sable, sturgeon and lox—or sandwiches made with similar contents, plus fresh caviar, chopped herring salad, cheese blintzes, borscht and other such specialties. During the week, it's less frenzied. Credit cards are taken on bills of $25 or more only.
✚ 244 B4 ✉ 541 Amsterdam Avenue between West 86th and 87th streets ☎ 212/724-4707 🕐 Tue–Fri 8.30am–4pm, Sat–Sun 8.30am–5pm 🖐 L $18, D $25 🚇 86th Street (1) 🚌 M7, M86, M104

Opposite Rosa Mexicano on Columbus Avenue serves delicious, authentic Mexican food

CAFÉ BOULUD

www.danielnyc.com

Many diners consider this casually smart 1930s-style Parisian neighborhood restaurant their favorite Daniel Boulud restaurant. Three Daniel muses inspire the menu—classics, seasons and ethnic cuisines. You will find a pot-au-feu and a good bouillabaisse; and entrées inspired by Tuscany, Morocco, Vietnam, Spain and the Caribbean. The 450 wine selections are categorized by varietal.

➕ 244 D6 ✉ 20 East 76th Street, between Fifth and Madison avenues ☎ 212/772-2600 🕐 Tue–Sat 12–2.30, 5.45–11, Sun 11.30–2.30, 5.45–11, Mon 5.45–11 ✋ L $40, D $70, Wine $25 🚇 77th Street (6) 🚌 M1, M2, M3, M4, M79

CAFÉ DES ARTISTES

www.cafenyc.com

Intimate and romantic, this classic French restaurant dates to 1917 when it was favored by artists. Today Lincoln Center theatergoers often dine here before or after the performance. The decor is artistic, the waiters experienced and the food is worth splurging on. Try the Dover sole with brown butter sauce, or the roasted duck. Desserts like chocolate bread pudding and hot-fudge Napoleon are notable.

➕ 244 C6 ✉ 1 West 67th Street, between Columbus Avenue and Central Park West ☎ 212/877-3500 🕐 Mon–Fri 12–3, 5–11.45, Sat 11–3, 5–11.45, Sun 10–3, 5.30–11 ✋ L $25, D $45, Wine $40 🚇 66th Street (1) 🚌 M5, M7, M10, M11, M66, M104

CALLE OCHO

www.calleochonyc.com

Calle Ocho has brought an extensive menu of very good Latin cuisine to the Upper West Side. The atmosphere is trendy and cozy, with a brightly lit high-ceilinged dining room and an intimate lounge serving sherry, brandy, port, cognac, single malts and blends. The Nuevo Latino fusion cuisine provides tantalizing flavor combinations reminiscent of Miami's Little Havana. Start with one of the refreshing ceviches (say, lobster with lemon, lime and jalapeño) or appetizers like *arepa* with spicy braised short ribs. Fish and meat dishes are tasty, both the coffee-glazed tuna or the basil *chimichurri* chicken with roasted almond sauce. The dinner breads and muffins are delicious. The weekend Latin brunch with five kinds of all-you-can-drink Sangria is very popular, with excellent entrées.

➕ 244 B5 ✉ 446 Columbus Avenue, between West 81st and 82nd streets ☎ 212/873-5025 🕐 Mon–Thu 6–11, Fri 6–12, Sat 5–12, Sun 11.30–3, 5–10 ✋ D $45, Wine $22 🚇 81st Street (B, C) 🚌 M7, M11, M79

CESCA

www.cescanyc.com

At this popular Italian trattoria turning out fine cuisine, settle into a booth and order the veal meatballs in broth or the roasted oysters under a spicy tomato zabaglione and crisp pancetta. Settle into a plush booth surrounded by softly lit ivory walls and cast iron lamps. The food is tasty and eminently affordable, and an extensive Italian wine list complements the Italian cuisine.

➕ 244 B6 ✉ 164 West 75th Street (at Amsterdam Avenue) ☎ 212/787-6300 🕐 Mon–Thu 5–11, Fri–Sat 5–11.30, Sun 12–3, 5–10 ✋ D $55, Wine $25 🚇 72nd Street (1, 2, 3) 🚌 M7, M11, M104

COMPASS

www.compassrestaurant.com

Chef Neil Annis worked with Alain Ducasse in Paris before taking charge of the kitchen here. He has maintained its traditions of serving fine contemporary American cuisine with influences (just like New York itself) from all over the world. Dishes like corn risotto and rack of Berkshire pork with Italian prune show how the kitchen brings these tastes together superbly.

➕ 244 B6 ✉ 208 West 70th Street at Amsterdam Avenue ☎ 212/875-8600

🕐 Mon–Sat 5–11, Sun 5–10 ✋ D $55 Prix Fixe 3-course menu $35 Wine $24 🚇 72nd Street (1, 2, 3) 🚌 M5, M7 M104

DANIEL

www.danielnyc.com

Lyons-born chef Daniel Boulud opened this restaurant in 1993. It has all the romance of an Italian Renaissance palazzo, and dining here is a joyous experience. Signature dishes include the creamy oyster velouté with lemongrass and caviar, roast squab stuffed with foie gras and black truffle, and chocolate fondant with nougatine. Warm madeleines, home-made chocolates and petits fours conclude the meal. The predominantly French wine list offers more than 1,600 selections. Jacket and tie are required.

➕ 244 D7 ✉ 60 East 65th Street at Park Avenue ☎ 212/288-0033 🕐 Mon–Sat 5.45–11 ✋ D 3-course prix fixe $105, tasting menus $165–$185, Wine $30 🚇 63rd Street/Lexington (F), 68th Street (6) 🚌 M1, M2, M3, M4, M66

JEAN-GEORGES

www.jean-georges.com

Jean-Georges Vongerichten is the toast of the town. He has developed a signature cuisine that is intensely flavored and highly textured, based on vegetable and fruit essences, oils, vinaigrettes and broths. Stellar examples are the peekytoe crab and English pea fondue with rhubarb gelée and shiso purée, and the veal tenderloin with fricasee of mushrooms, fava beans, and Meyer lemon with liquid Parmesan. It's usually hard to snag a table here, so consider the less formal Nougatine at the same address. There's a 700-plus wine list and terrace dining in summer.

➕ 244 C7 ✉ Trump International Hotel Tower, 1 Central Park West, between 60th and 61st streets ☎ 212/299-3900 🕐 Mon–Thu 12–2.30, 5.30–11, Fri 12–2.30, 5.15–11, Sat 5.15–11, closed Sun ✋ L $45, 3-course $24 (in Nougatine), 2-course $28; D $60, prix fixe 4-course menu $98, prix fixe 7-course menu $148, Wine $22 🚇 59th Street/Columbus Circle (A, C, B, D, 1) 🚌 M7, M10, M20

LONDEL'S

www.londelsrestaurant.com

The South has given the United States its most distinctive cuisine, and this restaurant serves some of the best, from the Southern fried chicken and barbecue back ribs to the blackened catfish. Order collard greens or candied yams on the side, and bread pudding with rum sauce. You'll have had a feast. Live music on Friday and Saturday.

✚ Off map 244 C2 ✉ 2620 Frederick Douglass Boulevard, between 139th and 140th streets ☎ 212/234-6114 🕐 Tue–Sat 11.30am–midnight, Sun brunch 11–5 🍴 L $18, D $30, Wine $25 🚇 145th Street (A, B, C, D) 🚌 M10

MASA

www.masanyc.com

Currently the Holy Grail of dining in Manhattan. Here, sushi chef Masa (from Tokyo via Los Angeles) holds forth behind his hinoki counter creating whatever he has selected as the freshest and best from around the world. It seats only 26 (10 at the sushi bar) and sushi lovers swear it is nirvana.

✚ 244 C7 ✉ Time Warner Center, 10 Columbus Circle, 4th Floor ☎ 212/823-9800 🕐 Wed–Fri 12–1.30, Tue–Sat 6–9 🍴 $400 prix fixe ($200 penalty for cancellations within 48 hours of reservation), Wine $50 🚇 59th Street/Columbus Circle (A, B, C, D, 1, 9) 🚌 M5, M7, M10, M20, M104

MAYA

www.modernmexican.com

Sophisticated Mexican cuisine is the draw here. The chile relleno stuffed with seafood and Gouda cheese is a palate-pleasing combination and the guacamole, served in the stone pestle in which it's made, is among the best in the city. The pork tenderloin marinated with onion-orange salsa is ultra tender and richly flavored—a winner. Credit cards are not accepted.

✚ 245 E7 ✉ 1191 First Avenue, between East 64th and 65th streets ☎ 212/585-1818 🕐 Sun–Thu 5–10, Fri–Sat 5–11 🍴 D $52, Wine $32 🚇 Lexington Avenue/63rd Street (F), 68th Street (6) 🚌 M15

OUEST

www.ouestny.com

This lively, entertaining restaurant helped raise the Upper West Side's culinary reputation with Tom Valenti's fresh seasonal menu. Settle into one of the cherry-red booths and order the luscious short ribs, one of the braised or roasted meats such as the roast free-range chicken with garlic jus, or a fish dish such as seared tuna with white bean purée, black olive-lemon compote and red pepper coulis. The nightly specials attract crowds, especially on Monday, when the kitchen turns out the chef's signature braised lamb shanks. Desserts are Italian-inspired.

✚ 244 B5 ✉ 2315 Broadway, between West 83rd and 84th streets ☎ 212/580-8700 🕐 Mon–Thu 5.30–10.30, Fri–Sat 5–11.30, Sun 11–2, 5–10 🍴 D $55, also prix fixe 3-course menu $34, Wine $35 🚇 86th Street (1, 9) 🚌 M 104

PER SE

http://perseny.com

The room has urban chic and fine views, but diners come to taste the superlative cuisine of Thomas Keller, whom many consider America's finest chef. He arrived from the Napa Valley with his famous French Laundry. The menu changes daily, but diners can expect perfectly prepared dishes right down to the finest details. His "oysters and pearls" (oysters, tapioca and osetra caviar) and his "macaroni and cheese"(lobster mascarpone in a lobster broth topped with a wheel of crisp Parmesan) are legendary signature dishes. The wine list has 500 selections. It's hard to snag one of the 16 tables.

✚ 244 C7 ✉ Time Warner Center, 10 Columbus Circle, 4th Floor ☎ 212/823-9335 🕐 Fri–Sun 11.30–1.30, daily 5.30–10 🍴 Prix fixe tasting menus $275, Wine $30 🚇 59th Street/Columbus Circle (A, B, C, D, 1) 🚌 M5, M7, M10, M20, M104

PERSEPOLIS

www.persepolisnyc.com

Thai chef San Sethachutkul had to master the art of Persian cooking when he took over the kitchens at

Persepolis, but there is a similarity in the way the cuisines blend and contrast flavors. The Vermont lamb shank served with almond, raisin and herb couscous is just one example of this Middle Eastern cuisine at its finest, followed by typical desserts like roasted pineapple or baklava.

✚ 245 E6 ✉ 1407 Second Avenue, between 73rd and 74th streets ☎ 212/535-1100 🕐 Daily 12–11.30 🍴 L $20 3-course prix fixe menu, D $40, Wine $35 🚇 Lexington Avenue (6) 🚌 M15

PICHOLINE

www.picholinenyc.com

The Mediterranean cuisine at Picholine is superb. Among the entrees, the licorice-lacquered squab is exquisite, perfectly complemented by foie gras, glazed turnips and spiced rhubarb marmalade. The wild mushroom and duck risotto is a perennial favorite. It's easy to fill up with delicious entrees and main courses—but be sure to save room for one more course. Picholine also has one of the city's most fabulous cheese trays.

✚ 244 C7 ✉ 35 West 64th Street between Central Park West and Broadway ☎ 212/724-8585 🕐 Mon–Thu 5–11, Fri–Sat 5–11.45, Sun 5–9 🍴 D $80, tasting menu $125, light dinner $45, Wine $45 🚇 66th Street (1) 🚌 M10, M20

PIO PIO

www.piopionyc.com

This is the Peruvian version of the Boston Chicken chain. Order a quarter, half or whole chicken, marinated in secret spices. Then add some ceviche tostones, red beans or yuca frita and a beer, and you've got yourself a tasty meal. Amex credit cards only are accepted.

✚ 245 E4 ✉ 1746 First Avenue, between East 90th and 91st streets ☎ 212/426-5800 🕐 Daily 11–11 🍴 L$15, D $35, Wine $25 🚇 86th Street (4, 5, 6) 🚌 M15

ROSA MEXICANO

www.rosamexicano.com

A waterfall studded with sculptures of Acapulco-style divers, among other decorative notes, sets a flashy

scene at this authentic Mexican eaterie. The guacamole, which is made at the table, is fragrant with cilantro (coriander) and oregano, and the menu offers unusual regional dishes such salmon *al guajillo*, beef short ribs marinated in lime and beer and *budin Azteca,* a flavorsome tortilla pie.

✚ 244 C7 ✉ 61 Columbus Avenue at West 62nd Street, NE corner ☎ 212/977-7700 ③ Mon 11.30–10, Tue–Fri 11.30–11.30, Sat 11.30–2.30, 4–11.30, Sun 11.30–2.30, 4–10.30 🖐 L $28, D $45, Wine $24 🚇 59th Street/Columbus Circle (A, B, C, D, 1) 🚌 M5, M7, M11, M104

SARABETH'S
www.sarabeth.com
Sarabeth Levine is most famous for her luscious baking and breakfasts, but that does not mean that she can't turn out equally wonderful lunch and dinner fare. Try her short ribs in Zinfandel or her hazelnut-crusted sea bass, and you'll be a fan. At breakfast, don't miss the cinnamon French toast or the pumpkin waffles—and plan on a light lunch afterwards.

✚ 244 D4 ✉ 1295 Madison Avenue, between East 92nd and 93rd streets ☎ 212/410-7335 ③ Mon–Sat 8am–11pm, Sun 8am–9.30pm 🖐 L $25, D $45, Wine $32 🚇 96th Street (6) 🚌 M1, M2, M3, M4

TAVERN ON THE GREEN
www.tavernonthegreen.com
Visitors are drawn to this bauble of a restaurant at the edge of Central Park, shaded by stately trees outlined after dark by thousands of twinkling fairy lights. The view from the Crystal Room and the summer dining terrace creates a certain magical, festive look. Against all odds, the Tavern delivers a memorable dining experience—despite its stature as a prime visitor destination, despite its size, and despite the breadth of its menu, which ranges from prime rib with Yorkshire pudding to sautéed rainbow trout in brown butter sauce. The wine list boasts a huge selection, a 1999 Chateau Petrus among them. From May to mid-October you can dance under the stars in the garden areas from 9pm.

✚ 244 C7 ✉ Central Park West at 67th Street ☎ 212/873-3200 ③ Mon–Fri 7–9.30, 11.30–3, 5–9.30, Sat 5–10, Sat–Sun 10–3, Sun 5–9.30 🖐 L $40, prix fixe menu $39, D $65, Wine $32 🚇 66th Street (1) 🚌 M10

Above *The water wall at Rosa Mexicano spans both levels of the contemporary restaurant near the Lincoln Center*

PRICES AND SYMBOLS

Prices are the lowest and highest for a double room for one night. Breakfast is included unless noted otherwise. All the hotels listed accept credit cards unless otherwise stated. Note that rates vary widely throughout the year.

For a key to the symbols, ▷ 2.

AFFINIA GARDENS

www.affinia.com
The suites at this well-located hotel have fully equipped kitchens, tranquility kits and guest laundry. There's also a fitness center.
🛗 245 E7 ✉ 215 East 64th Street, between Second and Third avenues, 10021 ☎ 212/355-1230 ✋ Doubles and suites from $350 ⓘ 131 ▼ ⊕ 68th Street (6) 🚌 M15, M72, M98, M101, M102, M103

CARLYLE

www.thecarlyle.com
This is a striking art deco building. The rooms boast large bathrooms and every conceivable amenity. Bemelman's Bar has charming murals and in the café pianist Bobby Short plays.
🛗 244 D5 ✉ 35 East 76th Street, between Madison and Park avenues, 10021 ☎ 212/744-1600 ✋ $650–$950, suites

from $1.050 ⓘ 181 rooms and suites ⚐ ▼ ⊕ 77th Street (4, 5) 🚌 M1, M2, M3, M4

EXCELSIOR

www.excelsiorhotelny.com
One of the few hotels on the Upper West Side, near the Natural History Museum, the Excelsior offers spotless modern rooms equipped with cable TV, dual-line phone with data port, and bathrobes.
🛗 244 C5 ✉ 45 West 81st Street, between Columbus Avenue and Central Park West, 10024 ☎ 212/362-9200 ✋ $299–$499, suites from $399 ⓘ 199 rooms and suites ▼ ⊕ 81st Street (B, C) 🚌 M7, M11, M10, M79

GRACIE INN

www.gracieinnhotel.com
Slightly off the beaten track, this inn attracts long-term guests. Each room has a kitchenette, plus TV and phone with data port. The penthouses have waterbeds, whirlpool tubs and sundecks. Breakfast delivered to your room is a welcome indulgence.
🛗 245 F5 ✉ 502 East 81st Street, between York and East End avenues, 10028 ☎ 212/628-1700 ✋ Studio $139–$179, 1-bedroom suite from $189 ⓘ 12 rooms, 2 suites ⊕ 77th St (6) 🚌 M15, M31, M79

JUMEIRAH ESSEX HOUSE

www.jumeirah.com
This landmark art deco hotel was thoroughly renovated in 2007 by the Dubai Hotel Group Jumeirah. The sparkling lobby retains its classic art deco look with black-and-white marble floor, columns and classic decor. Cream-colored sofas in a burgundy-draped alcove provide a relaxing environment. Guest rooms are decorated in neutral tones, with plush carpeting, modern furnishings and art deco highlights, HD LCD flat-panel TV, touch-screen controls and mood lighting.
🛗 244 C7 ✉ 160 Central Park South, between Sixth and Seventh avenues, 10019 ☎ 212/247-0300 ✋ From $709, suites from $959 ⓘ 515 ⊕ 57th Street (N, R, W, Q) 🚌 M5

LUCERNE

www.thelucernehotel.com
This hotel, in a 1903 landmark building, is a bargain. Rooms are spacious and have marble bathrooms. The suites have sitting areas as well as kitchenette with refrigerator and microwave.
🛗 244 B5 ✉ 201 West 79th Street, between Broadway and Amsterdam Avenue, 10024 ☎ 212/875-1000 ✋ From $280,

Opposite The art deco Carlyle hotel

🏢 142 rooms, 42 suites 🍴 🚇 79th Street (1) 🚌 M7, M11, M79

MANDARIN ORIENTAL

www.mandarinoriental.com

This hotel soars majestically above Columbus Circle commanding views of Central Park, the Hudson River and the Manhattan skyline from floors 35 through 54 of the new Time Warner Center. Rooms are sumptuously furnished. Bathrooms have deep tubs and glass wall showers plus flat panel TVs. Asiate (▷ 238) is Asian-inspired fine dining. MO Bar (on the 35th floor) has been attracting a lot of buzz. Facilities include a two-story spa, and a fitness center with 75ft (23m) lap pool. The hotel has access to all the facilities in the Time Warner Center.

➕ 244 C7 ✉ 80 Columbus Circle at West 60th Street, 10023 ☎ 212/805-8800 ✋ From $895, suites from $2,400 🏢 202 rooms, 46 suites 🚊 🍴 🚇 59th Street (A, B, C, D, 1, 9) 🚌 M5, M7, M10, M104

NEWTON

www.thehotelnewton.com

This reliable hotel caters to the workers in the entertainment industry who appreciate the value of the rooms here. They are equipped with cable TV and phone, and some have microwaves and refrigerators. There is WiFi access throughout.

➕ 244 B4 ✉ 2528 Broadway, between 94th and 95th streets, 10025 ☎ 212/678-6500 ✋ $145–$250 🏢 98 rooms, 12 suites 🚇 96th Street (1, 2, 3) 🚌 M104

ON THE AVE

www.ontheave-nyc.com

A few blocks from the Natural History Museum, this small hotel built in 1922 is part of the Citylife Hotel Group. The rooms, furnished in sleek modern style, feature vibrant paintings by Alfonso Muñoz. There are three floors of penthouse suites.

➕ 244 B5 ✉ 2178 Broadway at 77th Street, 10024 ☎ 212/362-1100 ✋ Doubles from $299, suites from $459 🏢 250 rooms, 16 suites 🚇 79th Street (1) 🚌 M79, M104

PIERRE

www.tajhotels.com

Overlooking Central Park, this 41-story hotel, built in 1930, is the quintessence of luxury. A complete renovation was finished in 2009. The hotel is renowned for its premier service and fabulous guest rooms, many with city or park views. The oversized bathrooms have large soaking tubs and showers with multiple jet sprays. Le Caprice serves eclectic international cuisine.

➕ 244 D7 ✉ Fifth Avenue at 61st Street, 10021 ☎ 212/838-8000 ✋ From $476, suites from $1,068 🏢 140 rooms, 49 suites 🚇 59th Street/Fifth Avenue (N, R, W) 🚌 M1, M2, M3, M4

PLAZA ATHÉNÉE

www.plaza-athenee.com

The hotel is on a quiet, tree-lined street one block from Central Park. All rooms are furnished with antique-style European furniture with Belgian linens and writing desks. All rooms also include CD players and high-speed internet, while some of the suites have their own dining rooms with atriums and balconies.

➕ 244 D7 ✉ 37 East 64th Street at Madison Avenue, 10065 ☎ 212/734-9100 ✋ Rooms $795–$1,250, suites from $1,790 🏢 114 rooms and 35 suites 🚇 Lexington Avenue (F) 🚌 M1, M2, M3, M4

RITZ-CARLTON

www.ritzcarlton.com

This 33-story hotel has magnificent views. The lobby sets an opulent tone with its limestone walls, inlaid onyx floor and Samuel Halpert paintings. The rooms are luxuriously decorated and amenities include flat-screen TVs, DVDs, and park-view rooms have telescopes for birdwatching. Bathrooms have deep tubs with neck pillows, Frederic Fekkai toiletries and Frette candles. Pratesi linens and Bang and Olufsen stereos grace the suites. The Ritz-Carlton is famous for its exceptional service. BLT Market offers fresh seasonal dishes and The Star Lounge specializes in elegant afternoon tea and classic cocktails. La Prairie spa (▷ 237) is full service.

➕ 244 D7 ✉ 50 Central Park South, 10019 ☎ 212/308-9100 ✋ $600–$1,300, suites from $995 🏢 259 rooms, 47 suites 🍴 🚇 59th Street/Fifth Avenue (N, R, W), 57th Street (F) 🚌 M5, M6, M7

SHERRY-NETHERLAND

www.sherrynetherland.com

This hotel is a building cooperative— the owners individually decorate their units. The number of guest rooms fluctuates between 100 and 150. The building dates from 1927 and much of its luxury detailing was taken from a Vanderbilt mansion. It has European style and a Harry Cipriani restaurant.

➕ 244 D7 ✉ 781 Fifth Avenue, between 59th and 60th streets, 10022 ☎ 212/355-2800 ✋ $425–$820, suites from $650 🏢 150 🍴 🚇 59th Street/Fifth Avenue (N, R, W) 🚌 M1, M2, M3, M4

TRUMP INTERNATIONAL HOTEL AND TOWER

www.trumpintl.com

The location is superb, with views of Central Park and easy access to the Lincoln Center and Midtown. The rooms, located between the third and 17th floors, are stylish, and each has plasma TV, VCR, CD and DVD; suites have whirlpool tubs and even telescopes. The restaurant Jean-Georges (▷ 239) is another draw.

➕ 244 C7 ✉ 1 Central Park West at Columbus Circle, 10023 ☎ 212/299-1000 ✋ Doubles from $595, suites from $845 🏢 38 rooms, 129 suites 🚊 🍴 🚇 59th Street/Columbus Circle (A, B, C, D, 1, 9) 🚌 M10, M20

WALES

www.hotelwalesnyc.com

The Hotel Wales is a study in old-fashioned luxury on the quiet Upper East Side near Museum Mile and Central Park. The rooms have plush chairs and luxurious beds. Sarabeth's (▷ 241) and Joanna's Italian Restaurant are bonuses.

➕ 244 D4 ✉ 1295 Madison Avenue, between 92nd and 93rd streets, 10128 ☎ 212/876-6000 ✋ Doubles from $286, suites from $386 🏢 46 rooms, 42 suites 🍴 🚇 96th Street (6) 🚌 M1, M2, M3, M4, M96

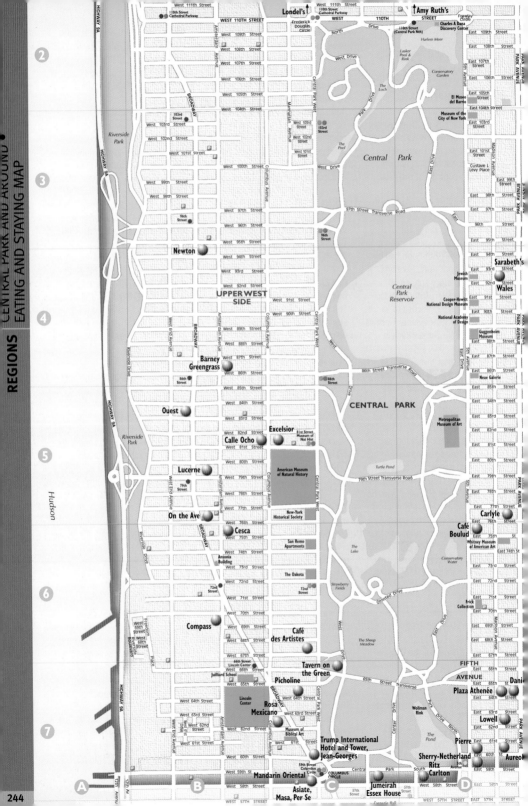

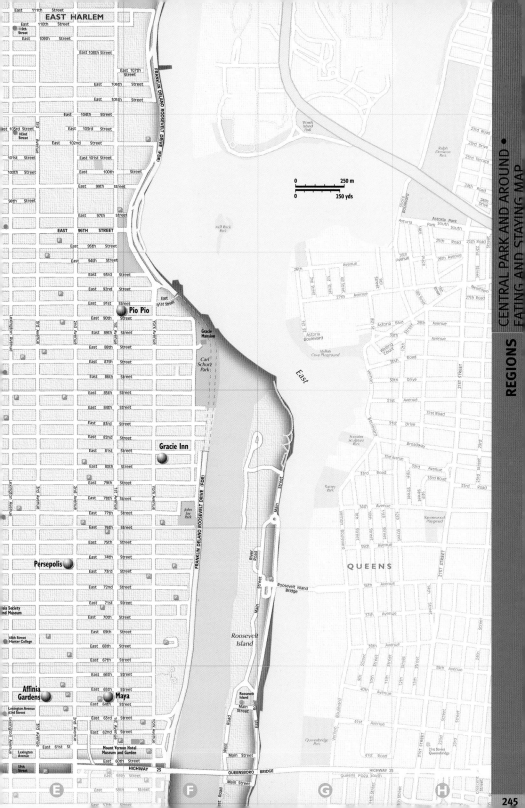

EAST HARLEM

East 111th Street
East 110th Street
East 109th Street
East 108th Street
East 107th Street
East 106th street
East 105th street
East 104th Street
East 103rd Street
East 102nd Street
East 101st Street
East 100th Street
East 99th Street
East 98th Street
East 97th Street
EAST 96TH STREET
East 95th Street
East 94th Street
East 93rd Street
East 92nd Street
East 91st Street
East 90th Street
East 89th Street
East 88th Street
East 87th Street
East 86th Street
East 85th Street
East 84th Street
East 83rd Street
East 82nd Street
East 81st Street
East 80th Street
East 79th Street
East 78th Street
East 77th Street
East 76th Street
East 75th Street
East 74th Street
East 73rd Street
East 72nd Street
East 71st Street
East 70th Street
East 69th Street
East 68th Street
East 67th Street
East 66th Street
East 65th Street
East 64th Street
East 63rd Street
East 62nd Street
East 61st Street
East 60th Street
HIGHWAY 25
East 59th Street
East 58th Street

Lexington Avenue
3rd Avenue
2nd Avenue
1st Avenue
York Avenue

FRANKLIN DELANO ROOSEVELT DRIVE (FDR)

Pio Pio

Gracie Mansion
Carl Schurz Park
John Jay Park
Gracie Inn

Persepolis

Asia Society and Museum
68th Street Hunter College

Affinia Gardens
Maya

Lexington Avenue 63rd Street
Mount Vernon Hotel Museum and Garden
Lexington Avenue
59th Street

Mull Rock Park

East River

Wards Island Park

Ralph Demarco Park

Astoria Park
Astoria Park South

Astoria
Astoria Boulevard
Hallets Cove Playground
Welling Court
Socrates Sculpture Park
Rainey Park
Ravenswood Playground

QUEENS

Roosevelt Island
Roosevelt Island Bridge
Main Street
River Road
West Road
East Road

Roosevelt Island
Main Street

Queensbridge Park
Queensboro Queensbridge

QUEENSBORO BRIDGE
Queens Plaza South
HIGHWAY 25
Main Street

0   250 m
0   250 yds

E   F   G   H

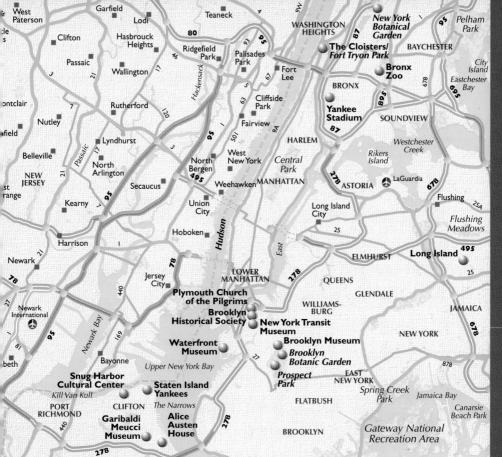

EXCURSIONS

Beyond Manhattan there are four more boroughs that form the largest part, about 73 percent, of New York City in both land mass and population. Many New Yorkers live here in residential neighborhoods, far from the hustle and bustle of congested Manhattan, which is often referred to as "the city". There are many fine attractions here, including museums, the city's largest zoo, gardens and huge sports arenas.

The Bronx, north of Manhattan, is best known as home to the New York Yankees and the city's largest park, Pelham Bay Park, with the Bronx Zoo and New York Botanical Garden. Here too is the public garden at Wave Hill, fine seafood and Italian dining, and the Bronx Museum of the Arts.

To the east of the city, Queens boasts the most ethnically diverse population in the world. If you crave ethnic food, there are many small neighborhood restaurants that feature Indian, Peruvian, Greek, Korean and many other regional foods. Here, too, are amazing modern and contemporary art collections at Queens Museum of Art, P.S. 1 Contemporary Art Center, Socrates Sculpture Park and the Noguchi Museum.

South of Queens and southeast of the city, Brooklyn is the place to go for atmospheric neighborhoods like DUMBO (Down Under the Manhattan Bridge Overpass) and Williamsburg for the arts, or the specialty shops and boutiques in the young-professional neighborhoods of Brooklyn Heights, Prospect Heights and Cobble Hill.

Take the Staten Island Ferry to Staten Island for sweeping vistas that include the Statue of Liberty and the harbor. On the island, explore the harbor area and dine in a local café before heading to Snug Harbor for the Cultural Center, Botanical Garden and the Staten Island Children's Museum.

Just beyond the city lies Long Island fringed with miles of beaches along the Atlantic Coast, historic towns, museums and state parks. To the north of the city, the scenic Hudson River Valley, especially beautiful in the fall, offers splendid historic mansions, museums and West Point Military Academy.

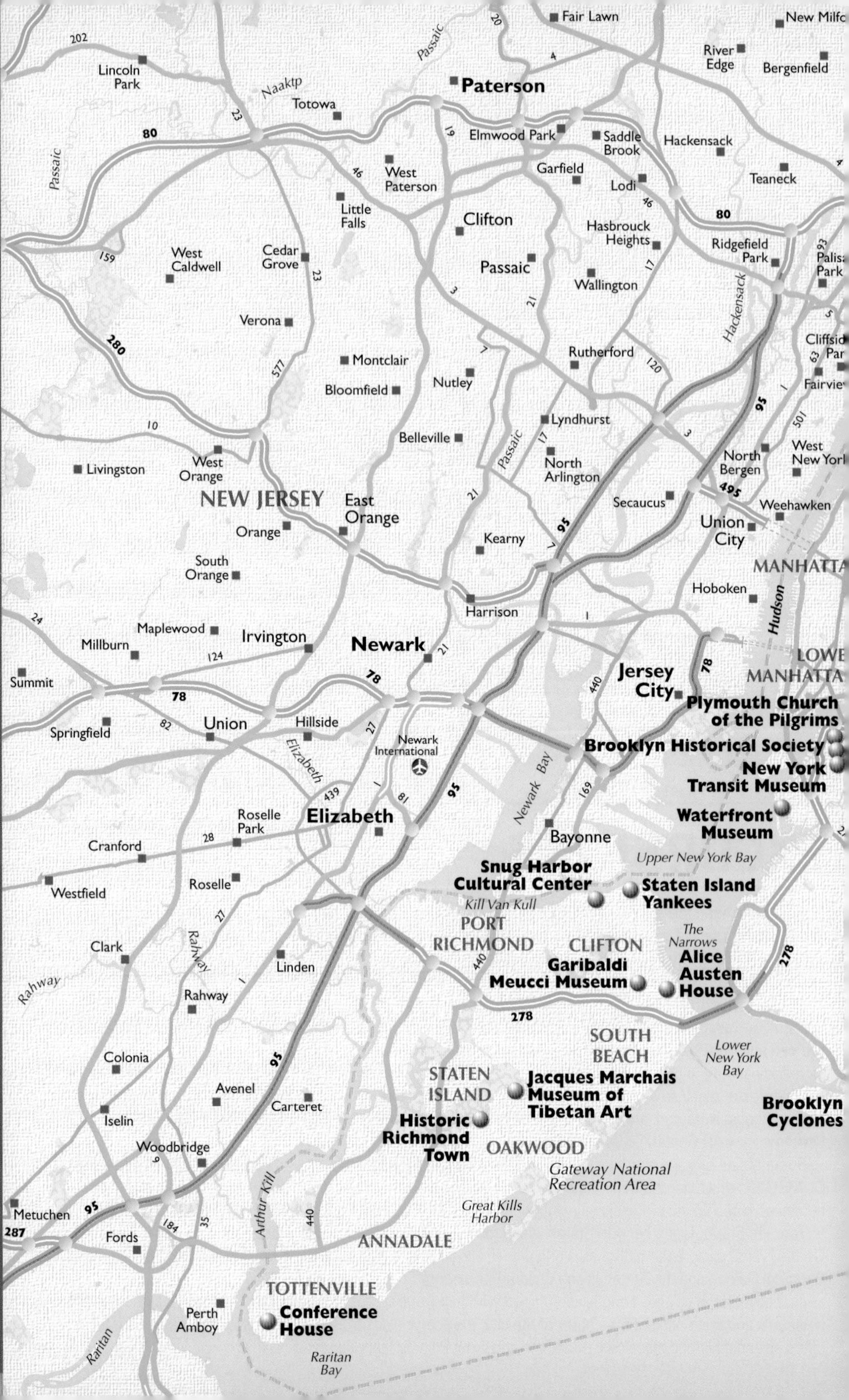

202
Lincoln Park
Naaktp
Passaic
Fair Lawn
New Milfc
River Edge
Bergenfield
Paterson
20
Totowa
80
23
Passaic
159
19
Elmwood Park
Saddle Brook
Hackensack
Teaneck
46
West Paterson
Garfield
Lodi
80
Little Falls
Clifton
Hasbrouck Heights
Ridgefield Park
93
Palisa Park
West Caldwell
Cedar Grove
23
Passaic
17
46
Cliffsid Par
280
577
Verona
3
21
Passaic
120
Rutherford
63
Fairvie
Montclair
Nutley
7
95
501
West New Yorl
Bloomfield
Belleville
Lyndhurst
17
North Bergen
10
Livingston
West Orange
NEW JERSEY
East Orange
Passaic
17
North Arlington
3
495
Weehawken
Orange
21
Secaucus
Union City
South Orange
Kearny
7
95
MANHATTA
24
Harrison
1
Hoboken
Hudson
Maplewood
Irvington
Millburn
Newark
21
Jersey City
78
LOWE MANHATTA
Summit
124
78
Plymouth Church of the Pilgrims
Springfield
82
Union
Hillside
27
440
78
Brooklyn Historical Society
New York Transit Museum
Roselle Park
Elizabeth
Newark International
81
95
169
Waterfront Museum
Cranford
28
Elizabeth
439
1
Bayonne
Upper New York Bay
2
Westfield
Roselle
27
Snug Harbor Cultural Center
Kill Van Kull
Staten Island Yankees
Clark
Rahway
PORT RICHMOND
CLIFTON
The Narrows
278
Linden
440
Garibaldi Meucci Museum
Alice Austen House
Rahway
Rahway
1
278
SOUTH BEACH
Lower New York Bay
Colonia
95
STATEN ISLAND
Jacques Marchais Museum of Tibetan Art
Brooklyn Cyclones
Avenel
Iselin
Carteret
Historic Richmond Town
OAKWOOD
Woodbridge
9
Gateway National Recreation Area
Metuchen
95
184
35
440
Great Kills Harbor
287
Fords
ANNADALE
Arthur Kill
TOTTENVILLE
Perth Amboy
Conference House
Raritan
Raritan Bay

Hudson River
Valley

Tenafly

Yonkers

Milton Harbor

Long Island Sound

Mount
Vernon

New
Rochelle

Wave Hill

Englewood

Hudson

New York
Botanical
Garden

WASHINGTON
HEIGHTS

Pelham
Park

Glen
Cove

Hart
Island

The Cloisters /
Fort Tryon Park

Fort
Lee

BAYCHESTER

City
Island

Bronx
Zoo

Eastchester
Bay

BRONX

Long Island Sound

Port
Washington

Yankee
Stadium

Bronx
Museum
of the Arts

SOUNDVIEW

HARLEM

Westchester
Creek

Central
Park

Rikers
Island

Noguchi
Museum

ASTORIA

LaGuardia

DOUGLASTON

Long Island
City

Museum of the
Moving Image

Flushing

North New
Hyde Park

Westbury

Flushing
Meadows

Mineola

PS 1 Contemporary
Art Center

New York
Hall of
Science

ELMHURST

Long Island

Garden
City

Floral
Park

Uniondale

QUEENS

GLENDALE

QUEENS
VILLAGE

Hempstead

Franklin
Square

West
Hempstead

WILLIAMSBURG

JAMAICA

Elmont

Brooklyn Tabernacle

NEW
YORK

ST ALBANS

North Valley
Stream

Roosevelt

Brooklyn Museum

Valley
Stream

Brooklyn
Botanic Garden

EAST
NEW YORK

Rockville
Centre

Baldwin

Prospect Park

ROSEDALE

Lynbrook

FLATBUSH

Spring Creek
Park

Jamaica Bay

John F Kennedy
International

East
Rockaway

Oceanside

BROOKLYN

Canarsie
Beach Park

Woodmere

Powell Creek

Gateway National
Recreation Area

Head of Bay

East Rockaway
Channel

Garrett Lead

SHEEPSHEAD
BAY

Far
Rockaway

Broad Channel

Middle Bay

New York
Aquarium

Bergen
Beach Park

BRIGHTON
BEACH

Long Beach

Coney
Island

Atlantic Beach

Rockaway Beach

Rockaway
Point

0   5 km

0   3 miles

INFORMATION

www.visitbrooklyn.org

ℹ Brooklyn Tourism and Visitors Center, Historic Brooklyn Borough Hall, 209 Joralemon Street, Ground Floor
☎ 718/802-3846 ⓒ Mon–Fri 10–6

WHAT TO SEE

BRIGHTON BEACH

The influx of Russian immigrants to this area on Brooklyn's Atlantic-pounded shore has earned it the nickname Little Odessa by the Sea. You'll appreciate why as you stroll along the ocean's-edge boardwalk and Brighton Beach Avenue. The dozens of supermarkets and delicatessens are stocked with caviar, knishes, vodka, sausages and foods you just don't see back home unless home is Russia. The nightlife recalls Las Vegas, with its scantily clad dancers crowned with elaborate plumage.

✉ Southern tip of Brooklyn 🚇 Q 🚌 B1, B68 🍴 ☕ 🎁

BROOKLYN BOTANIC GARDEN

www.bbg.org

These 52 acres (21ha), planted with more than 13,000 varieties from around the world, are a place for a quiet stroll when you've had enough of Manhattan. There are water-lily ponds, stately old trees and flowering shrubs, a local plantlife section and a conifer collection. The Cranford Rose Garden shelters more than 1,000 varieties of rose. The stunning Cherry Esplanade draws large crowds in May for the blooming season and the Japanese hill-and-pond garden is one of the best of its type in the country. The Palm House, designed by McKim, Mead & White in 1914, and the greenhouses added in 1987, offer additional spaces. You can see everything in the Botanic Garden in two or three hours.

✉ 1000 Washington Avenue, Brooklyn, 11225 ☎ 718/623-7200 ⓒ Mar–end Oct Tue–Fri 8–6, Sat–Sun 10–6; Nov–end Feb Tue–Fri 8–4.30, Sat–Sun 10–4.30 💲 Adult $8, under 12 free. Free to all Tue and Sat 10–noon 🚇 Q to Prospect Park, 2, 3 to Eastern Parkway 🚌 B41, B43, B47, B48, B71 🗣 Guided tours weekends 1pm ☕ 🎁

Above *At the southern tip of Brooklyn, broad and sandy Brighton Beach draws New Yorkers on summer weekends*

BROOKLYN CYCLONES

www.brooklyncyclones.com

This minor-league club has the fans cheering, because going to the game here is the way baseball used to be. Sitting in the bleachers at this waterfront stadium is just the ticket, especially for old Dodgers fans.

✉ Keyspan Park, 1904 Surf Avenue between 17th and 19th streets, Coney Island ☎ 718/449-8497 ⚐ $8–$15 (single tickets available mid-Apr) Ⓜ Stillwell Avenue/Coney Island (W) 🚌 B36, B64, B74 (Stillwell/Surf Avenue)

BROOKLYN HISTORICAL SOCIETY

www.brooklynhistory.org

The Brooklyn Historical Society is a museum, library and educational center dedicated to preserving and exploring Brooklyn's heritage. It occupies a landmark Queen Anne-style building (1881) designed by George B. Post, who embellished the interior with Minton tile floors, elaborately carved black ash, and stained glass by Charles Booth. Post applied bridge engineering techniques to create an open and dramatic two-story space in the center of the building. The museum has a collection of 9,000-plus objects relating to local history. They are used in shows such as *Brooklyn Works,* which traced the history of working people from early farming days through the industrial era (when Brooklyn was the fourth-largest city in the US) to today. The shows are accessible and include fascinating oral history. Prints and Dodger memorabilia are strong elements, too. The society also offers walking tours of Brooklyn neighborhoods and a boat tour of the working waterfront (prices vary). The library (open by appointment) has a premier collection too, including a first edition of Walt Whitman's *Leaves of Grass.*

✉ 128 Pierrepont Street, Brooklyn, 11201 ☎ 718/222-4111 ⏰ Wed–Fri, Sun noon–5, Sat 10–5 ⚐ Adult $6, members and under 12 free Ⓜ 2, 3, 4, 5 🚌 B51 weekdays only ⚑ Guided tours available

BROOKLYN MUSEUM

www.brooklynmuseum.org

The second-largest art museum in New York City, and one of the largest in the country, attracts half a million visitors every year. The Brooklyn Museum is housed in a grand Beaux Arts building designed by McKim, Mead & White in 1897, with an addition by Polshek Partners completed in spring 2004.

The museum prides itself on its fine collection of Egyptian, Classical and Ancient Middle Eastern Art. It holds the third-largest collection of Ancient Egyptian artifacts dating from predynastic times to the Roman conquest. The renovated Morris A. and Meyer Schapiro Wing contains objects from 1350BC, in the reign of Akhenaten and his wife Nefertiti, through to the time of Cleopatra. Jewelry, reliefs of major deities, decorated sarcophagi, coffins and a 2,600-year-old mummy are on display.

The Arts of Africa, the Pacific and the Americas galleries have astonishing collections. An ivory gong from the Edo people of Benin, works from Polynesia and Indonesia, and important textiles from the Andes are just some of the fascinating items. The Arts of Asia collection has objects from China, India, Iran, Korea, Japan, Tibet, Thailand and Turkey.

The collection of decorative arts, costumes and textiles features a 17th-century Dutch farmhouse and a 20th-century art deco library and fashions of 19th-century America and Europe.

Paintings, sculptures, prints, drawings and photographs include works by Gilbert Stuart, Thomas Cole, George Caleb Bingham, Winslow Homer, Auguste Rodin, Edgar Degas, Camille Pissarro, Edward Steichen and Paul Strand.

First Saturdays of the month are enormously popular. A free program of art and entertainment, with food and drinks supplied, attracts thousands. For example, the entertainment may start with spoken-word artists and members

WHERE TO EAT
BLACK SHEEP PUB

www.blacksheepbrooklyn.com

The Irish owners pour a good pint of Guinness at this neighborhood bar that doesn't look too promising from the outside but is a lively place when you get through the doors. The bar food— burgers, sandwiches, salads, and fish and chips—is great value. There's a pub quiz Wednesday nights, movies on Tuesday, sports on TV most other times, and a good price on beers.

✉ 428 Bergen Street at 5th Avenue, Brooklyn ☎ 718/638-1109 ⏰ Mon–Wed 4–4, Thu–Fri 2pm–4am, Sat–Sun noon–4am Ⓜ Bergen Street (2, 3), Atlantic Avenue-Pacific Street (D, M, N, R)

THE GUTTER

www.thegutterbrooklyn.com

Gutter is a new bar with an old 1950s kind of a feel, and eight bowling lanes. Vintage bowling memorabilia decorates the bar, which looks out over the bowling lanes and also has 12 craft beers on draft, but you can get pitchers.

✉ 200 North 14th Street at Wythe Avenue, Brooklyn ☎ 718/387-3585 ⏰ Mon–Thu 5–4, Fri 2pm–4am, Sat–Sun noon–4am ⚐ $7 a game for bowling Ⓜ Nassau Avenue (G), Bedford Avenue (L)

THE LEVEE

www.theleveenyc.com

New Yorkers who know their beer rate this place, which has a few dozen bottled ales as well as six draft brews and a full bar. The Texan owner has made sure there's a friendly Southern feel, and there's a jukebox, pinball and pool table, and a basic bar menu is served until 4am. No frills but a great place to kick back.

✉ 212 Berry Street at Metropolitan Avenue, Brooklyn ☎ 718/218-8787 ◷ Daily noon–4am 🚇 Bedford Avenue (L)

SUPERFINE

Chef Laura Taylor came from Santa Fe, and her innovative seasonal cuisine is Mediterranean inspired. The affordable menu changes daily to take advantage of fresh, organic meat and produce from local markets, and usually offers a main course salad, pasta, steak, chicken and seafood entrees. The restaurant is housed in a casual neighborhood setting with a view of the bridge through the glass doors. Credit cards are not accepted.

✉ 126 Front Street at Pearl Street, DUMBO, Brooklyn ☎ 718/243-9005 ◷ Tue–Fri 11.30–3, 6–11, Sat 3–11, Sun 11–3, 6–10 🍴 L $18, D $32 🚇 York Street

of the Brooklyn Philharmonic in Shakespeare Live alongside a program of Hands-on-Art that allows you to create your own Egyptian-inspired necklaces.

✉ 200 Eastern Parkway, Brooklyn, 11238 ☎ 718/638-5000 ◷ Wed–Fri 10–5, Sat–Sun 11–6, first Sat of the month (except Sep) 11–11 🍴 Adult $10, under 12 free; 1st Sat each month free 5–11 🚇 2, 3 🚌 B41, B69, B71 🎧 Audiotour of permanent collection, $3 🍴 Museum Café Wed–Fri 10–4, Sat, Sun and holidays 11–5 🏛 Museum shop Wed–Fri 10.30–5.30, Sat–Sun 11–6, until 11pm on First Saturdays

BROOKLYN TABERNACLE

www.brooklyntabernacle.org

Housed in the renovated old Lowes Metropolitan Theater building, this non-denominational gospel church in the heart of downtown Brooklyn has a congregation of nearly 10,000 from all walks of life. The tabernacle is one of the most renowned inner-city churches in the country. Pastor Jim Cymbala is a powerful orator, and his services are attended by members of all ethnic and national origins as well as visitors from all over the world who come to listen to the 275-voice gospel choir. His wife, Carol, is the choral director of the four-time Grammy award winning Brooklyn Tabernacle Choir, which frequently sings for the 9am and 12pm services.

✉ 17 Smith Street between Fulton and Livingston streets, downtown Brooklyn ☎ 718/290-2000 ◷ Services: Sun 9am, noon, 3.30pm, Tue 7pm 🚇 Jay Street/Borough Hall (A, C, F); Hoyt Street (2, 3); Borough Hall (4, 5); Lawrence Street (M, R)

CONEY ISLAND

www.coneyisland.com

Known as the Playground of the World, Coney Island is a New York treasure, though it's seen tough times. It lost its Thunderbolt roller coaster and Kensington Hotel in 2000; Steeplechase Park was closed in 1964; Astroland Park closed in 2008. In spite of this, the New York Aquarium (opened in 1957) is going strong, the world-famous Cyclone and Wonder Wheel are open and the broad sand beaches remain. The Mermaid Parade, a summer solstice staple, is a "must-see." Nathan Handwerker opened his hot-dog emporium here in 1916, and his famous hot dogs are now sold all over New York. Keyspan Park is the $39-million home of the Brooklyn Cyclones baseball team. It is located behind Parachute Jump on the Boardwalk.

✉ Southern tip of Brooklyn, 11224 🚇 F, Q, W 🚌 B36, B74 🍴 🍺 🏛

NEW YORK AQUARIUM

www.nyaquarium.com

There are daily dolphin and sea lion shows in summer at this small park, which also houses penguins, walruses, Beluga whales, sharks and seals—300 species in all. Most exhibits are outside. In the Discovery Center kids can pick up starfish, crabs and other small sea creatures.

✉ Surf Avenue and West 8th Street, Coney Island, Brooklyn ☎ 718-265-3400 ◷ Memorial Day–Labor Day, Mon–Fri 10–6, Sat–Sun 10–7; Apr–Memorial Day and Labor Day–Oct 31 Mon–Fri 10–5, Sat–Sun 10–5.30; Nov–Mar daily 10–4.30 🍴 Adult $13, child (2–12) $9, under 2 free 🚇 Stillwell Avenue (D), 8th Street (F, Q) 🚌 From Manhattan, call 718/330-1234

NEW YORK TRANSIT MUSEUM

www.mta.info/mta/museum

The New York Transit Museum occupies a decommissioned subway station in downtown Brooklyn. The permanent and temporary exhibitions explore the history of buses and trolleys in New York City. Highlights are the vintage subway and trolley cars.

✉ Boerum Place and Schermerhorn Street, Brooklyn, 11201 ☎ 718/694-1600 ◷ Tue–Fri 10–4, Sat–Sun noon–5 🍴 Adult $5, child (under 17) $3 🚇 2, 3, 4, 5 🏛 Gallery annex and store at Grand Central Terminal (▷ 157) ☎ 212/878-0106

PLYMOUTH CHURCH OF THE PILGRIMS

www.plymouthchurch.org

The Plymouth Church of the Pilgrims, built in 1849, was the first Congregational Church in Brooklyn and a focal point of the anti-slavery movement at the time. Abraham Lincoln worshiped here twice in 1860, and many eminent writers have spoken here. Elegant and beautiful stained-glass windows by Tiffany adorn this otherwise modest church, and in the courtyard next to it is a superb bronze statue of Henry Ward Beecher (1813–87) with slaves, sculpted by Gutzon Borglum (famous for his work on Mount Rushmore). Beecher, the most famous preacher in America, preached from this pulpit for 40 years, often speaking out against slavery.

✉ 75 Hicks Street, Brooklyn, 11201 ☎ 718/624-4743 ◐ Guided tour only (1hr 30 min) Mon–Fri 10–4, Sun 11–2, advance reservation required ✋ Phone for prices ⓠ 2, 3, A, C

PROSPECT PARK

www.prospectpark.org

Designed by Frederick Law Olmsted and Calvert Vaux, the designers of Central Park (▷ 208–213), this 526-acre (213ha) park is a pleasant place to spend a day. At the main entrance at Grand Army Plaza are a triumphal arch and a monument to President John F. Kennedy.

In Leffert's Homestead is a museum for children. A zoo, skating rink, boathouse and pond, playgrounds, and a lovely 1912 carousel (open same hours as museum; $1.50) are very popular with children, too. The northeast corner has a rose garden, Japanese gardens, a sculpture garden and the Brooklyn Museum (▷ 251). Events throughout the year draw large crowds.

The Audubon Center provides maps and guides for self-guiding tours, as well as free guided nature walks and other programs.

✉ Flatbush Avenue at Grand Army Plaza. Information: Prospect Park Alliance, 95 Prospect Park West, Brooklyn, 11215 ☎ Information: 718/965-8999; Lefferts Homestead Historic House Museum: 718/789-2822; Audubon Center: 718/287-3400 ◐ Daily 5am–1am. Museum: late May to mid-Sep Thu–Sun 12–5. Also open weekends and school holidays mid-Sep to late May. Audubon Center: late May–Nov Thu–Sun 12–5; Dec–late May Sat–Sun 12–4 ✋ Free ⓠ 2, 3, F, Q 🚌 B41, B69, B71, B75 🗟 🖭 ⌗

WATERFRONT MUSEUM

www.waterfrontmuseum.org

An unusual museum in the last surviving railroad barge, the Waterfront stages a summer music series on Saturday nights in July featuring blues to swing and country artists, and a program of Circus Sundays in June. The barge was designated by the UN in 1998 as the Regional Craft of the International Year of the Oceans. Day visitors learn about New York Harbor, barge history and how this barge was rescued.

✉ 290 Conover Street at Pier 44, Brooklyn, 11231 ☎ 718/624-4719 ◐ Thu 4–8 ✋ Free ⓠ F, G 🚌 B77

Above *The Audubon Center in leafy Prospect Park is the place to go for maps and self-guiding tours*

Below *Ancient Egyptian artifacts on display in Brooklyn Museum*

BROOKLYN HEIGHTS TO MANHATTAN WALK

If Brooklyn were not part of New York City, it would be America's sixth-largest city. Historic Brooklyn Heights, with its many landmark churches, fine brownstones and leafy streets, remains one of the city's most distinguished residential areas. The walk across Brooklyn Bridge provides stunning views of Lower Manhattan.

THE WALK

Distance: 2.5 miles (4km)
Time: 2 to 2.5 hours (allow time to enjoy the view of Manhattan from Brooklyn Bridge)
Start at: High Street/Brooklyn Bridge subway station
End at: Brooklyn Bridge/City Hall subway station

HOW TO GET THERE

Subway A or C from Manhattan to High Street or Brooklyn Bridge subway stations.

★Leave the High Street/Brooklyn Bridge subway station. As you come out of the station, you see Cadman Plaza Park, with its tall trees, paths and benches. On the right side of the park is Cadman Plaza West. Walk south on this street the length of the park.

❶ Stop for a moment at the large stone monument on your left, dedicated to the Brooklyn men and women who fought during World War II. With its trees and benches, this park is a pleasant place to sit.

Continue on Cadman Plaza West, crossing Tillary Street. Pass the Korean War Veterans Plaza on your left and continue to the Federal Building and the Romanesque Revival US Post Office and Courthouse. Cross Johnson Street.

❷ The enormous building on the left is the Supreme Court of New York. Pause to admire the statue of Christopher Columbus in front of the building and the bronze bust of Senator Robert F. Kennedy, the assassinated brother of President John F. Kennedy.

❸ Straight ahead is an elaborate fountain and behind it is the Greek Revival Brooklyn Borough Hall, built in 1848.

Just past Borough Hall is Joralemon Street. Walk west on Joralemon a block and a half to Sidney Place, on your left. Look down this little street to the big red church, St. Charles Borromeo Roman Catholic Church, built in 1849. Three blocks farther

west on Joralemon, turn right on Hicks Street. Walk one block north.

❹ Grace Church, at 254 Hicks Street, is one of many New York City churches designed by Richard Upjohn; it dates from 1849. Visit the charming entrance court off Hicks Street and cool off in the shade of the enormous elm tree.

Continue a block north on Hicks to Remsen Street, and turn right. Go one block east and cross Henry Street.

❺ On your left is Richard Upjohn's Cathedral of Our Lady of Lebanon, the first round-arched, Early Romanesque Revival ecclesiastical building in the United States. Notice the medallions on the entrance doors. Originally the dining room doors on the French luxury liner *Normandie*, they were bought at an auction in 1945.

Continue another block east on Remsen, and turn left on Clinton

Street. Walking north, as you cross Montague Street, look at St. Ann and the Holy Trinity Episcopal Church, a major work of James Renwick, Jr., on your left; it is one of the most important Victorian Gothic churches in the United States. At the end of Clinton Street, turn left on Cadman Plaza West, left again on Clark Street and then right on Henry Street. Walk two blocks to Orange Street and turn left.

❻ The Plymouth Church of the Pilgrims, built in 1849 on Orange Street between Henry and Hicks streets, was the center of anti-slavery sentiment during antebellum days. Abolitionist minister Henry Ward Beecher preached against slavery here. Abraham Lincoln worshiped here twice, and the building was a key part of the Underground Railroad, which helped get escaped slaves to freedom in the north. Beautiful stained-glass windows adorn this otherwise modest church, and in the courtyard next to it stands a bronze statue of Henry Ward Beecher by Gutzon Borglum, who sculpted the famous four presidents' heads at Mount Rushmore, South Dakota.

Return to Henry Street and turn left. There are many cafés, restaurants and delis along here. At the traffic lights, turn right on Middagh Street and, at Cadman Plaza West, take the path ahead across the park. On your left is a plaque with information about the peregrine falcons that often roost here. At the fork in the path, keep left and you'll come to Washington Street. Turn left, and just before you come to the traffic lights at Prospect Street, go up the steps on your left.

❼ You now leave Brooklyn Heights across Brooklyn Bridge (▷ 68–69), on the wide wooden pedestrian walkway. In 1883 Brooklyn Bridge became the world's longest suspension bridge, spanning the East River and connecting Brooklyn to Manhattan. This spectacular bridge, with its web of steel cables, remains as much a marvel today as it did when it was first built.

When you reach the other side of the bridge you'll see the Brooklyn Bridge City Hall subway, from where you can access lines 4, 5, 6, J, M, Z.

WHEN TO GO

Any day of the week, morning or afternoon, but the walk across the bridge is especially romantic as the sun slowly sets behind Liberty Island and Lower Manhattan's city lights begin to twinkle.

WHERE TO EAT

Henry and Montague streets have a wide selection of cafés and restaurants.

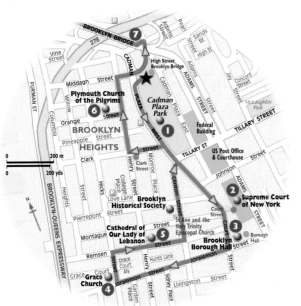

EXCURSIONS WALK

INFORMATION
www.ilovethebronx.com
🛈 The Bronx Tourism Council, 198
E. 161st Street, Suite 201, Bronx
☎ 718-590-3518

Above *Bronx Zoo is a fantastic destination
for a family day out*

WHAT TO SEE

BRONX MUSEUM OF THE ARTS
www.bronxmuseum.org
Founded in 1971, the museum maintains a permanent collection of 20th- and
21st-century works in all media by artists of African, Asian and Latin American
descent. The permanent collection of more than 800 works also includes artists
for whom the Bronx has been a key component of their artistic development
or practice. Exhibitions focus on contemporary and historical cultural issues
related to the Bronx, and past exhibitions have featured African-American artist
Romare Bearden and photography by Harlem-based Jamel Shabazz.
✉ 1040 Grand Concourse at 165th Street, Bronx ☎ 718/681-6000 🕐 Thu, Sat–Sun 11–6, Fri
11–8 ✋ Adult $5, child $3 🚇 167th Street/Grand Concourse (D, B)

BRONX ZOO
www.bronxzoo.com
The largest metropolitan wildlife park in the country, Bronx Zoo has more than
4,500 animals representing 55 species housed on 265 acres (107ha). This
wonderful and hugely popular zoo has no fewer than three names—Bronx
Zoo, New York Zoological Park and International Wildlife Conservation Park. The
animals, including endangered and threatened species, are well cared for and
their surroundings are as near as possible to native habitats.
One of the most impressive areas is the Wild Asia Complex, where you
can see Indonesian tigers and Asian elephants, but only from the Wild Asia
Monorail. JungleWorld's indoor re-creation of an Asian forest will envelop you,

and it's home to leopards, lizards, tree kangaroos and white-cheeked gibbons, among other exotic wildlife from jungles around the world. In the Himalayan Highlands there are rare snow leopards as well as red pandas.

The Congo Gorilla Forest is a 6.5-acre (2.6ha) re-creation of an African rainforest; among the treetop lookouts, wooded pathways and lush greenery are 400 animals, including western lowland gorillas, who can be entertaining. You'll also see okapi and red river hogs.

In the Butterfly Garden (Apr–end Oct) the size of some of the butterflies might surprise you, not to mention the enormous variety and beauty of these complicated insects.

The World of Darkness, as you might imagine, is devoted to the lives of nocturnal creatures, such as fruit-eating bats.

The Children's Zoo (Apr–end Oct) has wonderful activities—kids learn to see like an owl and hear like a fox—and a petting zoo.

The Wild Asia Monorail (late Apr–end Oct) is a 25-minute narrated ride above the roaming Siberian tigers, Indian rhinoceroses, Asian elephants, and other animals of the Indian subcontinent. It's a good way to see a lot without wearing yourself out. Other rides include the Skyfari aerial tram, camel rides and the Zoo Shuttle (Apr–early Nov).

In summer it can get crowded, and if it is a very warm day the animals retreat from open sunny positions and it can be hard to see some of them. If you are planning to visit for a day, you would be advised to eat early or late or bring a picnic and drinks. Lines for the food stands can be long and slow on a busy, hot afternoon.

✉ Bronx River Parkway and Fordham Road, Bronx, 10460 ☎ 718/367-1010 🕐 Apr–Oct Mon–Fri 10–5, Sat–Sun 10–5.30; rest of year Mon–Fri 10–4.30, Sat–Sun 10–5 💲 Thu–Tue adult $15, child (2–12) $11, under 2 free; Wed suggested donation. Congo Gorilla Forest, Children's Zoo, Bug Carousel, Zoo Shuttle, Butterfly Zone $3 each. Camel rides and monorail $5. Pay-One-Price ticket that includes admission and all rides except camel rides: adult $27, child $21 🚇 2 or 5 to Pelham Parkway or East Tremont Avenue 🚌 Liberty Lines Bx11 from Madison Avenue ☎ 718/445-3100 for details 🎫 Tours by Friends of the Zoo ☎ 718/ 220-5141 🍴 🛒 🏛

NEW YORK BOTANICAL GARDEN
www.nybg.org
One of the greatest botanical gardens in the world encompasses 250 acres (100ha) of beautiful landscape, gorgeous gardens and extensive collections of more than 1 million plants. There are 50 indoor and outdoor display gardens, a waterfall, wetlands and 50 acres (20ha) of virgin native forest as well as special programs exhibitions and a range of activities.

The Victorian-style Enid A. Haupt Conservatory glasshouse displays plants from around the world in 11 distinct habitats, including misty rainforests, exotic aquatics and spectacular deserts. In spring and fall the lovely, fragrant Peggy Rockefeller Rose Garden displays antique roses, hybrid teas, floribundas and shrub roses, while every summer the Daylily Garden showcases blooms in rainbow colors. The 12-acre (5ha) Everett Children's Adventure Garden offers the boulder maze for climbing, aquatic plant touch tank and an indoor laboratory with hands-on activities.

✉ Kazimiroff (Southern) Boulevard at 200th Street, Bronx ☎ 718/817-8700 🕐 Tue–Sun 10–6 💲 Prices vary with exhibitions. Grounds only adults $6, child (2–12) $1 🚇 Bedford Park Boulevard (B, D, 4) then walk, or take Bx 26 bus 🚌 Bx 19, Bx 26 🚉 Botanical Garden Station (Metro North)

WAVE HILL
www.wavehill.org
The setting of this park in the Riverdale section of the Bronx is spectacular. This former private estate offers sweeping views of the Hudson River and the New Jersey cliffs as well as 28 delightful acres (11ha) of beautiful intimate gardens,

WHERE TO EAT
DOMINICK'S RESTAURANT
Family-style Italian meals are served in a fun, old-style noisy and casual restaurant with no menus. Just tell the waiter what you want for dinner, and listen for today's options. No reservations are accepted and there is almost always a line here. Many tables are communal, and payment is cash only.

✉ 2335 Arthur Avenue near 184th Street, Bronx ☎ 718/733-2807 🕐 Wed–Sun, 12–12 💲 D $45 🚇 182nd Street (B, D)

MARIO'S
www.mariosrestarthurave.com
Five generations of the Migliucci family have prepared food from scratch to order in this family casual eatery known for its authentic recipes. The Neapolitan pies are legendary; pizzas are crusty and bubbling hot, with fresh tomatoes, olive oil, basil and mozzarella cheese. The menu also includes excellent lamb, veal and pasta entrees.

✉ 2342 Arthur Avenue near 184th Street, Bronx ☎ 718/584-1188 🕐 Tue–Thu, Sun 12–9.30, Fri–Sat 12–10.30 💲 L $18, D $35 🚇 182nd Street (B, D)

SPORTS AND ACTIVITIES
BRONX EQUESTRIAN CENTER
www.bronxequestriancenter.com

Located near the lovely Pelham Bay park, there's an opportunity at this equestrian center to go trail-riding through the woods or enjoy pony and hay wagon rides too.

✉ 9 Shore Road, Bronx ☎ 718/885-0551 🕐 Daily 9–7 ✋ Lessons $40 per half-hour, trail rides from $30 per hour, $5 for three pony rides 🚇 Phone for directions

VAN CORTLANDT GOLF COURSE
www.nycgovparks.org

The oldest public golf course in the US is not exactly grade A, but it will do. Eighteen holes, 6,122 yards, with clubhouse.

✉ Van Cortlandt Park South and Bailey Avenue, Bronx ☎ 718/543-4595 🕐 Dawn–dusk ✋ $16.75–$39.50 plus $8 for non-NY residents 🚇 242nd Street (1)

Below *The new Yankee Stadium, opened in 2009, was built to resemble the original 1923 structure*

a cultural center that stages art exhibitions, greenhouses full of plants from around the world, a herb garden and gracious wooded paths. On weekends, there's often an imaginative Family Art Project scheduled.

✉ 675 West 249th Street at Independence Avenue, Bronx ☎ 718-549-3200 🕐 Tue–Sun 9–5.30 (Oct 15–Apr 14 until 4.30) ✋ Adult $6, child $2, under 6 free (free Tue and mornings on Sat) 🚇 231st Street (1, 9), then Bx 7 or Bx 10 🚌 Bx 7, Bx 10 🚆 Riverdale (Metro North ☎ 212/532-4900)

YANKEE STADIUM
http://newyork.yankees.mlb.com

Yankee Stadium, America's first triple-decker stadium, was the home of the New York Yankees from April 18, 1923, until April 3, 2009, when the new Yankee Stadium, located next door, opened with a victory over the Cubs (7–4). The most famous player of them all, Babe Ruth, hit a three-run homer on that inaugural day in 1923 in front of 74,200 fans and the Yankees were victorious (4–1). After that, the stadium quickly became known as The House That Ruth Built. The stadium was first powered by electric lighting in 1946 and the first electronic message board was installed in 1959. After CBS became its new owner in 1967, the Yankees spent two seasons at Shea Stadium while their own stadium was renovated. Upon their return to Yankee Stadium, the Yankees went on to host the World Series.

The new stadium is designed to resemble the original Yankee Stadium and incorporates many features in honor of the Yankees' history. Groundbreaking ceremonies occurred on August 16, 2006, the 58th anniversary of Babe Ruth's death. The exterior closely resembles the original 1923 stadium, and the modern ballpark interior features a playing field very close in size to the former Yankee Stadium. The new stadium boasts the latest technology and the inside walls are decorated with hundreds of photographs that portray the history of the Yankees.

There are several main entrances, so make a mental note of where you enter to avoid confusion when you leave. Make sure that you have no reason to leave once you are inside, because you cannot re-enter the stadium using the same ticket. Arrive an hour and a half before the game Mondays to Fridays, two hours ahead on weekends to watch the batting practice. It can take some time to get through the entrance, so allow plenty of time to see the beginning of the game.

To get a behind-the-scenes tour it is best to buy advance tickets, but you can take a chance and go to the Advance Ticket window or any of the Clubhouse stores on the day of the tour. The tour covers Yankees' history and you can get a good look at the field, the dugout area, the press box, the Clubhouse and Monument Park.

Alcohol is sold up until the seventh inning of each game, but drunkenness is not tolerated; you can ask to sit in an alcohol-free section when you buy your tickets. Other rules ban bottles, cans, coolers or containers, large bags and briefcases, noisemakers, laser pens, beachballs, firearms and knives; and there's no smoking.

✉ 161st Street and River Avenue, Bronx, 10451 ☎ 718/293-6000 🕐 Baseball season Apr– Oct ✋ Tickets for games $14–$400 ☎ Ticketmaster 212/307-1212 or visit http://newyork. yankees.mlb.com 🚇 4, B, D 🚌 Bx6, Bx13, Bx55 ℹ 45-min behind-the-scenes tour: visit the website to purchase advanced tickets, or buy tickets from Ticketmaster or any Clubhouse store. Tours daily 12–1.40, except when the Yankees play at home. Adult $20 🍴 🛍 Upscale NYY Steak is open till 11pm daily; snacks and drinks throughout the stadium 🎁 Three gift shops and an art gallery. The largest selection of Yankee merchandise is at the Home Plate Store in the Great Hall. Yankee Clubhouse stores have five Manhattan locations; get the location details and opening hours from the website

VAN CORTLANDT PARK

The Caribbean communities brought cricket to New York City, and this is the best place to find a cricket game in progress.

✉ Van Cortlandt Park, Park South and Bailey Avenue 🕐 Dawn–dusk in summer ✋ Free 🚇 242nd Street (1)

YONKERS RACEWAY

www.yonkersraceway.com

One of the premier harness racing tracks in the nation is in the city, just north of the Bronx. The track celebrated its centennial in 1999. The most illustrious race run here is the Night of Champions, with a $1.2 million purse.

✉ 810 Yonkers Avenue, Yonkers ☎ 914/968-4200 🕐 Mon–Tue, Thu– Sat, 7.10pm post time ✋ $2.25–$4.25 🚇 Woodlawn (4) and Beeline 20 bus

Above *Yonkers Raceway is one of the United States' premier harness racing tracks*

INFORMATION
www.metmuseum.org

✉ 99 Margaret Corbin Drive, Fort Tryon Park, 10040 ☎ 212/923-3700

🕐 Mar–end Oct Tue–Sun 9.30–5.15; rest of year Tue–Sun 9.30–4.45

🎫 Adult $20, under 12 free. Ticket includes same-day admission to the Metropolitan Museum of Art 🚇 A

🚌 M4 🍴 The Trie Café on the lower level in the Trie Cloister; May–Oct Tue–Sun 10–4.15 📷 Free guided tours Tue–Fri and Sun 3pm; audioguide adult $7, under 12 $5 🎧

TIPS
➤➤ Take the subway ride if you are in a hurry. Get off at 190th Street and take the elevator to street level. Enter Fort Tryon Park and walk up the Promenade to the Cloisters.

➤➤ In summer there is a direct bus from the Metropolitan Museum of Art—more expensive than public transportation but quicker.

Above *Designed in the style of a fortified monastery, the Cloisters commands stunning views over the Hudson River*

INTRODUCTION

Perched high above the Hudson River, the Cloisters is in delightful Fort Tryon Park in Washington Heights, at the northern tip of Manhattan, with spectacular views across the river to the steep rock-faced cliffs known as the Palisades. The Cloisters opened in 1938 as a branch of the Metropolitan Museum of Art and is devoted to the art and architecture of medieval Europe. The building includes large sections transported from five 12th- to 15th-century cloisters in southern France and Spain.

WHAT TO SEE
THE COLLECTION

The collection is based on medieval sculptures and segments of architecture acquired by American sculptor George Grey Barnard during trips to Europe, and includes 5,000 sculptures, tapestries, illuminated manuscripts, paintings, stained glass and other priceless objects. He brought them to New York and exhibited them in a brick building on Fort Washington Avenue. In 1925, John D. Rockefeller donated a large sum of money to the Met to purchase the Barnard collection. Then in 1930, Rockefeller gave his beautiful Fort Tryon estate to the Met, stipulating that the Cloisters be built to house a medieval collection.

HIGHLIGHTS OF THE COLLECTION

On the main floor is the Fuentidueña Chapel, whose 1160 apse comes from the Church of San Martín in Castile, Spain. The capital on the right side depicts Daniel in the Lions' Den, while the one on the left shows the Adoration of the Magi. The Virgin and Child fresco in the semidome came from a small Catalan church in the Pyrenees. The Romanesque doorway in the nave of the chapel was carved in about 1175 in Tuscany. Also on this floor is the Saint-Guilhem Cloister, whose imposing covered walkway is from a Benedictine abbey near Montpellier, France. The columns have intricately carved capitals and date from the 12th to 13th centuries. In the center of the main floor is the Cuxa Cloister, from a Benedictine monastery near Prades, France. The cloister was abandoned during the French Revolution and was later sold off in parts. Barnard managed to collect about half the original capitals, 25 bases and 12 columns. In the Nine Heroes Tapestries Room are some of the oldest surviving tapestries from a set dating from 1385.

FORT TRYON PARK WALK

Go to Fort Tryon Park for fresh air, a walk in the woods, spectacular views of the Hudson River from Manhattan's highest natural point, gardens and a medieval-style monastery.

THE WALK

Distance: 1.5 miles (2.4km)
Time: 1.5 to 2 hours
Start/End at: Margaret Corbin Circle at 190th Street subway station

HOW TO GET THERE

Subway A to 190th Street or bus M4 to 190th Street.

❶ One of the earliest battles of the American Revolutionary War was fought here on November 16, 1776. General George Washington's troops lost to the British, who named the fort for the colonial governor, Sir William Tryon. Frederick Law Olmsted, Jr. designed the 62-acre (25ha) gardens to recall medieval Europe, using more than 250 species of plant, stone walls, arches and terraces. Margaret Corbin Circle is named for a woman who fought in the Fort Tryon battle. On the west side of the circle stands the gatehouse for the Billings estate. Cornelius K. G. Billings spent more than $2 million building his Tryon Hill mansion between 1901 and 1905.

Make your way through the huge stone gateway ahead and onto the Promenade. Turn immediately to your left onto this walkway.

❷ The 3-acre (1.2ha) Heather Garden enjoys a breathtaking view across the Hudson River to New Jersey's Palisades and the George Washington Bridge. With its many heathers, brooms, perennials and shrubs, this garden is one of the largest heather gardens on the east coast. By May, 5,000 bulbs are in full bloom, with more than 30 varieties of daffodils and tulips; 1,000 lilies are in flower from June to September.

From the Heather Garden, return to the Promenade and follow it to Linden Terrace.

❸ In 1909, Billings erected a stela in Linden Terrace as a memorial to the Continental Army's defense of the site. There are benches, parapets and splendid river views. At the northeast corner, a flight of steps leads to a flagpole on the highest natural point in Manhattan.

Return down the steps to the Promenade, which veers to the left and down some stone steps. At the bottom of the steps continue along the path to your right.

❹ You can see the Cloisters straight ahead to the north. Stroll northward with the river on your left and, if you wish to have a quick look inside the museum, cross the road at the crosswalk (pedestrian crossing) on your right and go straight ahead.

Continue north on the path you left to visit the Cloisters and stroll through the woods and lawns. If you stay on the path closest to Margaret Corbin Drive you'll come to the New Leaf Café (tel 212/568-5323; Tue–Sun), an enterprise of actress Bette Midler's New York Restoration Project.

❺ The café's stunning location, good food and affordable prices, make it a pleasant rest stop. Proceeds support ongoing work in the park.

The path from the café leads back to the park's main entrance.

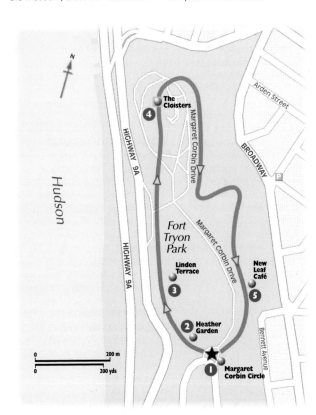

INFORMATION
HISTORIC HUDSON VALLEY
www.hudsonvalley.org
☎ 914/631-8200

HOW TO GET THERE
🚃 Most of the valley north of New York City is easily visited by train. From Grand Central Terminal, take the Metro-North Hudson Line to the closest station; local taxis meet trains at most stations, or you can book one through Rivertowns Taxi (tel 914/478-2222)

🚗 Follow the West Side Highway to the Henry Hudson Parkway and then the Saw Mill River Parkway (all one road, really, but with three different names). It's best to get specific directions from the Saw Mill by phoning each sight

🚢 The New York Waterway offers day-long excursions (late Oct–end Nov only) up the Hudson River, leaving from Pier 78 on Manhattan's west side (tel 1800/533-3779, www.nywaterway.com)

INTRODUCTION
The Hudson River flows 315 miles (507km) from the Adirondack Mountains to New York and out into the Atlantic. The splendor of the valley can be seen in 19th-century paintings by the Hudson River School artists, and today the area is lovely, especially in the fall, when the colorful foliage brightens the shoreline.

WHAT TO SEE
HUDSON RIVER MUSEUM
The Hudson River Museum (511 Warburton Avenue, Yonkers, tel 914/963-4550; Wed–Sun noon–5, Fri noon–8) is built around a historic house and a modern addition. Collections encompass art and history, and there's a planetarium. At the Museum Café, you can have a light lunch with splendid views of the Hudson River and the Palisades in New Jersey. Take Metro-North to Yonkers, then grab a cab (about $5).

SUNNYSIDE TO LYNDHURST
Sunnyside, a National Historic Landmark, was the home of Washington Irving, who wrote *The Legend of Sleepy Hollow* and was America's first internationally known author. The cottage (tel 914/631-8200; Apr–end Oct Wed–Mon 10–5; Nov–Dec Sat–Sun 10–4) was built in the 18th century and enlarged by Irving in 1835. Guided tours of the house and grounds are available up to one hour before closing time. There is a visitor center, museum shop and seasonal café. From Grand Central Terminal, catch a train to Tarrytown, where taxis wait.

Lyndhurst, a spectacular Gothic Revival-style mansion (tel 914/ 631-4481; mid-Apr to end Oct Tue–Sun 10–5; rest of year Sat–Sun 10–4), was the home of railroad tycoon Jay Gould. The surrounding lawns have amazing Hudson River views. You can call a cab to take you to Sunnyside, or walk on the footpath.

PHILLIPSBURG MANOR AND KYKUIT
Phillipsburg Manor, on Route 9 in Sleepy Hollow, is a restored colonial farm once owned by the Phillips family (tel 914/631-3992; Apr–end Oct Wed–Mon 10–6; Nov–Dec Sat–Sun 10–4). Guided tours are available and buildings are staffed by interpreters in costume who explain early Hudson River Valley life.

Kykuit is a National Trust Historic Site that was home to four generations of the wealthy Rockefeller family. The sumptuous mansion is filled with priceless antiques and works of art, and sculptures fill the landscaped gardens. Guided

Above *Wisteria adorns the east facade of Kykuit, the Rockefeller family home*

tours (mid-May to end Oct Wed–Mon 10–3) begin at Phillipsburg Manor; tickets go on sale at 9am and are issued on a first-come, first-served basis (children under 10 are not admitted).

VAN CORTLANDT MANOR
This 18th-century Hudson Valley mansion belonged to the Van Cortlandt family for more than 260 years. Pierre Van Cortlandt was the first lieutenant-governor of New York State. The house has original furnishings, and the kitchen is a tour highlight with its original hearth and beehive oven (tel 914/271-8981; Apr–early Sep Wed–Mon 10–5; Oct–end Dec Sat–Sun 10–4).

WEST POINT, FRANKLIN D. ROOSEVELT NATIONAL HISTORIC SITE TO VANDERBILT MANSION
Farther upstate, there are several other landmarks on the eastern banks of the Hudson, most notably West Point Military Academy. Nearby is Cold Spring, a charming riverfront town known for its antiques shops and garrison, home to another 19th-century mansion **Boscobel** (tel 845/265-3638). Beacon is a riverfront town that is being revived with the help of DIA Arts. Farther north are two sites associated with the Roosevelts. The best way to visit is by car.

The United States Military Academy at **West Point** (tel 845/938-2638) has turned out great generals, presidents and astronauts. The museum displays guns, uniforms, medals and flags from conflicts, and the grounds are beautiful.

Franklin D. Roosevelt National Historic Site (tel 800/337-8474; daily 9–5) was the Depression-era president's birthplace. The house, library and museum have a large collection of family memorabilia. Franklin and his formidable wife, Eleanor, are buried in the rose garden; a marble monument marks their graves.

From this point a shuttle bus will take you to the **Eleanor Roosevelt National Historic Site** (daily 9–5) in the grounds of the Roosevelt estate.

Vanderbilt Mansion (tel 800/337-8474; daily 9–5, visit by guided tour only), 2 miles (3.2km) north of the Roosevelt Historic Site, is the lavish Beaux Arts mansion of the grandson of railroad magnate Cornelius Vanderbilt. Inside you will see Renaissance to rococo furniture and works of art. The gardens are exquisite, and there are several walking trails that skirt the river.

WHERE TO EAT
In Tarrytown there are three good places to find something to eat: Equus Restaurant, The Castle (914/631-3646); Horsefeathers, 94 North Broadway (914/ 631-6606); and Striped Bass, 236 Main Street (914/366-4455).

NATIONAL PARK SERVICE
☎ 845/229-9115

NATIONAL TRUST FOR HISTORIC PRESERVATION
☎ 914/631-4481

Below *Portrait of John D. Rockefeller (1917) by John Singer Sargent, flanked by Meissen birds of prey in the dining room of Kykuit*

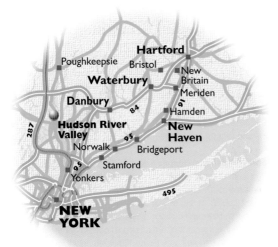

INFORMATION

www.discoverlongisland.com

🛈 Long Island Convention & Visitors Bureau and Sports Commission

☎ 877/FUN-ON-LI

HOW TO GET THERE

🚉 Go to Pennsylvania Station on 7th Avenue between 31st and 33rd streets. From here catch a Long Island Railroad train to the town nearest the place of interest

🚗 From New York, travel from Manhattan east on the Long island Expressway (I-495). Buses and trains are often a better way to get to Long Island, but you usually need a car to get around the various sights, so it's best to take your own wheels

Above *Steps leading to the South Terrace of the Charles II-style Westbury House in Old Westbury Gardens*

INTRODUCTION

Long Island is 125 miles (201 km) long and between 12 and 23 miles (19 and 37km) wide. It lies east of New York City and is washed by the Atlantic Ocean on the south and Long Island Sound on the north. The rocky northern shoreline, scalloped with beaches, coves and bluffs, and sometimes called the Gold Coast, has attracted the affluent since the late 19th century. The Hamptons, at the east of the island, on the Atlantic shore, has become the playground of wealthy families, who have built fine summer houses and mansions. The delightful Atlantic-pounded beaches along the southern shore offer an escape from city heat in summer. The western part of the island, which consists of the Manhattan boroughs of Brooklyn and Queens, is densely populated, but the farther east you go, the more rural it becomes. Here are historic homes, fishing ports, historic whaling towns, museums and state parks.

WHAT TO SEE

OLD WESTBURY GARDENS AND SAGAMORE HILL HISTORIC SITE

Old Westbury Gardens (tel 516/333-0048) was the home of financier John S. Phipps (1874–1958), his wife Margarita and their four children. The Charles II-style manor house is furnished with English antiques and decorative arts. The surrounding 160 acres (65ha), with 88 breathtaking acres (36ha) of formal gardens, walkways, architectural follies and woodlands, are dotted with ponds and lakes. The gardens are between the Long Island Expressway and Jericho Turnpike (Route 25). By car, take Exit 39 (Glen Cove Road) off the I-495. Follow the service road east for 1 mile (1.6km), turn right on Old Westbury Road and continue for half a mile.

Sagamore Hill National Historic Site is northeast of Old Westbury, the home of President Theodore Roosevelt from 1885 until his death in 1919. The house is furnished as it was when he lived here (tel 516/922-4788; Memorial Day–Labor Day daily 10–4; rest of year Wed–Sun). Tours last half an hour and are on a first-come, first-served basis. They are limited in size, so arrive early if possible (by noon in summer they are often sold out). To get there by car, take Exit 41N (Oyster Bay) off I-495 onto Route 106 North. Travel for 4 miles (6km) to Route 25A, where you will turn right and travel 2.5 miles (4km) to the third traffic light. At the bottom of a long hill, turn left onto Cove Road and continue for 1.5 miles (2.4km). Turn right onto Cove Neck Road for 1.5 miles (2.4km).

WALT WHITMAN BIRTHPLACE TO OLD BETHPAGE VILLAGE

Walt Whitman (1819–92) was one of America's finest poets and essayists. At his birthplace (tel 631/427-5240; Jun 15–Labor Day Mon–Fri 11–4, Sat–Sun 12–5; rest of year Wed–Fri 1–4, Sat–Sun 11–4), south of Sagamore Hill, you will see Whitman memorabilia, including photographs and excerpts from his writings and letters. To get there from I-495, take Exit 49N onto Route 110 North. Turn left onto Walt Whitman Road in Huntington Station. As the site is very popular with school groups, you may want to phone ahead.

Old Bethpage Village (tel 516/572-8400; Mar–end Oct Wed–Fri 10–4, Sat–Sun 10–5; Nov–Dec Wed–Sun 10–4) is an area of shops, farms, a one-room school-house, a church, gardens and homes filled with antiques, staffed by costumed interpreters explaining about life on Long Island in the 19th century. Special events are lively and fun.

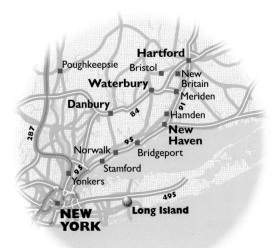

Above *A pergola lies at the end of a pretty avenue in the Walled Garden of Old Westbury Gardens*

INFORMATION

www.discoverqueens.info

ℹ️ Queens Visitor's Center, Queens Center Mall, 90-15 Queens Boulevard, Elmhurst, 11373 ☎ 718/592-2082

US OPEN TENNIS CHAMPIONSHIP

www.usopen.org

www.usta.com

This two-week tournament is one of four in the sport's Grand Slam. Tickets to any session admit you to matches played in Arthur Ashe stadium, and to other courts. You can see more tennis if you buy daytime tickets, since many of the outer courts are not used at night. Tickets go on sale at the end of April; most are sold via subscription and what remain are usually in the stratosphere—but for day sessions most of the action takes place on outer courts. ✉️ USTA National Tennis Center, Flushing Meadows–Corona Park, Queens ☎ 718/760-6200 or 516/354-2590 🕐 Late Aug–end Sep 🚇 Willetts Pt/ Citi Field Stadium (7) 🚉 LIRR to Citi Field Stadium

WHAT TO SEE

MUSEUM OF THE MOVING IMAGE

www.movingimage.us

Dedicated to the art, history, technique and technology of motion pictures, video and television, this fascinating museum doubled in size in 2009. The main exhibit, *Behind the Screen*, illustrates the processes involved in producing and exhibiting moving images, using more than 1,000 artifacts, interactive experiences and demonstrations. There are also exhibits featuring movie stars' wardrobes, memorabilia and special effects. Interactive exhibits offer the opportunity to dub your voice, or add sound effects, into a actual movie. ✉️ 35th Avenue at 36th Street, Astoria, Queens ☎ 718/784-4520 🕐 Tue–Fri 10–3 👐 Adult $10, child $5 🚇 36th Avenue at 31st Street (N, W)

NEW YORK HALL OF SCIENCE

www.nysci.org

This museum was one of the first hands-on science museums in the US. The entire basement is filled with interactive exhibits. Permanent exhibits demonstrate biology, chemistry and physics, and special shows explore such topics as Optical Illusions. There's also a large outdoor science playground. ✉️ 47-01 111th Street at 48th Avenue, Flushing Meadows–Corona Park, Queens ☎ 718/699-0005 🕐 Sep–Mar Tue–Thu 9.30–2, Fri 9.30–5, Sat–Sun 10–6; Apr–Jun Mon–Thu 9.30–2, Fri 9.30–5, Sat–Sun 10–6; Jul–Aug and hol weekends Mon–Fri 9.30–5, Sat–Sun 10–6 👐 Adult $11, child (2–17) $8 (free Sep–Jun Fri 2–5, Sun 10–11) 🚇 111th Street (7) 🚌 Q23, Q48

NOGUCHI MUSEUM

www.noguchi.org

Sculpture in clay, metal, stone and wood by noted 20th-century artist Isamu Noguchi are displayed in 13 galleries along with his *Akari Light Sculptures*, and a garden displays some of his major granite and basalt works. Housed in a renovated photo engraving plant, the museum offers public programs to provide an in-depth look at Noguchi's work.

✉ 9-01 33rd Road at Vernon Boulevard, Long Island City, Queens ☎ 718/204-7088
🕐 Wed–Fri 10–5, Sat–Sun 11–6 ✋ Adult $10, child $5 🚇 Broadway (N, W)

P.S.1 CONTEMPORARY ART CENTER
www.ps1.org
Dedicated to cutting-edge contemporary art, the museum offers 50 original exhibitions each year, including the prestigious International and National Projects series. The museum's exhibitions showcase emerging artists from throughout the world. P.S.1 Contemporary Art Center has been affiliated with the Museum of Modern Art (▷ 162–163) since the millennium, working together to promote the enjoyment and appreciation of contemporary art. *Warm Up*, the museum's summer music series, is one of New York's favorite summer venues. Performances are held in or near the winning entry of the museum's annual Young Architects Program.

✉ 22–25 Jackson Avenue at the intersection of 46th Avenue, Long Island City, Queens
☎ 718/784-2084 🕐 Thu–Mon 12–6 ✋ $5 donation 🚇 45th Road/Courthouse Square (7)

BELMONT PARK
www.nyra.com
This beautiful 430-acre (174ha) racecourse is the largest in North America. In June, it hosts the Belmont Stakes, the third leg of the Triple Crown.

✉ 2150 Hempstead Turnpike and Plainfield Avenue, Belmont, Queens ☎ 516/488-6000
🕐 May–end Jul, Sep–end Oct Wed–Sun, 1pm post time ✋ $2–$5 🚉 Long Island Railroad's Pony Express from Penn Station

MORE TO SEE
NEW YORK METS
www.mets.com
When the Brooklyn Dodgers left New York in 1957, the Mets in effect replaced them. Even though they haven't won a championship since 1986 and often finish at or near the bottom of their league, they continue to draw fans to their games. You can usually obtain tickets unless they're playing local rivals the Yankees or the Boston Red Sox. The new Citi Field stadium, right underneath the landing approach path to LaGuardia airport, is noisy.

✉ Citi Field, Flushing Meadows–Corona Park, Queens ☎ 718/507-8499 ✋ $8–$60
🚇 Willets Pt/Citi Field Stadium (7) 🚢 On Sat–Sun only: New York Waterway (tel 800/533-3779) operates from the South Street Seaport, East 34th Street or East 90th Street for $18 round trip. Reservations recommended

WHERE TO EAT
CHRISTOS STEAK HOUSE
www.christossteakhouse.com
Prime aged steaks, fresh seafood and savory Greek dishes come together in this casual restaurant with indoor and outdoor seating. The steaks are prepared to perfection in classic American steakhouse style, while the salads, sides, appetizers and desserts are influenced by traditional Greek cuisine.

✉ 4108 23rd Avenue, Queens
☎ 718/777-8400 🕐 Mon–Sat 4–12; Sun 3–12 ✋ D $60 🚇 Astoria Boulevard West (B, Q, E)

LA FLOR BAKERY & CAFE
Small and charming, this Mexican-fusion café serves real food and exceptional bakery to long lines of hungry folks. Dinner specialties such as grilled snapper with julienne vegetables are offered alongside traditional Mexican favorites like mole enchiladas. Save room for dessert, and pay in cash.

✉ 53-02 Roosevelt Avenue at 53rd Street, Woodside, Queens ☎ 718/426-8023 🕐 Daily 8am–10pm ✋ L $15, D $30 🚇 52nd Street (7)

Opposite *The New York Mets playing the Colorado Rockies at Citi Field*
Below *The P.S.1 Contemporary Art Center*

INFORMATION

www.visitstatenisland.com

SINY Inc., 1110 South Avenue, Suite 57, Staten Island, 10314

☎ 347-273-1257

WHAT TO SEE

ALICE AUSTEN HOUSE

www.aliceausten.org

This unique museum is the Victorian house and garden of Alice Austen (1866–1952), one of America's early female documentary photographers. A visit here is fascinating for the quality of Austen's photographs, but also for the idea it gives of what middle-class life was like at the turn of the 20th century. The house was declared a city landmark in 1971.

The photographs give you a glimpse into the world of a well-traveled young woman, who taught herself to operate the camera, develop heavy glass plates and make prints. Alice took her equipment with her everywhere, despite it weighing as much as 50 pounds (23kg), and photographed the world around her, including New York street scenes, using visual satire to create the effect.

Exhibitions and events take place throughout most of the year and often feature works by other local artists. Take the Staten Island Ferry from Manhattan, then catch the S51 bus to Hylan Boulevard.

✉ 2 Hylan Boulevard, Staten Island, 10305 ☎ 718/816-4506 ⏰ Mar–end Dec Thu–Sun 12–5 ✋ Adult $2, child free ⛴ Staten Island Ferry 🚌 S51 to Hylan Boulevard

CONFERENCE HOUSE

www.theconferencehouse.org

Originally called the Billop Manor House, Conference House was built around 1680. On September 11, 1776, Benjamin Franklin, John Adams and Edward Rutledge (a South Carolina governor and signatory to the Declaration of Independence) came here for a meeting with Admiral Lord Howe, the Commander of Her Majesty's Atlantic Squadron. Howe hoped to persuade the colonists to give up their fight for independence, but the visitors made it clear that they were not interested in his offer.

The two-and-a-half-story house has furnished period rooms and offers a look at life in colonial America. Special events take place throughout the year.

✉ 7455 Hylan Boulevard, Staten Island, 10307 ☎ 718/984-0415 ⏰ Apr–mid-Dec Fri–Sun 1–4, guided tours only ✋ Adult $3, child $2 ⛴ Staten Island Ferry 🚌 S78 to Craig Avenue

Above *Snug Harbor Cultural Center*

GARIBALDI MEUCCI MUSEUM

www.garibaldimeuccimuseum.org

The Italian national hero, and one of the founders of unified Italy, Giuseppe Garibaldi (1807–82) spent two years in this 1840s house after fleeing the conquering republicans in Italy. It was the home of one Antonio Meucci (1808–89), who in fact was the inventor of the telephone. He invented a prototype several years before Alexander Graham Bell got into the picture, but, as he failed to patent his idea, he never got the credit.

After Garibaldi's death in 1884, a committee decided to commemorate his stay in Staten Island and a plaque was placed on the house. After Meucci's death, the house was given to the Italian community to preserve as a memorial to Garibaldi.

Today the house is owned and operated by The Order of Sons of Italy in America and displays artifacts about the lives of these two men.

✉ 420 Tompkins Avenue, 10305 ☎ 718/442-1608 ◷ Tue–Sun 1–5 ✋ Adult $5 ⛴ Staten Island Ferry 🚌 S52, S78

HISTORIC RICHMOND TOWN

www.historicrichmondtown.org

About 15 historic buildings are spread out over 100 acres (40ha) at this museum complex. It stretches across three centuries of daily life and culture on Staten Island, from its earliest days as a rural crossroad to its incorporation into Greater New York. The quaint atmosphere and helpful staff make the whole experience a very pleasurable day out. Special events take place throughout the year, including summer fairs, concerts and costumed re-enactments.

✉ 441 Clarke Avenue, Staten Island, 10306 ☎ 718/351-1611 ◷ Sep–Jun Wed–Sun 1–5; Jul–end Aug Wed–Fri 10–5, Sat–Sun 1–5 ✋ Adult $5, child (5–17) $3.50, under 5 free ⛴ Staten Island Ferry 🚌 S74 🎫 Guided tours Wed–Fri 2.30, Sat–Sun 2 and 3.30 🍴

JACQUES MARCHAIS MUSEUM OF TIBETAN ART

www.tibetanmuseum.org

This lovely museum is one of New York's best-kept secrets. The Dalai Lama, when he visited in 1991, attested to the likeness of the stone cottage on Lighthouse Hill to a Tibetan mountain temple, with its peaceful terraced sculpture gardens and an attractive fish pond. The museum exhibits Tibetan, Nepalese and Mongolian art from the 17th to the 19th centuries. The Nepalese metalwork, encrusted with jewels, and the metal figures of deities and lamas, are exquisite. Informative explanations help you understand the significance of the jewelry, dance masks, ritual objects, incense burners, paintings and many other items from the world's Buddhist cultures. Special exhibitions and activities enhance a visit.

✉ 338 Lighthouse Avenue, Staten Island, 10306 ☎ 718/987-3500 ◷ Wed–Sun 1–5 ✋ Adult $5, child under 6 free ⛴ Staten Island Ferry 🚌 S74 to Lighthouse Avenue 🏛

SNUG HARBOR CULTURAL CENTER

www.snug-harbor.org

Snug Harbor, a National Historic Landmark District, spreads out over 83 acres (34ha). Its 26 buildings, a fine collection of Greek Revival, Beaux Arts, Italianate and Victorian architecture, housed "decrepit and worn-out" old sailors during the 1880s. By the 1960s, the buildings had fallen into disrepair. After a vast restoration project, however, they are now a focal point of Staten Island cultural life, with art exhibitions in the Newhouse Galleries (Wed–Sun) and other activities. Be sure to see the Main Hall (Tue–Sun), the oldest building, and its lavish ceiling mural, towering skylight dome and gilded weathervane.

✉ 1000 Richmond Terrace, Staten Island, 10301 ☎ 718/448-2500 ◷ Grounds daily dawn–dusk. Gallery Museum: Tue–Sun 10–5 ✋ Gallery adult $5, child (under 12) $3. Grounds: free ⛴ Staten Island Ferry 🚌 S40 🎫 💻 🏛

SPORTS AND ACTIVITIES
STATEN ISLAND YANKEES

www.siyanks.com

This minor-league team plays in a stadium overlooking the harbor. It's fun to take the trip on the Staten Island Ferry.

✉ Richmond County Bank Ballpark at St. George ☎ 718/720-9265 or 718/720-9200 ✋ $9–$13 🚇 South Ferry (1) to Staten Island Ferry ⛴ Staten Island Ferry

New York offers more tours than any city in the world. There are walking tours, bicycle tours, harbor tours, art and theater tours, behind-the-scenes tours, bus tours, limo tours, train tours, multilingual tours and special-interest tours such as ethnic, food and shopping tours. The list of tour operators below is a small sample of what's available.

BICYCLE TOURS

CENTRAL PARK BICYCLE TOURS
www.centralparkbiketour.com
Rent a bicycle and ride around Central Park with a knowledgeable guide for two hours. Tours daily at 10am, 1pm and 4pm.
✉ 203 West 58th Street ☎ 212/541-8759 👆 Adult $49, child (under 18) $40. Rental only: $30 for 2 hours, $40 for 3 hours, $65 all day

BUS TOURS

ON LOCATION TOURS
www.screentours.com
Coaches depart from different locations and reservations are recommended. New York TV Tour is a 3 to 3.5-hour tour to 40 locations; *Sex and the City* Tour is a 4-hour tour; the *Sopranos* Tour is 4 hours.
☎ 212/209-3370 👆 New York TV tour: adult $36, plus $2 ticket fee. *Sex and the City* tour: $40. *Sopranos* tour: $42

A SLICE OF BROOKLYN TOURS
www.asliceofbrooklyn.com
These 4.5-hour bus tours are led by a New York native. There are several tours, but the most popular is the Pizza Tour which includes top Brooklyn attractions like the Brooklyn Bridge, Fulton Navy Yard and Coney Island. You'll visit film locations for *Saturday Night Fever* and *The French Connection*. Best of all, there are two stops for pizza (with no waiting in line), including Grimaldi's for Neapolitan pizza and L&B Spumoni Gardens for Brooklyn Sicilian Pizza.
☎ 212/209-3370 👆 Adult $75, child (under 12) $65 (includes pizza and soft drinks). Advance tickets required

HELICOPTER TOURS

Helicopters leave from the Downtown Manhattan Heliport at Pier 6 and South Street and from the VIP Heliport at West 30th Street.

LIBERTY HELICOPTER TOURS
www.libertyhelicopters.com
Fly over Manhattan's skyscrapers, New York Harbor and the five boroughs.
☎ 212/967-2099 👆 $120, 6–8 min; $150, 12–15 min; $215, 16–20 min

RIVER TOURS

CIRCLE LINE
www.circleline42.com
Cruises from the Circle Line (Pier 83 at West 42nd Street/12th Avenue or Pier 16, South Street Seaport at Fulton Street and East River) are worth every penny. Take the 3-hour Full Island cruise, the 2-hour Semi-Circle cruise, 75-minute Liberty cruise, or a combination of packages. Combos are more expensive. Cruises with live music (adults only) operate from May to September. In spring and fall remember that it's at least 10 degrees colder on the water—and more when you consider wind chill in a moving boat.
☎ 212/563-3200 👆 Adult $24–$36, child under 12 $16–$24. Cruises $35–$50

WALKING TOURS

Here are a few that are highly recommended. Call ahead for up-to-date schedules.

BIG APPLE GREETER
www.bigapplegreeter.org
Big Apple Greeter is a free public service. The greeters—volunteer New Yorkers—are matched with visitors according to languages spoken and areas of interest. Give at least a month's advance notice (longer during peak season).
☎ 212/669-8159

BIG ONION WALKING TOURS
www.bigonion.com
Guides for these two-hour tours have degrees in American history.
☎ 212/439-1090 🕐 Wed–Mon, times vary 👆 Adult $15, child $12

GRAND CENTRAL PARTNERSHIP
www.grandcentralpartnership.org
Show up outside Grand Central Terminal at Philip Morris at 42nd Street and Park Avenue for free tours of Grand Central Terminal.
☎ 212/883-2420 🕐 Fri 12.30

NEW YORK LIKE A NATIVE TOURS
www.nylikeanative.com
These fast-paced walking tours are designed for energetic folks who are willing to hop aboard public transportation along the walk. Learn more about Brooklyn than an average tourist tour provides.
☎ 718/393-7537 👆 $15–$20

THEMED WALKING TOURS

MUNICIPAL ARTS SOCIETY
www.mas.org
Architects, historians, educators and writers guide tours of Grand Central Terminal and other sites, including Ground Zero, Madison Avenue and Rockefeller Center.
☎ 212/439-1049 👆 Adult $15

NEW YORK GALLERY TOURS
www.nygallerytours.com
Tour ten modern art galleries in two hours in Chelsea and SoHo.
☎ 212/946-1548 👆 Adult $20

PATRIOT TOURS
www.patriottoursnyc.com
Historical walking tours of Lower Manhattan specialize in the events and people of the Revolutionary War and Civil War eras.
☎ 212/209-3370 👆 Adult $23

PRACTICALITIES

Practicalities gives you all the important practical information you will need during your visit from money matters to emergency phone numbers.

WEATHER

New York City is in the northeast United States. Four of the five boroughs that comprise New York City are islands. Manhattan, the most populous, is bordered on the east by the East River and on the west by the Hudson River. The narrow Harlem River separates it from the Bronx to the north, and Long Island Sound separates it from Long Island to the south. The city has a waterfront of 580 miles (930km). The surrounding landscape is flat, although the highest point, at Todt Hill on Staten Island, is the highest point on the Atlantic coast south of Maine at 409ft (125m).

During the Ice Age, most of New York State was covered by glaciers, with southern Long Island and Staten Island being the exceptions. The movement of the glaciers produced nine distinct physiographic regions. The four seasons are very distinct in this region, and New Yorkers endure, without too many complaints, the cold, damp winters and hot, humid summers.

NEW YORK
TEMPERATURE

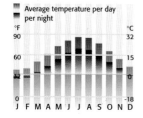

RAINFALL

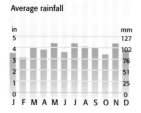

WEATHER REPORTS

» Radio and television news end with a weather report and a short-range forecast (▷ 283).
» Visit www.weather.com, the Weather Channel's 10-day forecast.
» Visit www.cnn.com/weather for CNN's eight-day forecast and satellite pictures.

DAYLIGHT HOURS

Be aware of the number of daylight hours you have when planning your days out. There are some areas, away from central tourist areas, that are best avoided after dark.

TEMPERATURE

Below left are the average daily maximum and minimum temperatures for New York City. Precipitation in December, January, February and March can fall as snow.

WINTER

The city's average annual snowfall is 29.2 inches (74cm), most of it falling in January and February. However, even after heavy snowfall, plows quickly remove the snow and disruptions are minimal. The strong winds, more pronounced as you approach the East or Hudson rivers, make it feel colder than it really is.

SUMMER

In July and August, the hottest months, humidity can be as high as 90 percent, and the sun can be fierce. Avoid these months if you suffer from the heat. If you do decide to visit then, make sure to wear sunscreen during the day both in the city and at the beaches.

THE BEST TIME TO VISIT

The most pleasant time to visit, and therefore peak season, is May to early June and September to mid-November. From May to early June, the days are comfortable and the evenings cool; showers are always a possibility. From September to

TIME ZONES

CITY	TIME DIFFERENCE	TIME AT NOON IN NEW YORK
Amsterdam	+6	6pm
Berlin	+6	6pm
Brussels	+6	6pm
Chicago	-1	11am
Dublin	+5	5pm
Johannesburg	+7	7pm
London	+5	5pm
Madrid	+6	6pm
Montreal	0	noon
Paris	+6	6pm
Perth, Australia	+13	1am
Rome	+6	6pm
San Francisco	-3	9am
Sydney, Australia	+15	3am
Tokyo	+14	2am

AVERAGE SUNRISE/SUNSET TIMES

	SUNRISE	SUNSET
Jan	7.15	4.45
Feb	6.50	5.30
Mar	6.10	6.00
Apr	5.15	6.30
May	4.30	7.00
Jun	4.30	7.30
Jul	4.35	7.30
Aug	5.00	7.00
Sep	5.30	6.00
Oct	5.30	5.20
Nov	6.35	4.45
Dec	7.15	4.30

late October, days are still warm but evenings start getting cooler. The leaves change to gold and red in mid- to late October, pretty but less spectacular than New England. By November, days are much cooler and there is more rain and wind.

TIME ZONES

New York is on Eastern Standard Time, five hours behind GMT. Daylight Saving Time, four hours behind GMT, is from early March to November 1.

DOCUMENTATION FOR NON-US VISITORS

SECURITY

Since 9/11, 2001, security in the US has been stepped up. Restrictions are tight on what baggage you can check in and what you can carry on board, both for domestic and international flights (see www.tsa.gov for the latest information). At airports allow plenty of time to clear security checks and check the current situation before you travel.

Expect your belongings to be searched at airports, at museums and at the entryways of many office buildings. Prohibited items may be confiscated. If you are carrying bottled water, you may be asked to take a sip of it, or, more likely, dispose of it altogether. Co-operation will facilitate easy access. For the most up-to-date information on security in and around the city, contact multilingual visitor information counsellors (tel 212/484-1222) or New York City non-emergency government agencies (dial 311 or tel 212/639-9675).

VISA AND PASSPORT REQUIREMENTS

Canadian citizens, like all other nationalities, must have a machine-readable passport to enter the United States. Non-resident foreign visitors must show their machine-readable passport, their visa if required, and their round-trip ticket when entering the United States. Upon entry, all visitors should expect to be fingerprinted and photographed.

For up-to-date information on visa requirements and how to obtain one, it is vital that you contact the American embassy in your home country months before your journey. Passport and visa requirements can change at short notice so always check before you travel.

CUSTOMS ALLOWANCES

Visitors arriving in New York from outside the country are required to fill in a Customs Declaration before landing in the United States, and they must declare everything except personal effects, which include either 200 cigarettes or 50 cigars or 2.2lbs (1kg) of smoking tobacco, providing you are 21 or older. You may also bring in 1 liter (33.8fl oz) of alcohol. Visitors are not allowed to bring in any fruits, vegetables, plants, meat or meat products, firearms or ammunition.

If you have any questions, contact your nearest United States consulate or embassy before departing, or visit www.cbp.gov and click on "Travel." If you are bringing more than $10,000 into the country, you must declare it on the customs form given to passengers during your inbound flight. You may bring into the country only $100 worth of gifts duty free, however.

WHAT YOU CAN TAKE HOME

If you buy expensive items, you can often avoid paying New York City's 8.375 percent sales tax by having the items shipped back to your home. Ask when making the purchase, but before paying.

Because rules vary for each country, contact the customs service in your home country.

TRAVEL INSURANCE

The US does not have reciprocal healthcare arrangements with other countries. Ensure you purchase full travel insurance in your country before departing. Check that it covers cancellations, lost luggage and medical expenses up to at least $1 million, including dental care. Medical costs in the US are high, so make sure you have good medical coverage.

The cost of insurance depends on your age, health, type and length of your trip. One-year coverage is very economical if you are planning more than one trip per year. Family coverage can also be very good value if you are traveling with a spouse and children.

US EMBASSIES AND CONSULATES ABROAD		
COUNTRY	**ADDRESS**	**WEBSITE**
Australia	Moonah Place, Yarralumla ACT 2600, tel 61 2 6214 5600	http://canberra.usembassy.gov
Canada	490 Sussex Drive, Ottawa, ON K1N 1G8, tel 1 800 283-4356 or 613 238-5335	http://ottawa.usembassy.gov
France	2 avenue Gabriel, 75382 Paris, tel 33 1 43 12 22 22	http://france.usembassy.gov
Germany	Pariser Platz 2, 10117 Berlin, Federal Republic of Germany, tel 030 83050	http://germany.usembassy.gov
Ireland	42 Elgin Road, Ballsbridge, Dublin 4, tel 353 1 668 8777	http://dublin.usembassy.gov
Italy	via Vittorio Veneto 121, 00187 Roma, tel 39 06 46741	http://italy.usembassy.gov
New Zealand	29 Fitzherbert Terrace, Thorndon, Wellington, tel 644 462 6000	http://newzealand.usembassy.gov
Spain	Calle Serrano 75, 28006 Madrid, tel 91 587 2200	http://madrid.usembassy.gov
South Africa	PO Box 9536, Pretoria 0001, 877 Pretorius St, Pretoria, tel 27 12 431 4000	http://southafrica.usembassy.gov
UK	24 Grosvenor Square, London, W1A 1AE, tel 020 7499 9000	http://london.usembassy.gov

ESSENTIAL INFORMATION

PRACTICALITIES

MONEY

TAXES

In New York City an 8.375 percent sales tax is added on purchase of goods, except clothing and footwear. The hotel tax is 13.875 percent, plus $2 per room per night. The parking garage tax is 18.25 percent.

TIPPING

You must tip people in the service sector because their livelihood depends on tips. If you tip less than expected, you are sending a message that the service was poor.

» In restaurants, tip waiters, waitresses and bartenders at least 15 percent of the bill. Tip 20 percent in expensive restaurants, and always round up for good service. The head waiter in upscale restaurants expects 5 percent and the cloakroom attendant expects $1.

» In taxis, tip the driver 15 to 20 percent, more if the journey is short.

» In hotels, tip the bellboy $1 or $2 for each suitcase he carries. The chambermaid expects $2 for a few nights' stay. The hall porter expects $1 or $2 for getting you a taxi.

» At the airport or train station, tip the porter $1 or $2 per bag.

FOR NON-US VISITORS

Changing money

Change money before you leave home so that you can pay taxis, trains or buses on arrival. The commission at airport bureaux de change is higher than in most banks. Dollar bills of more than $20 may not be accepted by taxi drivers. There are bureaux de change throughout Manhattan, but you get better service in banks and at the visitor center in Times Square

(▷ 168–169). There are ATMs all over the city. Expect to pay up to $3 per transaction if you are using a bank other than your own.

» American Express Travel Services has many offices in the city, including one on the mezzanine level at Macy's in Herald Square (tel 212/695-8075).

» Travelex has some offices (tel 212/935-9935 or www.travelex.com).

» Chase Manhattan Bank (tel 800/935-9935 or www.chase.com) has more than 400 branches with bureaux de change.

How to get money

Most people use credit cards to pay for hotels, restaurant meals and shopping. However, some restaurants accept only cash. If you rent a car, a credit card is essential. MasterCard, Visa and American Express are the cards most often accepted (but occasionally Amex is not accepted). Diner's Club and Carte Blanche are accepted by most restaurants and many hotels. Discover, enRoute, Eurocard and JCB are also often accepted.

Traveler's checks in US dollars remain a safe way to carry money. Keep a copy of the serial numbers separate from the checks and record the ones you cash, so that any lost or stolen checks can be replaced quickly. Checks from American Express (tel 800/528-4800 or www.americanexpress.com) are the most widely accepted. Most restaurants and large stores will accept traveler's checks as payment but will ask to you to produce your passport. Most banks will cash them, but charge between 1 percent and 4 percent

on the value for doing so. American Automobile Association members can avoid fees by purchasing checks from an AAA office.

Stolen cards or traveler's checks

If your credit card is stolen, report the theft to the bank so that charges can be blocked. Also notify the police. It's a good idea to photocopy every card, or at least write down the numbers you need to report a loss, and keep this separately.

Exchange rates

For the latest market conversion rates, visit www.oanda.com or www.x-rates.com.

MONEY-SAVING TIPS

» CityPass (tel 888/350-5008, www.citypass.com) is a book of discounted tickets to six attractions and will save you hours of waiting in line at attractions, as well as on two-hour Circle Line harbor cruises (▷ 270). The CityPass costs $79 ($59 for ages 12–17) and can be purchased at any attraction. It is good for nine days.

» New York Pass (250 West 49th Street, New York 10019, tel 877/714-1999, www.newyorkpass.com) an all-inclusive passport to New York City that gets you discounted admission to more than 50 attractions. Passes cost $75 ($55 children 2–12) for one day, $110/90 for two, $140/120 for three or $180/140 for seven days.

» "Pay-what-you-wish" lets you decide how much you will pay for museum entry. Some museums are free one day a week.

MONEY VOCABULARY

$	dollar
¢	cent
a penny	1 cent
a nickel	5 cents
a dime	10 cents
a quarter	25 cents
a half dollar	50 cents
5 bucks	5 dollars

LOST OR STOLEN CREDIT CARDS

American Express		
800/992-3404	www.americanexpress.com	
Diners Club		
1800.234-6377	www.dinersclub.com	
MasterCard		
800/627-8372	www.mastercard.com	
Visa		
800/847-2911	www.visa.com	

10 EVERYDAY ITEMS AND HOW MUCH THEY COST

Takeout sandwich	$8
Bottle of water	$2
Cup of tea or coffee	$1.50
Pint of beer	$6
Glass of wine	$10
Daily newspaper	25¢–$1.25
20 cigarettes	$7.75
An ice cream	$3.50
A gallon of fuel (petrol)	$2.50–$4.50

IN CASE OF EMERGENCY

Dial **911** for fire, police and ambulance

Poison Control 800/222-1222

Rape and Sexual Abuse Hotline
212/267-7273 (24-hour)

Crime Victims' Hotline 212/577-7777

Dentists 212/677-2510

Emergency Medical Service (EMS)
718/999-2770

HEALTH

New York City has some of the best hospitals and doctors in the country, so if you should be in need of care, you have come to the right place. But make sure you have full insurance (▷ 273).

INOCULATIONS

If you are arriving in the United States from Canada or from a European Union member country, you will probably not need inoculations. However, check with your travel agent or with a US consulate or embassy (▷ 273). All visitors to the United States are advised to be fully immunized against tetanus and diptheria.

WHAT TO TAKE

If you will be in New York during the summer, make sure to have sunscreen, which you can easily purchase from any pharmacy upon arrival. You should bring any medication you require with you and, if it is prescription medicine, pack it in your in-flight baggage. Take copies of your prescription to be on the safe side. If your medication

gets lost or stolen, the copy of the prescription will make it easier to get a replacement.

If you require medication containing habit-forming drugs or

narcotics, such as some cough medicines, diuretics, heart drugs, tranquilizers, sleeping pills, anti-depressants, stimulants, etc., make sure they are properly labeled and that you have a prescription or written statement from your doctor confirming that you are taking these under a doctor's direction and that you require them while traveling.

If you suffer from any sort of heart problems, epilepsy or diabetes, it is a good idea to wear a Medic Alert Identification Tag so that the doctor can easily get access to your medical records through the 24-hour hotline in case of an emergency. You can obtain this tag by phoning 888/633-4298 or visit www.medicalert.org.

HEALTHY FLYING

» Visitors from Europe, Australia or New Zealand may be concerned about the effect of a long-haul flight on their health. The most widely publicized concern is deep vein thrombosis (DVT). Misleadingly labeled "economy class syndrome," DVT is when a blood clot forms in the body's deep veins, particularly in the legs. The clot can move around the bloodstream and can be fatal.

» You are most at risk if you are elderly, pregnant, using the contraceptive pill, smoke or are overweight. If you think you are at increased risk of DVT, see your doctor before departing. Flying increases the likelihood of DVT because passengers are often seated in a cramped position for long periods of time and may become dehydrated.

» Other health hazards for flyers are airborne diseases and bugs spread by the air-conditioning system on board. These hazards are largely unavoidable but if you have a serious medical condition, seek advice from a doctor before flying.

To minimize risk:
Drink water (not alcohol)
Don't stay immobile for hours at a time
Stretch and exercise your legs periodically
Do wear elastic flight socks, which support veins and reduce the chances of a clot forming

Exercises

1. Ankle rotations	**2. Calf stretches**	**3. Knee lifts**
Lift feet off the floor. Draw a circle with the toes, moving one foot clockwise and the other counterclockwise	Start with heel on the floor and point foot upwards as high as you can. Then lift heels high keeping balls of feet on the floor	Lift leg with knee bent while contracting your thigh muscle. Then straighten leg pressing foot flat to the floor

DRINKING WATER
The tap water in New York is safe to drink, as is water from public water fountains. However, bottled water is sold throughout the city in stores, restaurants and vending machines.

BUYING MEDICATIONS
The 24-hour pharmacies listed below are all located in convenient places.

Travelers from abroad may require a prescription in the United States to purchase certain medications, such as birth control pills, inhalers and codeine, that they can buy over the counter in their own country. Pharmacies are generally open from 9am to 5pm and can be recognized by signs in the window—either a mortar and pestle or a caduceus (a staff with two entwined snakes and two wings at the top, which symbolize a physician).

FINDING A DOCTOR
If you need to find a doctor in New York, contact any one of the health services listed below. They are reputable healthcare providers accustomed to treating visitors.

DOCS at New York Healthcare (55 East 34th Street between Park and Madison avenues, tel 212/252-6001) is a walk-in medical center for non-emergency cases. New York University Downtown Hospital (tel 212/312-5000) offers referrals. N.Y. Hotel Urgent Medical Services (952 Fifth Avenue between 76th and 77th streets, tel 212/737-1212, www.travelmd.com) was set up by a New York City doctor to treat visitors. Whether you need a prescription, a medical examination or a dentist, a specialist will come to your hotel room. He or she will produce appropriate identification. The hotel visit fee is $350 to $400, with higher rates at night and on weekends. You can also go to the office for a fee of $175–$200—either drop in or phone for an appointment. Emergency rooms (ER rooms) in some hospitals have walk-in clinics where you can go for non-emergencies (and pay a slightly lower rate than in the emergency area), but you will

probably have to wait for a long time. Or you can always ask the hotel staff to suggest a doctor.

IF YOU HAVE TO GO TO THE HOSPITAL
Before you go, phone your travel insurance company's emergency number to find out which hospitals accept your insurance. You will need to show your insurance card at the hospital before any treatment will be given.

INSURANCE FOR NON-US VISITORS
Although you are not required to have health insurance in order to visit the United States, it would be extremely unwise not to. The US does not have reciprocal health agreements with other countries and the cost of healthcare is very high, whether you need a doctor's

visit or dental care or have a medical emergency. An emergency room visit usually carries a minimum charge of $500, and that's before you begin receiving treatment. Make sure that you have a good insurance policy that covers all healthcare, including dental care (▷ 273).

PHARMACIES OPEN 24 HOURS
NAME	ADDRESS	TELEPHONE
Duane Reade	224 West 57th Street/Broadway	212/547-9708
Duane Reade	1279 Third Avenue	212/744-2668
Duane Reade	2765 Broadway	212/799-3172
Rite Aid	408 Grand Street/Clinton	212/529-7115

OPTICIANS
Lenscrafters has several Midtown locations. Go to 542 Fifth Avenue at 45th Street, tel 212/302-4882 www.lenscrafters.com

Cohen's Optical has numerous locations in Manhattan, including 2565 Broadway, tel 212/666-2615 and 2 West 14th Street, tel 212/989-3937 www.cohensfashionoptical.com

ALTERNATIVE MEDICINE
Alternative medical treatments are widely available in New York City.
American Academy of Medical Acupuncture www.medicalacupuncture.org
Chiropractic Federation of New York 64 East 34th Street, tel 212/532-0185
North American Society of Homeopaths www.homeopathy.org

Chinatown offers a wide selection of herbal and alternative treatments, including acupuncture. You will find, among others:
Grand Meridian Herbs, Acupuncture and Massage 211 Grand Street, New York 10013, tel 212/965-1503
Kamwo Herbs 209 Grand Street, New York 10013, tel 212/966-6370
Zon Foo Acupuncture and Medical 36 East Broadway, 2nd Floor, New York 10002, tel 212/925-2501

BASICS

CLOTHING

Casual clothing is acceptable in restaurants, museums and attractions throughout New York City. In summer, men must wear a shirt to enter most restaurants, although only a handful of places require men to wear a jacket and tie. Of course, there is no shortage of stores where you can buy any clothing that you may have forgotten to bring with you. In public places, you will be expected to wear shoes (no bare feet), and men are expected to remove their hats in churches.

Comfortable walking shoes are a must. In winter, you will need a hat or earmuffs, scarf, gloves or mittens, boots, a sweater and a warm coat or jacket. If you want to go ice skating or sledding in Central Park, you can either bring your own gear or rent skates once you're there.

In spring, bring a sweater and a spring coat or jacket. In summer, prepare for hot, humid weather, and be sure to bring a sun hat or cap and sunglasses. In the fall, pack a sweater and a light jacket or coat as well as lighter clothes in case of warm weather. Rainwear and an umbrella, however, are a must all year round.

SHOPPING

Don't overpack. Shopping in New York is fun, and you can readily find anything you may need—umbrella vendors seem to materialize on almost every significant street corner when it rains (you can pick up an umbrella from $5), and you can readily acquire sunglasses on the street on fine days.

Clothes, accessories, electronic equipment and many other items come in wider selections than in most of the rest of the United States and are cheaper than in many European countries.

For every shopper, bargain-hunting can be rewarding. Be aware, however, that the "Going out of business" sales advertised on posters at electronic equipment stores in the Theater District are bogus—these "sales" are a come-on to attract naïve customers. Before buying, get the model number of the product you want and check other retailers' prices online or you will almost certainly pay too much; if you're spending a significant sum of money, it's better to patronize a reputable specialist retailer. In vintage and second-hand shops it is always worthwhile to ask for a better price—sometimes you will get it.

Keep in mind that many stores close on public holidays; SoHo is fairly closed on Mondays and the Lower East Side is shuttered on Saturdays and very slow on Friday afternoons.

MEASUREMENTS

If you are more used to metric measurements than imperial, the conversion table below will be very useful.

VOLTAGE AND ADAPTERS

The power supply in the US is 110/120 volts AC (60 cycles). American plugs have two-prong flat pins, so you will need an adapter if you have plugs with two round pins, or three pins.

It is best to buy an adapter before departing or in the airport shop as they can be difficult to find in the US, although some department stores and pharmacies stock them. You will also need a voltage transformer for European appliances.

COMFORT AND ETIQUETTE
Public restrooms

Restrooms are normally labeled "Women" and "Men" or use a male/female symbol. You may notice that they are labeled in Spanish as well as English in airports, some restaurants and clubs.

Public restrooms are found in visitor centers (▷ 282) and in Grand Central Terminal (▷ 156–157), but

CONVERSION CHART

FROM	TO	MULTIPLY BY
Inches	Centimetres	2.54
Centimetres	Inches	0.3937
Feet	Metres	0.3048
Metres	Feet	3.2810
Yards	Metres	0.9144
Metres	Yards	1.0940
Miles	Kilometres	1.6090
Kilometres	Miles	0.6214
Acres	Hectares	0.4047
Hectares	Acres	2.4710
Gallons	Litres	4.5460
Litres	Gallons	0.2200
Ounces	Grams	28.35
Grams	Ounces	0.0353
Pounds	Grams	453.6
Grams	Pounds	0.0022
Pounds	Kilograms	0.4536
Kilograms	Pounds	2.205
Tons	Tonnes	1.0160
Tonnes	Tons	0.9842

New Yorkers stop in hotels, large bookstores, department stores or cafés—theoretically restrooms in eating places are for patrons only, but in some restaurants it's an option. Restrooms in public buildings are wheelchair-accessible and may offer facilities for baby-changing. Restrooms in most parts of the city are clean and well supplied with soap, hand-dryers and paper. A few in Chinatown are substandard.

Traveling with children

New York is family-friendly for the most part, with special discounts for children, special prices for meals and plenty of attractions to keep them happy. Many hotels let kids stay for free and most museums do not charge for young children.

Look for special things to do in the "Weekend" section of the Friday *New York Times*, *New York* magazine's "Cue" section and in *Time Out New York*. Special performances can sell out or fill up early, so expect to plan ahead.

For babysitting services there's the Baby Sitters' Guild (tel 212/682-0227 or www.babysittersguild.com).

Laundry services

Most hotels either offer laundry services or will recommend one. Before you make your reservation, check what the hotel offers.

Smoking

When smoking in New York was banned in all public places, including restaurants, clubs, bars and anywhere an employee may be exposed to a patron's smoke, it was very controversial. Today it is widely accepted throughout the city.

People who want to smoke must go outside. There is no smoking on buses, subways or trains, but you may smoke in the privacy of your hotel room—providing it is a designated smoking room.

Dealing with beggars

It is your choice whether to give money to beggars. If you would prefer not to, simply keep moving

PLACES OF WORSHIP	
Baptist	Abyssinian Baptist Church (132 Odell Clark Place at West 138th Street between Adam Clayton Powell Boulevard and Lenox Avenue, tel 212/862-7474).
Buddhist	New York Buddhist Church (Riverside Drive between 105th and 106th streets, tel 212/678-0305; www.newyorkbuddhistchurch.org).
Greek Orthodox	Holy Trinity Greek Orthodox Cathedral (319 East 74th Street, tel 212/288-3215; www.thecathedral.goarch.org).
Interfaith	Cathedral of St. John the Divine (1047 Amsterdam Avenue at 112th Street, tel 212/316-7490; www.stjohndivine.org).
Jewish	Temple Emanu-El (1 East 65th Street at Fifth Avenue, tel 212/744-1400; www.emanuelnyc.org) is reform.
Muslim	Mosque of Islamic Brotherhood (130 West 113th Street, tel 212/662-4100; www.mosqueofislamicbrotherhoodinc.org).
Roman Catholic	St. Patrick's Cathedral (960 Madison Avenue, tel 212/753-2261; www.saintpatrickscathedral.org).

if a beggar approaches you on the street and asks for money. Don't make eye contact and don't engage in conversation.

On the subway, you may come across beggars who deliver a monologue or present you with a written notice about their hard times and about how your donation will help their family. Again, if you prefer not to give, don't make eye contact, and shake your head to indicate "no" if you are approached by them personally.

On subways

If all seats are taken, move to the center of the subway car so you don't block the doors. If a senior citizen, an adult with a young child, a pregnant woman or person with a disability gets on and there are no available seats, offer yours. This is polite and it's the civilized thing to do.

GAY AND LESBIAN NEW YORK

The Stonewall Riot on Christopher Street in Greenwich Village is credited with starting the gay liberation movement in New York City in 1969.

Today, gay and lesbian visitors will find New York a welcoming and easy place to stay. The West Village, especially Christopher Street, is full of shops, restaurants and services with a gay orientation, as is Chelsea, on Eighth Avenue from 16th to 23rd streets.

Finding help

» **The International Gay & Lesbian Travel Association** (tel 800/448-8550 or 954/630-1637, www.iglta.org) is a specialist travel agency.

» **Lesbian, Gay, Bisexual & Transgender Community Center** (208 West 13th Street, between Seventh and Eighth avenues, tel 212/620-7310, www.gaycenter.org) is an excellent source of information on what's happening in the city and where to stay.

» **Gay and Lesbian Switchboard** (www.glnh.org) offers peer counseling and information on events.

What's happening

For current gay and lesbian nightlife options, pick up a copy of *Metro*, *Go*, *HX*, *New York Blade*, *Next* and *Village Voice*, all of them free publications. *Time Out New York*, available at all street news-stands and many other retail outlets, has an excellent section on what's on in and around the city for gay and lesbian visitors.

PLACES OF WORSHIP

With its rich cultural mix, this city of immigrants offers a place to worship for every kind of belief. A selection of places of worship is listed above. Listings in newspapers note the topic of the current week's theme. For the most extensive list of churches, temples, synagogues and mosques, look in the Yellow Pages.

FINDING HELP

The crime rate in New York has plummeted over the past 10 years and it is now one of the safest large cities in the United States. However, it is big and crowded, and crimes do occur, so always be aware of your surroundings and people around you. If someone does try to steal your property, let them take it, then report the crime to the police.

PERSONAL SECURITY

» Do not keep all your money, credit cards and traveler's checks in the same place.

» Do not carry large sums of money with you. Use the hotel safe if you have brought valuables or have large amounts of cash.

» Do not walk alone at night in deserted areas, and do not go into parks after dark unless there is a concert and a large crowd is there.

» If someone "falls" in front of you, be aware that this may be a ploy to distract you while an accomplice picks your pocket.

» Wear shoulder bags and cameras over one shoulder and across your front—in bandolier style. Do not let your handbag dangle from the back of your chair in restaurants; put it on your lap rather than risk making it an easy target.

OBEY THE LAWS

» Drinking laws are strictly enforced in New York. It is against the law to drive with an open container of alcohol in the car and also, of course, to drive while intoxicated.

» Smoking in all public places, such as restaurants, museums, on public transportation or in public offices, is illegal in New York. You must smoke outside—as you will see many New Yorkers doing.

IF YOU ARE ARRESTED

» Remember that New York has been on high security alert at different times since 9/11 and that even when these alerts are not in effect, there is a high police presence in the streets, at public places, in airports and at other metropolitan locations. Never joke about matters of security—it's considered a crime.

» Visitors from abroad need to be aware that the police can arrest you if you break the law, if they have a strong suspicion that you have been involved in a crime, or if your behavior or activities make them suspect that you are involved in criminal activities.

» If you are arrested, you have the right to remain silent, to make a telephone call, and you have the right to contact a lawyer.

» Anything you say can be used as evidence against you. Your best option is, as soon as possible, to contact your embassy or consulate (see below and right) and ask for their assistance.

LOST AND FOUND TELEPHONE NUMBERS

MTA for buses or trains 212/424-4343	
Taxi and Limousine Commission for taxis 311	
Police property clerk (lost for more than 48 hours) 646/610-5906	

LEGAL AGE

To purchase tobacco	18 years
To gamble or play the lottery	18 years
To purchase/consume alcohol	21 years
To rent a car	25 years

CONSULATES FOR VISITORS FROM OVERSEAS

Australia	212/351-6500
Canada	212/596-1628
Ireland	212/319-2555
New Zealand	212/832-4038
United Kingdom	212/745-0200

Below *New York City police officers*

EMBASSIES FOR VISITORS FROM OVERSEAS

COUNTRY	ADDRESS	TELEPHONE	WEBSITE
Australia	1601 Massachusetts Avenue, NW, Washington DC 20036	202/797-3000	www.usa.embassy.gov.au
Canada	501 Pennsylvania Avenue, NW, Washington DC 20001	202/682-1740	www.canadianembassy.org
Ireland	2234 Massachusetts Avenue, NW, Washington DC 20008	202/462-3939	www.irelandemb.org
New Zealand	37 Observatory Circle, NW, Washington DC 20008	202/328-4800	www.nzembassy.com/usa
United Kingdom	3100 Massachusetts Avenue, NW, Washington DC 20008	202/588-6500	www.britainusa.com

COMMUNICATIONS

TELEPHONE CHARGES

Public pay phones

Local calls cost 20 to 50 cents for the first three minutes. Even if you are making a local call, one that has the 212 or 646 area code, you must still dial 1, then the area code, before the seven-digit number. This includes calls from Manhattan to other boroughs (area codes 718 and 347).

All calls that are not local are so-called long-distance calls, which cost more; for these, you again have to dial 1 followed by the area code and seven-digit number.

Paying by card

Prepaid calling cards, sold at many convenience stores and news-stands in various denominations, are the easiest and probably the cheapest way to phone home. Public pay phones throughout New York City take phonecards. Airport public telephones all accept MasterCard, Visa and American Express credit cards.

TELEPHONES AND NON-US VISITORS

Telephone numbers

Local and long-distance calls: dial 1 + area code + 7-digit number

Word telephone numbers:
Some numbers are made easy to remember by using the letters on the dial rather than the numbers, for example, 1-800/ WHITNEY. Find the appropriate letters on the dial to call these numbers.

Toll-free numbers

There is no charge for telephone numbers with area codes 800, 888 and 877. The 911 emergency number is also free.

High-toll numbers

Telephone numbers with area codes 700 and 900 are chat lines, dating services or other specialized services that can charge anywhere between 95¢ and $15 per minute.

Cell phones and laptops

If your cell phone is not equipped to make calls from the US, you may as well leave it at home.

If you plan to use a laptop while traveling, make sure that the battery is fully charged before you leave home. At airport security, you may be asked to take the laptop out of the case. Security officers may ask you if it is yours, if it is new and if anyone else has been using it. Make sure that you have an adapter for your laptop, and a converter for voltage if necessary, if it does not have a US two-prong, flat-pin plug and does not work on 110/120 volts. If you plan to use it a lot, bring an extra battery.

EMAIL

Go to www.mail2web.com and type in your email address and password to retrieve your email from any web browser. You can also open a free email account via www.hotmail.com or www.mail.yahoo.com.

You can check your email from most hotel lobbies, at internet cafés or FedEx Office outlets (www.fedex.com/us/office), which are found throughout the city.

Alternatively, use the free terminals at the Times Square Information Center at 1560 Broadway (▷ 282).

CYBER-CAFÉS

There are more and more of these around town (see below for two well-known cafés).

POST OFFICES

The main post office is at 441 Eighth Avenue between 31st and 33rd streets (tel 212/330-3002). Throughout the city there are numerous branches, which are listed in the Yellow Pages. Most branches are open Monday to Friday 8, 9 or 10am to 6pm. A few open Saturday 9am to 4pm.

TIP

Hotel-room phones may be convenient but they are costly, because most hotels impose a high surcharge on calls dialed from rooms. To avoid these surcharges, use a public pay phone. Many hotels have internet access in the lobby, so you can email, as long as you have a credit card.

COUNTRY CODES FROM THE UNITED STATES

Dial 011 followed by the country code, the city code, then the telephone number

Australia	(011) 61
Belgium	(011) 32
France	(011) 33
Germany	(011) 49
Greece	(011) 30
Ireland	(011) 353
Italy	(011) 39
Netherlands	(011) 31
New Zealand	(011) 64
Spain	(011) 34
Sweden	(011) 46
United Kingdom	(011) 44

USEFUL TELEPHONE NUMBERS AND WEBSITES

Emergency (Police, Fire, Ambulance) 911
Traveler's Aid 718/656-4870 or 518/463-2124; www.travelersaid.org
US Postal Information 800/275-8777; www.usps.com
Directory Assistance 411

POSTAGE RATES

A regular letter costs:
Within the US, minimum of 44 cents
Across the border to Canada or Mexico, minimum of 75 cents
Overseas, minimum of 98 cents

CYBER CONNECTIONS

FedEx Office
60 West 40th Street
Tel 212/921-1060
www.fedex.com/us/office
Wed–Mon 24 hours, Tue 6am–midnight. Also at many other locations

Cybercafé
250 West 49th Street at Broadway/ 8th Avenue
Tel 212/333-4109
Mon–Fri 8am–11pm, Sat–Sun 11am–11pm

OPENING TIMES AND PUBLIC HOLIDAYS

New York never sleeps. The working week is Monday through Friday, 9am to 5pm, but some banks are open on Saturday mornings and many stores are open longer hours; most stores are open all weekend. Some pharmacies are open 24/7, as are some coffee shops and bureaux de change.

Always phone in advance if timing is critical or if you're making a detour to visit a particular place.

PUBLIC HOLIDAYS

On public holidays many museums, some restaurants and all public office buildings close. New Year's Day, Christmas and Thanksgiving are the biggest, most widely celebrated holidays, when most New York businesses grind to a halt. Airports and train stations are particularly busy in the period leading up to these holidays, when many New Yorkers travel out of town to be with family or friends.

However, it is also a time when the city is festive and celebrations are enjoyed by visitors as well as New Yorkers (for a list of parades ▷ 290–291). Much of the city closes down or slows during the Jewish High Holidays—Rosh Hashanah and Yom Kippur—in September and early October.

Above *View of the Chrysler Building and the "city that never sleeps" from the Empire State Building*

OPENING HOURS

	OPEN	CLOSED	COMMENTS
Stores	Mon–Sat, 10–7		Many closed Sun Upper East
	Sun noon–6		Side, Sat Lower East Side
Banks	Mon–Fri 9.30–3.30	Sat–Sun	Some close at 3, some open
			Sat morning
Offices	Mon–Fri 9–5	Sat–Sun	
Museums	Tue–Sun		Some open Mon or close
			another day
Galleries	Tue–Sat 10–6	Mon	
Doctors	Mon–Fri 9–5	Sat–Sun	▷ 275
Pharmacies	Daily 9–7 or 9–9		Shorter hours and Sun closing in
			commercial neighborhoods,
			some 24hrs
Grocery stores	Daily 7am–9pm		As above
Restaurants	Daily (see listings)	Some close one	Many serve until 11pm or
		day a week	midnight, a few between 4pm
			and 5.30pm

PUBLIC HOLIDAYS

January 1	New Year's Day
3rd Monday in January	Martin Luther King Day
3rd Monday in February	Presidents' Day
Last Monday in May	Memorial Day
July 4	Independence Day
1st Monday in September	Labor Day
2nd Monday in October	Columbus Day
November 11	Veterans' Day
4th Thursday in November	Thanksgiving Day
December 25	Christmas Day

TOURIST INFORMATION
EVENTS AND PARADES

Lively events worth planning a trip around take place throughout the year. If you are in New York during a parade, don't miss it. The two biggest are the St. Patrick's Day Parade and the Macy's Thanksgiving Day Parade, which is televised nationwide. The crowd scene is almost as entertaining as the parade. Check local listings for dates, times and parade routes, and plan to show up early for either of them to get a choice viewing spot.

TOURIST OFFICES

Major visitor centers, listed below, are well worth visiting on your first or second day. Many brochures offer discount vouchers, which will save you a few dollars at attractions or restaurants. In addition, most hotels offer a good selection of maps and free brochures.

Times Square Information Center

(1560 Broadway between 46th and 47th streets, tel 212/768-1560, www.timessquarenyc.org, daily 8–8) This is New York's central tourist office and has free brochures, maps, helpful staff, a Broadway Ticket Center and a Metropolitan Transportation Authority that sells MetroCards (▷ 45), as well as providing ATMs, currency-exchange machines and free internet. It's worth visiting even if you think you don't need to. Some of the free walking tours start from here.

PARADES

January
Three Kings' Day
Martin Luther King Day Parade
March
St. Patrick's Day
March or April
Greek Independence Day Parade
Circus Animal Walk to Madison Square Garden
Easter Parade, Fifth Avenue between 44th and 59th streets
June
Puerto Rican Day Parade
Lesbian and Gay Pride Parade
October
Columbus Day Parade
Halloween Parade in Greenwich Village
November
Macy's Thanksgiving Day Parade

NYC & Company Visitor Information Center

(810 Seventh Avenue between 52nd and 53rd streets, tel 212/484-1222, www.nycgo.com, Mon–Fri 8.30 to 6, Sat–Sun 9–5) Smaller than the Times Square complex, this information center has free brochures and leaflets.

The interactive terminal with touch-screen access to visitor information is extremely useful. Buy advance tickets to major attractions here and your CityPass (▷ 274), and pick up a copy of the *Official Visitor Guide*. It contains discount vouchers for hotels, stores, restaurants, cruises and museums.

The center provides an ATM (cashpoint), plus telephones that

EVENTS

January or early February
Chinese New Year in Chinatown
April–October
Baseball season
May
Ninth Avenue International Food Festival
June
Metropolitan Opera park concerts, Museum Mile celebration
July
Independence Day fireworks over the East River
July–August
Shakespeare in the Park
August–September
Lincoln Center Out-of-Doors Festival, Harlem Week
September
Feast of San Gennaro, in Little Italy
September–October
New York Film Festival
Early November
New York City Marathon
December
Tree lighting at Rockefeller Center, New Year's Eve celebrations

are directly connected to American Express offices.

Lower East Side Visitors Center

(70 Orchard Street between Broome and Grand streets, tel 866/224-0206 or 212/226-9010, www.lowereastsideny.com, daily 10–4) Provides pamphlets covering local shopping, dining and nightlife entertainment.

Below *The Christmas tree at the Rockefeller Center is ceremoniously lit in December*

USEFUL WEBSITES

ACCOMMODATIONS
» All New York Hotels
www.allnewyorkhotels.net
Search for a hotel (including discount hotels) by name or criteria
» Hotel Conxions
www.hotelconxions.com
Finds great deals on city hotels
» Manhattan Bed and Breakfast
www.bedandbreakfast.com/
manhattan-new-york.html lists inns and bed-and-breakfast options
» Central Reservation Service
www.crshotels.com
A central reservation service for independent hotels in New York City
» YMCA Guest Rooms
www.ymcanyc.org
Main YMCA site with links to YMCAs around Greater New York

BROADWAY AND OFF-BROADWAY TICKETS
» Playbill's Online Theater Club
www.playbillclub.com
A membership club that gives discounts to top shows
» TeleCharge www.telecharge.com
» Broadway.com
www.broadway.com
» TheaterMania
www.theatermania.com
» Ticketmaster
www.ticketmaster.com

MONEY
» Travelex Worldwide Money
www.travelex.com

NEW YORK CITY INFORMATION
» Alliance for Downtown New York
www.downtownny.com
Everything you need to know about Downtown, including links to a free bus service and an interactive map
» The Bronx Tourism Council
www.ilovethebronx.com
» Brooklyn Tourism Council
www.visitbrooklyn.org
» Citysearch
www.newyork.citysearch.com
Attractions, events, hotels, real estate, restaurants and shopping
» Customs information for entering New York City
www.cbp.gov

» New York Convention & Visitors Bureau
www.nycgo.com
» NYC.com
www.nyc.com
» Times Square Business Improvement District
www.timessquarenyc.org
The official site for Times Square and what's going on there

NEWS, REVIEWS AND WHAT'S ON
» *New York*
www.nymag.com
New York magazine website
» New York Today
www.nytoday.com
The *New York Times* site, a guide for New Yorkers and visitors to what's on and what to do
» The *New York Times*
www.nytimes.com
» The *New Yorker*
www.newyorker.com
» *New York Press*
www.nypress.com
A free weekly newspaper
» *Time Out New York*
http://newyork.timeout.com
» *Village Voice*
www.villagevoice.com
A culturally hip publication

RADIO
New York City is the top radio outlet in the United States. The radio bandwidths are literally cacophonous, and if you live in an area without a similar level or choice, just turning on the radio and flipping the dial is an experience. A few top stations are:

» WNYC-FM 93.9 (820-AM)
www.wnyc.org
» 1010 WINS-AM Radio
www.1010wins.com
» WBGO-FM 88.3 Radio
www.wbgo.org
» WQXR-FM 105.9 www.wqxr.org
Classical music station
» WFAN-AM 660 www.wfan.com
Sports and news talk
» WOR-AM 710 www.wor710.com
Venerable NYC talk radio

TRANSPORTATION
» Airports
www.newyorkairports.com
» Trains
www.amtrak.com
» Airtrain Newark
www.airtrainnewark.com
An on-airport service and shuttle from Newark Liberty International Airport Train Station to Newark Liberty Airport
» American Automobile Association
www.aaa.com
» Subways and buses
www.mta.info

GENERAL
» The Baby Sitters' Guild
www.babysittersguild.com
For child care at any time
» Weather
www.weather.com
www.cnn.com/weather
A comprehensive weather service

Below *Cyber Café on West 49th Street, just off Broadway and Times Square*

MEDIA

At the newspaper stands on many streets throughout the city, you can buy newspapers in English, Spanish and, at some, a few other languages, as well as a wide variety of magazines.

NEWSPAPERS

» The **New York Times** is the city's most widely read daily (www.nytimes.com), published seven days a week. The Sunday edition includes a magazine and special sections for sports, travel, real estate, etc.

» The **Daily News** is a tabloid published seven days a week and offers a large quantity of Sunday supplements.

» The **New York Post** is another tabloid published daily.

» The **Wall Street Journal** is the much-respected New York-based national financial newspaper.

» The **New York Observer** is the pink-hued weekly full of media and political gossip.

MAGAZINES

» The **New Yorker** (www.newyorker.com) is a national literary and news magazine with New York listings and reviews as well as articles; published every Monday.

Above The New Yorker *magazine has listings and reviews*

» **New York Magazine** (www.nymag.com), published every Monday, is a good source of information on restaurants, theaters, movies, books, art, television and bargains around town.

» **The Village Voice** (www.villagevoice.com) is published weekly every Tuesday, with extensive listings of music, clubs, arts and entertainment.

» **Time Out** (http://newyork.timeout.com) is a very good comprehensive weekly magazine with plenty of listings on just about everything going on around town.

To buy newspapers from other countries, go to **Universal News & Magazines** (234 West 42nd Street between Seventh and Eighth avenues, tel 212/221-1809; www.universalnewsusa.com) and nine other locations around Manhattan.

MAJOR TV STATIONS

On cable, NY1 is all about New York, and more than 50 stations on cable, available in most hotels, supply movies, weather updates and home shopping. If you're traveling with kids, ask whether the Disney Channel is available.

NATIONAL TV STATIONS

2 (CBS)
4 (NBC)
5 (Fox)
7 (ABC)
9 and 11 (independent)
13 (PBS)

MAJOR RADIO STATIONS

www.nyradioguide.com

AM:	
Sports	660 (WFAN)
News and Talk	820 (WNYC feeds from NPR and; the BBC World Service)
Multi-ethnic	930 (WPAT)
News	1130 (WBBR)
News around the clock	880 and 1010 (WINS)
FM:	
Classic and talk	93.9 (WNYC-FM)
Classical	105.9 (WQXR)
Top 40	100.3 (also known as Z-100).

BOOKS, MAPS, MOVIES AND TELEVISION

BOOKS

Non-fiction

The Historical Atlas of New York City: Eric Homberger, Henry Holt and Company, New York, 1998
A fascinating book on the history of New York, always a pleasure to read. Excellent graphics, maps and photographs.

New York City (A Short History): George J. Lankevich, New York University Press, New York, 2002
A fascinating look at New York's political and social history from the first settlers to the election of Mayor Michael Bloomberg.

New York: Songs of the City: Nancy Groce, Watson-Guptill Publications, New York, 1999
A delightful musical journey through New York's five boroughs, with anecdotes and facts about people in the music industry, lyrics of old tunes about New York, and beautifully reproduced music sheet covers and posters.

Fiction

Novelists and short-story writers have always been attracted to New York, and many American classics have been set here. For short stories pick up O. Henry's **The Voice of the City** (1908) or Damon Runyon's **Guys and Dolls** (1932). Novels such as F. Scott Fitzgerald's **The Beautiful and the Damned** (1922), John Dos Passos's **Manhattan Transfer** (1925), J. D. Salinger's **The Catcher in the Rye** (1951) and Truman Capote's **Breakfast at Tiffany's** (1958) are all popular reads. More recent novels include Tom Wolfe's **Bonfire of the Vanities** (1987) and **The New York Trilogy** (1988) by Paul Auster.

MAPS AND OTHER PUBLICATIONS

Fodor's 25 Best
Focuses on the top 25 must-see sights. It breaks the city into five areas and recommends the best sights, shops, entertainment venues, nightlife and restaurants.

Fodor's New York City Information on where to go, what to see and how to get there, written by New York City-based shopping experts, restaurant critics and other specialists. It includes detailed descriptions of hundreds of restaurant and hotel choices, information on sights, and listings of stores and sports opportunities. Useful web links and smart travel tips help in planning.

AIA Guide to New York City: Norval White & Elliot Willensky, Three Rivers Press, New York, 2000
The American Institute of Architects' guide to parks and buildings in all five boroughs is truly a treasure store of acknowledged architectural knowledge and informed opinion. Arranged in geographical order, it's fun to have at hand as you amble around town, but it's hefty.

Guide to New York City Landmarks: New York Landmarks Preservation Commission 2008
This guide to the city's landmarks and historic districts is ideal for walking tours.

MOVIES

New York has been the setting of great movies by some great directors. Why not watch a few of them before you visit?

42nd Street (1933), Hal Wallis
King Kong (1933), Merian C. Cooper
Guys and Dolls (1955), Samuel Goldwyn
Breakfast at Tiffany's (1961), M. Jurrow, R. Shepherd
West Side Story (1961), Robert Wise
Mean Streets (1973), Martin Scorsese
Taxi Driver (1976), Martin Scorsese
New York, New York (1977), Martin Scorsese
Saturday Night Fever (1977), John Badham
Manhattan (1979), Woody Allen
Broadway Danny Rose (1984), Woody Allen
The Cotton Club (1984), Francis Ford Coppola
Desperately Seeking Susan (1985), Susan Seidelman
Radio Days (1987), Woody Allen
When Harry Met Sally (1989), Rob Reiner
A Bronx Tale (1993), Robert De Niro
Pollock (2000), Ed Harris
Gangs of New York (2002), Martin Scorsese
The Devil Wears Prada (2006), David Franke
Sex and the City: The Movie (2008), Michael Patrick King

TELEVISION

High drama, farce and comedy are played out on the streets of New York daily, and on the screens in people's homes throughout the world when they tune into the following popular TV shows set in or about New York City. Many of them can also be seen on video or DVD.

Friends (now in rerun)
Law & Order
NYPD Blue (now in rerun)
Seinfeld (now in rerun)
Sex and the City (now in rerun)
Will & Grace (now in rerun)
30 Rock

SHOPPING

They say that you can buy anything you want in New York City, and it's true. New York's shopping ranges from large opulent department stores to tiny one-room boutiques. Many visitors come to New York just to shop, especially pre-Christmas, uptown at the flagship designer stores that line Madison and Fifth avenues, or downtown at the cutting-edge designers in SoHo and NoLita. More moderately priced wares can be found at stores around Herald Square and 34th Street, or in the branches of national chains. There aren't any malls of note. Many stores open seven days a week (with late-night hours usually on Thursday). European visitors should note that American sizes differ from British and European sizes. Note too that the sales tax (added at the cash register) is 8.375 percent. There is no tax on clothing or footware. Credit cards are accepted virtually everywhere.

SALES

The largest sales take place in January and July, and also around legal holidays—Presidents' Day, Memorial Day and Labor Day, for example.

To keep abreast of current and forthcoming sales check the relevant sections of *New York* magazine and *Time Out* or go online to www.dailycandy.com or http://nymag.com/shopping/articles/sb/. Some of the best deals are found at sample sales, usually held in the spring and fall. Designers and manufacturers hold such sales to make space for their new design samples. Shopping fiends find out about them by subscribing to S & B Report (tel 843/579-0222) or going online at www.lazarshopping.com. Online subscription is $75 a year. For visitors the best way to locate these sales is to go to a favorite designer or store and ask if they hold them. Or try walking around the Garment District, where people often give out flyers announcing them. Bring cash and note you may not be able to try items on. There are no refunds available either.

MARKETS

Unlike European cities, New York has few outstanding markets, although one or two are worth visiting. At the African Market at 2278 Eighth Avenue, textiles, jewelry, bowls made from gourds, wooden stools and other artifacts from Africa are for sale. The Annex Antique Fair and Flea Market in the parking lots at Sixth Avenue and 26th Street (tel 212/243-5343) is very popular. Get there early for the best pickings (it opens at 5am). The Sunday Columbus Avenue market (between 76th and 77th streets) is also fun. In summer, expect small neighborhood street fairs at which people sell all kinds of bric-à-brac, clothing, CDs, food and books. Green markets have become very popular. The most storied is at Union Square (▷ 126), but there are smaller ones around town in Abingdon Square in the West Village or Tompkins Square in the East Village, for example.

Savvy New Yorkers also shop the thrift stores and consignment shops. Some of the best are: Housing Works, 143 West 17th Street (tel 212/366-0820) and 306 Columbus Avenue (tel 212/579-7566), Encore, 1132 Madison Avenue (tel 212/879-2850) at 84th Street, and the Salvation Army, 112 4th Avenue (tel 212/673-2741).

Below *Fifth Avenue is one of New York's most prestigious shopping streets*

ENTERTAINMENT AND NIGHTLIFE

The city's performance scene reflects the diversity of the metropolis. Theater patrons will find an array of options. There are 39 or so Broadway theaters, plus 450 non-profit theaters operating in the city. New Yorkers take their nightlife very seriously. You can always find a "scene" somewhere in the city that never sleeps, with the party shifting from bar to dance club and back, and then to the Meatpacking District at dawn.

BARS
There are bars to suit every taste. Great saloons with antique bars often have a lot of history attached. The King Cole Bar claims to have invented the Bloody Mary, while P. J. Clarke's has long been associated with Damon Runyon types. In swank hotel bars such as the St. Regis's King Cole or the Carlyle's Bemelman's you can lounge in luxury. Rooftop bars are spectacular trysting places. Specialty bars serve up every liquor (beer, wine, champagne, vodka and sake). You'll find an extensive gay scene catering to different crowds, concentrated mainly in Chelsea and Greenwich Village. Many lounges now have DJs spinning music, but some don't allow dancing because they lack a cabaret license.

CINEMA
The city is a veritable cinema paradiso. Numerous art houses operate, frequently showcasing individual directors or focusing on particular themes or eras. First-run movies are shown all over town in grand movieplexes.

CLASSICAL MUSIC, DANCE AND OPERA
Musical riches abound, led by the Metropolitan and City Operas and Carnegie Hall and the New York Philharmonic. All kinds of smaller groups and orchestras, plus independent opera companies, play at diverse venues—museums, music schools and churches. The New York City Ballet and American Ballet Theatre are leaders of the traditional dance scene, while Merce Cunningham, Mark Morris, Alvin Ailey, Paul Taylor and Martha Graham are the leading modern dance companies.

CLUBS
Some New York City clubs have a great deal of attitude. At the hottest dance clubs, there's a competition to get in, and people dress à la mode to ensure that they get past the velvet rope and the bouncer at the door. And there's always a VIP room and an A-list for guests (although you can often get on the list by calling in advance or going to www.sheckys.com). So tough has it become to gain entry to the most fashionable clubs, that even a $1,000 bribe will not work. Hence PartyBuddys (tel 866/856-2748, www.partybuddys.com), which promises to shepherd visitors on a nightlife tour for a fee, starting at $350 per person. Still, there are plenty more casual clubs available, especially the gay spots (see *Next*, *HX*, *Metro Source* and *Go* for listings), which are often a lot more fun.

COMEDY, POETRY AND THE SPOKEN WORD
The spoken word can be heard throughout the city, as the intellectuals and literary lights meet, greet and sign at bookstores, lecture at the 92nd Street Y, or deliver their poetry at poetry fests and St. Mark's-in-the-Bowery. And don't forget stand-up comedy, a unique American cultural contribution, celebrated in New York City clubs, which gave birth to such brilliant comedians as Jerry Seinfeld, Jay Leno, Woody Allen, Rosie O'Donnell and Joan Rivers.

CONTEMPORARY LIVE MUSIC
Cabaret is flourishing in alluring rooms at the Carlyle and the Algonquin hotels. Musically, uptown tends to be more traditional; downtown leans to the avant-garde. Indie rock clubs abound on the Lower East Side and in the East Village. Cool jazz and other exotica can be heard at the Knitting Factory and Tonic. Jazz continues to thrive as it has always in New York. The leading venue is still the Village Vanguard, now under the watchful eye of Lorraine Gordon, but it has

been joined by the $140 million Jazz at Lincoln Center in the Time Warner building on Columbus Circle. World music programming is featured all over town at Town Hall, Zankel Hall at Carnegie and Symphony Space.

THEATER

The Great White Way attracts the most visitors with its brightly lit marquees and gilded theaters named after such luminaries as Ethel Barrymore, David Belasco and Eugene O'Neill. The Public Theater and BAM are the shining lights of off-Broadway. The first, founded by Joe Papp, also delivers free summer Shakespeare in the Park, while BAM is famous for its New Wave Festival. Off-Broadway has nurtured many playwrights too, such as Wally Shawn, Lanford Wilson and

Tony Kushner, and several Broadway hits have emerged from here, notably *Rent, Avenue Q, A Chorus Line* and the *Heidi Chronicles*. off-off-Broadway stages quirky experimental showcases in tiny theaters with less than 100 seats, but it has nurtured such players as Eric Bogosian and Laurie Anderson.

PRACTICALITIES

Most box offices open from Monday to Saturday, 10am to 8pm, and Sunday from 11am to 6.30pm. Tickets can be purchased here without paying a fee. Standing Room Only tickets, when available, go on sale on the day of the performance.

Tickets can also be purchased through Telecharge (tel 212/ 239-6200) and Ticketmaster (tel 212/ 307-7171).

Best performance listings are found in *Time Out, New York* magazine, the *Village Voice* and the Friday edition of the *New York Times*. A good website for listings is http://newyork.timeout.com.

The city's nightlife hot spots are Harlem, Chelsea, the East and West villages, and the Lower East Side. There's also plenty of action across the East River in Williamsburg, which now draws its own crowd from Manhattan. Drinking age is 21 (always carry a picture ID). British visitors should note that whiskey is rye, not Scotch.

Above *The Ed Sullivan Theater on Broadway is now a television and radio studio, home of* Late Show with David Letterman *since 1993; tickets are available for show recordings*

SPORTS AND ACTIVITIES

New York City is a major sports destination, whether you fancy watching a game of baseball, football, basketball, ice hockey or tennis. If you want to take part in something yourself, try jogging in Central Park or working out at one of the many gyms.

PROFESSIONAL SPORTS
Local and regional rivalries drive the professional sports scene. In baseball it's the Yankees (Bronx) versus the Mets (Queens). In addition, whenever the Yankees play the Red Sox, it's a grudge game because Boston has never forgiven New York for stealing Babe Ruth.

The biggest sports are football (Giants and Jets) and basketball (Knicks and New Jersey Nets). Ice hockey has fanatical fans too, supporting the Rangers, Islanders and New Jersey Devils. Despite the American women's global success in soccer, women's professional sports struggle for audience support, although such teams as basketball's Liberty have loyal fans.

Sports seasons are: baseball April–end October; basketball November–end April; soccer March–end October; football and ice hockey September–end April.

TICKETS
Most seats are sold in advance by subscription to corporations and individuals. Tickets are available without fee at the box office; there's an extra fee for phone and online orders. Agencies like TicketMaster (tel 212/307-7171 or www.ticketmaster.com) usually charge a fee of from $4 to $8 per ticket.

Tickets to any of these sports are tough to get and/or expensive, but you can always take a seat in one of the many raucous sports bars around town and see the action there, or at the large ESPN Zone in Times Square.

EXERCISE AND ACTIVITIES
New Yorkers go to the gym, walk, run, cycle, skate, rollerblade and play tennis, softball and street basketball. Equestrians can ride in Central Park. They have also rediscovered the waterfront and now enjoy kayaking and sailing from several downtown piers. The more sedentary count bowling and pool as sports.

HEALTHY AND BEAUTY

Almost every neighborhood in New York has a selection of health clubs with fitness equipment, classes and assorted frills—sometimes a pool. Massages, nutrition consultations and personal trainers may be available by appointment. Most offer day passes for visitors for a price (anywhere from $15 to $50). It's best to go at off-peak hours–between 12 and 2 and from 5 till 8 the clubs may be so crowded you have to sign up to use the machines.

WHAT'S ON OFFER
The city has always had yoga studios and fancy hair salons, but it has seen an enormous growth of day spas and other pampering facilities. Some are world-class, like La Prairie in the Ritz; others cater to New Age constituencies, while still others hustle passers-by for a quick back massage. The Brazilian nail salons are considered extra-special.

FOR CHILDREN
With its towering buildings, vibrant streets, sights and sounds, New York is for kids. Even a ride on the subway can be exciting.

FAMILY-FRIENDLY
A few family-friendly institutions are listed under the individual regions in this book. Also check the Sports and Activities sections and the Shopping sections (especially Niketown and the Disney Store).

In addition, many seasonal events appeal to kids—performances of the Big Apple Circus and the *Nutcracker* at Christmas as well as the Radio City Christmas Spectacular; the Ringling Brothers' circus in spring; and the parades and fairs that take place throughout the year.

SPECIAL EVENTS
As you research your visit, it's worth calling concert halls and museums in advance to find out what special events will be on while you're in town; reserve ahead for those that interest you.

Note that the Convention & Visitors Bureau often has information about these events. Call 212/484-1222 or check www.nycgo.com. Other useful websites are www.nyc.com and www.nyctourist.com.

JANUARY

NEW YORK WINTER ANTIQUES SHOW
www.winterantiquesshow.com
The city's most prestigious antiques fair in the Park Avenue Armory.
☎ 212/987-0446

FEBRUARY

CHINESE NEW YEAR
www.chinatown-online.com
Firecrackers blast and dragon and lion dancers sashay through the streets of Chinatown.
☎ 212/484-1222 🕓 Depends on the lunar calendar

WESTMINSTER KENNEL DOG SHOW
www.westminsterkennelclub.org
About 2,500 canines strut their stuff at Madison Square Garden.
☎ 212/213-3165 🕓 Dates vary

Above *Street decorations in Little Italy*

MARCH

ST. PATRICK'S DAY PARADE
www.saintpatricksdayparade.com
Bagpipers and bands, politicians and New York's finest march down Fifth Avenue from 86th to 44th streets celebrating the patron saint of Ireland.
☎ 212/484-1222 🕓 March 17

MARCH–APRIL

EASTER PARADE
People with a bent for fashion design stroll along Fifth Avenue between 49th and 57th streets showing off their often wacky and wonderful hats.
🕓 Depending on when Easter falls

NEW YORK INTERNATIONAL AUTO SHOW
www.autoshowny.com
www.javitscenter.com
Heaven for car enthusiasts.
✉ Jacob Javits Convention Center
☎ 800/282-3336 🕓 Late March/early April

APRIL

MACY'S FLOWER SHOW
More than 30,000 varieties of flower are arrayed in the store in celebration of spring.
☎ 212/494-4495 🕓 Last two weeks of April

CHERRY BLOSSOM FESTIVAL
www.bbg.org
A range of traditional Japanese activities and performances take place against a backdrop of gorgeous pink cherry blossoms in the Brooklyn Botanic Garden.
☎ 718/623-7200 🕓 Late April, depending on when trees flower

MAY

NINTH AVENUE INTERNATIONAL FOOD FESTIVAL
Between 37th and 57th streets, Ninth Avenue is lined with stands selling food of all kinds. Musical entertainment, too.
☎ 212/484-1222 🕓 Second or third weekend of May

FLEET WEEK

The tall ships, active military ships and aircraft carriers sail in a majestic parade into New York Harbor and up the Hudson River. The festival includes military demonstrations, tugs of war and cooking fests, and culminates in a Memorial Day celebration. Posses of sailors roam New York City streets in their crisp white uniforms.
☎ 212/245-0072 ◷ Third week of May

WASHINGTON SQUARE

www.nycgv.com
The streets around Washington Square are lined with artists, photographers and craftspeople selling their work.
☎ 212/982-6255 ◷ Outdoor Art Exhibit Memorial Day weekend

JUNE
BELMONT STAKES

www.nyra.com
The last leg of the horse-racing Triple Crown is run at Belmont on Long Island.
☎ 516/488-6000 ◷ First weekend in June

PUERTO RICAN DAY PARADE

www.nationalpuertoricandayparade.org
The city is awash with Puerto Rican flags.
☎ 718/401-0404 ◷ Second weekend in June

LESBIAN AND GAY PRIDE PARADE

www.nycpride.org
The flamboyant parade from 52nd Street to Greenwich Village, via Fifth Avenue, is the culmination of a week of gay-oriented celebrations.
☎ 212/807-7433 ◷ Last Sunday in June

JULY
INDEPENDENCE DAY HARBOR FESTIVAL AND FIREWORKS

New York City celebrates the nation's birth with a festival in Lower Manhattan and some spectacular fireworks launched from barges on the East River.
☎ 212/484-1222 ◷ July 4

AUGUST
HARLEM WEEK

www.harlemdiscover.com
A host of Harlem events—film, jazz and food festivals among them—start mid-July and the "week" runs into September.
☎ 212/862-8477 or 212/484-1222
◷ Most of August

LINCOLN CENTER OUT-OF-DOORS FESTIVAL

www.lincolncenter.org
Over 100 free performances on the plazas at Lincoln Center, including music, dance, theatricals and more.
☎ 212/546-2656

SEPTEMBER
WEST INDIAN PARADE AND CARNIVAL

www.carnaval.com
Thousands flock to Brooklyn to see the dancers and bands sashaying along to reggae, soca and calypso. Caribbean food adds to the festivities.
☎ 212/484-1222 ◷ Labor Day

FEAST OF SAN GENNARO

www.sangennaro.org
The patron saint of Naples is paraded down Mulberry Street at this fiesta, with all kinds of Italian food and street entertainment.
☎ 212/226-6427 ◷ Eleven days in mid-September

NEW YORK FILM FESTIVAL

www.filmlinc.com
The Film Society of Lincoln Center organizes this major film festival. The hub is the Walter Reade Theatre.
☎ 212/875-5600 ◷ 17 days in late September or early October

OCTOBER
BLESSING OF THE ANIMALS

www.stjohndivine.org
At churches throughout the city, animals are blessed on St. Francis Day. The biggest event takes place at the Cathedral of St. John the Divine. People bring their pets.
☎ 212/316-7490 ◷ First Sunday

HALLOWEEN PARADE

www.halloween-nyc.com
What started as an impromptu procession of drag queens in Greenwich Village has become a huge event with big-name sponsors. The costumes are amazing, but line up early to get a glimpse.
☎ 212/484-1222

NOVEMBER
NEW YORK CITY MARATHON

www.nyrrc.org
Thousands of runners thunder across the Queensborough Bridge into Manhattan and race for the finish in Central Park.
☎ 212/860-4455 ◷ First weekend in November

MACY'S THANKSGIVING DAY PARADE

Families line the route from 77th Street and Central Park West to Herald Square to see the immense helium balloons.
☎ 212/484-1222 ◷ Last Thursday

DECEMBER
LIGHTING OF THE CHRISTMAS TREE

www.rockefellercenter.com
It's a media event, usually starring popular singers. Stake out your place early—or avoid the area altogether because crowds make it impossible to get through.
✉ Rockefeller Center ☎ 212/332-6868
◷ Usually the first week in December

RADIO CITY SPECTACULAR

www.radiocity.com
Busloads of revelers come to see the Rockettes kick up a storm in a stylish chorus line for this seasonal show, which always includes a Parade of the Wooden Soldiers.
☎ 212/247-4777 ◷ Through December 30

NEW YEAR'S EVE CELEBRATION

Times Square fills with thousands of partyers who show up to watch the ball drop announcing the official start of the next year.
◷ December 31

You can dine around the world in New York City and you can spend a pittance or a fortune or somewhere in between. The choice is yours. Some New Yorkers dine out every night, others save the top-class choices for special occasions. Dining trends change from season to season. Whether dining at a deluxe restaurant or a casual eatery, healthier, locally grown food is growing in popularity.

RESERVATIONS, DRESS CODES AND OTHER NOTES

In general, it's wise to make a reservation for dinner, especially on weekends. Indeed, top-class restaurants require reservations and will ask you to provide a telephone number for confirmation. If you want a table at Jean-Georges, Le Bernardin, Gordon Ramsay or similar, call well in advance. Sometimes, at these "famous" restaurants, it can be tough to get through even to the reservation desk. Just keep trying. If you're on your own and want to eat on the run, you may be able to eat at the bar in one of these fancy restaurants. Note that some restaurants do not take reservations for parties under six people. In Midtown, luncheon reservations are also essential.

The United States is a more casual culture than most and strict dress codes have disappeared. Nonetheless a few places still do require a jacket and tie at dinner so remember to ask when making a reservation. In general, casual smart is the way to go.

Smoking is not allowed in public spaces, period. The majority of restaurants have full bars; some sell beer and wine only, and a few have no liquor but will allow you to bring your own. At premier BYO (bring your own) restaurants, there will be a substantial corkage fee if you bring your own wine.

Vegetarians will find a welcome. Many top-class dining rooms offer vegetarian menus, and fast-food joints are offering more healthful options on their menus these days.

Breakfast may be served all day at coffee shops and diners. Otherwise, the normal breakfast hours are from 7 to 11am. Lunch usually runs from 11.30am to 2 or 2.30pm and dinner from 5pm to 10 or 11pm, depending on the day of the week. Most top-class restaurants close for

lunch on Saturday and Sunday. Many restaurants offer brunch on Sunday or both Saturday and Sunday.

TAXES, TIPPING AND OTHER FINANCIAL CONSIDERATIONS

A sales tax of 8.375 percent will be added to your dining bill. Americans tip more generously than most other nationalities. The minimum (with good service) is 15 percent; many people double the tax for a 16.75 percent tip. Many restaurants offer prix-fixe menus, which often provide good value. In January and late June, a special promotion offers a three-course menu at reduced rates for lunch and dinner at numerous restaurants; this promotion is often extended so it's always worth checking if it's available.

DESSERT AND COFFEE

Greenwich Village has been famous for its coffeehouses since the 1950s. Of the few that remain, Caffe

Reggio (119 MacDougal Street, tel 212/475-9557) is one of the best, a genuine Italian coffeehouse where you can idle away an afternoon over a few espressos. Le Gamin (132 West Houston at Sullivan Street, tel 212/475-1543) is a similar French version. Bean Coffee and Tea (446 Sixth Avenue, tel 212/777-0402) is a small, cozy coffee shop serving great coffee, mocha, latte and chai along with delectable cupcakes, muffins, cookies, tarts and fancy pastries. The Paris-inspired Payard Patisserie & Bistro (1032 Lexington Avenue, tel 212/717-5252) displays the creations of former Restaurant Daniel pastry chef, François Payard. The pastry case displays all kinds of gems plus handmade chocolates; sorbets are also available. Crowds make their way to the tiny storefront Magnolia Bakery (401 Bleecker Street, tel 212/462-2572) to taste the cupcakes iced with thick ultrasweet buttercream. In the East Village, Veniero's (342 East 11th Street, tel 212/674-7070) has been making and selling delicious Italian pastries for aeons.

TRADITIONAL AMERICAN FOOD

The United States of America is a nation of immigrants. Traditional American food has evolved out of the traditions of the immigrant populations—German, Jewish, Italian, Scandinavian, Latino, Asian—plus Native American and African-American. Each group has contributed its ingredients and techniques to the current food scene. The Germans brought sauerkraut, sausages and pumpernickel; the Hungarians goulash and stuffed cabbage; the Cubans black bean soup and Cuban sandwiches; the Irish corned beef and cabbage; the Japanese sushi and teriyaki; the Jews chopped liver pastrami and knishes; the Greeks kebabs; the Lebanese baba ganoush and falafel; the Mexicans salsa, tacos and refried beans; the Moroccans couscous; the Russians blinis and caviar; the Spanish tapas, chorizo and paella; the Swedes gravlax; and the Welsh leek and potato pie. Many of these dishes (or American modifications) have become common fare on all-American menus at standard American restaurants and even at lowly diners. The United States also boasts some distinctive regional cuisines, most notably Southern, Cajun, Southwestern and Tex-Mex.

DRINKS

The New York bar scene is extremely varied. Bars range from cheap dives charging a few dollars for a drink to luxury lounges charging anywhere from $10 for a cocktail. Despite the campaign against drinking and driving, most bars offer happy hours when they charge half price for drinks or offer two for the price of one. Note that American bartenders expect to be tipped (at least 10 percent). As far as drinks go, international beers and microbrews are readily available; cocktails are in vogue and every day brings a new concoction to light. Food is always available. It ranges from burgers and wings to more sophisticated fare. Most bars open from mid-morning to anywhere from 1am to 4am. Note that the drinking age is 21; expect to be "carded" (to show a photo ID), so carry an identification with photo. Buy wine and liquor at a liquor store; supermarkets sell beer only.

SOME NEW YORK DINING INSTITUTIONS

New York does have some unique dining institutions. The most famous is the deli. Among delis, the most traditional is the Jewish deli, which sells a variety of smoked fish and meats, plus items such as bagels, pastrami and corned beef sandwiches, chopped liver, pickles and knishes. The word deli is also used for small neighborhood grocery stores, often operated by Korean merchants. They sell coffee, bagels, sandwiches, salads and other grocery items.

The coffeeshop/diner is another traditional dining haven. It will have counters and stools as well as table service. Here people secure endless cups of coffee, and breakfast, lunch or dinner selections taken from a vast (usually laminated) menu. The city has plenty of fast-food outlets, too (McDonald's, etc). Look for street vendors also. They sell everything from hot salty pretzels to soups, hot dogs and ethnic snacks. The pizza parlor is also endemic to New York. The most visible coffee vendor is Starbucks, which seems to be on every street corner, but there are plenty of independent cafés, especially in the West and East villages.

LATE NIGHT/24-HOUR

Despite New York's reputation as a 24/7 town, it's not that easy to find food in the small hours. Among tried-and-true late-night oases, the hip but strangely unpretentious Blue Ribbon (97 Sullivan Street, tel 212/274-0404) draws clubbers and workers, including many chefs for sesame-glazed catfish, tofu ravioli, paella, and oysters on the half shell. It's open from 4pm to 4am daily.

The Coffee Shop (29 Union Square West, tel 212/243-7969), which looks like what you'd expect, is like nothing you'd find in Peoria with its Brazilian ownership and varied fare.

At Empire Diner (210 Tenth Avenue, tel 212/243-2736), you'll pay for the stylish chrome-and-black art deco setting as well as for the classic egg dishes, sandwiches and meat loaf. It's open around the clock except on Tuesday.

At the intersection of SoHo and NoLita, Delicatessen (54 Prince Street at Lafayette Street, tel 212/226-0211) offers international comfort food with Italian, French and American twists. The slick, modern restaurant features a steel and glass wall that opens in warm weather.

Singles can almost always eat at the bar in Manhattan. If the place is full, or if you want to eat on the run, just ask.

Bagel An unsweetened dense eggless bread cooked in water and then baked. It's shaped with a hole in the middle

Boston baked beans Navy beans flavored with molasses and salt pork

Chicken-fried steak Batter-dipped steak

Chowder Thick soup traditionally made with clams or corn

Cobbler Fruit pie topped with a biscuit-style crust

Egg cream A thick drink made with chocolate syrup, milk and seltzer

Eggplant Aubergine

Eggs over easy Fried eggs turned over so they are cooked through
Eggs sunnyside up Fried eggs that have not been turned over

French toast Bread coated with beaten eggs and sautéed. Served with maple syrup

Grits Corn kernels with the bran and germ removed

Hero An extra-large long roll

Key lime pie Made with a special lime variety from Florida

London broil A particular cut of flank steak

Lox Cured salmon

Meat loaf Ground beef, turkey and pork combined with breadcrumbs and egg and baked

New York cheesecake Jewish-style dense and creamy cake, which may be plain or topped with fruit

On the rocks With ice

Pot roast Braised beef

Pretzel A long bread, twisted into a knot, sprinkled with coarse salt and sold warm from carts

Salisbury steak A beef patty

Scotch Scottish whisky

Stack of pancakes Three or four thick batter cakes served with maple syrup

Sub Short for submarine; another name for an extra-large long roll

Straight up No ice

Waldorf salad Apples, celery and walnuts in mayonnaise; first created at the Waldorf Astoria

Whiskey American rye

Above *Piles of pretzels on a stand*

RESTAURANTS BY CUISINE

American contemporary
Annisa
Aureole
Blue Hill
Blue Ribbon Bakery
Compass
Craft and Craftbar
Cru
Eleven Madison Park
Gotham Bar & Grill
Gramercy Tavern
The Harrison
Ouest
Per Se
Prune
Red Cat
Sarabeth's
Tavern on the Green
Town
Union Square Café
Veritas
WD-50
American traditional
'21' Club
Asian
Asiate
Spice Market
Barbecue
Blue Smoke
Virgil's Real Barbecue
Burgers
Corner Bistro
Caribbean
Negril Village
Chinese
Dim Sum Go Go
Shun Lee Palace
Continental
Four Seasons
Deli
Barney Greengrass
Katz's Deli
Eclectic
Spotted Pig
French
Artisanal
Balthazar
Bouley
Brasserie
Café des Artistes
Café Boulud
Chanterelle
Daniel

DB Bistro Moderne
Fleur de Sel
Gordon Ramsay at the London
Jean-Georges
Odeon
Paradou
Pastis
Greek
Molyvos
Periyali
Indian
Banjara
Dawat
Devi
Hampton Chutney
Tabla
Tamarind
Italian
Babbo
Bar Pitti
Bread
Cesca
Felidia
Gnocco
Gonzo
I Coppi
Lupa
Naples 45
Peasant
Japanese
Bond Street
Masa
Nobu
Sugiyama
Sushi Yasuda
Tomoe Sushi
Korean
Cho Dang Gol
Woo Lae Oak
Latin American
Calle Ocho
Pio Pio
Malaysian
Nyonya
Mediterranean
Picholine
Mexican
Crema Restaurant
Dos Caminos
Hell's Kitchen
La Palapa
Maya
Mesa Grill
Pampano

Rosa Mexicano
Sueños
Zarela
Middle Eastern
Persepolis
Noodle shops
Big Wong King
Pizza
John's Pizzeria
Otto Enoteca Pizzeria
Russian
Uncle Vanya Café
Scandinavian
Aquavit
Seafood
Aquagrill
Blue Fin
Esca
Grand Central Oyster Bar
Le Bernardin
Mermaid Inn
Pearl Oyster Bar
Soul
Amy Ruth's
Londel's
Spanish
Casa Mono
Pipa
Steak
Mark Joseph Steakhouse
Strip House
Thai
Holy Basil
Pam Real Thai
Vegetarian
Angelica Kitchen
Vietnamese
Le Colonial
Nam

HOTELS WITH EXCEPTIONAL DINING ROOMS
Algonquin
Carlyle
Four Seasons
Le Parker Meridien
Mandarin Oriental
Mercer Hotel
New York Palace
Plaza Athénée
Ritz-Carlton (Central Park South)
St. Regis
Sherry Netherland
Trump International Hotel
W New York – Times Square

Traditionally the priciest hotels in New York have been relatively traditional, formal places. However the last two decades have seen a number of ultra-chic hotels open around the city, offering guests luxurious amenities in modern, stylish settings. The restaurants, lounges and bars in these places also attract trendy New Yorkers, as well as visitors to the city. There are plenty of hotel rooms, but it is hard to find a comfortable room under $150. If money is no object, reserve a room at the Carlyle or the Four Seasons.

For less expensive options, check out the inexpensive chains—Red Roof, Super 8 and others. The city also has some bed-and-breakfasts, which charge less than the average hotel and provide good-value extras. Hostels are the least expensive lodging options (see below).

It used to be that all the best hotels were in Midtown but that has changed dramatically. Now, there are first-class luxury hotels downtown in SoHo, Greenwich Village and the Financial District. Still, there are more bargains away from Midtown. New York City hotels range in size from vast 2,000-room monstrosities to smaller establishments with 250 rooms or less. If you stay at a large convention hotel, expect to find crowded lobbies, more lines and slower service.

Most hotels have similar amenities. The average hotel room comes with air conditioning, private bathroom, cable TV, telephone, coffeemaker, hairdryer, iron and ironing board. The level of luxury and the quality and range of the service are the real distinctions between hotels. Top-class hotel rooms boast luxe fabrics and linens, high-tech electronics and telephony, and high staff-to-guest ratios, which guarantees prompt, courteous service. Space is at a premium in Manhattan, so expect rooms to be on the small side. Double-glazed windows, which are usually standard, help reduce noise. Most hotels have complimentary coffee/tea service, and newspapers in the lobby or delivered to your room.

HOTEL ROOM RATES

Today there is no such thing as a standard rack rate. Prices fluctuate with customer demand. To get the best rate on a hotel room, always call the hotel directly and ask for the best available rate and what special discounts are available. Alternatively, go online to such discount services as www.hotels.com, www.quikbook.com or www.hoteldiscount.com to secure the best rates. Winter (Jan–end Feb) and summer (Jul–end Aug) are the least expensive seasons. Depending on the hotel, weekend rates may be higher or lower than midweek. Parking charges of $35 and up will add substantially to any bill. Note, too, that 13.875 percent will be added to your bill, as well as additional occupancy taxes of a dollar or two which are charged for each night's stay.

HOSTELS IN NEW YORK
BIG APPLE HOSTEL

www.bigapplehostel.com

296 D18 ✉ 119 West 45th Street, between Sixth and Seventh avenues, 10036 ☎ 212/302-2603

CHELSEA CENTER HOSTEL
www.chelseacenterhostel.com
➕ 296 D19 ✉ 313 West 29th Street,
between Eighth and Ninth avenues, 10031
☎ 212/643-0214

CHELSEA INTERNATIONAL HOSTEL
www.chelseahostel.com
➕ 296 D20 ✉ 251 West 20th Street,
between Seventh and Eighth avenues, 10011
☎ 212/647-0010

HOSTELLING INTERNATIONAL
www.hinewyork.org
➕ 294 C12 ✉ 891 Amsterdam Avenue at
104th Street, 10025-4403 ☎ 212/932-2300

WHITEHOUSE
www.whitehousehotelofny.com
➕ 297 F22 ✉ 340 Bowery between
2nd and Great Jones streets, 10012
☎ 212/477-562

YMCA OF GREATER NEW YORK
www.ymcanyc.org
➕ 294 D16 ✉ 5 West 63rd Street,
between Central Park West and Broadway,
10023 ☎ 212/875-4100

HOTELS BY AREA
LOWER EAST SIDE
Off-SoHo Suites

GREENWICH VILLAGE/
MEAT MARKET/CHELSEA
Abingdon Guest House
Chelsea
Chelsea Lodge
Hotel Gansevoort

The Inn on 23rd
Larchmont
Maritime Hotel
Washington Square

SOHO/TRIBECA
Cosmopolitan Hotel-Tribeca
Hotel Azure
Mercer
SoHo Grand
Tribeca Grand

UNION SQUARE/FLATIRON
DISTRICT/GRAMERCY PARK
Gershwin
Giraffe
Inn at Irving Place

MADISON SQUARE PARK/
MURRAY HILL
70 Park Avenue
Avalon
Grand Union
Hotel Chandler
Marcel
Morgans
Thirty Thirty
Wolcott

MIDTOWN WEST/
THEATER DISTRICT
Algonquin
Americana Inn
Belvedere
Blakely
Casablanca
Dream Hotel
Hudson
Le Parker Meridien

Mansfield
The Michelangelo
Moderne
The Muse
Royalton
Shoreham
Travel Inn
Warwick

LINCOLN CENTER/
UPPER WEST SIDE
Excelsior
Hotel Roger Williams
Jumeirah Essex House
Lucerne
Mandarin Oriental
Newton
On the Ave
Ritz-Carlton
Trump International Hotel and Tower

MIDTOWN EAST
Beekman Tower
Benjamin
Edison
Elysée
Four Seasons
Kimberly
Library
Metro
New York Palace
Peninsula
The Pod Hotel
Renaissance New York Hotel 57
St. Regis
Sherry-Netherland
W New York – Times Square
Waldorf-Astoria Hotel and Towers

UPPER EAST SIDE
Affinia Gardens
Carlyle
Gracie Inn
Pierre
Plaza Athénée
Wales

PRACTICALITIES | STAYING

Opposite and left *The New York Palace hotel
on Madison Avenue in Midtown*

New York is divided into the five boroughs of Manhattan, Brooklyn, the Bronx, Queens and Staten Island, each with their own distinct character.

MANHATTAN

Attractions, many of them world famous, line the streets of Manhattan, the area stretching from Battery Park at its tip to Harlem in the north, beyond Central Park.

FINANCIAL DISTRICT

The oldest part of the city and the nexus of the securities industry anchored by the New York Stock Exchange and Wall Street. It's still primarily a business district, although residents have moved in over the last decade.

BATTERY PARK CITY

A 92-acre (35ha) complex, built on landfill from the creation of the World Trade Center in 1974. It includes housing, commercial and retail space, plus a marina and the Museum of Jewish Heritage.

TRIBECA

It means *Tri*angle *Be*low *Ca*nal and is defined by Canal and Barclay streets and Broadway and the Hudson River. In 1980, the Odeon restaurant opened and pioneer residents followed, settling into the warehouses and manufacturing buildings. It now has the highest real-estate values in the city and plenty of celebrity cachet. Home to TriBeCa Film Center, it's still a mixed-use neighborhood of gritty warehouse lofts, loft-style restaurants and low-end retail.

CIVIC CENTER

The focal point of city government, incorporating the courts, police and immigration. City Hall is at the center of the area. It's dwarfed by the Municipal Building, designed by McKim, Mead and White.

CHINATOWN

In the 1840s, Chinatown was just eight blocks. Today it includes about 30 blocks, from Kenmare and Delancey streets to East Broadway and Worth Street, and from Broadway to Allen Street. Shop for fish, meat, vegetables and herbal remedies or dine in the many affordable restaurants.

LITTLE ITALY

Little of this once vibrant community survives. Most of the Italians have moved to the suburbs and Chinese residents have replaced them. It consists largely of Mulberry Street, which is lined with tourist-oriented restaurants, plus genuine delis.

NOLITA

It stands for *No*rth of *Li*ttle *Ita*ly. The narrow streets around St. Patrick's

Opposite Chinatown has a wealth of colorful and exotic shops and restaurants

Cathedral, once the heart of the Italian community, are now lined with hip designer boutiques.

SOHO

In 1973 the 20 blocks between Houston, Canal, West Broadway and Broadway were designated a Historic District, protecting the best stock of cast-iron buildings in the city. Artists had already begun reclaiming the manufacturing and warehouse spaces and pioneering a loft lifestyle. Today the artists and most galleries have moved on; the area is now an ultra-expensive, chic shopping mall crowded with non-residents on weekends.

BOWERY

A long street connecting Chinatown to the East Village, it was once the city's Skid Row, lined with flophouses and numerous stores selling kitchen supplies and lighting fixtures. Today it is being gentrified.

LOWER EAST SIDE

The traditional gateway for every wave of immigrants, from the Jewish and the Italians to the Puerto Ricans, this was the last Manhattan neighborhood to be updated. Today, young professionals and artists occupy the tenements and congregate at the clubs and bars along Orchard, Clinton and other streets. Remnants of the Puerto Rican community survive, and so does the bargain bazaar on Sunday along Orchard Street. The boundaries stretch from 14th Street to Fulton and Franklin and from the East River to Broadway, incorporating Chinatown, Little Italy and the East Village neighborhoods.

GREENWICH VILLAGE/ WEST VILLAGE

This area stretches from 14th to Houston streets and from the Hudson River to Bowery and Fourth Avenue. Originally a poor neighborhood housing the workers

and stevedores who worked the waterfront, it became a bohemia around 1900, attracting a mixture of artists, writers and anarchists. Today, it's a mixed neighborhood. The gay population has mostly moved to Chelsea, and now "successful" singles and families occupy the town houses and apartments. Small boutiques line the west end of Bleecker Street. The southern section around Bleecker Street and Sixth Avenue still has an Italian flavor.

MEATPACKING DISTRICT

Sandwiched between the West Village and Chelsea around 14th Street, this gritty neighborhood is being redeveloped. Restaurants, bars, clubs and stores are opening, and hotels too.

NOHO

Between SoHo and Greenwich Village (from Houston to Eighth Streets and Mercer to Bowery/ Third Avenue), this youth-oriented neighborhood has plenty of fashionable shopping, bars and restaurants. The acronym stands for *North of Houston.*

EAST VILLAGE

This was originally an extension of the Lower East Side, settled by Jewish and Ukrainian/Polish communities. In the 1960s–70s it became the center of the counter-culture. East Village has been rapidly redeveloped and is now filled with restaurants, bars and a young street scene.

ALPHABET CITY

It refers to avenues A, B, C and D between Houston and 14th streets. In the 1970s, First Avenue marked the DMZ and the streets east of First were considered dangerous drug supermarkets. Gentrification began in 1983 when Operation Pressure Point started cleaning up the drug trade, and buildings on Tompkins Square became co-ops. Today young professionals occupy the tenement apartments; there's

a thriving dining and bar scene, including a substantial number of gay bars and clubs. The original Hispanic population has been dispersed.

GRAMERCY PARK

This genteel and dignified neighborhood radiating from the eponymous gated garden square remains primarily residential. It stretches from 18th to 23rd streets and from Park Avenue South to Third Avenue.

UNION SQUARE/ FLATIRON DISTRICT

This hot new neighborhood, leading south from the Flatiron Building on 22nd Street and around Madison Square, has plenty of bars, restaurants and clubs. The Green Market at Union Square is a must on Saturday. The former Ladies' Mile along Sixth Avenue between 15th and 24th streets is now occupied by large national chain stores. The boundaries are 14th and 23rd streets, and Park and Sixth avenues.

CHELSEA

Today Chelsea is the center of the gay community and the new focus for contemporary art anchored by numerous warehouse/garage galleries around and along 24th Street. It has a lively club and restaurant scene. The boundaries stretch from 14th to 30th streets and from Sixth Avenue to the Hudson River.

MURRAY HILL

A quiet residential neighborhood between 34th and 40th streets and Madison and Third avenues. It is becoming increasingly commercial on the fringes. The Morgan Library and the Episcopalian church, where the Roosevelts worshiped, set the tone.

MIDTOWN

The commercial heart of the city, between 34th and 59th streets on the West Side and from 40th to 59th streets on the East Side.

It includes major attractions, shops, restaurants, theaters, TV studios, Nasdaq and corporate offices.

TIMES SQUARE/ THEATER DISTRICT

The old peep shows, hookers and junkies have been displaced, and the area around 42nd Street and Broadway is now occupied by an array of major corporations and national chain stores—Condé Nast, Reuters, ESPN Zone, Toys R-Us and many others, who share the area with new hotels, clubs and theaters.

CLINTON/HELL'S KITCHEN

Real-estate developers have rediscovered this neighborhood from 42nd to 59th streets between Eighth Avenue and the Hudson River. It was formerly known as Hell's Kitchen and was the site of slaughterhouses, freight yards and factories.

UPPER EAST SIDE

It stretches from 59th to 96th streets from Fifth Avenue to the East River. The section from 59th to 78th streets between Fifth and Park avenues is often referred to as the Gold Coast, where those who can afford it live. Farther east it was not always elegant, but it became more so in 1956 when the Third Avenue "El" was demolished and Madison Avenue became an ultra-chic shopping street. Today it is filled with private clubs, consulates, art galleries, restaurants and fine residences. Museum Mile extends along Fifth Avenue from 81st Street north past the Metropolitan Museum of Art.

YORKVILLE

High-rise apartments line the streets of what was formerly the German section between Lexington and Third avenues on 86th Street.

CARNEGIE HILL

Between 86th and 96th streets and Fifth and Third avenues, this is primarily a low-key wealthy residential district, anchored by the Carnegie mansion (now the Cooper-Hewitt National Design Museum). The area is home to such prestigious private schools as Dalton, Spence and Horace Mann, plus the Guggenheim and the Jewish Museum.

EAST HARLEM/SPANISH HARLEM

From 96th to 142nd streets, between Park Avenue and the East River, this area is still home to El Barrio, the community established by the Puerto Ricans, who first arrived at the end of World War I and increased in numbers after World War II. Today it's a mixed neighborhood of Italians, African-Americans and Hispanics.

LINCOLN SQUARE

The square is the area around the Lincoln Center. Wealthy individuals, many of them successful performers, occupy the towers, and the area buzzes with bars, restaurants and stores. The ABC and CNN studios are a major presence.

UPPER WEST SIDE

Broadway cuts right through this section that extends from 59th to 125th streets between the Hudson River and Central Park West. The blocks around 72nd Street were the center of an old German/East-European, primarily Jewish, liberal intellectual community. In the 1970s and 1980s, Columbus and Amsterdam avenues were gentrified and the old single-room occupancy hotels returned to handsome residences. Today, it's often referred to as a Manhattan suburb, because of its family orientation, although it has become more fashionable recently, as new chic restaurants have opened. Central Park West is lined with expensive cooperatives overlooking Central Park. Notable attractions include the American Museum of Natural History.

MORNINGSIDE HEIGHTS

Columbia University dominates this neighborhood, along with Barnard, Teachers College, the Cathedral of St. John the Divine and the Union Theological and Jewish Theological seminaries.

HARLEM

Stretching from 110th Street to the Harlem River and from Fifth to St. Nicholas avenues, Harlem is the city's most famous black community. Originally a suburb for the wealthy, it was settled in the late 19th century by Jewish immigrants from Germany. When the subway arrived in the early 20th century, most of the black community moved in from midtown Manhattan and also from the southern states, and it drew black artists, writers and musicians. In the 1920s the Harlem Renaissance brought whites and blacks together to the clubs, theaters and jazz joints. Later it became a blighted community, destroyed by the riots of the 1960s. Today it has been rediscovered by the middle classes and increasingly by whites in search of reasonably priced houses. The restaurants and churches attract visitors.

WASHINGTON HEIGHTS/ INWOOD

This is the last stop in Manhattan. It has been home to many different immigrant groups. Today, it's largely a Dominican community, although young professionals are moving in. It's also home to the Cloisters and Fort Tryon Park.

BROOKLYN

With the highest population of the five boroughs (2.5 million), Brooklyn is a healthy rival to Manhattan. It's full of world-class museums, spacious parks, landmark buildings and lively neighborhoods.

GREENPOINT

This is an old Polish neighborhood where young professionals have moved in because of its proximity to Manhattan.

WILLIAMSBURG

Primarily a Jewish and African-American neighborhood, recently Williamsburg has been discovered by the young and hip. Its ambience is now reminiscent of 1950s Greenwich Village.

DUMBO
One developer alone has created this neighborhood (Down Under the Manhattan Bridge Overpass) by renting to artists and musicians. Today it is becoming a "hot" neighborhood à la SoHo with expensive lofts.

BROOKLYN HEIGHTS
This is a former premier residential neighborhood. The Promenade offers magnificent views of the Manhattan skyline.

COBBLE HILL
Cobble Hill is another affluent residential neighborhood where the streets are lined with elegant brownstones. Atlantic Avenue supports a major Middle Eastern community.

PROSPECT PARK
The Brooklyn Botanic Gardens are in Prospect Park and the Brooklyn Museum of Art is adjacent to the gardens.

CARROLL GARDENS
Fine brownstones made this primarily Italian neighborhood an attractive residential area for those who could not afford to buy property in Manhattan.

FORT GREENE
After it was designated a historic district in 1978, professionals started buying the handsome brownstones. It's home to the Brooklyn Academy of Music.

PARK SLOPE
Brooklyn's "alternative" village on the western edge of Prospect Park. The main commercial streets are 7th and 5th avenues.

CROWN HEIGHTS
The city's largest West Indian community, plus a thriving Hasidic Jewish community.

BRIGHTON BEACH/ CONEY ISLAND
Often called Little Odessa due to its Russian Jewish community, Brighton Beach has a boardwalk, clubs, restaurants and stores servicing the Russian community. Next door, Coney Island was the city's great blue-collar playground from the late 1890s to the early 1930s. In the 1960s it became drug infested and dangerous. Today it is being revived. It's home to the New York Aquarium.

QUEENS
An international melting pot, Queens has the most diverse population of the five boroughs, and is also the largest. Named for Queen Catherine of Braganza, Charles II's wife, it is a good place to go to sample ethnic life and cuisine.

ASTORIA
The old Greek neighborhood has survived. Astoria was also a film-making area and some of the studios have been revived, including one that houses the American Museum of the Moving Image.

LONG ISLAND CITY
This is Queens' most industrialized area. The gritty waterfront area is being revamped.

FOREST HILLS
This wealthy, largely Jewish enclave, only a short commute from Manhattan, has handsome apartment houses, and good restaurants and social services.

JACKSON HEIGHTS
There is a major South American and Indian enclave on 82nd Street.

CORONA, CITI FIELD AND FLUSHING MEADOWS PARK
The Citi Field stadium is the home of the Mets. The park has the National Tennis Center, the New York Hall of Science and the Queens Museum of Art. Corona is mainly a Dominican, Colombian and Mexican community.

FLUSHING MEADOWS
This is an area populated by Chinese, Koreans, Vietnamese, Malaysians and Japanese.

THE BRONX
The Bronx was once an expensive retreat for the wealthy. Development in the 1920s brought more well-heeled residents, then it got a reputation as a crime-laden area, and now has been turned into a much more tourist-friendly borough, with plenty of attractions and some beautiful parks.

FORDHAM
The Bronx Zoo and the New York Botanical Garden are in this neighborhood. Arthur Avenue is a colorful Italian area.

RIVERDALE
The most desirable residential neighborhood in the borough and the location of Wave Hill, an 1843 estate once home to Mark Twain and Teddy Roosevelt and now a public garden and cultural center.

VAN CORTLANDT PARK AND WOODLAWN CEMETERY
Many famous people are buried at Woodlawn, including F. W. Woolworth, Irving Berlin and Duke Ellington. Van Cortlandt Park is a delightful space with forests and hills to explore.

CITY ISLAND
New Yorkers come to this historic fishing community for fresh fish.

STATEN ISLAND
Staten Island is more than twice the size of Manhattan. Its residents are largely blue collar, still living a fairly autonomous, rural life away from busy Manhattan. Attractions include the Alice Austen House, Snug Harbor Cultural Center and Historic Richmond Town.

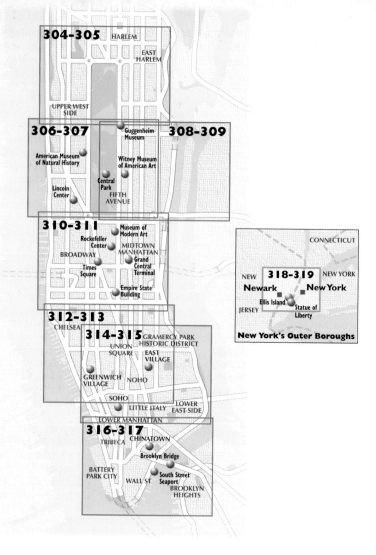
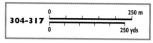
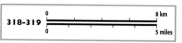
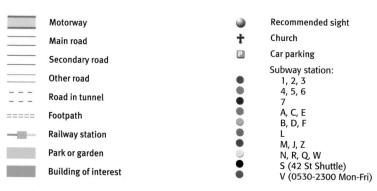

MAPS

Map references for the sights refer to the individual locator maps within the regional chapters. For example, the Empire State Building has the reference ✚ 147 D10, indicating the locator map page number (147) and the grid square in which the Empire State Building sits (D10). These same grid references can also be used to locate the sights in this section. For example, the Empire State Building appears again in grid square D10 within the atlas, on page 311.

Marcus Garvey Park

East 121st Street

Sylvian Court

Sylvian Place

121st Street

D

E

F

HARLEM

Mt Morris Park West

East 120th Street

PARK AVENUE

PARK AVENUE

East

East 120th Street

2nd

Street

East 119th Street

East

East 119th Street

Avenue

Street

East 118th Street

East

East 118th Street

Street

I

East 117th Street

East

East 117th Street

Street

Avenue

116th Street

East 116th Street

East

116th Street

East 116th Street

Street

116th Street

East 115th Street

East

East 115th Street

Street

Malcolm X

East 114th Street

1st Avenue

Pleasant

Boulevard

East 113th Street

East 112th Street

Jefferson Park

STREET

Frawley Circle

EAST 111th Street

EAST HARLEM

110th Street
Central Park Nth)

Charles A Dana Discovery Center

East 110th Street

East 110th Street

East 109th Street

East

East 109th Street

Harlem Meer

Lasker Pool & Rink

East 108th Street

East 108th Street

2

FRANKLIN DELANO ROOSEVELT DRIVE (FDR)

Conservatory Garden

PARK AVENUE

East 107th Street

East 107th Street

5th Avenue

East 106th Street

East 106th Street

East 105th Street

East 105th Street

El Museo del Barrio

East 104th Street

East 104th Street

Museum of the City of New York

East 103rd Street

East 103rd Street

East 103rd Street

103rd Street

3rd

P

East 102nd Street

ark

East Drive

East 101st Street

Madison Avenue

East 101st Street

East 101st Street

Gustave L Levy Place

East 100th Street

East 100th Street

Avenue

East 99th Street

PARK AVENUE

East 99th Street

3

East 98th Street

East 98th Street

East 97th Street

East 97th Street

P

East 96th Street

96th Street

96th Street

EAST 96TH STREET

P

East 95th Street

East 95th Street

East 94th Street

P

East 94th Street

East 93rd Street

East 93rd Street

Jewish Museum

East 92nd Street

P

East 92nd Street

4

East 307

East 91st Street

Cooper-Hewitt National Design Museum

308

East 91st Street

East 91st Street

D

East 90th Street

PA

Lexington

3rd

E

P

2nd

1st

East 90th Street

F

Central Park

reservoir

National Academy of Fine

305

SIDE

304

West 90th Street
West 89th Street
West 88th Street
West 87th Street
West 86th Street

86th Street

West 85th Street
West 84th Street
West 83rd Street
West 82nd Street

81st Street Museum of Nat Hist

West 81st Street
West 80th Street
West 79th Street

American Museum of Natural History

West 78th Street
West 77th Street
West 76th Street

New-York Historical Society

West 75th Street

San Remo Apartments

West 74th Street

Ansonia Building

West 73rd Street

The Dakota

West 72nd Street

72nd Street

72nd Street

West 71st Street
West 70th Street
West 69th Street
West 68th Street
West 67th Street

66th Street Lincoln Center

West 66th Street

Juilliard School

West 65th Street
West 64th Street

West 64th Street

West 63rd Street

West 63rd Street

Lincoln Center

310

Museum of Biblical Art

West 62nd Street
West 61st Street

West 61st Street

West 60th

West 59th Street

59th Street Columbus Circle

BROADWAY
West End Avenue
Amsterdam Avenue
Columbus Avenue
Central Park West
Riverside Drive

Riverside Park

Riverside Drive

HIGHWAY 9A

Hudson

Freedom Place
West 69th Street
Riverside Boulevard
West 68th Street

West End Avenue
West Drive
West 61st Street
West 62nd Street

Amsterdam Avenue
Columbus Avenue
Central Park West

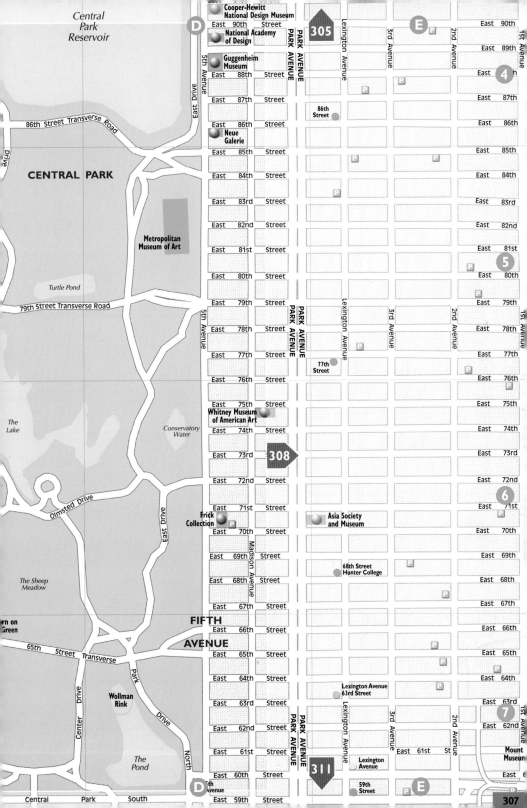

Central
Park
Reservoir

Cooper-Hewitt
National Design Museum

East   90th   Street

National Academy
of Design

East   89th   Street

Guggenheim
Museum

East   88th   Street

East   87th   Street

86th
Street

East   86th   Street

Neue
Galerie

East   85th   Street

East   84th   Street

East   83rd   Street

East   82nd   Street

East   81st   Street

East   80th   Street

East   79th   Street

East   78th   Street

East   77th   Street

77th
Street

East   76th   Street

East   75th   Street

Whitney Museum
of American Art

East   74th   Street

East   73rd

East   72nd   Street

East   71st

Frick
Collection

East   70th   Street

Asia Society
and Museum

East   69th   Street

East   68th   Street

68th Street
Hunter College

East   67th   Street

FIFTH

East   66th   Street

AVENUE

East   65th   Street

East   64th   Street

Lexington Avenue
63rd Street

East   63rd

East   62nd   Street

East   61st   St

Lexington
Avenue

East   60th   Street

59th
Street

Central   Park   South

East   59th   Street

86th Street Transverse Road

CENTRAL PARK

Metropolitan
Museum of Art

Turtle Pond

79th Street Transverse Road

The
Lake

Conservatory
Water

Olmsted Drive

The Sheep
Meadow

rn on
Green

65th   Street   Transverse

Wollman
Rink

The
Pond

East Drive

5th Avenue

PARK AVENUE

PARK AVENUE

Lexington Avenue

3rd Avenue

2nd Avenue

1st Avenue

Madison Avenue

East Drive

Center Drive

Park Drive

North

Mount
Museum

East   6

305

E

4

5

308

6

7

311

E

D

D

307

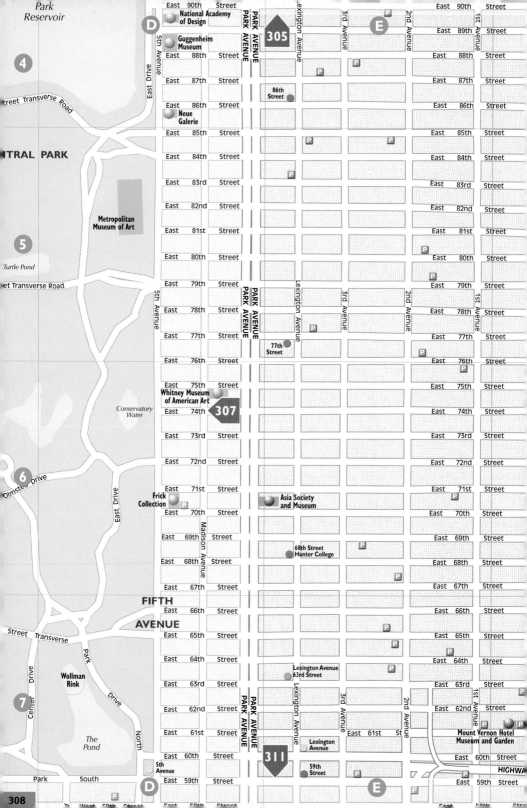

F

Gracie
Mansion

Carl
Schurz
Park

G Astoria
Boulevard

Hallets
Cove Playground

H Astoria Blvd
29th Avenue
30th Avenue

Welling
Court

30th Road

30th Drive

31st Avenue

31st Road

31st Drive

Socrates
Sculpture
Park

Broadway

33rd Avenue

33rd Avenue

33rd Road

33rd Road

33rd Road

Rainey
Park

34th Avenue

Ravenswood
Playgroud

35th Avenue

QUEENS

FRANKLIN DELANO ROOSEVELT DRIVE (FDR)

John Jay
Park

River Road

Main Street

Roosevelt Island
Bridge

36th Avenue

37th Avenue

*Roosevelt
Island*

38th Avenue

39th Avenue

9th Street

10th Street

11th Street

12th Street

13th Street

Roosevelt
Island
Main
Street

40th Avenue

West Road

East Road

Main Street

41st Avenue

Queensbridge
Park

41st Road

21st Street
Queensbridge

22nd Street

23rd Street

21ST STREET

21ST STREET

Vernon Boulevard

Vernon Boulevard

Vernon Boulevard

9th Street

10th Street

11th Street

12th Street

13th Street

14th Street

14th Street

12th Street

25

QUEENSBORO BRIDGE

Main Street

F

Queens Plaza South

G

HIGHWAY 25

H

East

4

5

6

7

309

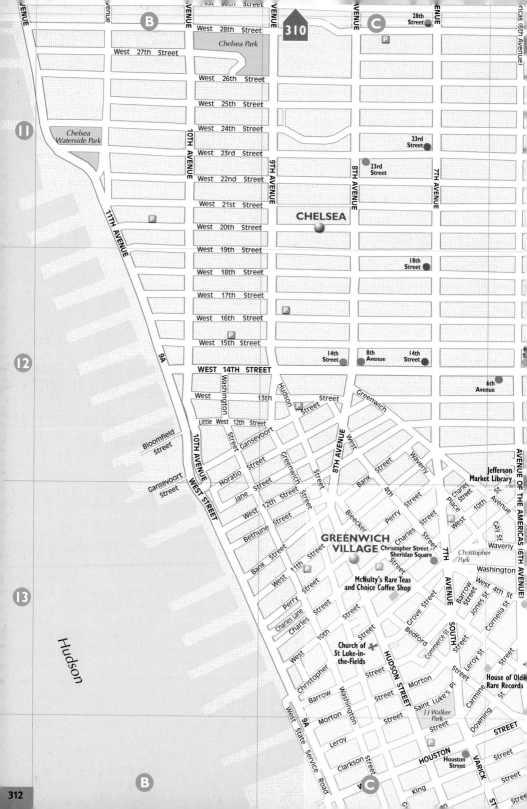

West 22nd Street · East 22nd Street · **GRAMERCY PARK HISTORIC DISTRICT**

West 21st Street · East 21st Street · Gramercy Park North · Gramercy Park · Gramercy Park South

West 20th Street · East 20th Street · Theodore Roosevelt Birthplace · Block Beautiful

West 19th Street · East 19th Street

West 18th Street · East 18th Street · 18th Street

West 17th Street · East 17th Street · Irving Place · 3rd Avenue · Rutherford Place

West 16th Street · East 16th St · **UNION SQUARE** · Union Square · 3rd Avenue

West 15th Street · East 15th Street

14th Street · **WEST 14TH STREET** · **EAST 14TH STREET** · 14th Street Union Square

8th Avenue · 14th Street · 14th Street · 6th Avenue

West 13th Street · East 13th Street · Forbes Magazine Galleries

West 12th Street · East 12th Street

West 11th Street · East 11th Street · Grace Church · St Mark's Church-in-the-Bowery

West 10th Street · East 10th Street · **313** · BROADWAY · 3rd Avenue · Stuyvesant Street

Jefferson Market Library · West 9th Street · East 9th Street · 5TH AVENUE · Wanamaker Place · Astor Place

West 8th Street · East 8th Street · 8th Street NYU · Astor Place

Mac Dougal Aly · Washington Mews · **GREENWICH VILLAGE** · Christopher Street · Sheridan Square · Christopher Park · WASHINGTON SQUARE NORTH · Ukrainian Museum

McNulty's Rare Teas and Choice Coffee Shop · Washington Place · Washington Square Park · **NOHO**

Church of St Luke-in-the-Fields · West 4th Street · WASHINGTON SQUARE SOUTH · West 4th Street · Merchant's House Museum

HUDSON STREET · West 4th Street - Washington Square · West 3rd Street · Great Jones Street · Bond Street · Bowery

Minetta Lane · Minetta St · Bleecker Street · Bleecker Street

House of Oldies Rare Records · Bleecker Street · La Guardia · Mercer · Broadway · Bleecker Street · Mott Street

J J Walker Park · **WEST HOUSTON STREET** · Broadway-Lafayette Street · **EAST HOUSTON** · Elizabeth Street

Houston Street · Prince Street · Prince Street · St Patrick's Old Cathedral · New Muse Contempora

VARICK STREET · King · AVENUE OF THE AMERICAS (6TH AVENUE) · Sullivan Street · West Broadway · Wooster Street · Greene Street · Mercer Street · Singer Building · Spring Street · Spring Street

New York City Fire Museum · Charlton · Vandam · Spring Street · Crosby · **SOHO** · Haughwout Building · Kenmare · **LITTLE IT**

WEST STREET · Dominick · Broome Street · Children's Museum of the Arts · Broome Street

American Numismatic Society · Watts · Grand Street · Museum of Chinese in America

Renwick St · Spring · Canal Street · Canal Street · CANAL · **316** · VARICK · **CANAL STREET** · Canal Street · Howard Street

Washington · Watts · Desbrosses · Canal Street · Hester

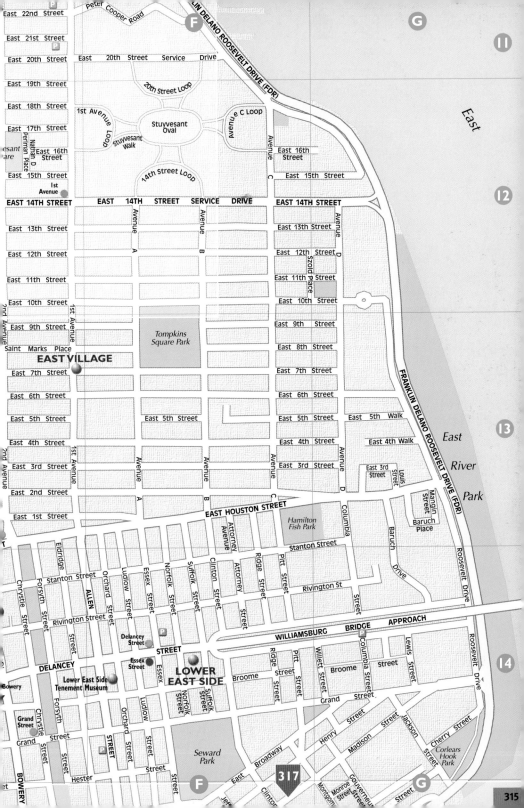

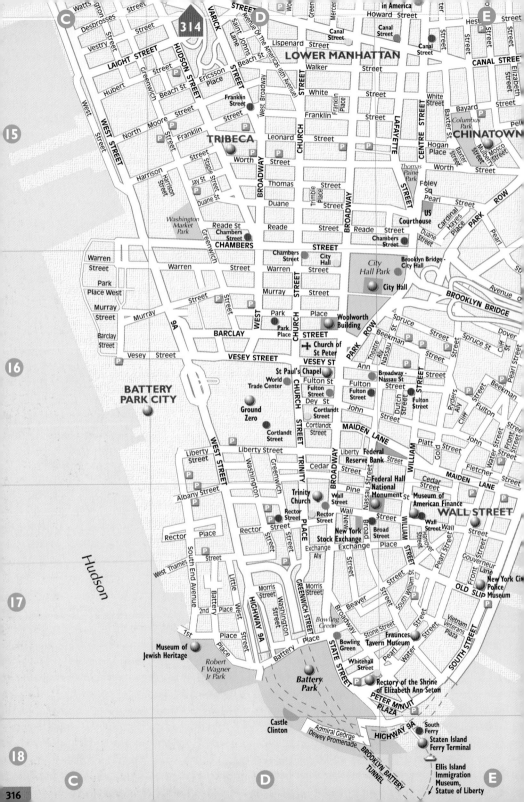

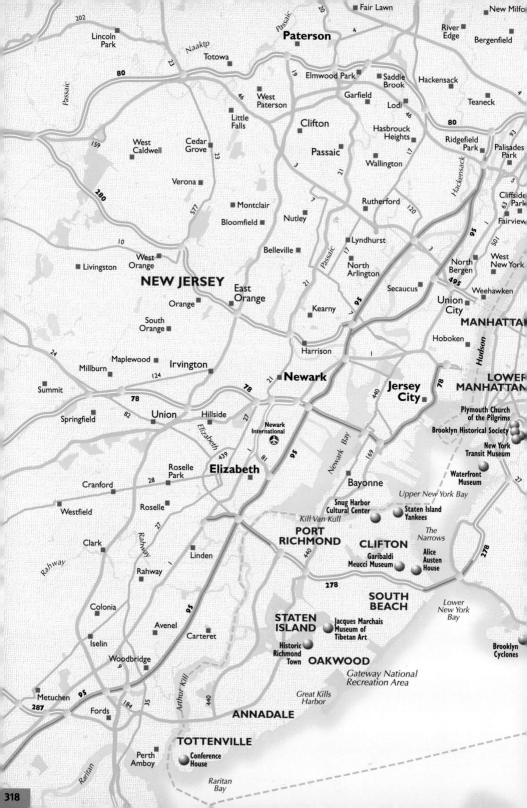

202

Lincoln
Park

Totowa

Naaktp

23

80

Passaic

Fair Lawn

New Milfo

Paterson

River
Edge

Bergenfield

20

4

19

Elmwood Park

Saddle
Brook

Hackensack

West
Paterson

Garfield

Lodi

Teaneck

46

Little
Falls

Clifton

Hasbrouck
Heights

80

West
Caldwell

Cedar
Grove

Passaic

Ridgefield
Park

Palisades
Park

159

23

Wallington

17

93

5

Verona

577

3

21

Rutherford

120

Cliffside
Park

63

180

Montclair

7

Fairview

Bloomfield

Nutley

Lyndhurst

North
Bergen

West
New York

501

10

Belleville

17

1

West
Orange

Livingston

North
Arlington

Weehawken

495

NEW JERSEY

East
Orange

21

Secaucus

Union
City

MANHATTAN

Orange

Passaic

Kearny

3

Hoboken

South
Orange

Harrison

1

24

Maplewood

Newark

Jersey
City

**LOWER
MANHATTAN**

Millburn

Irvington

95

78

Hudson

Summit

124

78

440

Plymouth Church
of the Pilgrims

82

Union

Hillside

21

78

Brooklyn Historical Society

Springfield

27

Newark
International

New York
Transit Museum

Cranford

Roselle
Park

439

81

95

169

Waterfront
Museum

28

Elizabeth

Newark Bay

Westfield

Roselle

Bayonne

Upper New York Bay

27

Clark

27

Linden

Snug Harbor
Cultural Center

Staten Island
Yankees

*The
Narrows*

Rahway

Rahway

Kill Van Kull

**PORT
RICHMOND**

CLIFTON

278

Colonia

Avenel

440

Garibaldi
Meucci Museum

Alice
Austen
House

Iselin

1

Carteret

278

**SOUTH
BEACH**

*Lower
New York
Bay*

Woodbridge

9

**STATEN
ISLAND**

Jacques Marchais
Museum of
Tibetan Art

Brooklyn
Cyclones

Metuchen

95

35

Historic
Richmond
Town

OAKWOOD

287

Fords

184

Arthur Kill

440

ANNADALE

*Gateway National
Recreation Area*

*Great Kills
Harbor*

TOTTENVILLE

Perth
Amboy

Conference
House

Raritan

*Raritan
Bay*

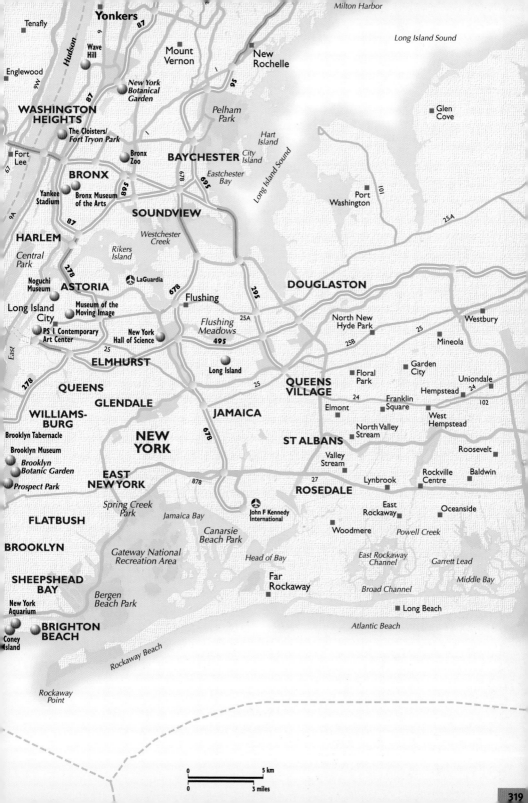

Milton Harbor

Long Island Sound

Tenafly

Yonkers
87

Wave
Hill

Mount
Vernon

New
Rochelle

Glen
Cove

Hudson

Englewood

New York
Botanical
Garden

Pelham
Park

Port
Washington

101

**WASHINGTON
HEIGHTS**

87

Hart
Island

The Cloisters/
Fort Tryon Park

Bronx
Zoo

BAYCHESTER

City
Island

25A

Fort
Lee

878

Eastchester
Bay

BRONX

895

695

Long Island Sound

Yankee
Stadium

Bronx Museum
of the Arts

SOUNDVIEW

9A

87

Westchester
Creek

HARLEM

278

Rikers
Island

25A

Central
Park

Noguchi
Museum

ASTORIA

LaGuardia

678

Flushing

295

DOUGLASTON

North New
Hyde Park

25

Westbury

Long Island
City

Museum of the
Moving Image

258

Mineola

East

PS 1 Contemporary
Art Center

New York
Hall of Science

Flushing
Meadows

495

25

Long Island

Floral
Park

Garden
City

Uniondale

ELMHURST

25

**QUEENS
VILLAGE**

24

Hempstead

24

102

278

QUEENS

GLENDALE

Elmont

Franklin
Square

West
Hempstead

Roosevelt

**WILLIAMS-
BURG**

**NEW
YORK**

678

JAMAICA

North Valley
Stream

Brooklyn Tabernacle

ST ALBANS

Brooklyn Museum

Valley
Stream

Rockville
Centre

Baldwin

Brooklyn
Botanic Garden

878

ROSEDALE

27

Lynbrook

Prospect Park

**EAST
NEW YORK**

FLATBUSH

Spring Creek
Park

Jamaica Bay

John F Kennedy
International

Canarsie
Beach Park

East
Rockaway

Oceanside

Woodmere

Powell Creek

BROOKLYN

Gateway National
Recreation Area

Head of Bay

East Rockaway
Channel

Garrett Lead

**SHEEPSHEAD
BAY**

Bergen
Beach Park

Far
Rockaway

Broad Channel

Middle Bay

New York
Aquarium

**BRIGHTON
BEACH**

Long Beach

Coney
Island

Atlantic Beach

Rockaway Beach

Rockaway
Point

0   5 km

0   3 miles

INDEX NEW YORK

PICTURES

The Automobile Association would like to thank the following photographers, companies and picture libraries for their assistance in the preparation of this book.

Abbreviations for the picture credits are as follows – (t) top; (b) bottom; (c) centre; (l) left; (r) right; (AA) AA World Travel Library.

2 AA/J Tims;
3t AA/J Tims;
3c AA/J Tims;
3b AA/J Tims;
4 AA/J Tims;
5 AA/J Tims;
6 AA/J Tims;
7 AA/J Tims;
8 AA/J Tims;
9 AA/D Corrance;
10 AA/J Tims;
11 AA/J Tims;
12 AA/J Tims;
13bl AA/J Tims;
13tr AA/J Tims;
14 AA/J Tims;
15tl AA/J Tims;
15br AA/J Tims;
16 AA/J Tims;
17bl AA/J Tims;
17br AA/J Tims;
18 AA/J Tims;
19t AA/J Tims;
19b AA/J Tims;
20 AA/J Tims;
21tl AA/J Tims;
21tr AA/J Tims;
22 AA/J Tims;
23bl AA/J Tims;
23tr AA/J Tims;
24 AA/J Tims;
25bl AA/J Tims;
25br AA/J Tims;
26 AA/J Tims;
27 AA/J Tims;
28 AA;
29bl Mary Evans Picture Library;
29br Mary Evans Picture Library;
30 AA/C Sawyer;
31 AA;
32 Mary Evans Picture Library;
33tl AA/J Tims;
33br AA/J Tims;
34 Mary Evans Picture Library;
35bl AA;

35br AA/J Tims;
36 AA/J Tims;
37bl AA/J Tims;
37tr AA/J Tims;
38 AA/J Tims;
39tl Stephane de Sakutin/AFP/Getty Images;
39br Bettmann/Corbis;
40 AA/J Tims;
41 AA/J Tims;
42 Digitalvision;
44 AA/J Tims;
48 AA/J Tims;
49t AA/J Tims;
49b AA/J Tims;
50 AA/J Tims;
51 AA/J Tims;
53 AA/J Tims;
55bl AA/J Tims;
55cr AA/Clive Sawyer;
56 AA/J Tims;
57 AA/J Tims;
58 AA/J Tims;
59 AA/J Tims;
60 AA/E Rooney;
64 AA/J Tims;
65 AA/J Tims;
66 AA/J Tims;
67 AA/J Tims;
68 AA/J Tims;
69bl AA/J Tims;
69br AA/J Tims;
70 AA/J Tims;
71 AA/J Tims;
72 AA/J Tims;
75 AA/C Sawyer;
76 AA/J Tims;
77 AA/J Tims;
78 AA/J Tims;
79 AA/J Tims;
80 AA/J Tims;
81bl AA/J Tims;
81br AA/S McBride;
82 AA/J Tims;
83 AA/J Tims;
84 AA/C Sawyer;
85 AA/J Tims;
86 AA/J Tims;
87 AA/J Tims;
88 AA/J Tims;
89 AA/C Sawyer;
90 AA/J Tims;
92 AA/J Tims;
94 AA/J Tims;
95 AA/C Sawyer;
97 Jon Kamantigue;
98 Resurrection Vintage;

100 AA/J Tims;
101 AA/J Tims;
102 ImageState;
105 AA/J Tims;
108 AA/J Tims;
112 AA/J Tims;
113 AA/J Tims;
114 AA/J Tims;
115bl AA/J Tims;
115br AA/J Tims;
116 AA/J Tims;
117 AA/J Tims;
119 AA/J Tims;
120t AA/J Tims;
120b AA/J Tims;
121 AA/J Tims;
122 AA/J Tims;
124 AA/J Tims;
134 AA/S Collier;
139 AA/J Tims;
140 AA/J Tims;
144 AA/C Sawyer;
148 AA/J Tims;
149 AA/J Tims;
150 AA/J Tims;
151t AA/J Tims;
151b AA/J Tims;
152 AA/C Sawyer;
153 AA/J Tims;
155 AA/J Tims;
156 AA/J Tims;
157 AA/J Tims;
158 Pierpont Morgan Library/Art Resource/Scala, Florence;
159 AA/J Tims;
160 AA/J Tims;
161 Stephen Finn/Alamy;
162 MOMA, New York/Scala, Florence;
163 AA/J Tims;
164 AA/J Tims;
165 AA/J Tims;
166bl AA/J Tims;
166br AA/J Tims;
167 AA/J Tims;
168 AA/J Tims;
169 AA/J Tims;
170 AA/J Tims;
171 AA/C Sawyer;
172 AA/J Tims;
174 AA/C Sawyer;
175 AA/J Tims;
176 AA/J Tims;
186 Ingram;
190 AA/J Tims;
193 The New York Palace;
194 AA/C Sawyer;

198 AA/J Tims;
202 AA/C Sawyer;
203 AA/J Tims;
204 AA/J Tims;
205 AA/J Tims;
206 AA/J Tims;
208 AA/J Tims;
209 AA/J Tims;
210t AA/J Tims;
210b AA/J Tims;
211 AA/J Tims;
212 AA/J Tims;
213t AA/J Tims;
213b AA/J Tims;
214 AA/C Sawyer;
215 Michael Bodycomb;
216 AA/J Tims;
217 Sylvain Grandadam/Robert Harding;
218 AA/J Tims;
219bl AA/J Tims;
219br AA/J Tims;
221 AA/J Tims;
222 AA/J Tims;
223 Whitney Museum of American Art;
224 Whitney Museum of American Art;
225 Whitney Museum of American Art;
226 AA/J Tims;
227 AA/J Tims;
228 AA/J Tims;
230 AA/J Tims;
237 AA/J Tims;
238 AA/J Tims;
241 AA/J Tims;
242 AA/J Tims;
246 AA/J Tims;
250 AA/J Tims;
253t AA/J Tims;
253b AA/J Tims;
254 AA/J Tims;
255 AA/J Tims;
256 AA/J Tims;
258 New York Yankees;
259 Photorush/Photolibrary;
260 AA;
262 Mick Hales/Historic Husdon Valley;
263 Historic Husdon Valley;
264 Vince Kish, Courtesy of Old Westbury Gardens;
265 Vince Kish, Courtesy of Old Westbury Gardens;
266 G Fiume/Getty Images;
267 Rick Shupper/Photolibrary;

268 AA/J Tims;
271 AA/J Tims;
275 AA/J Tims;
277 AA/J Tims;
279 AA/J Tims;
281 AA/J Tims;
282 AA/C Sawyer;
283 AA/J Tims;
284 AA/J Tims;
285 AA/J Tims;
286 AA/J Tims;
287 AA/J Tims;
288 AA/J Tims;
290 AA/J Tims;
292 AA/J Tims;
294 AA/C Sawyer;
296 The New York Palace;
297 The New York Palace;
298 AA/J Tims;
303 AA/J Tims.

Every effort has been made to trace the copyright holders, and we apologise in advance for any accidental errors. We would be happy to apply any corrections in the following edition of this publication.

CREDITS

Managing editor
Marie-Claire Jefferies

Project editor
Lodestone Publishing Ltd

Design
Drew Jones, pentacorbig

Cover design
Chie Ushio

Picture research
Alice Earle, Lesley Grayson

Image retouching and repro
Sarah Montgomery, James Tims

Mapping
Maps produced by the Mapping Services Department of AA Publishing

Main contributors
Coleen Degnan-Veness, Paul Franklin, Nancy Mikula, Marilyn Wood

Updaters
Paul Franklin and Nancy Mikula

Indexer
Marie Lorimer

Production
Lorraine Taylor

See It New York City
ISBN 978-1-4000-0498-0
Fourth Edition

Published in the United States by Fodor's Travel and simultaneously in Canada by Random House of Canada Limited, Toronto.
Published in the United Kingdom by AA Publishing.
Fodor's is a registered trademark of Random House, Inc., and Fodor's See It is a trademark of Random House, Inc.
Fodor's Travel is a division of Random House, Inc.

Color separation by AA Digital Department
Printed and bound by Leo Paper Products, China
10 9 8 7 6 5 4 3 2 1

Special Sales: This book is available for special discounts for bulk purchases for sales promotions or premiums. Special editions, including personalized covers, excerpts of existing books, and corporate imprints, can be created in large quantities for special needs. For more information, write to Special Markets/Premium Sales, 1745 Broadway, MD 6-2, New York, NY 10019 or e-mail specialmarkets@randomhouse.com
Important Note: Time inevitably brings changes, so always confirm prices, travel facts, and other perishable information when it matters. Although Fodor's cannot accept responsibility for errors, you can use this guide in the confidence that we have taken every care to ensure its accuracy.

A04025
Maps in this title produced from cartographic data © Tele Atlas N.V. 2003   Tele Atlas
Transport map © Communicarta Ltd, UK
Weather chart statistics supplied by Weatherbase © Copyright 2003 Canty and Associates, LLC